Enigma

Enigma

The Life of Knut Hamsun

Robert Ferguson

Farrar, Straus & Giroux
New York

Contents

	Introduction	1
1	Childhood, Restless Adolescence and the Start of a Mini-Career	5
2	1879–1882: Bjørnson and the End of the Mini-Career	27
3	1882–1884: The American Experience I	47
4	1884–1886: Convalescence and Valdres	67
5	1886–1888: The American Experience II	81
6	1888–1890: The Breakthrough: *Hunger*	99
7	1890–1893: Controversy: *Mysteries*, the Lecture Tour and the 'Clenched Fist' Books	122
8	1893–1895: Paris, *Pan* and Strindberg	142
9	1895–1898: Persecution and Marriage: *Victoria*	163
10	1898–1906: Restless Middle Age, Depression and Divorce	182
11	1906–1911: The Sage: Retrospection, Introspection and Marie	199
12	1911–1918: Marriage and the Return to the Roots: the *Segelfoss* Books and *The Growth of the Soil*	220
13	1918–1927: The Quiet Years: Family Man and Psychoanalysis	260
14	1927–1933: The Height of Fame: the *August* Trilogy	290
15	1933–1940: Hamsun's Politics	324
16	1940–1945: Hamsun's War	350
17	1945–1948: Internment, Examination and Trial	387
18	1948–1952: The Last Years: *On Overgrown Paths*	411
	Notes	423
	References	424
	Select Bibliography	434
	Appendix: Knut Hamsun's Complete Works	438
	Index	439

Acknowledgements

Thanks to John Townsend; Torbjørn Støverud; Rolf Nyboe Nettum; the late Ronald Popperwell; Professor T. K. Derry; Rolf Normann; Sigurd Abusdal; Arild Hamsun; Tore Hamsun; Terence de Vere White; Suzanne Palme; the staff at the following libraries: Oslo University, Bergen University, The Royal Library, Copenhagen, The Deichmanske Library, Oslo; the staff of the Riksarkiv, Oslo; archivist Elisabet Trier at *Aftenposten*; the archivist at the Post Office Museum, Olso; the archivists at NRK TV and Radio; the Secretary, the English P.E.N. Club; the archivist at the Munch Museum, Olso; the archivist at the Vigeland Museum, Oslo; Erik Charlesson; Henry Andersen; the staff at the Harry Ransom Humanities Research Centre, Texas; Jan and Liv Marstrander; Harald S. Næss; Michael Meyer; Per Amdam, Lars L'Abée – Lund.

Thanks also to Gyldendal Norsk Forlag, Refotografert, Pressesbild, Norsk Telegrambyrå AS and Universitetsbiblioteket, Oslo for their kind permission to reproduce the photographs appearing between the text.

Particular thanks to Sten Sparre Nilson; Oskar Mendelsohn; Ellinor Ringstrøm and Eva Lie-Nielsen at Gyldendal Norsk Forlag; Knut Thomas Dederick Charlesson; Th. Myklestad; Erik Petersen at The Royal Library, Copenhagen.

Especial thanks to Lars-Frode Larsen for so generously sharing his extensive knowledge of the by-ways of Hamsun's life with me; and to Nina, for her support, encouragement and everything else.

The presence of a name on this list naturally does not imply any agreement with the statements made or conclusions reached in this book. These remain my own responsibility.

One upon a time I was like my comrades. They have kept pace with the times, I have not. Now I am like no one. Unfortunately. Thank God.

Knut Hamsun

Introduction

If they've heard of him at all, people tend to know two things about Knut Hamsun: that he wrote *Hunger*, and that he met Hitler. Those who know a little more know that in *Hunger*, *Mysteries*, and *Pan*, he produced novels that have had a decisive effect on European and American literature of the twentieth century. Ernest Hemingway tried to write like him; so did Henry Miller, who called him 'the Dickens of my generation'; 'never has the Nobel Prize been awarded to one worthier of it' Thomas Mann wrote in 1929. Hermann Hesse called him 'my favourite author'. Russian writers like Andre Bely and Boris Pasternak read him keenly in their youth, and André Gide thought him arguably superior to Dostoevsky. They all read him – Kafka, Brecht, Gorky, Wells, Musil. Rebecca West described him as the possessor of 'qualities that belong to the very great – the completest omniscience about human nature', and Isaac Bashevis Singer stated that Hamsun was quite simply 'the father of the modern school of literature in his every aspect – his subjectiveness, his fragmentariness, his use of flashbacks, his lyricism'. Singer, in his foreword to *Hunger*, goes on to state that 'The whole modern school of fiction in the twentieth century stems from Hamsun.' Yet in discussions of the history of modern literature, Hamsun's name is rarely mentioned. His reputation, which probably reached its height around 1929 with the world celebrations of his seventieth birthday, was in ruins by the end of the Second World War. Alone among major European writers, he had supported Hitler. Brazenly alone, he had hailed the rise and bemoaned the fall of the epitome of spiritual tyranny in recent history.

An episode from 1955 illustrates well the strange situation this left Hamsun's admirers in. One might say that his literary reputation was in a critical state just at that time, three years after

his death and only seven years after his trial and conviction for
treason, and it was in an attempt to ensure its survival that a
woman named Hilde Fürstenberg proposed to start a Knut
Hamsun Society in her native Germany. Her aims were entirely
literary, not political, and she solicited the support of two of
Hamsun's most notable German admirers, Hermann Hesse and
Thomas Mann, for her undertaking. Hesse turned down the
invitation to attend an inaugural meeting of the Society on the
grounds of age and ill-health, but he wished it all good luck:

> The great writer has paid enough for his astonishing political
> mistakes; we no longer bear him any grudge, and even though
> we stood on opposing sides, I have never for one moment
> doubted the greatness of Hamsun's literary work.

Mann was less well-disposed towards the project:

> I will not have anything to do with the formation of a Knut
> Hamsun Society. I know quite well that the stigma of his politics
> will one day be separated from his writing, which I regard very
> highly; and as a close student of both his work and his persona I
> recognise the inevitability, however regrettable, of his conduct
> during the Nazi-era. But the wretched, and really wicked things
> he constantly said, wrote and did are still too fresh in my mind
> for me to find the time right for the formation of such a society.

Mann's profound unease, and Hesse's careful statement that 'we
stood on opposite sides' are understandable just ten years after the
war. But even now, forty years afterwards, Hamsun's literary
reputation is still struggling to throw off the shadow of his politics.
The label 'Nazi' has stuck, and in the absence of any detailed
account of Hamsun's life, including his special relationship with
Germany and the Germans, it remains – for the English-speaking
world at least – the decisive description of the man. Part of my aim
in writing this book has been to provide such an account, in the
hope that it will prove enlightening; Hamsun, after all, is only an
extreme example of that curious tendency in art for great creative
revolutionaries to be personally reactionary and anti-liberal. In
literature names like Faulkner, Eliot and Lawrence spring to mind,
with Ezra Pound and Louis Ferdinand Céline closer to Hamsun's
extreme example.

My personal involvement with Hamsun began when I first came
across *Pan*, some sixteen years ago. There was a hypnotic intensity

about the prose style, even in translation, that fascinated me, and I read the book three times in succession before going on to devour whatever else of Hamsun I could get my hands on. In those days it was the early novels – *Hunger*, *Mysteries*, and *Victoria* – that were most readily available. I read these with great excitement, and a mounting curiosity about the author. English publishers of Hamsun's novels have tended to be reticent about his last years, however, and it was quite some time before I found out about the association with Hitler.

From the first, the information fascinated rather than repelled me. Could the sensitive, dreaming genius who had created beautiful love stories like *Pan* and *Victoria* really have been a Nazi? The remarks he was reported to have made after publishing his necrology for Hitler in May 1945, that he had not liked the man, and had written the necrology 'as a courtesy, nothing more', merely increased my curiosity about Hamsun, and strengthened my suspicions that there was more to the case than met the eye. My desire to read him in the original, and to find out more about him, eventually led to my enrolling as an undergraduate student of Norwegian at UCL in 1976, where I was able to make a special study of his life and works.

There has never been a full-length biography of Knut Hamsun in English, and the damage to his reputation after the war has meant that there has been no new biography of him in Norwegian either. The subject has simply been too sensitive. His widow Marie produced two volumes of memoirs, and Tore Hamsun has produced several editions of a fascinating and well-written account of his father's life; but in both cases the close personal involvement of the writers with their subject precludes objectivity.

Was Hamsun a Nazi, or was he not? Did he know what he was doing and saying, or not? Was he really senile, as the psychiatrists who examined him after the war declared; or was he so bitter, cynical and disillusioned that he genuinely wished for the triumph of the jackboot? Or was he – another possibility – a misunderstood and misinterpreted patriot? Not only is it possible to argue every case, but there are times when to do so seems the only hope of getting anywhere near the truth. One thing is certain: Hamsun was a multiple paradox; a living riddle; a human question-mark.

It was in some hopes of satisfying my curiosity about the man that I arrived in Oslo in 1983 on a scholarship from the Norwegian government, and began researching Hamsun's life. Living in Norway, I often found that in the course of a conversation I would eventually be asked, in that attractively shy but direct way Norwegians have, what I was doing in their country. My reply would frequently provoke a thoughtful silence, and then the calm and ever so slightly challenging response, 'But he was a Nazi, wasn't he?' No matter how often I was asked this, a wholly satisfactory answer never sprang to my lips, and I would usually end by muttering something about 'complicated man' and 'nothing being black and white'. This book is an attempt to elaborate on that mutter.

Chapter 1
Childhood, Restless Adolescence, and the start of a Mini-Career

In October 1945 Knut Hamsun sits writing in his room in the Psychiatric Clinic at Vindern, Olso. He is being examined there by two psychiatrists, Dr Gabriel Langfeldt and Dr Ørnulv Ødegård, who are to pronouce on his mental state and his fitness to stand trial on a charge of treason. He is eighty-six years old and extremely deaf. After a number of tragicomic attempts at verbal communication the psychiatrists have adopted the procedure of submitting written questions to him. Their report to the Public Prosecutor contains the following exchange:[1]

Question: Please give here a short description of how you now view your childhood and upbringing. Mention particularly relationships and experiences which you think have had a lasting effect.

Answer: My home was poor, but full of warmth. Each time I was allowed to go back there from my uncle's I cried and thanked God. He starved me, and ruled over me. And I used to beg to be allowed to go up in the hills and mind the animals, even when it wasn't our day for it. I sat out and talked to myself, whittled flutes and wrote rhymes on scraps of paper, like any other peasant boy. I was no different from anyone else, a bit quicker than the others maybe. We children respected our father, and our mother was kind and patient. She kept the scraps of paper I wrote on, and showed me them again when I was grown-up. Her voice was soft and musical. But we spoke more with our father than with her. He taught us more. We brothers fought and forgave one another, just like other peasant boys. We loved and respected our eldest sister, although our other sister was cleverer. None of my brothers and sisters is alive now. I couldn't help my eldest sister. She died young. I couldn't even help myself in those days. It pains me when I think that I was unable to help her.

It was my uncle who made the deepest impression on me. He was not without good qualities, but he had no idea how to treat children. He helped us with the farm, small and wretched as it was. But we never owed anything to anyone. Nor must I forget our grandfather on my mother's side. He was a warm and honest man, always kind and good to us children. I am not as good a grandfather as he was.

Hamsun answers the question, yes – but one feels somehow that the easy, dream-like, subjective flow of this memoir is not quite what the psychiatrists were hoping for. There seems no *opening* for them; Knut Hamsun was the master of the artful confession. In a literary career that spanned seventy-two years and included novels, short stories, travel books, newspaper articles and plays he had improvised with a dazzling and faithful consistency over a single theme: his life.

The Pedersen family – the name Hamsun was to come later – came originally from Lom, in the Gudbrandsdal, in central south Norway. His father Per was born on 28 March 1825, at Skultbakken in Vågå, a remote farm settlement now wholly deserted. Per's father, also called Per, was unable to make a living from the small farm, and in order to support his family had to travel locally as a 'bygdetusenkunstner', a sort of jack-of-all-trades. Among his other talents he was a smith capable of fine, delicate work. Ymbjør, his wife, brewed the liquor locally, until the law forbade it. Tailoring was a local tradition in Skultbakken, and in his youth the younger Per wandered away to Ålesund, and apprenticed himself to a tailor there for five years, returning to Skultbakken a craftsman, and setting up in business there. A photograph taken late in life shows him with a dome-like head and long white whiskers, a wistful look in his eyes; as a young man he was said to have been supple and strong, with a wry sense of humour which made him particularly attractive to girls. On one occasion he delivered a pair of trousers in which he had deliberately forgotten to sew an opening at the front to a bridegroom shortly before the wedding ceremony.

Per Pedersen was highly regarded locally as a skilled and hardworking tailor. He would travel around Lom and Vågå with his scissors and his pressing iron, and cut and press the cloth, and his assistants would follow on behind and make up the clothes. It was in the course of his work that he met Tora Olsdatter Garmotraedet, whose father Ole farmed a smallholding on the west side of the Vågå lake, next to the village church. The couple married in Vågå church on 14 October 1852, by which time they were already the parents of a seven-month-old son Peter. Per was then twenty-seven and Tora twenty-two. Again, the only extant photographs show her as an old woman, her mouth puckered and toothless, but with clear, strong eyes, and kempt white hair drawn in at the back of her head. When young she was said to have been tall and dignified, and very beautiful. 'You should have come before', she is reported to have murmured to one journalist who came to photograph her.

While the Pedersens from Skultbakken were common working people, the Garmo family from Lom could claim to be one of the oldest families in the Gudbrandsdal, with roots going back 900 years to Torgeir the Old who, according to local tradition, built the church at Garmo at the direct request of the Saint – King Olaf himself. Another tradition also claimed descent from Harald Fine-Hair, a Norse chieftain who vowed not to cut his hair until he had brought about the unification of Norway, a goal he finally achieved in the latter half of the ninth century. Whatever the truth of these traditions, the fact is that by the time of the marriage the wealth and power of the family were long gone, and the subject only of nostalgic and longing gossip from the living bearers of the name.

The Pedersens lived mostly at Garmotraedet with Tora's parents, and added to their family. Per took over most of the running of the farm from his father-in-law Ole, but times were hard, and even with the additional income from clothes-making it was a constant struggle to provide for them all.

Norway was slowly becoming industrialised. Railways, roads and canals encouraged the drift to the cities, where factories were springing up. The emigration to America had begun already in 1825, when the *Restoration*, with forty-five Norwegians on board, sailed from Stavanger. The motives of these original emigrants were religious, but their immediate successors, under the organisation and leadership of Cleng Peerson, were attracted by the hope of better living conditions. Eighteen thousand Norwegians emigrated to America between 1825 and 1850, a modest enough number compared with later years, but nevertheless an indication of restlessness and change in a society that had survived in a remarkably unchanged form for almost a thousand years.

Those who felt that the old ways were disappearing, and yet did not wish to abandon them wholly, had a third option open to them besides the cities or America – they could try to make a fresh start by moving to the north of Norway. Even before Tora's marriage to Per Pedersen, her brother Hans Olsen had moved up to Hamarøy in Nordland, about 200 miles north of the polar circle, and had established himself economically and socially in the village of Presteid. With the birth of Knut, on 4 August 1859, the fourth in a family that eventually totalled seven children, Per's economic problems became desperate. A market slump the following year released another wave of migrations, and in 1860 he travelled north to visit his brother-in-law, to try to find out whether a move to Hamarøy was practicable. He was not an educated man, and the message he sent back to Tora was copied out for him by his brother Hans:

> . . . next time I will write to you myself, when I have had more time to practise. For now please forgive me. It is not that I am ill after the journey, just that I am so unused to writing after such a long journey. Have faith in God, from whom all good things come, and do not forget to test the boys in reading. If the Almighty continues to keep us all in good health, then I hope now that the worst times are behind us. Please give everyone my warmest wishes, which I send most especially to you, my dear wife, and our boys, Peter, Ole, Hans and Knud.
>   yours sincerely, Peder Pedersen.[2]

Hans Olsen, who was to play such a decisive part in Knut Hamsun's life, had been born in Lom in 1827. He was an industrious and sober man, in many ways the opposite of his brother Ole, nicknamed Vetltraein, or 'little one', a charming wastrel who liked drinking and reminiscing more than work. Hans Olsen lived in the rectory in Presteid, and ran a small farm there. He did some tailoring – a skill taught him by his brother-in-law Per – as well as buying and selling clothes, and ran the village post office and supplied and organised the local library. He was a well-respected man in Hamarøy, and his circle of friends included the priest and the sexton. Perhaps it was in his mind, when he bought the small farm at Hamsund, three miles up the road from Presteid, that his brother-in-law and his family could be tempted to run it. He must have known that the pressures of his own work would never allow him to do so. It was this farm that Per Pedersen came to see in 1860 and to which he finally moved, making the long journey by horse and wagon from Vågå to Trondheim, taking the steamboat north from Trondheim, and arriving by rowboat at Hamsund on 24 June 1862.

One would not expect Hamsun, then not quite three years old, to retain any strong impressions of Lom, and of the wide, peaceful Gudbrandsdal valley where he spent the first days of his long life, although there is a fragment from *The Growth of the Soil* in which the mercurial and flawed 'god' of the book, Geissler, speaks of a remembered smell coming to his senses, from a time when he was eighteen months old and stood leaning down from the barn-bridge at Garmo.[3]

Hamarøy was a very different world, with its wild, mountainous beauty and its long sea views, a landscape that could seem both intoxicating and threatening at the same time. This was Hamsun's real childhood home. Here he was to absorb influences which left a lasting mark on him, and on his fiction. Up until the age of nine he seems to have been happy, in spite of the family's poverty, and the cramped living accommodation – in addition to the seven children, both of Tora's parents were living with them. Vetltraein had made the trip too, leaving a wife and family behind in Gudbrandsdal. Even when, soon after the move, Tora's mother died, and the men built a new house not far from the old one, the living space was limited. Per continued to travel locally as a tailor, and spent the rest of his time running the farm and trying to extend it by breaking new soil. He had a horse, five cows, some sheep and some goats, and the farm was self-sufficient in corn and potatoes. But with so many mouths to feed his was a life of endless toil which only the love of God, the love of his own family, his sense of humour and powers of endurance made tolerable.

A sketch of Hamsun's earliest childhood in Hamarøy, artless beyond the calculations of art, recalls it as a lost paradise, where the children lived in close harmony with the animals on the farm and the nature around them. They spent their money on little bells for the goats and the sheep; and when unknown dogs came by, tired and hungry from long travelling, the children would steal food from the larder to give to them. One day they found a deer and made a pet of it. After a while it was shot but, 'so that it should not die like a dog among us', Knut wrote a little verse in its memory.

There is an idyllic and magical remoteness about the life he describes in *Among the Animals*. But it is entirely characteristic of him that without altering the tone or the pace of his description of these innocent days he also includes a long account of the hanging of an old and sick cat which his mother asked him to kill. The cat twists and turns for five minutes before dying. Paradise was not without its shadows.

A special friend of these early days was his uncle, Vetltraein. He was a children's man, impractical and irresponsible, but a great dreamer and vivid talker. He claimed to be able to skate prodigious distances backwards across the frozen Vestfjord on his home-

made wooden skates, and told Knut that the two of them came
originally from the stars, and that their sojourn in Hamarøy was a
purely temporary affair. Like the other members of the uprooted
family, he hankered after the imagined joys of the good old days in
Lom, and he liked to turn the fireside conversation in the evenings
to the vanished glories and lost nobility of the Garmo family.

If a link to the childlike, the fantastical, and the sense of longing
in Hamsun the writer might be traced through his early contact
with Vetltraein, a link to the darker side of his literary personality
might also be evident in his relationship with his other uncle, Hans
Olsen. 'Big Hans', the Pedersen family called him, the reference
being to his power, not his size. Hamsun was sent to live with
Uncle Hans at Presteid in 1868, when he was nine. As his
statements to the psychiatrists some eighty years later indicate, he
retained vivid memories of his five years at the rectory, and
regarded Hans as one of the decisive influences in the shaping of
his own character. The story that Hamsun grew up with and
passed on to his own family is that the uncle came visiting the farm
at Hamsund one day and after a few stiffly exchanged courtesies
began demanding payment of the money the Pedersen family
owed him for the farm. His sickness was beginning to affect his
work, he argued: he wasn't earning as much as he used to, and
now he needed the money. He knew, presumably as well as the
Pedersens did, that there was not the slightest chance of their
being able to pay him back. They told him as much. He seemed
unimpressed, and gave them a week in which to pay. While they
were digesting the news he picked up one of Knut's schoolbooks
and began flipping through it. He remarked on how neatly the boy
wrote, and then made a suggestion that had perhaps been at the
back of his mind the whole time: that they might forget about the
debt on condition that Knut came and lived at Presteid with him,
and helped him with his work. They had no realistic choice in the
matter.[4]

Authors notoriously exaggerate the horrors of their own childhood, but in Hamsun's case there seems some justification for it.
Uncle Hans was forty-two when Knut moved in with him. The
sickness which led him to think of using the boy as his assistant
was a paralysis agitans which had left him lame, and obliged him to
spend much of his time seated. His right arm shook uncontroll-
ably, and though he had taught himself to write with his left hand,
the sickness was of a deteriorating kind. With an iron discipline, he
tried to mould the boy into a tool for the use of his own feeble body.
Fear and physical violence were the means he used. As Knut
copied down the figures in the post books, his uncle would sit by

him with a long ruler in his hand which he would bring down on the boy's knuckles at the slightest mistake. Not infrequently he drew blood, and once broke the ruler over Knut's head. When Knut overslept, he would wake him by inserting the crook of his walking stick under his arm, and then jerking it swiftly upwards. He was made to work long hours keeping the books, helping on the farm, chopping wood, delivering mail, and quickly came to hate and fear his uncle. In later life he consistently claimed that he was underfed at Presteid, and that for five years he went to bed hungry every night, with the result that he became – according to his own diagnosis – a 'neurasthenic'. The short story *A Ghost*, published in 1898, eight years after Olsen's death, paints a compelling picture of his loneliness and unhappiness at the rectory in Presteid:

> Several years of my boyhood were spent with my uncle at the rectory in Nordland. It was a hard time for me, a lot of work, a lot of beating, with seldom if ever a free hour. My uncle controlled me so strictly that after a while the only recreation left to me was to steal away and be on my own. I would go off into the woods, or up to the churchyard, and wander between the crosses and gravestones, dreaming and thinking and talking out loud to myself.

Up here among the gravestones he one day finds a tooth which he slips into his pocket, intending to use it to decorate a wooden figure that he's carving. Then the ghost of the owner of the tooth begins to haunt him, a red-bearded seaman who appears at his bedroom window and stares at him. In fear the boy returns to the churchyard, and, hardly daring to return the tooth to the place indicated by the apparition gliding along in front of him, he throws it as hard as he can and runs back to the house. Still the red-bearded man haunts him, dominating his inner world and turning his daily life into a hell in which the only pleasant thought is of running down to the River Glimma at high tide and casting himself into the water. After a while he begins to acquire a harsh courage which enables him to meet the ghost's stare. One day it touches him on the forehead. He removes the hand, and orders it to leave. Finally the ghost appears before him and the boy notices that at last the tooth is in place again. The haunting ceases, but the marks of the experience remain with him:

> This man, this red-bearded messenger from the realm of the dead, with all the indescribable pain and unhappiness he

brought to my childhood, has done me much harm. Since then I
have had more than one vision, more than one encounter with
the strange and the inexplicable; but nothing has affected me as
he did. And perhaps after all it was not only harm that he did
me. I have often thought about this. It occurs to me that my
experiences with him led to my learning how to bite my lip, and
make myself hard. In later years I have sometimes needed to be
able to do this.

One may imagine that it was some years before Hamsun was
able to see his experiences in this light, and to forget the crude
harshness of his life with Olsen. On one occasion he tried to run
away, and was found half frozen to death on a neighbouring farm.
Later he deliberately hacked at his own leg with an axe while
chopping wood. He was put to bed, and his mother sent for, but
the desired result – to be allowed to go home – did not materialise.

More than anything he seems to have hated the loneliness and
isolation that his uncle's regime imposed on him. When he was not
working on the farm or in the office he would often be called upon
to read from the Bible to a small group, followers of the Stavanger
evangelist Lars Oftedal. In a series of newspaper articles from 1889
Hamsun savagely attacked Oftedal and his joyless pietism,
mingling his contempt with bitter personal memories of those
days:

The first impression of Lars Oftedal I have is in a strangely
intense way connected to a Sunday afternoon in my childhood.
A Sunday afternoon, with blue sky and still, still air. A spring
evening, with the black grouse calling in the east, and a great
yellow dog barking in the hills in the north, and a blood red sun
burning over the fjord in the west. I had looked forward so much
to that afternoon. Two boys from the farm next door stood
outside waiting for me to come out – but I had been ordered to
read. A new magazine had appeared in the house – the *Biblical
Messenger* – from Stavanger. Countless issues of it. I read
Oftedal. I sat in a small, hot room, with people in dark clothes,
people who had just come from church and now sat gloomy and
thoughtful, listening to the Holy Spirit calling in their hearts.
Directly in front of me stood a great black oven with terrifying
dragons on the doors, and this was the first time I'd ever noticed
anything unpleasant about these doors. Outside the light
streamed down, hectic and brilliant, from the Lofoten skies.
Sunlight coloured the pages under my fingers. At each full stop I
heard the grouse up in the hills. At the start of each new line I

saw the yellow dog farther and farther away. And each time I took up a new issue of the magazine I seemed to hear the voices of my friends, whispering so clearly my name, and I saw them creep forward and peer in through the windows. And there I had to sit.

I read. Seven people sat and listened to me. An hour passed. Two, three hours. . . . I read and read. It seemed endless. Big, harsh words which swelled in my mouth. Long, difficult sentences which left me gasping for breath, which buzzed around inside my head and then flew out into the room, echoing and bouncing off the walls. God, how that unknown man in Stavanger tormented me. I would not love him. I would never read his magazines when I grew up. He was a thick and dark and broad man who tormented flies when he was alone. God, how I detested him. He blocked out the sunlight . . .[5]

And when the boy is eventually allowed out, the sun has gone, and his friends have long disappeared. Presumably Hans Olsen meant well, but clearly, as Hamsun told Langfeldt and Ødegård, he had no idea how to treat children.

Knut derived other benefits from his years with his uncle besides the grimly appreciated power to be hard and to endure. For one thing, his close association with such an important man and with the mysteries of bookkeeping must have given him considerable status among his playmates. The relationship also provided him with a first taste of the world of books. The only reading matter at his parents' home had been the psalm-book and a couple of newspapers to which his father subscribed. At Uncle Hans' he had a whole local library at his disposal. Here he would have come across books by writers like P. A. Munch and Jacob Aall, the fairy-tales of the Grimm brothers, Bjørnstjerne Bjørnson's early stories of peasant life like *Synnøve Solbakken* and *Arne*, as well as books and magazines containing sentimental popular fiction.

The library also contained books on geography, natural history, and history, and it was from the history books he read that Hamsun received[6] an early and unpleasant impression of the English, which was to have important consequences for him in later life. Two incidents in particular seem to have struck him: he read of the bullying and arrogant way in which the English authorities had dealt with Norway in the so-called 'Bodø Case' of 1818. Here, a British export firm which had been carrying out large-scale smuggling operations in the Nordland town of Bodø made their escape by the use of violence when approached by the Norwegian authorities. Safely back in England, the firm then presented inflated claims for damages and loss to the Swedish government. The British government took up the firm's case, refusing to have any direct contact with the Norwegians at all, since Norway was a colony of the Swedish crown. The outcome of the discussions, which were carried on at cabinet level, was that the British smugglers were awarded a hefty sum in compensation for their 'losses' by an agreement of 1821. Nor was the injustice righted twelve years later, in 1833, when it came to light that the documents on which the claim for compensation had been based were forgeries which the smugglers had obtained with the assistance of a man who was then a police inspector in Glasgow.

The other incident from his reading which stuck in Hamsun's mind was the occasion in 1807 when a British fleet bombarded Copenhagen day and night for seventy-two hours, in an attempt to persuade the Danish government not to ally themselves with Napoleon. Hundreds of civilians were killed during the bombardment, and houses, public buildings, churches, and the University were extensively damaged. When the Danes eventually surrendered, it turned out that British suspicions of their intentions to join the French were quite unfounded.

The two incidents together were to form the basis for what was at first an idiosyncratic dislike, and finally a passionate and intense loathing for England and the English way of doing things.

His schooling also began in the same year that he moved to his uncle's, in January 1868. It was a primitive education, sporadically acquired: he was taught at a travelling school which made the rounds of isolated communities, setting up makeshift classrooms wherever there was room enough for them. The aim was sixty-nine days' schooling per child per year, but with the competing claims of farmwork on the children the goal was not always consistently achieved. Knut received just eleven days' schooling in his first year, was normally present for the next two years, and did not finish the final year. In 1872, at the age of thirteen, he went into full-time schooling, which lasted just under two years. His examination results for 18 September 1873, his last year at school, show the following marks: Bible History 2, Religious Instruction 2+, Reading 2, Writing 1½. This last mark, for handwriting, is the best mark gained for any subject, for any pupil, in the whole period of Hamsun's schooling, and he is the only one who has achieved it.[7] All his life he was proud of his handwriting, and there is a curious irony in the fact that it was precisely this talent which drew him to the attention of his uncle, and was the indirect cause of the unhappiness of his childhood. There is also something touching in the idea of an innocent connection forming in the boy's mind between the ability to write neatly and the ability to write well, to write expressively. There was, after all, no tradition of education in the Pedersen family, let alone any literary tradition.

Hamsun's will was always strong, and in spite of his tactics, Uncle Hans failed to subdue him as he had subdued others living and working with him. Hamsun's closest boyhood friend Georg Olsen recalled that Knut never seemed cowed or beaten, that he was on the contrary always good company, and liked to laugh a lot.

As Knut approached adolescence, a change seems to have taken place in the relationship with his uncle. Hans Olsen's sickness grew steadily worse. At times Knut would have to spoon-feed meals to him. But as his uncle grew weaker, his own strength increased. Soon he realised that his uncle's physical superiority over him was gone. Olsen realised it too, and tried another tactic to keep the boy in thrall. Knowing what an impressionable child he was, with a vivid imagination, he would detain him for hours on end with Oftedal-inspired visions of hell-fire and the torments of the sinful and the disobedient. They did indeed frighten Knut; but not enough. The boy began practising a dumb insolence. The relationship between Per på Bua and his son Theodor which Hamsun created in the novel *Segelfoss Town*, published in 1915, might give us some idea of how the two conducted themselves in the last few months before Knut finally left. Theodor does not rush from minding the store when he hears his crippled father's imperious rapping with his stick on the wooden floor above. He comes when he is ready, and listens unaffected to the ranting tirade of abuse he receives for not coming immediately, retaining the presence of mind to station himself in front of the window in the sensible belief that his father will not risk valuable glass by throwing something at him. Knut and Hans Olsen finally parted company in 1873, but the effect of those five years on Hamsun was to last throughout his life. One can see it perhaps in the almost pathological hatred for all forms of authority which characterises his behaviour until well into middle-age; and it is perhaps most noticeable of all in the way in which he treats the old and the crippled in his writing. Almost invariably they are objects of contempt and horrified disgust. At times he manages to restrict himself to a black humour which can be amusing; but just as often he overshoots the mark and his descriptions, like those of Mons and Fredrik Mensa in the novels *Benoni* and *Rosa*, border on the hysterical.

From Presteid, Knut returned for a while to the family home at

Hamsund. Vetltraein had died of nerve-fever in 1869, but the many tales he had told the boy of the glories of Lom lingered, and he felt a desire to revisit his birthplace. The restlessness which was to characterise him for the whole of his long life made its first appearance now as he sat down and composed a letter to his godfather Torstein Hestehagen, the proprietor of the village store. In reply he received a letter of welcome, and enough money to pay for the journey; in the autumn of 1873 he sailed, alone, on the steamboat from Presteid. He had just turned fourteen.

At Lom he lived with his godfather's family and worked in the store while studying for his confirmation. He seems not to have been a particularly diligent student, but had a notable power for improvising answers to the priest which somehow obscured the point of the question. He was big for his age, and strong, and a natural leader among the other boys. In one story from this time he appears in the uncharacteristic role of working-class champion. Boys from the neighbouring community of Fossbergom considered themselves a cut above the boys from Vardalen, Hamsun's friends, and accordingly always occupied the first benches in the confirmation classes. One day, before the priest arrived, Knut rolled up his sleeves and set about systematically dragging the Fossbergom boys from the benches; as soon as a place was vacant one of the Vardal boys would jump up and occupy it until presently the whole seating arrangement was reversed. Confirmation itself took place at Lom church on 4 October 1874. A photograph of Hamsun shows him wearing a special confirmation suit, staring off to the right of the camera with arms folded, his hair standing up in an enormous broken wave across his forehead. There is a tremendous obstinacy and firmness about the eyes and the set of the jaw. It is already the face of a man.

He was probably almost ungovernable in his new-found freedom. Within a year he and his godfather had fallen out, and Knut announced that he wanted to go back to Hamarøy. When Hestehagen refused either to let him go or to provide him with any money for the trip, he calmly produced the original letter of invitation from Lom in which his godfather categorically undertook to provide his fare back home if the boy was not content. Hestehagen conceded.

Back home in Hamarøy again, Knut found work in Walsøe's store in Tranøy, on the north side of the Hamarøy isthmus, about five miles from Hamsund. Tranøy was the busiest trading centre for miles around, and for the boy to work there was yet another rung up the social ladder. In the owner of the store, Walsøe, Hamsun encountered for the first time the patriarchal squire-figure who was to play such a decisive part both in his own personal fortunes and in his fiction. The Norwegian language had various names for such a man – 'enevoldskongen', 'matadoren', 'handelskongen', 'nessekongen'. He was a small-town aristocrat, the local squire, the financial power-centre, the great employer. Everyone was dependent on him, from the farmer to the fisherman. He equipped the fishermen and bought their catch from them, dried or salted it and packed it in barrels before sending it down the coast to Bergen. As often as not in Hamsun's fiction he exercised a kind of droit de seigneur over the local women, married or single.

As the junior assistant Knut was used mostly to do the fetching and carrying in Walsøe's store, but he was sometimes allowed to serve behind the counter, and on rare occasions even asked by Walsøe to help him with some bookwork. Like the other assistants he lived in, up on the second floor, and ate his meals with the family. He seems to have been popular with the adults, who were amused by his wit and his pretensions to maturity. A photograph of a family gathering outside the store at Tranøy shows him posing stylishly in a dark, three-piece suit – probably the confirmation suit made for him by his father a year earlier – with a fine watch chain slung across his waistcoat and a soft hat perched rakishly on his head. Again, his facial expression is oddly grim and determined for one so young. Sometimes the adults would tease him by asking him the time, obliging him to show forth the watchless chain and explain that he was still saving up for the watch. And like Johannes the miller's son in *Victoria*, he was already establishing a reputation among his friends for his interest in the macabre. A lifelong fondness for graveyards began at Presteid, and while at Tranøy he became fascinated by the phenomenon of delirium. A peasant boy was dying of typhus, and Knut used to visit him in his room for a short while each day, and listen to his wild speech and tormented psalm-singing.

A degree of mystery surrounds his departure from Tranøy in 1875, at the age of sixteen. It is usually believed to have been as a direct result of the fact that in the same year Walsøe went bankrupt and had to sell his store and release his staff. This seems a reasonable explanation, particularly in the light of Hamsun's later consistent use in his fiction of the bankruptcy of the 'enevoldskongen' as an event of shattering local importance. But there is a persistent local legend in Hamarøy that Knut and one of Walsøe's daughters, Laura, were sweethearts, and that Knut was actually fired by Walsøe in an attempt to break up an over-intense relationship. Certainly all of Hamsun's fiction shows a respectful awareness of the painful intensity of feeling of which children in love are capable. A short-story, *Carnations Small*, from 1912, stresses that 'adolescents, even children, can experience the strangest passion for one another'. Even more striking is the fact that Hamsun, in both of his first two attempts at fiction, chooses as his theme the love between a peasant and a princess, which is more or less how Walsøe might have regarded the relationship between his daughter and his cellar-boy. Most striking of all is that in the second of these two works, *Bjørger*, written in 1879, the eponymous hero of the tale falls in love with the daughter of 'enevolds-kongen' Moe, a girl who just happens to be called – Laura. The whole idea is aesthetically preferable to that of Knut's simply being laid off with all Walsøe's other workers on account of bankruptcy, but the truth of the matter cannot be known now. Nevertheless, Hamsun's fascination in all his early work, his juvenilia as well as his great novels of the 1890s, with the tragic fate of love which attempts to cross the barriers of social class might indicate a deep personal experience of the problem. Laura was long thought to have married a telegraphist and settled down to family life locally, information that stemmed from Hamsun himself. However, recent researches have shown that it was her sister who married. Laura, by a tragic irony which links her fate to that of the girl in *Bjørger*, really did die young, at the age of twenty-three, and lies buried in the churchyard at Tranøy.

There now follow two years in which information on Hamsun's activities is sparse, and subject to various conjectures. The only certainty is that not long after he left Walsøe and Tranøy, a man from his birthplace Lom came by, an older man named Ole Trykket, and that the two of them decided to pool their resources, invest in various small goods, and seek their fortunes as travelling pedlars. In one version of what follows, that of Hamsun's son Tore,[8] the two agreed that Hamsun would take the north and Ole Trykket the south, and arranged to meet again in Bodø to sort out their money and buy more goods. Hamsun begins travelling between Tromsø in the north and Helgeland in the south, and thrives. He and Ole Trykket meet for the great market at Stokmarknes, in the Lofoten Islands. They set up a stall selling everything from button thread to oilskins. Things go so well that for the first time Hamsun is able to send money home to his parents. He profits in experience too, moving in this fantastic world of conjurers and fortune-tellers, organ-grinders and watch-sellers. Here is the world of August and Edevart, the charlatan and the innocent abroad of the *August* trilogy (1927–1933), a world so extensively described in those books as to suggest long and intimate knowledge of it.

The version Hamsun gave to the psychiatrists Langfeldt and Ødegård is rather different.[9] He dismisses the period with the remark that it probably lasted no more than two months, that he was a poor salesman, and that he failed to make enough even to feed himself. Is Tore Hamsun creating after the fact of the *August* books, improvising slightly on the facts in order to arrange the years more neatly? Or had Hamsun, at eighty-seven, forgotten the details? After a lifetime of creating for himself alternative destinies and experiences hauntingly close to his own, the line between factual and fictional adventures may have become blurred. Particularly the early years of his life are characterised by an extreme restlessness, a wanderlust and a seeking out of new experiences which he often afterwards improvised on in his novels. Even when what he wrote was pure fiction, the intense subjectivity of his narrative technique persuaded many early commentators that what they were reading was autobiography.*

Hamsun's whole background was so thoroughly unlikely for a literary genius that anything could be, and indeed was, believed of him. And, naturally enough, in his later years of fame he did nothing to halt the spread of rumours of his dark exoticism. The lack of hard facts from this period is regrettable, for the appearance of his first prose effort in 1877 suggests that it was important and influential for him. The style and content of *The Enigmatic One*, mixing elements of sentimental popular fiction, fairy tales, and his own experiences, might hint at a compromise description of the period: that he spent a great deal of time sitting down reading the cheap, colporteur literature which, along with all the other goods he carried on his back, he was supposed to be peddling.

At some point around this time his parents seem to have felt that it was time for the boy to begin to show some sense of responsibility, which in their eyes meant learning a trade. Perhaps because he had so little daily contact with his father, Hamsun preserved a lifelong respect for him, and the aggression and rebellion which is so often the lot of the father of a headstrong boy with a strong sense of personal destiny was instead directed towards Hans Olsen and Torstein Hestehagen. Knut agreed to his parents' suggestion, and was dutifully apprenticed to a shoemaker called Bjørnsen who lived in Bodø. Bjørnsen was a distant relative of his father's, and an old family friend. Here he was one of a staff of eleven or twelve

---

* Early biographers commonly – and quite erroneously – described him as having worked for three years on a fishing boat off the coast of Newfoundland, solely on the evidence of his first-person short story *On the Banks*, published in 1891.

men, and in the usual course of events he would have spent a six-month period on trial, before proceeding to an apprenticeship proper, lasting five years. Bjørnsen recalled him as a pleasant, capable youth and a conscientious worker. He was not given to chatter, and did not attempt to cultivate the friendship of the other apprentices, but kept himself to himself.[10] The years since Hans Olsen had given him a taste for independence, which made the daily routine of apprenticeship and the submission to a master difficult. Additionally, one might imagine that he did not share his father's faith in the usefulness of a trade – after all, his own trade of tailor had scarcely provided enough to support the Pedersen family. After just four months' shoemaking he left, and found work in a shop again. He liked the sense of life there; of being at the heart of a community, with plenty of coming and going, plenty of gossip and rumour. There was something that appealed to his sense of the exotic about working in a place that sold absolutely *everything*, from coffee to women's knickers, as these stores were obliged to. He was to work in shops again on both of his trips to America in the 1880s, and in the novels of his old age, the trilogy about August the wanderer, it is the local store which functions as a kind of fixed point around which the fragmentary plotting of the tales whirls.

When Knut's parents found out that he had abandoned his apprenticeship, they renewed their appeals to him to become respectable and settle down. He travelled to the Lofoten Islands, and there came into contact with the priest at Bø, on Langøy, August Weenaas. Weenaas was responsible for the administration of schooling in the area, and in spite of Hamsun's youth he was impressed by his idiosyncratically extensive learning, and gave him a job as a teacher at the local school in Hjørundfjord.[11] This was a mark of great faith on the part of Weenaas, and Hamsun never forgot him for it. Without money and social status, he was totally dependent on such gestures.

As a teacher at the Hjørundfjord school he had a class of seven or eight pupils of about eight years of age. According to a former pupil, he was an unusual, popular and entertaining teacher who preferred to stimulate his charges' imaginative powers with strange and exciting tales rather than drill them in their ABC. He dispensed his own eccentrically beautiful versions of geography and history, and told the children about Africa, and the negroes there, whom he called the best people on God's green earth. When directly challenged as to the source of this information since he had never been to Africa, he replied that, on the contrary, he travelled to Africa every night in his dreams. Children do not easily forget such breathtakingly logical answers. He also introduced the study of botany, and took them out on field trips on which he showed them and named for them all the plants that grew wild there – giving them their local names, of course, not their Latin names. He also painted at this time, landscapes usually, which he gave away to people whom he liked. Weenaas gave him a testimonial, dated 27 November, 1878:

> Hr Knut Pedersen has been employed for about a year as acting teacher in the travelling school in Bø, and in this post he has fulfilled his duties to the complete satisfaction of all. He combines considerable ability in the arts of writing with punctuality, sobriety, and conscientiousness, and I can safely recommend him for that post for which he now wishes to apply.[12]

The clerical skills which Hans had beaten into him now stood him in good stead. After his year schoolteaching he applied for and got a job at Bø as assistant to town clerk Nordahl. He developed a good relationship with Nordahl, and with his daughter Inger. The town clerk was a literary man, with his own library, something of a rarity in those parts and in those times, and Hamsun was allowed free access to the books there. Here he would have seen the works of the great Norwegian poets Wergeland and J. S. Welhaven, as well as the folk-tales gathered by the collectors Asbjørnson and Moe. He might have seen Ibsen's verse dramas *Brand* and *Peer Gynt*, as well as the classics of antiquity. Certainly he read Bjørnson here again, and a book by a follower of Bjørnson's, Kristofer Janson, entitled *Torgrim*, which made a powerful impact on him. The process of self-education through familiarity with the world of books, begun at Hans Olsen's, continued here.

These were the years of Hamsun's first literary efforts, a kind of mini-career he pursued, which spanned a three-year period before fizzling out into ten years of tough anonymity. The first of the three publications involved appeared when he was eighteen years old. Called *The Enigmatic One*, it was published in the northern town of Trømso by a rather roguish publisher named Mikkel Urdal. The book had a subtitle – 'A Love Story From Nordland' – and the author styled himself Kn. Pedersen. Already in that rather unnatural abbreviation of his christian name is a hint of the almost mystical belief Hamsun had in the importance of names. In the thirteen years that were to elapse between the publication of this novella in 1877, and the appearance of *Hunger* in 1890, a constant feature is the experimenting with a bewildering variety of names, and permutations of forms of his own name.

The story itself is banal, a child's attempt to reproduce the popular sentimental fiction of the time. Nevertheless, it contains in essence the seeds of some of Hamsun's most fruitful developments. In thirty-one pages and eight short chapters it tells the story of a 'husmann', a member of the lowest class of Norwegian peasant society, who appears one day with his father in a strange town. The boy's name is Rolf Andersen, and shortly after their arrival in town the boy's father dies. He gets a job working on the farm of the richest man in the area, Ole Aae. Ole has a daughter Rønnaug, aged fifteen, and she and Rolf fall in love. This all seems fairly straightforward and conventional, until it gradually begins to emerge that Rolf is something other and more than he seems to be. The dialect in which he speaks, for example, seems to be some form of disguise. There are times when it slips, and when he suddenly begins speaking in the well-modulated tones of a rich, educated boy from the big town. The beauty of his handwriting, too, astonishes Ole Aae. Finally the whole truth emerges, that Rolf is not a simple peasant boy after all. His real name is not even Rolf Andersen, but Knut Sonnenfeld, an altogether more rarefied name. Nor is he even really poor, but the inheritor of a large secret fortune from his dead father. Ole Aae's initial opposition to the affair dissolves in the face of this. He gives the lovers his blessing, and they marry and travel to the city, where Knut becomes a successful businessman. Here, in this crude, adolescent caricature of a man who is not quite what he seems to be, we meet the original of the hero of Hamsun's greatest novels, *Pan*'s Lieutenant Glahn, Johan Nilsson Nagel from *Mysteries*, and the writer Johannes from *Victoria*.

The Enigmatic One was probably sold as colporteur literature, the kind of book Hamsun himself might have sold during his brief career as a pedlar. No records exist of its sales, but they can't have been terribly encouraging: Urdal was said to have tried to get rid of remaindered copies of the book by wrapping them in paper and selling them as 'surprise packs'.[13]

In the following year, 1878, Hamsun persuaded a Bodø publisher, A. F. Knudsen, to print his poem *A Reconciliation*. This time he chose to style himself Knud Pedersen Hamsund, following a Norwegian tradition of assuming one's place of origin within one's name when away from home. This poem is undoubtedly the strangest of Hamsun's adolescent literary efforts, and its publication perhaps more than anything else a tribute to his powers of persuasion. In the course of the poem we learn of an old German hermit living in a cave on the coast of Norway. He is half-mad with guilt for having murdered his lover long ago. Now a great storm rises up, and the body of a young woman is washed ashore. He rescues and revives her, and thereby atones for his crime. Seventy years later, in 1950, the Norwegian Eli Krog was editing a book of the first published efforts of a number of well-known Norwegian authors. In his reply to her enquiry, Hamsun named a poem *The Secret Island* as his first publication, but was unable to provide a copy of this, nor suggest where one might be found. The old man, then ninety-one years of age, perhaps made a mistake, and was actually referring to *A Reconciliation*. Yet Hamsun wrote and wandered so much in his youth that it is not impossible that a local newspaper from one of the many towns he passed through has *The Secret Island* printed on one of its pages.

Knudsen of Bodø was again responsible for the printing of Hamsun's next work, the short novel *Bjørger*, but this time the title page bears the words 'Published Privately', indicating that Hamsun himself had had to pay for the publication. Knudsen probably regretted his investment in *A Reconciliation*, and the two came to an arrangement whereby 1200 copies of *Bjørger* were printed, of which 300 copies went to Hamsun as his fee, the remaining 900 copies being Knudsen's fee and his profit. The book did not sell well, and the bulk of the edition went in the end to a travelling pedlar for ten øre per copy.

Bjørger, from 1878, although distinctly juvenilia, is an altogether different proposition from both the previous works. It runs to a respectable 124 pages, and is written clearly and patiently, with here and there flashes of the highly distinctive style Hamsun was to bring to maturity in *Hunger* twelve years later. In form and content it bears witness to the extent of the influence of two writers on him during this early period, both of whom he was later to meet personally – Kristofer Janson, and Bjørnstjerne Bjørnson.

Bjørnson (1832–1910) is now largely forgotten outside Norway. A writer of plays, poems, novels and short stories, and an inveterate and inexhaustible polemicist, he is a figure in many ways dearer to Norwegians than Ibsen, who lived most of his life abroad, and is the property of the world rather than of any particular nation. Unlike the shy and taciturn Ibsen, Bjørnson was a visible and dramatic figure, a passionate orator who threw himself into the cultural and moral debates of his society. From the very first, he was Hamsun's ideal, initially as literary stylist, and later as public man. His peasant tales such as *Arne* and *A Happy Boy* introduced a new genre and a new hero into Norwegian literature. They introduced a new style too; the short, lapidary sentences which Bjørnson revived from the language of the Old Norse sagas. It is curious to think how it was the almost forgotten Bjørnson who introduced

Hamsun to a style which he studied, and refined, and took to such heights of mastery that the young Ernest Hemingway apprenticed himself to him, and thus introduced into American literature that 'hard-boiled' quality which Raymond Chandler and Dashiel Hammett, for example, were to exploit so successfully.*

Bjørger is the eponymous hero of the tale, a peasant boy who, with his brother Thor, is taken in by foster parents after his mother dies and his father commits suicide. Thor, the elder brother, is unbalanced by the tragedy and runs away to the mountains to become a hermit. Bjørger finds work in the local store, and he and a girl called Laura, daughter of the store's rich owner, fall in love. But the progress of this affair is far from the untroubled fairy-tale cliché of *The Enigmatic One*. Already in the relationship which develops, that element of doomed coquetry appears, the helpless crossing and recrossing of the borders between harmless flirtation and psychic war which characterises even the mature Hamsun's view of sexual love. *Bjørger* contains his first description of this intellectual perversion of spontaneous love which finds its most vivid expression in *Pan*. The impossible situation is resolved when Laura dies in Bjørger's arms. The theme obsessed Hamsun, and he returned to it again and again in novels, short stories and plays. The novel *Victoria*, written when he was thirty-nine, is effectively a mature restatement of *Bjørger*. Another interesting link between the young and the mature artist can be found in his treatment of the two brothers. Thor and Bjørger have many qualities in common: both find solace in being alone; both are given to brooding; both feel a need to write down their thoughts. Even at nineteen years of age, Hamsun seems to have made the fairly sophisticated literary attempt to describe different sides of the same character by splitting him in two.

Hamsun was always disparaging about these early works. In the foreword to a facsimile edition of *The Enigmatic One* published in 1959, the head of the Gyldendal publishing house, Harald Grieg, quoted part of a letter Hamsun once sent to him about them:

> I would never have published things like *A Reconciliation*, *The Enigmatic One*, and *Bjørger* if it had not been each time to show my brothers and sisters that they should not mock me. I wrote

* Hamsun's publisher Harald Grieg met Ernest Hemingway in Cuba, and asked him what he thought of Arthur Koestler's observation that there was much of Hamsun to be found in Hemingway. Hemingway replied that this was undoubtedly true, Hamsun was one of the writers to whom he was most deeply indebted.[14] And in Hemingway's short story *Summer People*, Nick Adams speaks of his desire to 'write like Hardy and Hamsun'.

none of these things at home, but sent them all proudly back to Hamarøy afterwards.

All three books were comprehensively overlooked at the time, being treated and marketed as colporteur literature. Both *The Enigmatic One* and *Bjørger* were listed in the Norwegian Catalogue of Books in Print 1873–1882, although the compiler, Feilberg, lists them separately, and was unaware that Kn. Pedersen and Knud Pedersen Hamsund were one and the same person.

Hamsun was an exceptional case of a man obsessed by the desire to be a writer, and in looking for hints as to what it was that gave him the fanatic courage and endurance to hold out over the next ten years, until he achieved a real breakthrough, one must take into account this mini-career of his (which was not quite over yet) and the fact that at the early age of eighteen he had held in his hands a book with his own name on the cover. For a young writer, the psychological value of this would be priceless, and the experience, repeated three times in the course of two years, perhaps encouraged him in the belief that he could go all the way.

Greatly encouraged by his own successes, it seemed to him that the time was now ripe for him to make his assault on the wider literary world outside Nordland. He needed money to do this effectively, and, having none, he did what many another ambitious Nordland peasant boy before him had done, and wrote a letter to the most powerful 'enevoldskongen' of the whole county, Erasmus Benedikter Kjerschov Zahl. He put on his best prose style for the occasion:

Hrr Zahl, Kjerringøy, Folden.

With the deepest respect I venture to ask you to read the following: as a twenty-year-old youth, though not born with a silver spoon in my mouth, and with no more than ordinary schooling, I have nevertheless, through a course of rigorous self-instruction, and with outstanding abilities which can be testified to by those authorities before whom I have submitted work, brought my soul, thirsting for knowledge, a little further than that of others as equally without means as myself. I have also as a writer, in the domain of literature, which in the opinion of many is my mission in life, won a name as the author of the book *Bjørger*, and of the collection of poems *Sverdgny*. The former was published in the provincial town of Bodø last Christmas, and has been lavishly praised in a Danish magazine, by an anonymous critic. His only regret about the book was that it was published in Bodø, and not by one of the country's largest publishers. *Sverdgny* has not been published yet, but it has been read in manuscript form by a respected and discerning critic here, who is sufficiently impressed by it to recommend unconditionally and immediately a trip to Copenhagen to the largest bookdealer and publisher (Gyldendal or F. Hegel) to arrange the printing and presentation to the public of the above-mentioned poems. Now, as a twenty-year-old, without material advantages, I lack the resources for such a trip, and I therefore, in the name of art and progress, implore you, hrr Zahl, as the greatest businessman in Nordland, for the gracious loan of 1600.00 – sixteen hundred kroner (£88) – against the guarantee of a life assurance policy with the Idun Assurance Company worth 2000.00 – two thousand kroner. That you in lending a helping hand on this occasion to a poor but upward-striving person do not run any risk in the light of this guarantee I venture to confirm thus: that as soon as I have sold my book, I will repay you, and that if I should die in the meantime, you have merely to cash in the policy to the appropriate sum. Should you require me to travel personally to Kjerringøy, I would be only too pleased to do so, since I have often heard you spoken of as a patronising and humane man, to whom even the most wretched might apply. If, that is, I can be spared from the office where I am now working. In any case, I feel it is right that I do this, bringing with me confirmation of the statements made here. If you wish, I will send you a copy of *Bjørger*.

I respectfully await your decisive reply in this matter; I shall await it with a keen longing, and put my faith in the belief that a helping hand extended at the right time brings happiness, and a joy that lasts forever.

Bø, Vesterålen, 26.april 1879,

> sincerely,
> Knud Pedersen Hamsund.

This was a prodigious amount of money Hamsun was asking for, something like three times the annual wage he would have been receiving at Nordahl's office. But he had chosen his man well. Zahl, a multi-millionaire by modern standards, had arrived in Kjerringøy in 1846, twenty years old, owning little more than the clothes he stood up in. By dint of hard work, good business acumen, and by marrying his boss' widow, he had built up a personal fortune so extensive that debts for 200,000 kroner were wiped out while he lived, and for a further 50,000 when he died. Hamsun's letter, which came to light in the Nordland County Archive in 1977, bears Zahl's footnote:

Answered 1.5.79 and promised him 1600 kroner.[15]

Chapter 2

1879–1882: Bjørnson and the End of the Mini-Career

With this exchange of letters there begins an interlude in Hamsun's life which lasts just over a year and which has, save for its outcome, all the ingredients of a fairy-tale.

Hamsun himself seems to have experienced the events which followed on his contact with Zahl with a strong sense of their unreality, and at times seems to act and write as though he were a character in a story rather than an independent being. His next contact with Zahl suggests that from the outset he sensed that his personal fortunes were in some intimate way involved in the larger, impersonal flowing of fate: he chose to write it on Norwegian National Day, 17 May, a day of great patriotic significance, and since the brief and passionate career of the poet and nationalist Henrik Wergeland (1808–1845), one with curiously strong literary associations in the public mind. It was perhaps a hint to the patriarch Zahl that in supporting the aspiring writer he was also showing his faith in the future of his country:

(Bø, Vesterålen, 17 May 1879)
Dear Hr. K. Zahl,
Receipt of your of its kind extravagant, rare, and for my future profession so decisive written answer of the 1st is hereby confirmed, in spite of the fact that I can hardly believe my eyes, nor fully grasp the implications of its contents. I have, however, recapitulated the letter repeatedly and have, originally having doubted the possibility of my application succeeding, finally achieved sufficient clear-headedness to proclaim you a rare and generous spirit of the most superior sort. These thanks, which I have not yet personally extended to you, I do hereby in ardent gratitude lay before your throne.

Immediately on receipt of your letter I began to fill out the application forms for the life insurance policy, and have today been examined by the doctor who is responsible for filling out the so-called 'Confidential Declaration By A Doctor', and he finds the strongest possible grounds for recommending me for acceptance. The application has been sent off, but I cannot expect the policy to arrive for another three weeks or a month yet, when the declarations on the various applications are checked, according to the company's regulations, by their medical superintendent Professor Hjalmar Heiberg, Christiania.

In the meantime my employer's young daughter is to travel to Namsos in *c.* fourteen days' time (that is, early in June), and her parents have asked me to accompany her part of the way south. Although there is no question of any relationship between the daughter and myself, a refusal here would undoubtedly be interpreted as an affront to my employer, to whom I owe gratitude, in addition to the performance of my duties. Therefore I am obliged, in spite of consequent fisculary loss, to go along with the said suggestion.

My real purpose in writing is to enquire whether you, herr Zahl, will allow me in *c.* fourteen days' time to visit you, not bringing with me the life-insurance policy, inasmuch as this is not expected to arrive for a month yet, but with a declaration from the company's agent to the effect that I am indeed an applicant for a policy with 'Idun' on my life to the value of 2000.00, and inasmuch as the agent, who is also the bailiff, guarantees that the policy will be forwarded to you as soon as it arrives. My aim is to economise on the cost of travel, and I hope that you will acquiesce in my suggestion, so that I may receive and receipt the agreed 1600.00 which you, alone in the face of the majority's hostility towards me, have, with your fatherly helping hand, in my hour of need, offered me.

I presume with due humility and respect to request you, herr Zahl, to give me your answer at the first available opportunity. And when I have the honour and pleasure of thanking you in person, as much for the faith already shown in me as for the trouble gone to on my account, I shall bring a copy of *Bjørger* with me, as well as a number of references which it might please you to read.

yours faithfully,
Knud Pedersen Hamsund.

He adds a postscript: 'My condolent sympathies to you, Herr Zahl, on the death of your wife.'

If Zahl had ever entertained any doubts about the wisdom of sponsoring the youthful Hamsun quite so extravagantly, this letter must surely have terrified him into submission. A receipt for 5 June 1879 shows that the visit took place and that the money was duly handed over. Hamsun promised to pay Zahl back, and then returned to Bø to prepare for his trip to Copenhagen, and for the succeeding inevitabilities of the fairy-tale: the publication of his manuscript, fame, wealth, the princess and half the kingdom.

But now Hamsun did a slightly curious thing. Having said goodbye to his parents, whom he was not to see again for over twenty years, instead of travelling to Copenhagen he made his way to a small coastal town on the Hardanger fjord, called Øystese, and settled there for a few months. In answer to an enquiry from his publisher Harald Grieg in 1934, he said that it was the romantic picture of the area created by Wergeland in his poems that had decided him on Hardanger. He may also have recalled conversations with certain Hardanger skippers who used the fish-drying grounds up in Hamarøy, particularly one skipper, Knut Aga, who worked there for three years in the early 1870s. Most of the Pedersen family did casual work for him in the drying season, including Knut, who would have picked up a vivid impression of the Hardanger area from his talk.[1]

There may have been other reasons why Hamsun did not wish to go directly to Copenhagen. Perhaps the collection of poems *Sverdgny*, mentioned with such breezy confidence in the first letter to Zahl, did not exist in quite the finished form that he had led people to believe. Or possibly there was a slight failure of nerve at the last minute, a feeling that he was still not quite ready for the awe-inspiring step he believed he was about to take, from self-taught peasant boy to professional writer. For Hamsun, being a writer was not simply about the physical act of putting words on paper; it involved a whole way of being, a way of speaking and acting and dressing, a complete commitment to a role. He might have felt that his interpretation of this social side of the role was still far from satisfactory, and that he needed to put in some practice in the decent obscurity of Øystese before he was ready for the larger stage of Copenhagen.

Certainly his behaviour at Øystese suggests that he was trying very hard to make an impression. Having rented a room in the house of a Captain Flatabø, he set about the difficult business of reinventing himself; bought expensive new clothes, took to wearing a lorgnette, and smoked a superior brand of tobacco. He paid for grammar lessons, and invested in costly books. The experimenting with various forms of his name continued too, as he searched for his identity. To Zahl he had been both Knud Pedersen Hamsund and Knud Pedersen before the move to Øystese. After the move he became Knut Pedersen, the *t* and *o* replacing the *d* and *e* to give his name a more specifically Norwegian rather than Danish sound and appearance. A name had for Hamsun a kind of potential, a magical power quite independent of its banal function as label – as indeed words themselves did – and he exercised as much care in the choice of his own name as he did in the choice of names for his fictional characters.

Hamsun continued to work while at Captain Flatabø's, dividing his time between poetry and a book for which he had great hopes, called *Frida*. He also took a first step into journalism, and casually started a fierce newspaper debate which lasted for two months in the pages of the *Søndre Bergenhus Folkeblad*. His subject was the quality of the psalm-singing in the two local churches at Øystese and Vikøy.

The first of Hamsun's two letters appeared in the newspaper on 28 August. In it he expressed surprise at the lack of an organised choir in the parish, which was the more to be regretted in view of the fact that neither church possessed an organ. He then went on to criticise the singing style of the congregation, which he described as 'wild'. The blame for this he laid squarely at the feet of the schoolteachers, the church elders, and what he called the 'decrepit old farmers' who ran the town, and who insisted on singing the psalms to traditional, local melodies instead of in the style of Lindeman (as they do at home in Hamarøy, he might have added, but did not). He claimed to have tried to sing the psalms 'correctly' only to find himself the object of 'idiotic stares'. To save embarrassment all round he had resorted in the end to speaking them. In concluding he quoted the Roman proverb *Abusus non tollit sum*, and piously hoped that God would arrange a satisfactory solution to the problem.

It would be nice to think that the whole thing was no more than an irreverent practical joke, and that Hamsun was chortling away to himself at his own pomposity. However, this kind of subtlety was to come later, and his interest in the psalms was perfectly genuine. The psalm book had been his earliest experience of reading, since it was the only book in his father's house at Hamsund, and he continued to take an active interest in the successive revisions of it for the rest of his life. The editor of the *Folkeblad* knew good copy when he saw it, and put the letter on the front page with a footnote in which he wrote that, 'for obvious reasons', he had omitted the Latin quotations with which the young writer had 'armed' his piece. The readers did the rest, and letters came in attacking Hamsun furiously as big-headed, know-all and naïve.

The fury of the attacks was probably no more than he expected, but one which might have impressed him was a drily witty response from Jon Skaar, brother of the editor Nils, in which he mocked the author's cockiness and his 'book-learning', and added that 'when a learned man has spoken thus to us, should we presume to doubt any longer?' This was precisely the kind of folksy, cunning use of intelligence that Hamsun himself came to prize as he grew older. His reply to his critics in a letter of 9 October was calm, and he maintained that his criticisms had been sincerely meant, and that personal attacks on him were beside the point. The whole episode was a curiously prophetic example of Hamsun's talent for arousing opposition to his personality, and is in a way a tribute to that obstinate courage and faith in himself which shored him up in the years of disappointment and hardship that lay ahead of him. At the end of *An Enemy of the People*, Ibsen's Dr Stockmann declares the strongest man in the world to be, 'the man who stands most alone'. Hamsun had, and tested, this strength throughout his life. It was a kind of obsession with him, a psychic need which removed him ever further, and finally fatally far, from the people around him. Of his five opponents in the debate, only one had signed his name.

He had a sweetheart in Østensjø, a girl called Marta Flatabø for whom he bought presents, and complimented sweetly. He told her once that there was 'sunshine in her face', and she never forgot him for it. Compliments were perhaps as far as he went with her – another girl who went out with him during fairs week at Stokmarknes recalled that the young Knut had given her a dress, and taken her into the woods with him. There he simply sat and brushed straw off his clothes. 'He was a real dry fish when it came to lovemaking and stuff like that', she said. Hamsun was probably too preoccupied with *Frida* to pay much more attention to Marta.[2]

As work continued on the new book, Hamsun soon found that he was in need of more money. A couple of days before his first letter to the *Søndre Bergenhus Folkeblad*, he had received a letter from Zahl, and on 20 September he wrote to thank him, and to try to arrange for more money:

In writing to you now it is first of all to thank you for your friendly letter of the 26th of last month which has relieved me in

several ways, above all in leading me to feel that I have in you a
father and a protector whose goodwill towards me has in no way
weakened. And secondly – (Oh please, do not lose patience, I
shall never trouble you again!) – *I ask you for 400 kroner.* My book
is almost finished now, and soon I shall travel to Copenhagen
where I expect to get it published together with my poems – and
then I will pay you back first of all these 400 kroner – Yes, believe
me, Hrr Zahl! I shall pay you back then. I would not lie to you for
anything in the world, you who have shown such faith in me,
and just as surely as I sent my life-insurance policy to you, so
shall I keep my promise to you.

I will tell you how I have used the monies earlier received from
you, if you wish, and you will see from this that I have not let you
down at all. They have been used to provide the necessities of
life for me, and to give a helping hand to my dear, grey-haired
parents of whom I am so very fond. As I say, if you would like a
detailed account of my expenditure then you may have one,
since I have kept a record of everything.

Now that everything is finally organised, now, that is, that I
have got the books which I as a writer need, these being neither
few in number, nor cheap, and the clothes, as well as the
grammar lessons, now that all this is organised it means that I
have no other outgoing than the cost of my keep, which is forty
kroner a month – oh how much, how very much you help me!

When you shook my hand, and allowed me so feebly to thank
you for the best I have yet encountered among people, at the
same time you led me to hope that I might on a later occasion also
count on your help. When I ask now, it is because I am driven by
need, and I put my faith in that hope you gave me at the moment
of our parting.

And in promising you never again to ask for money from you,
but from now on only advice, and to pay you back at the earliest
opportunity, Oh Zahl! – I wait with hope, wait, in the name of
Jesus!

Your son in spirit and hope,
Knut Pederson.

Yet again this shameless mixture of boldness, innocence and
sentimentality struck a chord with Zahl, and a month later the 400
kroner were telegraphed through from Kjerringøy to Øystese.
One wonders whether Zahl was really taken in by these letters of
Hamsun's, or whether he simply liked him, and having once
decided to sponsor him would continue to do so, come what may.
That Hamsun could write a simple, straightforward and effective

prose is evident from many passages in *Bjørger*; but there was something in the relationship with Zahl that seemed to draw him back into the world of *The Enigmatic One* of 1877 and the role of a Rolf Andersen, intent on proving that he was in reality Knud Sonnenfeld.

Hamsun could quite well have tried to get his book published in Norway – an independent Norwegian publisher, Aschehoug, had been in existence in Christiania since 1872 – but cultural snobbery determined that books published in Norway would not be read by the people who counted. Additionally the four most famous and influential Norwegian writers of the time, Ibsen, Bjørnson, Kielland and Jonas Lie, were all published by the Danish firm, Gyldendal, and it was to the company's offices on Klareboderne, Number 3, that Hamsun travelled, probably some time in November 1879. One might imagine that there were many among the Øystese inhabitants who wished him a hearty tumble at the end of his long journey.

The head of Gyldendal in those days was Frederick Hegel, a dapper, small-featured man with a slightly clerical air about him who received Hamsun's manuscript personally, and told him to come back the following day for a decision. How Hamsun spent the day and the night on this first visit to Copenhagen we don't know. Perhaps he drank in a café, or visited a museum, or spent time looking round a bookshop. Copenhagen was the artistic centre of Scandinavia, and close enough to Munich, Berlin and Paris to absorb and reflect their cultural influences – for Hamsun simply to *be* there at the age of twenty would have been occupation enough.

When he returned to Klareboderne the following day the same Hegel handed his manuscript package to him with the letter 'P' written in one corner. This stood for 'Pederson', and meant that Gyldendal were not interested in publishing the book. Hamsun heard Hegel make some ironic passing reference to Bjørnson's wealth – a new edition of his play *The New System* was about to be published – and then he was out in the street again, with *Frida* still in his hands.[3]

A disappointment is not always necessarily a surprise, but whatever else Hamsun felt, the disappointment – after all the effort that had gone into the construction of his extensive dream – must have been great. He went looking for a second opinion, and visited Andreas Munch. Munch was a hero of the old national-romantic movement, and in the 1850s and '60s, in the lacuna between Wergeland and Welhaven, and Ibsen and Bjørnson, was probably the best of the Norwegian poets. He was part of the extensive colony of Norwegian exiles living in Copenhagen. In the next of his reports to Zahl, Hamsun describes the results of this visit.

Copenhagen. 2 January 1880. Herr K. Zahl, Kjerringøy, Salten:

After having been here in Copenhagen for about one month I feel it my duty to inform you, my patron and my benefactor, that I have unfortunately not at this particular time of the year been able to get my book published. Most recently it has been read by Baron Munch, who has given me the following recommend-ation: 'After having read hrr Knut Pederson's story *Frida*, I would like to recommend this young author as a man of considerable literary ability' etc etc. The fact of the matter is, that my writing is somewhat along the lines of Bjørnson's, and just at the moment Bjørnson has no friends, only enemies, here in Copenhagen. Now I shall send my manuscript to Christiania and present it for publication there. As a matter of fact I am convinced it will be published there, a view which also hrr Munch (professor) has expressed. Book sales are at their strongest here in the spring, and I have come at an unfortunate time. But I did not know this before I came.

Now I am afraid it looks as though I have no positive economic results to show for my trip here. But as soon as I have settled down again I intend to write a few character sketches of some of the people I have met on my journey. As I say, I have no tangible and direct results from this trip to Copenhagen. But on the other hand I have collected enough material to keep me writing for at least a year, and I have acquired a much greater insight into people, and a wider perspective on life in all manner of new directions. This will naturally be of use to me in my future career as a writer, if I live long enough to carry on with it, my one, my only delight. Similarly I have acquired a little knowledge of the stage, and have been studying the theatre world here. As a Norwegian author, I have been allowed in free to performances. I am quite satisfied with all this, and could I but feel sure that you, hrr Zahl, will be understanding with me a little longer, then I will show you that with God's help I shall go on to greater things than this. I was convinced that I would not leave here without having paid you back at least the 400 kroner you gave me. Now that hope must be abandoned. But if you wait awhile, you will not be disappointed – I will sell my books back, if necessary, so that I can pay you at least something. In the meantime good luck, good health, and a Happy New Year,

Do not lose faith in yours sincerely,
Knut Pederson.[4]

The style of this letter is quite different from that of previous correspondence with Zahl. The cocky, baroque quirks are gone, and real, recognisable feelings are conveyed. And behind the disappointment one senses that stubbornness and that refusal to be broken by reversal, which together make up one of the most important and impressive sides of Hamsun's personality.

He did not linger in Copenhagen. Shortly after writing to Zahl he returned, with the manuscript of *Frida*, to Norway. Not content with the judgements of Hegel and Andreas Munch, he had decided to submit his book to the highest authority he knew of.

Munch's comparison of his style with Bjørnson's, perhaps intended as a gentle hint, may only have served to flatter Hamsun. By means of a dramatic, upswept hairstyle he was already practising a physical impersonation of his idol as well as a literary one, and was not displeased to be occasionally taken for an illegitimate son of Bjørnson's. It was to Bjørnson's mansion at Aulestad that he now travelled, journeying much of the way on foot.

Perhaps the thought of meeting his idol in person was too much for him, or perhaps, as he said later, he slipped on the ice on Bjørnson's front-door step; whatever it was, the maid thought he was drunk when he arrived, and told him to go away. Bjørnson, anyway, had company, and Hamsun had to spend the night on a neighbouring farm. The next day he returned, again with *Frida*, and this time was admitted. The tension must have been considerable as he waited and watched Bjørnson flipping through the pages of his book. The ideal response, of course, would have been for him to stop suddenly, arrested by some small, devastating turn of phrase, and begin to read the book line by line, page by page, sitting down, forgetting the passage of time, and some hours later closing it with a profound look on his face. Of course, he merely flipped through the book as fast as he decently could and with that insensitivity somehow curiously characteristic of 'great men', suggested that a tall, good-looking young man like Hamsun ought to be a natural for the stage. He gave him a letter of personal recommendation to his friend, the Christiania actor Jens Selmer, and that was the end of that, apart from a handshake and an admonition not to hesitate to seek help again should he need it.

It gives some indication of the esteem in which the young Hamsun held Bjørnson that he did not take the rejection personally, and as a lesser spirit might have done sourly console himself by rejecting the hero who had rejected him. Instead, he returned to Christiania and, against his own better judgement, began to take acting lessons. He lodged at Tomtegaten II (ie eleven) in the slum district of Vaterland, near the docks and the railway station, where his landlord was a hair-buyer named Werschowski. The hero of *Hunger* also lives at Tomtegaten II, and this winter of 1880 sees the beginning of that life and those wretched experiences which Hamsun was later to use as the raw material for his novel.

On 24 January 1880 he wrote a tactful letter to Bjørnson describing his progress as an actor:

When we parted company you were kind enough to give me permission to apply to you again should I encounter any great difficulties in my planned stage-career. And although I know full well that you are a very busy man, I do ask you once again for your help, this time in the form of a letter of recommendation to one of your acquaintances in Christiania. For your use and information I append references.

Selmer was extremely kind to me, and told me what he thought quite candidly. This he did by pointing out to me those particular qualities which would seem to make it clear that I am not, after all, 'called to the stage'. He realised, of course, that I am not really cut out for the theatre. He then advised me to find some paid work which would enable me to afford to go to the theatre, so that I could then find out for myself whether I really wanted to be an actor with all my heart.

On Selmer's advice I then went to see the editor Wullum and asked for a job. He replied that he did not have a job for me, and furthermore that it seemed more suitable to him for me to apply to the manager of the theatre, since my interests lay in this direction – and so on and so on. But in this particular play, it seems to me that Selmer knows his lines best.

Things are a little tight for me at the moment; it is all in any event a very different story now from that evening I spent in the Café 'Hell' in Copenhagen – I drank the landlady's health twice, and called her mon cher ami!

If you could help me to get some job or other, hr Bjørnson, I would never forget that it was *you* who helped me. But soon!

Sincerely,
Knut Pederson.

He enclosed four carefully copied-out testimonials from his most respectable employers of recent years – his uncle Hans Olsen from Presteid, O. C. D. Bugge from Bodø, Weenaas the priest who took him on as a schoolteacher in Bø, and Nordahl the bailiff in Bø. And in case Bjørnson was suspicious at the sight of these glowing reports in Hamsun's own hand, Hamsun eased his mind by assuring him, in a postscript, that he was 'aware of the seriousness of forgery, and I hope that you believe me'.[5]

Bjørnson did help him, in a very indirect way, but not yet, and not in quite the way that Hamsun might have hoped. His obsession with the idea of being a writer continued to dominate his thoughts, and we get some insight into his plans and hopes from the next of his 'reports' to Zahl:

Christiania 24 March 1880, Hrr K. Zahl, Kjerringøy in Salten
My benefactor!
I am almost ashamed to write to you, but I think I have delayed long enough. I have not written to you since sometime around Christmas, in Copenhagen – I left and came here, where I have still not managed to get my book published. Now please allow me, Hrr Zahl, to transcribe for you what certain authoritative persons have said about me. These are testimonials from Munch and from Skavlan, both of whom are professors.
'After having read Hrr Knut Hamsunn's story *Frida*, I am forced to concede that this (young) writer has considerable literary talent, although his work is altogether too closely modelled on Bjørnson's *style*, so that he will have to try a little bit harder if he is to achieve completely satisfactory results.'
– And another:
'My opinion of Knut Hamsunn, who has shown me a poem and a story, is much the same as Hrr A. Munch's – But it is indeed remarkable that such a young and self-taught man could reproduce the style of another author in this way. It is particularly remarkable that he has carried this off in such a thoroughly consistent manner. This implies an undeveloped but undeniably *very considerable literary talent*. There is something about Hamsunn that makes a *good* impression. It would be a shame if this writer, young as he is and with so many varying interests, were to be prevented from realising to the full his potential'.
You can see for yourself, Hrr Zahl, that I have basically everything necessary to ensure that I will one day make a name for myself in our literature; but this time things have not worked out for me. The great writer Henrik Ibsen didn't manage to get his first book published either, but now he is the one that all the other great writers look up to.
The worst of it all is that it puts me in such a bad light with you, who have been so kind and generous to me. You may rest assured of this, that one day I shall pay you back for your great goodness to me. Until that day I ask you in all sincerity not to be angry with me because I am as yet still not able to start paying

back what I owe you. One day I will bind my name in with yours and raise it up – I am totally and unshakeably convinced of this. Until then: patience. Dear Zahl, if only you won't turn against me now, I shall work all the harder.

I am thinking about writing a new book, and in this one I shall be on my guard against the Bjørnson style. I should in any case have had more lessons in grammar, but I don't see how I can now. But God will look after me, I know! You said that you would be taking a trip to Holland this spring. If you come this way, I will be able to greet you. Perhaps I might come with you as a kind of interpreter and secretary – I speak a little English. Until then, look after yourself. Be my friend still, and don't be angry with me,

> yours
> Knut Hamsunn.

He adds a note that Zahl is not to worry about the life-insurance policy, one way or another he will continue making the payments on it. But Hamsunn, as he now signs himself, is clearly in a bit of trouble. Life refuses to imitate Art, and the plot of *The Enigmatic One* begins to look as though it is going badly wrong. No matter how he styles himself, Rolf Andersen/Pedersen does not become Knud Sonnenfeld. The successive transformations still fail to awake the magical power of the name, and the peasant boy remains obdurately a peasant boy.

Hamsun made one last great effort to rescue the fairy-tale. The Swedish King, Oscar II, was on a state visit to Norway, and Hamsun went to see him at the castle on Karl Johansgate. In his last known report to Zahl, Hamsun describes the visit, and in the shadow of its magnificence slips his benefactor the saddest bit of news yet:

Roadworks, Undliden – Boverbro, nr Gjøvik, 31 May 1880.
    It is my duty to tell you that I have found it necessary to move from Christiania. I had applied in person to the Lord Chancellor during His Royal Highness' recent visit there, and when I had delivered my message to him he promised that he would help me to find a job, and I have indeed been given a job – but imagine! – working as a navvy! (see address above) I have an hour off at the moment, and I will use this hour to write to you. Since you arranged to meet me at the 'Royal' in the event of your coming to Christiania, it is best I do not mislead you and deceive you into waiting for me.
    My handwriting is what you might expect of a navvy. My

arms are swollen, and my hand shakes. I am ashamed to send you such a letter, but you have always been so kind and so tolerant, and I hope you will forgive me also this now.

No matter how much I might wish to meet you personally at the 'Royal', Hr Zahl, I am afraid I have to say that it is not possible. I know that if I could have stayed in Christiania just until you came you could have used your influence on my behalf, and I could have found a more suitable job. Now in God's name I must just make out the best I can.

But I am happy to be able to report that the King is taking a personal interest in me. What I did was to present a written request to the Lord Chancellor for help and influence, and the letter, which it took me a whole day to write, was read out to the King, who praised it warmly (Naturally, one took into account the fact that I was twenty-one years old, and an autodidact). My latest book *Frida*, which I have unfortunately not managed to find a publisher for, has been read by the Chancellor personally; his opinion was that the person who wrote this has undoubted literary talent. But since I wrote it à la Bjørnson, and the Chancellor being a conservative monarchist, the fact of the matter is that he does not like a Republican like Bjørnson!

While I am working here I shall try to revise my book, and it may be possible to get it published sometime during the summer (when I hope my luck will have turned).

Until then, God give us strength and courage! And if you do travel, Hr Zahl, then good luck, and safe journey home again! Look after yourself!

Gratefully yours,
Knut Hamsunn.

So ended Hamsun's first career as a literary sensation. The surprising claim that King Oscar II was taking a 'personal interest' in him has never been verified, although the young Hamsun's innocent boldness was such that he probably had the necessary audacity to seek an audience with a king if he thought it might help him to become a writer. An incident in *Hunger* makes a wryly ironic reference to the whole business. The narrator of the novel lives, like Hamsun, at Tomtegaten II, where he sleeps rent-free on the floor of the living room. He spends his days trying to write a visionary verse-drama, and wages a desperate battle to maintain a degree of self-respect in the face of considerable difficulties. One day a servant girl at the house teases him by saying that she saw him coming out of the palace, and asks 'Were you invited to dinner up there?' The narrator, terrified of being evicted, makes no reply, and sits in morose contemplation of his impotence. 'What if I had come out of the castle?' he asks himself, 'Did it harm her?'[6] The question of the royal visit cropped up again in 1909, during an interview in the Norwegian-American immigrant magazine *Eidsvold* with R. B. Anderson, Professor of Scandinavian Studies at the University in Madison, whom Hamsun was to meet shortly in America. He told the paper that Hamsun had 'appeared before King Oscar and showed him his poems. Of course, the King liked them, or at any rate, he felt obliged to say he did. He handed Pedersen twenty kroner as a kind of consolation.' Hamsun denied Anderson's version of events, and said that he had never spoken with the King: 'I requested an audience, but got no further than the chancellor.' As for the claim that it was through the intercession of a king that he had got the job as a navvy at Gjøvik, the more likely tale is that it was through the influence of Bjørnson. Hamsun had done occasional clerical work for a Christiania apothecary named Thaulow during the winter of 1879–80. Thaulow had introduced him to a builder named Krag, who was a friend of Bjørnson's, and it was probably thus that Hamsun found himself at Gjøvik. Whoever and however it was, one thing was certain – it had nothing to do with fairy-tales any more.

Hamsun had informed Zahl that he intended to try to revise *Frida* for publication in the summer of 1880, but this is the last we hear of the manuscript. In all probability it was destroyed. Judging by the various references Hamsun makes to the book in his letters, it seems clear that it was simply another peasant tale in the style of Bjørnson's early works, and as such it is not difficult to see why it failed to find a publisher, even though it may have been an adequate example of the genre. Simply in producing it at all, Hamsun showed how out of touch he was with prevailing literary fashion. These peasant tales, idealisations of country people, were already old-fashioned by the time he came across them in the bookshelves at bailiff Nordahl's home in remote Bø, and social realism was now the dominant concern of the major Norwegian writers.

The Danish literary apologist Georg Brandes had begun publication in 1871 of his account in five volumes of nineteenth-century European literary trends, in which he defined the value of literature thus: 'The proof that a literature lives lies in the fact of its willingness to debate controversial matters.' This was a view previously expressed in Norway by the historian Ernst Sars, but it did not become fashionable until taken up by the Danish cultural authority Brandes. The so-called 'four great men' of Norwegian literature, Ibsen, Bjørnson, Lie and Kielland, all soon produced work which in one way or another discussed the problems of individual freedom and responsibility within society. Bjørnson had returned from Rome and moved into the house at Aulestad in 1875 and in the same year produced two plays, *The Editor* and *A Bankrupt*, which Strindberg later described as the 'rocket signals' for the new literary direction, with their attacks on moral, religious, and bureaucratic hypocrisy. *The New System* followed in 1878, a play which foreshadowed Ibsen's *An Enemy of the People* in discussing the difficulties of telling the truth in a small community. Ibsen's *Pillars of Society* appeared in 1877 and achieved immediate and widespread popular success, and in 1879 came *A Doll's House*, the play which was to make him internationally known. These plays defined the literary mood of both Copenhagen and Christiania, and as Hamsun himself probably soon realised, a book like *Frida*, planned and written in the cultural isolation of Nordland and Hardanger, was unlikely to interest anyone either intellectually or as an economic proposition any more.

Hamsun worked for two years on various road-making projects around Toten, and in spite of the dismay with which he reported the move to Zahl probably found it a relief to be temporarily released from the burdens of his ambition. He could relax and be an ordinary person again, take part in social life and be one of the crowd. He was still poor, of course – a letter to his shoemaker cousin Knudsen in Christiania written in June 1880 contains an elaborate plea for a pair of cheap shoes to be supplied on credit –but it was not the neurotic, isolated, urban poverty described in *Hunger*. He was working hard, getting paid, and eating regularly. He lodged with Torger Kyseth and his wife Torger-Maria in one of the old workers' houses in Raufoss, consisting of one room and a kitchen in which, during the day, Torger-Maria ran an eating-house for local workmen.[7] Hamsun slept on a bed in the kitchen after the café was closed and Torger-Maria looked after him. She said that when he came to Toten he had five shirts which he wore all at the same time, and she persuaded him to go over to a system of wearing one shirt at a time, and changing it every Saturday. He was 'terrifyingly learned', she remembered. His intelligence and reliability soon earned him a form of promotion, from navvy to 'gruskontrollør', where his job was to keep a note of the number of barrowloads of grit that were used on the road in a day. This was almost an office job, and gave him plenty of time to read, so he would borrow books from the library at East Toten, and read with the indiscriminate freedom of the self-taught man. Eugene Sue's

Mysteries of Paris was among the books he came across there.

Hamsun undoubtedly enjoyed his time at Toten. In the *Wanderer* novels from 1906 and 1909 the narrator, tired of celebrity, civilisation and the unnatural city life he has been living for so long, sets out on a fictional voyage of return to the scenes of his youth. He wanders about the countryside doing casual farm-work while he tries to rediscover what he has lost.* One day he falls in with someone who turns out to be a workmate of his from the old days at Skreia:

> I go up to him and introduce myself and start talking.
>
> It's many years now since we were navvies together, Grindhusen and I. It was in the bright days of our youth, when we danced along the road in our beat-up old shoes and ate what we could get our hands on when we had the money for it. And if we had any extra over then we danced with the girls all Saturday night, and all our workmates would be there too. And the lady of the house sold us coffee and made a fortune out of it. Then we got stuck in and worked hard for another week, longing for Saturday to come round again. Grindhusen was a red-haired wolf when it came to the women.
>
> Could he remember the days at Skreia?
>
> He looks at me and weighs me up. He won't give anything away, and it takes me a little while before I can get him to reminisce along with me.
>
> Yes, he remembers Skreia alright.
>
> And do you remember Anders the File, and the Screw? And Petra?
>
> Which one?
>
> Petra. The one who was your sweetheart.
>
> Oh yes, I remember her alright. I settled down with her in the end.

A couple of days later Grindhusen calls to him while he is out fishing. Grindhusen's shout comes to him across the water, 'and a ray of warmth pierces me through and through, like a summons from my youth, from Skreia, a lifetime ago'.

The qualities that the older Hamsun found most unattractive in old age, and which he fought so hard to resist in himself – the husbanding of life, of resources, of time and money, the belief that age implies wisdom – were all gloriously mocked in these days. The fortune from Zahl was gone within six months. Even allowing

---

* The narrator's name is Knud Pedersen, Hamsun's own original name.

for the cost of the long journeys, the lorgnette, the fine clothes, the grammar lessons and expensive books, what became of it all is a mystery. Maybe Hamsun lost much of it in gambling. He had a lifelong fondness for cards, and enjoyed playing recklessly, so that at times a whole week's wages at Toten would disappear in the course of a night. He liked to gamble as a matter of principle, and would explain that the attraction of it lay neither in winning nor in losing, but in the thrill of the risk itself.

Hamsun was a popular man, and a natural leader among his workmates. Once, when trouble broke out between the travelling workers in the road-gang and the resident local workers, he was elected to speak for the migrants, and smoothed the trouble out. His special friends were his landlord Torger Kyseth, Per Saugstad, and an adventurer named Ernst Sengebusch. Sengebusch worked in the local match factory where another friend, Nils Frøsland, was the manager. The two met when Frøsland stopped to give Hamsun a lift one day, and the friendship developed quickly. In his free time Hamsun sometimes helped Frøsland with his paper-work at the Raufoss factory, and became a regular visitor to the Frøsland home. Something worthy of note in these friendships is that they span the social scale; Hamsun's charm meant that he could move easily from the kitchen café at Torger-Maria's to the drawing room of a socially prominent family like the Frøslands. This mobility was an important asset to him.

The only known published writing from this period of Hamsun's life is a newspaper article, 'From Vardal', which appeared in *Gjøviks Blad* on 6 July 1880 under the signature 'Ego'. The article was again characterised by that insolence which had caused such uproar at Østensjø. His target this time was an elderly lay preacher, Hans Pedersen Lingjerde, whom Hamsun had heard speak locally, and who had irritated him both on account of his message and the incompetence with which it was delivered. Mindful of the personal nature of the opposition aroused by that previous article, on this occasion Hamsun opened his attack with a few seductive dissimulations to the effect that this was just a few thoughts about Lingjerde from a mere worker, a little philosophising from the ditch. In part, his concern was to attack the joyless and punitive bigotry of Lingjerde's Haugian theology, a hell-fire puritanism that might perhaps have reminded him unpleasantly of his uncle Hans, and those sunny afternoons spent reading from the *Biblical Messenger*. He was also aesthetically affronted by Lingjerde's style of preaching, which he called uneven and jumpy, and his use of language 'in which he does not forget to enrich his biblical quotations with constructions and formulae entirely of his own devising'.

In spite of the disarming opening, the impression left by Hamsun's article, as he goes on to criticise Lingjerde for being old, having a squeaky voice, and using a crude and ridiculous language, is of an inappropriate aggression that probably worked to arouse sympathy for the preacher as the object of an unfair and personal attack. At first glance this might seem merely a tactical error on the part of the young writer. In fact, as Hamsun's subsequent long career as a journalist shows, his aim was probably quite specifically the expression of his aggression and irritation, with little regard for what people might think of him or his cause. This is an important point, bearing in mind that the popular image of Hamsun as a Nazi sympathiser is based almost entirely on his journalism during the 1930s and the war. The labour over a work of art like a novel seems to be in itself a civilising factor, and Hamsun exhibited throughout his life a profound ambivalence about whether or not he wanted to be civilised at all. Journalism – brief, ephemeral and simplistic – offered him an important outlet for the uncivilised side of his personality.

No matter how much he enjoyed the healthy, outdoor life at Toten, the girlfriends and the card games, the drinking and dancing, and the walks in the beautiful, thickly-wooded countryside around Vardal, Hamsun knew all along that this was not the life for him, and that sooner or later he would have to cut himself loose from ties again, and take the risks that mattered.

Ever since his oldest brother, Peter, had gone to America during the first great wave of Scandinavian emigrations in the mid-1860s, the thought of trying his own luck out there had probably had a place in Hamsun's mind. Conversations with his friend Ernst Sengebusch, who had also been there, perhaps made the idea more pressing. To add an extra prompt, there was also a great deal of public encouragement to prospective emigrants in the form of letters home and newspaper articles from satisfied settlers in the Norwegian national newspapers. *Gjøviks Blad* for 12 December 1880 carried an article that might have had a special appeal for Hamsun, being a discussion of the need for native-language writers and lecturers to serve the needs of the Norwegian communities in the mid-western states.

Bjørnson had been on a lecture tour in the winter of 1880–81, and his enthusiastic reports home were featured prominently in the newspapers. Kristofer Janson, the unitarian preacher and author who, along with Bjørnson, was Hamsun's first stylistic influence, lectured at Gjøvik, near Toten, shortly before emigrating to

Minneapolis, and in August and November of 1881 Bjørnson himself spoke at public meetings at Valheim and at Augelands Bridge, at least one of which Hamsun seems to have attended. His ambitions and hopes for himself soon fired his friend Nils Frøsland, and already in September 1881 Frøsland had written to the ubiquitous Bjørnson, a family friend, and asked for his help in getting Hamsun over to America. On 29 September[8] he wrote to his mother urging that the family pay Hamsun's fare, and Hamsun's foreman on the roadworks, Captain Moestue, also wrote a letter to Bjørnson asking him to use his influence to help Hamsun in America. All these efforts soon paid off when Bjørnson wrote back on 29 November promising to recommend the young man to his good friend Professor R. B. Anderson in Madison, Wisconsin.

Anderson was an interesting character. A man, like Hamsun, from an unpromising background, he had by the age of thirty established and held a chair in Scandinavian Studies at the University of Wisconsin. Bjørnson wrote to Moestue that few could match Anderson in his ability to help a promising man, but added the warning rider, that this was 'if this chap (Hamsun) meets with his approval. And this is a very big "if", especially in America, where personal impression counts for everything.' Nils Frøsland could then write to his mother on 12 December that Bjørnson had written to Anderson recommending that Hamsun 'be made a professor or something equally big. Bjørnson thinks it's marvellous of you and I to help him, poor and talented as he is. One day he may be world-famous. We're relying on the fact that you will be able to lend him the money for his fare; if you can, I'll stand guarantor for him, so you can't lose anything by it. Pedersen and I will both be coming home for Christmas. If he gets the money then, he'll travel straightaway. Poor Knut Pedersen! I've never felt so sorry for someone of my own age before.'

The Christmas gathering at Fru Frøsland's home at Torpa was a great success all round. Fru Frøsland found Hamsun charming, and his rendition of Ibsen's dramatic ballad *Terje Vigen*, delivered standing on a stool, was said to have moved some of the ladies present to tears. Fru Frøsland, perhaps because of her enthusiasm for Kristofer Janson's unitarianism, made a brief attempt to divert him in the direction of the ministry while promising, in any case, to pay the fare over to America. In addition to 400 kroner from her, he received another fifty kroner from Captain Moestue, and a further letter of recommendation to Professor Anderson in America, written on the back of Bjørnson's letter. Hamsun could 'turn his hand to anything', the Captain wrote. 'He is used to heavy work,

and has been roadmaking with me for over a year and a half.'
Neither referee nor protégé were aware of the fact that academic
success had turned Anderson into a rather snobbish man who
would not necessarily find this kind of adaptability suitable in an
aspiring writer.

In January 1882 Hamsun bought himself a new set of clothes and
then travelled to Hamburg to take the steamship *Oder* to New
York. Before sailing he presented himself at the offices of the
shipping-line, North-German Lloyd, and suggested that he
might travel free in return for a journalistic account of the voyage
he was about to make. This was not an unheard-of procedure for
emigrants, but he was still delighted to find his suggestion
accepted, and even more delighted when the manager threw in the
cost of a train ticket to his brother's home in Elroy. Hamsun was
twenty-two years old at the time of this first trip to America.

Chapter 3
1882–1884: The American Experience I

Hamsun's very first impressions of America were no different from those of the 29,000 other Norwegians who emigrated in the record year of 1882. He was overwhelmed:

> Torger, you should have been with us in New York and seen the fantastic things there. The railway goes up in the air above the people's houses, and there are telegraph and telephone wires by the thousand stretching between the houses. The bridge from New York to Brooklyn is about three-quarters of a Norwegian mile; that's where the railway goes, and above that thin wires are threaded together in a kind of net, and that is where the pedestrians go. This bridge is the greatest engineering feat in the world, and it's so high that you come up into another layer of the atmosphere when you walk over it, and there's a terrible wind up there. And you should've seen the houses. I saw houses in New York thirteen storeys high, with two of them under the ground. One day I went to the 'New York Post Office' (ie posthuset) with a letter for Frøsland and I was shot up to the fourth floor in a kind of swaying contraption; I decided to walk down, and thought I would never get there.[1]

Chicago impressed him as much. He and his travelling companions were astounded by the new city hall, 'the most *handsome* building I've ever seen', with stone so highly polished that they could stand there and see themselves reflected in it. He submitted two poems to the magazine *Norden* which were immediately accepted for publication;[2] and as he travelled on with his letters of recommendation in his pocket to Professor Anderson's house on North Carroll Street in Madison he must have felt that the great adventure had got off to a fairly auspicious start.

Anderson had created for himself an important role in the establishment and maintenance of cultural links between the old world and the new, a role he carried out with a perhaps necessary degree of aggressive pioneering bluster. He was a tireless propagandist, not only for himself, but for all Scandinavian cultural achievements, translating saga literature, writing on Old Norse mythology, and insisting upon the Viking discovery of America. He translated Bjørnson and Andreas Munch, and in spite of his personal disapproval of the 'new' drama was mainly responsible for bringing Ibsen to the attention of Americans for the first time.* Among Norwegian writers, America had swiftly established itself as a lucrative market where good money could be earned – Bjørnson's winter lecture tour of 1880–81 earned him 10,000 dollars – and many of those anxious to take advantage of this kept Anderson in constant correspondence. Hamsun, with his background, was an unusual candidate for his help. Anderson described their meeting several times and in several different moods, but most extensively in his *Life Story of Rasmus B. Anderson*, published in 1915:

> One day during the summer of 1882, I think, while my family and I were seated at the dinner table we heard the doorbell ring. The maid being engaged in the kitchen, I went to the door myself. On opening it there stood before me a tall, slender, smooth-faced young man with a large growth of hair on his head. You could not look at this youth with a forest of brown hair without thinking of Bjørnstjerne Bjørnson in his palmiest days. This young man held his hat in one hand and with the other handed me a letter, after asking if I was Professor Anderson. I opened the letter and found it was written to me by no less a personage than Bjørnstjerne Bjørnson himself. . . . I asked Knud Pederson to walk in and learning that he had not had any dinner that day a place was found for him at the table. At the dinner table, after some conversation, I put the question to Knud Pederson:
>
> 'Well my young friend, what do you intend to do in this country?'
>
> He replied at once: 'I have come to write poetry for the Norwegians in America. Bjørnson told me that his countrymen here needed a poet, and I have come to supply this want.'

* 'They seem to me mere twaddle, and all the symbolism which they are said to contain I regard as a mere opinion of his readers and admiring critics', he wrote in his autobiography.

According to the account, Hamsun then went on to tell Anderson about his past, 'and the fact that he had only attended the elementary schools struck a responsive chord in me as I knew well by experience what it meant to be an autodidact, or self-taught scholar'. The discussion then turned to the question of names as Anderson was in the middle of an energetic campaign to persuade Norwegians to drop all their 'Olson, Larson, Johnson, Peterson and the whole aggregation of "sons" ' and substitute the name of the farm in Norway from which they or their families came. In line with this he suggested that 'Pederson' change his name to 'Hamsund', a suggestion which apparently so delighted Hamsun that he immediately took to styling himself thus. The meeting between patron and protégé concluded with Anderson sending Hamsun on to an acquaintance of his, a Norwegian store-owner in Elroy who needed a clerk, with the usual letter of recommendation.

Anderson comes across as an ingenuous, patient and helpful person in this 1915 extract. His earliest account, in the magazine *Eidsvold*, in 1909, had been rich in an impatient and arrogant and unforgiving distaste for Hamsun: he referred to 'this peasant from Norway', 'this tramcar conductor' (a later job) 'this greenhorn'. He spoke mockingly of him to two visitors to the house as 'a young man who has come to this country with a view to becoming President of the United States'. All just details, of course, but Hamsun was fanatic about details, and several times replied with a point-by-point refutation of every claim made by Anderson: he had had no letter with him from Bjørnson to Anderson, but Bjørnson's letter to Moestue of 29 November 1881, promising to write to Anderson about Hamsun; he was not invited to eat in the house, but on the contrary directed to a lodging house in town; and his older brother Peter had been using the farm-name Hamsund for many years, so that Anderson's suggestion was not the decisive one he claimed it to be. (Hamsun might also have pointed out that he himself had been using the name occasionally at least since 1879, as in his first letter to Zahl.) Hamsun wrote to his Toten friend Ernst Sengebusch shortly after the meeting:

> Prof. Anderson was not the man to come to if it was a question of standing up to him at all costs. He cut the whole thing short and said that I would have to help myself. 'In America everybody has to help themselves'[3]

thus confirming what Bjørnson had written in that note to Moestue – that Anderson's unrivalled capacity to help a man was highly conditional on his liking him, 'especially in America, where personal impression counts for everything'.

After his night in the Madison lodging house Hamsun used the rest of his train ticket to take him to his brother's house in Elroy, some time in the middle of February. Brother Peter Pedersen Hamsund, seven years older than Knut, had emigrated to America at the age of sixteen in 1868, and at twenty married a woman of higher social class, as his father had done. He followed his father in his trade of tailor, too. The family had moved to Elroy just before Knut emigrated, and letters home gave the impression Peter was doing well. The circumstances of their childhood meant that the brothers would be practically strangers to one another, but all the same, Hamsun must have had hopes that the contact would be a useful and supportive one.

On arrival he worked very briefly for a Norwegian store-owner in a town named Moe, and in the evenings, as arranged with the North-German Lloyd Line, began trying to write an account of the crossing. In the letter already quoted to his friend and former landlord in Raufoss, Torger Kyseth, besides enthusing over the achievements of American city dwellers he advised Kyseth to look out for an article in *Gjøviks Blad*, but warned that it would be some time yet; it was going so slowly and he was unused to this kind of writing. The article never in fact appeared. Hamsun's Swedish biographer John Landquist mentions other articles that were sent to German newspapers, but neither did these appear. Presumably the editors were satisfied with accounts of the emigrant experience from contributors writing in German.

If the academic Anderson's indifference to Hamsun was a disappointment to him, so was the encounter with his brother, though of a different kind. Hamsun soon found out that things were not going quite as well as they had seemed to be from the letters. Peter Pedersen, besides being a tailor with a distaste for work, was also a splendid musician with a fondness for drink, traits which he found difficulty in harmonising. He was another like their uncle Vetltraein, and had not managed to establish himself as a respectable member of the Elroy community. The family connection was of no great use to Knut. Never a man to hang around in an unpromising situation, he moved on and by April was working on a farm outside Elroy, a tiny holding with two horses and four cows run by a couple named Loveland who were about as wealthy as he was. It was heavy work, but he regarded it as temporary. He was right: soon the Lovelands laid him off, unable even to pay him. According to his account in *On Overgrown*

Paths, written over sixty years later, he then went to work for some German immigrants named Spear, after a chance encounter in town. On his first day on the farm Spear gave him a spade and told him to dig a hole at the edge of a wood, and when it was done he came out carrying a tiny coffin which he laid in the grave. No words were said over the coffin; there was no ceremony at all.

The Spears' was a better managed farm than the Lovelands', and Spear himself looked after the animals while 'Nut' worked out in the fields. He found the couple strange, but came to like them. Once they weighed him on an old steelyard scales, and were delighted and proud when he proved so heavy that he broke the mechanism and brought the yardarm down on his head. Mrs Spear laughed a lot, and taught him English words. But the word 'homesick' he had already learned from Mrs Loveland. Hamsun, always an emotional man, suffered badly and cried a lot.

Moving on from there he was offered a variety of jobs and had to be on his guard against confidence tricksters looking to exploit the simple 'Swede' – he soon found out that all Scandinavian immigrants were 'Swedes', it was useless to protest otherwise. Hamsun turned down an offer to rent a farm, as well as a suggestion that he hire a couple of horses and a wagon on credit and start a haulage business. These dubious offers, intended to trap him into debt, might have had success with others who found themselves in a position like Hamsun's, ostensibly adrift, broke, homesick and unable to speak the language; but for all his impulsive and extravagant behaviour, Hamsun had also a prudent streak in him which distinguished clearly between relevant and irrelevant rashness.

He kept friends back home posted on the state of his love-life, and on Easter Saturday 1882 wrote to Ernst Sengebusch that he had 'only been in love three times in the last two months'. There was no desperate passion at the moment, he said – 'their teeth are too black, their shoulders too narrow'.[4] There were no princesses in America, apparently.

He was nearly snapped up by a girl, directly after being laid off at Loveland's farm. In *On Overgrown Paths* he calls her Bridget. She was the daughter of a local widow, who waylaid him on his way into town one day and tricked him into going back to the farm with her, clearly hoping that he would settle down and begin to run the place for them. He had no idea how to manage a farm, and confined himself to muck-spreading and chopping great quantities of wood, and was probably greatly relieved when one day the widow tired of his efforts and rode into town herself and came back with a Finn, an altogether more capable man who took over the

running of the farm. That was the end of Bridget's advances. The
long short story *Vagabond Days* from 1904 contains an interlude
which improvises on the same thematic material. Here 'Nut' is
passed over for the German charmer Fred by a girl named Alice
Rodgers.

In the autumn of 1882 Hamsun was back in town after his season
of farm work. An Englishman named Hart, owner of the largest
store in Elroy, was extending the property, and Hamsun was taken
on as a hod-carrier. His vertigo made the job more difficult as the
building got higher, and Hart noticed him, swaying about on the
ladder with his hod, his monocle incongruously dangling from a
thin gold chain. He gave him a job down on the ground, as a
delivery boy, and after getting to know him slightly better
promoted him to counter assistant. Now at last Hamsun could
shine, and use the experience gained as a youth in his godfather's
store in Lom, and at Walsøe's in Tranøy.

He enjoyed the sociability of the job, and soon demonstrated his
considerable talent for selling: one day when the owner Hart was
away Hamsun took it on his own initiative to buy up a stock of
ladies cuffs of an unusual design from a travelling salesman. When
Hart returned and saw the cuffs he was convinced they would
never sell. On the contrary, a short while later a society lady was
persuaded by Hamsun into buying the entire stock. And his
English, which had been such an embarrassment to him in his
dealings with 'Bridget', also improved when he began sharing
lodgings with W. T. Ager, a teacher at Elroy High School, and
taking lessons from Ager's colleague Henry M. Johnston.[5]

Ager, his room-mate on the top floor of the Northwestern
Railways Hotel in Elroy, was a fan. An article he wrote and
published in *Kvartalskrift* in January 1916, 'Incidents In The Early
Life of Knut Hamsun' makes this clear, and in doing so gives us an
interesting and amusing picture of their lives during that 1882
autumn. Hamsun was:

> . . . tall, broad, lithe with the springing step of a panther and
> with muscles of steel. His yellow hair, which he wore long,
> drooped down upon his shoulders and imparted to his clear-cut
> classical features something of a liolene appearance difficult to
> define.

The ceiling of Room 15 was so low that Hamsun could draw on it,
and he covered a third of it with a pencil drawing of the Angel of
Night spreading a veil of darkness over the world which their
landlord George Hopper used to show proudly to new guests at

the hotel. Another of his drawings showed the life-size figure of a man with a hole in the plaster for his mouth. He stuck a cigar stub in it one day, to terrify the chambermaid. And underneath a self-portrait he wrote, in English:

> My life is a peaceless flight through all the land. My religion is the Moral of the wildest Naturalism, but my world is the Aesthetical literature.

This was a credo that had particular appeal for him, and he reproduced it in Hart's son Harry's autograph album at Christmas, along with a drawing of a schooner. His humour could sometimes be rather melancholic, and he enjoyed unsettling his friends. Sometimes Ager would arrive home to find Hamsun asleep, and neatly laid out for him a cigar and a knife with an accompanying note asking him kindly to smoke the cigar and stick the knife into his heart. A thoughtful PS added that 'this note will be your defence in court'. He smoked a pipe himself, and set fire to the bedding one night when he fell asleep with it in his mouth. To avoid a repetition he rigged up a long stem to the pipe, and wedged the bowl between some stones on the floor.

By means of such behaviour, he created a striking image of himself among his friends. His was indeed a genuinely unusual personality; but from his adolescence onwards one suspects that he was also very highly conscious of the effect of his eccentric behaviour on others, and that he often deliberately cultivated it in order to observe its results both on himself and his friends. He also supplemented his natural exoticism with fanciful improvisations on the exact nature of his own past. In his memoir of their days together, W. T. Ager wrote:

> I learned from him that he had published a book at the age of eighteen after submitting the manuscript to the great Bjørnson, who consented to give it his indorsement by writing the foreword. He remained for two weeks a guest in the home of this great author, and the counsel and instruction he there received exerted a powerful influence on his future life.
>
> Bjørnson advised him to lay aside the pen until he was thirty years of age; to travel in all lands; to see and become familiar with all conditions of life in so far as it was possible for him to do so. To become conversant with the characteristics of all people, and to study their language and their modes of living. Truly a Herculean task to be undertaken by a youth of eighteen without means, affluent relatives or influential friends on whom he

could rely for assistance, but he followed Bjørnson's advice, and it was in pursuance of this course after having travelled extensively in Germany and France and visited many of the famous art galleries of those countries that we find him in America at the date we have mentioned.[6]

Thus the brief hop from Gjøvik to Hamburg to take the boat over to America has become 'extensive travel in Germany'. The disaster with *Frida* and Bjørnson's indifference to it have been converted into a triumph, and the brief encounter has become a two-week residency at Aulestad. Conceivably Ager became confused over the details of what Hamsun told him about his past, but it all seems rather too detailed for confusion. In the gentlest possible way, Hamsun was stuffing him full of lies.

In spite of the improvements in his English brought about by his contact with Ager, Hamsun was never very happy about speaking a foreign language. Ager records that he studied from a sense of duty rather than for pleasure. Perhaps the close attention which he routinely paid to words in his own language made him too conscious of the terrible imprecisions which even great familiarity with a foreign language will always involve.

Hamsun illustrated the frustrations of the situation well in his impressionistic short story *On the Banks* from 1891, about a crew of all nations fishing on the Newfoundland banks. English is the common tongue, and when the yarning begins in the evening a Dutchman named Van Tatzel always attempts to make the same contribution, a story about a society lady who followed him home from a beer hall one night. Always at the same point in his narration, the most intense, exciting, and linguistically demanding point, his jobbing English fails him, he begins to stammer and stutter, and in despair explodes back into his native language, finishing his tale in a great swarm of strange words 'which not one of us understands except his fellow countryman who lies in another bunk, snoring'. Ager experienced Hamsun several times in this 'explosion', borne out of verbal impotence. Nor did Hamsun's habitually literal examination of language help matters. He laboured long to understand what possible meaning could reside in the formula 'How do you do?', and Ager records a splendid incident of confusion over the correct way of referring to the Virgin Mary:

One evening he interrupted the course of our study to tell me about his sister in Norway whom he described as a very beautiful girl whom he loved devotedly. I asked her name and he replied that it was Marie. He repeated it several times. Marie, Marie, as though not sure of the English pronunciation, then asked me how we pronounced the name of the Mother of Jesus. I replied, Mary. Well, said he, It is the same. Then you would call her Mary. After a moment's pause he asked if it would be proper to say Miss Mary. Supposing that he had reference to his sister, I replied in the affirmative when an unutterable look of disgust passed over his features, and he exclaimed, No, no Ager, it can't be so. I know that you have many crudities of speech, but surely you do not refer to the Mother of Jesus as 'Miss Mary'.

I hastened to tell him that in our language we referred to the Mother of Jesus as 'The Virgin Mary', and asked him how she was called in his language. His look of disgust changed to a smile as he answered leisurely: Well, if we had such a (– –) language as you have I suppose we would call her Mrs Josephson.

It was to his old room-mate and teacher Ager that Hamsun later sent his only known attempt to write fiction in a foreign language, a 'romance in broken and bleeding English' of which he could but haltingly follow the thread of the story. It was entitled *A Vignette Picture*, and Ager was asked to edit it into decent prose, a task which he declined on the grounds that it 'required a Hercules, and had been assigned to a Lilliputian'.

The friendship and respect of Ager, Johnston, the Hart family and others, encouraged Hamsun to think seriously about his writing again, and he finally got under way with his career as a lecturer in October 1882 with a lecture in Elroy schoolhouse on Bjørnson. It was enthusiastically received in the local press. Hamsun was praised for his insight into the subject, and his talent as a reciter was again noted as he rounded off the evening with a recitation of Ibsen's *Terje Vigen*, just as he had done at the Frøsland's house the Christmas before. All Scandinavians living in the vicinity were exhorted to catch Hamsun should he appear again, the more so, the reviewer brightly concluded, since admission was free. An unnecessary remark like this might have made Hamsun wince slightly, but he was naturally excited by the review. Shortly after Christmas he wrote to Rasmus Anderson drawing his attention to it and soliciting his advice and encouragement to go on with his lecturing. In April he spoke again on Bjørnson at nearby Stoughton, this time with less success. There were fewer than twenty people present, as he bitterly reported to Anderson in a letter dated 21 April:

. . . the Stoughton story is soon told. Filthy weather kept the country people at home on a Saturday afternoon, and the townspeople weren't interested in a lecture either. All they know about is drinking. The place is a dump. The worst places in Norway are better than Stoughton.[7]

Later in 1883 Hamsun had a short holiday with Ager at his parents' home at Lake Mason in Adams County. Here he delivered a third lecture on Bjørnson. Ager, who spoke no Norwegian, attended the lecture, and it is a testimony to Hamsun's powers as an orator that Ager could sit for two hours, understanding nothing, but fascinated by his friend's stage presence, 'a rare blending of grace and power, of tenderness and passion'. Ager also noted that Hamsun's 'gestures and facial expressions covered the whole broad range of human emotions'.

After the holiday Hamsun resumed work at the store in Elroy, and one day had a rather frightening experience there. While unloading a barrel of salt from a freight car into a dray wagon he felt something 'tear loose' in his chest, which resulted in bleeding in the lungs. He gave up heavy work for the time being, and recovered. But it was an ominous sign.

Changes were taking place around him. Hart's store was taken over by the Wightman family, though Harry Hart continued to work there and effectively run it. His friend Henry Johnston had moved away in the high summer and started a timber business in the prairie town of Madelia, and Ager was considering a move to Nebraska which he eventually made in the spring of 1884. A romantic affair with a girl called Anna Johnson was also causing him trouble. He was involved in a project to establish a public library in the town, but Elroy was not the intellectual environment he needed in which to develop. He had made himself an enemy there too – a Pastor Ruh, who warned people against attending his lectures for the mild heresy that any defence of Bjørnson at that time involved in the wake of Bjørnson's attack on Christianity and the established church. But Hamsun struggled to keep his mind alive, and pressed his friends into debate and discussion, challenging them with his bold and original suggestions. On 12 December 1883 he wrote provocatively to his friend Sven Tveraas, a local farmer:

. . . as regards 'walking on the water', according to your beliefs is not this against the law of gravity, a defiance of science? Or is it against your beliefs? Do you perhaps believe that there was once a man who walked on the surface of water? There is something incomplete about your beliefs that bothers me, Sven.[8]

The whole thrust of the letter is an exhortation to Sven to examine and to analyse his own beliefs, and to try to find the real reason why he has abandoned the orthodox faith: was it in the search for truth, or merely from a desire to contradict? The question was a curiously central one for Hamsun, and one imagines that he also frequently examined his own behaviour in the light of it.

Hamsun was restless, and when he received a letter from Henry Johnston asking if he were free, and interested in moving to Madelia to work for him, he accepted the offer. He left Elroy probably just after Christmas, and travelled extensively before reaching the Johnstons'. He spent a week in a place called Red Wing, where he wrote a long article on 'The God of the Moses Books' which he hoped to deliver as a lecture in Madelia. He also had plans to lecture in Red Wing which he abandoned for economic reasons.

Having made the move from Elroy, Hamsun did not regret the decision. He felt he had been there too long, stagnating. In Madelia he enjoyed the lively debate that was going on between the Unitarian Kristofer Janson and the orthodox Lutherans. He thought deeply about issues, but was always aware of his own limitations. Any religious faith that involved blind acceptance of certain received 'truths' was an impossibility for him. He was a seeker who before long came to see the meaning in the search itself, and regarded revelations, findings and syntheses as the claims of a comfortable cowardice.

The short story *Fear*, published in 1897, is based on Hamsun's three-month stay in Madelia. It gives a dramatised account of a frightening experience he had one night while the owners were away and he was minding the store and living in the house alone. The Johnstons had gone east on business, and before leaving had presented him with a gun. To begin with all went smoothly. Hamsun moved out of the room assigned to him and into the living room, where he could keep a better eye on the house. He minded the store, sold wood and furniture, and at the end of the day banked the takings and got his receipt. A pan of gruel he had cooked for his evening meal had boiled over, settling and hardening into a thick stodge on the table-top. In the evening he would hack off a wedge of this, boil it up with some milk, and eat. Afterwards he would settle down to write. The house was some distance from town and stood alone, but he had no particular reason to be afraid, and when on successive nights he heard what he thought was someone fiddling with the latch of the door he took a lamp and went to investigate without the gun. On the third

night, after a particularly long day in the shop had meant that he
could not bank the takings, he heard the sound again. It was about
two in the morning, and he was still up writing. Immediately
afterwards he heard the front door being violently forced, and then
voices whispering. Beside himself with fright he took the money
and hid it in the bedroom under the bedclothes. He took the gun,
and shouting through the living room door – first in Norwegian, in
his confusion, then in English – threatened to shoot anyone who
came in. He heard someone swearing at him. He went over to a
window and opened it, and saw something, a dark shape moving
against the snow. He took aim and fired. Click. Nothing. Fired
again. Click. He went round the whole barrel and at last a bullet
popped out. Fortunately for him it made a noise loud enough to
scare off an accomplice who had still been hiding in the house. He
stayed up and at first light went to town and banked the money.
   'Do you remember that I, one night in Madelia, was broken into?
I do not blame you even if you doubted this occurrence . . .',
Hamsun wrote later about the incident to Johnston. He certainly
never forgot it, nor that feeling of uncontrollable fear when he
heard the front door crash open, and his heart was suddenly
beating in his throat, and he could not breathe. Like many of his
short stories, *Fear* is an autobiographical sketch in the 'yarning'
tradition of writers like Mark Twain, W. W. Jacobs, Damon
Runyan and Ambrose Bierce; fact with fictional trimmings. In the
case of *Fear*, Hamsun tells his Norwegian readers that all this took
place in the town of Madelia, the very same town where Jesse
James, 'bloodiest and blackest of villains', was finally caught and
killed. In fact it was not James but the Younger brothers who were
caught and killed there.
   Hamsun's main hope was still that he would be able to make a
name and a living for himself as a lecturer on literature. His letters
to Sven Tveraas, a Norwegian immigrant who farmed a small-
holding just outside Elroy, are full of details of lectures prepared
and given, or about to be given, or not given at all. On 3 February
he had spoken in Madelia on 'The Jews from Abraham up to the
Present Time'. An audience of one hundred encouraged him to
think finally of charging for admission, because money was always
a problem. He asked Sven for the loan of twenty-five dollars which
he hoped to pay back from the proceeds of his next lecture, at St
James. But in this he was disappointed. Not enough people turned
up to cover the cost of hiring the hall, and he had to cancel the
lecture. It was all a far cry from Bjørnson and his 10,000 dollars, but
in terms of the thorough experience of disappointment it was
priceless for the themes and attitude of his future work. But he was

getting tired of it, nevertheless. He wrote to Sven that after cancelling the lecture, he swore that that would be the end of it all. And a new possibility had arisen with the impending visit of the Unitarian Minister and writer Kristofer Janson to Madelia. Janson was the author of the peasant-tale *Torgrim* which had exerted considerable influence on Hamsun during the composition of *Bjørger*, and Hamsun looked forward to meeting him. He also hoped to persuade him to look at a new work in progress, a book to be called *Across the Sea*. He promised to write and let Sven know the result of the meeting.

As a writer Janson is now largely forgotten, but to his contemporaries he was a not inconsiderable literary figure. Apart from the years of his ministry in America, he was in receipt of the 'diktergasje' from the Norwegian Parliament, an annuity for honoured writers. He was a rare man; hard-working, honest, open and generous. Bjørnson used him as the model for Pastor Stang in his best play *Beyond Our Power (I)* as a symbol of boundless faith, and even a cynic like Rasmus Anderson could say that, 'with all his faults I love him still'. He had come to America the year before Hamsun at Anderson's suggestion and established a Unitarian mission in Minneapolis which he ran with zeal and an imagination which sometimes got him into trouble with the orthodox church. Besides Minneapolis he took care of Unitarian communities in Underwood, in St Paul, in Hudson Wisconsin, and in Brown County. Madelia was the station Janson used when he was travelling to Brown County, and it was there in late February 1884 that he and Hamsun met. It is interesting to read the account of their meeting as Janson recalls it in his memoirs *What I Have Experienced*:

I met him by chance. . . . I noticed a tall, straight-backed man wearing gold-rimmed spectacles, with an intelligent, aristocratic face. He was working in a timber-yard there. He spoke Norwegian. We fell into conversation. It was a Sunday, and he had time to go for a walk with me in the wood. I asked him if he was content to work there and shave planks:

'No, of course I'm not content – but what is one to do? A man must live.'

'Would he prefer working with his mind?'

'Of course – but how?'

I told him that I needed a secretary who could help me to translate for *The Sower*, and give lectures for me. I asked him if he were religious.

No, he said he had no religious beliefs whatever.

I told him about Unitarianism, that it was the very opposite of all the dogma which seemed to him so tasteless and immoral.

Janson's observation that he met Hamsun 'by chance' is interesting, bearing in mind how keenly the young writer had been looking forward to meeting one of his early heroes. Hamsun was an ambitious man, capable of considerable personal charm when he wanted, and he had clearly mastered the art of making people meet him. And even though Hamsun had no religious beliefs whatever, Janson offered him the job as his secretary in Minneapolis. In his autobiography he admits that he had hopes of raising Hamsun's religious consciousness – but in this he was to be sorely disappointed. 'He developed an ever greater distaste for everything that had to do with theology', he noted sadly.

They arranged that Hamsun would lodge with the Janson family, and receive 500 dollars a year and free travelling expenses, and then Janson travelled on to Brown County. On 29 February Hamsun wrote to tell Sven Tveraas the good news. He mentioned that he had also been offered work as a shepherd in Nebraska, perhaps through the influence of his friend W. T. Ager; but in spite of better money, and free board and lodging, not to mention the romantic appeal of the job, he had turned it down. He needed contact, stimulation, discussion, talk. He needed people. He was especially excited at the prospect of exploring Janson's library.

Shortly afterwards, Hamsun travelled to Minneapolis, moved into the house on Nicollet Avenue, and by mid-April was deeply involved in all the practical aspects of Janson's mission. The work consisted mostly of the constant fund-raising required to keep the mission going, and this Janson did in a variety of ways. There were bazaars, auctions, minor entertainments, comedies and sketches that he wrote, and living tableaux in which his own children played 'the Siamese twins', 'the leopard man' and 'Hannah with the big foot'. They charged ten cents to see 'the giant water snake' which turned out to be a hose coiled up in a box, and another ten cents to see 'the enemies of the people' through a stereoscope – a flea and a bug. Hamsun certainly took part in all this. He loved children and always delighted in their company, and the respect and affection of the Janson children was mutual. When they baked for the dolls in their doll's house, there was always a cake or pudding baked for him too. He also captivated Janson's wife Drude. According to Rasmus Anderson, who knew the family well, she once said that it was 'bracing and invigorating both mentally and physically to be in the same room with Knut Hamsun'.

On the literary front Hamsun was soon active in the newspapers defending his new employer against a series of bitter personal attacks. Janson's unorthodox habit of using drama to spread the Word had upset the Lutheran establishment. In addition to his own works he would read from new plays by Bjørnson and Ibsen to a packed audience in the Nazareth Hall. The orthodox Lutherans accused him of trying to turn people away from the Bible and to encourage them in the Unitarian rejection of the doctrine of the Trinity and the Divinity of Christ.* He was also accused of perverting through his preaching Paul's doctrine of female subservience, and of bringing shame on the calling of priest by mixing stagecraft and worship. A reading of his own play *Children of Hell* at Nazareth Hall provoked a protest letter signed by five Lutheran priests; and another attack came from a Dr Julson in the 25 March issue of the community newspaper *Skandinaven*. It was to this attack that Hamsun replied, in the same paper, on 22 April.

Apart from the two poems printed immediately after his arrival in America in the Chicago magazine *Norden*, this is Hamsun's only known publication from his first period in America. It is a defence of his new friend and employer, in the tradition of the two newspaper contributions discussed earlier, against the psalm-singing in Hardanger in 1879, and against Hans Lingjerde's Haugian theology in *Gjøviks Blad* in 1880. He uses a modified form of the same aggressive technique as before, suggesting that Julson is quite simply not intelligent enough to understand either what Janson is trying to say or what he is trying to do; Julson, with his long contribution, has 'plagued *Skandinaven* out into a special number'; the doctor lacks 'even the rudiments of psychological understanding . . . and ought to admit it, and not get in such a state simply because you do not understand'. He is advised to ask for an explanation of what he has failed to understand, instead of shouting out 'Nonsense'. Janson's *Children of Hell* will be coming out in book form soon, Hamsun declares, and Julson is advised to study it again, but to make sure to find someone to explain it to him this time. The style is combative and taunting, infuriating after the style of the previous journalism.[9]

As agreed, Hamsun also gave lectures for Janson. He spoke twice at Harrison Hall, on 'The Religion of the Ancient Egyptians', and on the 'History of Unitarianism' before Janson decided to give

---

* This rejection of the doctrine of the Trinity and the Divinity of Christ in favour of the unipersonality of God was the fundamental tenet of Unitarianism. The strict scripturalism of the Lutherans made the two factions natural opponents.

up using the hall. The owners also hired it out as a 'dime museum', and as Janson wrote, it was neither pleasant nor inspiring to preach in front of a curtain depicting 'the fattest woman in the world', or a buffalo charging a steam-train. Hamsun avoided controversial topics while working for Janson, and chose subjects which would not compromise his own lack of religious faith. He had once before lectured on St Paul in Elroy, and was sensitive to Sven Tveraas' criticism on that occasion that this was hypocritical of him, in spite of claiming that the lecture had been largely meant as an objective examination of the pillars of the orthodox church. The heat in the conflict between the liberals in the Unitarian camp and the orthodox Lutherans was probably as much social as religious anyway; Janson felt that the Lutheran church was doing its utmost to insulate and isolate the Norwegian communities in the mid-west from the influence of America, while the Lutherans regarded Unitarianism as a corrupting American heresy that would in time destroy the Norwegian character of these communities. Hamsun's sympathies were clearly on the liberal side, but his attitude towards Unitarianism remained one of sympathy, not commitment. When Janson had to travel in the West for three weeks, Hamsun took over the congregational duties, and spelled out his position in a letter to Tveraas:

> . . . since basically I cannot accept the Unitarian faith, I will only give cultural-religious lectures about different countries, and in that way I shall avoid the question of belief.

His policy here would not give any offence. An article by his friend Krøger Johansen in *Dagbladet* on 16 January 1891 makes it clear that the contemporary American priest was willing to talk about anything in his sermon, 'railway strikes, the reform of Congress, political administration, the schools, the tax system, on everyday topics of every kind'.

Hamsun read voraciously in Minneapolis. Both Jansons were broad-minded and intellectually curious, and their large library was stocked with everything from the great Russian novelists to the thinkers of India and ancient China, as well as a wide selection of current American literature. Hamsun spent hours in front of the shelves. Janson noticed his habit of standing and browsing in a book for minutes on end before replacing it on a shelf in favour of another, and on the basis of his discussions later with Hamsun concluded that he was a man like Bjørnson, with the happy knack of picking up the essence of a book on the basis of these fleeting examinations. The two men talked a great deal together, discussing theology and philosophy, and they also talked as writers, analysing how particular effects could be achieved by the use of unusual adjectives. Hamsun soon realised that he was a vastly more gifted writer than his former mentor, but he retained a degree of respect for Janson's talent that was not merely an expression of the gratitude he felt towards him for all his help and encouragement in these early years.

Drude Janson also encouraged him unstintingly. She wrote a little herself, and seems to have been a more complex and emotional person than her husband. Hamsun showed her his writing, and she praised it, but advised him to wait before trying to have it published or translated into English. She seems to have been deeply touched by Hamsun's situation, and attracted to him; so deeply serious, but with a child-like sense of fun, so hungry to educate himself, proud of what he had achieved already but still painfully aware of the gaps in his learning. Their conversations moved her to tears sometimes. Hamsun retained for her also a strong sense of loyalty and affectionate gratitude. The dramatic turn that his life now took involved Drude in a way that shows the considerable degree of intimacy that existed between the two.*

That incident at Elroy when Hamsun felt something 'tear loose' in his chest while lifting a barrel of salt had indeed been a warning: one day, as he was acting as auctioneer at a church bazaar, he began coughing blood again. The Norwegian Dr Thams was called to the house on Nicollet Avenue where he examined Hamsun, concluded that he was suffering from galloping tuberculosis, and gave him three more months to live. He offered a faint hope of remission if Hamsun recovered sufficiently to be able to get away from the Minnesota climate.

In the weeks that followed, Drude Janson nursed Hamsun as he tried to come to terms with the prospect of his own death. He recalled his own state of mind in a letter to the Danish novelist Erik Skram in 1888:

I felt a desperate desire to go to a whorehouse in town and sin.

* Any possibility of an affair between the two, however, seems to be excluded. The Jansons later divorced, Kristofer to marry a spiritualist, and Drude to write a *roman-à-clef* called *Mira* which caused quite a sensation when it became known that the author 'Judith Keller' was actually Drude. Hamsun found the scandalous whispering about his old friends and patrons tasteless and in a letter to *Dagbladet* on 10 February 1898 he was at pains to point out that 'Judith's' use of the word infidelity in her description of the marriage referred to a purely platonic betrayal.

Have you ever heard anything so crazy? When I was on the point
of dying! I wanted to sin magnificently, to die in the act, to die in
sin, whisper hurrah and breathe my last. I'm ashamed to admit
it. But I was burning up so violently. And all my life I'd been so
strict with myself – what was the point of it all, if I was going to
die now anyway? I was furious.

I told Fru Janson openly what was on my mind, and she must
have been human herself once, she told me that she could
understand. Imagine that. That was what she said to me. She
was so indulgent with me around that time. She indulged me
more than I deserved, it was embarrassing.

I sold my watch to pay for the visit, secretly ordered a cab,
because I was too ill to walk, and made ready to go. Then it
transpires that the lady cannot 'understand' after all, and when
she hears about it she cancels the cab.

So it all came to nothing. And I don't regret it, not now. I know
I would have died on the spot.

But can you understand how a young man could be so crazy
with a death sentence hanging over him? I didn't give a damn for
the consequences 'on the other side'. Didn't even consider
them, even though in those days I believed in a half-hearted way
in the 'wages of sin'. A professor of theology visited me around
that time, a kind and lovable man who had known me since I
was a child. I behaved badly to him, and offended him, without
meaning to.

I was in a state of extreme agitation. An evening passed. A
night. A morning. Then, to put it plainly, I was offered the
chance to sin right there in the very house in which I was living. I
received a specific offer.

I did not accept.

Can you understand that? This is something that has haunted
me for years. That I was once offered the key to a door – a red
bow in the curtain, a particular hour, a tap on the door – and I
would not accept. Had I actually *asked* for the key, anything
might have happened. So much can a small detail mean to me.
Are there many like me, or am I the only idiot in the world?[10]

Frustrated in this way, his sexual lust turned aside and he went on
to describe to Skram how he had developed an erotic passion for
light – sunlight, torches, flares, even humble daylight. Drude
Janson thought he had gone mad. She was shocked when she
entered his room one day and found that he had set fire to his
curtains and was watching them burning. The sight of the flames
brought him an intense erotic release, and he told Skram that for

the first time, he had been able to understand Nero's joy in watching Rome burn. The incident, and subsequent letter, throw interesting light on Hamsun's sexual personality as a young man, especially the comment that he had been so 'strict' with himself in his life. For all his precocity, and the adventurous rough and tumble of his early years, he seems to have guarded his innocence fiercely. Elsewhere, for example, he claimed never to have touched whisky until his thirtieth year.

His condition improved over the summer, but did not stabilise. The Jansons organised a collection to pay for his fare back to Norway, where there was hope for his recovery if he could get plenty of country air. He was presently well enough to travel unaccompanied, and so determined to live that he climbed on to the roof of the train and for long stretches of the three-day journey from Minnesota to New York sat there and let the cold air rush down into his lungs.

On the journey home he probably travelled the normal route, across the Atlantic from New York to Belfast, then to Liverpool and by train across England to Hull, and so to Norway. A letter to Sven Tveraas of 23 September 1884, from Aurdal, indicates that he delayed in Christiania long enough to visit the offices of *Aftenposten* and *Verdens Gang*, and to present a letter of introduction to *Dagbladet*'s editor, Lars Holst, from Kristofer Janson in an effort to try to sell some articles he had brought with him from America. He had also arranged for the bookseller and publisher Albert Cammermeyer to send him new books,[11] which he would review for *Aftenposten*. But he was still unsure whether he would live or die, and sometimes it seemed to him that it would not matter much either way. He told Sven:

I have travelled up here to Valdres to see if the air here can make me well again. I have now only spat blood once since crossing the Atlantic, and I hope I can shake it for good now. But I don't know how likely this is. The doctors in Christiania didn't think I would die this winter, they seem agreed that next spring is more likely. Anyway, I have done what I can, and now things must just go as they please. I don't regret anything. Of course, I would like to have lived a little longer, but if I don't, then I don't. The worst of it is the money I owe you. This was not how I intended to repay you for your friendship, that you should lose through me; but just now I see no way in which I can settle the debt. Now some explanations:
I have hired a place here in Aurdal, but though I'm supposed

to pay forty kroner in fourteen days I have no idea where I'll get them from. Because I cannot work. I'm just too ill, I'm wasted away.

Hamsun felt wretched, alone and friendless, and his thoughts went back to Elroy. Now it seemed to have been a golden time, when he always had money and friends, and good company. He asked after A . . . (probably Anna Johnson), and all his old friends:

Now I've got nothing. When I consider it all, I think I'd rather die than live. I've had to sell the few things I owned to pay for doctor's and chemist's bills. The doctor in Christiania (Dr Bull, the best in Norway) said that if I survived through to next spring then it would be alright for me to travel back to America again. And I think I will, if I live. And this time I will get myself a job where I don't have to push myself so hard, and I will save every cent.

And if he ever regretted having once thought of being a writer, he knew it was much too late to do anything about it now:

If I could avoid all the strain that thinking and writing causes me I know I would be better. But I have to write for my food, so you see, I must do it.

Chapter 4
1884–1886: Convalescence and Valdres

The Valdres valley where Hamsun was now living is one of the loveliest parts of eastern Norway, wide and flat, with countless lakes studded with small islands, surrounded by pine woods. The valley walls are steep and green, and in Hamsun's day were farmed way up to the heights. In the west the main valley climbs through the settlements at Vang to the watershed dividing east and west at Filefjeld, and in the north it passes through Østre Slidre to the lake at Bygdin, 1060 metres above sea level. In those days the main roads connecting east and west Norway ran right through the valley, so that particularly in the summer there was plenty of life in the hotels and settlements along the way.*

Hamsun's first lodgings were in the south of the valley, with the widow Dahle at Østre Sørum. Here he was no more than eighty kilometres or so from Gjøvik, where he had worked on the roads before emigrating. He had friends there who would have spared him the loneliness of which he complained to Sven Tveraas, but in fact he seems to have chosen to isolate himself in order to write. The uncertainty over whether he would recover his health or not imparted a feverish urgency to his efforts, as he set about writing a novel set in the Christiania Bohemian milieu. Its theme, he told a friend, was to be 'the tragedy of people going to the dogs'. In one memorable day and night session he produced fifty sides, working in the grip of a hallucinated synaesthesia in which he saw 'tones, notes, rhythms floating in the air not far away from me, like lines of light which I can hear'. But the novel's progress was halting and frustrating, and was impeded by the constant need to earn money.

As arranged with Albert Cammermeyer, he read and reviewed

* The development of the railways, particularly the building of the Christiania-Bergen line in the 1890s, moved the focus of attention away from the valley.

books sent to him in *Aftenposten*, though the fees here were hardly likely to keep him in food and lodging. He had better hopes for three newspaper articles which he had brought back with him from America and had submitted to *Aftenposten*. These were bought, and appeared in January and February of 1885 under the pen-name 'Ego' which he had used for the first time in his Gjøvik article of 1880.

The three articles together were a lengthy and not quite formless series of impressions of America, a theme which suggested itself as a money-spinner to Hamsun several times in the course of the next few years as emigration fever continued to run high in Norway. In them he writes with a breezy confidence about such subjects as American women, American industry, American mores, speech and literature, his attitude varying between one of wide-eyed innocence and wary cynicism. Generally speaking he was a good deal more tolerant than he was to be in his caustic and dismissive book *On the Cultural Life of Modern America* three years later, written after his second visit there. The articles also give a glimpse of the future novelist at work: at one point Hamsun describes his meeting with the inventor of an electric psalm-book, one of the many unusual claims to fame of the extraordinary Johan Arndt Happolati in *Hunger*.

Inevitably, Hamsun also treated his own fraught situation in literary form, and wrote the short story *Fragment of a Life* shortly after his return. Romantically signed as from the hand of 'A Young, Unknown Author', it consists of a farewell letter from a young man to an actress for whom he feels a hopeless and unrequited love. The writer has, like Hamsun, been given a sentence of death by his doctors – by two doctors, in fact – who disagree about the origins and progress of the disease. He tries briefly to persuade himself that it might be possible to survive the illness by an act of will, but eventually abandons hope. The writer ends his love letter with the news that he has decided to take the boat to America, although he is careful to suggest to the girl that he will certainly not land there alive. Hamsun's prose contains much striking and precise observation, and sudden unnerving shafts of self-insight which again point forward to the mature novelist, but there is too much sentimentality in it, indicating that there was still something of the author of *Bjørger* and *Frida* in him.*

The editor of *Dagbladet*, Lars Holst, bought the story and published it in the paper on 12 December 1884. In a letter to

* 'My, how this boy weeps!' Hamsun heard Bjørnson mutter as he thumbed through the ms of *Frida*.

Hamsun he said that it showed 'great talent', and Hamsun, much encouraged, sent him what he considered himself to be a far superior piece of work.[1] This, alas, Holst would not take, telling Hamsun that it was 'too strong' for a daily paper.

In Aurdal Hamsun had met Erik Frydenlund and struck up a friendship with him. Erik and his mother Kari ran the hotel further up the valley at Frydenlund, and soon Hamsun moved in with them and began helping out. He and Erik shared a room on the upper floor of the hotel, Room 14. Hamsun had realised by this time that he was not dying of 'galloping tuberculosis' after all – in fact, it turned out to have been a severe attack of bronchitis – and as though by way of celebration he now entered one of the happiest phases of his life.

The Frydenlund's hotel was on the main Christiania-Bergen road, and was run to a standard that met the exacting demands of rich Norwegian and German tourists, and was also deemed acceptable by the English who made up most of the hotel's clientéle. Hamsun's observations of them, arriving stiff and unapproachable in their Bennett's carioles, imperious in their dealings with the locals, did little to improve the uneasy impression he had formed of them from his boyhood reading at Uncle Hans'. However, they were merely background figures to the social circle in which he now moved.

The tourist traffic gave Frydenlund a status locally as the home of the Valdres élite. The valley's businessmen and administrators all lived nearby, and the hotel itself had a small extension built on the side to house the post office. Erik ran this – which made him an important man in the community – and Hamsun, with his experiences of postal work from Hamarøy, was his assistant. Through Erik he also gained entry into a circle of friends whose ready acceptance of him meant a great deal. One friend was the district doctor, Andreas Aabel, who lived next door to the hotel at Frydenlund. He had a fine singing voice, and was the leading light of the local glee club which Hamsun was soon persuaded to join. The doctor was also an amateur poet like two other members of the circle, Jul Haganes and Ola Olsen. Olsen was a shoemaker, and Hamsun developed the habit of dropping in on him for a chat and helping out at the bench, keeping alive the skills he had picked up in his apprenticeship as a sixteen-year-old in Bodø. Olsen was also a fine performer on the Hardanger fiddle, a folk instrument with four melody and four drone strings which produces music of great and haunting beauty. But the real musician among them was a man named 'Ulrik from Jens' place', whom Hamsun probably met at the house of the animal-doctor, Bolleng, the first vet in the valley and a man who had managed to overcome to a great extent the local hostility among the peasant farmers to his 'college' background. Bolleng was a great democrat and deflater of pretension, and a fine storyteller. He had two rooms at 'Jens' place', and the friends would often meet there to socialise. Bolleng had a special jug there called 'Goldsides', which would be filled with moonshine at such gatherings and passed from hand to hand. It had magical properties which could cure melancholy and sadness. Whoever drank from it would presently be overcome by a desire to tell a story or a joke. Ulrik played at dances for them, and in among the local dance tunes he would slip a few of the exotic numbers Bolleng had brought with him from his student days in Stockholm – Rhineland Polkas, Mazurkas, the Figaro, the Waltz. Hamsun showed the dances that he'd learnt in America and the jigs and reels taught to him by the Irishmen he'd met over there. There was a lot of card-playing in this circle too, and walking trips up into the mountains. Hamsun also had a fondness for the local 'black sheep', an irreverent, hard-drinking miner and stone-breaker named Asgjer-Timann, and the pair of them once went off into the mountains together for ten days and did some contract hay-making for a farmer up there.[2]

In the middle of 1885, Erik Frydenlund was called-up to do his military service, and Hamsun took over the running of the post office.[3] Trouble arose with the Head Post Office in Christiania straight away, and Hamsun's letter of explanation on 10 June to Erik gives us a splendid picture of how he was diversifying his time in Aurdal, taking care of post-office business – just – and battling on, in the face of huge indifference, with his career as a great lecturer. He encloses a copy of a long, pained reply he has made to complaints from Head Office about some registered letters that turned up loose in the mail, and then brings Erik up to date on happenings in Aurdal:

> Right then, there's a little something for the label-scholars of the Norwegian Postal Department. If they want more, all they have to do is write to me again. But what about that bloke Jonsrud?! I mean, if he *really* wants to do business . . . Anyway, that's enough about that.
>
> During my last lecture on Bjørnson I had to have a very severe word with the Honourable Herr Halvorsen right in the middle of proceedings. He turned up, the only true blue there, and without being aware of my stipulations from the previous lecture coughed, cleared his throat, grunted and whispered so

loudly and showed in general such a keen desire to 'express himself' (as you would put it) that I had to call him publicly to order. So we had quiet again, whether from anger or fear, or even intelligence, I don't know. All I know is that for once I lost my temper. And that was fine, because it went like a house on fire afterwards. Hot stuff alright. Once I just managed in time to stop myself from saying 'Jesus wept' – you know how I can get carried away sometimes. Next time it will be Ibsen; that should all go off quietly enough. But Bjørnson is another matter; according to Kjørstad I 'burned my boats' in my last lecture on him. But Christ, it's so ridiculous to have to listen to criticism on subjects like rhetoric and aesthetics from a man like Halvorsen. It isn't as if I'd never had an audience before either. Christ . . .

Are you my friend, Erik? I like you so much. And your mother – oh, I'm mad about her. Actually I love everybody. They're all so good to me, everybody's so good to me. Even though I'm a man who's strayed into the wilderness. God I feel such a fantastic urge to say – phew – !

How are things 'down there', under the circumstances? And Heyerdal? Say hello to him from me. I liked that man. There was nothing calculated about his way of speaking, he spoke quite openly, the way a man should speak –

I'm brimming over with stuff I should be writing – there's a short story besides the novel – full of stuff. And have you ever seen a more luscious human being than Lina Tandberg? Well yes, I probably have; but not many, – I tell you, the race is dying out. What we have to do is begin lower down in nature again, if we want to find really beautiful people. Look at the upper classes, they aren't beautiful. Overcivilisation, my boy, it's cultural dynamite. I'm telling you.[4]

Hamsun, as is evident, was well aware that there was a comic side to these local lectures of his; a note to his friend Ola Aaberg in the magistrates office about another mini-series of literary lectures confirms this:

Lecture (for what it's worth) at Storengen (if I can find a room) at six o'clock in the evening (if that's not too late) on Friday (health permitting) and Saturday (likewise) on Kielland (that sinner) and Strindberg (that brute).[5]

He was also continuing with his journalism. Of particular interest is a two-part article that *Aftenposten* published early in May 1885, in which Hamsun described a visit he had made with a schoolteacher friend – possibly W. T. Ager – to an Indian camp outside Briggsville. Here he had met a man named Louis Remman, the son of an Indian woman who was raped by a white man. Remman was later claimed by the whites as one of their own, carried off and given an education and a civilisation. What fascinated Hamsun was that Remman had then consciously rejected the white world with its 'measurement and algebra, ritual, scheme and liturgy', and gone back to the Indians to live a life that followed the natural dictation of the appetites. The problem of the tensions between nature and culture, a theme later examined in *Pan*, clearly occupied already an important place in his thinking.

An article published in March the same year in the *Ny illustreret Tidende* was important for other reasons. Hamsun's parenthetical comments in his letter to Ola Aaberg indicate that he already possessed in high degree the ability to ironise over himself. This was clearly a vital talent for a young man of his pretensions who was prepared to make such apparently extravagant claims for the importance of his own views on contemporary literature – especially since he lacked all orthodox qualifications for making such claims. One of the most important influences on him in this respect was his discovery of Mark Twain, the subject of his article. Twain was the one American writer for whom Hamsun felt real respect, and even love. With considerable acumen for an immigrant with a limited grasp of English he had managed to penetrate the 'folksy' exterior of Twain's style to discover that he was in fact a literary master of great subtlety:

> It takes more to be a good comic writer than the ability to use colossal and grotesque exaggeration in one's language, and considerably more than the simple ability to be able to write pathetic and atmospheric descriptions of life in the mining towns.

He praised the originality and the richness of language in *Roughing It*, and enjoyed Twain's use of the technique of which he himself later became a master – the ability to knit some small, personal, often idyllic memory suddenly, but fittingly, into a prose passage dealing with some quite other time and place and mood. He felt the kinship of the self-educated man with Twain:

> The fact that he has been out in the world himself, and suffered his way towards his experiences, enables him not only to feel artistically sure of himself, but also to make correct judgements.

Twain's faith in personal experience, his courage in not letting himself be overawed by his lack of learning, gave great encouragement to Hamsun, who never quite managed to shake off a deep sense of unease about his own lack of a formal education. The resumés Hamsun goes on to give of Twain's *Innocents Abroad* and *The New Pilgrim's Progress* both sound strikingly like descriptions of the kind of book he himself was to produce on America just a few years later – violently subjective, crude, irreverent, witty and fiercely prejudiced – and suggest that Twain was a very important influence indeed on Hamsun during these days of his literary apprenticeship. Above all, one feels that in his frequent portrayal of himself as the ridiculous, pretentious, slightly clownish figure, Twain taught the over-sensitive young Hamsun a vital lesson in the art of literary self-portraiture: that it is possible – with care – to laugh at oneself and survive. Hamsun submitted this article to the *Ny illustreret Tidende* under the name of Hamsund. A printer's devil knocked the *d* off, so that the name appeared in its now familiar form – Hamsun. Though he had occasionally used this spelling before, the misprint here struck him as auspicious, and he stuck to this form for the rest of his life. Humour and a degree of self-ridicule are so very much a part of Hamsun's literary personality from now on that it seems appropriate that the search for an identity, suggested by all the experimenting with different forms of his name, should finally cease in connection with an article on one of the finest self-debunkers of them all.

Hamsun's health was now fully recovered. Local reports of this, his first stay in Valdres, depict him as a boisterous, sociable man fond of singing and dancing, joking and talking and visiting people, and going for long walks in the hills. He revelled in his own fitness after the desolate months of sickness, and acquired a mystical belief in the healing properties of the air in Valdres. The valley was to remain important to him. Already a committed wanderer, he found a temporary home at Aurdal, and a family in the community there. The friendship formed with Erik Frydenlund was one of the few deep and lasting ones of his life. But the contentment and affection he found there were not enough to blot out the bitterness he sometimes felt about his predicament. In a letter to Nikolai Frøsland, a brother of his Gjøvik friend Nils, he describes his life as a climb, a gruelling step-by-step process, and envied Nikolai his mother, saying that with a mother like her, 'all those talents which were stifled in my upbringing would have been encouraged, and I would be somebody by now'.[6] His need to escape the chains of his birth, to reinvent himself completely,

continued to be the driving force within him. Abruptly, towards
the end of 1885, he returned to Christiania.

Once again, as in 1880, he had experiences which were to
become the raw material for *Hunger*. 'I looked for work', he wrote,
'but nothing came up for me. I was very poor. Now and then I
earned a few kroner for a newspaper article.'[7] He also decided on a
serious attempt to make a name for himself as a lecturer on
literature, no doubt feeling that he had served his apprenticeship
both in America and in the villages around Valdres. He spent the
winter and spring of 1885–86 putting the lectures together and
planning a tour of larger Norwegian towns. In April he returned
briefly to Valdres, and then began in earnest at Gjøvik on 8 May,
with a lecture on Strindberg. Perhaps he chose Gjøvik in hopes that
former workmates and acquaintances would be persuaded out to
support their old friend and comrade, and so get the tour off to a
rousing start. But apparently no one there remembered the former
navvy Knut Pederson, or if they did, didn't really care much what
he had to say about Strindberg – five people turned up. He tried
again two days later, and this time drew a crowd of seven.
Undaunted, he managed to get *Dagbladet* to mention his projected
tour in the issue of 14 May. According to the report, he was going
to begin with towns along the Christiania fjord, continue along the
west coast speaking in the larger towns there – Kristiansand,
Stavanger, Bergen – and finish off up in his home county,
Nordland. The paper called him Herr Homsum.[8]

The novelist Alexander Kielland was at the time the subject of a
heated political debate in Norway. His status in the country was on
a par with that of Ibsen, Bjørnson, and Jonas Lie, but a suggestion
to the government – sponsored by his great contemporaries – that
he be allocated one of the coveted annual literary stipends to
established writers had been controversially thrown out. Certain
reactionary parliamentarians, among them Lars Oftedal, the bane
of Hamsun's boyhood summer, did not approve of his 'attitude'
towards life. Hoping to capitalise on interest in the case, Hamsun
spoke on Kielland at Horten on National Day, 17 May, then
travelled further south to Tønsberg for a lecture on the 21st, and on
to Sandefjord on the 23rd, where he delivered two lectures on the
same day on Kielland and Strindberg. From Tønsberg he wrote to
give Erik Frydenlund an account of his progress:

> No luck at all Erik, no luck at all. I spoke at Horten on 17 May, I'm
> speaking here tonight and at Sandefjord on Sunday. The people
> just don't come. The few who do turn up are enthusiastic, but
> there are so few of them.

I can't think what the hell to do. I ought to try the big towns on the west coast, Stavanger and Kristiansand and Bergen. But if it doesn't go any better there then I can't see any point in continuing with this damn thing at all.[9]

His pride was hurt. He admitted to Erik that he did not like writing letters as long as he was not earning any money – and he had run up debts which he now realised he was going to have difficulty paying off. Hamsun was particularly worried about a large debt of 200 kroner that he owed to Erik's uncle, Nils Frydenlund, but the improvement he hoped for did not materialise, and he returned to Christiania deeply dispirited, and tried to work out a next move. He had mentioned in his letter to Erik the offer of a job on the staff of a Christiania newspaper which he thought he might fall back on if the worst came to the worst; but now that it had come to the worst, he decided there was nothing to be gained by falling back on it. Instead he sat down and turned failure into art, and wrote a short story about the whole heartbreaking farce.

In *On Tour*[10] Hamsun found his real voice for the first time. It is a description of a journey he makes by rail from Christiania to Drammen to deliver one of his literary lectures. He travels third-class, pretentiously reading Daudet and puffing on a cigar, in his luggage a bag of dirty washing and 500 business cards with his name incorrectly printed on them. At Drammen he finds that the main hall has already been booked by an anti-spiritist conjurer who adds spice to his act by exhibiting a troupe of monkeys. The only other venue available is the Park Pavilion, and Hamsun makes his way there on foot to meet Carlsen, the man in charge of hiring out the pavilion. 'It wasn't far', he claims, 'I was there within a few short hours.' Carlsen feels sorry for him, and tries to persuade him to abandon the lecture on the grounds that competition from the anti-spiritist conjurer will be too strong. He warns him that a Swedish student once before tried a similar thing, bringing culture to Drammen in the form of a lecture, and he lost money on it.

Hamsun will have none of it, and dismisses as absurd the suggestion that he might lose money. Carlsen then upsets him still further by saying that he will have to put the matter to the committee in charge of the pavilion, which might take a couple of days. This leads to an irritated and mocking aside from Hamsun as he delivers his opinion of such committees, forever debating whether or not to cut back the trees in the park half a centimetre; or the advisability of allowing children into the pavilion in their ordinary shoes; or whether money can be spared for the purchase of a long-handled broom to sweep the pavilion with. According to him, they should be addressing themselves to higher matters altogether, conducting learned debates there on whether Petofi wore brown or grey socks, and on the inheritability or otherwise of poetic talent. The tone of the whole place should be higher, and the flag fly at half-mast whenever Parnell has belly-ache, or a member of the French Academy dies. He haughtily declines to wait two days while some park committee or other votes on his fitness to lecture in their premises, and returns to Christiania cold, tired and dispirited, glumly smoking one of his foul-smelling five-øre cigars. The reality, of course, is that he had no money to pay for his keep for an extra two days.

The whole story observes a beautiful distance between the narrator's attempts to persuade others that he is something more than he is, and the clear indifference of others to these attempts. He wastes precious money paying a porter to carry his bags between the station and the hotel rather than have the boy think that he is too poor to afford him. Terrified of being seen through, he is also comically aware that he is effortlessly seen through. *On Tour* is a marvellous portrait of the self as 'ridiculous man', and its narrator distinctly related to the aspiring young tyro of *Hunger* and his absurdly ambitious projects to write full-scale refutations of Kant, and visionary verse dramas set in the Middle Ages. The story is a witty satire on the subject of his own anonymity, a humorous victory over his own self-importance which shows real character, besides being a neatly-turned and well-deserved piece of self-advertisement:

> I am a young genius with a name so unfamiliar that no advertising editor has yet been able to spell it right in the columns of his newspaper. It is altogether a name which no one seems to remember having read anywhere, and one of the worst names in the world to make famous. *Hamsun*! I seem to spend at least five minutes every time I write down these so-and-so letters to make it quite clear to people that it cannot possibly be Hansen, or Hansum, or Hammersund, but simply *Hamsun*.

The increasing difficulties of his life in Christiania now seem to have made it clear to Hamsun that the recognition which he so desperately wanted was going to exact an almost mephisthophelean price of him. Two other short stories written at the same time indicate the extent of his despair, while confirming his determination to go on. One entitled *Sin* he wrote explicitly to show that 'thieving under certain conditions, thieving from *need*, is not sin at all'. He meant need in its most basic sense – need for shoes, warmth, food. The story *A Liar* had an even more unusual purpose, namely to show that 'lying is not sin, but *talent*'; a perfect credo for a writer perhaps, but still, not an idea one can ever be wholly comfortable with. Hamsun was proud of all three stories, and rightly so. But there seems a trace of unease, or apology, in the words with which he follows these controversial assertions in his letter to Erik Frydenlund – 'you see, Erik, I was driven to the very edge in Christiania'.[11]

How great must his distress have been, then, when *Dagbladet* refused *On Tour*. It was undoubtedly a disaster when what he knew quite well was not merely the best thing that he personally had ever written, but something that was also new to Norwegian literature in so many ways, not least in its experiments with language, was rejected. During a similar crisis six years earlier he had sought out Bjørnson with the manuscript of *Frida*, and asked for a writer's opinion on it. Now, with his confidence shaken, he went to a writer again.

He chose his man well this time. Arne Garborg, eight years older than Hamsun, was already an established literary figure. He was a public supporter of young writers and had openly protested the banning, for alleged obscenity, of books by Hans Jaeger and Christian Krohg in this same year, 1886. His courage lost him his government job in the Treasury Department. He was also involved in the debate over Alexander Kielland's grant. Hamsun went to see this brave and principled man on 12 June, but the meeting did not go well, and Hamsun explains why in a letter written the following day:

> I would like to ask you not to be offended by my behaviour of yesterday. The fact is that when you kindly offered to read my manuscript the day after Whitsunday, and I hesitated, it was because I was so tired, so very tired. And I had forgotten that we are already in Whitsun now.
>
> For nearly five years now, people have been telling me to 'come back in a few days' time'. Five years. Suddenly I was so very tired of it yesterday. I know that now I have told you this, you will understand. And besides, one has so little to live on during these 'few days' times'. No, I'm not starving, I still have almost two untouched loaves left. But my appetite is another matter . . .
>
> I wish to tell you: I have come to you now looking for a final judgement. Please give this to me. I realise now how dangerous it is to occupy oneself with something one feels passionately about, other than as a diverting hobby. If you say to me that I

should give up now, then I will, – then I will [*sic*] give up now. I
only regret to think that I have brought you my *last* work; I know
I could have found you something better. And I want to ask you
also why it is precisely those words and those turns of phrase
which I have taken the most trouble with, expressions involving
colours and sounds, that the editors underline with their
pencils, and put question marks against. This has surprised and
hurt me. For example (manuscript, first page): 'the *dirty* wind
from the sliding windows'. Sub-editor Pettersen has underlined
'dirty'. I would have thought that anyone who has ever travelled
on a train would have understood this description. But now I
want to know what you think.

Five years. Why haven't I given up before now? Because I
have had such a deep faith in my mission as a writer. And I have
had tremendous encouragement sometimes. Bjørnson, for
example. Janson and Fru Janson. I actually lived for quite a long
time with Janson, and we really *talked* about things. But to give
you an example of what happens to me: I wrote a sketch* for
Dagbladet in the winter of 1885, some desperate something or
other about a man with a rotting spine or something; and yes,
Holst sends me a postcard, an encouraging word up to Valdres,
where I was living then. He even used the expression 'great
talent' about my story. Of course, I was delighted, and wrote
him another story which *I* thought was much superior. But that
one he couldn't use. It was too daring, he said, it would be more
suitable for 'The New Magazine'. So I sent it to Skavlan. Still
haven't had an answer. Nothing, since the winter of 1885. It is
clear to me that since it has never been printed, it cannot be used.
This is how it is, all the time. I go from one to the other. Either I'm
told to 'come back in a few days' time' or else: this cannot be used.

Now I want to hear what you think. I ask you to be as honest as
possible when you tell me what you think of my writing, and I
apologise for giving you this task. But it is too late now.

I thank you so much for your kindness in helping me like this.
I know it must be boring for you. Forgive me.[12]

This plea to Garborg did the trick. He was a personal friend of the
editor Holst, and *On Tour* duly appeared in *Dagbladet* for 4 July.
Holst also bought *Sin* and *A Liar*, as well as some articles on
American literature, thereby giving Hamsun confirmation, if he
needed it, of the element of corruption involved in literary success.

It all seems to have happened just a little too late for him,

---

* *Fragment of a Life.*

though. And for someone of his high ambition a short story published in a newspaper, no matter how good the story, was no longer the great thrill it had once been. He had been submitting successfully to magazines and newspapers in Norway and America for over four years now, and he must have known that the real problem was still his failure to produce a large-scale work. Nothing had come of his novel on the Bohemians in Christiania, and the tragedy of people going to the dogs. The problem was not one of willingness to work – Hamsun had that in abundance – but his inability to control the novel, to keep it in a consistent focus. He was bewildered and frustrated by the rapid changes in his own relationship with it. There were times, he wrote to Nikolai Frøsland, when he felt that he had his hand on the pulse of the book, and saw effortlessly all the way through to the end, only to find that the following day the vision was gone. It left him feeling hopeless, with a sense that the whole thing was a waste of time. The fact that he had also to force himself to think about how to raise money all the time angered him. His own perfectionism frustrated him as well; he was pitifully sensitive to the question of style in his writing, and complained pathetically to Nikolai of how much of the book he had crossed out:

It was my hope, my downright obsession, that this book should change things ever so slightly for the better, for myself and for others; but I can never finish it.[13]

Then there was the fiasco of the lecture tour, the mounting debts that he could see no way of repaying, and the humiliation of sub-editors questioning his attempts to do something new with the language. Hamsun had reached the kind of impasse from which only one mighty bound could free him, and summoning up all his courage he leapt, dashing off a telegrammatic missive of explanation to Erik Frydenlund in mid-flight:

Dear Friend,
I am going to New York again. It is quite impossible here at home.
Expect a letter from NY.
Ask your mother not to be angry with me.
Are we still friends?
Say hello to everyone!
                    Your Knut H.
On board *Geisir* off Kristiansand, 20 Aug. 86[14]

He had persuaded both *Dagbladet* and Ola Thommesen on *Verdens Gang* to give him press cards as a roving reporter, while Lars Holst and a businessman friend of Holst's named Dobloug paid his fare. The story Hamsun had written to show that 'lying is not sin, but *talent'* was never published. Perhaps, like the follow-up to *Fragment of a Life*, it went too far for Holst to publish it in a daily paper. *Sin*, the story which he wrote to show that 'theft under certain circumstances, theft from need' was not a sin, appeared while Hamsun was still at sea, a harbinger of more explosive and enigmatically provocative things to come. One who didn't expect to hear any more from him was the compiler of Halvorsen's Lexicon of Norwegian Authors. He closed off the entry on 'Knud Pedersen Hamsund' with the succinct line 'Emigrated to America, 1886'. But of course, it was not 'Knud Pedersen Hamsund' who sailed on the *Geisir*, but Knut Hamsun. *On Tour* was the voice he'd been looking for.

Chapter 5
1886–1888: The American Experience II

The *Geisir* docked in New York on the afternoon of 3 September after what Hamsun described as a 'pig' of a crossing. He stayed overnight in the city and then made straight for Chicago, with the intention of heading on into the west as swiftly as possible. He may perhaps have entertained rather grandiose plans about how much could be got out of being a roving reporter for two of Norway's most important newspapers in America; and as such he could travel for half-fare on the American railways.[1] However, as soon as he arrived in Chicago he changed his mind, and began to look for a steady job. For two weeks he answered advertisements in the *Chicago Tribune*, and roamed the streets looking for work. Perhaps initially he hoped to avoid the usual fate of the poor Scandinavian immigrant – a labouring job involving hard, physical work and low pay – and tried to find himself something for which his abilities fitted him, office work of some kind. But finally he cursed his luck, and as though to an inevitability applied for a job on the railways. The work was on the open street, in the heart of the city, and the weather was hot. He sent a report to Erik Frydenlund:

We are a crew of some five to six hundred men, and it's punishing work. I've been promised a brilliant future when I begin on the cable-cars in about a month's time. Let me tell you about it: they have trams here that go through the streets by themselves – no horses, no engines – you just see a row of carriages coming towards you, and you can't see what it is that drives them along. In fact, there's a kind of thingammujig under the ground that propels the carriages along, a cable several English miles long, and all along the route there is a slit in the road about half an inch wide, where an arm connecting the carriages to the cables runs. In about a month's time I'll be given a job on one of these trains. I'll only be a reserve to begin with, at a salary of about fifty to sixty dollars a month; but come the spring, when I get my own route, I'll be able to push the money up to around 100 dollars. This is a job with a future. It's a question of keeping in with the right man. I hope I can do it. There are hundreds of people after jobs like this: but I have the Superintendent's own word for it that I will get the job – he's made a note of my name – whoopee!

So I've taken ordinary labouring work in the streets, because otherwise it would seem to me a long time without work. But God help us it's hard. Farmwork's got nothing on it. Three men to carry an iron rail weighing 1200 pounds; one man to carry a barrel of cement weighing 400 pounds; likewise a barrel of screws, 450 pounds; the cement is the worst – it gets in my eyes. And the heat! It's been up to 100 degrees F in the shade. We work half-naked . . .[2]

He had his hair cut in the 'American' style, cropped to the scalp, and had begun to grow a small moustache for which the barber had prophesied a great future. As ever, the fascination for Hamsun of new experiences, and the enthusiastic interest with which he viewed life in those days, overrides the temporary physical discomforts of the job. Even so, the recent past of his experiences in Christiania seems to have set a special mark on his mind. Through the long letter to Erik he comes back to them, relating the details with a kind of eerie wonderment, as though in actual fact it all might have happened to somebody else. A man who had met Bjørnson, and talked literature with Kristofer Janson in the shadow of his bookshelves – could such a man really have slept rough and starving for several nights in a deserted tinsmith's shop in Møllergade? Just as Elroy, seen from across the Atlantic, had seemed to him in the lonely first few weeks back in Norway in 1884 to have been a homelike place, full of friends, with plenty of money about, so now Valdres is the place that seems like a lost home to him. And the feeling for Valdres was stronger. He asks Erik to remember him to Anne, Olea, Anton – everybody, and to tell him if anybody in Valdres is angry with him. A strange refrain that sings through all the letters from the years of his struggle are these anxieties for the opinion of others, and pleas for forgiveness for unspecified crimes – imagined slights, failures and boasts, sins committed in the driven pursuit of his destiny. The debt to Nils Frydenlund weighs on his conscience. Hamsun was terrified Nils would begin selling his prized collection of books in order to

redeem his money, and urged Erik to convince him that the debt
would be repaid, if only Nils would wait. He knew quite well that
one day he would be able to repay him. He knew that he would be
back in Valdres, and see them all again. It was all part of the one big
thing, 'Because I most emphatically do not renounce my dream of
getting my book finished one day'.

The next year in Chicago is one of the blank spots in Hamsun's life
story. We know that he lodged for a time at 3737 Langley Avenue,
with some people named Nelson, and that he established contact
with relatives; an old photograph, so worn and faded that half of
Hamsun's left leg and his foot have disappeared, shows him
posing with his cousin, Marie Andersen, in a photographer's
studio. Another photo shows him after his promotion on to the
cars. The moustache has arrived, and his hair grown out from the
summer crop of September, and he looks remote, contained, and
not very happy. Later, he wrote a short story about his winter and
spring on the Chicago trams, a gruesome thing, about a man under
one of the cable-cars whose head is ripped off by the claw of the car
as it passes over him. *Victory for the Woman* contains a number of
interesting details of Hamsun's life as a conductor.

He worked first on the Halstead Line, which ran from the middle
of town out to the cattle-market. This was still horse-driven, and
was known as a rough line, especially problematical on the night-
shift. One night over Christmas 1886 a mob of drunken Irish
workers from the cattle-market clambered on board and refused to
pay their fares. They had been paying fares all year, they
complained, and now it was Christmas, and the company should
treat them. In spite of his fears of company spies, Hamsun
diplomatically agreed with them.

After a while he was transferred to a cable-car line, the Cottage
Line, where his passengers were a more genteel lot, villa-dwellers
from whom he collected his five cents wearing gloves. He soon
missed the excitement of the Halstead Line, and found the new
route and its customers boring. His hopes of pushing his wages up
to around 100 dollars a month had to be adjusted considerably
downwards – he was in that hard winter unable to afford warm
clothing, and as a protection against the bitter wind that whipped
through the city streets adopted the tramp's habit of wearing a
layer of newspaper next to his skin. His fellow-workers thought
this was highly amusing, and greatly enjoyed making him crackle
by poking him with their fingers. The few anecdotes from this
time, mostly originating from Hamsun himself, suggest that he
was generally eccentric in his behaviour, notably in his habit of

reading Aristotle and Euripides between stops. This habit, coupled
with his weak eyesight, meant that he was poor at keeping track of
the various stops, especially at night. Hamsun was never a man
who liked to admit himself at a loss (at least, not to anyone but his
readers), and with commendable optimism would continue to sing
out the stops in their correct order, to the consternation and
confusion of passengers.

That winter he wrote a long, two-part description[3] of the voyage
over on the *Geiser* which *Dagbladet* published in November. In
among his subjective and novelistic flourishes – among the least
credible of which is the claim that he lost all his notes for the article
in a great storm off the Newfoundland banks – he gives a
convincing picture of the conditions of travel these hopeful
emigrants had to endure. Discipline was military. Passengers were
all to be abed by a certain hour, and when one night some younger
passengers defied the curfew, the captain armed his crew and sent
them on deck, and delivered a fierce warning speech. It was very
much a 'human interest' kind of journalism, often funny and
illuminating, but sometimes striving a little too hard for effect. The
description is also too long; but that may simply have been to get
paid for two articles instead of one.

One wonders why such a prolific writer produced just this and
nothing else for publication throughout the late summer, winter
and spring of this period. Clearly, as a stranger in Chicago, he
would be far from his literary and journalistic contacts, and to
make new contacts in a city the size of Chicago would need much
more time, effort and luck than was necessary in Christiania. The
indications, primarily the absence of anecdotes, suggest that he
kept a very low profile. Perhaps the hours he worked gave him no
time for writing and socialising, and it is possible that he was still
trying to get his novel of Bohemian life finished – he spoke later to
Kristofer Janson of a novel that he had ripped up. In fact, it seems
equally likely that Hamsun simply wrote nothing for a while. Tired
of small successes, conscious of the fact that the further pursuit of
them was not only financially pointless, but might also represent
an actual dissipation of his talent, perhaps he had decided to let the
material of his experiences grow undisturbed for a while.

Hamsun lasted nine months on the cars. For a man who was
determined to be a writer it was a long time to be a tram conductor,
and he may have felt it was time to get going again. He decided to
leave Chicago and, as usual, had no money to pay for his fare. His
solution to the problem was not as simple as the tram driver Pat's
solution in *Victory for the Woman* – a contract murder – nor was it
nearly so lucrative. It was, however, highly characteristic. Hamsun

recalled the circumstances in a newspaper article written for the American *St Louis Post-Dispatch* in 1928:

> I wrote a short letter to a famous American and asked – *asked* for twenty-five dollars which I could not promise to pay back. I took the letter myself, and walked the long way out to his slaughter-houses, asked around and was directed to the man's office. It was a huge place, and ugly, and looked like some kind of outhouse. It was swarming with office-workers. I gave my letter to the young doorman, and watched him take it to a man sitting on a platform and working with some papers. It was Armour (Philip Armour, the meat millionaire). From this moment on I daren't look up. I felt a little ashamed maybe, and afraid, because my letter would in all probability be rejected. The doorman came swiftly back, and before I knew what was happening he had shoved twenty-five dollars into my hand. I took a little while to recover, and asked like an idiot: Did I get them? Yes, smiled the man. What did he say? I asked. He said that 'your letter was worth it'.[4]

Hamsun recalled that it was written in certainly the most wretched English Armour had ever read, and that the comment about its being 'worth' twenty-five dollars was surely ironic. However, forty-two years earlier, twenty-seven years old and broke, he didn't much care whether it was ironic or not. Armour's generosity was an important confirmation of the faith Hamsun had in the patriarch, grounded in Zahl from Kjerringøy. With the money he was able to leave Chicago and return to Minneapolis, where he had lived happily in 1884. Though it left little visible trace in his fiction, Hamsun's stay in Chicago, and his months on the cable-cars, remained an oddly bright point in his mind. This was one of the few jobs which he specifically mentioned whenever asked for biographical details, after he had reached that peak of fame and respectability at which an unruly and chaotic past is once and for all shaped into a suitably compact form; symbolic, quotable, portable.

Back in Minneapolis, he met Kristofer Janson again. Yes, he was able to tell Janson that was still writing – as a matter of fact, he had ripped up a novel just the other day . . . Janson offered Hamsun a room rent-free in his house on Nicollet Avenue so that he could write without worrying about where the money for his keep was coming from. In fact, after his hibernation in Chicago, rather as he had done after that first winter in Valdres, he seemed to explode back into life in the spring, and did little writing. He fell in with a group of young Norwegian-American Christians who ran a small teetotal newspaper called *The Password* who were, in spite of their distrust of alcohol – or perhaps, who knows, because of it – a lively group of young men who liked a good laugh, and shared Hamsun's taste for irreverent humour. John O. Hansen and Hallvard Askeland were the journalists, and Yngvar Laws their friend and sympathiser; Laws ran a drugstore, and kept a small stock of Norwegian books. At their invitation Hamsun mounted the podium again on 17 May for an evening of patriotic 'speeches, duologues, music, song and refreshment' promoted by The Norwegian League for Abstinence. Sandwiched between a 'Piano Solo by Miss Gelmeyden' and 'O Lovely Month of May' sung by the choir, he delivered a characteristically controversial speech on the illusory nature of individual freedom in American society.[5] Always quixotically himself, he openly disagreed with Askeland and Hansen's desire to close the saloons, deeming this a blow against freedom, but was quite willing to accept them, prejudices and all, if they reciprocated. Hamsun even wrote for their paper *The Password*, although he avoided preaching or even mentioning 'the cause' of Prohibition.

One is reminded of his willingness to speak to Kristofer Janson's Unitarian congregations in Janson's absence, during his previous stay in Minneapolis, while avoiding subjects that might involve him in hypocrisy.* He also involved himself briefly in a debate currently running in the pages of the Minneapolis magazine *Budstikken*.

Norwegian immigrant communities followed with a passionate intensity the various cultural and political developments taking place back home in Norway, and the uproar in the literary world in Christiania over the banning of books by Hans Jaeger and Christian Krohg in 1886 echoed loudly in Minneapolis. A Mr Kallum had been giving a series of readings from Krohg's *Albertine*, and one of his audience had written in criticism of the venture to *Budstikken*, using the *nom de plume* 'Dixi'. Hamsun took both Kallum and 'Dixi' to task in a good-tempered and amusingly patronising letter of 18 May to the magazine. He criticised 'Dixi' for calling the book 'boring, protracted and unbelievable' when authorities like Brandes, Janson and Garborg had praised it as a work of considerable merit and importance. And he criticised Mr Kallum for not having understood the kind of language and dialect

---

* One such contribution was an article entitled 'Flies', inspired by the droning sound of Pastor Gjertsen's sermon which he had heard one Thursday afternoon when he had gone down to the Conference Church with Askeland, to pump up the organ for him.

Krohg had used in the book, and for his poor rendering of the different dialects in his readings from the stage. Above all, he criticised him for his habit of banging and joggling the lectern all the time. Mr Kallum is wrong to state that the book is written throughout in the Vika-dialect (a working-class Christiania dialect), Hamsun wrote, adding that it is written in a *phonetic* Norwegian.

But the main point of the letter is to praise Mr Kallum for his initiative, and to ask 'Dixi' to show more tolerance:

> We are not so rich here that we can manage without all the cultural stimulation we can get. And as Norwegians we ought to think very carefully before dismissing the opportunity of hearing a public reading of a Norwegian book which has created a stir across three countries, and which it is no longer possible to get hold of.[6]

In the main, Hamsun continued to produce little in this period, strengthening the idea that he had perhaps come to see in his previous prodigality a danger of dissipation. Kristofer Janson had just started publishing his Unitarian magazine *Saamanden*, and Hamsun was supposed to be contributing to his keep by translating articles from Norwegian into English for the paper. But Janson soon found that his grasp of the language was so poor that he had to go over Hamsun's work afterwards. In fact, Hamsun's written English, which he later had to use in correspondence with Germans, Russians, Poles and others, was to develop into an instrument of considerable charm, although it always remained grammatically chaotic.

The outstanding picture we have of Hamsun from this summer of 1887 is as a friend. Most of his comrades at this time wrote memoirs of him after his climb to fame, and all of them are warm and positive in praise of his generosity, his honesty, and his courage, if they do at times give way to a tendency to idolatry. Another friend from this period was a young Swedish journalist named Victor Nilsson, an assistant editor on *Svenska Folkets Tidning*. He met Hamsun often at Janson's house, and talked about books with him. Hamsun spoke enthusiastically to him of Balzac, Strindberg, and the Dane J. P. Jacobsen. Jacobsen's novel *Niels Lyhne* from 1880 seemed an especial favourite. This portrait of a young man who has lost faith in the past, denies all received forms of wisdom, but is yet unable to find anything to replace the vacuum left by disillusion, might have seemed to Hamsun to come fairly close to describing his own situation.

Nilsson and Hamsun also talked about the great Russians, all of whom were well-represented on Janson's bookshelves, and the Swede recalled lending Hamsun a copy of Dostoevsky's *Crime and Punishment*, although he could not say for sure whether Hamsun read it or not. The degree of Hamsun's familiarity with Dostoevsky, when and where he first read him, was to assume prominence in an uneasy little interlude in 1892 when an accusation of plagiarism was raised against him.

Nilsson was a serious man. He saw clearly the darker side of Hamsun's desperate ambition, and made the acute and unusual observation that he was 'a lonely man, who was not much affected by all the people and scenes he came across in the world'. He wrote that Hamsun 'repelled many because of his eccentricities. He could of course conduct himself in an extremely refined and considerate fashion when he wished to; but his behaviour could also on occasion arouse contempt.'[7]

Hamsun's habit of sometimes going barefoot in the Janson's house could upset the more conservative visitors, especially when by way of explanation all he would say was that his shoes 'troubled him'. And perhaps it would take a good friend like John Hansen to appreciate a situation into which Hamsun 'dropped him' one day without warning. They were visiting the house of an important and wealthy woman who had artistic pretensions. While she was out of the room getting some coffee, the two young men examined some of her works which were hanging up on the wall. One of them, Hamsun maintained, was a painting of a dog. When the artist returned with the coffee, Hamsun took a sip, and with a nod of his head indicated the painting:

> About that lion, he began – it *is* a lion, isn't it – ?
> Why yes, of course it was a lion . . .
> Yes, he went on, I thought it was a lion. Hansen here kept trying to tell me it was a *dog* . . .[8]

For all the refinement of which he was now capable, he knew – and could never forget – that he was a peasant. At gatherings like the soirées at the Jansons' house on Thursday evenings, Hamsun must have cut an odd figure, tall and powerfully built, with his swathe of chestnut-red hair and his pince-nez, slightly pigeon-toed, with his huge hands thrown into prominence by a jacket too tight and too short for him. At these soirées Janson would talk on literature and art, and sing songs by Schubert, Kjerulf and Grieg while his wife accompanied him on the piano,[9] and Hamsun would stand, observing people, observing himself observing people. To Askeland he played the philistine, and told him that the only kind of music he had any time for was barrel-organ music. Janson would explain him to interested visitors by describing him as a writer. He told them that Hamsun practised writing his sentences over and over again, like a girl practising her scales at the piano, in search of the perfect form of expression.

In July the Jansons closed up their house on Nicollet Avenue and made their annual summer journey to Brown County, and Hamsun had to decide whether to stay in Minneapolis or move on in search of further adventure. He toyed briefly with the idea of making money by cutting hair, a skill he had picked up while an apprentice shoemaker in Bodø, but soon changed his mind and decided to go looking for seasonal farm work. He wrote to Janson from Casselton on 16 July:

> We left Minneapolis looking for railroad work out here, and towards morning they dropped us off in the middle of the prairie. Three canvas tents pitched nearby, that was all we saw. Pah – we wouldn't stay there! We shouldered our packs and tramped on to the next town, where we took a train to another town, looking for farm work. No luck. On to Fargo, where we slept the night in an empty boxcar standing alone on the tracks. In the morning I shaved under the bridge that goes over to Moorhead. An old woman rinsing clothes in the river stood watching and laughing at me. We didn't get any farm work in Fargo either, so we travelled down here to Casselton in Dakota, and again we slept in an empty boxcar. On the 4th of July we celebrated – there were three of us – as best we could with a bottle of beer and a hunk of rye bread. We moved on again on the 5th, trudged six miles inland and found work on a so-called 'bonanza-farm', which we were driven away from anyway after two days because we wouldn't stand for the way they talked to us. So again down to Casselton, then a further six miles in another direction where we found another job, and where we are now.[10]

In an article printed in *Verdens Gang* on 10 November, Hamsun painted a graphic picture of life on these huge 'bonanza farms' where he had worked for a time.

Oliver Dalrymple's farm in the Red River Valley was a monstrous operation involving a workforce of 1200 to 1400, with its own general store, smith, wagon-maker, its own painters and carpenters. The workers, mostly Scandinavian, Irish and German, were drummed up to breakfast at 3.30 am, and worked a fifteen-hour day. There was no shade to be had from the burning sun, and the hot earth scorched their feet. On one particularly hot day, a mule collapsed with sunstroke. The animal was left simply lying where it had fallen, and another mule sent for. A few minutes later this one too collapsed. Only then did the foreman order all hands to stop work and take shelter under the shade of the wagons until the worst of the heat was over. Scandinavians, especially newly-arrived immigrants, were particularly favoured by those recruiting for wheat-kings like Dalrymple because of their reputation as men willing to endure the gruelling regime without complaint, and in his article Hamsun explicitly and urgently warns intending immigrants to avoid such farms at all costs. The demands of the factory workers in the east, the 'Eight-Hour Movement', have not yet penetrated to the west, he adds wryly. Characteristically, he finds a flash of heaven in this hell, a moment's transcendant ecstasy, and this is the final image he chooses to leave the newspaper's readers with:

> . . . the most distressing sight in Dakota is the treatment of the mules, and the deep wounds that form under the chafing rings around their necks. The loveliest sight, the most beautiful in the world, is the sunset, when the horizon foams in blood and gold.

Significantly, it is the plight of the mules that touches Hamsun, not that of the men, and his reaction to the conditions he describes is not to call for reform but simply to advise men to avoid the work. His unusual and varied experiences of life seem already to have created a deep fatalism in him, a total acceptance of man's inhumanity to man as something quite natural. Three short stories, written much later, which use the events and experiences of this summer as thematic material, all confirm this harsh, passionate stoicism, and the inevitability and indeed sanctity of naturally-arising justice.

In *Zacheus* a silly argument over a borrowed newspaper blows up between the cook, Polly, and the eponymous hero of the story. Zacheus later loses a finger in an accident at work. The cook steals the finger from him, and to take his revenge on Zacheus, serves it up to him in his evening meal, nail and all. The rest of the crew find Zacheus' outraged astonishment hilarious; but when shortly afterwards he kills and buries his tormentor, there is general agreement that justice has been done.

On the Prairie and *Vagabond Days* similarly depict men living in harsh, primitive societies where the notions of written law and organised law enforcement are simply irrelevant. Hamsun's descriptions of these societies, written from the inside and sometimes as an active participant in the quarrels that arose, never offer moral judgement. He developed instead a sympathetic fondness for the tramps and migrant workers he met during his years in America. 'Derailed existences' he called them, and knew that all that separated him from them was his literary talent. This he shared with them too, telling stories, and helping them to read and write their letters in the evenings.

Hamsun's greatest sympathy was reserved for the figure of the life-gambler. *On the Prairie* gives us a picture of an Irishman, Evans, who came to fascinate him, with his dignified bearing, his faded silk shirts, and his absolute refusal to discuss whatever 'tragedy' in his personal life it was that had turned him into a wanderer. At the great drinking feast that gets under way once the harvest is in, and the gang prepares to break up, Evans, slightly drunk, gambles away all the money he has sweated to earn through the long summer. A fellow countryman, O'Brien, refuses to lend him a stake, lying that he has not enough money. Evans applies to Hamsun and, misunderstanding Hamsun's offer to lend him travel money, takes the entire contents of his wallet and begins to play with it. His luck changes, and a marvellous winning streak begins. Meanwhile, the cautious and selfish O'Brien has been run over and killed while trying to hop a freight out of town. Evans repays the loan from Hamsun, but when he goes the following morning to collect his winnings from the banker, he finds that he has left town. 'And Evans took this as calmly as he took everything else', writes Hamsun. 'It seemed almost as though it didn't matter to him at all.' His admiration for Evans' oriental disdain is evident. Personally, however, he was too crudely driven by ambition to reach the philosophical heights of an Evans, and while the Irishman moved on to spend the winter chopping cord wood in his silk shirt in the mystical obscurity of the Wisconsin forests, Hamsun took the crooked road back to the city, from nature to culture, and resumed his pursuit of refinement, and the visible successes of fame. These tramps continued to haunt him however, and it was perhaps of Evans, or someone similar, that he was thinking when he spoke in later years with such contempt of being 'a writer', and tried to convince himself, and others, that he was ashamed of the occupation.

Hamsun returned to Minneapolis in the late autumn, bringing with him other souvenirs besides his experiences. Hallvard

Askeland was on his way to the offices of *The Password* at 430 Cedar
Avenue one morning when he saw Hamsun coming towards him.
He had just left the train, and was still carrying his carpet-bag.
Askeland went forward to greet him, but Hamsun motioned him
to stay back. He was infested with fleas, he explained.

He could probably have had his old room with the Jansons on
Nicollet Avenue again had he wanted it, but this time he rented a
room of his own at Number 4 North Street. Perhaps he wished to
insist on his independence, and be free of any constricting that the
role of aspirant in the house of his mentor might have worked on
him. He now felt, as he told another friend, the radical journalist
Krøger Johansen, that he understood literature better than anyone
else in Minnesota.[11]

To prove it to himself, and to his friends – and in hopes of
making some money – he spent the early winter preparing a series
of lectures on different writers and literary topics. There were
eleven of them in all, and they were delivered at the Little Dania
Hall on consecutive Sundays, starting on 11 December and going
right through, with lectures on Christmas Day and New Year's
Day, to 12 February 1888. Victor Nilsson reviewed, or summarised,
all of them in the *Svenska Folkets Tidning*, and other friends
encouraged Hamsun with their presence. Kristofer Janson and his
family turned out every week in loyal support, and the lectures,
generally delivered between 4–5 pm, seem to have been well-
supported – as well they might have been, with an admission fee
set tactfully low at ten cents per person. Back in 1883, at Lake
Mason in Adams County, in his Elroy days, Hamsun had delivered
a lecture on Bjørnson which his American friend W. T. Ager had
attended. 'I admired him before,' wrote Ager, 'now I revered him'.
And Askeland wrote that, after these Minnesota lectures, Hamsun
became at once the local great man, lionised wherever he went.
These tributes were no doubt sincerely meant, but both of them
look back through the inevitably distorting mist of fame which
settled over Hamsun's name in later years, before it in turn was
distorted by the violent moral disturbances caused by his attitude
towards Nazi Germany in the 1930s and '40s.

So many of these personal memoirs of Hamsun before his
breakthrough partake of this hero-worship that it is refreshing to
come across the testament of Mr G. E. Loftfield. He was not an
intimate of Hamsun's (no one was an *intimate* of Hamsun's really,
not even Kristofer Janson), and his description of the writer in
1887/1888 seems serviceable, and honest. His Hamsun wore thick
grey woollen socks, his trousers were worn, and too short, and his
jacket likewise too short. He wore it tightly buttoned. His hair was

long again, and he wore lorgnettes attached to a yard-long band of silk. Loftfield's description of his style of delivery is striking:

> He seemed to have a great deal to say, but had difficulty in expressing himself. Often he bit his lip, started as though in surprise, and then a salvo of passionate phrases would come literally tearing out of his throat.[12]

Hamsun began with lectures on Balzac, Flaubert, and Zola; came nearer home, and perhaps nearer his Scandinavian audience with talks on Bjørnson, Ibsen, Kielland, Lie and Janson; spoke again on August Strindberg; and concluded with two general lectures, on 'Impressionism' and 'Criticism'. Victor Nilsson's brief reports in the *Svenska Folkets Tidning* (permitted by the editor only on condition that they were 'as concise as possible') indicate that Hamsun, for all his wide reading and understanding of literature, did not yet feel confident enough to go openly on the attack against the literary establishment, and there is little evidence of the passionate disapproval with which he spoke of the 'four greats' on his sensational lecture tour of Norway three years later.

Hamsun's attitude towards Strindberg at this time is of particular interest. Nilsson quoted him as saying in his lecture that Strindberg was 'no learned man, no great thinker, but a great original genius'. The distinctions were important and encouraging to Hamsun. Strindberg's *Son of a Servant* had just been published, and quite apart from his sympathy with Strindberg as a thinker ('the will is the backbone of the soul'), Hamsun must have also found positive encouragement in Strindberg's violent struggle to assert himself in the world against his feelings of social inferiority.

Hamsun himself was actually never very happy on the lecture stage. It seems to have been something that he drove himself to do. One feels that he was making a colossal effort to seem self-assured with performances of this kind, while knowing all along that the roots of healthy self-assurance were not to be found in him, either because he was born that way, or because his childhood was not conducive to their growth. A disinterested member of the audience voiced the general bafflement with which those outside his circle viewed Hamsun's enterprises at this time when he remarked to Loftfield that 'the big chap is either somebody really special, or just a bloody fool'.

Hamsun's impatience with everything was increasing: impatience with his poverty, with his inability to produce something uniquely new, interesting and unusual, and with America. He spoke often to Janson and other friends of a particular book he wanted to write. He described it as an 'autobiography', and now that the lectures were behind him he felt he ought to have another go at it. But still the material wouldn't come, or wouldn't come right. Krøger Johansen wrote that he made himself ill, staying up all night, never resting, that he was so 'intent on creating a form which was different from everybody else's that he would not tolerate anything that resembled the work of others, and drove his desire for originality out into extremes of affectation'. Hallvard Askeland described how, at Hamsun's insistence, he once locked him in his office and went away for three hours. Returning to release his friend, he found that Hamsun had produced fifty-four lines, of which fifty had been crossed out.

Eventually Hamsun decided that he must return home. He arranged a farewell lecture which he hoped would help to raise money for the trip back to Norway, and wrote to Victor Nilsson on 18 March, inviting him to attend:

> The lecture will be two hours long, and I doubt if it will be boring. I hope to see you there. I like to see you in front of me. Sit near the stage, because of my short-sightedness. I hear the hall is fully booked, which is good news. The topic will be life here in Minneapolis, and I shall be speaking frankly.

A discussion of what Hamsun meant by 'speaking frankly' about America belongs properly in the next chapter. His views were in fact so extreme, so witty, so shocking and so intensively subjective that he decided to develop them into a book, *On the Cultural Life of Modern America*, published in 1889.

These lectures were never the money-spinners Hamsun hoped they would be, and shortly after the lecture on 28 March he left Minneapolis again and worked as a minder of pigs for a few weeks to raise money, returning to town again in time to speak at the Norwegian National Day celebrations on 17 May. One suspects that he again expressed anti-American views in his speech: he was still wearing the black ribbons which he and Kroger Johansen had adopted as a gesture of sympathy for the Chicago anarchists condemned to death, in openly corrupt trials, after the famous bomb outrage in the Haymarket in 1887. He was already disillusioned with America, and regarded the country's much-vaunted 'liberty' as a myth.

As the time for his return to Europe drew near he discussed a publishing strategy with Victor Nilsson. Nilsson took a keen interest in the field, and subscribed to the new literary magazines from Stockholm, Copenhagen and Christiania. Within a couple of years he was to take his bibliophile leanings seriously, and become a librarian. He advised Hamsun against the soft option of trying publishers in Christiania, and encouraged him to try Copenhagen again.

Copenhagen was still the cultural capital of Scandinavia, Georg Brandes was there, and literature was taken seriously both by writers and by publishers living in the city. It also happened to be currently rather fashionable to be a Norwegian writer in Copenhagen – much as London regularly has fashions for Liverpudlian, Irish, or female writers – so that it made tactical sense to go there. Nilsson showed Hamsun the early issues of a new magazine he had been subscribing to called *Ny Jord*. It was published by Gustav Philipsen, under the editorship of Carl Behrens, and the list of contributors was bound to excite Hamsun: the Brandes brothers, Georg and Edward, August Strindberg, and Strindberg's friend Ola Hansson. In addition the magazine contained the first translated extracts from Nietzsche which Nilsson had ever come across.

As usual, Hamsun had not managed to save enough money for his trip home, and friends and acquaintances rallied round, as usual, to help him out. Askeland got him a free ticket from a friend who worked on the railways, and together with John Hansen he travelled back to Chicago. Here he sold an article on Strindberg which Laws had translated into English for him to the magazine *America*, for which he received fifteen dollars. Hansen then went with him to the offices of the shipping company and helped him to arrange a free passage over to Copenhagen. They spent a few days together in Chicago. Hamsun used his press-pass to get them into a theatre one night, and before travelling on alone to New York, he went to see a Professor N. C. Frederiksen, who also loaned him money. Hamsun seems to have regarded the larger sums of money he received from wealthy men as gifts, probably reasoning that they could afford to be generous; but he kept a careful track of smaller sums received from friends. He was never the spongeing 'artist' imperiously demanding to be kept by 'lesser' mortals, and fully intended to pay back those who had helped him. Frederiksen was to hear from him again.

Hamsun sailed home on the *Thingvalla*, the oldest of the Denmark-America boats. He travelled third class, and in the same boat, travelling first class, was his old acquaintance from Madison Professor R. B. Anderson. Anderson was returning, with his wife, from a short holiday in America, and was now in the last year of a four-year stint as legation secretary at the American Embassy in Copenhagen. He accompanied the *Thingvalla*'s captain one day on his tour of inspection of the ship, and on the bottom deck they came across a group of four young men, dirty and clad in rags, who were playing cards for money. One of the group looked up, saw him, greeted him by name, and to his astonishment Anderson recognised Knut Hamsun. They chatted briefly. Hamsun had a thick, grubby manuscript with him which he showed to Anderson, who glanced through it, didn't think much of it, and handed it back. He noticed the black ribbon in Hamsun's jacket, and asked sympathetically whether Hamsun had been bereaved. No, Hamsun replied, and told him that he was wearing the ribbon in sympathy with the executed Chicago anarchists, and the innocent idealist John Parsons. They then parted company. When the *Thingvalla* docked in Copenhagen, Anderson went straight to the police and reported the presence in the city of a dangerous anarchist, and Hamsun was then, unbeknownst to him, shadowed by the security forces day and night. When he tried to use the American Embassy as a forwarding address for important mail he was expecting from America, Anderson refused him the facility, sending a servant girl out with the message. He also warned the consul, Ryder, against having anything to do with Hamsun.

This was Rasmus Anderson's version of events, which he first produced in a magazine interview in 1908, and subsequently refined for his autobiography published in 1915. Hamsun's credo was already that 'Subjectivity is Truth', but he seems to have found Anderson's interpretation of the gospel a little too advanced even for his tastes. His own more prosaic account of what happened appeared in *Dagbladet* on New Year's Day 1909:

> In fact, I travelled home second class, and I could hardly have been playing cards when Anderson 'appeared', since he never set foot in the second class the whole way over. He was legation secretary, after all . . . However Fru Anderson and another lady came down one day to have a look round: but at that time there was only a Danish passenger and myself in the forward compartment, and we were not playing cards. I did not then have the 'manuscript for a large, finished work' with me, nor did I show Anderson a single written line while on board. When he then relates how he 'leafed through an appallingly dirty and slovenly manuscript', which did not in fact exist, it is therefore quite likely that he 'did not think much of it'.

According to Hamsun, the two men met by chance on deck. He goes on to concede that they exchanged remarks about the black ribbon, but dismisses as ridiculous the suggestion that he was watched day and night once he landed in Copenhagen. The Embassy, he agrees, was closed to him. The explanation for this, and for all of Anderson's many subsequent attempts to belittle Hamsun, seems to be that he had become fiercely jealous of him, and bitterly resentful of his success. He hated him as man and as author. 'There are passages in his books', he wrote in his autobiography, 'too coarse and indecent to be read aloud, even where only men are present. Such writers as Hamsun are a disgrace to the country that tolerates them'. Anderson's reaction to Hamsun provides valuable evidence of the forcefulness of Hamsun's personality. People tended to respond violently to it, adoring him, or being repelled by him. Few of those who knew him could remain indifferent.

Once ashore, he pawned his raincoat, and with the six kroner rented the cheapest room he could find, an attic at Number 18 St Hans Gade, in the working-class stretch of Copenhagen between Nørrebro and Østerbro, and began writing immediately. One may imagine he felt a little uneasy. Here he was just one year short of his thirtieth birthday. As a boy of twenty he had visited Hegel at the publishers Gyldendal, a rather flashy youth fresh from his sensational participation in a heated newspaper debate about psalm-singing in small town on the west coast of Norway. Hegel had been unimpressed, either by his lorgnette or by his manuscript *Frida*, and had sent him away. Here he was again nearly ten years later, and very little about him was different. Or so it seemed on the outside. He still had no home, no family, no job, no reputation and no money. He had no way of knowing whether this pathetic, dangerous and ridiculous poverty of his was a strength or a weakness. He sent a cheerful greeting to his friends on *The Password* in America, but in truth his uncertainties and material difficulties had never been greater.

Following Victor Nilsson's advice he got in touch with Carl Behrens on *Ny Jord* and sold him an article on Kristofer Janson which earned him a few kroner. But the real stuff was crackling and sparkling away in his head all the time now, jangling and flashing through his nerves. He wanted to write about the smell of his clothes, the feel of his breath on his own hands, the rasp of a struck match across his hearing. To ward off the intolerable and insoluble problems and fears of real, daily life he wrote constantly – about the intolerable and insoluble problems and fears of his real, daily life. It was as though he finally stopped running, and, turning round, held out the cross of Art against whatever demon of failure and perfectionism it was that had been pursuing him through all the years and the struggling, the inner and outer forces that combined with such calm efficiency to prevent his ever achieving his goal – the book of himself, the single act of extraordinary self-revelation of which he knew he was uniquely capable.

In a fever he wrote some thirty pages of completely new stuff, and took it to Edward Brandes, editor of the newspaper *Politiken*, and the brother of Georg. He told Hamsun he would look at the piece, and that he was to come back in twenty-four hours for a decision. As Hamsun thanked him and left, his shabbiness, and the intensity with which he burned inside his shabbiness, must have affected Brandes: he reached spontaneously into his pocket and gave him five crowns.[13] The incident appears disguised in the full version of *Hunger*. Brandes read the story Hamsun had given him – substantially part two of *Hunger* – was profoundly impressed by it, and was able to tell him when he returned the following day that it was too long for *Politiken*, but that he was getting Carl Behrens to publish it in *Ny Jord*.

This November issue of *Ny Jord* caused a sensation in literary circles in Copenhagen and Christiania, and sold out within three days. Everyone was talking about the piece. But the extraordinary thing is that Hamsun – obsessed by fame and the desire to imprint his name on the world – had insisted that the story be published anonymously. No one therefore knew who the author was.

Chapter 6
1888–1890: The Breakthrough: *Hunger*

The question of anonymity, and Hamsun's lifelong violent ambivalence towards the concept and consequences of personal fame, brings us at once up against one of the central paradoxes of this strange man. So far, we have met a Hamsun who was a tireless promoter of himself as personality and writer, keenly and noisily airing his views in newspaper debates, bringing himself through personal letters to the attention of editors and writers, famous and influential strangers. The Norwegian memoirist Peter Egge wrote that he first heard of him through a journalist colleague of his, Arne Dybfest, who told him that when in America, he had met in a newspaper office a man 'who ceaselessly advertised himself, and who was a consummate bluffer both in what he said and what he wrote'. Those repelled by Hamsun's personality found in his decision to publish the *Hunger* extract anonymously one more example of the calculated coquetry on which his whole approach to his reader was based.

For years Hamsun had been preoccupied with the form and the *idea* of his name, progressing from Knud Pedersen to Knut Pederson to Knut Pederson Hamsund to Knut Hamsund to Knut Hamsun. He had used this preoccupation with making his name famous as the subject of self-mockery in the short-story *On Tour*. He also experimented with the use of the author's anonymity as part of the technical apparatus of his story *Fragment Of A Life*. The tear-jerking short-story from 1884 carried the romantic ascription 'By a Young, Unknown Writer'. When now in the early winter of 1888 he took a short trip to Sweden, and from there sent to *Dagbladet* an appreciation of Julius Kron's painting *The Queen of Sheba*, he signed his review 'By a Norwegian Author'. Now surely this anonymity was coy, as the anonymity of the *Hunger* extract was coy, and the purpose behind it all simply to whip up enough curiosity about the author's identity to make the revelation of it a good newspaper story. So, more or less, ran the argument based on coquetry. The Christiania newspapers certainly reacted as though this had been the idea: between 19 and 30 November, *Verdens Gang* ran a series of five articles, enthusiastically discussing the extract from *Hunger* and speculating on the identity of the author. In the last article they were able to reveal that he was Knut Hamsun, 'currently living in America, from where, as our readers will recall, he has on several occasions sent articles to us'.

Hamsun's whole style of authorship, his insistence on ambiguity, his rejection of certainty, his juggling with lies that turn out to be true, and truths that turn out to be lies, his recognition and reproduction of the calculating nature of the mind's voice, has always repelled certain readers, and created in them a distrust of Hamsun both as man and as writer. His grimly cheerful description of the aim of his unpublished short story *A Liar*, from 1886, as demonstrating that lying is not sin but *talent*, shows well enough how easy it is to face the phenomenon of Hamsun the man with suspicion. We shall see, throughout the 1890s, how violently his attitude towards the truth affected his contemporaries. However, in the specific case of *Hunger*, the small fact that *Verdens Gang* described him as 'currently living in America' suggests that Hamsun was not in any way involved in the leaking of his 'story' to the press. Even more important than this, there are contained in letters to friends and acquaintances concerning both the partial and the complete appearance of *Hunger*, explicit statements that seem to express a genuine ambivalence towards the business, not merely of being famous, but of being famous as the dreadful and shocking author Knut Hamsun. Resuming his correspondence with his honoured and trusted friend Frydenlund after the break of his second American trip, Hamsun apologises for not having written, 'but you know, one feels a little sensitive about it, when things seem to be turning out badly, and so one does not write'. He then goes on to report that at last he has been having some success:

> The piece that was in *Ny Jord* is actually just a part of a whole. I had to publish it early for the sake of the money. The whole will consist of a series of analyses, and will be published in the autumn. I have a publisher for it already. But it will be published anonymously. So you must not mention it to anyone. I would have given a great deal not to have been revealed as the author when that extract was published. Some wretched Swedish

newspapers leaked the news first, and that was that. But I will never admit publicly that it was I who wrote it. You know, it is quite something to reveal oneself as nakedly as I did there. And in the remaining parts of the book it will be worse. But I permit myself to think it will cause a nice little stir when it comes.[1]

The confusion of emotions is characteristic: deep down, Hamsun did not know whether he was ashamed or proud of what he had done. The tensions that this uncertainty produced were to give rise to much of the sense of strangeness and inspired disharmony of the full version of the novel, and were to remain vital elements of his literary personality.

Once it became public knowledge that Hamsun was the author of the piece in *Ny Jord*, things began happening very swiftly around him in Copenhagen. He was introduced to the literary world of cafés and parties by Erik Skram and his wife, the Norwegian novelist Amalie Skram. The Danish Erik was active in defence of young Norwegian writers generally at this period, when many of his countrymen were beginning to react against the craze for Norwegian art and artists which had persisted in the capital througout the 1880s. This was in part a cult of the Norwegians as the pure, uncorrupted members of the family of Scandinavian peoples, which received further impetus from the European successes of Ibsen and Bjørnson. Even though it was fading by the early 1890s, it undoubtedly benefited the careers of younger Norwegian writers too, like Hamsun and his contemporary, Gabriel Finne.[2]

Hamsun began to frequent the circles that met in the café Bernina, where Norwegian expatriates like Kielland and Thaulow, Garborg, and Hans Jaeger had previously assembled groups of artists and writers around them. He found himself lionised, and invited out to parties. He spent Christmas with the Skrams, and was invited to spend New Year with the prominent Winkel-Horn family, but refused, feeling already that the frantic socialising, though necessary for his career, was keeping him from his work. Already the whole circus seemed slightly ridiculous to him; he was sure, he wrote to Skram, that he did not deserve the honour of being invited to the Winkel-Horns, and with a jib at the current hysteria over Fridtjof Nansen's achievement, added that it would all be much more understandable if one happened to be someone who had just walked over the polar cap.[3]

The new life was costing him money, and in spite of the fact that he at once treated established writers like the Skrams as literary equals, he was still living the material life of the character from

Hunger, in a loft 'nine ells from the moon'. The publisher Philipsen, on the advice of Edward Brandes, had already advanced Hamsun 100 kroner towards the full version of *Hunger*, but most of this had gone on a short holiday trip to Sweden in the autumn, and by December he was broke again. He sat down and wrote a long letter to Johan Sørensen, a rich publisher whose ambition was to produce cheap editions of great books for the education of the masses. He introduced himself as the author of the *Hunger* story, and asked for practical help. Sørensen replied enclosing 200 kroner within a week of receiving the letter. Once again, Hamsun's faith in the patriarch had been rewarded. In three more letters, all in this same month of December, he thanked his patron, and as in the short series of letters to Zahl some ten years earlier, described graphically and persuasively his faith in himself and his hopes for the future. In these letters Hamsun laid great stress on his determination to be true to himself:

> I do not seriously believe that Philipsen will try to put pressure on me as regards the form and content of my future production. In any case, I would not agree to this. If any attempt is made to prevent me from writing the way I believe I ought to write, then I shall consider myself morally free from Philipsen.[4]

Philipsen had indeed given Hamsun a mild warning against ignoring 'the masses' in his writing, explaining that without their interest and support, it was not possible for an author to live. But Hamsun was not interested in writing for 'the masses'. He was quite obsessed by the desire to pursue the psychological literature he had started to explore with *Hunger*. It was the inner world that fascinated him, the depths and darknesses, the bright places, the cities and mountains, the remote universes and small flowers of his own mind.

But in December 1888 the finished novel was still eighteen months and a great deal of irrelevant journalism away. Yet time and again the mood of the book suddenly bursts out into private letters, showing how constantly it was in his mind. One detail from a letter to Sørensen went directly into the book, the observation that 'for the past six weeks I have had to write with a cloth bound round my left hand, because I could not stand the touch of my own breath on my skin'. He describes also how he has to strike his safety matches under the table, because he cannot stand to see the flaring of the match. He felt himself that these sensitivities were absurd and ridiculous; they were nonetheless real, and a vital part of the swarming mass of trivia which made up the mosaic of reality he was determined to try to record.

A second large sum of money, boldly begged from Sørensen in December, enabled Hamsun to make the symbolic move away from the slum quarters on St Hans Gade to a new address at Number 25, Nordvestvej, and to clothe himself properly. He was particularly pleased to be able to buy decent clothes: Copenhagen University students had invited the new sensation to lecture at their Union Building. 'Only intelligent people will be there', he wrote to Sørensen, with a touching faith in the intelligence of university students, 'so it is good that I will not have to feel ashamed on account of my clothes.'

He gave two lectures, the first on 15 December, and the second on 12 January 1889. He had originally been invited to speak on the American philosopher Henry George, but saw his chance to turn the occasion rather more to his own advantage and suggested instead that he lecture on his views on America, based on his personal experiences there. These were in violent contrast to the optimistic views of America usually presented to the Scandinavian public, either by a writer like Ibsen in *The Pillars of Society*, or by such as Bjørnson who had been on lecture tours there, and written extensively in the press of his good impressions of the New World. Ibsen had never been to America, it was only a symbol of freshness to him; and Bjørnson's America was a place of civic receptions, bunches of flowers and brass bands at the local railway stations of small towns where his arrival was regarded as a major event. Hamsun's, however, was the working man's experience of America, a harsh place where anonymity, insecurity, rootlessness and poverty formed the common fate. It was the land of disappointment and disillusionment which had sucked his brother Peter under, and he was deeply cynical about it as the society of the future. He also felt to a high degree the Old World's arrogant contempt for the cultural aspirations of the New, an anti-democratic stance that went down extremely well in a Copenhagen still buzzing from Georg Brandes' seminal lectures there on Nietzsche in May. The response to Hamsun's first lecture was tremendous. Already the publisher Philipsen realised that he had a controversialist of rank on his hands, and without waiting to hear the second lecture he commissioned Hamsun to write a book on America.

Hamsun worked at breakneck speed on his commission throughout the winter and early spring of 1889, for the moment setting aside the completion of *Hunger*. He had two full sections of it still to write while the beginning of it was already going through the printers, but managed to finish it in time for publication on 3 March 1889. The speed with which he produced the book reflects three things: the fact that it was based on material and attitudes familiar to him from his two Copenhagen lectures plus the farewell lecture in Minneapolis in March 1888; the fact that he had to or chose to write most of it without troubling the reference books; and the fact that he did not really want to write it. Writing about America and playing cultural historian bored him, and kept him from his real work. But having contracted to do the book for money, he made sure that he got it out of the way as quickly as possible. He called the book *On the Cultural Life of Modern America*, and prefaced it with a motto – 'Truth is neither objectivity nor the balanced view; truth is a selfless subjectivity' – which is at once both justification and excuse for what follows. For as well as a book about America, it is a very entertaining book about Hamsun, crackling with irrational prejudices, some hilarious, some considerably less so. America pleases him not. Not its politics, not its language, not its women, not its sensationalist press, not its crass materialism, not its analphabetism, not its literature, not its painting, nor yet its theatre.

As one might imagine from the circumstances of its composition, *On the Cultural Life of Modern America* contains many fine examples of waffle. This, for example, on the famous actor Edwin Booth: 'One can see him intoxicated. But he acts superbly, as long as he does not lapse into carelessness.' It also contains striking observations: he writes of American painting, that 'Where American literature speaks with dashes, American art speaks with clothes.' He sees acutely some of the absurdities and incongruities in the American version of individual freedom; an immigrant's tobacco knife will be taken from him at the customs, he observes, but as for his revolvers, he is welcome to keep both of them if he wishes, 'for the revolver is the national murder weapon'. He despises what he sees as the 'despotic' freedom of democracy, its tendency to level down and encourage a mob response to issues and events. Returning to a matter in which he had felt a personal engagement, he discusses the anarchist bombings in the Chicago Haymarket in 1886. The mob's unfocused clamour for revenge seems contemptible to him 'when not one in a hundred, not one in a thousand, knew what Anarchism was'. The subsequent trials demonstrate only too clearly what it is that most frightens an American – 'those crimes that do not occur every day, those that the mob is incapable of understanding – the crimes of ideals'.

But, he asks, what else can one expect of a land where the highest morality is money, where the meaning of a work of art is reduced to its cash value, where Woman calls the tune, 'tending her nerves in the morning, painting works of art until two o'clock, reading *Uncle Tom's Cabin* until six o'clock, and strolling in the evening until eight'? There is practically nothing he will admit to liking about the country, and had there been, he would have been obliged to leave it out, since the aim of the book is so very clearly to provoke. Writing of American literature, for example, Hamsun avoids any extended discussion of a writer whom he adored, and learnt much from, Mark Twain, and concentrates instead on a lengthy attack on Walt Whitman ('A rich human being rather than a talented poet. He can't write at all; but he can feel.'), and a treatment of Ralph Waldo Emerson which is mainly a critique of Emerson's Unitarian philosophy.*

Discussing the mixed nature of American society, he writes that 'cohabitation with the blacks was forced upon the people. Inhumanity stole them away from Africa where they belong', a statement that would have pleased Marcus Garvey himself. He also describes the war against slavery as in reality a war against aristocracy, and draws attention to the hypocrisy of capitalists in the northern states who maintained immense landholdings in the south – what kind of morality was that for a democrat? But from such discussible points he veers suddenly away, and concludes that 'Instead of founding an intellectual élite, America has established a mulatto stud-farm.'

There are certain passages in the book, notably the entire last section entitled 'Black Skies', in which the writing itself reaches heights of visionary intensity and the kind of hallucinated surrealism one associates with Céline and Henry Miller; but generally speaking it descends too often into adolescent crudity, with what he hopes are shocking jibes about 'black half-apes', to sustain any degree of sympathetic attention from a modern reader.

'Childish' was the word Hamsun himself always used on the several occasions in later life in which he dissociated himself from the book.[5] It does not appear in his *Collected Works*, and while he lived he refused to allow it to be republished.† He knew too well that in it he was still consciously playing the role of *enfant terrible*, the brilliant brat who sees through the emperor's clothes, the wise child who, along with drunks, always tells the truth. And it was a role he was getting tired of.

Even so, he made a conscientious effort to promote the book, with copies despatched with requests for reviews to critics at home and abroad. He hoped that it might create a scandal of the kind that

* Emerson had been a Unitarian minister at Boston from 1829 to 1832.
† Although in 1899 he offered to make a thorough revision of it for Gyldendal, saying that '*Amerikas Aandsliv* is a lively book, and can be read as a novel'.

had operated so favourably for Christian Krohg's novel *Albertine* in 1885. In letters to friends he indulged himself in a scenario in which Bjørnson would signal a general attack on him by denouncing the book, with Georg Brandes and Arne Garborg jumping to his defence and a great debate ensuing.[6] But Bjørnson remained silent, as did Garborg.

Brandes, who had heard Hamsun's second lecture in January, and had seen and lavishly praised the book in proof copy, reviewed it for *Verdens Gang* on 9 May. His original enthusiasm had waned, and now he praised the author's talent as potential rather than actual. Hamsun hoped for a translation into German, and a second edition, but his real opinion of the book always remained that it was unworthy of him. He did not regard it as 'real' writing, and complained to Philipsen of how he constantly had to curb inspiration when he felt it rising up in him. He was in fact almost finished with his American hackwork, and after two more articles in 1890 and 1891 he dropped the whole subject for the next twenty years. What pleased him most about the book, naturally, was the money. He received 960 kroner, far and away his biggest payday to date; and, as he proudly wrote to Victor Nilsson, the same advance as both Ibsen and Bjørnson received.

One of the book's fans – and it *did* have fans, and continued to do so – was August Strindberg. Hamsun was at this time quite obsessed by Strindberg. His letters to the Swede Nilsson in America are full of gossip about him, wondering tales of his mercurial personality, his expressed fears of incipient lunacy, his prodigious industry ('he makes Balzac look like a dwarf'). He had already sent to Strindberg an article written on him in America and published in English on 20 December 1888 in the magazine *America*, though the text had been so mutilated and 'edited' that he half-expected an angry reply from Strindberg. When now he came across *On the Cultural Life of Modern America*, Strindberg was impressed. He was another like Hamsun, a man willing to express his opinion on anything under the sun – and in his case, on most of the things beyond it – and the book's violent subjectivity appealed to him. In April 1890 he wrote to Brandes that 'all the opinions I've suffered half to death for over the last five years' were 'openly and frankly expressed' in Hamsun's book.[7]

Hamsun was already very conscious of the fact and form of his growing fame. He wanted to meet the writers he admired, and had written to Arne Garborg asking him to put him in touch with Strindberg's friend and ally in Nietzsche, Ola Hansson. He was also keen to meet Strindberg himself – but not yet. He wrote to Victor Nilsson in January 1889:

I look forward to meeting Strindberg one day. I was invited to a party one evening at which he was to be present, but I did not go. I am proud, in my way.

Hamsun realised that *Hunger* was the key to his whole future. He wanted fame, and the respect of the Strindbergs and Ola Hanssons; but only the deserved fame, the warranted respect, that the writing of an exceptional novel would bring him. His wish to be famous, though compulsive to the point of obsession, was nevertheless not the desire for fame at any price, and he was not deluded by the intense local fame created in Copenhagen and Christiania by his magazine and newspaper articles, and his hastily written demolition job on American civilisation, into thinking that he was now worthy of Strindberg's attention.*

In the Spring of 1889 Hamsun returned to Norway. Johan Sørensen had prepared a room for him at his house in Fagerstrand where he could write in peace, and sent his assistant Olaf Huseby to meet Hamsun off the Copenhagen train at Christiania station on Good Friday. Sørensen took his duties as patron seriously, and when Hamsun arrived was able to inform him that he had arranged a house-party consisting of the historian Ernst Sars, and the newspapermen Lars Holst and Ola Thommessen, three of the most influential names in contemporary Norwegian cultural life. Hamsun and Sørensen talked alone for a while, and suddenly a full-scale quarrel erupted: Hamsun had dared to speak his mind about Sørensen's household gods, Bjørnson and a language reformer named Knud Knudsen. Hamsun admired and respected Bjørnson, but was never guilty of the idolatry so many of his fellow countrymen practised towards him; it was typical of Hamsun's courage, and his almost fanatical insistence on independence, that instead of retreating when he saw that he was treading on his benefactor's toes, he trod all the harder. Sørensen was not a man used to being crossed, and the two men argued long into the night and Hamsun eventually left the house rather than sleep the night there. He returned the next day to collect his suitcase, and that was the end of the association with Sørensen.[8]

In June he moved into a flat on the fourth floor at Number 18 Torvgaden, just around the corner from the Grand Hotel on Karl Johans gate, the 'Bernina' of the Norwegian capital, where famous and would-be famous artists met to drink and talk. Still he did not finish *Hunger*. The lure of controversy proved too great for him,

---

* Their meeting, when it did take place in Paris some five years later, was electric with misunderstandings, with Strindberg at the height of his inferno crisis, and Hamsun doing his best to help him.

and over the next few months he produced a number of newspaper articles, most of them on non-literary topics, which performed the undeniably useful function of making his name better known and providing him with a small independent income.

The first of these was an article for *Dagbladet* on Fridtjof Nansen, whose achievement in walking east to west across Greenland had made him a national hero in Norway. Nansen's popularity never penetrated to the Christiania smart-set; they felt that his habit of going about the streets of the capital ostentatiously wearing his 'famous explorer's clothes' was in poor taste. Hamsun's attitude to what he called the 'hysteria' surrounding Nansen was also one of superior disapproval. For him, the writers were the aristocrats of a society, the natural recipients of its highest forms of praise, status and attention. He did not so much begrudge the explorer his fame as find it incomprehensible and slightly ridiculous. The fame of sportsmen affected him in the same way. He called the whole business 'humbug', a word that was to whizz around his own head like a boomerang over the next few years.

His next target was Ibsen. In August 1889 Hamsun reviewed August Lindberg's production of *Ghosts* at the Christiania National Theatre for *Dagbladet*, and the article appeared on the front page – as indeed everything he wrote appeared on the the front page in the year of his Norwegian breakthrough. Here he voiced for the first time – at least publicly – the aesthetic and artistic doubts about Ibsen which he developed as the subject of one of the lectures he was to deliver on his sensational national tour of 1891. This early attack on a man who was already, like Bjørnson, a demi-god among his countrymen, was controlled. He praised some of the acting, shook his head over Fru Alving's relentless capability, and questioned some of Ibsen's dialogue:

> There are one or two lines in the last Act that I do not quite understand, although they apparently went down very well in England and Germany. To mention but one, Osvald's line 'Mother, give me the sun'.

Hamsun was being ironic: he understood the lines only too well. He found Ibsen simplistic and obvious, and was baffled and irritated by his reputation as a difficult writer. He felt that Ibsen had betrayed his talent in switching from the verse-dramas of his early period like *Brand* and *Peer Gynt* to the dogged prose realism of plays like *Ghosts*, a possibility that Ibsen himself hinted at in his last play, *When We Dead Awaken*.*

Next up: Lars Oftedal. Oftedal was a pietist politician, editor, and moral agitator, one of the most feared men in Norwegian politics. Hamsun had an old score to settle with him: he was the man whose teachings had captured the dark imagination of his uncle Hans Olsen up in Hamarøy in the 1860s. Now, with re-elections to the Norwegian parliament looming, Hamsun produced a series of articles for *Dagbladet* which he hoped would destroy Oftedal's chances. 'I shall make Oftedollops of the man', he wrote gleefully to Erik Frydenlund.

The eleven articles[11] appeared throughout October 1889, and they gave Hamsun a taste of something that was to be rare for him in the coming decade – widespread public popularity. He fully expected – perhaps even hoped – to be sued by Oftedal, for the style was as ever personal and unashamedly subjective. But Oftedal did not. Instead, the articles were read with approval, and his name noted in circles which would not normally have cared about a writer. It was also one of the few times in his life in which he publicly and unequivocally stood on the Left.

The amount of attention the articles attracted induced a small publisher in Bergen, Mons Litleré, to publish them in book form in December. Hamsun received a further 250 kroner for this, and the number of works published before the full version of *Hunger* appeared now rises to five. *Lars Oftedal* continued to have a local, Scandinavian reputation: the Danish writer Jeppe Aajaer recalled[12] that in the 1890s it came 'crashing like a rock through the windows of the mission houses', and, in writing his own *Master and Mission* against pietism in 1897, used Hamsun's book as his model.†

In September Hamsun took a short holiday in Valdres. He warned Erik that he would be bearing with him a number of eccentric gifts – hats 'the like of which you have never seen – one for each of us. Individually styled to accommodate the unique architecture of our heads to my express specifications.' He must have enjoyed himself up there – he managed to lose a short story

---

* Characteristic of the terms of opposition in which Hamsun conceived even literary reputations was an elevation of Bjørnson at the expense of Ibsen. 'How refreshing to read Bjørnson again', he wrote in 1890. 'We have had enough, thank you, of the supremely enigmatic writing that began with *The Wild Duck* and has lately reached new heights of lunacy with *The Lady from the Sea*.'[10]
† Oftedal did take a tumble – in 1891 – but not as a result of Hamsun's book. He was involved in a scandal that also involved several young women which effectively ruined him as a church figure. Even so, there were loyal parishioners who refused to believe the stories, and his career as a politician continued.

about 'an extremely unusual horse' which he wrote in the Valdres cariole.[13] It turned up in time to make the Christmas Eve number of *Dagbladet*, a marvellous comic vignette about a horse making a fool of a man.

Back in the capital he moved again, in November, to a fourth-floor apartment at Number 3 Waldemar Thranes gate. The flat cost him forty kroner a month, and was a decent distance from the centre of town and the attractions of the Grand Café; he was now quite determined to get *Hunger* finished. Bjørnson had offered him free board and lodging at his house at Aulestad for a year, but he turned it down, knowing that with a human whirlwind like Bjørnson around he would never get his writing done. He was also receiving repeated offers of the job of theatre director at Bergen's National Stage, the second-most important theatre in Norway after Christiania's National Theatre. This was a post both Ibsen and Bjørnson had occupied in their time, and the temptation must have been considerable. And at 4000 kroner a year, the money was tremendous. Nevertheless, he appears to have turned it down with a minimum of soul-searching, explaining to friends that he did not know enough about the theatre to take it on. Another reason may have been that he feared further postponements on *Hunger*.

Hamsun worked hard throughout the winter, putting together the scraps of the novel he had been assembling ever since the autumn of 1888. Finally, in the spring of 1890, with the end of the book in sight, he moved back to Copenhagen, and just as he had done with *On the Cultural Life of Modern America*, wrote the final sections of it while the earlier parts were already going through the printers. The full version finally appeared on 5 June 1890.

Hunger is one of the great novels of urban alienation, on a par with Kafka's *Castle*, Dostoevsky's *Notes from the Underground*, and Rilke's *Notebook of Malte Laurids Brigge*, and what gives it its peculiar authority is that it was in many ways Hamsun's own story. In writing it he drew on the experiences he underwent during his two most desperate periods in Christiania in the winters of 1880–81 and 1885–86, and probably also drew on the experiences of his winter in Chicago in 1886–87. The many small correspondences of fact and fiction – the narrator's visit to the castle, for example, and his address at Tomtegaten II – as well as the autobiographical details that crop up in letters to Erik Frydenlund and Johan Sørensen, indicate that the book is Hamsun's self-portrait in fiction. From America Victor Nilsson wrote asking him whether the events described in *Hunger* had really happened to him: 'Yes, all of it, and much more, right here at home', replied Hamsun.

The novel describes a period of months in the life of a young stranger who lives in Christiania while trying to make a name for himself as a writer. The absurdly ambitious nature of the subjects he writes about – appreciations of Correggio, denunciations of Kant, a verse drama set in the Middle Ages – means that he is rarely in luck with the editors of the newspapers where he tries to sell his stuff. Most of his time is spent in the effort to keep body and soul together. Always hungry, often homeless, he wanders the streets of Christiania, an emaciated human consciousness in rags, looking for work, begging for food, becoming involved in a series of preposterous encounters with policemen, tramps and whores, strange beings who are nevertheless not half so strange as he. Like the protagonist of *On Tour*, he is pitifully and absurdly keen to keep from a surrounding world always perceived as hostile the catastrophic extent of the gap between the pretensions and the realities of his life. It's a grim theme, but the novel's great triumph is that in Hamsun's careful hands, it doesn't finally seem grim at all. As the hero's vivid torments continue, we begin gradually to suspect something that Hamsun undoubtedly wanted us to suspect; namely that what looks at first like a dogged *inability* to do anything about his plight is in reality a dogged *refusal* to act. He does not in actual fact want release, and is in some perverse way enjoying his predicament, savouring to the full the bizarre sensations of homelessness, hunger, insecurity, and the attendant forms of isolation, social, cultural, sexual, economic. We get the curious feeling that the whole thing is willed; a life-game that the hero is playing, to see how far it can go, how far he can let it go, how low he can sink, how long suffer. It is a prolonged flirtation with death and madness which the narrator can indulge in only because he knows he has the strength to withdraw from the game before it claims him. The novel has no plot – plot is replaced by this tension created by the struggle between the narrator's strong mind and the attracting forces of total personal annihilation. Few things are better suited to break down and render anonymous a human personality than prolonged want of the most primitive kind – want of love, money, warmth, food, a place of one's own – and the narrator's secret victory, always achieved, is that he remains hugely and quixotically himself through the worst deprivations and humiliations that befall him. When on the last pages he joins a ship bound for England, and sails away both from the novel and the city with which he has wrestled so desperately, it is clearly no retreat, but only a temporary withdrawal.

Hamsun was proud of the book. Fifteen years and a great deal more disillusionment later, he described it with a wry fondness as 'My first book, written in the days when the way of the writer seemed to me the most honourable in the world.'[14] Yet even at the time, he was aware that the book had faults – eight of them, 'or rather, lacks',[15] as he specified on more than one occasion, leaving one with the curious impression that he had worked from some kind of list of psychological states to be described. We get the same impression from a comment to Georg Brandes which also shows again how extremely competitive Hamsun's attitude towards literature was: 'If we were to count them', he wrote, 'I do not think that we would find a greater number of spiritual fluctuations in for example *Raskolnikov** or in *Germinie Lacerteux* than in my book.'[16] On several occasions he protested vigorously that *Hunger* was 'not a novel', and ought not to be treated as such. 'The book plays on just one string', he pointed out, 'but tries to draw hundreds of notes from it – no doubt with a varying degree of success, naturally.'[17]

The book's fame and its status as one of the central texts of modern European and American literature confirm that he achieved in fact a consistently high degree of success. Save for a few external details, such as the presence of horse-drawn carriages in the streets, *Hunger* remains eerily and thrillingly undated. Hamsun's concern, after all, was with the workings of his mind, and in *Hunger* he produced perhaps the first novel to make consciousness itself a hero. In so doing he signalled the voyage inwards towards introspection which in our century probably reaches its furthest point in Samuel Beckett's work, via Kafka, Joyce, and Virginia Woolf.† The achievement was largely the result of his own talent and genius; yet a look at the literary background in Europe against which Hamsun produced his novel indicates that he was also, inevitably, a child of his own time.

The sensation created by *Hunger* on its publication – and its enthusiastic critical reception among writers rather than critics – reflects a literary world in a process of dramatic change affecting every artistic capital of Europe, and the figure of Georg Brandes was central to this process of change and development. A Dane who was also a European, he made it his business to introduce the

---

* The title by which *Crime And Punishment* is traditionally known in Norway.
† Beckett's short story *The End* has striking parallels with *Hunger*. A tramp wanders pointlessly round a city, alternately comforted and tormented by the voice in his own head. He has the same fleeting, slightly ridiculous contact with people as the narrator of *Hunger*, and the story ends in his taking to a boat just as Hamsun's tormented hero does.

most important European thinkers to Danish minds. In his *Main Currents in 19th Century Literature*, published through the 1870s, he had written on Taine, Renan, John Stuart Mill, and called for a utilitarian literature of social debate. The rise of Ibsen and Bjørnson was closely connected with his championing of them, and especially with the spread of their reputation and influence across northern Europe. Then in the 1880s Brandes came across Nietzsche. The two corresponded, and Brandes became convinced of Nietzsche's genius. The series of lectures he delivered on him in Copenhagen in May 1888 effectively signalled Nietzsche's 'breakthrough' as a major philosophical and literary influence on the younger generation of European writers. These lectures served in a sense to crystallise for literature a host of large and small indices which had been confusedly abroad in European literary circles since the middle of the century. This was the sense that somehow, somewhere, something had been shattered. Between them, Darwin and Nietzsche put an end to God and the old certainties. This 'shattering' of the soul in a curious way echoes the shattering of the atom by physicists, and Strindberg was one of the first to try to accept and reflect and live out these new understandings. His preface to the published version of his play *Miss Julie* in 1888 sounded the keynote of the new vision. In it, he wrote of 'modern characters, living in an age of transition more urgently hysterical at any rate than the age which preceded it', and as a response to this claimed to have created in his play characters who were 'split and vacillating'. He described the human soul as something 'patched together'. This essay had a particularly strong effect on Hamsun, whose own theoretical justifications for his writing often make points similar to those made here, notably in the aversion to the idea of 'characters', whether on stage or in a novel, who are in fact merely clichés, exhibiting Taine's 'dominant characteristic', and repeating at regular intervals short catch-phrases or exclamations by means of which audiences and readers might readily recognise them.

'Aristocratic radicalism' was Brandes' term for the new stance, a term embraced by Nietzsche himself. It struck a chord at once among his audience of young poets and novelists bored by the fustian literature of naturalism and social utilitarianism, and ushered in a decade of proudly individualistic and defiantly 'useless' writing. Hamsun arrived back from America just too late to hear Brandes' lectures in May 1888, but Nietzsche continued to be the talk of the Bernina in Copenhagen and the Grand in Christiania. He was 'in the air', as Dostoevsky was in the air, and Hamsun could not have failed to pick up the ideas. In view of his sympathies for Fascist regimes in the 1930s and during the Second World War, it is natural to wonder to what extent he was influenced by Nietzsche in his youth, and whether this influence was decisive. Certainly the concept of 'aristocratic radicalism' must have appealed to him; deprived of the satisfaction of being a 'real' aristocrat by reason of his social background, his own unusually strong personality, and not least his achievement in writing a masterpiece like *Hunger* seemed to demand some sort of explanation. The kind of problems Hamsun had to face merely in being Hamsun were probably unusual: physically strong, brave, handsome, clever and quick of mind – the possession of such qualities can easily destroy a person. Where one is always effortlessly superior, the fun disappears; one ceases to bother to compete at all, but rests in the certain knowledge of one's mere superiority. These problems of the laxness of arrogance were something Hamsun had successfully surmounted. In seeking therefore to understand his own personality and success, the idea of the 'born' or 'natural' aristocrat implicit in Nietzsche's teaching, the concept of the 'spiritual aristocrat' must have seemed to provide an ideal explanation. Or perhaps more correctly, an ideal intellectual justification for something he had known instinctively all along – that in terms of the game of life, in terms of the rat race of society, he was born 'better' than the others. There were few, after all, who could have made the journey – largely unaided – from a dirty little farm in Hamarøy to the lecture hall at the Students' Union in Copenhagen. Nietzsche did matter to him, but hardly taught him anything he didn't already know.

When the novel was published, Hamsun set about its energetic defence and promotion. Reviews by Irgens Hansen in Bergen, and Carl Ewald and Edward Brandes in Copenhagen pleased him, and his friend Erik Skram, in the Bergen magazine *Samtiden* and the Danish *Tilskueren*, wrote enthusiastic appreciations of the book. But the one review he would really have liked – Georg Brandes' –he did not get. He presented Brandes with a copy, and perhaps rushed him for a response – 'you cannot have read enough of the book yesterday afternoon, and not enough in context', he retorted when Brandes described the book as 'monotonous'. The long letter of defence which this criticism fired off tells us a lot about what Hamsun was trying to do as a writer:

> I have been thinking about what you said about my book. I had not expected such a view from *you*. In the first place, the action takes place in the space of just a few months, and in such a limited space of time not a great deal more usually happens than

that which I have described; secondly, I have avoided all the usual stuff about suicidal thoughts, weddings, trips to the country and dances up at the mansion house. This is too cheap for me. What fascinates me is the endless motion of my own mind, and I thought I had described in *Hunger* moods whose very strangeness should strike one as being precisely not monotonous. . . .

My book must not be considered as a novel. There are enough authors who write novels when they write about hunger – from Zola to Kielland. They all do it. And if it is a lack of the 'novelistic' that possibly makes my book monotonous, then that is in fact a recommendation, since I had made up my mind quite simply not to write a novel.[18]

Hamsun was noticeably more guardedly technical in his discussions of the book with literary men like Brandes, and in contrast to his attitude towards friends like Frydenlund and Nilsson seemed anxious to play down the autobiographical element. In letters to the Swedish critic Gustaf af Geijerstam he carefully distanced himself from 'the man in the book' and 'the I of the book'. The general reaction of shocked excitement which *Hunger* created among the reading public at home in Norway must have confirmed him in his belief that he had succeeded at last in his ambition to produce something startlingly new and unusual in literature. Technically he had achieved this by his artful confusion of two forms, the autobiography and the novel. In succeeding experiments with the new genre over the course of the next ten years he was to discover that the public found this deliberate confusion of fact and fiction teasing, not a little disorienting, at times downright enraging, but always – fortunately for him – fascinating.

He was nervous and overworked after the last strenuous spurt on *Hunger*, and with the anodyne of hard work removed he felt loneliness keenly. Half-jokingly he asked Erik Frydenlund to look out for a woman for him, complaining that he was tired of travelling around without a single person he could turn to, without a home or any permanent place, from hotel to hotel, from country to country. He knew that he should rest, but felt that he could not afford it. He had received 2100 kroner for *Hunger*, but was spending money 'like a pig'. As he turns over in his mind the possibilities for the summer, for the first time the idea of a trip to the near East comes up; he wanted to travel to Constantinople, a two-month sea voyage via Antwerp, Tunisia, Piraeus, Salonika and Odessa.[19] This is the first direct expression of a more than passing interest in the Orient – which in those days meant the near East – an interest that was probably fostered by his reading of Confucius and certain Buddhist scriptures which he would have found in Kristofer Janson's library in the course of his energetic progress towards self-education. Hamsun writes of this trip as though it had been firmly planned in his mind, and only circumstances had contrived to put it off for what he described as 'at least a couple of months'. In fact, he had to wait another ten years before he made it. He lived on the wing during these days, constantly changing his address, making and abandoning plans with a bewildering, whimsical rapidity in which we recognise again the character portrayed in *Hunger*.

He looked round for a small place where he could settle down for a few months quite anonymously and work; he had a collection of 'curious short stories' which he was hoping to add to and publish in time to catch the Christmas book market in Christiania. Sometime in June he moved into a hotel room in the small Norwegian coastal town of Lillesand,[20] on the south coast between Kristiansand and Grimstad. From here he continued his efforts to promote *Hunger*; the first edition of 2000 was selling poorly after the original sensation, and his publisher Philipsen was only 'reasonably pleased'. He quickly abandoned his idea for a short-story collection and thought of another novel: 'I'll write a new book which will stir things up for the four prophets here at home, so help me God I will', he wrote to Erik Skram in Denmark.[21] It was the idea of the competition that thrilled and inspired Hamsun most in the early days, the thought of killing kings and capturing citadels. It was not enough for him just to write and be published – nothing short of a complete victory over all other writers, sealed by some kind of crowning ceremony, was going to be enough for him.

His room had a large balcony overlooking the sea and the Saltholmen lighthouse,[22] with numerous potted plants and creepers, and he spent hours walking back and forth here trying to get started on the new book. A neighbour whom he described as a 'mad musician' disturbed his concentration with his violin playing. Hamsun soon found that he did not like the town. 'Fillesand' he called it punningly – Ragtown – and complained that it was a wretched little town whose only inhabitants were one priest and a lame tailor. The pleasures of the graveyard, which had brought him such comfort when a boy in Uncle Hans' house, and which had often soothed him during his worst times in Christiania,*

---

* The narrator of *Hunger* is often to be found sitting on benches in the cemetery at Our Saviour's Church.

exerted their old attraction on him here in Lillesand, and he frequently took the walk to Molands Church where he would 'amuse himself' by reading the different inscriptions on the gravestones, counting them, and sorting them by motto.

A distraction of a different kind was the visit of a young Englishwoman named Mary Dunne, a writer herself and already at twenty-nine a rich widow. Having come across Hamsun's *Hunger* in a bookshop, she had become infatuated with him, and wrote to him suggesting that she translate the book into English. What correspondence the two may have had has been lost, but from references Hamsun makes to Mary Dunne in letters to friends, and using Mary Dunne's own lightly fictionalised account of their relationship in her short story *Now Spring Has Gone*,* it seems clear that when she visited him that summer in order to discuss the translation, she fell in love with him. Hamsun was slightly flattered, slightly amused, and – apart from the possibility of being translated into English – distinctly not interested: early in September she visited him at Arendal and presented him with a photograph of herself which he carefully wrapped in a hand-kerchief and placed in the bottom of his yellow leather suitcase.[23] According to Hamsun she actually proposed to him,[24] an assertion that the tone of her story of the meeting lends credibility to. Clearly he wanted *Hunger* to appear in English, and occasionally permitted himself to dream of the riches an appearance in what he called the 'beef-language' would bring him; but Mary Dunne had difficulty in finding a publisher for her work, and his interest in the project soon disappeared.

Unable to get on with his novel, Hamsun eventually did the next best thing and produced a statement of intention for it which he called *From the Unconscious Life of the Mind*, published in the Bergen literary magazine *Samtiden*. It provides an interesting footnote not only to *Hunger*, but to all the fiction he was to produce throughout the 1890s:

We have an old proverb: There are many things hidden in Nature. For the attentive, searching man of today, fewer and fewer of these secrets remain hidden. One after another they are being brought forth for observation and identification. An increasing number of people who lead mental lives of great intensity, people who are sensitive by nature, notice the steadily

* In the collection *Keynotes*, London 1894, under the *nom de plume* she also used for her translation of *Hunger*, George Egerton. The collection carries a dedication to Knut Hamsun.

more frequent appearance in them of mental states of great strangeness. It might be something completely inexplicable – a wordless and irrational feeling of ecstasy; or a breath of psychic pain; a sense of being spoken to from afar, from the sky, or the sea; an agonisingly developed sense of hearing which can cause one to wince at the murmuring of unseen atoms; an unnatural staring into the heart of some closed kingdom suddenly and briefly revealed; an intuition of some approaching danger in the midst of a carefree hour . . .

It was this vision of the unguessed-at complexity of the human mind – or at least, its under-representation in literature – that concerned Hamsun. He wanted a literature that would redefine normality and abnormality, that would in effect expand the known territory of consciousness and give a more vivid and accurate picture of what it's really like to be a human being.

Hamsun was proud of his article. To a friend he wrote that he felt he had gone 'as far as a sane man can go – except the Russians, who can go as far again'.[25] But if we ignore for a moment the chirpiness and look at the article itself, we find that it casts interesting and probably unintentional light on the author's personal life at this time, confirming his essential loneliness, his sense of isolation, and indeed his slight paranoia. Describing his walk home from the Molands Church one day, he writes that he 'met a number of people walking in the town . . . It interested me that all these good people I met glared so indignantly at me, as if the mere fact that also I was walking there was the height of impudence. I was used to these looks and scowls. I recognised them all again.'[26] He also mentions how he looked through an old newspaper trying to trace the source of an image that cropped up in his dreams; finding it, he realises that he did not register it consciously on the earlier reading because he was on that occasion searching its pages for something else, namely an attack on him which he 'assumed' the paper would contain – he apparently regularly received from America copies of any newspapers which contained attacks on him for his book *On the Cultural Life of Modern America*. He also mentions five anonymous, threatening letters received from America in connection with the book.

Later in the year the novel began to move a little. Nevertheless he knew that it was going to be a large book, and that he could not expect to see money for it for some time yet. He simply had to find a way to finance himself. One of the most important results of the publication of *Hunger* in June was the speed with which the book was taken up in Germany. Within one month of publication in

Norway the book was being translated into German for the Berlin publishing house of S. Fischer. Although it did not relieve his immediate financial needs, the importance of this for Hamsun's career as a writer, for his economic future, and for his future attitude towards Germany cannot be overestimated. Without it, Hamsun might have gone the way of many another author from a small linguistic community, and simply disappeared along with all his works. And this goes not merely for authors, but for all artists: it is hard to think of a single known Norwegian artist from this period – or indeed from succeeding periods – who did not come to European prominence through German enthusiasm. The most well-known examples are the most obvious – Ibsen, Grieg, Edvard Munch and Hamsun himself.

The traditional links between the lands were strong: Germany gave Denmark–Norway her religion, her kings, her aristocracy, her military, her schooling. And just as there was an intellectual cult of 'Norwegianness' prevailing in Copenhagen which helped to make *Hunger* such an immediate critical success, so there was a corresponding cult of Scandinavianism in Germany around the year 1890 which ensured that the book received immediate attention, and subsequent translation. Ibsen and Bjørnson were the founders of this cult of Scandinavianism, but as the influence of Nietzsche and Dostoevsky spread among the younger writers it was names like Strindberg and Hamsun that came to the fore. The cult reached its heights in Berlin, where a group led by the Polish writer and musician Stanislaw Przybyszewski and his Norwegian wife Dagny Juel, Ola Hansson and Strindberg, and including Edvard Munch and the writers Arne Garborg and Andreas Aubert, set a frantic intellectual and social pace which only the most dedicated of romantics could follow. Hamsun was never a member of this group – he visited Germany only once, and briefly, in the early part of his life – but he profited by its existence. Ola Hansson wrote a critical study of him in German, and Harald Hansen reviewed *Hunger* for the influential magazine *Freie Buhne*. The magazine also printed *Hunger* prior to its publication in book form in 1891. Hamsun was of course delighted at this response to what was effectively his first novel. He could also inform Erik Skram that he had received further requests for authorisation to translate the book from Proznan in Poland, from Marienbad, from Vienna, as well as from England.

For the most part, however, this impressive list of successes was a matter of prestige and status rather than money. Hamsun corresponded energetically with a German translator named Marie

Herzfeld throughout his stay in Lillesand, sending her short stories as well as his programme article *From The Unconscious Life of the Mind*. He exhorted her to read an imminent German translation of his American book by a Dr Hans Kurella (it never materialised), and enquired about the quality of the translation her colleague Maria von Borch had produced of *Hunger* for *Freie Buhne*. He was particularly pleased with the violence of the blasphemous outburst that appears in the last part of the novel, and when Fischer's edition appeared, wrote anxiously to Marie Herzfeld asking her to check that it had been included. He sent her a long short-story *Chance*, written in the summer of 1889 though not published in Norway until Christmas Eve. Apparently she had trouble placing her German translation of it. He wrote to her on 26 November 1890:

> I am sorry you have had such problems with *Chance*; it was wrong of me to send it. Next time you must simply refuse me when I send you poor quality stuff. In any case, I do not write like that any more; it does not interest me.

Nevertheless, she eventually managed to persuade *Freie Buhne* to take it in 1891. It was a small success, and one which Hamsun may later have wished undone in view of the storm which broke out over the story in 1892.

With the money earned from *Hunger* Hamsun was now able to start repaying some of the debts he had amassed in the course of the previous few years. He was particularly pleased to be able to pay off Nils Frydenlund the 200 kroner outstanding from 1886, plus a payment for interest on the money. But typically, no sooner had he repaid it than he had to start borrowing again. A man from his home county of Nordland had written to him describing the hard time he was having looking after his family of five children and wife. Hamsun knew the couple – had even been in love with the girl once himself – but this man had won her. Now he found that he had written promising the man 100 kroner in October, money which he no longer had, having just lent 100 kroner to a schoolteacher in Lillesand. This money, he was informed locally, he was unlikely to see again. He wrote in some embarrassment explaining the problem to Erik Frydenlund and, as usual, Frydenlund did not let him down.[27]

Money, the new novel, and how to make sure that the new 'psychological' literature continued to make progress, and did not wither in the shadow of Norway's ageing 'great men' – Ibsen,

Bjørnson, Kielland and Lie; these were the three problems uppermost in Hamsun's mind during his six months' stay at Lillesand. And at some point he hit upon an idea which seemed to offer a partial solution to all three: a lecture tour of Norway's major cities in which he would both promote the new literature and explicitly condemn the old. The controversy would ensure the financial success of such an undertaking, and between lectures he would be able to continue work on the new book. By September 1890 he was already wholly committed to the idea, and had ceased work on the novel in order to prepare the lectures. In December he returned to Christiania to put the finishing touches to them, and in February 1891 took them with him to Bergen to begin one of the most controversial years of his long life of controversy.

Chapter 7

1890–1893: Controversy: *Mysteries*, the Lecture Tour, and the 'Clenched Fist' Books

Hamsun began his lecture tour at Bergen, from the house of a journalist friend Bolette Pavels Larsen. It was a wise move to begin there, where he had already established a circle of friendly contacts which included the writers Gerhard Gran and Just Cato Frøchen, the young publisher Mons Litleré who had published his articles on Lars Oftedal, and the editor of the city's leading newspaper, Olav Lofthus. It was through the influence of these people that the tour got off to an auspicious and exciting start.

The three lectures he had prepared were on Norwegian litera-ture, on psychological literature, and on cult literature; and they were delivered on separate evenings at a cost of two kroner for the series, or one krone per lecture. Published for the first time in 1960, they amount to a wide-ranging development of the points first made in *From The Unconscious Life of the Mind*. In his opening remarks Hamsun warns his audience that he will be 'as aggressive and destructive as possible this evening, but I will also make an attempt to build something as well'. He asks them not to be too insulted by his demolishing and clearing work, his aim is only to make room for something for which at present there is no place – psychological literature. Throughout the three long lectures, of which the second is the most considerable, he returns again and again to this point. The lectures are fundamentally a plea for tolerance in literature, a warning against the stupefying effects of 'schools' of writing, a warning against the state of cliché into which writers of fiction seem to fall with such relief. His strongest criticism is reserved for the kind of clichéd psychology which he accuses all his contemporaries, older and younger, of practising. No one is praised in these talks – just as in his book on America, praise is not the idea. Not even the previously admired Zola survives the fanatic upsurge of self-conscious certainty that invests these lectures, a sense that Hamsun was speaking from a vision of how literature *ought to be*. All the heroes of antiquity, ancient and modern, are dismissed, including Shakespeare, Plato and Dante, for Hamsun maintained that the work produced by these authors had passed beyond the state of literature, and become in effect not books, but symbols, and the authors themselves no longer writers, but authorities. As the tour progressed, and word-of-mouth reports of these heresies spread through the Norwegian literary establishment, the adverse reactions began. More outrageous even than the attacks on dead writers were the attacks on the living, particularly Ibsen. According to Hamsun, no other writer had dedicated himself more thoroughly to the creation of 'types', characters with a simple, static psychology, beings who were wholly explicable in terms of Taine's theory of the 'dominant character trait' to be found in each person. He regarded Ibsen as a creator of devices, representing concepts and ideas, and not of real human beings. He also detested Ibsen's self-importance, which he found as ridiculous as his reputation for being 'difficult' and 'enigmatic'.

Ibsen's great contemporaries were also criticised, including Bjørnson, and all were found wanting; old men standing still, tramping the earth on a well-worn track, repeating themselves over and over again. He rejected completely their insistence that an art should be democratic, and address itself to social problems. He rejected, too, the notion of writers as the moral doctors of their society, and preached the gospel of total individuality, with authors dedicated to the creation of works which – if necessary – would only be comprehensible to a tiny proportion of the population. An author was for him a thoroughly subjective being, a pair of eyes, a heart, someone who created from passion, not a pseudo-rational pseudo-scientist creating characters after the latest scientific theories of human personality. 'I will make my hero laugh, where sensible people think he ought to cry', he proclaimed, 'and why? Because my hero is no character, no "type" who laughs and cries according to the theories of some School, but a complex, modern being.'

This was all, of course, a passionate justification of his own work: if *Hunger* was 'not a novel', then the concept of the novel must be shattered and re-defined in order to admit *Hunger*. In a passage which gives the key to Hamsun's subjective and instinct-driven work from the 1890s he declared:

I will therefore have 'contradictions' in the inner man considered as quite natural phenomena, and I dream of a literature with characters in which their very lack of consistency is their basic characteristic – not the only, not the dominating characteristic; but central, decisive.

This, then, was the basic message of these lectures. Taken in their entirety, they are balanced and reasonable, and every outrageous judgement is well and wittily defended.

Hamsun insisted that he was not hoping to experience some kind of triumph for the new literature at the expense of the old, but that he hoped for a literature that had within it a place for every kind of writing; even the artistically worthless cult successes of sexually outrageous writers like Hans Jaeger and Christian Krohg ought to have their place. 'Because everything in life has a place', he concluded, 'everything should have a place in literature.'

Between February and May 1891 Hamsun travelled with these lectures to Haugesund, Stavanger, Kristiansand, Sandefjord, Drammen and Fredrikstad, coastal towns reached by steamer, a form of travel which he came to dread, being an unusually bad sailor. News of the nature of his views preceded him and created plenty of interest. People came to 'gawp at the animal', a phenomenon he had become familiar with as the 'mad' protagonist of *Hunger*. He played up to the image, too, having learnt from his years in America the importance of ballyhoo. One simple example was in the several irrelevant swipes the lectures took at the powerful and burgeoning Women's Movement in Norway. The noted feminist journalist Aasta Hansteen wrote as early as March 1891 an article attacking him in *Dagbladet* – he was so arrogant, she prophesied, that soon he would break the bounds of gravity altogether and go into orbit. Appearances to the contrary notwithstanding, his feet were firmly on the ground. Although sincere in his hopes for the triumph of the new literature – and meaning at least most of what he said – he kept a wryly humorous perspective on the whole circus: from Stavanger he dashed off a note to Bolette Larsen announcing that he was 'just off to play the clown again for the second time today'.

Hamsun's strong views, and the provocative way he expressed them, polarised people: the feminists from the first scented a deadly enemy – and yet over half the audience at Hamsun's lectures were women. His sexual charm was visible and powerful. Arne Garborg, soon to become an enemy, described him as 'a handsome man, dangerous for all women, interesting and striking', and when he wrote to Bolette Larsen in Bergen to ask

how many conquests Hamsun had made there, 'God, he con-
quered them all,' Bolette replied, 'all the women, all of them were
at his feet.' Not the least of his charms was openly on display in the
lecture hall, a voice of great manly beauty which all who met him,
men and women alike, commented on. Yet probably the most
striking polarisations were into 'old' and 'young', and 'famous'
and 'unknown': with great courage, Hamsun was affronting a
whole establishment of old men with big reputations. Even lesser
lights, middle-aged local successes like Amalie Skram, Christian
Krohg and Hans Jaeger who might have provided useful moral
support were cheerfully alienated by remarks to the effect that they
were 'not real writers at all'. Those who really loved what Hamsun
was doing were in the main powerless unknown writers much
younger than himself, like Peter Egge and Arne Dybfest. But
those who had been pleased to patronise an interesting, self-
educated farm-boy, men like Bjørnson, the newspaper editor Ola
Thommessen, and the Brandes brothers, found their protégé's
breathtaking arrogance and impudence a wholly unacceptable
departure from the script, and were already separately planning
their reactions.

Hamsun took a break in the summer, and for three months
stayed in a hotel in Sarpsborg and worked hard on his new novel.
Then he steeled himself in preparation for the climax of the tour in
Christiania in October, at the famous Hals Brothers Auditorium,
where he spoke on the 7th, 9th and 12th. With considerable cheek
he had personally invited Ibsen to attend, and Ibsen, curious, no
doubt, to find out what all the fuss was about, came to all three
lectures, sitting prominently and magisterially in the first row, in
company with Edvard and Nina Grieg. Fridtjof Nansen was there
too. The house was full every night; the lectures had become social
'musts', and Hamsun, although visibly nervous, delivered the
same implacable mixture of heresy, paradox and passion as he had
done so many nights before in the course of the year.

But the establishment was ready for him now, and the
Christiania press turned on the new hero. Ola Thommessen in
Verdens Gang reacted most violently. In an attack which Hamsun
could never forget nor forgive he described the lectures as 'a course
in ignorance, superficiality, and cheek'. Hamsun had 'crushed
Europe's foremost authors in the same way that a year or two ago
he crushed the United States, of which he did not know much
more than that they could manage perfectly well without him,
thank you. America is still standing – and so are our writers.'[1]

Ola Thommessen was the model for the character of the
'Commander' in *Hunger*, the newspaper editor whose patience

and charity towards the desperate young writer are such an encouragement to him, and Hamsun took the desertion badly. He would take his revenge, in his own way.

Hamsun's naïve courage had very quickly led him from the beaten tracks, and out into the wilderness. He was not choosing the easy way up. In fact, he could not, because he did not know the easy way. But if the establishment thought that a few thick ears might put him in his place, they had a great deal yet to learn. A young writer friend, Hans Aanrud, met him in Christiania around this time, and was at once struck by Hamsun's combative response. As they walked the streets of the city together late one night Hamsun talked a great deal about his career so far, how influential liberal people had patronised him after *Hunger*, and had tried to nurse him along, and give him good advice. Now when he had shown that he did not wish to be nursed along, did not wish to take well-meant advice, these same people had turned on him. 'They think they can break me', he told Aanrud, 'But when I am finished with the book I am writing now, they won't be able to get me any lower than on my knees.'[2]

'The book I am writing now' was *Mysteries*, the second in the quartet of masterpieces Hamsun was to produce in the 1890s. More even than *Hunger* it is probably the book he had been dreaming of writing all along, the 'autobiography' of which he had spoken so often to friends in America. His son Tore confirms that it is as close to unadulterated self-portraiture as Hamsun ever came in fiction.

An unpublished manuscript in Hamsun's hand in the library of the University of Oslo, dated 1894, contains his own description of *Mysteries*. The objective tone of the writing suggests that it was intended for promotional purposes, perhaps for inclusion in the catalogue of his German publisher Albert Langen:

> The hero of *Mysteries* is a poseur, a pathological phenomenon who is part madman and part genius, pursued through 516 pages, never once out of sight. Every hour of his day is described. Hr Hamsun has both verbally and in writing attacked 'character' psychology . . . He presents Nagel therefore as a split and divided person, bursting with contradictions, full of inconsistencies. . . . There are twenty characters in the book, but nineteen of them are there only to cast light on the poseur Nagel.
>
> The plot of *Mysteries* revolves round Nagel's love for Dagny, the daughter of a priest, a refined and educated flirt who ensnares him through her beauty. Disappointed in his love for this woman, torn apart by a sense that life is meaningless and banal, he goes mad, has visions, and loses all contact with life.

He ends by drowning himself in the sea.

On every single page of this thick book Hamsun has tried to amass and compress meaning. But the book cannot be described in précis; it consists of subtleties.

The book does indeed consist of subtleties, and can hardly be described in précis. To fill out the picture a little, however, we can say that it opens with the arrival of the stranger Johan Nagel in a small Norwegian coastal town in which he settles for a few weeks. Here his unusual personality and behaviour soon bring him to the attention of the townspeople, and he is given entry into the town's higher social circles. He proves an uncomfortable guest, however; provocative and unpredictable in his views, alternately charming. and repellent in his utterances. Three relationships in particular develop. The first is his obsessive passion for the priest's daughter Dagny Kielland. She is already engaged to another man and contrives – just – to resist Nagel's desperate attempts to seduce her. Nagel next turns his attention to a middle-aged spinster named Martha Gude; in spite of her unassuming personality and plain appearance, he has sensed the powerful eroticism in her. He uses Martha, partly to console himself for Dagny's rejection of him, partly to try to arouse Dagny's jealousy. The inscrutable observer of all this is the grotesque and crippled Minutten, the town clown in whom Nagel displays from the first an eccentrically intense interest. Minutten appears to embody all the Christian virtues in his response to the bullyings and humiliations he has to put up with from the townspeople. Soon a second obsession grips Nagel: to unmask Minutten and expose him as a fraud, an actor. He achieves none of his goals, however, and drowns himself in the sea. In a short coda a few months later, Dagny and Martha walk together and reminisce about Nagel. It seems as though he was right about Minutten all along: Dagny mentions that the cripple has come to a bad end, and refers to something – clearly something terrible – which he did to Martha. Precisely what he did remains one of the books many mysteries, but a reasonable guess would be that he raped her.

Hamsun's own synopsis of *Mysteries* lays stress on the fact that it is a love story, and in the light of this it is interesting to consider something that he wrote in trying to account for what he considered a fault in the book – that he had worked on it 'in Sarpsborg, in Christiania, in Copenhagen, while on the move, while in love, while poor – hence the sense of disconnection in many of the scenes'.[3] In fact, there is some evidence that while engaged in writing the book he experienced two quite serious disappointments in love.

The first of these involved a girl named Caroline. Hamsun met her in Sarpsborg, during his summer break from the lecture tour in 1891. She worked as a chambermaid at Kristiansens Hotel, where Hamsun was living. His conduct of the affair was unusual. He would apparently follow Caroline about wherever she went. He accompanied her to church, and waited outside until she came out again. When she went to the Glåma to wash clothes he would go with her and wait beside her while she worked. His landlady tried to persuade him there was no future in the relationship, but he insisted that he was in love with her. Caroline apparently became quite impossible in the face of all this attention, and ended up refusing to work and demanding to be waited on herself. Finally her employer sacked her, ignoring Hamsun's protests on Caroline's behalf.[4]

The reactions of the inhabitants of Sarpsborg to Hamsun's conduct of the affair were divided in much the same way that the inhabitants of the 'small Norwegian coastal town' divided themselves over Nagel's behaviour. Some thought that he was mad, others that he was making some kind of study of the girl, and still others that for obscure reasons of his own he was making a fool of her. No one seems to have believed that he was genuine in his love for her. The only firm indication that he was, and that the failure of the relationship was a disappointment to him, comes from an unusual source which one has to approach with some care. A few years later, an authoress named Anna Munch wrote a letter to Hamsun's first wife Bergljot, shortly after Bergljot and Hamsun became engaged in 1898: 'So you think you've done well? Well, a couple of years ago your lover wanted to marry a chambermaid in Sarpsborg named Caroline. But the girl was sensible enough to turn him down, and your writer grieved for a long time over it.' Why one must approach Anna Munch's testimony with care will become apparent later. It is sufficient to point out here that the information contained in the letter is so oddly precise about an obscure period of Hamsun's life as to suggest that he might have been the source of it himself.

The other possibility is that in describing *Mysteries* as having been written 'while in love', Hamsun was referring to his affair with a woman named Lulli Lous. After the finale of his lecture tour in Christiania, Hamsun settled in the west coast town of Kristiansund and continued work on the book. Here he became friendly with a brother and sister named Hans and Kalla Neeraas, and through them met their friend Lulli. Like all of Hamsun's friends in these days, the Neeraas were professional people at the upper end of the social scale. Hamsun and Lulli Lous were powerfully attracted to one another, but the very great gap between the conventional and strictly brought up young lady and the radical young literary firebrand proved too much for the relationship, and when Hamsun moved on from Kristiansand in the spring in order to put the finishing touches to *Mysteries* and see it through publication, he was also trying to put some distance between himself and another disappointment in love. His determination to forget all about it and get on with his life is evident in a letter to the Neeraas from Copenhagen in that summer of 1892:

> Why does Frøken Lous refer to it as a sorry business? What is there so specifically sorry about it? She got what she wanted. There is no shame in my having wanted her, it doesn't invalidate her chances for the rest of her life. There was a girl I wanted once before – that didn't necessarily make the whole thing a matter of life and death. But it's alright! I've recovered already. I can't see that there was anything 'sorry' about it though. Now for God's sake please do me a favour and don't talk to her about me again, and let her forget the whole 'sorry business', and that I was ever in Kristiansand at all. And one more thing: as I asked you before – *don't write to me about her*. I need peace.[5]

Lulli Lous has sometimes been mentioned as a model for Dagny Kielland. Certainly the suspicions Hamsun entertained of her motives, in saying that 'she got what she wanted', correspond with his own attitude towards the character of Dagny as a 'refined and educated flirt who ensnares Nagel'. One might imagine that she entered Hamsun's life rather too late to act as model for the leading female character in the book; but he did, after all, write it 'while on the move', and the sense of disconnectedness he himself remarked in it strengthens one's suspicion that *Mysteries* was in many ways an inspired act of literary improvisation into which Hamsun wove and developed incidents from his own life almost as soon as they happened.*

Whatever, he had, as he wrote from Copenhagen, recovered already: in another letter to the Neeraas' from his lodgings at Number 17 Bredegade he mentions that his landlady has two daughters, 'one of whom is incredibly beautiful and collects

---

* In connection with a legal matter Hamsun's lawyer went to see Lulli Lous in 1935. She had never married, and confirmed for Fru Stray – an old friend – that the break with Hamsun had been 'her life's tragedy'. On being told this, Hamsun expressed surprise, and said that he had never really believed that she loved him.[6]

stamps (I have given her my collection as a keepsake), and the other goes to the Royal Theatre Ballet School'.[7]

Mysteries, of course, was his real love, and his anodyne. In letters he referred to the book as 'she'. He was thrilled and puzzled by 'her', and felt at times that he did not understand 'her' at all. At other times he wrote as though he were pregnant, and *Mysteries* the child he was expecting. Regularly he worked himself into a trance-like state of exhaustion:

> I wrote without stopping from five in the afternoon until three in the morning. I forgot about the clock, forgot to eat, burned my lamp dry, and still my head wasn't empty. God how good it is when it goes like that! I wrote a whole chapter, at least ten printed pages. You'll notice it in the book, Chapter XIX, one of the most desperate chapters in the whole novel.[8]

Then came the reaction:

> Imagine a row of fishes' heads, gaping mouths, indescribably dead-eyed, in which every process of thought has simply ceased, leaving just dumb dullness – and there you have my head.[9]

At such times he would leave his work and wander into town, and hide himself away in a theatre, or drink in an obscure bar.

Mysteries was published on 16 September, and Hamsun threw himself into the social side of the business with relieved abandon. 'I am completely wrecked by ceaseless visits to Circus, and the Tivoli, and parties with my publisher and a number of literary young ladies. My hands are shaking like a sinners,' he wrote to Kalla Neeraas,[10] and complained woefully over the vast sums of money he was getting through. He was also not at all sure what kind of reception the novel would get:

> How can I fool myself into thinking people will understand my book? In fact, I don't. On the contrary, I've felt sure all along that people will not find a single good thing to say about me . . .[11]

But he knew that the book, which by a fairly crude act of insertion contained many of the heretical views he had associated himself with on the lecture stand, might also attract a good deal of scandalised attention. To Marie Herzfeld, who was working on some German translations of short stories he had sent to her, he wrote:

I discuss named Norwegians and other European great men in a pretty savage way. In Norway there is just Ibsen now, just Ibsen. I've already had a go at him in my lecture, but in the novel it's much worse.[12]

'Much worse' it was indeed. Besides a personal attack on Ibsen, Nagel dismisses him professionally as the purveyor of 'dramatised pulp'. Hamsun even feared – or perhaps hoped – that Ibsen might take him to court.

As he had expected, the book was badly received. Christiania newspaper critics used their reviews to chastise Hamsun for being Hamsun, and to put him in his place after the lectures. It was not difficult for them to do, since they were also genuinely baffled by the novel: determinism, and the law of cause and effect, had such a strong hold over minds in those days. Critics were puzzled: the perverse and peculiar mind which the state of hunger seemed satisfactorily to 'explain' in the first novel was here presented again, in a more refined and tortured perversity, but this time without any seeming excuse or explanation at all.* The most interesting criticism, in *Aftenposten*, linked the novel with an exhibition of paintings then causing a sensation in Scandinavia in which Edvard Munch and the Dane J. F. Willumsen exhibited together. 'Of the two', the reviewer wrote, 'the latter is the most entertaining and accomplished.' As for Munch, he and Hamsun were bracketed together as purveyors of a new cult of perversity and mysticism: 'One can no longer speak here of Nature, only of twisted imaginations, atmospheres swimming in delirium, sick and feverish hallucinations.'

The parallel with Munch is striking: at about the same time that Hamsun was producing his apologia *From the Unconscious Life of the Mind*, Munch, four years younger, formulated his 'St Cloud Manifesto', in which he announced an end to the painting of people 'reading and knitting. There will be living people, who breathe, feel, suffer, and love.' Munch's *Evening on Karl Johan*, in which a ghoulish throng tramps a city pavement while a single figure on the right-hand side of the canvas walks alone in the opposite direction, is an excellent visual evocation of the mood of Hamsun's *Hunger*, and of the struggle both artists were having to be accepted in their native country.

* Hamsun had realised that hunger would be used to explain the behaviour of the narrator of *Hunger*, but knew that this was not the real explanation. 'Everybody thinks that the crazy things "Andreas Tangen" does are as a result of his hunger. But this is not true, unfortunately.' He confessed that the real explanation lay in his own bizarre personality.[13]

The *Aftenposten* reviewer called Nagel 'a fantastic personification of the author's own thoughts, visions and dreams' and described Hamsun as 'oppositional to the point of fanaticism, with an almost pathological desire to be independent, and a compulsion to contradict that often drives him into expressing the wildest paradoxes. . . . What he hates is authority in any form; the accepted truth; the politeness of the bourgeoisie; the doctrinaire pronouncements of the academic; and the judgement of the masses.'[14] Edward Brandes, who had some claim to be Hamsun's discoverer, shook his head in *Politiken* over his wayward protégé, and complained not so much at a lack of tension in the book as at the perverse form the tension took. In so doing he attacked Hamsun at one of the points where his influence on the narrative techniques of twentieth-century writers has been most decisive, complaining that 'tension arises from the fact that the author does not give correct information about the characters, not the reasonable information one has, after all, the right to expect from an author.'[15] In a word, the author's preferring subjective to objective truth in fashioning his narration.

Mysteries is an extraordinary novel. More than any comparable work of the last hundred years, perhaps more even than Joyce's *Ulysses*, it gives us a sensation of being actually and physically close to another consciousness; close enough to hear it whirring and ticking, to register sudden explosions of light within it, and consuming surges of darkness and obscurity. There is a powerful naturalness about the novel, a careering inevitability, tremendous technical and psychological subtlety and withal a sense that the whole thing is in fact a dazzling and half-conscious act of literary improvisation. Literature has no genuine equivalent to the primitive painter, but in the force with which Hamsun writes, in the eerily successful ineptness with which he wields the third person in what is essentially a first-person story, one is reminded sometimes of a great primitive painter like Rousseau, imposing a vision on the world in defiance of all the known laws of technique out of a divine conviction that *this is how it is*. What upset Hamsun most about the criticism was that his critics made the simple equation Nagel=Hamsun, and accepted the weird foolery and mental games and double bluffs as simply showing-off. The extravagance of his ambition in trying to display consciousness itself as the hero of his novel, and the thrilling nature of the results, went completely over their heads. That simple equation, plus a demonstrable coincidence of views between character and author, obscured the true nature of the achievement. Hamsun could only resign himself to the fact that the book had sunk. He wrote to Erik Skram with a wry contempt for the criticisms:

> It is obvious that in a novel one does not put forward one's ideas systematically; one has to hop about too much. But in any case, I cannot accept personal responsibility for Nagel's opinions. The question is whether or not he hangs together with his other self, Minutten, while exhibiting such a disunity within himself that he is practically falling apart.*[16]

And in a postscript to this letter he reveals the extent to which in writing the book he was all along the conscious artist:

> Nagel astonishes a small town with his opinions, and in that small town he *is* astonishing. But people are twisting this to make it seem as though *I* am trying to astonish *them* with *my* opinions, to make myself seem important. This is definitely a mistake. In the small town in which Nagel appears, naturally, he astonishes. But I could hardly have given him a line to say: 'Of course, in Copenhagen I would not have astonished anybody.'[17]

Before leaving *Mysteries*, one ought to say of it that, like *Hunger*, it simply does not strike a modern reader as a hundred-year-old book. Again this is largely due to the acuteness of Hamsun's psychological insight, both into himself as Nagel, and into those around him. Hamsun's concerns in the novel, what he described as Nagel's sense that 'life is meaningless and banal', remain the concerns of twentieth-century existentialists. His narrative techniques are remarkably undated: in a series of monologues which give us access to Nagel's thoughts he uses free association and techniques of stream of consciousness at least twenty years before writers in English discovered them. He also takes the 'name as descriptive label' technique an interesting stage further than most of his contemporaries: the wildly paradoxical nature of Nagel's personality is implied in the fact that it involves an anagram in Norwegian of 'en gal' (a madman) and in English of 'angel'.

In later years Hamsun named the greatest influences on his younger self as Nietzsche, Strindberg, and Dostoevsky. Nagel has been described as a 'small-town Zarathustra', but the character is really too subtle to fit the description. For all his admiration for the

---

* A passing reference to Nagel as an 'unprepossessing dwarf' in Hamsun's next novel, *Editor Lynge*, confirms that Nagel and Minutten were conceived of as two different sides of the same personality.

ideas of the born leader, and the spiritual aristocrat – an admiration which he shared with Nagel – there was too much of the self-mocker in Hamsun, and to call him a Nietzschean ultimately misses out more than it contributes. Additionally, as his confidence in himself as an artist grew – which it did, in spite of the press attacks – so, proportionately, his anti-academicism increased, as did his passionate belief in the superiority of the wisdom of experience over the wisdom of book-learning. Nietzsche, a university professor at the age of twenty-five, and a man with a very limited practical experience of life, was not really the stuff of which Hamsun's heroes were made.

As for Strindberg, one feels always that it was the staring eyes and the bristling moustache that Hamsun admired above all. He loved Strindberg for his egomania, for the fearless violence of his subjective pronouncements, for his anti-feminism. He set great store by Strindberg's theories of the nature of contemporary consciousness, and of the inadequacy of established and conventional forms of art to convey this; but as writer, as technician, and as artist he must have realised fairly soon that he was superior to him. Dostoevsky alone of these three heroes seems to have shone with an undiminished brightness for Hamsun. He began reading him at some point in the late 1880s, and praised him without reservation on many occasions throughout his life. In Dostoevsky's books he found one of the greatest joys that the practice of reading novels has to offer – sudden recognition of oneself. In a letter to Marie Herzfeld in 1892 he wrote:

> He felt as I do – I realise it now – and even in some ways thought as I do, only infinitely richer and better and greater, because he is the great writer. But the strange thing is that even before he taught me anything, even before I ever heard the man's name, one might say that Dostoevsky had a decided influence on me.[18]

Besides being the great writer, Dostoevsky was the great psychologist for Hamsun, the explorer of the irrational, the expounder of the psychology of the unique individual who brought new and vital insights into literature. Sixty years later, Dostoevsky's importance was still clear to him:

> The so-called Naturalists, Zola and his contemporaries, wrote about people with single dominant characteristics. They had no use for a psychology of nuance – people had a 'ruling characteristic' which controlled their behaviour.
> Dostoevsky – and others – taught all of us something different about people.[19]

By 1892 he had read most of what was available in Norwegian translation of Dostoevsky, which included *The Brothers Karamazov* and *Crime and Punishment*. Even his readings of the lesser-known works were shattering physical experiences for Hamsun; in an undated letter to Bolette Larsen he tells her that he has read *The Insulted and the Injured* 'and it just about murdered me. I went for a walk afterwards and came back shaking all over my body.'

How very disturbing it must have been for him, then, when in June 1892, just as he was working on the last pages of *Mysteries*, he received from Germany a copy of a magazine article in which he was accused of having plagiarised *The Gambler* with his own short-story *Chance*, written in the summer of 1889 and published in a Christmas edition of *Verdens Gang* the same year. This was the story that Marie Herzfeld had had such trouble finding a home for back in 1890, but which she had eventually placed in *Freie Buhne*. It was there that Felix Hollander's attack now appeared. Hamsun replied at great length to the accusation in a private letter to his translator.

The Gambler had been published for the first time in Norway in 1889, and as soon as he read it, Hamsun realised the similarities between the two works, and tried to get *Verdens Gang* to return his story to him. But he was too late; the story was already printing. Among other things he explained to Marie Herzfeld the very great similarities that any two stories about the specialised milieu of the roulette table are bound to have. He thought that perhaps someone had once described the story to him, and that he had reproduced elements of it unconsciously in his own work. He deeply regretted all this, but felt no guilt about it. His response to the accusation tells us a great deal about his character at this time: he insisted that this extremely lengthy private response to Marie Herzfeld be kept private:

> You say that I ought to defend myself. But I would rather not. I never reply to attacks on myself – why should I do it now?[20]

There is a tremendous pride in this attitude, this determination not to break under any form of attack. The accusation was, after all, a major blow to his nascent reputation in Germany. *Freie Buhne* was an important new magazine devoted to the encouragement of new writers and writing, and was an important showcase in Berlin for the talents of Norwegian writers striving to break through in a major European language. *Hunger* had been serialised in it in the year of Norwegian publication; and when the Berlin publishers of *Hunger*, S. Fischer, now declined the offer to publish *Mysteries*,

Hamsun privately attributed this directly to the blow dealt his reputation by Hollander.

He became totally convinced that the article had been written at the instigation – and with the direct assistance – of the clique of Norwegian writers then living in Berlin as a revenge for the attacks made on them in his lectures. He suspected particularly Arne Garborg, the man to whom he had gone for help in 1886 after the rejection of his story *On Tour*. In reviews of *Mysteries*, Garborg had been used as a stick with which to beat the jumped-up Hamsun. *Mysteries* was compared unfavourably with Garborg's own novel from 1890, *Tired Men*, a possibility Hamsun had rather gloomily foreseen, since Nagel does not go to a priest in the end as does Garborg's hero. Garborg was promoted as the 'decent' alternative to Hamsun, and hailed as a serious thinker in comparison to the superficial Nagel/Hamsun. Garborg was, in fact, a fundamentally decent type who did not think it right of Hamsun to criticise his fellow writers; but whether or not he had anything to do with Hollander's article cannot be said. Two factors probably led Hamsun to the conclusion that he did; one, that Hollander's hearsay references to the lectures indicated that he had heard about them from someone who violently disapproved of them; and two, that the article in effect involved a double accusation of plagiarism by mentioning the entirely superficial thematic similarities between Hamsun's *Hunger* and Garborg's novel *Peasant Students*.*

Both of Hamsun's novels so far show the secretive nature of his personality, and like the narrator of *Hunger*, and Nagel, he was a man given to thinking repetitively about things, searching for hidden meanings, and the key to secrets. This suspicion, that his contemporaries and brother writers, as well as the press, were dedicated to the aim of destroying him, marks perhaps the real beginnings of a state of mind never far from paranoia which reveals itself over and over again within the next few years. Hamsun became totally committed to the idea of himself as a man working alone in the face of a universal hostility. It gave him a fanatic strength, a determination to triumph over the imagined odds in a stratospheric sense, and by the exercise of his talent alone force the establishment to hail him as a great writer whether it wanted to or not. 'Let the article in *Freie Buhne* stand,' he told Marie Herzfeld, 'I will give my own reply in the course of time, in book after book

---

* The novel, published in 1883 and usually regarded as Garborg's best, is a naturalistic study of the corruption and decline of a peasant boy who comes to the city to study. Hamsun was familiar with the novel: in 1885 he presented an inscribed copy of it to a friend in Valdres as a Christmas gift.

after book after book.'*

After the publication of *Mysteries*, and after having spent most of the 3000 kroner he received for the book in cafés like the Bernina, the Achen, and the A Porta, Hamsun suddenly disappeared from the scene, without telling anyone where he was going, and took up residence on the island of Samsø, in the Danish Kattegat. Here he began work on not one, but two of these books that he had promised himself, and the world.

It has been suggested that *Mysteries* was written as a kind of apology for the storm aroused by the lectures of 1891; that in creating the character of Nagel, Hamsun went a long way towards admitting that there was some truth in the accusations that he was a bluffer, a charlatan, an intellectual con-man and literary acrobat; and that in embracing the description of himself as charlatan *in part* he was in fact extending a hand of reconciliation to those he had affronted. If such were the case, no one was interested in his peace-making, and he travelled to Samsø with an enormous chip on his shoulder.

The winter of 1892–93 was harsh and cold on Samsø – at one point the island was cut off by ice from the Danish mainland, and received no post for eleven days – but work on the new novels continued. Presently one of these claimed his urgent attention, and the other was put aside until later. That which pressed hardest on him was *Editor Lynge*, a book which, he told Bolette Larsen, was going to be 'as hot as hate'. It was, in fact, a supremely personal and considered act of revenge on the editor of *Verdens Gang*, Ola Thommessen, for his review of Hamsun's lectures. Hamsun, understandably, does not refer to this aspect of the book in his own description of it for Langen's catalogue in 1894:

> A political polemic, violent, and as a piece of writing different from all of Hamsun's previous works. Hamsun has been accused of not writing novels like other novelists, novels with beginnings and ends, with recognisable characters in them; he has been accused of being incapable of writing such novels. Thereupon Hr Hamsun publishes *Editor Lynge*, a book in which one finds, in prominent degree, the required qualities. Hr Hamsun will probably not write more than one book in this style; but he wished to do so on this one occasion, simply to show that he could.

* Hamsun later substantially rewrote *Chance* and under the title *Father and Son* included it in his short story collection *Brushwood* (1903).

Ola Thommessen, the model for Hamsun's editor Lynge,* had taken over the Christiania newspaper *Verdens Gang* in 1878, and had made it into a leading organ of radical opinion in the capital. As the century drew towards a close, the central political issue of debate, and the touchstone of a newspaper's politics, was the attitude towards the question of Norway's seceding from the union with the Swedish crown, to become an independent nation. And as a radical paper *Verdens Gang* was originally an unequivocal supporter of independence. Hamsun, who followed keenly the major issues of the day, was not alone in entertaining a suspicion that Thommessen, as the 1890s progressed, was editing his newspaper in an inconsistent fashion, and that his standpoint on particular issues, including independence, was dictated increasingly by considerations of money, social prestige, and even sexual advancement, rather than principle. It was this side of his attack on Thommessen that Hamsun stressed, claiming that he had written *Editor Lynge* 'to oppose the editor of one of Christiania's leading newspapers', and that 'the book flays with scorn this political renegade'. In a not wholly convincing attempt to stress the disinterested nature of the attack, he disclaimed political affiliations, calling himself 'a radical who belongs to no party, but is an individual in the extreme'.

He took an early Christmas in Copenhagen, and worked throughout the season itself. Feeling himself alone and friendless now, aware that the book he was writing would only create still more scandal and opposition, he turned to his friends from America as a source of comfort. He wrote to Halvard Askeland, thanking him for his loyalty, joking that it was obvious that he didn't read the Scandinavian newspapers over there in America, or he would surely also turn against him. He complained morosely that, among all his other troubles, he was suffering from sycosis, and that he looked 'gruesomely leprous'.

In March 1893 Hamsun returned to Copenhagen and presented his finished manuscript to Philipsen. While it was being printed he delivered another lecture at the Students' Union which was again unrepentantly critical of older and younger contemporary writers. The students, of course, loved it. But it was a professionally suicidal course Hamsun was embarked on now. Back home in Christiania, Garborg reacted to his lecture with a sarcastic article called 'One Helluva Bloke'. No doubt Garborg was offended by Hamsun's lack of ethics; he may also have felt that Hamsun was

---

* This was his second sitting – he had previously appeared as the kindly 'Commander' in *Hunger*.

'queering the pitch' for his fellow Norwegians in Copenhagen, where literary fashion still set some premium on Norwegianness. Garborg and Hamsun had preserved, mostly through letters to third parties, an uneasy mutual admiration ever since the publication of *Hunger*, and Hamsun retained his respect and admiration for Garborg. But on the publication of *Editor Lynge* Garborg was finally convinced that Hamsun was a lost cause. *Verdens Gang* commissioned him to do the hatchet job on the novel, and in his review of 22 April he did so, describing the book as 'a lampoon', and concluding with the damning accusation that the book was 'one for the mob'.

'One for the mob' it was indeed: *Editor Lynge* sold sensationally well, and went into a second edition within a month of publication. Understandably, in view of the parochial nature of its theme, the book is one of the least translated of all Hamsun's major works; but it is also the weakest of his novels, in the crudeness of its psychology betraying the faint contempt for the traditional nature of the form in which it was written, simply to prove that he could more or less toss off this kind of stuff at will, if that was what 'the mob' really wanted.

Philipsen had paid Hamsun well for the novel – 2100 kroner – but in writing it Hamsun forfeited the last of any residual goodwill the establishment might have had left for him as the talented working-class provincial author of *Hunger*. Most of the newspaper reviews were along the lines of Garborg's, although the general condemnation of the book was not exclusively moral; the reviewer in the *Norske Intelligenssedler* made the valid point that Hamsun's polemic intentions were realised 'at the expense of art and psychology'.[21] And in private letters to one another, outraged pillars of Norwegian literary society vied with each other in expressing the extent of their disapproval of Hamsun. Bjørnson, who had reacted to Hamsun's lectures by calling him 'a know-nothing' and 'narrow-minded', was even more upset by the novel. In a letter to Amalie Skram he conceded that 'with talent it preaches honesty and responsibility', but went on to describe it as 'the most dishonest and irresponsible book in Norwegian literature'. Fru Skram, who along with her husband Erik had been one of Hamsun's first supporters in Copenhagen in 1888, wrote back to tell Bjørnson that she had liked Hamsun enormously to begin with, 'but since I have found out what a casual relationship he has to truth, I have been unable to bring myself to talk to him'. His book, she declared, was 'vile'.[22] Hamsun had his own suspicions about such reactions from fellow writers: he had met the Skrams back in May 1892 and found Amalie 'very cool' towards him, and in a letter to Bolette Larsen surmised that this was because he had used her in his lectures in 1891 as an example of what he called 'altsaa' literature – the literature of characterisation by catch-phrase.[23]

All the fuss did not stop Hamsun celebrating the publication of the novel in April with his Copenhagen friends. The years between 1888 and 1893, when he was very often in the city, laid the basis for his reputation as a drinker and hell-raiser of legendary powers. Aage Welblund's book on the Copenhagen literary cafés crowns him undisputed King of Bohemian life-celebrants and hard drinkers. The code of unflinching stoicism, the ability to grit his teeth and endure which he had learnt in Uncle Hans' care, and his own fierce sense of competition turned him into a drinker who as a matter of pride would outdrink and outlast anyone who cared to challenge him.

In a letter of 1890 to Bolette Larsen, Hamsun described for her what he called his 'ambition', which was to appear suddenly on a scene, astonish with his behaviour, and disappear again as abruptly as he had come.[24] And the life of a writer, as he lived it, was peculiarly well-suited to the achievement of such an 'ambition', with its long periods of withdrawal from the world, followed by abrupt returns when the work in hand was completed, followed in turn by another disappearance when a new project announced itself. The drinking and fantastic escapades at cafés like the Bernina were not the desperate substitutes for work and inspiration that they were for many a lesser artist, but gargantuan gulps of society which functioned also as calculated 'appearances' during which he would indeed astonish. He also deliberately used these bouts of social drinking as a means of destroying the unusable remains of a finished work in his head and clearing space for the next one. As *Editor Lynge* was going through the presses, Hamsun sent a story to the editor of *Samtiden*, urging him to use it soon 'while there is still a bit of heat around my novel – because there's sure to be an outcry about it'; the brief card accompanying the story also includes the information that he is 'hungover, a nervous wreck, half-dead. The last five weeks drunk to bed every night. Now I stop.'[25]

Now, indeed, he did stop, and began planning his next disappearance; he had half a novel waiting to be completed. The immediate popular success of *Editor Lynge* had put money into his pocket which not even his five-week binge could exhaust, and for the first time he was free to travel where he chose.

For all the courage and daring of Hamsun's fierce swipes at the establishment, for all the pride in the fact that he had educated himself up from nowhere to a position in which he was one of the most discussed young writers in his country, he continued to suffer from a profound sense of intellectual and social uncertainty. It accounts for those sudden lapses into 'contemptible behaviour' which Victor Nilsson remarked on in America – his insistence on going barefoot in the Janson's house, for example. Many people will come to remark on similar sudden and often aggressive demonstrations of bad manners in Hamsun. But such behaviour was inevitable in a man who was living out the anarchist's dream, a life of total subjectivity in which he made his own laws and was answerable only to himself.

Or so it seemed; in fact, beneath the pose of heedless primitive a part of him seemed to be clinging to a hope that the transfiguration of which he'd dreamed so many years ago in *The Enigmatic One* might still take place, and the frog turn into a prince. As often as he publicly flaunted his indifference to civilisation and refinement he privately longed to master the arts. It was in pursuit of civilisation and refinement that he sailed for France on 13 April 1893,[26] in company with the Danish playwright Sven Lange. French was the language of a cultured man, and Hamsun was going to Paris to learn French, and turn himself into a cultured man.

Chapter 8
1893–1895: Paris, *Pan* and Strindberg

Paris of the 1890s was still *the* cultural centre for most European artists, and Hamsun, travelling across Europe by train from Antwerp, went to join an already extensive colony of Scandinavians living there. Jonas Lie and his family were the focal point for the Norwegian community, which at one time or another during these years included Bjørnson, Alexander Kielland, Edvard Munch, the sculptor Gustav Vigeland, the composers Edvard Grieg and Christian Sinding, and the literary Krag brothers, besides dozens of young students of music and painting. Yet they were a peculiarly insular crowd,[1] and only Grieg, Munch and Sinding crop up as members of the famous artistic circles of those times, such as that which grouped around Paul Gauguin and William Molard. Most of the Norwegians kept company with each other at their own apartments in the streets around the Luxembourg Gardens, or at meeting places like the Café de la Régence.

Sven Lange had been in Paris before, and had useful contacts. He introduced Hamsun to the Danish painter Willy Gretor, who let him live free in the room underneath his studio at 112 place Malesherbes[2] until he could find somewhere of his own. Gretor was to become one of Hamsun's companions; his strange, amoral character fascinated the connoisseur of personalities in Hamsun. Besides original work, Gretor also produced expert copies of works by names such as Rembrandt, Frans Hals, Teniers and Van Gogh, which he sold in good faith, for huge sums of money, to his rich friends. He was also implicated in the suicide of a young painter who may have been his collaborator and homosexual lover, and may even have murdered him; the case was never solved. He was a man with a passport to every important house and salon in Paris, capable of extraordinary public charm, and great private cruelty.

He aroused violently contradictory opinions among those who came across him. The playwright Frank Wedekind described him as the most fascinating man he had ever met, hailed him as a genius, and dedicated his play *Earthspirit* to him. To Strindberg, however, he was a 'scoundrel', while Hamsun described his adventurous life as 'human and inspiring, a novel'.

Whatever else he may have been, Gretor was of vital importance for Knut Hamsun professionally. It was he who set Hamsun on the road to a major European reputation by introducing him to a young playboy millionaire from Munich, Albert Langen, who was to found the large Langen publishing concern which still flourishes in Germany. Langen had come to Paris hoping to be a painter, or a writer, and had come to a kind of gentleman's agreement with Gretor – the Dane would introduce him to all the interesting and important people in the art world, and he would foot the bill for the process. Langen soon realised that he was no artist himself; but he was not stupid, and he loved literature, and at twenty-three years of age he was looking hard for his destiny. Gretor and Hamsun between them showed it to him.

Hunger had sold poorly for its publisher, S. Fischer, in German translation, and Fischer had shown no interest in translating and publishing *Mysteries*. Undoubtedly the accusation of plagiarism in *Freie Buhne* had contributed to this lack of interest. Langen and the ten-year older Hamsun got on well immediately, with the result that Langen put up the money for a German publication of the book. Gretor and he formed the Albert Langen Buch und Kunst Verlag for the express purpose of publishing *Mysteries*, which duly appeared in Maria von Borch's translation in 1894.

This publishing event marks the definitive beginning of the lifelong mutual love-affair between Hamsun and the German reading public. Here at last, after the false start with *Hunger* and the problem with *Freie Buhne*, was Hamsun's real and irreversible entry into the European sphere, and access to the wealth a literate and literary people like the Germans could bestow on him. Langen died in 1909, but the gamble he took on Hamsun paid off for both of them. His company flourished, and continues as Hamsun's publishers right through to the present day, while Hamsun was to remain largely dependent for the financing of his life-style on royalties from the German market for the next twenty-five years.

After a few weeks at Gretor's Hamsun moved to a cheap hotel catering for students at 8 rue de Vaugirard, one of the oldest and longest streets in central Paris, just around the corner from the Luxembourg Gardens and the Hotel des Americains, another favourite lodging for Scandinavians. Hamsun took two rooms up on the first floor; a front room with a balcony overlooking the street, and a tiny bedroom at the rear. He had come, he told the newspapers,[3] to learn French, and so as not to bog himself down in the tedium of grammar books he kept the company of a young language student, Brede Kristensen, taking his meals and walking the streets with this man, listening to his French in hopes of picking up the language as painlessly as possible. Alas, the technique did not work for him, and after one patient year he abandoned his attempt to acquire the tool of refinement which he considered the French language to be. Hamsun's pronunciation of the few words he knew was splendid, but he had not progressed far enough even for the reading of French newspapers. Rather than indicating a lack of linguistic talent, however, this is more probably explained by the tremendous strain imposed in spending one's days and nights thinking and writing in one language, and then going out with a head weary of the whole business of words and trying to summon an almost equally great effort in the service of mere light conversation. It was another aspect of the same problem that had hampered his attempts to learn English in America. He was also – naturally – already hard at work on another novel, the half-completed work he had brought with him from Samsø, which he had set aside to write *Editor Lynge*.

Hard work made an isolated man of him, and the circles he might have relaxed in were closed to him, or at least, un-welcoming, owing to the fact that the leading lights were Jonas Lie and the painter Fritz Thaulow. Lie had no particular reason for making Hamsun feel at home after he had dealt with him in his lectures of 1891, and Lie's friend Thaulow, an extremely robust person who had no time for the new 'neurotic' art, regarded Hamsun with profound suspicion. He had to find companions outside the main groups, where the stigma attached to his name was irrelevant. Thus he was often together with Danes, like Gretor and Lange, or the homosexual Herman Bang. He helped Bang with money, and felt sorry for him at first, until he discovered that his jeremiads were a constant part of his personality which his own friends and helpers had long since grown tired of. He helped other writers too, like the Swedes Ola Hansson and Adolf Paul. He put Paul in touch with Mons Litleré, the Bergen publisher of his own *Lars Oftedal*, but advised Litleré not to mention his name in connection with the book on the grounds that this would ruin its chances.[4] He also went to great lengths to help a man he hardly knew, Frank Wedekind, and arranged a translation of Wedekind's book into Danish on receipt of what he thought was enthusiastic interest from Edward Brandes, only to find Brandes coolly dissociating himself from the project once the work was ready for publication.[5]

In experiences like this, Hamsun inevitably saw evidence of what he took to be a full-scale plot against him on the part of the Norwegian literary establishment. Whatever he did seemed to make matters worse. He wrote an article for the Parisian *Revue des Revues* on trends in modern Norwegian literature which angered the pundits back home who felt that the absence of any lengthy discussion of 'star' names like Garborg, Amalie Skram and Gunnar Heiberg amounted to a deliberate insult to those writers. He protested in vain that he was writing about the movement, not individuals, and complained to Bolette Larsen that Bjørnson, when in adversity in his youth, had always had at least one newspaper supporting him, whereas he seemed to be the target for all of them.[6] He was feeling the draught on all sides. To Victor Nilsson he wrote that since coming to France 'I have been unable to say or write one word without getting a hail of curses rained over me from Norway, Denmark and Sweden'.[7] To another correspondent he claimed that he couldn't open his mouth without people like Edward Brandes, Arne Garborg and a host of others accusing him of being a cheap self-promoter who never tired of reminding people that he had been in America. He found that Brandes had gone back on his original enthusiasm for *Hunger*[8] and now regarded it too as a dishonest book written to publicise its writer. When an article by Octave Mirbeau appeared enthusiastically praising *Hunger*, Hamsun believed that he was suspected of having solicited the article, and publicly denied it. 'The hate to me must be very high,' he wrote to Langen, 'Thaulow did not believe me and he went to Mirbeau.'[9]

It is difficult to tell just how real this atmosphere of hostility was, and just how much of it was Hamsun's own fevered imagination. He complained that he had been excluded from the press in the wake of the scandals over his lecture tour and *Mysteries*, but late in 1892 claimed that 'those newspapers which have given me the hardest time have come to me the day after and offered me good money to write for them. The whole thing is just humbug.'[10] And *Morgenbladet*, the conservative newspaper to which he referred as 'my greatest enemy', praised an article he wrote for the *Social Democrat* on the assassination of the French President Carnot in the summer of 1894.* The important thing is that he *believed* himself to

---

* In his article Hamsun criticised Norwegian newspapers, including *Morgenbladet*, for trying to turn Carnot into a great man simply because he had been murdered.

be the victim of a plot dedicated to the hindrance of his career, whether it existed or not. He seems to have had a need to conceive of his life as a war in which he fought alone against a host of unscrupulous enemies, a conception which became a total necessity for the successful functioning of his literary personality. This state of mind, rooted in the very real unpopularity he had experienced ever since 1891, erupted at the end of October 1893 when he came across a fiercely critical reference to himself in a book review in *Morgenbladet*, and in a long letter to Bolette Larsen he poured out his heart:

> Please let me talk to you this afternoon; it is not merely that I am sad, but I am actually in despair. Partly this must be due to the fact that I have been grossly overworking, and I am exhausted, not mentally, but physically. I have been lying face down here on the sofa almost all afternoon, and been shaking. I can't make it out. I've read twenty-six pages of proofs today, but unfortunately, there are still more. And when my book is published people will say that now I can just reel the stuff off with the greatest of ease, when in fact many a night I have worked through until eight, nine in the morning, and started work again at midday. And I've kept at it, and not wasted a single day.
>
> No, but that isn't what I wanted to talk to you about. I want to ask you to give me your honest answer to a question, because I just don't understand this anymore, it's all beginning to go right over my head. But as you can see from my handwriting, I am calm now, and I'll write as calmly as anyone could ask.
>
> It's like this: I strolled over to the Café de la Régence today, and read the following in *Morgenbladet*:
>
> 'The Apostle of humbug in Norwegian literature, the arch con-man of the "new writing", Knut Hamsun, is herein accurately described as the "living embodiment" of the inconsistencies and the hollowness of Norwegian cultural life.'*
>
> This was in a review of *Young Norwegians*, and signed – 8 – which is Nils Vogt.
>
> But this is becoming impossible now. They will take everything from me in the long run, honour, talent, decency. I don't understand it any more. Surely it has never before happened that an author can be attacked in this extreme way. It's almost as

---

* The description of him as 'arch con-man of the "new writing"' imprinted itself on Hamsun's mind. Over fifty years later, during the course of his psychiatric examination, he was able to recall the contents of this paragraph almost word for word.

though I were not a person anymore. And so this is what I want to ask you about: there *must* be something about me and my writing which makes it possible for people to treat me like this, something which I don't notice myself, but which others see? It cannot simply be that I have used Thommessen as a model in one of my books, there must in addition to that be something dishonest, untrustworthy and false in everything I do, for how otherwise could I be called an impostor and a con-man? I don't understand it. I put everything, all my strength, all my heart, into every chapter. I have sat here and wept and suffered with my characters so many nights throughout the summer, and the same with *Mysteries* and *Lynge*. . . . It *must* be something else. It is no longer simply *one* man, *one* paper, *one* party that condemns me, but *everybody*, everybody seems agreed on it. The slightest thing I do is considered as merely another piece of cheap dishonesty, and yet it is exactly cheap dishonesty that I am attacking myself, and believe myself to hate with every fibre of my being! . . . I don't understand it. If I recognised, myself, that in this or that case I had behaved dishonestly and dishonourably, without believing with every drop of blood in my veins in what I wrote, then I would tell you. And now, in return, you must tell me what it is that causes everyone to agree about me that I am a bad man. Tell me, please, if you can work out what it is, or if you've already known what it is for a long time and have not wanted to tell me. As I lay here today I began wondering if perhaps there might not be some monstrous lie about me circulating in Christiania, a lie, something monstrous and secret, that everyone believed. That possibility occurred to me, but I know nothing about it. Maybe you have heard something? . . . Please give me your honest answer. . . . I haven't a soul to turn to. You are not to interpret this as whining, I am not whimpering, but I really am in despair, and I am beginning to wonder whether there might not be something wrong with me. Maybe I never should have left the prairie.[11]

Characteristically, one week later and feeling stronger again, he wrote to the Larsens bitterly regretting the letter, 'and I have wished and wished that I had never sent it'. He told them he had stopped going to the Régence 'because quite frankly, I am beginning to be afraid of meeting people'.

Bolette Larsen was not able to help him much. She could find no dark, secret reason for the antipathy, and she may privately have puzzled over how a man like Hamsun, to whom aggression came so naturally, could have so little understanding of aggression in

others. What she had been able to find out was that the people who
attacked him did so generally because they felt that he was
'uncultured'. Clearly, his attacks in 1891 on such as Shakespeare,
Goethe, Schiller, Ibsen and Hugo had been interpreted in certain
quarters as not merely ill-judged, but as genuinely shocking acts of
cultural heresy. Such is the nature of culture, after all; even in our
day, reviewers of productions of Shakespeare's plays are expected
to confine themselves to comments on the idiosyncrasies of
production and acting style rather than on the meaning or content
of the plays. All Hamsun did was to treat Shakespeare as what he
was – a writer. He did not know that, to quote Ibsen's Judge Brack,
'One doesn't *do* that kind of thing'.

To the Larsens, Hamsun simply dismissed the impossible
unfairness of an attitude that criticised him as 'uncultured':

> . . . that I am not a learned man is, of course, quite correct. Or
> partly correct, at least. As a matter of fact, I know quite a lot. But
> because I am a self-taught man, there is a unity lacking in my
> knowledge. Anyway, I can't do anything about it now.[12]

Nils Vogt's attack in *Morgenbladet* reached Hamsun just one month
before the publication of the new novel on which he had been
working so hard. *Shallow Soil* was published by Philipsen in
Copenhagen on 30 November, to a howl of critical disapproval, if
possible, louder than that which had greeted *Editor Lynge*.

Having already alienated the older establishment, he now set
about the younger in this novel. Like *Lynge*, it is a *roman-à-clef*, a
damning critique of the kind of vapidly arrogant and talentless
artists who spend most of their time drinking and showing off in
cafés, and who expend most of their words on expressing
contempt for 'businessmen'. He intended it as a corrective to all the
decadence that he saw about him. Formally, it is another 'proper'
book like *Lynge*, although technically speaking a much better shot
at the literary norm than the latter represented. He described it as
being 'about Norwegian youth', and admitted that it was 'full of
symbolism, but so little Ibsenish, I hope, that it can be understood'.[13]

The novel contrasts the lifestyle of a group of artists, portrayed
as arrogant wastrels,* with that of two industrious young
businessmen whose charity and support they sneeringly accept.

---

* The theme of the novel, and the fact that Hamsun could describe it as 'already
half-finished' by December 1892, suggest that it may possibly have used material
from the novel set in a Bohemian milieu about 'the tragedy of people going to the
dogs' which he had abandoned in 1886.

On every count, the businessmen win: in hard work; in daring enterprise; in stoical acceptance of reverse; in personal loyalty and generosity. As in *Lynge*, a love story is what holds the book together. Hanka Tidemand, the wife of one of the businessmen, is a liberated and modern woman of the type Hamsun strongly disapproved of. Having insisted on her right to be herself, and to express her freedom, she has found no better use for it than to throw herself into the arms of a cynical, womanising poet, Irgens. Irgens soon becomes tired of her, and finds a new ambition in the person of Aagot Lynum, a lovely and innocent country girl whom the other of the two businessmen, Ole Henriksen, has brought to Christiania and hopes to marry. Irgens triumphs, and introduces Aagot to the corrupt and cynical crowd that meets at the Grand Café. Irgens' behaviour comes as a revelation to Hanka Tidemand. She re-examines her values, and finds that her proud and hard-working husband, the father of her children, is worth far more than the dramatic, but shallow artist. Her divorce is imminent, her freedom beckons; but it is the sight and thought of her own children that really re-awaken her love for her husband, and with due pride and contrite reserve, she asks him to take her back. They, at least, end happily.

To invoke the name of Ibsen, and the closing scene of *A Doll's House*, is not far-fetched here. Both *Editor Lynge* and *Shallow Soil* are books of a 'socially improving' nature, curious little throwbacks to the kind of literature Georg Brandes prophesied and Ibsen and Bjørnson practised in the 1870s and '80s. Hamsun detested the feminist movement, and regarded Ibsen's play as a piece of opportunist bandwagon-hopping. And in *Shallow Soil* he wrote what he would probably have described himself as the 'correct' conclusion to the play.

To write such a book, at such a time, was, of course, pushing the knife further into his own back. As in the case of his other 'clenched fist' novel,[14] the reviewers were willing to praise his talent, but execrated his use of it. The most cutting remarks of all appeared in *Politiken*, where Hamsun was accused of sucking-up to the business community, and of having written the book for money alone. The reviewer, Peter Nansen, stated categorically that Hamsun was without talent, and was no artist.

Why did he do it? Once again, one can only imagine it was because of his compulsion to stand alone, to be 'oppositional to the point of fanaticism', as *Aftenposten*'s reviewer of *Mysteries* had described him.

Peter Egge, a young writer for whom Hamsun had helped to find a publisher in 1891, lived for a time in the same hotel as Hamsun, and was often in his company. He noticed that whatever he said, whatever opinion he held, his friend would not be satisfied until he had looked around and found exactly the opposite opinion, and then argued that case. Hamsun did not like being agreed with. Egge was a socialist, Hamsun contemptuously anti-democratic, and he enjoyed Egge's company very much indeed. Hamsun was a provoker, a champion of the riddle and the paradox: the idea of being a writer oneself, member of a greatly admired, even adored, élite, and writing a book expressing contempt for that same élite, must have made enormous appeal to this paradoxical side of him. He meant it as well: his boyhood dream of literature as a noble calling was already in tatters. 'Wait till you read my book',* he wrote to Victor Nilsson in 1892, 'You'll see that I have a very low opinion of writing. It's just humbug.' He even wrote that if he had a steady job, he wouldn't bother writing any more, though he was honest enough to doubt that he could really give it up: 'It's probably in the blood', he shrugged.

And no matter what he thought of writing, the books he wrote sold. People bought them, and read them, and talked about them.

Hamsun seemed to reserve for correspondents his expressions of anxiety and sorrow. His troubles, real or imagined, were never foisted on those he met in daily life. Peter Egge has left a splendid picture of Hamsun at this time which shows how effectively he managed to hide his feelings:

> He was always the uncompromising and distinctive man, proud and hard, but always and ever honest, always true to his word in matters both large and small, honest to the point of pedantry. And moreover unselfishly kind and helpful. And on top of all this, a man with a superabundance of high spirits, full of laughter and good humour, a wild-spirited man full of charm, bursting with invention. And in his prime also an unusually handsome man, beautiful in a manly way, not *too* beautiful. In the afternoons we often walked together to the Régence to read the Scandinavian newspapers. I noticed then the way in which the people we passed noticed him, the sudden way in which they became aware of him. He went about in a thick fur coat, because the winter that year was hard, the coldest since the war-winter of seventy–seventy-one. . . . In the café the women

* *Mysteries.*

looked long after him, and the waiter rushed to get him just those papers which he knew Hamsun read.

In our hotel lived also the Danish writer Sven Lange who was for many years the astute theatre critic for *Politiken*. Often we four Scandinavians ate our main evening meal together in a little restaurant not far from our hotel. And then Hamsun, with his hilarious remarks about the menu, the food, and the service (sheer childishness, of course) would make us laugh until we choked. The calm, pale and melancholic Sven Lange struggled not to make a scene. Once, in a helpless paroxysm of laughter, he lost his lorgnette. Luckily for him, it had a safety-loop on it. He prayed for mercy: 'No, Hamsun, please stop now!'

Sometimes Hamsun, Castberg and I played three-handed whist at home at the hotel. Easy-going type that I am, I have always been a wretched card-player, and have never been able to work up any enthusiasm for cards. Hamsun was the opposite. He was a brilliant card-player, and was furious whenever I made a mistake, and scolded me as though I were ten and he twelve years old.[15]

With *Shallow Soil* out of the way Hamsun cleared his head with another short, fierce bout of drinking, and in the first week of January 1894 began work on *Pan*. He had looked forward to it in his long letter to the Larsens of 30 October: 'It will be so beautiful, and will take place in Nordland, a still, red love-story. There will be no polemic in it, just people, under a strange sky.' In fact, it was a book that had been in his mind before he left for France: the short story he had submitted to *Samtiden* in April, where his accompanying letter spoke of having gone to bed drunk every night for the last five weeks, was called *Glahn's Death*, and, minus a slight narrative framing device used there, it forms the last section of the novel. Now, tired of dealing in aggression, his own as well as other people's, tired of the feeling that for three years now he had been breathing, eating, sleeping, writing and thinking with clenched fists, he was ready to write it. Perhaps it was the sheer strangeness of the experience of living in a genuinely foreign country, and the intense homesickness of which he wrote to the Larsens, that created in him the deep sense of loss and longing that pervades the book, and led him to write about places that he had not seen since he left his Nordland home fifteen years before, in 1879. And the isolation which the fierce loyalty to the truth of his own instincts had caused made its own indispensable contribution to the mood in which he began the book, that passionate sense of longing caught by the simple repetition in the opening line: 'These last few days I have thought and thought of the Nordland summer's endless day.'

His correspondence with Albert Langen,[16] written in a powerful and idiosyncratic English, provides an illuminating record of his progress on the book, from its beginning in early January to its completion at the end of October. The Larsens were also kept informed. On 21 February he wrote of the difficulties of getting under way; telling them that he had been sitting over one and a half pages for the last five weeks, 'And now today it bursts, if I can put it like that, a great flood of it.'

To Langen in March he wrote:

Work, work and work bad, slowly, night and day, and gitting nervous, angry and 'gejl' [ie lustful] for the spring. Hard time!

In April he took a week at Ville d'Avray, a small village just outside Paris where the richer artists had their retreats. Delius, who was friendly with so many Norwegian artists, kept a house there; and Erik Lie, son of Jonas Lie, whom Hamsun had met and liked, also stayed there while working on a book on Balzac. Hamsun probably stayed with Lie, fishing, drinking and writing, before returning from this 'paradise' to 8 rue de Vaugirard.

Langen supported him throughout the year of *Pan*. There are constant, shorter and longer notes passing between the two about money. The record for the briefest is probably Hamsun's of 26 April:

Dear Langen,
    what about that 100 francs?
    For God's sake tell me if you are unable,
                                    yours Knut Hamsun.

while the most trickily charming is a note of 21 March in which he thanks Langen for 300 francs which he borrowed to help his friend the soldier-artist Segelcke, and with a bold disdain for the proximity of the two sentences adds that, 'I was drunk last night, or else I would have wrote this to you long ago, today I am ill, have of course bad conscience. Thank you!'

Hamsun fell deeply into Langen's debt in the course of this year, but his faith in his own earning potential was profound, and he never hesitated to ask when in need. In one letter he remarked on the frequency of his own borrowing, adding, with a devastating directness, 'But Langen, you are a rich man.' As usual, he kept his own personal records of his debts, knowing that in time he would pay the money back.

In June homesickness and restlessness overtook him again, and he returned impulsively to Norway, taking the novel with him. His aim was simply to be in Norway again, and hear Norwegian spoken all around him, and he settled for the next five months in Kristiansand, a town on the south coast. Seasickness dictated his choice – he simply went ashore when he couldn't stand any more of it.[17]

He worked well here. The finished product is clearly recognisable in a letter to Langen on 22 July:

> I write, go on slowly, but I hope good. It is hard to tell the title. Think of the Nordland in Norway, the regions of the Lapper, the mysteries, the grand superstitions, the midnight sun, think of J. J. Rousseau in this regions, making acquaintance with a Nordland girl – that is my book. I try to clear some of the nature-worshipping sensitivity, overnervousness in a Rousseauian soul. Wait till I send the correcturs, I hope to be ready in a month or little more. The book I think will touch new things.

He was quite convinced that the book he was working on was unique: 'O, I shall furnish a queer book this time, unexpected, unknown. Punktum!', and a month later was still pleased with it:

> Excuse me for not having written before; I work hard and work good now. Thank you for the money, very many thanks. I have got my dress [Nw=suit] and am now a fine boy. Good God, I owe you too much money now. But now we will see, I think I can judge about just, and if the book I now write is not my best, I don't understand literature at all. I write a small chapter per day, the chapters are very small, but I think havey of thoughts and fantasi. I never was so contented.

He was beginning to think in terms of a title, something which caused him bother throughout his career:

> The girl in my book will be a new one, her name is Edvarda; but I don't like her name for the title of the book, I must find something else.

In September he changed his mind:

> 'Edvarda' is in itself a good title in Norwegian too, but I don't exactly know yet if it strikes the head-point in the book. 'Mittnachtsonne' what is that? Mittnachts – what?

But in the same letter, without realising it himself, Hamsun had found the title:

> The reason why my book is not yet finished is that every chapter is a poem, every line worked hard on. There is no dialogues, only a few replics; if I say that every chapter has made me a week's work, I don't lie, although the chapters is so short. There is vissions, adventures, symbolisme all over. I am content for finishing in a month.
>
> 'Pan bless you, yours for ever'
> Knut Hamsun.

Langen continued to press him for a title, since a German publication was planned as soon as Philipsen's edition was printed in Copenhagen. But by 1 October he had still not decided:

> I received your dispatch tonight and I answered Yes, I call the book *Edvarda*, but after all I can judge now, it will not be called *Edvarda* in the Norwegian edition, because it is not all about Edvarda (the heroin), on the contrary it is less about Edvarda then about the Hero.

And sometime within the next week he decided it should be called *Pan*, because, as he told the Larsens, 'there are such strange things in it'.

The story of *Pan* is soon told. The hero Glahn, bearing the title of lieutenant, lives as a stranger in a small fishing community in the far north of Norway. He occupies a hut on the edge of a forest, and uses the settlement only to buy necessary supplies and powder for his gun, content in the freedom of his solitude. At night he lies alone, talking to his dog, listening to the sounds of the birds calling in the forest. Now and then a burst of natural ecstasy wells up in him, and produces in him moods of profound pantheistic identification with the nature around him.

One day he meets a girl from the settlement, Edvarda, the daughter of the local fishing magnate, Herr Mack. The two experience a spontaneous physical attraction for one another. Glahn visits her at home sometimes and she comes to him in his hut at night. For a brief period – no more than three or four weeks – their happiness is of an ecstatic, uncomplicated kind. Then intellect begins to play its part; pride, calculation and the considerations of power. The relationship between them develops into a psychic war and neither one of them is able, or willing, to perform the necessary acts of submission which might turn intense romantic eroticism into a stable, practical relationship of love. Their playing with one another reaches fantastical, grotesque heights: Glahn, imagining that his rival is a lame doctor, deliberately shoots himself through the foot so that he will be the equal of the doctor in Edvarda's eyes. She flirts with and finally becomes engaged to a Finnish aristocrat, a delicate, asexual academic man whom she does not love.

The love story has passed through all the stages of the natural year: the short and thrilling spring; the long stasis of summer; the irrevocable decline of autumn; and ends with the coming of winter. Glahn prepares to leave the settlement. Edvarda asks him for the gift of his dog as something to remember him by, and before the steamship sails, he goes to his hut, shoots the dog, and pays a man to take the corpse to Edvarda. Glahn travels to India, and Edvarda marries the Baron. She continues to press herself into Glahn's thoughts with letters to him while he pursues a life of drink and sexual degeneracy in his attempts to forget her. Finally he solicits his own death at the hands of a fellow-hunter, openly seducing a young native girl whom this man loves, and then challenging and tormenting him until the man shoots him with his gun.

Pan is one of the most beautiful short novels ever written, an experience rather than a book, written in a controlled prose so tight, so exact, that translation cannot diminish it. Hamsun's prose here has an almost hypnotic effect, an effect heightened by the form of the chapters which often begin in a floating, unspecific, dream-like way. There is not a single word in excess, nor a word lacking here; this is a seamless Art, complete, invisible, displaying a total mastery of the unsaid thing, infinite and massive in the implications of its silence, illuminating whole oceans and forests of feeling in the flashing light of a single line. Like Hamsun's two previous masterpieces *Hunger* and *Mysteries*, this is again a book that reaches effortlessly and deeply into the soul and epitomises the literature of the twentieth century in its subjectivity and its fragmentation.

Still sensing an intense opposition to himself and his works, Hamsun panicked slightly around publication time, 6 December 1894, and tried to persuade Philipsen to publish *Pan* anonymously. Langen wanted to use a photograph of him in the German edition that Fru von Borsch was now busily translating, but Hamsun pleaded with him not to: 'It will be used in the Scandinavian press against me, it will be said that I use all means in order to make reklame [Nw=advertise) – I know it all.'

At first it looked as though he might be right. *Verdens Gang* wrote that 'The new book is characterised by the same cheap phoneyness which has marred so much of what Hamsun has written', and the reviewer only gave grudging praise to some of the nature descriptions in the book. *Morgenbladet* not only declined to review the new book by 'the arch con-man of the "new writing"', but did not even include it in the monthly listing of new fiction. All Hamsun's fears that he had become a permanent victim of the Norwegian literary establishment seemed to be justified. He felt that he was 'paying with a vengeance for *Shallow Soil*', he told Bolette Larsen.

In fact, he turned out to be wrong. Hamsun's sheer talent as a writer of fiction, and the extraordinary melancholic charm of this novel, turned most of the tide of hostility against him. Christofer Brinchmann in *Dagbladet* was first to express an unreserved admiration for the book, followed by Carl Naerup in the literary magazine *Kringsjaa*. From this point on, Hamsun's literary ascent, which has so far often looked strangely like plummeting, becomes an established fact; and the enemies he has to face from now on come only from classes that consider themselves either above the values of literature – the church – or below them, those with personal vendettas bent on revenge. But most of all, Hamsun remains his own worst enemy, the passionate disturber of his own peace, and still the battleground for the ever-more sharply focused war between nature and culture in which Lieutenant Glahn, wholly unable to choose, finally lost his life.

For over ten years now, Hamsun had been fascinated by August Strindberg. He had lectured on him on several occasions, written articles on him in both Norway and America, and had contributed to a book on him which the young Swedish writer Birger Mörner was editing for publication in 1894. Here he wrote of him that 'For me he is his country's, perhaps his age's most remarkable literary personality: an arrogant and superior talent, a brain on horseback, riding his own way and leaving most of the others behind in his wake.'[18] Strindberg was a giant in his eyes. He once wrote to the Larsens that 'Compared to Strindberg, little Hamsun and Heidenstam and Garborg are nothing but tiny dolly-men.'[19] He regarded him not only as the great theoretical apologist for the new psychological, personality-oriented literature, but as a polar opposite to the dreary and unexciting Ibsen. Strindberg in his prime was also a leader of fashion, and in Paris Hamsun, along with a thousand others, cultivated the fierce Strindbergian moustache, flattened and flared to give the face the look of a jungle cat. He wanted to meet Strindberg, and could have done so in Copenhagen in 1889 at a party which in the end he decided not to attend: his pride demanded further achievements of him before he could allow such a meeting to take place.

Strindberg, meanwhile, had early on become aware of Hamsun. He wrote admiringly to Georg Brandes about *On the Cultural Life of Modern America*, and must have noticed the murmur of excitement that was building around Hamsun's name and personality during the 1890s. He got his address from Birger Mörner and wrote to him in Kristiansand in August, asking for a rendezvous.

Strindberg was, in fact, another of the inspirations for *Pan*, besides Rousseau. 'He calls himself an animal that longs to be back in the forest', Hamsun wrote of him, 'Civilisation, overcivilisation – year after year Strindberg has preached the same wisdom, that Man has alienated himself from Nature, and thereby destroyed in himself the fundament of an organic, whole way of life.'[20]

The brief, disastrous relationship between these two was then inaugurated at a meeting shortly after Hamsun's return to Paris from Norway in November 1894. He wrote to Langen that Strindberg was 'childish and genial [Nw=genius] a remarkable writer, a queer man'. Strindberg, approaching the height of his 'inferno' crisis, may well have thought much the same of Hamsun.* They tried to strike up a friendship, and the young Norwegian writer Johann Bojer, author of *The Last Viking*, was a wide-eyed observer of it all. He was with Hamsun at the Régence one evening when Strindberg walked in:

> He and Hamsun are friends, and he joins us at our table. And behold the change in my companion; the modesty is abandoned, and a friendly sparring match takes place between the two.[21]

But it was not quite as friendly as the impressionable Bojer thought. Hamsun, with his strong personality and his massive ego, was nevertheless usually willing to accept other peoples' massive egos, and was capable of open and spontaneous recognition of talent in other artists where he believed it to exist. Strindberg had less of this tolerance, and found Hamsun's personality uncomfortably strong.[22] And even at the age of thirty-six, Hamsun had something of the 'young gun' about him, and probably challenged his hero in a way that Strindberg could have done without.

---

* Between 1894–96, Strindberg had a series of experiences, sometimes paranoid and sometimes mystical, from which he emerged a follower of the Swedish visionary Emmanual Swedenborg. He wrote and published his own account of the crisis under the title *Inferno* in 1897.

The relationship lasted throughout the winter. The two often went on long walks together. Sometimes Strindberg would talk non-stop. At other times he would walk in total silence. On one of their more relaxed evenings the two men worked out a plan to busk their way back across Europe to Sweden, with Strindberg playing his guitar, and Hamsun singing.[23] Strindberg's poverty touched Hamsun, who thought it unjust that the greatest writer in Europe should be walking the streets in rags and having to borrow money to pay for his drinks. He persuaded Sven Lange to go to Jonas Lie and get Lie's support for a public appeal for money for Strindberg, and in due course a letter, written by Hamsun and signed by Lie, Lange, himself, and three others, appeared in leading newspapers throughout Scandinavia. The wording of the appeal was generous and unequivocal: this was money for the assistance of a great genius. But in his delicate mental condition Strindberg reacted violently to the offer of help, and turned on Hamsun. He perhaps felt that he was being patronised by someone whose patronage he was unwilling to submit to. But Hamsun was certainly sincere: if there was one thing he knew about it was the importance of money, and how crushing its lack is to the spirit.

Strindberg would have none of it though. He wrote angrily to the newspapers claiming that the fund had been started without his authority, and on 26 March he visited Hamsun, and informed him that he had given instructions that any monies collected were not to be given to him but forwarded directly to his children in Finland. Hamsun also found out that Strindberg's position was far from the desperate one he had given people to believe, and that he was already being handsomely supported by private donations. He felt let down by what he thought was hypocrisy on Strindberg's part, claiming that Strindberg had known perfectly well that an appeal was being planned, and had even personally thanked the instigators. All of this he had to explain in some embarrassment to the venerable Jonas Lie, sighing, 'I had not met S before the winter, but people tell me he is odder than ever now.'[24]

Matters got worse. He went personally to visit Strindberg with some money early in April, only to be told that he was away. He left a message on a card, and received in his turn a card on which Strindberg had written 'Keep your thirty pieces of silver and let us be finished with one another for life.' In anger Hamsun wrote back that 'if he did not come within two days to collect the money from me, I would send it back to the donors. Furthermore – I added – a man who had suddenly become such an important chap that he could afford to give away thirty pieces of silver in a tip ought first to have paid off his debts. And I reminded him that he had borrowed money from someone as poor as me.'

He visited him again on 17 April to try to hand over money, forcing himself to go, persuaded by a dogged streak of pure common sense that Strindberg *must* need money, if not for himself then for his children. Strindberg, pathetically involved in his experimenting with sulphur, refused to admit him. To his great credit, Hamsun continued to try to help him in his expressed desire to return to Sweden, suggesting to Lie that they get one of the Swedish artists, Albert Edelfelt or Anders Zorn, who had signed the original appeal to take over the handling of the difficult relationship. But the following day Strindberg left Paris, as Hamsun wrote with some relief to Langen:

> Strindberg has left Paris, it is reported to me. I can have no transactions with him more, he has broke definitely with me and without cause. Oh he is mad, crazy. As soon as he got some money (on the application in the papers) he got mad of proudness and would not speak to me anymore.[25]

Hamsun met other famous men during this period – Verlaine, whom he often met drinking absinthe at Procope's Cellar in the Latin Quarter, and described to the Larsens as 'an old boozer who's been writing poetry for at least twenty-five years but is still alive';[26] and Gauguin, back in Paris after his first visit to Tahiti. While in Christiania in October 1894 he drank the remains of *Pan* out of his head in company with his friend the wine-merchant Heinrich Martens, and Stanislaw Przybyzewski, his Norwegian wife Dagny Juel, and Edvard Munch,[27] the inner circle of the group that met at 'Zum Schwarzen Ferkel' in Berlin in the early 1890s.

A small biographical mystery surrounds the possibility of his having met the composer Frederick Delius in Paris, too. Delius mentioned later to his wife Jelka that he and Hamsun and a violinist named Halfdan Jebe had made a small, informal and alcoholic concert tour of several towns in the Norwegian Gudbrandsdal some time in the 1890s; but I have been unable to find any confirmation that the tour took place. Most of Delius' friends in Paris were Norwegians, and he could speak and write the language, and it seems hardly possible that the two men did not meet.*

---

* Hamsun's friend, the poet Vilhlem Krag, arrived in Paris the same week as Hamsun, carrying with him a letter of recommendation from the composer Christian Sinding to Delius.

But work is the story of these years, ceaseless work carried out according to a discipline of extreme rigour which was a source of wonder to those observing it. The legend of it even carried back to Norway; Bjørnson wrote to chide a young colleague who was living a riotous life and neglecting his work in Paris that he ought to take an example from the self-control of his competitor, Knut Hamsun. Even when struggling to manage the riotous relationship with Strindberg he kept at it, and between January and April 1895 produced his first play, *At the Gates of the Kingdom*, the first part of the *Kareno* trilogy of plays, so-called after their main character. The piece was the result of the following fanatic regime: in the evening between six and seven he would eat a main meal, then take to the streets and visit the Café de la Régence where he would read the newspapers until nine; then he would return to his room at 8 rue de Vaugirard, sleep until eleven, rise, and work through the night until six, seven, or eight the following day; he would then sleep until two, rise, eat breakfast, walk the streets and think about work until six or seven, eat his main meal, and begin the cycle again.[28]

Since his breakthrough in 1890 with *Hunger*, Hamsun had produced five novels and a play in five years. This was five years of constant and difficult work, during which he was also producing short stories, and, during the first years, a considerable amount of journalism. Throughout the period he had neither home nor stable family base. Periodically in letters to friends he had complained in fairly unspecific terms about problems with his 'nerves', the kind of terrible delicacy which causes the hero of *Hunger* to write with a cloth wrapped round his hand because he is unable to bear the feel of his own breath on his skin.[29] One feels sometimes that such horrible sensitivities were the refined torture of over-work, rather than the products of hunger or the expressions of mere temperament, and it looks very much as though the act of forcing the play out of himself in the winter and spring of 1895 finally brought him close to breaking point. Just two weeks before he finished the play, on 4 April, Hamsun wrote to Langen that he was 'desperately ill', that he could not work, that after half an hour's writing he would begin to sweat and have to go to bed:

> It seems to be the end of me. I have worked too hard and weared myself out. My humeur is awful, triste as the triste days in Paris, I don't speak to people.

The play was finished; but so, temporarily, was Hamsun. In the early summer he returned to Norway, and travelled directly to Lillehammer, at the southern end of the Gudbrandsdal, and took lodgings in a private hotel just outside the town at a place called Faaberg. He intended to regain his health here, and put his faith once again in the country air which had restored him to full vigour in Valdres, after he had returned from America in similarly broken down condition in 1884.

If one day in Faaberg he passed a few minutes in contemplation of his situation and his achievements, he might have experienced a degree of satisfaction. His reputation was won now, and he was accepted as the leading young writer of his generation. Having proved that he could write 'proper' books he had now proved, with *Pan*, that he could command respect on his own literary terms.

The novel was not only a critical but a public success: the first edition of 2000 copies had sold out, and Philipsen was printing a further 500 copies, by Christmas 1894. These modest numbers were in fact extremely good sales figures for a young Norwegian writer in those days. And as so often happens, the acclaim became in short order retrospective: within twelve months Bjørnson, in an article on 'Modern Norwegian Literature' published simultaneously in New York, Christiania, Copenhagen, Holland and Berlin, was calling the ridiculed *Mysteries* 'one of the great books in our literature – falling over us like an intoxicated snowflake'. And the descriptions of nature in *Pan* were for him 'the most sublime, the most exalted in all Norwegian literature'. A long way, indeed, from the wretched days of Hamsun's visit to show him *Frida* in 1880, and Bjørnson's advice to him to give up writing and take up acting instead.

His reputation was European now, and growing. *Hunger, Mysteries, Shallow Soil, Pan, At the Gates of the Kingdom*, had all appeared in German. *Hunger* appeared in French in 1895, and in the same year Octave Mirbeau published an article fulsomely praising the book and its writer. The Russians had begun to show an interest in him, too, and produced in 1892 a pirate edition of *Hunger* – they were not signatories to the Berne Convention. It was an interest that would build dramatically after the turn of the century.* England was lagging slightly: 'George Egerton', in spite of being disappointed in her love for Hamsun – or perhaps one should really call it infatuation – continued to try to find a publisher for her translation of *Hunger* into the 'beef-language'. Her version eventually appeared in 1899, and sank without trace. English

* A translation into Russian of *Shallow Soil* was banned by the Russian censor. The translator told Hamsun that the ban was on account of Coldevin's speeches to the young in the book. Another suggestion was that it contained information compromising for the government about the ban on the export of wheat.

interest did not return, and then only in a rather feeble way, until after the sanction of the Nobel Prize in 1920.

All in all though, Hamsun might well feel content. He thrived at Faaberg, and socialised extensively. Lillehammer, now a tourist town, was then a great centre for painters and artists generally. Bjørnson's estate, Aulestad, was not far away, and acted as a magnet for writers and rich cosmopolitans. The retreat at nearby Gausdal also attracted artistic types looking, like Hamsun, to restore their health, while those with more serious problems, mental problems often brought on by alcoholism, sought out the nerve-doctor Torp at his clinic at Suttestad. Hamsun was often in the company of a consumptive writer Henrik Jaeger who lived at the same hotel, and the two seem to have enjoyed themselves hugely there. Hamsun wrote asking a friend to join them:

> We've got thirty women here between twelve and fifty-seven, all types, all nations (in Scandinavia). And Frøken Lund will sing for them, and by God, I shall recite for them. And in the evening we'll cut loose – because I'm assuming you'll be bringing Port Wine and sherry with you. Whereupon I repeat that you absolutely must come. Straightaway.

A photograph of Hamsun from this summer, along with Frøken Lund and a couple of other friends, shows him looking well, and in good shape for a number of particularly silly evenings. Paris had given him a fairly hard time, and apart from a couple of short stories, left little physical trace on his writing. But he had worked well, and one must call these, after all, years of triumph. The refinement which he hoped to acquire, however, did not fully materialise. Success had happened too late for that, and had cost too much. The Swedish poet, Gustav Fröding, staying at Dr Torp's clinic in hopes of being cured of bouts of hallucination, observed him well:

> I like Hamsun. There is a chaotic magnificence about him, which is partly fake; but even about this fake side of him there is something curiously pleasing. One has to laugh inwardly at his insolence and his impressive attitudinising – he does have style, but it's a mixed style, part clumsiness, and part grace.[30]

This mixture of styles, the tension between the past and the present, the tramp and the prince, continued to bother, depress, amuse and fire the creative genius in him. However, their harmonising, which might have brought peace and reconciliation to his soul, and put out this fire within him, was never to occur.

Chapter 9
1895–1898: Persecution and Marriage: *Victoria*

After his convalescence at Lillehammer, Hamsun returned to the capital, and in the early winter of 1895 took a room at Frøken Hammer's private hotel in Ljan. His first impressions of the place were comically ridiculous. Among the other guests were two of the fattest lady schoolteachers he'd ever seen. He offered Bolette's husband Ole Larsen his pick of them should he ever come to Ljan on a visit. There was an elderly feminist who pestered him for a contribution to a new magazine she was starting, and various other spinsters, widows, and single women. Another guest was Henrik Jaeger, who had been with him in Lillehammer. Poor Jaeger's consumption finished him off by Christmas.

At about the same time as he moved to Ljan, Hamsun heard that the National Theatre had accepted *At the Gates of the Kingdom* for production. It must have been great encouragement to him as he set about writing a sequel to the play, to be called *The Game of Life*. In fact, he had decided from the start that he would be producing a trilogy of plays about the same main character, Ivar Kareno, as a young man, as middle-aged, and as old.

There are a number of reasons why Hamsun might have taken up the challenge of the stage play, not the least of them being economic. Ibsen, Bjørnson and Strindberg, the three Scandinavians whose work was most widely discussed and rewarded in Paris and Berlin as part of the continuing fashion in Europe for Scandinavian writing, were all primarily famous as writers for the stage. Hamsun must have noticed himself that during 1893, his first year in Paris, no fewer than eleven plays by Scandinavian writers had their premières there. And in spite of the critical success of his novels, he was still by no means wealthy. By 1897, of the edition of 2100 copies of *Hunger* printed by Philipsen in

Copenhagen in 1890, 517 copies were still unsold. Only forty-four
copies were sold in 1896. The foreign markets had opened up for
him now, thanks to Langen, but he was still only a cult success,
and in addition lived way above his means. A reputation as a
successful new dramatist might have seemed to him a short cut to
riches. Another reason might have been that his growing faith in
his own literary powers had persuaded him to challenge the
detested Ibsen on his own ground. He had read *Little Eyolf* in 1894,
and true to form found it 'thin and boring'; it was 'tragic', in
Hamsun's eyes, to see a man ending up like Ibsen.[1]

The so-called *Kareno* trilogy, completed by *Evening Glow* in the
spring of 1898, was his most extensive attempt to master the new
form. Approaching his forties, he chose the theme of ageing, and
the changes and softening that take place in a man when the
heedless and principled passion of youth gives way to compromise
and the lure of ease.

The hero, Ivar Kareno, is a young philosopher with fiercely
anti-democratic views which he utters quite unequivocally: 'I
believe in the born leader, the natural despot, the master, not the
man who is chosen but the man who elects himself to be ruler over
the masses. I believe in and I hope for one thing, and that is the
return of the great terrorist, the living essence of human power, the
Caesar.' He has written a book setting forth his ideas, a work which
has obsessed him to such a degree that he has not even noticed his
wife Elina's desperate flirting with an acquaintance as she
struggles for his attention. The couple are in financial trouble,
hourly awaiting the arrival of the bailiffs, and living in hopes that
Kareno's great work will be accepted for publication. An offer of
publication does come, but only on condition that Kareno makes
certain changes in the manuscript, changes which he proudly
refuses even to contemplate. A friend and colleague, Jerven, who
has made precisely such a bargain with a publisher, now comes to
Kareno hoping to salve his conscience by lending him enough to
pay his debts; but after reading Jerven's book Kareno denounces
him as a traitor, and returns his money to him. His wife Elina,
meanwhile, tired of his principles, has run off with her lover, the
cynical journalist Endre Bondesen. The play ends with the arrival
of the bailiffs to take away the Karenos' furniture.

The second play *The Game of Life*, takes place ten years later, with
Kareno, at forty, the tutor to a rich man's sons. He is still the
dedicated philosopher, with a passionate interest in the search for
truth which exerts a magnetic attraction on his employer's
daughter, Teresita Oterman.

The concluding play, *Evening Glow*, returns us to an altered version of the scene and characters from the first play. Kareno, now fifty, is the hero and hope of a generation of younger philosophers; his wife has returned to him, with a child Sara who is clearly the daughter of Endre Bondeson. Bondeson, now the editor of a major newspaper, and a powerful establishment figure, does all in his power to seduce Kareno away from his principles, and holds out to him the chance of a seat in the Norwegian parliament if he will openly dissociate himself from the party and the opinions for which he has worked so long and so hard. His advancement will also involve the fall of the 'traitor' Jerven, from the first play. Kareno's rejection of Jerven had caused Jerven's fiancée to break off the engagement; wherever possible since, Jerven has used his power to hinder Kareno as a means of revenging himself. Kareno now takes the step which at twenty-nine he would not take, and enters the 'gates of the kingdom'. His spirit bathed in the mellow light of the evening sun, he aligns himself with Bondesen, breaks with the party of youth, and clambers upwards at last over the body of Jerven. The play closes with him taking his step-daughter Sara on his knee and reading to her a fairy-story which begins, 'There was once a man who would never give in'.

The three plays throw interesting light on Hamsun the man, and illuminate the fears he felt himself of softening with the years and abandoning the principles of his youth. His rise to fame had been, after all, a long battle; now that he had finally won the victory, he may have worried about what was going to become of his fighting spirit. But apart from this biographical insight into the man, and apart from the obvious relevance Kareno's prophesying of the 'great terrorist' in 1895 inevitably has for those trying to fathom Hamsun's enthusiasm for Hitler in the 1930s and '40s, the plays have little to offer. Hamsun produced them with an ease that excited his own contempt, his exceptional ear for dialogue leading him on too quickly to produce plays that were all surface and no depth. The central idea of the trilogy, that to betray the ideals of one's youth is contemptible but inevitable, is not the organic heart of the plays it should be, and Kareno's agonising over his principles is a spoken and not an acted affair. The plays lack conflict and suspense, and utilise a number of rather obvious symbols; the dressing gown, walking stick and pot of tea, for example, which in *Evening Glow* symbolise the fifty-year-old Kareno's 'decrepitude'.

Nevertheless, everything that Hamsun did in this period aroused interest, and the first two plays in the trilogy were performed in sequence at the Christiania Theatre, *At the Gates of the Kingdom* being played twenty-one times, and *The Game of Life* sixteen times. The final play *Evening Glow* had a run of eleven performances there in October 1898. The critical reception was friendly rather than enthusiastic, and the plays had only a short stage life in Hamsun's native Norway. They continue to be regarded there as very much literary footnotes to his career as novelist.

The plays did rather better for Hamsun abroad, particularly in Russia and Germany. *At the Gates of the Kingdom* and *The Game of Life* were both performed at the Moscow Arts Theatre, and Stanislavsky was especially fond of *The Game of Life*. In his autobiography *My Life in Art*, he devotes a whole chapter to the play,[2] and describes his production of it in 1905 as 'a historical turning point in my artistic activity'. Weirdly, the play's scandalous success there was cheered by supporters crying 'Long live the Left!', while the Right opposed the performances with cries of 'Down with the decadents! Long live the old theatre!', providing ironic confirmation of one of Hamsun's major objections to the form of the drama – that it is not possible for a playwright to create psychologically unambiguous characters who are both actor-proof and director-proof.

Hamsun soon realised there was not going to be any fortune for him in playwriting, though he wrote several more times for the stage before finally abandoning the form in 1910. He found the experience aesthetically as well as economically unrewarding. The thing about drama, he explained to Bolette Larsen, was to omit all good writing.[3] That was the secret. He called it crude work, dock-work.[4] It seemed to be all part of a general dissatisfaction with literary forms which now afflicted him after having produced five novels in as many years. To a friend he wrote:

> God how I detest this scribbling. I am tired of the novel, and have always despised drama. Now I have begun to write poetry, the only kind of writing which is not both pretentious and empty, but simply empty.[5]

And to Bolette in Bergen he repeated the general dissatisfaction:

> Literature does not delight me any more. (Literally does not *delight* me.) Literature is just books.[6]

And when students at Christiania University invited him to deliver a lecture to them, he chose to warn them against 'The Over-estimating of Writers and Writing'. He spoke scathingly of the cult of the oracular writer, and rejected completely the idea that a writer might be an organised man, and a thinker. This was to confuse them with philosophers. He held fast to the romantic idea of the writer as confused and passionate failure, like Villon and Verlaine. Writers, he told the students, were men not born to settle, not born to pay tax; they had the souls of wandering tramps, their spiritual kin were the travelling organ-grinders. And he slipped in his annual swipe at Ibsen, still, to his profound personal irritation, publishing every other year his old man's books, scraping them together in an empty and passionless vacuum. All his life he would continue to hold Ibsen before him as an image of what he did not want to be – an old man, pretending to know what he was talking about.

Hamsun was becoming hot publishing property now: his friend Sven Lange wrote to him with a secret offer from Gyldendal to tempt him away from Philipsen. Gyldendal was the firm that had refused him in 1880, with *Frida*, and the offer must have tasted sweet, though it was still some time before that lifelong and successful partnership came into being. Lange, writing from Munich, was part of the group that Langen was building up around a new publishing venture, the radical, satirical magazine *Simplicissimus*. Langen had strengthened his already strong ties with Scandinavia by marrying Bjørnson's daughter Dagny, and now Bjørnson was visiting his new son-in-law; together they were determined that the magazine should get off to a strong start. Jacob Wassermann and Frank Wedekind were involved from the beginning. The Mann brothers Thomas and Heinrich were also a part of this Munich group while the magazine's first illustrators were Thomas Th. Heine and the young Norwegian Olaf Gulbransson, invited to Munich by Langen on Bjørnson's advice. And now Bjørnson, through Lange, extended an invitation to Hamsun to join them in Munich, perhaps hoping to interest Hamsun in a staff position on the magazine.

Hamsun travelled out there in April and remained until June, staying at Langen's house at 51A Kaulbachstrasse. Bjørnson's warm, at times embarrassingly warm public demonstrations of respect here were still further proof that Hamsun had breached the literary establishment. He did some work in Munich, producing the short-stories *The Call of Life* and *Slaves of Love*, and caused great interest among the younger German writers, for whom he had long been a hero as the author of *Hunger*. A good deal of this was the sycophantic attention which the power of his personality, and his own need to show it publicly on occasions, always invited from this time onward; the journalist Arthur Holitscher wrote in his memoirs that Hamsun was the idol and the sensation wherever he went, although he noted that Wedekind, whom Hamsun had helped in Paris, held himself aloof from the general hero-worshipping. In Munich, as in Copenhagen and Christiania, his passage left a trail of confused anecdotes in its wake. One incident in Langen's office which Holitscher claims to have witnessed also cropped up in Kafka's diary for September 1911; in Kafka's version it is the artist Kubin who claims to have been present when, in the vivid, and never-corrected English version of events, Hamsun, in the middle of a conversation, took out a pair of scissors, put his foot on his *neck*, and trimmed off the ragged edges of his trousers.

Back in Norway he followed a plan laid already in Munich, and returned to Valdres in the Gudbrandsdal valley again. From the sanatorium at Tonsaasen he travelled all over the area, visiting old friends like Erik Frydenlund, and the Mjøen family at nearby Gjøvik, where he had worked as a roadmaker sixteen years previously. This was a symbolic journey, and one that affected him deeply. The wanderer saw clearly what the anarchic freedom of his personal life was costing him when he met old friends again, and found their children grown men and women. The thought of ageing was on his mind.

In the two *Kareno* plays so far completed he had perhaps tried to chart his own progress: in pursuit of his passion for literature he had, after all, forfeited the personal joys of normal life, the stability and support of a loving relationship, the joy of familiar surroundings, familiar faces, the joy of children. Though only thirty-seven –and for reasons we shall come to later, passing himself off as thirty-six – he felt that the years were flying by.

Even in the early 1890s, when exchanging photographs with his correspondents, as was the rather nice custom in those days, he joked about the wrinkles visible on his face. What seems at first an idiosyncrasy reveals itself gradually as a pathology: Glahn is only thirty when he writes *Pan*, but contrives somehow to sound like a man bearing a far heavier burden of years. Coldevin, a relatively minor character in *Shallow Soil* who yet clearly engages more of Hamsun's genuine interest and sympathy than the overtly major characters, is described as 'old', being over forty. In *The Call of Life* the 'old' husband whose death leaves his young widow free to seduce the narrator turns out to be all of fifty-three. The eccentrically accelerated decrepitude in the Kareno character, white-haired at fifty, is the most striking example of this harsh and unusual view of when a man may be said to be finished.

It all gave him a great deal to think about when he returned to Frøken Hammer's hotel at Ljan after Christmas. The idea of settling down may well have helped to focus the already strong feelings he had towards another guest at the hotel. Her name was Bergljot Goepfert; a mutual friend had introduced the two of them one day at Hamsun's request.[7] According to Bergljot, it was love at first sight. Hamsun's response to the meeting was to write *Alvilde*, a love poem of almost terrifying erotic intensity.

Bergljot was twenty-two years old when she and Hamsun met. Born at Trondheim in north Norway, she was a rich woman thanks to her father's success as a consultant in the design of steamships, and money inherited from her recently deceased mother. In Vienna in 1893 she married an Austrian businessman, Eduard Goepfert, and the following year gave birth to a daughter Maria. The marriage was not a success, however. Goepfert was a philanderer, and soon Hamsun and Bergljot were talking of her divorce, and their own marriage.

Once the affair got seriously under way, Hamsun moved from Ljan to an apartment near the city centre at Welhavens gate 3, while Bergljot went back to live in the family home at Arbins gate. Hamsun's friend Hans Aanrud acted as their postman and go-between. The intention was presumably to avoid scandal; but it was all in vain, alas.

The story of a writer's love affair should ideally be the story of the letters that passed between the lovers. In Hamsun's case, none of them have survived. Instead, we are left with letters of a very different kind as a legacy of the courtship. A woman named Anna Munch made it her business to try to destroy the relationship, and Hamsun along with it, by flooding the couple's private and public life with poison-pen letters. It was a grotesque and pitiful case of hopeless love and imagined scorn.

Hamsun had been aware of Anna Munch's existence for years. She was a writer herself, a pathetic woman with a history of mental illness. Ever since she saw Hamsun lecture at Trondheim in 1891, she had been erotically obsessed by him. She followed him about, booked in at the same hotels as him, even followed him out to Paris. She convinced herself that Hamsun loved her too, and wrote him long letters suggesting that they live together. She even produced a novel, *Two People*, in which the leading characters are clearly based on herself and Hamsun, and on her own persecution of him.

For a long time Hamsun accepted Anna Munch as a natural phenomenon in a universe in which strangeness, intrigue, suspicion and jealousy seemed normal everyday states to him. Nor were hers by any means the only bizarre letters he received during the course of his controversial rise to fame. However, the start of his relationship with Bergljot seems to have triggered off something in Anna Munch – she had, not greatly to his surprise, booked in at Frøken Hammer's in Ljan soon after he did – and around Christmas 1895 she began in earnest her campaign to destroy him and the relationship. Hamsun put up with it for almost eighteen months before finally contacting the police on the matter. He wrote to the Chief of Police on 23 April 1897:

> I hereby humbly request the assistance of the police in protecting me against the persecutions of the authoress Anna Munch. For over a year now she has been sending anonymous letters to a number of ladies of my acquaintance, has written to their fathers, and, in the case of married ladies, to their husbands. These letters contain warnings, advice, and threats, and portray me as a seducer and a deceiver who deserves to be ostracised. For this behaviour which, apart from the injury caused to me, causes confusion and unease in many people, in many homes, I request that Anna Munch be detained, accused, and punished; and above all that her mental condition be examined.
>
> For years now I have had to put up with the fact that the lady cannot leave me in peace. I have put up with her endless letters and telegrams, and tolerated her having followed me to a foreign country, and travelling around after me to the various places where I have lived in Norway. I have even had to swallow that here in Christiania she has hired rooms in the same hotel as me, and stood waiting up for me and watching me when I come to my room at one o'clock in the morning. Time after time I have warned her and begged her to leave me in peace, but completely in vain. In the last few weeks her activity as a writer of anonymous letters has assumed such proportions that for the sake of the recipients of these letters I find that I must ask the police for their help.
>
> I would add that there has never been any form of sexual relationship whatever between Fru Munch and I, and that never in the six years in which I have known her have I made the slightest form of approach to her.[8]

He also wrote, slightly less formally, to Bolette Larsen about the business:

> Dear Bolette,
>   Fru M. has persecuted me by letter for six years, in the last year and a half anonymously. She is mad. I have reported her to the police, but no results yet. She's supposed to have been in

Copenhagen since Easter, but tirelessly sends anonymous letters to her helpers here who then distribute them. Hardly a day passes without some woman or other receiving an anonymous letter about me. I have never, never, not even in dreams desired Fru M. She lies at that point in her book – that night I had to *trick* her out of my room because she'd got in somehow and stood waiting up for me in her stockinged feet when I came home at one o'clock in the morning. What I've had to go through for that passionate maiden's sake! I have never, never tried anything with her, Bolette – I've never been *that* desperate – she looks like a fat, red hippopotamus.[9]

Anna Munch's letters, written without punctuation in a disjointed, hieroglyphic hand, claimed that Bergljot was pregnant, and that Hamsun had other married lovers besides her and lived off the money they obtained for him from their husbands. These were sent to the husbands and families of the women concerned. Some took the form of secret notes, allegedly from Hamsun to these women, suggesting meetings at which they were enjoined to bring money for an evening's drinking. Many were sent to Bergljot's father, Captain Bech, begging him to rescue his daughter from the clutches of the evil seducer Hamsun 'before it is too late'. Bergljot's husband Goepfert also received letters, as did politicians, theatres, the cafés Hamsun frequented, bookshops, newspaper editors, publishers and libraries. They described Hamsun as a lazy man who never worked, and claimed that he was not the real author of the books which had appeared under his name. Bergljot also received many letters taunting her with her promiscuity, and declaring her a good match for Hamsun.*

Hamsun knew perfectly well who the letter writer was – he named her in his letter to the police of 23 April. The police, however, in pursuing the matter complicated it beyond all bounds. They set their own handwriting expert on the case, a Captain Schmelk, who studied the letters and came to the surprising conclusion, on Christmas Eve 1897, that Hamsun had written them himself. No explanation was offered as to why he should have done this; but certainly Captain Bech believed it. Deeply opposed

---

* The information about the name of the chambermaid Hamsun was involved with in Sarpsborg in 1891, and the claim that he asked her to marry him but was rejected, is taken from one such letter. The dangers of using such a source are self-evident; yet I have decided to offer the information anyway. Over sixty of these letters are preserved in the Riksarkiv in Oslo. The letter containing the information is uniquely sensible; and the fact that there was such a relationship with a girl in Sarpsborg is confirmed from another source.

to the affair, he believed that Hamsun had done so in the first
instance to force Bergljot to get a divorce; and thereafter to try to
prevent the marriage, since Bech believed that Hamsun had
changed his mind and no longer wished to marry Bergljot.

Surprising developments like these show the destructive power
of Anna Munch's campaign: for Hamsun, a highly suggestible man
with a rich seam of fantasy running through his mind, now
allowed himself to doubt that she was his persecutor. He *knew*
quite well that she was responsible – the contents of the letters as
well as the contents of her signed letters to him, the evidence of her
novel, and all his long experience of her made it abundantly clear.
But now he found the subjective nature of this certainty running
up against a wall of official objectivity quite breathtaking in its
ruthless consistency. The police, naturally, had contacted Anna
Munch about the matter, and she had denied the accusations with
outrage. She dismissed out of hand the possibility that her book
might constitute evidence against her. On the contrary, she told
the police, 'personally I regard my book, in which I exonerate him,
and depict myself as his tormentor, as clear proof of my innocence'.

With the active assistance of Bergljot, Hamsun's fantasy now
took off. The pair identified followers everywhere; small boys;
grown men walking two by two; whole crowds of people, so many
people that Hamsun reasoned no one persecutor could possibly
afford to pay so many watchers, and suggested to the police that
the campaign had now been taken up by a league of some sort,
possibly the Theosophical Society, which he had attacked in the
newspapers. Members of Anna Munch's family were Theo-
sophists, Hamsun added as he tipped the police off about this, still
loth to accept their exoneration.

Any joy there should have been in the courtship became quite
swallowed up in the hellish grind of trying to track down the
author of the conspiracy. Hamsun collected and delivered samples
of the handwriting of all of his correspondents to the police, having
assured them that he was not the author of them. There followed
some grotesquely comic attempts by the police to identify the
'watchers', with Captain Waldemar Hansen riding slowly up and
down Kirkeveien on his bicycle, and Constable Vyborg standing in
a hole in the road, disguised as a workman with a shovel in his
hand while Hamsun and Bergljot sat talking on a bench. Once a
man was even seen to jump out from behind a bush and run away.
The sceptical Captain Hansen met Hamsun standing by a letter-
box on Karl Johans gate one day. Hamsun was 'extremely
agitated', and asked Hansen to help him retrieve a letter he had

seen someone posting in the box. Hansen stressed in his report to his superiors the disturbed state Hamsun was in, clearly indicating the feeling among the Christiania police that this strange man was indeed the author of a campaign aimed at his own destruction. The terrible irony of the whole business, of course, is that such a campaign was not unthinkably far from the behaviour of a Nagel, who sent himself telegrams containing false information about himself, then left them lying open in his hotel room so that gossip would spread the information through the town.

By 1898, Hamsun was weary of the whole business, and in a letter of great restraint he asked the police to drop their investigations: their suspicions had now moved on from himself to focus on Bergljot, and detectives had even secretly obtained samples of her handwriting from her father. He could hazard no guess as to where they might end up if they did not stop now.

1897 should have been a good year for Hamsun. Instead it turned out to be one of the worst of his life. Among her other projects, Anna Munch had made it her business to try to sabotage his application for a literary scholarship from the government. That he did not get it probably had little to do with her efforts; yet in the confused and tormented course of this year it seemed to him that his anonymous persecutor was responsible for every reversal and bad thing that happened to him.[10] The facts of the matter were slightly more prosaic.

Hamsun's struggles against the old guard in the early 1890s had almost single-handedly opened up a breach through which many a young writer had since gratefully passed. By now he had many friends and supporters among the up and coming literary establishment. At the instigation of Erik Lie in 1893, many of the country's leading writers had formed themselves into a Society of Authors for the protection and advancement of the rights and interests of authors. Hamsun had given the project his guarded blessing, but when directly approached, in June 1894, had declined to join, on the grounds that too many of his fellow members would be hostile to his membership. However, he promised to contribute to a pension fund, once *Pan* was published. One of the Society's first aims was to see that only the best authors were rewarded with the State Scholarship for writers, an award administered by the Department of Church and Education with, thus far, an unreliable nose for literary talent. They formed, therefore, a committee of writers who would sit in discussion of a number of applications for the award, before sending their professional recommendations on to the Department. It was understood that such recommendations wold not be binding; nevertheless they would carry considerable weight. Hamsun was acknowledged as the leading young writer in the country, and when he now sought a grant to enable him to finish his *Kareno* trilogy, his name was first on the list of those recommended by the Society to the Department. Exceptionally for a writer of his age, he had not sought any official funding before, and the award was felt to be a foregone conclusion. However, the departmental head, a former priest named Jakob Sverdrup, overlooked Hamsun's claims, and gave the full award of 1200 kroner to the second name on the list, a regional author named Vetle Vislie, little read then and unread now.*

The reason for the Department's decision to overlook his claims goes back to Hamsun's visit to Munich in 1896. Albert Langen had asked him for a contribution for *Simplicissimus*, and Hamsun had provided him with a short-story entitled *The Call of Life*. In the story, a narrator describes what happened to him one evening as he was out walking. Drifting the streets in the hope of something happening, he was picked up by a young woman who took him home with her. They spent the night making love, and in the morning, as he was about to leave, the narrator saw through an open door the body of an old man laid out and awaiting the arrival of the undertaker. He made no mention of the matter to the woman, but found his explanation later in the death columns of a newspaper: his mysterious lover was the widow of the man he saw lying in the apartment. The narrator ends his story thus:

> I sit a long while thinking about all this. A man has a wife who is thirty years younger than him. He lies ill for a long time, and then one day dies.
> And the young widow breathes out.

It was a typically provocative moral statement from Hamsun. In Germany it might have passed unnoticed; but Langen also had high hopes for a Danish edition of his magazine called *Basta*, which was practically a duplicate of *Simplicissimus*, and the story duly appeared in the Copenhagen magazine, from whence it came to the attention of a Norwegian politician named John Lund. Lund raised the alarm about the story, and tried to get *Basta* banned. Later in the same year twenty-six people signed a letter to a Christiania newspaper after the performance of Hamsun's play *The Game of Life* at the National Theatre. They complained that the character of Teresita was immoral. The two unrelated incidents

* Vislie was another, like Arne Dybfest, Peter Egge, and Hans Aanrud, who had received valuable encouragement and practical support from Hamsun in 1890–1.

together created enough of a scandal to cause Sverdrup to hop over Hamsun's name in favour of Vislie's.

The upshot was a fierce literary debate in the newspapers of the capital between the moralists and the writers. A protest was sent to the Department, signed by Bjørnson and Arne Garborg, among others – although the names of Ibsen, Kielland and Lie were conspicuous by their absence. One who did sign was Anna Munch. The Larsens in Bergen signed too, and Hamsun thanked them warmly for thus openly identifying themselves with 'bordello literature', as the critics called his writing. But the protests were to no immediate effect.

It is hard to imagine Hamsun's state of mind in 1897. He was in love, and the object, not of love letters, but hate letters. He published nothing of note, only the collection of short-stories which he called *Siesta*; it was, he said later, a 'fruitless siesta of a year'.[11] Quite apart from the competing demands on his attention of a love affair, and what one might call a hate affair, he was also deeply unsure about whether there was any point in writing at all. A standing joke in letters to friends is the threat to become a smith; or to marry and disappear to a small farm somewhere and keep cows and raise a family. To cap it all his physical health was bad; he was plagued with sciatica[12] throughout the winter of 1896–97, and for four months travelled into Christiania every day for electrical treatment and massage. There were times when he almost gave way to despair. 'I ought to shoot myself',[13] he wrote to a friend, 'but you need courage to do that, and I don't have much.' To the Larsens, in November, he wrote:

> You know, I drank a great deal of whisky in the spring and the summer. In three months, alone and at night, I drank sixty bottles, quite alone. I felt so broken down that I had to do it, to keep me going. . . . And then things began to get a little lighter for me, and I stopped.[14]

It did indeed look as if things might be beginning to get a little brighter for him in some ways: snubbed by the government, the Society of Authors determined to raise by appeal an equivalent sum for Hamsun. His old friend Peter Egge was put in charge of the fundraising; but all his best efforts could only muster 600 kroner, half the sum involved. The Society hoped to make up the balance with the proceeds from a calendar to be put on sale at Christmas.[15]

The Germans, however, came to Hamsun's rescue. Langen, hearing of his difficulties, had inserted an appeal in *Simplicissimus* which, by the time the fund closed in the summer of 1898, had raised the enormous sum of 1606,55 marks[16] – more than three times the size of the scholarship he had been denied, and proof of Hamsun's rapidly growing popularity in Germany.

Bergljot's divorce had finally come through as well, in spite of Goepfert's opposition: it was granted to her by Royal Decree on 13 November 1897, on the grounds of her husband's proven adultery. By a second Royal Decree of 19 March 1898 she was given permission to remarry, and the ceremony itself took place at St John's Church, where the best men were Hans Aanrud and the bookseller Christian Dybwad.

Hamsun's wedding-day present was a bound, handwritten poem to his new wife in five long sections, *To Bergljot*.[17] A notable aspect of it is the aggressive way Hamsun writes about her ex-husband, 'the Austrian dog' who has tried to stand in their way. Other verses put the marriage on an intensely romantic footing in which he casts himself as a peasant boy, and Bergljot as the fine lady who will have him, despite the fact that he has no castle and his clothes are rags.

After the ceremony the couple held a reception at Fru Bye's private hotel on Egertorvet. Hamsun seems by this time to have acquired the status of an early pop star: crowds stood waiting on the pavement outside the hotel, and cheered when the couple appeared on the balcony. An eye-witness reported that the writer 'looked embarrassed'.

Afterwards they travelled for their honeymoon to Fru Florelius' sanatorium at Oppegård. They hired a villa on the edge of the nearby lake, away from the main building, and on sunny days bathed naked together. To avoid the attentions of the curious they often rowed over the lake to Ski, where they were able to walk in peace. They had their own wine and champagne with them from Christiania which they drank from some of Bergljot's own beauti-ful cut glasses. She was, after all, an extremely wealthy woman.[18]

From there, the couple moved on to Valdres. The wedding, and especially the money from Germany, buoyed Hamsun up con-siderably. In ecstatic mood he wrote to thank Langen for the *Simplicissimus* collection – it was far more than he had hoped, he said, adding that 'it shows that Germany is a great country; here I get almost nothing'. The long-planned trip to the east, first mooted in 1890 and referred to several times in subsequent years in letters to friends as a kind of dream flight from all his troubles, seems to have been in his mind again around this time – he told Langen that he would *not* now be able to travel to Turkey, because he had just got married. 'Ho ho,' he chortled, 'I am healthy, I am young, I am rich! And now it is summer time.'[19]

Rich, young and healthy, married to his rich, dark-haired society beauty Bergljot, and with the flood of poison-pen letters reduced to a trickle, Hamsun found his taste for the novel returning among the convivial surroundings of Valdres. *Victoria*, the last of his four great novels from the 1890s, was written quickly, and was ready for publication by the end of September. Remarkably, as late as the end of July, the final form it would take was still not clear in his mind, and he wrote to Langen that the book he was working on 'consists of two, or perhaps three smaller romans [Nw=novels], and I hope it shall be good'.[20] He described it as 'a pendent to *Pan*, but less big', and said that while the older book was 'dark lilla', the new one would be 'light red'; the books, he explained, were 'two different pictures'.[21]

The labour of writing was not particularly enjoyable. There was too much rain, and too many English and American tourists rolling by in wagon after wagon on their way to look at the Jotunheim peaks.[22] The subject matter of his book depressed him too.

In the middle of September he prepared himself for a final session that would get it finished, and sent Bergljot back to Christiania while he worked on the closing pages. They put him in a strange mood. To Bolette Larsen he wrote:

> . . . it is unbelievably tiring to sit and write about sunshine, and the smell of a garden, when the mind feels only darkness.[23]

For *Victoria*, his honeymoon novel, was no celebration of the joys of love. It was more like a requiem for the death of love.

Johannes the miller's son loves Victoria, the daughter of the village squire. She loves him too, and is fascinated by his imagination and the stories he tells her. As long as they remain in the secret world of children, they can meet almost as equals, but with the coming of adolescence the barriers of class rise up firmly between them. Johannes goes out into the world, and decides to try to become a writer. Now and then he comes home again. On one such visit, while wandering in one of his old childhood haunts, he finds Victoria has been attracted back to the old place too. In spite of the coincidence, the pair observe the social distinction between them, and behave formally towards one another. Another accidental meeting takes place later, in the city. This time Victoria is spontaneous and open with him; she kisses him. Johannes is ecstatically happy; but at a third meeting between the two he finds her inexplicably cold and formal towards him again. Hurt and baffled, he retreats from the situation.

The abrupt change in Victoria's attitude has been brought about by her engagement to a rich young man named Otto – her father is facing economic ruin, and like a dutiful daughter she has agreed to a loveless marriage in order to save him. Victoria and Otto throw a large engagement party at the mansion house to which Johannes is invited. His instincts are to refuse the invitation, but he goes nevertheless, and Victoria introduces him to Camilla, a pretty young woman whom Johannes once saved from drowning when she was a baby. Victoria's intentions are clearly to bring the two together, in spite of her own feelings for Johannes. Her situation leads her to behave strangely at the party – constantly talking about Johannes to the irritation of her fiancé, and trying to disguise her feelings by being rude to Johannes in front of the other guests.

Camilla shows an interest in Johannes. She shyly chases after him, and with a fatalistic good grace he eventually proposes to her and is accepted. On the same day, Otto is killed in a hunting accident. Victoria's father, realising that his ruin is a fact, sends everyone away from the house, and ritualistically sets fire to it, committing suicide in the flames. Victoria is suddenly freed from all obligations which bound her, and she goes straight to Johannes and makes an open and complete declaration of her love. Johannes can do nothing – Camilla has already accepted his proposal of marriage.

Time passes, and Johannes, now a famous writer, makes no move to fix a date for the wedding. A feeling of indifference and impotence has come over him. After a while Camilla meets and falls in love with a young man of her own age, an Englishman named Richmond; in a torment of guilt and divided loyalty she manages to confess this to Johannes, and finds him strangely unmoved. He gives the couple his avuncular blessings. Though he is now free to marry Victoria, it is too late. She has tuberculosis, and is already dead by the time her old tutor hands over to Johannes the farewell letter she has written to him, a moving, beautiful, uninhibited declaration of love.

Victoria is substantially a mature rewriting of the short novel *Bjørger* that Hamsun wrote as an eighteen-year-old in Nordland, the story of the love between the peasant boy Bjørger and the daughter of the local rich man, Moe. In both novels the lovers alternately approach and retreat from one another, seemingly in the grip of forces beyond their control, and in both, the impossible situation is resolved by the death of the female lover.

This vision of love as beautiful but hopeless fascinated Hamsun.

In a sense it is true to say that he never grew out of it, that it remained for him the definition of all that human love was, of all that it could aspire to, and of its inevitable fate. The idea that first love is the only real love, and that it is by its nature doomed to disappointment is most clearly expressed by the old tutor who delivers Victoria's letter to Johannes:

> Let me ask you another little question: have you ever in all your days known a case of a man getting the one he should have got? I haven't. There's a legend about a man whose prayers were answered by God, so that he was given his first and only love. But that was all the joy he got out of it. Why, you're going to ask again, and if you wait, I'll tell you: for the simple reason that she died immediately after – *immediately* after, you see, ha ha ha, instantly. It's always the same story. Naturally one doesn't get the woman one should have had; but if by some damned freak of reason and justice it ever does happen, then of course, she dies immediately after. There's always a trick in it somewhere. So then the man has to find himself another love, whatever's available, and there's no need for him to die of the change.

Perhaps the attitude had a specific basis in personal experience; or maybe it was only a general expression of the disillusionment that inevitably takes place as one passes from adolescence to manhood. Laura Walsøe, the daughter of 'enevoldskongen' Walsøe in Tranøy, where Hamsun worked as a boy of fourteen, was born in 1860, just one year after Hamsun. Bjørger's sweetheart was named Laura; and Laura Walsøe, like the fictional Victoria, died young and unwed, of tuberculosis. The coincidences are suggestive, but no more. And whether *Victoria* was pure fact, or free improvisations on fact, is not really the point: the point is that in this novel, Hamsun once again presented his readers with an account, in the form of art, of yet another stage of his journey through life; and that like his earlier 'reports' – *Hunger, Pan, Mysteries* – his conclusions were the same: that love is about failure, loss and defeat.

Victoria, Hamsun's first book for a Norwegian publisher, Cammermeyer, proved to be his greatest commercial success to date. The extraordinary fairy-tale like charm of the story made it a favourite with both readers and critics; the first edition of 6000, sold so well on its publication on 29 October that a second edition was printed before Christmas.

The most notable dissenting voice was that of his 'old enemy',

Nils Vogt in *Morgenbladet*. *Morgenbladet* was a paper for the upper-class readership, and Nils Vogt wrote a review of the novel that showed that certain sections of society at least were still not prepared to accept the upstart Hamsun. He described the novel as a failure because Hamsun simply did not have enough experience of upper-class women to be able to describe one convincingly. He had made a similar point about Elina in the play *Evening Glow*. Bergljot felt herself personally affronted by the review, and in the wake of it all Hamsun's profound personal insecurities welled up and overflowed, and in a long letter to his old mentor Georg Brandes he defended his book, and tried to give some account of his personality and the difficulties his disadvantaged upbringing had caused him:

> . . . There is a great deal of talk about 'being cultured' these days, it's been commonplace for some years now, even the newspapers at home write about it now and then. And 'being cultured' means above all having made so-and-so many journeys, seen *this* many paintings, read *this* number of books, and generally speaking, to be able to use one's memory. 'Lack of culture' – that has nothing to do with speaking disrespectfully about John Stuart Mill – Nietzsche did that, after all, and he was what you might call a 'cultured' man – 'lack of culture' really means that one had parents who didn't make one a student, or a doctor, or something along those lines. 'Lack of culture' means to have been driven to America, to physical labouring in the prairie, so that later one was not in any position to acquire the accepted views of educated people on all the acknowledged great men and great works of art, in spite of all one's honest and diligent efforts to do so. I don't know if I understand what 'culture' is. But I think it might be something in the direction of the education of a *heart*. Back home in Norway I used to meet people, especially journalists, untrustworthy and dishonest people, with a more limited experience of life than mine, ungenerous people with only a limited love of truth. And these people could with their born and nurtured superiority turn their nose up at anyone who wasn't 'cultured'. And it occurred to me, that if I could acquire and hold a consistent view of life, then in my books I might try to attack those injustices which 'education' continued to support and respect, and I could do this without having to regret that I had never had the learning to take a university degree. But then, everyone knows about me, that I was born a peasant, that I don't have any exams to prove that I know things, and that I never had the money to enable me to sit

for fifteen to eighteen years and study philosophy; and it's such a help to know that, when it comes down to judging my views on matters of 'culture'.

In its length, and in its disturbed passion, this letter to Brandes was a unique statement of the uncertainties which his lack of education caused Hamsun. It throws considerable light on his personality, and helps to explain how easy it was for him to consider himself, for example, the victim of a deliberate plot on the part of a class-based, albeit literary, establishment during the early 1890s. It illuminates, too, much of the strange vehemence of his attacks on the famous and the powerful. Vogt's was an isolated and rather contemptible attack; yet Hamsun's response had been frantic.

In the year of *Victoria*'s publication, Hamsun was awarded the literary scholarship denied him by the Church and Education Department the year before. The 1200-kroner scholarship carried with it an obligation to spend the year abroad, and in the winter of 1898 Hamsun travelled to Finland. Friends thought that, in Bergljot, he was taking his Victoria with him. He may have persuaded himself that he was too – that in spite of the ill-will of the Vogts of the world, he had finally won his princess. After a year that he described to Langen as 'the most terrible year I have lived in my thirty-seven-year long life', in spite of the trials and scandals of Anna Munch's campaign of persecution, and the strangely dark moods that had overtaken him in the writing of *Victoria*, perhaps in the marriage to Bergljot he would succeed where all his fictional alter egos had failed, and find happiness in love.

Chapter 10
1898–1906: Restless Middle Age, Depression and Divorce

The Hamsuns travelled first to Helsinki, and put up at the Hotel Kleineh while they looked around for a suitable place to live. They soon found a rather run-down property on the island Råholmen, and Hamsun invested in a tool kit and set about helping the carpenters to get the place into shape. By about the middle of December they were able to move in.

Hamsun worked, Bergljot kept house and did some translating work, and in the evenings they socialised with artists and writers from Helsinki. Here Hamsun renewed contact with friends from Paris like the painters Axel Gallen and Albert Edelfelt. He also met Birger Mörner again, whose play he had translated into Norwegian. Jean Sibelius was another member of the group, and later on Hamsun met the Swedish caricaturist and humourist Albert Engström, a man who was to become one of his few lifelong friends. They liked Bergljot, and called her Alvilde, the woman to whom Hamsun's fierce *Fever Poem* is addressed. However, the more conservative local people were rather shocked by her: dresses without sleeves were considered very advanced in those parts. But in spite of their fondness for the couple, friends could not help noticing from the first that the relationship between the newly-weds was not good.[1]

Bergljot struggled, but she was desperately unhappy. Everything was wrong. The winter was bitterly cold, and their island home was surrounded by ice. They had to walk across it to go shopping in nearby Fölisön, and the prices in Finland were way above what they had expected. She was a refined city-girl, and she found herself washing clothes in a groove cut in the ice. She poured out her heart to her sister Alette:

Knut and I hate it so much here, it's driving us mad. It's still winter here, still snow. It's terrible, we're both sick in the mind from this unbelievably vile winter. Just sickness and wretchedness. Now we'll see if we can rent this place out and travel south and warm ourselves in the sun, ah. May I never again come to Finland in my life.[2]

A note from Hamsun to a journalist friend, Alexander Slotte, juxtaposing with characteristic rapidity lyricism and unease, gives hidden confirmation of the sense of something being wrong:

It is three o'clock in the morning, and I am walking about the room smoking and looking at the sun over on the far shore. How beautiful it is! But I cannot sleep these days.[3]

The pair sent letters to Hans Aanrud desperately trying to persuade him to come and visit them, and even offering to pay his fare. Bergljot added her fervent postscript to one of them: 'Say yes, please, so we'll have something to look forward to all through the winter.' Aanrud did say yes, but not quickly enough: the money Hamsun had set aside for his ticket was gone by the time he replied. Aanrud, who was, after all, being asked to organise his summer holidays in the middle of December, did not manage to get his reply to Hamsun before early February, and instead of apologising for going back on the offer Hamsun only ticked him off at very great length for not having replied 'at once'.[4] He complained that he and Bergljot had spent hours speculating on how they could possibly have offended him. It was no easy matter, being Hamsun's friend.

At the end of May the couple moved to a new address in town at Kasarngatan 23, a small, quiet place facing into a back yard. Shortly afterwards Bergljot travelled alone to Vienna, perhaps in order to spend some time with her daughter by Eduard Goepfert. It was the first of the many separations which were to characterise their marriage.[5] After her return they went ahead with their plans for a trip to Russia in the autumn. Hamsun looked forward to his visit to Dostoevsky's homeland, and he looked forward, too, to emulating Birger Mörner's feat of drinking tea with the Cossacks. Both Hamsuns probably hoped that the trip would put the bad memories of the winter behind them.

They left Helsinki early in September.[6] Hamsun's excitement, however, was probably tempered by a slight feeling of unease. The Russian Czar had recently sent a new governor general to the Finnish capital to carry out a Russification of the civil and military institutions there; most of Hamsun's literary friends were involved in an opposition movement, and as a gesture of solidarity with them he had delivered a lecture on 10 May from which the proceeds were to go to a fund started by the resistance leader, Baron Mannerheim. Hamsun was slightly anxious that news of the lecture – nothing political, only an adapted version of the one he had given to Christiania University students in February 1897, 'Against the Overestimating of Writers and Writing' – might cause him problems at the border, and he declined to allow the lecture to be printed in the Finnish newspapers. However, they crossed into Russia without incident, and began their journey.

Hamsun made this journey through Russia the subject of his attempt at another genre besides the novels, poetry, short-stories, and drama he had so far tried. *In Wonderland. Experienced and Dreamt in the Caucasus* was published in Copenhagen in March 1903, and is probably one of the most highly subjective travel books ever written. In common with Hamsun's early book *On the Cultural Life of Modern America* it has as its main interest not so much the overt theme of the book – Russia, America – as the unusual personality of the writer.

Their adventure began with a fifteen-hour train journey from St Petersburg to Moscow, during which Bergljot slept all the way. 'My wife left nothing else behind her except her coat', he remarks. Thereafter she is referred to solely as 'my travelling companion', on the few occasions on which she is mentioned at all. Thence by wagon from Vladikaukasus to Tiflis, and finally to the goal of their journey, Baku, on the Caspian Sea. There are the obligatory descriptions of architecture and unusual churches, but the real fun of the book lies in the mileage Hamsun gets out of being a stranger in a strange land, wholly unable to speak the language, or understand any of what is being said to him, and yet boldly finding little adventures and incidents wherever he goes. One of the richest passages is his account of a three-day wagon ride from Vladikaukasus to Tiflis. Restless and unable to sleep one night, he wanders round the small overnight station where they have just arrived. Some distance from the village, he comes across a group of men standing round a fire on which horse flesh is roasting, and some sort of alcoholic concoction brewing. They offer him the meat to taste, but he refuses, explaining he has a fever. Somehow or other they contrive to understand him, and assure him that horse flesh is actually precisely what he needs if he wants to be rid of his fever. He bites away at his steak, and takes hearty swigs of the unknown brew offered him, and then wanders on. Later in the evening, still restless, he steals a tethered horse, and rides it up into the mountains. Coming to a small, remote farm he disarms the suspicious farmer with his usual gesture of friendship, the offer of a cigarette, and presently is being shown round the house. Ridiculous ideas come into his head. He imagines himself a very serious, scientific person come to make a serious investigation of the house. A great desire to investigate the kind of roofs to be found in such houses overcomes him; but the sight of two women sleeping up under the roof distracts him, and he begins to fantasise about these two women. One of them is the farmer's favourite wife, actually a beautiful and alluring woman; he resolves to steal her from the farmer. But she refuses to go with him; she says he isn't her type. He avenges himself by making fun of her husband's hat, calling it the most ridiculous hat he's ever seen. In the midst of all this fantasising the farmer shows him into a room where two bear cubs are lying curled up in a nest of bracken, and offers to sell him one. 'From curiosity over the price of Caucasian bears', Hamsun engages in a kind of bargaining with him. The man's last offer is fifteen scratches in the ground with his knife. 'Fifteen scratches in the ground for one bear cub? Never!' cries Hamsun, and closes the adventure in disgust.

One of the joys of the book is Hamsun's absolute refusal to take himself seriously as a 'travel writer'. There is a splendid bit of comic writing involving a description of his visit to Alfred Nobel's oil-refining plant at Baku. He was told that for reasons of industrial security he would not be permitted to take notes. He therefore took notes in a book held behind his back, with the result that when he got home and examined them, the lines were all mixed up in a surreal and inexplicable dance which he struggled dutifully to decipher. '261 steam cauldrons', he writes – 'but forgive me, I don't know whereabouts they are, or what they're used for, or why they're kept constantly on the boil. Nobel was a rich man, and of course, he could afford a certain number of steam cauldrons. He liked steam cauldrons, and enjoyed heating them up.' Another confused note refers to 'thirteen varieties of indigo, in glass': a particularly astonishing fact concerning the number of different kinds of oil which could be refined from raw naphtha had caused his writing hand to jerk a line, and bring it into false relationship with a line concerning the distillation of indigo.

In among the irony and the self-mockery come darker moments. Throughout much of his journey Hamsun experiences a near-paranoid fear that he is about to be arrested for some unknown crime by a mysterious and corrupt police officer who seems to be following him from place to place. This villain is a Jew, and his appearance is described with the casual anti-Semitism so regrettably fashionable in those days. 'His face is unpleasant, Jewish', Hamsun writes; and 'his Jewish snout is unbearable'. The book is in fact a kind of repository of prejudices, small and large. At one point he turns on an Englishman who just happens to be standing nearby and begins to taunt and humiliate him, solely because of his nationality. Hamsun's anglophobia appears here for the first time in public, and in earnest.

Not all the digressions are dark, however. One of the book's joys is the technique, picked up from Mark Twain, and used to expert effect, of suddenly, in the midst of a description or train of thought, producing a reference from another world of his experience. A rainstorm suddenly reminds him of the rainstorms on the prairies of America, and a sight of the vastness of the Russian steppes, and the thought of the people living and growing up there causes him to burst out, in a famous passage:

> There is nothing, nothing in the world like being completely alone and away from everything, I think to myself. It's something I remember from my childhood, back home, where I used to watch over the animals. In fine weather I would lie on my back in the heather, and write with my finger across the sky, and they were blessed days. I would let the animals wander wherever they liked for hours on end; and when I had to find them again all I had to do was climb up a rock, or up a high tree, and listen out, with my mouth open . . . It was a wonderful life. . . . I have tried to write about it; but I have never managed to. I would try to bring a little art to the writing, in order to be understood, and then it would all glide away from me.
>
> When I was minding the animals I went in clogs, and when it rained naturally my legs would get wet. But the joy of feeling the good warmth of the wood under the soles of my feet, even though I was soaking wet, is worth any ten of the joys I've known in later life. It's probably because I knew no better in those days.

Another rambling divagation contained in the book is about Russian literature. Here Dostoevsky is praised for his fanaticism, and his willingness to tackle the very greatest subjects in his writing, while Ibsen and Tolstoy are censured for the pseudo-philosophic nature of their writing. He blames 'English philosophy, with its utilitarianism, and its striving after happiness', for the decline in the quality of literature and the creation of dull, practical, 'realistic' works of art. It is this which has produced a school of writers who feel themselves called upon to have opinions on all the social and scientific questions of the day – the Zolas, and even the Strindbergs – and Hamsun bemoans the way in which the public turn them into demi-gods. Even more he regrets the way in which such writers unblushingly take their place on high, 'without a protest, without a smile'.

The book's best joke comes near the end. In the course of a troubled and sleepless night he notices, in his moments of confused wakefulness, that his wife is reading a book. He can't imagine what it is: the whole time they've been away their only reading matter in Russia has been an old copy of a Finnish magazine they took with them. By now he's even read the stock market prices in it. Bergljot asks him, as they are getting up the following morning:

Who's this policeman you keep running into?

Policeman? Aha, so it was my notebook she was amusing herself with in the night! I had mentioned nothing openly about this policeman. I had spared others, and kept the secret to myself: didn't that deserve some kind of gratitude, or appreciation?

You really can't go round telling lies like that, I hear from over by her wall. And I don't believe a word about that ride up into the mountains from Kobi either.

Nor have I mentioned anything openly about this ride, either. I had undertaken that ride on horseback in the name of science; had willingly sacrificed a night's sleep in my efforts to support the Geographical Society, put up with all the hardships involved with silent and stoical heart, that being the way a real travelling explorer behaves.

In any case, continues my travelling companion, In any case I think you write far too much about trivial things.

That does it for Hamsun. The last thing he wants is someone trying to make him doubt his ability to write a good travel book. He strides out of the room in a huff, leaving the reader to wonder just how much of all this really did take place. In the sudden and casual upending of painstakingly created illusions of truth, this is a narrative stunt worthy of Nagel himself. It demonstrates, if demonstration were needed, how difficult it is to know where one is with a man who happens to be a writer whose interest in the truth of his fiction is far greater than his interest in the dully logical distribution of the same truth through a world of fact.

This book, and its satellite (a description of the continuation of the Hamsuns' journey through Turkey entitled *Under the Crescent Moon*), while not of great literary value, are nevertheless interesting self-portraits of Hamsun at this time. What comes over particularly clearly is the open expression of the reactionary tendencies which come increasingly to characterise his public utterances as he struggles and suffers his way into middle-age and beyond. He despises the technological, American-inspired hell of the oil-town Baku, and a disappointment during his midnight visit to the mountain farm at Kobi is the sight of a modern petrol lamp burning there. But the further east he goes, the more he finds to admire:

> The ancient races have left the life of chatter and cackle behind. They smile, and are silent. Maybe it's best that way. The Koran has created an attitude towards life which cannot be debated, or discussed at meetings. The attitude is simply this: happiness is to survive; afterwards things will be better. Fatalism.

Again and again Hamsun expresses this longing for certainty which fatalism provides, 'tried and proven, simple, like iron'. And another expression of the same longing for freedom from personal responsibility and the burden of individual consciousness occurs during one of several outbursts of enthusiasm for the Russian people: 'One obeys a man who is able to command. One obeyed Napoleon with a kind of ecstasy, because obedience is a joy. And the Russian still knows how to obey.' How little he really had seen of the country and the people, and how little understood, with his race-oriented attitudes, is clear from the fact that he makes no mention whatever of the rise of the militant workers' movements in Russia at this time, nor of the frequent outbreaks of rioting that made the industrialised areas around Moscow and Vladimir dangerous for foreigners to travel through.

They were back in Copenhagen by the end of September – the trip to the near-East had lasted no more than a month[7] – and after Christmas returned to Christiania. Then, in April 1900, with no particular warning, Hamsun travelled back home to Nordland, leaving Bergljot behind at her father's house. He went to Hamarøy, and saw his parents again for the first time in twenty-five years. One wonders what they thought of this son of theirs, this celebrated stranger with his aristocratic moustache and his fine clothes. There was a rumour, which Hamsun firmly denied, that he had had to prevent his father using the polite form 'De' (for 'you') in addressing him. The veneer of refinement was thick, but it was still only a veneer.

The trip was another step in Hamsun's efforts to try to keep track of who he really was; eleven years later, when he thought he knew, he would return to Hamarøy to settle. He lived at home with his parents for about a month, and helped with some wall-building and panelling on extensions to the house.[8] But he had also come to work, and presently he set about a project that he had been toying with ever since he finished *Victoria*. In his search for a new and satisfactory literary form he now attempted a verse drama, one of the most demanding of all forms, and already almost obsolete. There was a consistency in this decision: he had all along maintained that Ibsen's finest works were the early verse dramas, and that the realistic prose-plays with which he achieved world fame represented a talent in decline.

When he wanted to get on seriously with the new work Hamsun had to move away to find the necessary peace and quiet. With obvious pleasure, he described his new quarters to the seven-year-old son of his friend Alexander Slotte in Helsinki:

Dear Xavier!
 Now at last I can send you a photograph, as a thank you for the one you sent me last winter. Say hello to Anna Lise, and tell her that any day now she should be getting a photograph of Aunt Bergljot. Xavier, I'm living in such a funny place at the moment. It's a turf hut. There's just one room, with three of the walls dug out of a mound, and with a window and a door in the fourth wall. I live here, because it's so quiet here. It's a good place to work, being so far away from people. A few years ago a piece of the mountain behind the houses here fell down and nearly crushed them; that frightened the people, and they dug this house in the earth where they could come and live if ever things looked dangerous again. And this year there have been many avalanches. When we stand outside and watch them we can feel the wind from the rushing snow so strong on our faces that it nearly knocks us over. Aunt Bergljot is in Christiania, so I am completely alone here . . .[9]

Besides getting on with the play, *Friar Vendt*, he tried to order his still chaotic financial relationship with Langen, an intricate and rather fraught business which was not settled to their mutual satisfaction until December that year.

Towards the close of 1900 Hamsun returned to civilisation. It had been a long time since the success of *Victoria*, and the scholarship and *Simplicissimus* money were long gone by this time. Hamsun felt uneasy about living off Bergljot, and in the spring of 1901 took off again on a gambling expedition to Belgium in hopes of solving his financial problems. He booked in at the Hotel D'Harscamp in Namur and remained there for some weeks, dividing his time between the casino there and another one in nearby Ostend. He gambled heavily and lost heavily and repeatedly. The experience brought out the *Hunger*-hero in him, and in letters to Bergljot he indulged in long flights of blasphemous invective, interspersed with protestations that he had tried prayer, 'not just once, but on my knees, in the middle of the night in the Ostend streets for a month, or was it five weeks – and He heard me the way He hears everyone. Now I spit in His face for the rest of my life. He gave me this mind, it's His responsibility.' Bergljot had to bail out her husband in the end, and send him money to get back home.[10]

The long partings continued. In his own mind Hamsun had clearly decided that the marriage was a terrible mistake, and although the couple now owned a flat at Number 49 Theresesgade in Christiania, from this time on they led largely separate lives. Hamsun hinted at problems in his letter to the Larsens in December 1900, written at five in the morning and asking them to forgive him for not having written for so long:

> Bear with me for one more year, and perhaps things will sort themselves out. I am not trying to seem unusual or 'interesting' here: during the last two years, the last three years, I've been through a crisis. But now, I feel it beginning to resolve itself. Bergljot is at home visiting her father in Christiania.*

He told them how much he enjoyed the freedoms of solitude, staying up all night drinking coffee and cutting himself thick slices of bread, not answering when his doorbell rang. He was drinking heavily, too.

Friar Vendt was finished in June 1902. One of the least known of Hamsun's works, it was intended as the first part of a trilogy depicting the three stages of an individual's relationship to God – rebellion, resignation, and living faith. Its eight acts, interspersed with poems and songs, represent a triumph for Hamsun's will rather than any solution to his search for a new form. It won the awed admiration of the Christiania critics, but was far too long for performance on the stage, and the most concrete results of his

---

* This was one of the last times he was able to address himself to Bolette; she died of a heart attack in 1904, and with her death he lost one of the very few people who, to judge by the freedom with which he wrote to her (and it was really *her* he wrote to, in spite of formally addressing himself to both husband and wife), he trusted absolutely.

arduous labouring over the baroque intricacies of bound form were the several poems and songs sung by one of the characters, Sven Herlufsen, which Hamsun was able to include in a book of poems which he collected and published as *The Wild Choir* in 1904.

There was still a physical side to the Hamsuns' marriage, and some time around the new year of 1902 Bergljot became pregnant. Perhaps they both hoped that it would save the marriage, and that the addition of a child to the family would force Hamsun into the stability and responsibility which he was still so desperately avoiding. But even her pregnancy could not seriously dent his adolescent routines, and with *Friar Vendt* out of the way he was once again to be seen in the Christiania cafés, drinking with his cronies and weaving the stuff of the numerous legends about him which became a part of Norwegian literary mythology.

There are countless anecdotes of his behaviour from this disturbed period of his life. Drinking at the Grand, or the Theatre Café, or the Opplands Café, or in 'The Nook' on the corner of Stortings gate and Rosencrantz gate, he would follow up the wildest ideas that came into his head. Seeing a farmer pass by with a wagon load of hay one day, he ran outside, bought the wagon and load, and went on a pub crawl with it. It was an excellent day's business from the farmer's point of view: when he tired of the fun a few hours later, Hamsun made a present of his own wagon and load back to him. Another story relates how he bought a cow he saw being led past the window of the Grand, wrote a letter to a young lady who was staying up on the first floor, and had the letter delivered to her door wedged between the beast's horns. Many of the stories indicate his prodigious powers of endurance, drinking day and night for days on end. He often found himself alone in the middle of these binges, and would scribble notes to friends like Aanrud summoning them to join him at the Grand. They would almost always come, because they held him in a powerful and slightly awestruck affection. And when they didn't, or when they in turn had fallen by the wayside, he would carry on drinking with anybody who could manage to keep upright. The Danish actor Olaf Fønss relates how he kept pace with him for a couple of days, but in the small hours of one morning had to hand him over to a fat cab-driver they'd picked up somewhere in the course of it all. He watched them from his window, Hamsun sitting bolt upright on the box and the cabby swaying beside him as they rode away.[11] From somewhere or other in the middle of it all a rumour cropped up that he had committed suicide. The newspapers picked up the sensational news and he had to ask the Ritzhaus press agency to send out an official denial.[12] They were strange days for Hamsun.

The debt he owed to Bergljot after his gambling escapade of 1901 was still an embarrassment to Hamsun and accounts for the fact that he published three books in 1903; *In Wonderland*, which he had worked on in the late summer of 1902 at Aas, a play *Queen Tamara*, the theme of which he had picked up while travelling in Russia, and a second collection of short stories, *Brushwood. Stories and Sketches.*

Queen Tamara was written largely on the island of Samsø, a retreat Hamsun had first used when writing *Editor Lynge*. Bjørnson's son Bjørn was the director at the National Theatre when the play was performed in January 1904, and encouraged him in the hope that it would be the popular success Hamsun had written it to be. Full of pageantry and spectacle, and short, and with music specially composed by Johan Halvorsen, it nevertheless ran for only a disappointing twelve performances.

Brushwood was, like the earlier *Siesta*, a mixture of old and new. As *Victoria* demonstrates, Hamsun had the useful power of remaining creatively alive to material over a period of years, and four stories in this collection, including *On Tour* and *A Thorough Rascal* (formerly *Sin*) from 1886, are complete reworkings of old material. Another is a new version of the story *Chance* from 1889, which had led to the accusation of plagiarism against him in 1892. Here also are three stories set in America, and the controversial *The Call of Life* which had caused such a stir in 1896. *A Street Revolution* is a laconic account of some street-rioting Hamsun was caught up in during his stay in Paris, and *A Ghost* is the *locus classicus* of the story of Hamsun's harsh childhood years in the house of his uncle Hans Olsen.

In 1904 came the collection of poems *The Wild Choir*, the earliest of which is probably the *Fever Poem* already mentioned, from 1895, one of the handful of poems which have come to symbolise the collection. Another is the poem written to honour Bjørnson on his seventieth birthday in 1902, another step in Hamsun's gradual progression towards the throne of 'national bard' which the death of Bjørnson would leave vacant. Bjørnson was by now wholly won over by Hamsun, and no sooner had he heard this poem than he rushed to visit Hamsun in hospital, where he was recovering from a minor operation for the removal of piles.

Another well-known poem is the philosophic, fatalistic *In a Hundred Years It Will All Be Forgotten*, while the most notorious is the *Letter to Byron in Heaven*, in which the poet pleads with

Lord Byron to return and reform a society in degeneration, plagued by empty prattle about freedom and the howling of the women's liberation movement, hell-bent on a course of destruction, now that the 'worker scum' have taken control. The most popular poem is *Island Poem*, a beautiful, mystical, pantheistic poem in four verses. The very great human distance between these last two poems illustrates well the fierce polarity of Hamsun's personality; the violent and crude, the gentle and philosophical, horses always straining resolutely in opposite directions at the end of long tethers, with never a move in the direction of harmony or compromise.

Not only is the gentler side of Hamsun the more attractive, it is also beyond all question artistically the greater. Somehow typical of the clumsiness of most of his 'fierce' utterances is the fact that he does not seem to have known that the 'Lord Byron' to whom he directs his pleas for the restoration of aristocratic values was in fact a champion of just that political liberty which he so deplores in his poem. Perhaps it was simply inconceivable to him that a born aristocrat could write battle hymns for the Luddite worker-revolutionaries. No one seems to have noticed the howler until Nordahl Grieg pointed it out in 1936.[13]

However, to keep a sense of perspective on this side of his activities, it is worth pointing out that Hamsun was by no means alone among his contemporaries in his feeling that the times were out of joint, and that the horses, without their riders, were finding out that it is easier to pull downhill than to pull uphill: Strindberg, Garborg for a while, contemporary Danish writers like Helge Rode, Harald Bergstedt, Valdemar Rørdam, and Johannes V. Jensen, one of Hamsun's closest friends at this time, were all of a similar persuasion.

By now Hamsun had gone over permanently to Gyldendal as his Scandinavian publisher, and in 1903 the company's literary director Peter Nansen took the unusual step of directly commissioning a novel from him. This was to be part of a popular series called 'The Northern Library', aimed at a wide market. The commissioned work was to be short, and to avoid controversial scenes and subject matter. It was also to be well paid. In 1903 and 1904 Hamsun received the Houens Scholarship for travel, and used it to commute back and forth between Drøbak, a small town on the fjord south of Christiania which had become popular among artists and businessmen from the capital, and Hornbeck, a tiny town on the northern tip of Zealand, while he worked on *Swarming*. This slight work, finished at Drøbak on 1 June, and published to catch the Christmas book market on 12 December 1904, marks an important transitional stage in Hamsun's authorship.

Utilising narrative techniques and subject matter experimented with earlier in short stories like *Rejersen of the 'Southern Star'* and *Small Town Life*, he produced in *Swarming* a novel in which, for the first time, the hero was not the past-less and mysterious wanderer of the great fiction of the 1890s, and in which the community – a small northern settlement along the lines of Sirilund in *Pan* – is equally the object of the author's interest and attention. There are dozens of characters, and a plot with enough wrinkles and folds and sudden surprises to satisfy the demands of the most resolutely traditional consumers of fiction.

One of the most striking departures from the old style is in the total change of mood; gone is the atmosphere of intense, brooding melancholy; gone the bizarre explosions of inhibited passion; and gone the sense of loneliness, and the mystic pantheism in which the wanderer-hero found his solace and his ecstasy. In its place comes a folksy, ironic cheerfulness, somewhat reminiscent of the atmosphere created by Mark Twain in his descriptions of small-town doings and characters.

There are still recognisable elements from the lyrical style of the earlier books, however: the hero Rolandsen, a telegraphist, is in love with the proud daughter of the local great man, a brother of Ferdinand Mack from Sirilund, Glahn's great enemy in *Pan*, and his struggle to be worthy of her, and win her, makes up the main part of the book. He does become worthy of her, just as Johannes the miller's son in *Victoria* becomes worthy of the eponymous heroine: but whereas Johannes makes his name and fortune by becoming a writer, Ove Rolandsen makes *his* fortune by patenting a new process for making glue from fishes; and in that rude realism lies the whole difference between early- and late-period Hamsun. And apart from occasional reversions to the old style and mood, this is to be the direction of Hamsun's fiction from now on.

His third and last collection of short stories, *Striving Life*, published in May 1905, was a symbolic mixture of the old and the new. Some, like *Blue Man Island* and *Alexander and Leonarda*, are about the passions of youth, and deal with love, murder and suicide. Others, like the long and impressive *Vagabond Days* and *A Win for the Woman*, are set in America, while *Under the Crescent Moon* is an account of the trip to the near East in 1899. Of particular interest is the inclusion of *In the Sweet Summertime*, an account of petty intriguing in a mountain sanatorium which points directly into the future at novels like *The Last Joy* from 1912, and *Chapter the Last* from 1923.

Hamsun was not especially moved by *Swarming*, but he was clearly proud of it as a technical achievement. He realised now that he could, in time, return to the form of the novel without necessarily being condemned to the pathos of becoming an old man stuck with a young man's style, subject matter, and vision. To a writer colleague like Hans Aanrud he could say that he was 'twaddling away at a best-seller',[14] and to Peter Nansen he complained that the limitations on length had spoiled a good novel, regretting particularly that he had to abandon his plans to have the priest's wife seduced in a coming chapter – but he also asked Nansen to read *Swarming* himself:

> It's a cheerful book, and I don't think you will be bored. And not one line of it which is not suitable for family reading at Christmas . . . I notice that Budde has written two books for the series so far – does that mean I will be writing the next one?[15]

The birth of a daughter, Victoria, on 15 August 1902 proved, after all, not to be the salvation of the marriage. Bergljot minded the baby at home at Theresesgade, and Hamsun worked and went his own sweet way. The Bernina, the A Porta, the Dagmar and the Industrikafeen were the favourite haunts when in Copenhagen, and the Grand, Tostrup's and The Nook in Christiania. With a crowd like Sigurd Bøtker, Nils Kjaer, Carl Naerup and Hans Aanrud he would often get drunk and go back to Aanrud's house for late-night card-playing sessions. Another companion was Peter Egge, his friend and protégé from the days in Paris. On their evenings together Egge noticed that Hamsun spoke often of Victoria, but never of Bergljot. Once, after Hamsun had slept the night on Egges' couch, he asked him to come home with him in the morning, and tell his wife where he had spent the night. Egge, still loyal to a man who was his hero, agreed. Bergljot was sitting up in bed, and listened, her face completely expressionless, as Egge explained. Hamsun stood in the far corner of the room, bent over Victoria's cot while Bergljot said nothing whatever, and simply looked at Egge as he fumbled through his story. Her expression he later described as one of resignation, indifference. When he was done[16] Hamsun showed him to the door, and shook his hand.

Some of Hamsun's excesses shocked even himself. From Hornbeck in 1904 he wrote to Hans Aanrud expressing regret over a binge that had lasted for seven weeks, and swore that he would never do it again. 'I just make a pig of myself, and do so many wrong things. After this I'll limit myself to a few days, so that it's still possible to straighten up after. And that's enough about boozing.'

That the marriage was failing must have been an open secret in Christiania literary circles. Hamsun made little effort to hide his indifference. When Albert Langen wrote to him asking for some biographical details Hamsun replied, 'I can't even remember which year I was married in, but you could always write and ask my wife about it.' And in the spring of 1903 the sculptor Gustav Vigeland, who was making a bust of Hamsun, also received surprisingly direct evidence of the state of the marriage. His mistress Inger Sivertsen, who began life as his housekeeper and bookkeeper, tells the story in a short memoir appended to a list of Hamsun's sittings in her appointments book:

> When Hamsun did not come on 15 April, Vigeland was furious. He sent me with a letter to his house in Theresesgade, where his first wife lived. She answered that she had not seen her husband for several days! When he came to the studio on 16 April Vigeland mentioned this to him. Hamsun told him that he used to send a messenger home for his shirts, and change his shirt and tie in the WC at Tostrup's Cellar! – He was an extremely difficult model. Every day a hangover. Sometimes visibly drunk! It's a wonder that there was any bust at all!

And at some point in 1904, while in Denmark on his Houens Scholarship, he committed adultery. In a single reference to the episode, in a letter written in 1909, he said that the experience depressed and humiliated him. He does not name the woman, and says only that 'I cheated no one by it save for myself. It is the most wretched and miserable thing a man can do. No love, no sweetness, just sin.'[17]

Still the marriage struggled on. In the summer of 1905 Hamsun bought land at Drøbak, and organised the building of a house to his own design. He lived locally at Petersen's Hotel so that he could keep an eye on the work.' We have been so terribly alone, Bergljot,' he had written to her once, 'so stupidly, fearfully alone.'[18] And they continued to be alone: while he was in Drøbak, Bergljot stayed in Christiania and studied to become a midwife, a one-year course at what Hamsun described as Midwives University. He joked that it was 'a good job one of us will be an academic'. Victoria stayed in Lillestrøm with one of Bergljot's aunts.

His own early years as a manual labourer had not given Hamsun any great confidence in the honesty and diligence of the average working-man, and he watched his workmen all the time, timing their breaks, and demanding an account of every penny spent: hardly surprising, in view of the colossal sums of money he was now borrowing, both from Langen and from Gyldendal, to finance the work. At last, on 7 December 1905, he paid off the last builder, and the house 'Maurbakken' (the Anthill), was deemed habitable. Perhaps it was this very habitability, the custom-made home inviting at long last a definite statement of their commitment to life as a family, that crystallised for the Hamsuns the undeniable hopelessness of the marriage.

Bergljot was ill, Victoria had bronchitis, their maid had something wrong with her leg and couldn't walk. 'Never get married, Aanrud', said Hamsun in December 1905. He wrote again to his best man on 10 February 1906, praising at length a new book by Aanrud, and concluding: 'As for me, things go as well as can be expected. True enough, "I've got no worse than I deserved". I would like to have spoken to you, but.' And by 2 March he was staying at the Grand in Christiania, and the marriage was over. He sent Langen a short story for his consideration, and added:

Now I have built my lovely house. But just when it was finished, my home and my family broke up. How sad everything is in this world!

By a separation agreement of 20 April 1906, the couple agreed that Bergljot would have Victoria for four more years, during which time the child would spend the summer months with her father. In 1910, Hamsun would assume responsibility for his daughter. In the event of either of them marrying again, the remaining partner was to have the right to insist on the child. Hamsun kept the house at Drøbak, and assumed all responsibility for debts outstanding on it; in addition he promised to pay 130 kroner a month maintenance and rent to Bergljot and Victoria for as long as Bergljot remained unwed.[19]

Why did their marriage fail? In later years, Hamsun said that, even before the wedding, he had realised that he did not really love Bergljot, and that he had asked her to reconsider the relationship, before it was too late. Bergljot would not. She said that as far as she was concerned, there was nothing to consider:

And she said this in a way that made it clear that any move on my part to break the engagement would shed a very poor light on my 'character'. And so we got married. And we were without love – at least, I was. I felt destroyed and defenceless. I went into a depression that lasted four years . . .

was how Hamsun explained it to his second wife in 1909.[20] And he was indeed a man with a strong sense of personal honour. Bergljot had made a divorced woman of herself for his sake; she had suffered with him the fear and scandal of the poison-pen letter campaign, and Hamsun married her, and struggled, in his fashion, to make the marriage work, from a sense of obligation.

To have won Bergljot's heart back in 1895 was perhaps the last stage in the young Hamsun's furious storming of the bastions of class. He had courted and married a dream, a princess. He had even built the castle Maurbakken for her. But part of him knew all along that what he wanted was not an upper-class woman at all. Perhaps to his own surprise, he found that what he really wanted, after years of joking about it, was a woman who would help him find his way back to his roots; a peasant like himself, who could milk cows, and keep house, and raise children with him somewhere far away from the corrupt city. It was hardly Bergljot's fault that she was not this woman.

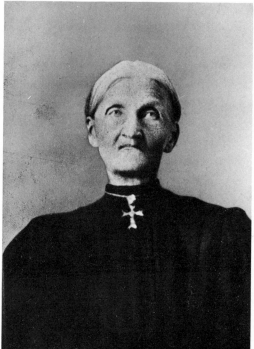

Knut Hamsun's
father, Per Pedersen
(1825-1907). He was a
tailor and
smallholder.

Knut Hamsun's
mother, Tora
Garmostraeet
(1830-1919).

Hamsun's uncle, Hans Olsen. Hamsun lived
with him for five years, between the ages of
nine and fourteen. His harsh treatment was
an enduring influence on the boy. In 1945,
eighty-six years old, he said: 'I still bear the
marks from where he hit me. I was afraid of
him, and went on tiptoe for years.'

The farm at Lom in Gudbrandsdalen in central Norway where Hamsun was born on 4 August 1859.

The house at Hamsund in Nordland where Knut Hamsun spent the happiest days of his childhood before being sent to work for his Uncle Hans in 1868.

Hamsun aged about fifteen, on the right. His sense of style was clearly already well-developed, although he was unable to afford a watch to go with the handsome chain. The photo was taken at Tranøy, in Hamarøy, while Hamsun was working for the 'enevoldskong' Walsøe.

A Confirmation photograph of Hamsun, wearing a suit probably made for him by his father.

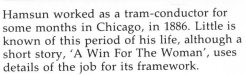

Hamsun worked as a tram-conductor for some months in Chicago, in 1886. Little is known of this period of his life, although a short story, 'A Win For The Woman', uses details of the job for its framework.

Bjørnstjerne Bjørnson (1832-1910), the poet, playwright, and patriot. A shameless and dramatic man, he was Hamsun's greatest idol. As a young man, Hamsun tried to copy his appearance and his gestures, and was not displeased to be sometimes taken for one of Bjørnson's illegitimate sons.

Henrik Ibsen (1828-1906) was the other dominant figure in Norwegian literature during Hamsun's literary adolescence. His vast reputation baffled and irritated Hamsun all his life. He was not the public figure Bjørnson was, and lacked his friend's flamboyant style. Nagel compares the two men in Chapter 13 of *Mysteries.*

August Strindberg (1849-1912). His moustache, his attitude towards women, and his dislike of Ibsen, as well as his attempt to convey in writing the fragmented nature of consciousness, all endeared him to Hamsun. In Paris, in 1894, the two were briefly and disastrously associated with one another.

Chapter 11
1906–1911: The Sage: Retrospection, Introspection and Marie

The end of the marriage came as a relief to Hamsun, though he missed Victoria very much. With a determined energy he turned to his trusted anodyne and in his first year on his own again produced not only the atmospheric and moving novel *Under the Autumn Star*, but also the opening chapters of two further novels – *Rosa*, completed in 1908, and *The Last Joy*, from 1912. He lived at a private hotel in Nordstrand, a pleasant and quiet suburb of Christiania, not far from Ljan where he had lived in the late 1890s.

Under the Autumn Star is a novel of great melancholic beauty, and marks a temporary return to the style Hamsun had used in *Pan*, with a first-person narrative, slow, introspective and dream-like, studded with sudden ecstasies and demonstrating well Hamsun's ability to find the miraculous in the small, the everyday, the overlooked. As in *Hunger* there is no plot to speak of, only the musings and doings of the wandering narrator. He came this time even closer to the genre of autobiography than in the namelessness of his first novel's central figure, and used his own original name for his narrator, Knut Pedersen. And the novel takes its theme and mood from that, a slow and hopeless searching for the man he once was, the peasant and working man he might have been had not ambition derailed him, and driven him to the city.

Through a landscape that is at once a symbolic picture of his own past, and of contemporary Norway, he wanders from farm to farm and job to job, trying to hide his refinement, constantly betraying himself with an educated word or inappropriate blush. Memories of his own past as a roadworker near Gjøvik twenty-five years ago come back to him. He even meets companions from the old days, like Grindhusen; changed men, like himself. With careful pleasure

he describes the kinds of work he does on his wanderings –
bringing running water to a farm, and logging on Captain
Falkenberg's estate. He also describes a saw he has invented which
enables men to fell trees while standing in an upright position, a
saw which Hamsun himself actually invented. 'A master of several
trades' he calls himself; but he knows that he's only playing a
game, and adds rather sadly that 'in my true calling, only my
second-best dreams came true'. He falls in love with the Captain's
wife, a secret love conjured and sustained by glances, accidental
touches, and words and acts with hidden meanings. When she
travels to the city at the end of the story he follows her, hoping
against hope that he can win her; but her courage fails. She gives
him the slip at her hotel, and, as usual, the Hamsun hero is left
with nothing from his experiences but memories.

Like so many of Hamsun's novels, *Under the Autumn Star* cannot
really be described, and seems to disappear between the words
one is trying to use to capture its essence. It is diffuse, with a centre
spread across the whole novel which is really only the personality
of the narrator himself. Reading it gives the curious effect
sometimes of overhearing something intensely private, as though
in opening its pages we suddenly hear a man singing a blues to
comfort himself, or a boy whistling to himself as he walks along a
darkening lane.

In 1907 Hamsun moved to Kongsberg, a town not far to the west
of Christiania, and lived at the Brittania Hotel there. He produced
nothing of note that year, although a lecture in April to the
Christiania students entitled 'Honour the Young' caused an uproar
in the press of a kind he had not experienced since the trouble over
his government scholarship in 1897. In this lecture he maintained
that the fourth commandment was wrong, and should be inverted
– fathers and mothers ought to honour the young. Churchmen and
concerned mothers protested vigorously at this heresy. It was
probably the last *deliberately* provocative outburst from Hamsun –
although by no means the last provocative one – and was mostly a
last, fond two-fingered salute from his own greatly protracted
adolescence. It was also a clear indication that he was determined
to avoid the fate of his own fictional creation Ivar Kareno, softening
and mellowing with age.

In Kongsberg Hamsun continued the process of reflection and
introspection. He did carpentry, and painted pictures.[1] One of
them was a fine primitive study of the view from his window, with
a big pile of logs in the foreground. He walked a great deal, and
was particularly fond of the town's bridge, where he liked to stand
and stare down at the water which boiled and foamed and swirled

as it dropped beneath. He loved the sound, as he had a curious passion for all soughing, seething sounds and derived a kind of ecstasy from listening to it, sleeping in a room that faced the waterfall, with his bedroom windows open.

He was still quite sociable, and sometimes played cards and dominoes with other guests at the hotel. That he was in a stocktaking mood is clear also from the fact that he talked a great deal of his parents to them. In March of 1907 his father died, eighty-two years old, and although they had never been close as individuals Hamsun had found himself coming increasingly to respect the values of toil and endurance that his father had lived by. But it is hard to think that he grieved over the death: he had seen so little of him during his life, as a boy being loaned out in the service of his uncle, and as a young man driven early from home by his own restlessness and ambition. In 1890 he told Bolette Larsen that his parents were in Nordland, 'I think – I know so little about them'. And to a guest at the hotel he said that he never wrote to his father, as he knew that he subscribed to a newspaper, *Norsk Intelligenssedler*, which regularly gave accounts of the whereabouts and state of health of the country's prominent people.[2]

In accordance with the separation agreement, Victoria arrived in the summer of 1908 to stay with her father in Kongsberg. The two of them walking together in the town became a familiar sight. Victoria had a nanny to look after her when Hamsun was working. He had been trying to write a play again, irritated by his failure to master the form, but had abandoned it again in disgust.[3] He made a start on a sequel to *Under the Autumn Star*, *A Wanderer Plays on Muted Strings*, but laid this aside as well. Chronically short of money, there had also been talk of a short season of lectures in Bergen, which came to nothing.[4]

Russia was becoming an ever more important market for Hamsun now.[5] He had begun selling in vast quantities there, as well as becoming a cult figure among young Russian authors; yet the Russians were not signatories to the Berne Convention, and he was receiving nothing for the sales. In order to prevent further pirating of his books, in 1908 he entered into an agreement with the Russian publishing house Znanije giving them exclusive rights to publish him in Russian. Maxim Gorky was Znanije's chief editorial adviser, and as a lifelong admirer of Hamsun it may well have been through his initiative that the arrangement came about.[6] Znanije preferred to get the professional relationship off the ground with a wholly new novel, not the continuation of *Under the Autumn Star*, and so Hamsun produced, in the winter and spring of 1907–08 the novel *Benoni*.[7]

Benoni and its companion novel *Rosa*, written and published later in the same year, are further steps in the direction of the orthodox novel – with modifications – first essayed in *Swarming*. *Benoni* follows the rise to local eminence of the eponymous hero, from postman to businessman, and the theme of dramatically changed fortunes in an individual's life was one which Hamsun would take up again, and more extensively, in his later novels. For obvious reasons it exerted a powerful fascination over him. *Benoni* is, like *Swarming*, charming, folksy and full of sly humour, and is set in a similar north Norwegian milieu, with a large cast of supporting characters. Love as a fatal disease has by now disappeared almost entirely from Hamsun's fiction, and instead of tragic princes his lovers are more clown-like and absurd, though still capable of great tenderness.

Rosa is the princess who was too good for Benoni before he moved up in the world; but by the time of her own novel *Rosa* she is glad to take him, and Benoni glad to marry her. *Rosa* is narrated by a mooning pierrot, the student Parelius who loves the heroine but fails to win her because he is too timid, and as Parelius' love story, it doesn't really come off. Like everything Hamsun wrote, it is full of interesting touches; but Parelius is too boring a person to arouse much emotion in the reader and represents a queer experiment on Hamsun's part to create a first-person narrator who is not subject to the extremism of his own personality.*

These are interesting novels for those who enjoy exploring a writer's literary universe, because Hamsun continued with his habit of introducing characters from his own previous fictions into new works, and shedding further light on their fate beyond the covers of the novel in which they originally appeared. This was something he had done for the first time with characters from *Mysteries* who pop up again in *Editor Lynge*; and characters from *Editor Lynge* who reappear in the *Kareno* plays. In *Editor Lynge* we find out how close *Mysteries'* Dagny Kielland really was to surrendering her heart to the suicidal Nagel, and in *Rosa* we meet Edvarda again, Glahn's lover from *Pan*. Her marriage to the Finnish Baron is over, and she is back living with her father at Sirilund, with her two little daughters. Unhappy and sexually

---

* He had made similar attempts before to write 'out of character'. A short-story from 1895, *Slaves of Love*, is supposed to be from the hand of a woman. The Epilogue to *Pan* is written in a style hardly distinguishable from Glahn's, and yet it is supposed to have been written by Glahn's killer. The novel *Shallow Soil* contains extracts from the work of the poet Øien, presumably for the purpose of satirising or ridiculing them – and yet the style and content bear close resemblances to Hamsun's own.

restless, she is sometimes still overpowered by the memory of Glahn. Munken Vendt, another peripatetic character who appears in *Victoria* as well as the play written about him in 1902, is one of her many lovers. And Hamsun takes pity on her in the end, pity of a kind, anyway – he arranges her engagement to a nobleman – a social superior, even if he does happen to be an Englishman.

A letter Hamsun wrote about *Rosa* to his Russian translator shows the mixture of God-like power and childlike glee he felt about the whole business of inventing people, and time, and worlds. The translator asked him if Munken Vendt was the same character as the protagonist of the verse-play:

> Yes, it's the same person. I needed him. But I've committed several such anachronisms in my books; no one has discussed them, or even mentioned them. What we can do is put at the beginning, instead of 1858, simply: 18—. And I'll also put this in the Norwegian edition to comply with the Russian. By the way, there is no question here of 'mistakes'. I knew quite well what I was doing.[8]

The translator was puzzled by the fact that Munken Vendt would be over one hundred years old by the time he was supposed to be Edvarda's lover in *Rosa*, if Hamsun were following real time in his fictional universe. To be accused of having made a 'mistake' must have been irritating to the artist in Hamsun, whose concern for the exactness and defensibility of his text was complete, even extending to the precise stipulations he made for line length and punctuation in the final printing of his books.

Hamsun had moved back to the city, back to Christiania, by the time he was at work on *Rosa*, living first at Keysers gate 9, and shortly afterwards moving to a room at the top of Dr von Hanno's house, in St Olavs gate 7. In explaining the relative dullness of the novel he once said that in writing it he had never managed to develop a 'real feeling of warmth' for Rosa. One good reason for his inability to do so was that, just as he had begun to write about her, he had fallen wildly and passionately in love with a real woman. Her name was Marie Andersen, born in Elverum in 1881, the daughter of a timber merchant. It is somehow typical of the paradox at the heart of Hamsun's nature that he should have fallen in love with someone who was practitioner of an art and denizen of a milieu for which he had long reserved one of the most passionate and contemptuous of all his prejudices: she was an actress. And as if that were not enough, she was an educated woman who had worked for three years as a schoolteacher before she heard the call to the stage.

In the spring of 1908 plans were afoot for the National Theatre to revive Hamsun's play *The Game of Life* under the direction of Vilhelm Krag. Marie Andersen, who had toured with a company under the leadership of one Dore Lavik before joining the National Theatre, had been told that she would probably be playing the part of Elina Kareno, and Krag had arranged a meeting between actress and author so that she could find out more about the character from Hamsun. She stood waiting for him at the appointed hour, and watched as he came up the theatre steps and walked over to the porter's lodge to ask for her. She went forward and introduced herself. There were many people there as he turned towards her and bowed slightly, but he was so overcome by her that he said aloud 'My God, child, how beautiful you are!' He invited her to go with him to the Theatre Café, a large, fashionable meeting place just over the road from the theatre. Try as she might she could not draw him into any discussion on the role of Elina. On the contrary he dedicated himself to amusing her, plied her with personal questions, and measured hands with her. The following day he sent twenty-six roses to her at the theatre, one for each year of her life.[9] Within a week the pair of them were hopelessly in love, and Hamsun had extracted a promise of marriage from her.

Hamsun was still living at Kongsberg at the time. His daughter Victoria was there, and he had made a start on *Rosa*, and after two weeks in Christiania during which he and Marie met every day, he returned to his obligations at the Brittania Hotel. From here he wrote to Marie daily; dramatic, passionate letters in which wild protestations of love were mixed with a pathological jealousy that fed on the difference in their ages, and on Marie's unresolved relationship with her old boss, Dore Lavik. She and Lavik had lived together for six years and she had taken Lavik's name; to her friends in the theatre world she was known as Marie Lavik.

All of this troubled Hamsun greatly. During the critical early days of his courtship of Marie, Lavik had been away on tour with his company, and although aware of what was happening, he was in no position to do anything about it. Like Hamsun, he was much older than Marie. He still loved her, and wanted their relationship to continue. Shortly after that first meeting at the theatre Marie had fallen seriously ill with nephritis, and was therefore bedridden when, on 15 June, she received the shock news of Lavik's death in hospital in Bergen, where he was being operated on for a stomach complaint. His sudden death filled Marie with a guilty sorrow, and she wept that 'he couldn't live without me'. She put a death-notice in the newspapers, and signed it Fru Marie Lavik. Hamsun would have absolutely none of it. He mocked her 'actress' grief', and told her that her first thought should have been that Lavik's death was the hand of providence, a sign from above that their love was meant to be. 'No, he couldn't live without you', he scoffed, 'Not when he had volvulus'. His immense *amour propre* was wounded by Marie's loyalty to the dead man. Like a detective, he wrote to a friend in Bergen, and asked for details of who had signed the announcements in the newspapers there. Thus Marie was very quickly acquainted with the two sides of the man she had promised to marry; the self-centred martinet fanatically in love with his own pride, and the tender and generous and deeply insecure and lonely man.

The relationship was characterised by extraordinary scenes. At one of their meetings in Christiania, Marie opened her handbag to get a handkerchief, and a letter fell out. In a deceptively mild voice Hamsun asked who the letter was from. It was from one of Marie's young admirers, and to show her indifference to the boy's attentions she ripped the letter up in front of Hamsun. He at once rose, paid the bill, and left. Later in the day a messenger arrived at the theatre and delivered a large envelope to Marie containing all the letters she had sent to Hamsun. She wrote back to him, a contrite letter begging for another meeting, and Hamsun agreed. They walked the streets of the capital, Marie holding on to his arm while Hamsun spoke at length of the corruptions that had been worked on her by her contact with the 'clown's milieu' (his word for the acting world). She realised that he had made a thorough investigation of her past in the grip of his terrible jealousy of her. A youth found their conversation interesting, and followed along behind in order to keep up with it. Without any warning Hamsun turned and struck him. The following day he returned to Kongsberg and sent his own letter of passionate contrition to Marie:

Darling, I am writing these words standing in the light of a lamp in the corridor in order to get this letter off to you straight away. When I left you today I was full of faith in you again, please believe me. Because you ignored your own wounded pride and came to me to make us both better again I love you and I thank you, Marie. My journey home was in a kind of ecstasy; I thought about everything, I have so much to ask for forgiveness for, and I sat and closed my eyes and begged you to forgive me. . . . I thank you on my knees because your heart was so great and warm and rich that you came to me and made us both well again. I will never forget it as long as I live. God above how happy you have made me. Just to be allowed to sit by you and take your hand and look at you is a joy greater than any I have ever known before. These are just poor, stupid words, maybe I'll be able to express myself better tomorrow. Even then they would only be the same wretched words. But as time goes by you will find out how much I love you, now and forever. Thank you, thank you for all the sweetness you have brought into my life. Remember that I will never be the one who leaves you, believe me. Please let me be yours, I beg you from the depths of my heart. Goodnight, my sweet.

Other letters during their courtship year – a necessary wait while Hamsun's divorce came through – constitute a sustained assault on Marie's personality which Hamsun was intent on remoulding nearer to his heart's desire. He asked her, politely, if she would mind very much no longer greeting certain people – certain actors and actresses – of whom he did not approve. He rebuked her for laughing at the jokes of a man he did not like. When she sent him photographs of herself he thanked her warmly, but advised her not to smile in photographs any more – this was all just a falseness cooked up between comedians and photographers. From the start he acquainted her with his horror of the city and its culture, and his determined longing to get away from it all and lead a life away from people, back on the land. Many times he asked her to give up acting, begged and threatened her to give it up, and go and live alone with him in the country. His own idea seems to have been that he had arisen in her life in order to save her from herself – she was still young enough, in his opinion, to be spared the corruptions he had been seduced into by city life, in spite of her acting years in what he called, among other choice phrases, 'the company of rats'.

But in among all this unappealing fanaticism there runs always that other song in these letters; sudden devastating admissions of loneliness and insecurity and need, lovely little compliments, and vast, passionate compliments, dreams, and more dreams, and touches of his charming humour. 'I know I am loving for the last time', he wrote, and told her of the jealousy he felt each time they were out together and a young man looked at her. Like Knut Pedersen in the *Wanderer* books he described himself to her as old, white-haired – even withered – which was all absolute nonsense. His hair was greying slightly round the ears, and he had a touch of deafness, but these were all the signs of age that Marie noticed. There were times during their courtship when she despaired of her ability to put up with his hysterical passions, and at one point, in a desperate attempt to escape her destiny, she even applied for the post of governess in the remote north of Norway. She got the job, and meant to go, but just a few moments' exposure to Hamsun's love and his charm were enough to dissolve that particular dream. Hamsun's iron will had decreed that he and Marie must marry: now there would be an end once and for all to the young man's life, rootless, wandering, irresponsible. The two of them must go back to the land, from whence they sprang; become peasants again, till the earth and raise a family far from the sick culture of civilisation and progress. And, of course, write books.

Hamsun was the one, to his own surprise, who was insisting that they make their union legal; Marie, with her 'rat's' morality, would have been happy for them merely to have lived together. The idea of marrying Hamsun must have frightened her. She had given up a whole career for him – what was she to do with her own ambition and her own talent? But she loved him, and he pressed and pressed her. A comment in one of his letters about marriage throws a great deal of incidental light on the fate of characters like Glahn and Nagel, Johannes and Victoria, and their lesser-known brothers and sisters who inhabit some of his short-stories:

. . . in any case, it seems upside-down to me that I am the one who is advocating marriage here, I who have had the theory for a long, long time now, and have advanced it both in writing and in speech, that marriage is the death of love.[10]

For Hamsun to have courted and married Marie must be accounted a tremendous triumph over himself. He was not good at being intimate, and was deeply afraid of falling in love. Like Strindberg, he felt keenly that it was a position of defencelessness, a fatal stage in the war between men and women which only the practice of an eternally vigilant dominance could prevent from becoming total disaster. Olaf Fønss, a drinking companion of Hamsun's from the wild days just before the break-up of his first marriage, wrote that he was 'always in love, and strangely enough, always unsuccessfully', and the legends of Hamsun as a lady-killer seem based largely on a number of grand, public gestures towards women.

When it came to the point, he was not a promiscuous man, and not a man who took love lightly. Always afraid of rejection and loss, his love for Marie and his need for her were so great that he drove onwards and beat his fears aside until he had won her. They were married at the Register Office in Christiania on 25 June 1909. Both had hoped for a church wedding, but their application was rejected on account of Hamsun's divorce, a rejection which caused him to leave the state church. And for all the ups and downs of their marriage, the two were well-suited to each other. Both, in their own way, were actors.

They had a short honeymoon at Lier before Hamsun, on 5 July, sent Marie off to stay with a sister at Drammen while he travelled to a place called Sollien where, as the summer before, Victoria was waiting for him with her nanny. Here he divided his time between entertaining his daughter, and carrying on with writing the sequel to *Under the Autumn Star* which he had set aside in 1907 for *Benoni* and *Rosa*. This was *A Wanderer Plays on Muted Strings*, another long, slow look at the process of ageing. Here Pedersen revisits the scene of the earlier novel after an interval of six years, lightly and unconvincingly disguised in a beard in order to hide his identity from Captain and Fru Falkenberg, on whose farm he again works, still wrestling with refinement, still sometimes forgetting his role:

> I had forgotten my cart-horse role, my shoes were too light. I had been corrupted by the refinements of many years, I must take a refresher course in being a peasant.

Marie Hamsun, in her book *The Rainbow*, wrote that she never failed to be surprised by the lack of apparent correspondence between the books her husband was writing, and the man he was and the life he was living at the time of writing them. Here the passionate and young fifty-year-old man she had just married writes with the mental detachment of some ancient sage of his profound indifference to life, his resignation to a future of memories, and the role of spectator at the drama of other people's lives which does not really penetrate the dim loneliness of his own old age. Eccentrically, as in the earlier *Kareno* plays, Hamsun placed the onset of emotional and intellectual impotence at fifty. Perhaps the pose was necessary for him in order to make the numerous limpid and beautifully 'wise' observations with which the book is studded:

> There's a large theatrical element in us all; we feel flattered at being taken for more than we are.

> How hard it is to judge people correctly, who is mad and who is wise. And may God preserve us all from being seen through.

> In old age we no longer live our lives, we merely keep on our feet with the aid of memories.

Pedersen is still in love with the Captain's wife, Fru Falkenberg. In fact, he is in love with the Captain as well, their way of life and everything they represent, and the decline observable in them after his six year absence pains him. The couple hold wild parties in their fine old house. Both have lovers, both wish somehow that their lives were not so, but seem unable to change anything. Fru Falkenberg has taken a young lover, a modern man, a technocrat and engineer whose large behind is only one of many signs that the author detests the way he is using the mistress of the house. The Falkenbergs almost manage to rescue their marriage; but when the Captain discovers that his wife is pregnant by the engineer he finds that he cannot take her back. Nor will the young engineer have her, and she takes her own life in the river. Hamsun makes quite clear what he takes to be the real cause of the failure of this marriage between a couple who at heart love one another: their failure to have children.

On a second level the novel is an extended commentary on the state of a Norwegian social and economic order breaking up after centuries of stability, under the irresistible pressures of industrialisation. The old patriarchs, the patrons and work-givers like Captain Falkenberg, are a class in an advanced state of decay. The flag-pole on the farm, the farm buildings themselves are shabby and worn and neglected. In an effort to alert the Captain into action Pedersen paints the house for him. And along with the farm-hand Nils he keeps the farm going, operating behind the scenes like a kind of benevolent providence, encouraging the Captain to get a grip on himself, realise what is happening and resume control of his own destiny.

Hamsun had been taking an increasingly 'responsible' interest in the progress of Norway since the declaration of independence from Sweden in 1905 and its birth as an independent nation. So much of what he saw horrified him: the coming of industry, the flight from the land, the rise of the city, the rise of organised labour and the decline of the old master. He looked uneasily at the agitation by the always advanced women's movement in the country for the social privileges traditionally reserved for men and to Marie's dismay hammered out his own aggressively unimproved opinion of women in the novel:

As for woman, she was what all wise men have always known her to be: a pauper in talents, but rich in irresponsibility, in vanity, in wantonness; with much of the child, but nothing of its innocence.

But Hamsun, in the role of Knut Pedersen, refugee from the city, and decrepit fifty-year-old sage struggling in the role of peasant, amused as much by his own pretensions as by his lack of them, knew that his protests were hopeless, and was content to withdraw from life with a lovely message of thanks to God as his final word:

It is wrong of a captain to ask God to forgive him – as he forgives God. He is simply dramatising. A wanderer who doesn't each day find food and drink, clothes and shoes, house and home provided, according to his needs, feels just the right degree of privation when all these splendours are absent. If one thing doesn't work out, another will. And if that other fails to work out also, he does not go around forgiving God but takes the responsibility himself. He puts his shoulder to the wheel of fortune – that is to say, he bows his back before it. It's a trifle hard on flesh and blood, it greys the hair horribly; but a wanderer thanks God for life, it was fun to live!

I might put it like that.

Why, in short, all these exacting demands? What have we earned? As many boxes of sweets as a sweet tooth could desire? Fair enough. But have we not looked on the world each day and heard the soughing of the forest? There is no splendour like the soughing of the forest.

There was a scent of jasmine in a grove, and a tremor of joy ran through one I know, not for the jasmine but for everything – a lit-up window, a memory, the whole of life. But when he was called away from the grove, he had already been paid in advance for this annoyance.

And there it is: the very favour of receiving life at all is handsome advance payment for all life's miseries, each single one.

This side of Hamsun, the lyrical, melancholic man, the emotional man still willing to affirm life in spite of all its disappointments – indeed, *because* of its disappointments – is the most attractive of all his many sides. These are indeed the words of a great master of life, a sage. Yet this kind of serene detachment only seemed possible for Hamsun in the still world between the covers of a book. Outside, in the real world, he became increasingly engaged in a struggle to hold back the tide of progress.

A Wanderer Plays on Muted Strings gives us our first sight, attractively blurred, of Hamsun at the start of his disastrous career as a patriot. All of his novels from this point on carry in varying

.

degrees of prominence a political message; namely that what passes for 'progress' in the modern world is in actual fact a failed and pretentious experiment which, by distancing ordinary people from their roots in the land, corrupts them. Sometimes, as in *The Growth of the Soil* from 1917, he tries to paint an attractive and heroic picture of the simple life lived close to the soil; but being a man who vastly enjoyed exercising his irritations, he wrote more frequently about the corruptions that progress brought with it. Why Hamsun came to feel that he had to write with a message for his readers is important for an understanding of his eventual fate, and can to some extent be explained by the political situation in Norway around the turn of the century, and the unique status writers had acquired in the land by that time.

For almost 500 years, until 1814, Norway had been a minor partner in a union under the Danish crown, administered from Copenhagen, in Danish interests, by Danish civil servants, in Danish. Norwegian national and cultural identity went underground. A change occurred in 1814, when the King of Denmark–Norway was forced under the terms of the Treaty of Kiel to cede Norway to Sweden. This new union, which lasted almost one hundred years, was characterised from the start by a powerful revival of nationalism in Norway. The outstanding figure of this romantic and passionate nationalism was the writer Henrik Wergeland (1808–45) who in his person came to symbolise the longing for an independent Norway. His spiritual heir was Bjørnstjerne Bjørnson, Hamsun's first and greatest idol. Bjørnson's tales of Norwegian peasant life were major contributions in restoring dignity and authority to the Norwegian language; additionally he was a natural public man, a great orator with a massive self-confidence. Norway had no native aristocracy – the national assembly had voted for the abolition of the nobility in 1821 – and this explains the unusual prominence writers had during the nineteenth century. In effect, in the mounting clamour for complete national independence, they assumed the mantle of an aristocracy. And by the time Hamsun was a young and impressionable man in the 1870s and '80s, Bjørnson, Kielland, Lie and Ibsen were widely accepted by government and people alike as a kind of collective conscience of the nation.

In the 1890s the political crisis arose which brought about the final break with Sweden. The Norwegians claimed that their interests were now sufficiently distinct from Sweden's for them to have their own Norwegian foreign minister to handle them. The Swedes disagreed. The crisis went through a number of stages, coming close to war on two occasions, before it was resolved in

1905 under an agreement whereby the Norwegians received full independent nationhood. A plebiscite on 13 August 1905 had confirmed that this was indeed the wish of the majority of the Norwegian people – the voting was 368,208 in favour, 184 against. Not one of the voters was a woman.

Hamsun played an active part in the struggle for independence. He was from its earliest days wholly in favour of the idea of the independent consular service, and beyond that, in favour of full national independence.* His 'clenched fist' novel *Editor Lynge* from 1893 was, according to him, written chiefly to punish the editor of the radical newspaper *Verdens Gang* for following a self- seeking and vacillating line on the question of full independence. He contributed patriotic poems to a political magazine *Strax* published by his friends, including a paean to the Norwegian military commander Oberst Stang. Stang was commander of the Norwegian frontier fortress at Oscarsborg, not far from Drøbak where Hamsun was then living and building his house 'Maur-bakken', and Hamsun enrolled as a volunteer rifleman under him.

Hamsun's visible patriotism did him no harm at all in the eyes of the social establishment which had never quite got over their suspicions of him. And as, after a while, his constant praising of Bjørnson began to be reciprocated by the older man, the curious possibility began to arise of the fierce and rebellious Hamsun actually being next in line for the crown of literary conscience of Norway. Apart from publicly praising Hamsun as a writer in 1896, and supporting him in the scandal over the state scholarship in 1897, Bjørnson had expressed particular delight over Hamsun's poem, written to honour him on his seventieth birthday in 1902. But the following year this smooth flow towards the handover of power received a severe jolt when Bjørnson suddenly began changing his signals about the independence issue, and counsell-ing caution and a conditional independence. Hamsun was not alone in thinking that this coincided rather nicely with the award to Bjørnson of the Nobel Prize for Literature in 1903. He was appalled to read accounts of his hero shaking hands with the Swedish King, and receiving the large cheque for the prize money. In a letter to his publisher Peter Nansen of Gyldendal he wrote:

* 'I want our own foreign minister and our own King', Hamsun wrote to the Larsens in 1893. 'We need our own King, or Norway will simply become a wretched republic, a spartan and penny-pinching republic.' The same letter contains one of his few positive remarks about the English; he praises them for being – in spite of their liberation and radicalism – 'monarchist from top to toe'. He adds that 'there is nothing finer than the sight of the Prince of Wales parading through the streets while the crowds cheer him.'[11]

That swine went over to the Swedes in his seventy-first year for 140,000 kroner. I could have done it, or his children, because they're only little Bjørnsonettes anyway – but not him. He owes a debt of responsibility to his whole past life.[12]

His outrageous poem *Letter to Byron in Heaven* was intended as a direct provocation to Bjørnson, and he looked forward to a fight if Bjørnson criticised it publicly.[13] He felt that Bjørnson was living out the fate of his creation Ivar Kareno, betraying in opportunist old age the principles of a lifetime, and Hamsun went on to attack him bitterly in newspaper articles of characteristic ferocity. 'You have become old, master. If only you had not become old', he wrote contemptuously, complaining that: 'Age thinks it becomes wiser and wiser; but the truth is that Age becomes more and more stupid.'[14]

The break was only temporary, however. He was back in Bjørnson's corner again in 1908. On 17 June he addressed a crowd from the balcony of the National Theatre on the occasion of the centenary of Henrik Wergeland's birth, and hailed Wergeland's successor Bjørnson, calling him the giant of Norwegian spiritual life and proclaiming him the glorious multiplication of all his predecessors. Bjørnson meanwhile, addressing a gathering at Fredrikstad, described Hamsun as the greatest living Norwegian poet and an altogether magnificent chap. The spiritual triumvirate of Wergeland–Bjørnson–Hamsun once again suggested itself as a distinct possibility in the national consciousness.

Hamsun's journalism, moreover, was now of an increasingly 'responsible' kind. 'Country Culture', a long newspaper article from 1908 in the form of an open letter to his Danish friend Johannes V. Jensen, took and discussed seriously Jensen's proposition that all of modern civilisation, from Newton and George Stephenson to Darwin and Edison, derives wholly from the nature-inspired imagination of the countryman. He took issue with what he saw as Jensen's romanticism of the cultural achievements of country people, and pointed out that his own cultural achievements were rather a product of his having left the country and gone to the city; however, he did not in his reply to Jensen give any direct indication of his own growing conviction that the fruits of his journey had been bitter. That was to come later.[15]

In a newspaper article from 1910, 'Theologian in Wonderland', Hamsun appeared as a champion of the north, and encouraged priests to stop regarding a posting to the north of Norway as the spiritual equivalent of being sent to Siberia. He described the beauties of the landscape to them, and tried to persuade them to

see God in the hard mountains and the mystic glory of the northern
lights.[16]

And later in the same year he wrote 'A Word to Us'[17] in which
he directly addressed himself to the whole of the Norwegian
people. His target was the growing and harmful effect of tourism
on Norway:

> We have turned our country into a ridiculous and meaningless
> Switzerland. We've turned the whole place into one enormous
> hotel for foreigners.*

Farmers sell their farms and start hotels. The peasant abandons his
fields to earn money acting as a guide for rich tourists. Father and
son race one another to open the gate for these same tourists, and
hold out their hands for their shilling afterwards. Hamsun found
shame and disgrace in this, and the concluding lines of his appeal
were unequivocal:

> A word to us:
> We've got to get our hands out of our pockets and start work
> again. In so doing we will avoid becoming an entire nation of
> hoteliers and waiters.
> We must drain the moors, plant trees, colonise the great
> Nordland. And in doing that we'll put an end to the emigrating.
> We must cultivate Norway's soil.
> And this is what we should write about in the papers. The rest of
> the stuff isn't worth a telegram. It's just passing whisps of
> tourism, and Americanism. And then the peasant can go back to
> work, and the valleys will be quiet once more.

Tourism in Norway, though confined to the summer months,
provided a much-needed extra source of income in many districts
like the western fjords where the possibilities for making a living
were otherwise very limited. Hamsun's was very much a luxury
gospel, though nevertheless sincerely meant, as Hamsun's own

---

* Switzerland was another of Hamsun's idiosyncratic prejudices. Three of his
novels, *A Wanderer Plays on Muted Strings*, *The Last Joy* and *Chapter the Last*,
contain disparaging references to the country and its people. As early as 1893 he
called the country 'culturally dead, if we except a saga-hero, a religious fanatic and
a few clock-makers'; and as late as 1922 he was still defending the prejudice in a
newspaper article. Most unfairly, he claimed that Arnold Böcklin, whom he
admired, was not 'really' Swiss. Switzerland with its large tourist industry always
epitomised for Hamsun the worst fate that could befall a small country and he
was desperately anxious for Norway to avoid a similar fate.

private life and his later fiction amply demonstrate. The article was also intended as a first spreading of his wings as the undisputed conscience of his people just three months after the death of Bjørnson, on 26 April 1910, in Paris. Hamsun cried when he was told the news. 'I feel we've become so alone', he told Marie.[18] The newspapers came to him for their tributes, and his poem on the death of Bjørnson is a classic state poem of the kind of innocent grandeur that no one would dare attempt in our day. In effect he assumed the role of Poet Laureate here. Some three months later the mantle was officially conferred on him by popular choice during the extensive newspaper celebrations of his fiftieth birthday. Some might say it was forcibly tied round his neck. The word 'fører' (leader) was applied to him in many of the celebratory articles. In a letter of thanks in the columns of *Verdens Gang* Hamsun referred to the '47 letters and 114 telegrams, in addition to books, paintings, flowers, press-cuttings, and a lock of golden hair from a child', which he had received in honour of the occasion.[19] Poems were written in praise of him. A feature of the tributes were the references to his rebellious early years: all was now forgiven; all was now understood. The patriotic tone of the celebrations was best caught by a poem in a local newspaper in which the poet asked, on behalf of a people still grieving for Bjørnson – Who will now take care of us? Who can now act as Norway's interpreter? Who will now reveal his spirit to Norway? And by the fifth verse he has answered his own questions: after travelling round the mountains and valleys, the questions have returned with the glad news that the saviour lives, that he will raise the people to the heights of spiritual glory, that the fatherland swells again, because Norway's future is his – Hamsun's – future.[20]

Not all contemporary journalism, however, greeted the new leader with equally simplistic fervour. One astute writer prophesied that Hamsun would probably make a strange leader, 'and not merely because one can never feel quite sure that one fine day the rebel in him won't kick the legs from under the whole business'.[21]

The Norwegian King, Håkon VII, through the Prime Minister, Konow, was prepared to offer Hamsun membership of the Order of St Olaf in honour of his half-century; but when the matter was raised with him Hamsun made it clear that he would on no account accept the decoration. He explained rather piously to Marie that it would be 'too hypocritical' of him. He may have been thinking that to accept would be to compromise the fierce independence of which he was justifiably proud. Another possibility is that he actually felt rather sheepish about the offer, because he was not in fact fifty at all in 1910, but fifty-one. Back in 1891 he had suddenly decided to lop one year off his age, and began telling people that he was born in 1860, not 1859.[22] Perhaps he had thought that his success at reinventing himself under a new name needed a new age to make it complete. For occasions when it mattered, however, such as filling in his personal particulars in the church book for his wedding to Bergljot in 1898, he remembered the correct date well enough. When challenged over the matter by a journalist in 1910, he published a pained admission of the truth in the press:

> I don't really know how I'm going to get out of this. I've heard of women who've lied themselves free of a few years, but in the first place I'm no woman, and in the second place, one year wouldn't be much use to me – I would need at least five before it made any difference to my age now. Because I am fifty-one.[23]

All the somewhat hysterical searching for a 'great man' which the press reaction to Hamsun's birthday revealed was in part a panic reaction, not only to Bjørnson's death, but to the deaths, within five years, of all of Norway's great men: Ibsen and Kielland died in 1906; Edvard Grieg in 1907; Jonas Lie in 1908, and Bjørnson two years later. Norway had a figurehead – the new King Håkon VII – but he had been voted in from the Danish royal family as part of the independence arrangements of 1905, and in five years had had little chance to make an impact on his people. Hamsun's reaction to Bjørnson's death, the sudden feeling of loneliness, was undoubtedly shared by a great many Norwegians – and in looking around to find a new focus for their patriotism they turned not to the King, but to Hamsun. Bjørnson, after all, had on a number of occasions publicly hinted that Hamsun was his spiritual heir.

Hamsun was an impressionable man, and despite his great psychological complexity, in many curious ways a simple man. He was also extremely vain, and in spite of the considerable struggle the ironist in him must have put up to protect himself from the 'great man' circus – something which he'd mocked so acutely in *Mysteries* – the fate that now came his way as the 'future of Norway' was something he found very hard to resist. The sombre authoritarian journalism of the succeeding decades, his political stance during the 1930s and his behaviour during the war may all be related to the quasi-official establishment of a relationship between a great writer and his public that occurred in 1910.

Hamsun was now earning considerable amounts of money from his writing, thanks largely to his success in Russia and Germany.

Between 1907 and 1910 three separate Russian publishing houses brought out editions of his *Collected Works*.[24] And the same years saw the appearance of the first of many such editions from Gyldendal, who had by now established an exclusively Norwegian branch of the company in Christiania. But he was keeping three families – Bergljot and Victoria, his widowed mother in Hamarøy, himself and Marie – and felt the pressures of money constantly. This was probably one of the main reasons for writing what turned out to be his last stage-play, *In the Grip of Life*. He finished it in May 1910 at Sollien, where he and Marie had rented a house, and the couple worked together on the dirty business of hectographing two copies of the play for simultaneous translation into Russian and German. And to prevent any piracy, Hamsun used the pseudonym Menz Føyen on the Russian editions.

In the Grip of Life was to become by far the most successful of his plays, artistically and financially. The première was in Christiania on 16 November 1910, and within five years it also had successful runs in Düsseldorf, Munich, Berlin, and at the Moscow Arts Theatre, where both *The Game of Life* and *At the Gates of the Kingdom* had already been performed under the direction of Stanislavsky. The Moscow Arts Theatre retained a fondness for the play, and revived it in 1932, and it has also been successfully revived at intervals throughout the century in Germany and Scandinavia. The play traces the twilight of the career of a once beautiful music-hall singer Juliane, now growing old with an attractively graceless passion. She betrays her rich old husband with a nasty young man, Alexander Blumenschøn, a man with a professional interest in antiques, only to lose him to a younger woman. Her downward spiral hurls her at the close of the play into the arms of an eighteen-year-old black servant, 'Boy'; not quite the unthinkable tragedy today perhaps that it was in 1910. As in Hamsun's other plays the strength is in the dialogue, and the weakness in the plot. There are also too many major characters for a theatre audience to digest, and Hamsun's adherence to the psychological truth of his characters makes them furthermore all too resolutely unusual. Yet the attempt to think dramatically and visually left a mark on his narrative technique as a novelist, and many of his later novels contain dialogue laid out almost in the form of a playscript, with the name of the speaker, a colon, and some parenthetical comment on the delivery of the spoken words that follow.

Besides Sollien, where *In the Grip of Life* was written, the Hamsuns also lived briefly at Elverum and Koppang. They considered settling at Elverum, where Marie had lived as a child, and rented a house into which they moved all the fine Regency furniture they had been buying and storing in Christiania since their wedding. But for some years now the idea of going back to his own old home in Hamarøy, and settling there for good, had been in Hamsun's mind. During his stay there in the spring of 1900 he had tried unsuccessfully to buy back the family farm from the present owner,[25] and since 1908 he had been in touch by letter with his boyhood friend Georg Olsen, who had stayed at home and become an important man in Hamarøy – steamship agent, postmaster, farmer, and owner of a small lodging house. Georg was to inform him when a suitable property came on the market. At the end of February he wrote to tell Hamsun that the farmhouse and farm 'Skogheim' were for sale, and that he thought it was exactly the sort of place the Hamsuns were looking for. The couple travelled north immediately, by train to Trondheim, coastal ferry to Bodø, then by the district steamboat to Presteide. They stayed the night at Georg Olsen's lodging house in Skautnes, and went with him the next day to look at Skogheim.

This was early in March, with the snow still thick on the ground, the fjord frozen, and the jagged Hamarøy peaks still swathed in arctic darkness most of the day and night. The house was in the centre of the settlement at Opeide, just an hour's walk from the isolated farm at Hamsund where the boy Pedersen had spent those five happy years between the move north from Gudbrandsdal in 1863, and 1868, when he was sent to live with his uncle. The River Glimma, which had once or twice tempted him with the prospect of a permanent release from the wretched bondage of his life with Hans Olsen, ran out into the sea at the foot of Skogheim's land. Ten minutes' walk away, in the direction of Presteid, was the cemetery where as a boy he had 'wandered between the crosses and the gravestones, dreaming and thinking and talking out loud to myself', as he wrote in his short story *A Ghost*. How much it must have meant to him to go back there, and to amaze all his old friends, and all the people who remembered him! To have wandered away from home at the age of fourteen with nothing but sharp wits in pursuit of the single dream of literary success, and be returning now a world-famous writer, rich, with a beautiful young wife; and to buy a big white farm right in the middle of the village, right by the main thoroughfare.

Maybe it seemed to people as though he had proved that it really could be done. A man – any man – could go out into the world, just put his faith in himself and God and pretend to be afraid of nothing at all. Go to America twice; come back a failure both times, and still not be beaten. Go to France and Germany, and Copenhagen and

Christiania; go to the heart of the city and plunder an education and make it his own; and then write books that gave back more than he could ever have plundered in the course of ten such lifetimes. And then come home again undestroyed, uncorrupted, having forgotten nothing, with his heart as simple and true as ever. Hamsun had done it. He was a King – it said so in the papers. He had gone all the way and back, and made a fairy-tale come true. They bought Skogheim the same day that they looked at it, for 6000 kroner.

Knut Gulliver Hamsun fylder femti!

Th. Krag   Nærup   S. B.   Tryggve Andersen
Kjær Wildenvey   Falkberget

Hamsun, Norges „Storegut“,
vi ser som Gjest i „Lilleput“.

A cartoon from 1910 celebrating Hamsun's fiftieth birthday. In fact, he was fifty-one, having knocked a year off his age in 1890. The Lilliputians attending him are contemporary Norwegian writers. The cartoon shows clearly the way in which certain sections of the Norwegian press idolised Hamsun and, with ultimately disastrous results, urged him to accept a role as national spokesman left vacant by the death of Bjørnstjerne Bjørnson.

Chapter 12

1911–1918: Marriage and the Return
to the Roots: The *Segelfoss* Books and
The Growth Of The Soil

Marie stayed behind in Elverum to organise the packing while
Hamsun travelled on ahead and began painting and decorating the
new house, measuring the rooms, ordering carpeting and wall-
paper, and new beams for the roof. They were each to have their
own bedroom, a lifelong practice that Hamsun insisted upon
because he often woke in the middle of the night with ideas that
had to be written down. He consulted his wife by letter about what
colour she thought best for his room:

> I've got wallpaper for the living room (if nine rolls are enough),
> the dining room and my room and your bedroom (a lovely red);
> but I can't find anything for my bedroom. I don't need much,
> since I want to extend your bedroom at the expense of mine, but
> I'd like to have it a decent colour. That yellow, for example, what
> do you think of that? It should be different from yours, which is
> red. We've got green in the dining room and my room, so maybe
> something yellow, or blue?

Soon after, Marie arrived with the clocks and the piano and the
paintings, and they settled in properly and began farming. They
took over the previous owner's three cows, and bought a fourth
from Hamsun's brother Ole, still living in the village and now
married with a family and working as a shoemaker. The cows were
rather disappointing milkers, but the Hamsuns liked them. They
also kept a piglet for fattening for the traditional Norwegian
Christmas pork, and sowed turnips, carrots and potatoes.
Hamsun made tentative enquiries about the possibility of buying a
cheap, second-hand car – he had hired one in Belgium in 1901 and

been much impressed – but the offers he got from the Christiania dealer were all too dear, and in the end they settled for a horse, and got friends in Christiania to buy a trap for them and ship it up north.

There was something of Benoni in Hamsun's childlike wish to return to his first home a 'great man', but the Hamarøy he returned to now was a much-changed place. His father was dead, and his mother now old, and very deaf. Hans Olsen had died in 1890, and his house, the house in which Hamsun had begun to learn about the harshness of the world, was pulled down in 1914.* Most of his childhood friends were either dead or had emigrated to the city or to America. Georg Olsen was still there, of course, and he often visited his favourite brother – Ole the shoemaker, who was modest, hard-working, stoical, asking little of life, and not being disappointed. Perhaps he found in his elder brother those qualities he had learnt to set store by in his father, and saw there an attractive contrast to his own ambitiousness and restlessness. Ole would need to be stoical too: he and his wife Stine had lost all their five children through tuberculosis.

The Hamsuns revelled in the physical challenge of taking the rather neglected small-holding and turning it into a model farm. Their land faced the sun, and lay on a slope down to the river, so that the snow ran quickly away. They saw now for the first time how uneven and rock-strewn the holding was, and with the help of some local hired hands set about the task of levelling the land. The feeling in the community generally seems to have been an expectation that the pair would make a mess of the undertaking, but the industry and efficiency with which they set about building up the farm quickly silenced the doubters.[1] As for the local working class, the Hamsuns developed a rather uneasy relationship with them. Hamsun perhaps hoped that in a small way he could play the role of 'matador', like Zahl of Kjerringøy, or Walsøe at Tranøy, but the day-labourers who worked for him at Skogheim were of a generation that was unwilling to cast itself in the role of serfs under a patriarch. Hamsun understood this well enough, and tried to handle his workers diplomatically; but the failure of the old ways was a source of the most profound regret to him, and was to provide a major theme for the fiction that he produced while living at Hamarøy. One local whom he got along splendidly with was an eccentric old wood-cutter and odd-job man, Marcelius Mollehaugen. The two of them used to sit and talk together for hours.

Buying and salvaging Skogheim had used up all the money the

* Oddly enough, Hamsun made an offer for it, but he was outbid, much to Marie's relief.

couple had. Indeed, Hamsun had now several large debts outstanding, including one of 10,000 kroner to Gyldendal.[2] From the very outset of his literary career he had lived beyond his means with a reckless confidence that he could write his way out of debt, and far beyond. 'A man lives *for* what he lives *from*', he had said in Sweden in 1893,[3] confirming a remark made at the beginning of his arduous lecture tour of 1891, that the only way to live was to 'earn one's bread in the sweat of one's brow'. Success and acclaim had not weakened this hard and proud attitude, and now he set about writing himself solvent again.

The novel he worked on was *The Last Joy*, nominally the last part of the *Wanderer* trilogy, concluding *Under the Autumn Star* from 1906 and *A Wanderer Plays on Muted Strings* from 1909. In common with the two preceding books *The Last Joy* plays on a deliberately close identification between the author Hamsun and the narrator Pedersen to create an effect of disturbing immediacy and intimacy, but the differences between this and the two other novels are so great that translation practice in England and America has been to keep them separate.*

The opening three chapters of the novel had in fact been written and published six years earlier, in 1906, the year of Hamsun's separation from Bergljot. The opening lines suggest that it was originally an attempt to capture the mood that the two *Wanderer* novels had already succeeded in catching; of a melancholic withdrawal from the world, an almost Asiatic quietism:

And now I've gone into the forest again.
Not because anything has upset me, or because I've become overly sensitive to mankind's cruelty; but when the forest won't come to me, then I must go to it. That's all.

This time I haven't gone out as a worker, or as a tramp. This time I'm rich, over-nourished, dull and sleepy with comfort and good fortune. Do you know what I mean? I left the world the way a sultan leaves his rich food and his harem and his flowers, and puts on his hair-shirt.

No doubt I could have made more fuss about it. Because I'll be doing a lot of walking here, and thinking, getting a lot of hot irons to glow. Nietzsche would probably have said something like this: My last word to the people found understanding and

---

* The first two novels were translated and published under the title *Wanderers* in 1922. W. W. Worster's translations were replaced by those of Oliver and Gunnvor Stallybrass when the two novels were republished in 1975 as *The Wanderers*. *The Last Joy* has appeared only once in English, as *Look Back on Happiness* in Paula Wiking's translation from 1940.

accord. The people nodded. But that was my last word, and I went into the forest. Because I realised then that I must have said something either very dishonest, or very stupid . . .

I said nothing of that nature, but simply went into the forest.

Before long the tone changes, and the unsuspecting reader finds himself the subject of a direct confrontation:

You have your home in the town. Yes, furnished with trinkets and pictures and books; but you've got a wife and a maid, and a thousand outgoings. Awake and asleep your life is one long race, and you never know a moment's peace. I know peace. Keep, you, your books and your art and your newspapers, keep your coffee and your whisky which only makes me feel ill anyway. Here am I in the forest, and I'm having a splendid time. And if you start asking me deep questions and try to trap me, then I'll answer you that God, for example, is the origin of all, and people are really no more than motes, flecks in the universe. And that's about as far as you can go as well. And if you want to go even further and ask me what eternity is, there again, you and I know about as much as each other, and I'll answer that eternity is just time that hasn't yet been created.

Little friend, come here. I'm going to take a mirror up out of my pocket and shine a little light on your face. I'm going to illuminate you, little friend.

The Last Joy may be seen as Hamsun's first extended shot at becoming the conscience of the nation, his first major work as Norway's unofficial Poet Laureate, a kind of 'state novel', written, as he reveals in the epilogue:

To you, the new spirit in Norway: I have written this in the midst of plague, and for the sake of plague. I cannot stop the plague, no, it's unstoppable now, it enjoys official protection, and the patronage of razzamatazz. One day it might stop. Until then I'm doing what I can against it. And you're doing the opposite.

The tone of humourless contempt Hamsun adopts shows how ill-suited he really was to this job of providing a national conscience. He attacks practically every aspect of modern life in Norway in the course of the novel; the rise of career theologians, the growth of a tourist industry, the changing status of women, the spread of education, while the plot itself concerns the fortunes of a restless young woman, Ingeborg Torsen, twenty-seven years old and a schoolteacher, as Marie Hamsun had once been. The narrator, an ageing and affluent man, like Hamsun, falls in love with her; but now the gap that had opened up in the earlier *Wanderer* books between the narrator and the characters around him has become impossibly wide, and this love is entirely platonic. In effect, it is the disinterested love of an author for one of his characters. He subjects Ingeborg to various tribulations, including a failed relationship with an actor, such as Marie Hamsun had had, before steering her to happiness in the arms of a manly farmer, Nikolai. The pair move to Nikolai's home in the north of Norway, settle and begin to farm the land and raise a family, again just as Knut and Marie Hamsun did. As plot, this is hardly more substantial than the vague unfolding of personal relationships which holds the first two *Wanderer* books together; but whereas in the earlier novels Hamsun's powerful narrative charm and the attractively defeated nature of his irascibility easily compensate for any feeling that, in fact, nothing much is happening at all, *The Last Joy* entirely lacks this charm, with the result that it is – along with *Editor Lynge* – one of the worst of Hamsun's books.

The Last Joy was, to Marie Hamsun's great relief, the last first-person novel Hamsun wrote. Ever since they had been together she had dreaded them. She could not understand why he should continue to wave tearful fictional farewells to his past in the midst of the happiness of falling in love with her. She was also distressed by the doings of his narrators, identifying them completely with Hamsun. In the first of the two books of memoirs she wrote about her life with him, she records the following exchange between them, which occurred while she was helping to correct the proofs of *A Wanderer Plays on Muted Strings*:

'And now here all of a sudden you've got this Ragnhild sitting on your lap! Couldn't you cut that out?'
'Me?' he replied, laughing.
'Yes, of course, You. Surely you know that everyone identifies you with the "I" of the book?'
The next time, two years later, there was another 'I' book, and again I was upset. But then he comforted me by telling me that this would be the last.[4]

Marie did manage to influence Hamsun in the composition of *The Last Joy*: she protested to him over the harsher fate Ingeborg had apparently met with in an early draft of the novel, and secured a better fate for her in the published version. Even more, she influenced the book by becoming pregnant and, in March 1912, giving birth to their first child, Tore. Hamsun the narrator had originally described the last joy as being 'to withdraw from the world, and sit quite alone in the forest, with plenty of good darkness all around one'. But by the end of the book he had come to describe it as something quite different: 'Children? A real miracle! And when old age comes, the only joy. The last joy.'

The Hamsuns had three more children in rapid succession, a second son Arild in 1914, a daughter Ellinor in 1915, and a daughter Cecilia born in 1917, and the joys of fatherhood became one of the few unconditional joys in Hamsun's life of strictly stoical happiness. Even so, the writing always came first, and for every one of the six years that the Hamsuns lived at Hamarøy he was away from home for at least three months, and sometimes more, as he tried to get started on his novels. His procedure was always the same: as the novel developed in his head the little piles of paper, one for each character, would mount up on the primitive desk in his workroom, a few boards nailed down onto two carpenter's donkeys and carefully covered with lining paper to save his shirt sleeves. Preparatory work of this kind was easy, and the problem arose when the time came actually to write the books. He tried Skogheim, but the lure of farmwork, and the temptation to interest himself in the practical problems of running the farm were too strong for him, and invariably he would pack all his notes and writing materials into a case and travel away, leaving the responsibilities of the farm behind him.

He sought out various places. For *The Last Joy* he tried Sortland, on one of the outer Lofoten Islands, staying at the Ellingsens' private hotel. Marie took the ferry-boat over to visit him once, to tell him that she was pregnant with Tore, and was alarmed to note the number of women living at the Ellingsens'. Already the tables were turning in the relationship, and now it was she who began to suffer from jealousy. He also tried Saltdalen for *The Last Joy*, a remote farm not far from the Swedish border, and again sought out wilderness farms for his novel from 1913, *Children of the Age*, and spent three months at Bardu, braving temperatures as low as −39° as well as tinned food – along with bicycles, one of the more idiosyncratic objects of his hatred of modern life and 'progress'. Later in the year he tried Kraakmo on the Sagfjord, and still later the Grand Hotel in Bodø, the town where his earliest literary efforts had seen the light of day more than thirty years previously.

He found that he could work well in this hotel, and used it frequently, solving the problem of neighbours by hiring three rooms on the top floor so that he could keep two of them empty while working in the middle room. Here he had one of those glorious ten-hour sessions, the fruits of which he valued so keenly all his life, loving the spontaneity and the passion of the out-pouring. A few sessions like this were worth the weeks of waiting for him. He wrote home:

> Just a short note to you, my dearest Marie. And forgive me if I offended you on the telephone last time we spoke when I said that you sounded so weary. Not easy for you to have a hysterical husband I know. But I love you and you're the only one I want in the world.
>
> Didn't sleep until five this morning and am a bit worn out, ah but, listen, I'm so happy, I feel like a hero, because I wrote more yesterday and last night than any other time during these last months. Worked for about ten hours yesterday, and today my hand is shaking.[5]

The young writer Johannes in *Victoria* describes such an onset of divine inspiration, and Willatz Holmsen IV, the composer in Hamsun's 1915 novel *Segelfoss Town*, also experiences true inspiration for his opera in ecstatic and compressed rushes such as these.

These prolonged absences from home were necessary for Hamsun. He needed to feel free from the concerns of running the farm, and as time went by needed also to feel certain that he would not be interrupted by the children – not so much because he disliked their attentions as because he liked them far too much. He was a loving and indulgent father, and could not listen to his children crying without going to pick them up. Yet the absences caused suffering to all parties, and he missed the children. He wrote to Marie from another of his Lofoten Island hermitages, Harstad:

> Tell Tore that I love him, and think often of him. Poor Tore, I regret now that I didn't look in his books every time he asked me to. I did look often, but not every time. I hope it didn't upset him too much. He's probably forgotten by now anyway. Tell him I'll bring lots of things for him when I come home. But I can't come yet, pappa must write and work and be very industrious now. And give Arild a hug from me. I can just see him now, lying on the floor. You won't get a rounder little bum than that. And how pretty he is. And Tore. And how pretty you are. And I kiss you and am yours.

At times Marie despaired of the irregularity of the relationship. She wrote to him during one of his stays in Bodø:

I wonder if you're managing to get peace to write there in Bodø? Oh, if only you could write here at home! God knows, I would cut off my hand if I thought it would make it any better for you to work here. I want nothing more in the world than to have you here, and for everything to be alright. I've tried so hard to adapt myself to your moods, but you've never been able to approve of me. It's been like that from the very beginning. Something or other about me was always wrong. And when I've tried to change and be different, it's only some other thing that's wrong.

Remember to send Tore a card or a letter, or ring him up on the 6th, his birthday. And live well, my darling, whom I miss so terribly, and long for always. I'm torn with jealousy, because you're always away from me, and I'm here alone . . .

She upset him profoundly, and had to explain herself at length, when in one of her letters she remarked that 'the little ones don't miss you very much any more, oddly enough'. They did try to solve the problem by erecting, in the summer of 1916, a small hut, away from the main farm buildings, where Hamsun could write, but as things turned out, he had little use of it.

The two books on which Hamsun worked most steadily during these years were *Children of the Age* and its sequel, *Segelfoss Town*. They represent the definitive start of the last long phase of Hamsun's authorship, a period encompassing twenty-three years and nine novels. All of these novels are written in the third person, all have large casts of characters, and all are in greater or lesser degree didactic. They are conventional in form, one might almost say Dickensian,* and resemble in many ways the kind of novels he himself had criticised so fiercely in his lectures of 1891, implicitly in his choice of form for *Hunger*, and explicitly in the views of the central character in *Mysteries*, Nagel.

For those readers coming to the works of Hamsun's late middle-age fresh from the intensity and the honest, confused passion of the great novels of the 1890s, the experience is disconcerting. The difference is not so much in the superficialities of theme – he was still writing about people, after all – but in the altered narrative stance. The author, the easily identifiable young man with a mania for guarded confession, Knut Hamsun under the name of Andreas Tangen in *Hunger*, Johan Nagel in *Mysteries*, Thomas Glahn in *Pan*, Johannes in *Victoria*, seems to have disappeared off the face of his fiction, to be replaced by a remote, slightly ironic God describing

* Among the books he read while trying to get started on *Children of the Age* was *David Copperfield*.

the goings-on on some far-off planet which happens to have attracted his attention one afternoon. It is as though Mark Twain's Mysterious Stranger were to have started producing novels instead of toy cities of clay inhabited by living human dolls. Yet this is not strictly the case. Hamsun the man, whose acute rendering of his unusual personality is in many ways the strength of the early works, is still vividly present in these novels, not as one readily identifiable individual, but shared out among a hundred characters. Between them they form a picture of a man in fascinated and animated debate with himself about the nature and meaning of life, of its profundities and, equally as important, of its trivialities. At times he writes as though he knew the answers, but as often his discussion ends in honest puzzlement about it all.

These later works are without firmly focused plots. Like high-quality soap operas, they roll on from incident to incident with an effortless naturalness which belies the torment their creation cost Hamsun, endlessly inventive, rarely dull, often funny, and suffused with that enigmatic mixture of sharp human intelligence, animal cunning, and unforced *naïveté* which is the hallmark of Hamsun's literary personality.

Nor are there any real heroes in these novels, heroes in the sense of 'protected species'. All of them are shot by their creator at least once, some with more regret than others, but all of them shot nevertheless, and all with the live ammunition of human frailty. They are accessible novels, and Hamsun probably kept them deliberately so, since one of the most important reasons he kept on writing was to earn a lot of money. With the publication of the *Segelfoss* books he was to become a best-selling author, like his friend Gustav Frenssen in Germany, and his admirers John Galsworthy and H G Wells in England. Yet success with the new style did not lose him his intellectually respectable admirers – Thomas Mann and Hermann Hesse continued to read him avidly, Ernest Hemingway and Franz Kafka did not distinguish too greatly between early and late Hamsun, and his legion of admirers in Russia, foremost among them Maxim Gorky, continued to hail him as a master.

The first *Segelfoss* novel, *Children of the Age*, was described by Hamsun as 'a novel about the war between the aristocrat and the peasant, or vice versa'.[7] Segelfoss itself was 'oppkomlingby', the town of the upstarts. The novel follows the fortunes of two rich men. One is the born aristocrat Willatz Holmsen, the squire of Segelfoss, which is a small coastal community in the north of Norway, somewhat along the lines of Sirilund in *Benoni* and *Rosa*.

The other is a local man, born a poor peasant, who has travelled out in the wide world and made his fortune (in Mexico), and now at the opening of the novel returns to his old home town, a fabulous and mysterious figure come home to find his roots again. Hamsun loved this story – it was his own, after all – and his sympathies with Tobias Holmengraa are evident. Yet the aristocrat Willatz Holmsen has in equal measure demonstrable similarities to Hamsun. The name itself contains a faint syllabic echo of his own, he is married to a much younger wife, is proud to the point of clownishness, pantheistic, and, like Hamsun, addicted to the playing of patience. The opening of the novel finds Segelfoss basking in the last hour of the long sunset of the late Middle Ages. Holmsen is the feudal overlord, effortlessly commanding in his relations with the local people, effortlessly respected by them. He sells a parcel of land to the returning Holmengraa, and on this land Holmengraa builds a large new mill, so that cereals can be refined locally, and the middle-men from Bergen cut out. His enterprise develops from this: he builds a quay to take larger ships to facilitate his trading contacts with the outside world, and as Segelfoss changes in character from a feudal to an industrial society it acquires a post office, a telegraph service, and its own bakery. Holmengraa's business success, and the fact that he is now the town's great employer, turns him into the economic power in Segelfoss. In the process he becomes – almost – a man fit to rank with Holmsen. Yet he carefully preserves his respect for Holmsen, even though Holmsen is soon dependent on his goodwill for the maintenance of his aristocratic lifestyle, and responsibilities: his son, Willatz IV, for example, receives higher education in both England and Germany. Holmsen the aristocrat produces nothing, however, and it is only by selling off his land and his rivers and his timber to Holmengraa that he is able to keep up appearances.

His son, now a music student in Germany, has inherited all his father's largesse of spirit. At an auction of musical instruments in Berlin he buys back for its owner a grand piano which poverty has forced him to put up for sale, and asks his father to send him the money. Willatz in turn has to go to Holmengraa – but his fortunes, too, are now in decline after a loss in speculation on a cargo of rye, and he has to disappoint Holmsen. The old aristocrat finally realises that the businessman actually owns the family estate. His wife Adelheid, having fled from a marriage which was a baffling web of incommunication and sexual unease, is reported to have drowned in a bathing accident in Germany, where she had travelled to be near her son. Holmsen, economically powerless, and isolated from the people around him by means of a rigid class system, begins slowly to wind down his affairs prior to dying, in the fashion of the heroes of Icelandic saga literature. Hamsun even uses a technique characteristic of saga literature to indicate to us that Holmsen is going to die soon, giving the reader a sudden close-up picture of the character, and remarking, 'He did not know what was about to happen to him.' But a fabulous and mysterious thing occurs, and Holmsen, digging in his garden, suddenly finds a great treasure trove buried by his father, Willatz II. It is enough to pay off all the debts, and to secure his son's future. The novel closes with his death.

The sequel, *Segelfoss Town*, follows the further social and economic fortunes of the townspeople but it is a more depressed and bitter book than *Children of the Age*, perhaps reflecting Hamsun's depression over the outbreak of war. His main concern is to try to show that power moves downwards in a society. From the autocrat Holmsen it had passed to the diplomat Holmengraa; now it passes to the democrat Theodor paa Bua, who runs the village store and provides the local people with all manner of fashionable modern nonsense, like false teeth, tinned food, and ready-made shoes, on which they can spend the money earned in Holmengraa's service. And Holmengraa in turn is plagued in this novel by his own inability to command the respect of his workers which a born aristocrat like Willatz Holmsen effortlessly enjoyed. Like so many Hamsun characters, he is obsessed with what people think of him. Hamsun picks out two of his employees, Aslak and Konrad, to paint a most unflattering portrait of the 'new worker', the industrial worker, the day-labourer, working for money alone, with no sense of personal loyalty to his employer. They humiliate Holmengraa, openly discussing the wisdom of his orders, doubting him, lazing and absenting themselves from work whenever they feel like it. 'So proud of their rudeness', Hamsun muses, 'and still not happy'. Holmengraa tries various ruses to persuade the workers that he has his own secret reserves of power and authority, among them pretending to have become a member of the freemasons, but by the end he realises what his true destiny on earth had been, 'that he had not been born to be a master of men, but only to come and go like a fairy-tale prince'. He is sharply aware of the social paradox he represents, knowing that he is 'a peasant, and yet not a peasant'. Hamsun likes him, and just as he had let Willatz Holmsen find his father's buried treasure, and settle up all his debts before dying, so he grants Holmengraa a magical and mysterious exit, leaving Segelfoss on the large ship which his sea captain son Felix has sailed to Norway from South America. Holmengraa's Mexican daughter Marianne agrees to marry

Willatz Holmsen's son, also called Willatz, and now a famous composer after his training in Germany. News of the impending marriage comes as a blow to Theodor the storekeeper; like the young Hamsun, he was fascinated by a woman higher up the social scale than himself, and had tried in vain to win Marianne himself.

The second half of the novel concentrates increasingly on Theodor, according to Hamsun's theory, the next spiral down in the movement of power. Hamsun shouldn't actually like him, yet the more he writes about him, the more he warms to him, in spite of the fundamentally meaningless way in which Theodor amasses his wealth. In fact, Hamsun's humanity touches every character at one point or another in the course of the novel; even the workers Aslak and Konrad; even the representatives of a class Hamsun hated above all, the professional middle class made up of doctors and lawyers which Holmengraa's enterprise in creating a modern town out of Segelfoss had attracted. Yet his favourite among all the characters is probably Baardsen, the alcoholic telegraphist who drinks 'not in order to have a better time, but to go on having a good one'. He is an artistic type who plays the cello, when he can be persuaded, and local rumour claims that he was once an unsuccessful writer of plays. Like Geissler in *The Growth of the Soil*, he is a figure somehow to be identified with providence, a man who can make a party out of nothing by producing a bottle of whisky at the right time. An intelligent and sensitive man, proud and generous, it is with his death that Hamsun chooses to close the novel. A spiritual aristocrat who, 'from his birth, had had a natural bias towards failure', Baardsen's mode of dying places him on the same plane as the born aristocratic Holmsen from *Children of the Age*: he gives away all his money to the destitute old shoemaker Nils, whose trade has been ruined by the arrival of the ready-made shoe industry, and also makes him a present of his own warm winter boots before wandering away from society to die alone and unseen, refusing to eat anymore, embracing his own death as the inevitable consequence of having strayed into a society and an age which seemed to him without meaning or values.

Hamsun was fascinated by such gifted, enigmatic failures. Extremism, oddness of any kind in a human being fascinated him, which is why the most sympathetic characters in these two *Segelfoss* novels are those at the very top and those at the very bottom. Less interesting to him, but still attractive, are characters on the move, like Theodor. Least interesting are those in the middle, self-satisfied members of the professional class like Doctor Muus, and the lawyer Rasch who take no risks with their lives, and devote all their efforts to staying exactly where they are.

After limited early attempts at the genre like *Swarming* and *Benoni* and *Rosa*, Hamsun showed with these two *Segelfoss* books that he could handle the epic, with its large cast of characters and its lengthy timespans, like a master. In a man of over fifty years of age, it was an impressive demonstration of his desire and his ability to renew himself artistically. It was also characteristic of the essentially paradoxical Hamsun that the vision that powered the renewal was a reactionary one.

The journalism Hamsun produced during his six years at Hamarøy was probably the most controversial of his whole journalistic career. With the outbreak of the First World War in 1914 he found himself, to his irritation, and to the detriment of his work on *Segelfoss Town*, involved in a lengthy newspaper debate with a Norwegian academic, Professor Christen Collin. The core of the debate was simply that Hamsun wanted Germany to win the war, while his opponents did not. Hamsun's pro-German feelings were to have such drastic consequences for him towards the end of his life that here is perhaps the right place to try to document their origins, as well as the equally important factor of his anti-Englishness.

Hamsun's reputation as a Nazi sympathiser is based on his statements and behaviour throughout the 1930s and the years of the German occupation of Norway in 1940–45, but a fair assessment as to how fervent a national socialist he was should also take into account the fact of his long-standing special relationships with both Germany and England.

As we have seen, Hamsun achieved his European breakthrough via Germany. He was at once recognised as a major European writer, and up until his popular success in Scandinavia with the Segelfoss books was largely dependent for his financial security on royalties from Germany. The first critical book about him, Carl Morburger's study from 1910, was German. Long before this though, he was expressing his admiration for the Germans. In 1894, while Hamsun was living in Paris, the accusations from 1892 that he had written a short story which plagiarised Dostoevsky came to Langen's attention, and Hamsun had wearily to explain the whole business again for his new backer. In despair at what he saw as only further evidence of the determination of his enemies among his fellow Norwegian writers to ruin his reputation he wrote:

> I wish I could leave Paris today and go to Germany and live there. I feel myself only as a Germanish soul, not as a Romanish, and these feelings are increasing the longer I remain here.[8]

And again, just before his marriage to Bergljot in 1898, when the Norwegian government passed him over for a travel scholarship on the grounds of the allegedly immoral short story *The Call of Life*, it was Langen, and the Germans, who gave him the financial security he needed to write *Victoria*. He wrote to thank Langen for the appeal in *Simplicissimus* which had saved him:

> The money was more than I hoped – far more; it shows that Germany is a great country; here I get almost nothing.[9]

The outbreak of war between England and Germany in 1914 focused for all time his pro-German feelings. 'As long as I can remember,' he wrote to Langens* in 1914, 'long before the war, I have expressed my fondness for Germany in both speech and writing, because I am German.'[10]

Other letters to his German publisher contain frequent messages of support and encouragement, and it was the publication of one of these private letters in the magazine *Simplicissimus* which prompted Professor Collin to open the debate in the Norwegian newspapers with an article in *Tidens Tegn* in November 1914. Collin was an academic, a widely-read man confident to the point of arrogance in his command of his learning, and able to wield statistics to devastating effect. Such men had always intimidated Hamsun, and brought out the worst in him as he struggled to overcome the sense that his own learning lacked unity. Collin demanded to know what Hamsun had meant by writing in his letter that a Germany victory over England was 'a natural inevitability'. Hamsun replied:

> Why is it nothing less than a natural inevitability that Germany will one day triumph over England? Because the Germans have, like the sound and flourishing people they are, a birth-boom. Germany needs colonies.[11]

He went on to doubt that Germany would necessarily win the war on this particular occasion, but affirmed that ultimate victory was inevitable:

> Not this time, perhaps, now that England has the help of half the world against Germany; and perhaps not for a long time, it all depends. But one day, Germany will punish the English to death.

* Albert Langen died in 1909. After his death the company continued under his name under the leadership of Korfitz Holm.

Herr professor Collin undoubtedly knows better. But no matter how much he or I 'know' about this matter, in the final analysis it is a question of intuition, and understanding. And even though Hr Collin has read half a million more books than I, in a matter like this my understanding has a greater value for me than his.

Hamsun dismissed English indignation over the fate of the Belgians and the destruction of Louvain, complaining that this was hypocrisy coming from a nation that bombarded the undefended town of Alexandria in 1882. He also mentioned with distaste the English treatment of the Boers, saying that the reason they refused to leave the Transvaal was solely because of the gold and diamond mines there; he quoted a half-remembered line from Kipling about the Boers, that the thing was to 'wear them down, those animals'. Talk of German militarism was a nonsense in the face of England's: 'The Briton has never made a move without it.' As for the alliance between the English and the Russians, a people whom he had admired both through their great writers, and through personal contact during his travels there in 1899, this was an 'unnatural friendship' which was bound to end soon. But in spite of his strong feelings, he tried to end on a conciliatory note:

In the course of any war one has one's sympathies and antipathies; he has his and I mine. Good grief, I don't want to make myself out to be any stupider than I already am; I am grateful to England, not only for 1905* and for her defence of small nations generally, but for the thousand other values which without England would never have become part of our common heritage. It should hardly be necessary for me to say so. Nor do I mention this with any intention of criticising Germany, which is, and will remain, closer to my Germanic head and heart.

This seems perfectly fair. Yet it is the phrase 'punish to death' (tukte til døden) which leaves the lasting impression. Hamsun had used exactly the same phrase in his novel *The Last Joy* from 1912 in closing his description of two repulsive English tourists he meets, members of that 'nation of athletes, wagon-drivers and perverts

* Public opinion in Norway had been gratefully aware of England's support for their independence struggle in 1905, and Edward VII was felt to have played a part in helping to get King Håkon on to the Norwegian throne. The City of London had also given Norway a loan of two million pounds on very favourable terms, which made it possible for the government to function during the difficult period between June and October 1905 while the new country's status remained uncertain.

which healthy Germany will one day punish to death'. It was a deliberately crude and ugly and violent phrase, a classic example of those sudden lapses of good taste of which Hamsun was capable. It was this phrase which Collin reacted to in his reply to Hamsun, quoting it several times; examining it, subjecting it to mockery before returning to his statistics. These he used to make a nonsense of Hamsun's claims that English women were on what Hamsun had called a 'forward march towards sterility' which accounted for England's dwindling population. On the contrary, Collin assured him, figures showed that Norway's women were on this same 'forward march'. Moreover, what he called 'new Malthusianism' was showing its effects on all nations, not excepting Germany – the percentage of births was sinking there, too. By this time William Archer, Ibsen's translator and apologist in England, had weighed in with two contributions. The first of them was a model of courtesy and restraint which won Hamsun's whole-hearted admiration after the 'unreadable' Collin. The second, alas, sank to the level of the Hamsun-Collin exchanges, a fact which curiously enough disappointed Hamsun who described it as unnecessary and 'strangely unEnglish'. Here Hamsun abandoned the attempt to match scientific pretensions with his opponents and let his case rest honestly in a plain statement of the subjective nature of their respective positions:

> As I indicated before, I do not doubt that Hr Archer and I could continue to 'answer' one another for a good while yet on this topic without ever getting anywhere. Here we are, each with our own point of view, one British, one German. We are in different camps.

Hamsun's point of view from the first had been the superficially rational one that the English had no problem with an expanding population, and did not need more colonies, or even all the colonies they already owned, whereas Germany – a nation in the throes of a population explosion – needed more land. But beneath the surface lay what was for Hamsun the real truth, the instinctive feeling that it was simply Germany's turn to be the dominant world power. Germany for him was always the coming land, the coming people, the young power seeking to challenge the stubbornly held might of the ageing English, and it is tempting to see in Hamsun's ready identification with Germany's situation on the outbreak of the war a parallel with his own personal experiences in the 1890s, when he felt himself young and strong and bursting with vitality and talent, and yet held down and held fast in the literary stranglehold of the old lions, Ibsen, Bjørnson, Kielland and Lie.

Hamsun adopted an assured, ironic, and often deliberately patronising approach in his contributions to the debate, which hid the fact that he took it terribly seriously. Challenged by William Archer to quote the source of the alleged poem by Kipling he was unable to do so, and furiously dashed off letters to literary friends in Norway whom he hoped might be able to help him. He asked Thom Vetlesen on *Morgenbladet* to check back-numbers of the newspaper[12] – 'It was towards the end of the Boer War. I seem to remember it was on the second page, last (or next to last) column' –promising that if he found the lines it would make him 'the happiest person in Nordland'. He wrote four separate letters to Vetlesen about the Kipling poem, driven by his need, part uncertainty and part arrogance, always to be in the right. Given the importance he seems to have attached to it all, it is hard to decide how one is to take an article found among his papers after his death which appears to have been intended as a contribution to the debate, in his own handwriting, but signed 'BM'. Here, in a voice quite different from his own, he humbly and calmly queries some of Professor Collin's statistical arguments, adding beguilingly that he does so because, 'even though my sympathies are with the English, and not the Germans, I have had difficulty in following him. I might conceivably end in complete agreement with him, if the professor will continue to explain the matter to us in further articles.' Perhaps it was a projected dirty trick, or an attempt to tease Collin into the bother of more work.

Every bit as important in trying to give an account of how Hamsun came to end up in the arms of the Germans in 1940 is the history of his hatred of the English. Indeed, of the two passions, it has the better pedigree. Its origins probably lie in the two historical incidents he had read about in his boyhood which cast the English in the role of bullies – the smuggling scandal known as the 'Bodø-affair', and the British naval bombardment of Copenhagen during the Napoleonic Wars. Ibsen's poem *Terje Vigen*, which Hamsun knew by heart and often recited publicly as a young man also casts the English in the role of villains. From Stockholm in 1944, the Norwegian writer Johan Borgen broadcast an oddly specific rumour to the effect that Hamsun's phobia was the result of a humiliating experience he had had with an Englishman during his adolescence, while serving behind the counter in Walsøe's store at Tranøy. If this were the case, it would indeed provide a strong early psychological motive for Hamsun's feelings – trifles, after all, played a supremely important role in his scheme of things.

Hamsun's years as a foreigner in American small towns might also have built up resentment at the automatically higher status that being English conferred on an immigrant. On returning to Norway, and during his convalescence at Frydenlund in Valdres he again met imperious Englishmen, tourists who strode about commandeering horses and hired hands and hotel beds. And what seems to have crystallised these impressions into a definite hatred was an incident that occurred during his visit to Munich in 1896. He recalls the incident in the travel book *In Wonderland*:

I saw an Englander once on a tram in Munich. He was an artist, probably, a painter, on his way to Schack's Gallery. We were travelling along at quite a speed. Suddenly a child, a little girl, was almost run over. She stumbled, and fell in between the horses, and was injured under their hooves; but we managed to pull her out alive. The Englishman, meanwhile, stood smoking his pipe. When we were all ready to set off again, and the driver had climbed back into his seat, the Englishman gives an anxious look at his watch. We look at him, some of us, but it's as though we're thin air to him. In his strange Englishman's German he asks for his money back, he says he wants to get off. A runover child is nothing to do with him. One of the passengers stretches out a hand and offers him his money back. He looks indifferently at the passenger, slowly and indifferently withdraws his gaze and does not take the money. He remains unaffected by the indignation which is now bubbling around him, and that firmness would probably have won the approval of all his countrymen: that's right, John, you stick to it! He remained standing all the way to his stop, and then got off.

Of course, when there's been an accident it's usually best if not too many people come rushing forward. But everybody ought to be able to forget to smoke their pipe. Everybody ought to look up. Everybody ought to manage a little shudder. Everybody. Surely.

If I were King of England, there's a little piece of advice I'd whisper in my people's ear. That even if my people were the most dignified people in the world . . .

In Wonderland appeared in 1903. Hamsun had previously mocked English liberal philosophy in both *Mysteries* and in his *Kareno* trilogy; but the attack in those books was an attack on ideas, an abstract attack. The criticism above, which is actually an appendage intended to justify a fairly long and – it might as well be

admitted – funny scene in which he has been tormenting an
Englishman, is Hamsun's first attack on the English *merely for being
English*.

The two novels *Benoni* and *Rosa* from 1908 both feature an
Englishman called Sir Hugh Trevelyan as a minor character. In
fact, he is a caricature rather than a character. Extremely rich and
extremely rude, he travels to Sirilund in the summer for the
fishing, drinks until he is stiff-eyed – though without ever
disgracing himself – and, by his purchase of land from him, turns
Benoni into a millionaire. The character of Sir Hugh suggests in fact
that Hamsun's attitude towards the English at that time, 1909, was
more deeply ambivalent than it later became. Like the man
Hamsun met in Munich, Sir Hugh treats the people around him as
though they were not there. He is depicted as infuriatingly and
insufferably rude, and Hamsun makes it plain that he is like this
simply because he is an Englishman. Yet he is allowed to win
Edvarda Mack and take her back to England with him.

The great crime, always, is the imperturbability. Yet that same
imperturbability among the orientals Hamsun met during his
travels in the near East was the quality that he prized most highly
in them. In fact, so many qualities that the British upper class were
traditionally associated with were qualities that Hamsun admired
and tried to cultivate in himself – the arrogant bearing, the
magisterial manner, the indifference to money – that one might
wonder sometimes if there were not somewhere in all this an
element of jealousy, a recognition that here was something he
wanted to be with all his heart, and yet knew he never could be.*
Hamsun loved to be loved, and loved to be hated: what was utterly
intolerable to him was to be ignored. At the risk of stretching the
psychological parallels which caused him to identify his own
personal fate with the fate of Germany one might here reflect on
the almost pathological nature of his dislike of Ibsen, whom he had
never met personally, and on the fact that Ibsen studiously and
completely ignored his existence throughout the years of
Hamsun's rampaging rise to fame, never once replying to
Hamsun's attacks on him, nor in any way acknowledging his
existence.†

* A theory first put forward by the writer Nordahl Grieg in his essay *Knut Hamsun*
in October, 1936.
† The only documented personal contact of any kind between the two writers is
Ibsen's presence at Hamsun's lectures in Christiania in 1891. To a companion who
expressed surprise at his insistence on attending all three lectures, Ibsen is said to
have replied, 'Surely you realise we must go and learn how we are to write.'
Ragnar Brovik, in Ibsen's *The Master Builder*, is sometimes thought to be Ibsen's
response to these lectures of Hamsun's.

Whatever the reasons for his orientation, Hamsun was a deeply patriotic Norwegian, and in a country which overwhelmingly supported the Entente powers it took courage to proclaim one's views so boldly. *Children of the Age* was selling well in Germany, and in September 1915 he wrote to Langens expressing the hope that this was because it was a good book, and not for any other reason:

> My pro-German attitude during the war is my way of trying to serve my country with all my heart, and is not dictated by personal motives.[13]

And he concludes the letter with a point of very great significance:

> There is nothing on this earth I fear more for my country than 'home-rule' from England.

The German defeat, when it came, hardly surprised him. But he saw it as only the postponement of the operation of an irresistible natural law for which he waited with a calm certainty. It was the only comfort he could glean from England's victory.

Hamsun's relationship to America and Americans developed along slightly different lines. In his thunderous attack on the burgeoning tourist industry in Norway, *A Word to Us*, he had lumped them together with the English as 'international Anglo-Saxons' whose fatuous pursuit of 'sights' and desire to see local people phonily attired in 'national dress' were major factors in the corruption and humiliation which he so feared for his small country. Another criticism levelled at Americans, in *In Wonderland*, was that they were the keenest advocates of a meaningless and trivial progress, in the pursuit of which they had taken the art of making a fuss to new depths of mastery. And right at the beginning of his career, in 1889, had come his wild and hilariously subjective book *On the Cultural Life of Modern America* in which he effectively denied that there was any cultural life there at all. As we have seen, this was a book he had consistently rejected in later years as being too childish, and no longer representative of his views; but American intervention in the closing stages of the First World War seemed to him to offer confirmation of some of the things he had written nearly thirty years ago about America, as a letter to Langens in 1917 shows:

And now comes this business with America. Had America not
supplied England and her allies with ammunition and weapons
this war would have been over eighteen months ago. Now when
America finds her deliveries being stopped by German U-boats
she threatens war!

Again and again I find that the major criticism I made of
Yankee materialism in that youthful book of mine is confirmed
by events.[14]

But the direct hatred which Hamsun already felt for the English
was never really part of his attitude towards America. Literary
America, in any event, was beginning to respond to Hamsun. In
1914 Scribner's Sons published the novel *Shallow Soil*, from 1893, in
a rather stiff and un-idiomatic translation by Carl Christian
Hyllestad. It seems a curious choice for a first publication to us
now, so thoroughly unlike the rest of the novels from that period
on which Hamsun's world reputation rests. One possible explanation is that Hamsun himself retained an eccentrically high
opinion of it for some time. To *Kringsjaa* magazine in 1904 he said
that he couldn't remember what it was about any more, but that
'for a long time, it seemed to me the best of my novels'. James L
Ford in the *New York Herald* for 14 March 1914 gave the book a full
page review, although the details of Hamsun's adventurous life
were what interested him more, leading him to give his readers a
rather misleading description of Hamsun as 'a sort of Norwegian
Jack London'.

Professionally, these were good years 'for Hamsun. The two
Segelfoss books had broken through to reach a far wider reading
public in Norway than any of his previous books had. The second
volume particularly had sold well, something for which Hamsun
himself could take the credit, since at his express suggestion the
book had been sold at an unusually low price in an effort to tempt
new readers. Gyldendal telegraphed to him in December 1915 with
the news that *Segelfoss Town* was being 'ripped off the shelves', to
which he laconically replied, 'Yes, I'm going cheap this year, I'm
on Special Offer'.[15]

In fact, he knew exactly what he was doing with these *Segelfoss*
books of his. His new lifestyle as farmer and father was proving
more expensive than ever his extravagant life as a wandering
bachelor had, and he was deeply in debt both to Gyldendal and to
private individuals. But, as he wrote to Peter Nansen at Gyldendal
in Copenhagen, in April 1913: 'With a few bestsellers I should
manage to pay off most of what I owe. And I am working on a
best-seller now.'[16]

A different kind of opportunity to improve his finances cropped up in 1914 when, probably in connection with the publication of *Shallow Soil*, he received an offer to make a lecture tour of America. He described the offer to Alette Gross, a sister of Bergljot's with whom he kept in touch, in a letter of November 1914:

> I might be making a quick trip to America in the early part of next year. They're offering me free travel, free accommodation, and a lot of money to make a flying tour of America, lecture in six towns, and fly home again. If I feel I can stand it, I'll go. But I've forgotten all the little English I once had, and this would have to be in fact in very good English.[17]

One feels that Hamsun was proud, and slightly flattered by the offer, but never seriously considered making the trip. He was too deeply involved in writing *Segelfoss Town*, and was anyway showing increasing signs of wanting personally to withdraw from the world and concentrate on his writing, his family, and his farm.

He took an active and constructive interest in all aspects of the publication of his books, however, and where disagreements arose he took a very firm line with his publishers. Gyldendal, which had already published an edition of his *Collected Novels* in 1907, in 1916 published a *Collected Works* in nine volumes, followed by a second edition in ten volumes in 1918. The contract they presented to him for the latter included the sentence 'The Publisher intends to publish the complete edition before the end of 1918.' Hamsun returned the contract to them with the wording altered to read, 'The Publisher will publish the complete edition before the end of 1918.' He also cut down the number of free copies that the contract proposed to allot him to five. Both his alterations were incorporated in the contract as signed on 10 October 1917. He also queried the sales tactics that Gyldendal proposed to employ for publication of the ten volumes; a proposal which meant that the last five or six volumes would all reach the shops at the same time, a mere three weeks before Christmas.

He interested himself in the appearance of his words on the printed page, expressly forbidding the use of italics, since 'Italic is a repulsive Franco-American nonsense that makes words look as if they're fading from the text', and insisted that his hand-written underlinings for emphasis were to be reproduced by wide spacing of the letters. A note to the printer of the first thirty chapters of *The Growth of the Soil* in October 1917 gave instructions that 'the dialogue in the opening is to be printed consecutively, with only dashes in between. And preferably pearl-face, not italic. Italic is an upstart on a printed page.'[18]

Gyldendal paid him 40,000 kroner for these *Collected Works*, more than enough to clear his debt to them, and to enable him to pay off debts to private individuals of 3000. One of these, a debt for 2000 to Thorvald Meyer, was outstanding from 1905. The other 1000 was to another businessman, Olaf Schou, whom Hamsun eventually traced by detective work to Switzerland. The sense of honour in money matters which had so astonished his Bohemian con-temporaries in Copenhagen and Paris in the 1890s was still intact.

The Germans, too, had been planning a *Collected Works*, but in 1916 Langens had had to inform him that war conditions made it impossible for them to go ahead as planned. *Hunger* and *Mysteries* appeared in a first volume in 1917, but a first edition of fourteen volumes did not appear complete until 1928. In connection with this German edition he asked Langens to be sure to use the new edition of his books from Gyldendal, because of certain changes and major reductions he had made in three of them, *Hunger, Editor Lynge* and *At the Gates of the Kingdom*.[19] Langens were rather lucky still to have him: his contract with them ran out in 1914, and with Albert Langen himself dead in 1909 Hamsun's sense of personal loyalty to the company was less intense than it had been. Fischer, who had been the first to publish Hamsun in Germany with *Hunger* in 1891, and whose rejection of *Mysteries* had led Hamsun to Langen, now campaigned intensely to win him back, approaching him directly with a tempting financial offer, and also engaging in a certain amount of back-door negotiating with Peter Nansen at Gyldendal, but in the end Hamsun's sense of loyalty to Langens led to his renewing his contract with them.

It seems clear that already by 1913 Hamsun was feeling some of the disadvantages of his self-imposed exile to north Norway. In answer to a questionnaire in June that year he described his new life as 'both more useful, and richer', but added that he missed the company of his friends from the city, and missed hearing news of them. In 1915, at the height of his newspaper debate with Collin and Archer, and while desperately striving to track down the elusive Kipling quotation, he had written to Vetlesen at *Morgen-bladet* apologising for bothering him with requests for assistance, and explaining rather pathetically that it was 'because I am living in the sticks, and feel myself wretchedly cut off'. One wonders if possibly this feeling of isolation might account for the dramatically provocative cast of his journalism from Hamarøy, as though the increased distance between himself and his opponents required spectacularly ugly formulations such as that England must be 'punished to death' if it were to be successfully achieved. Quite well aware that it had the force of a blow suddenly delivered below the belt in the midst of all his reasoned arguments about the German need for colonies, he had carefully repeated it in his successive contributions, as though deliberately flaunting his lack of concern for 'good taste'. It was a technique he used to equally upsetting effect on his opponents in another newspaper debate that took off just as the steam was going out of the debate on the war, a debate which caused much bitterness on both sides, and was long remembered and often used in attempts to prove that Hamsun lacked a basic humanity. He started the ball rolling with an article in *Morgenbladet* on 16 January 1915:

There was an article in *Morgenbladet* some weeks ago on a young girl who had been sentenced to eight months' imprisonment for having killed her own child. It did not say eighteen years, or eight years, but eight months. Were there unusual circumstances surrounding the case, or is eight months for killing a child now the normal sentence? There was nothing in the article to suggest that the girl had been deserted by the father of the child.

The girl was perhaps just another unhappy creature, and there must have been something wrong with her if she could murder a child, especially since it was her own child. A well-made child, breathing, but in the grip of its mother screaming less and less, until it was dead.

This girl, this mother, is undoubtedly of a type that Norway, and life, would be better off without. She is worth less than the child. She is without love, without responsibility, she has no call in life. The child, on the other hand, might have made something of itself. The article did not mention whether the child were boy or girl, but whatever, it might well have come to achieve great things; we have no way of knowing. At least there would have been hope for the child for many years, while it was growing up. But the mother is beyond hope.

We build palaces for the blind, the crippled, the old – but our Children's Homes are not palaces, our nurseries have to beg daily just to keep themselves in rags and food for the children. And when a young girl kills her child, she gets eight months. And then returns to us.

Murder should cost. We need to be able to afford living, well-made children.

But now, of course, the whole chorus starts up: society locked in the Middle Ages, rights to inherit of illegitimate children, special organisations devoted to helping mothers, the situation of the child's father avoiding all responsibilities – the whole chorus. And here we go, marching on the spot and getting nowhere. A mother like that and a father like that are hopeless – hang them! They have killed a child, a little child that was full of potential and might have gone on to achieve more than we have achieved. And besides, a child is a beautiful thing, and a lovely thing for us to have in our lives, a child plays with its small hands, and sometimes looks up. A child is filled with wonder when it goes from one room and finds itself in another. Imagine that actual moment when the murderess stood over her child and began to strangle it! There are mothers who have killed child after child after child, and are still living. But the children are dead.

Are they really so unprotected, these mothers? And does the father really get away with it? We're marching on the spot, and getting nowhere. Hang both the parents! Wipe them out! Hang the first hundred of them, because they are hopeless. Hang the first hundred. That might create a bit of respect. That might put a stop to these terrible goings-on. Let us do something. Let us deliver our children from the grip around the throat. From all this blood, and all these murders.

The article unleashed a storm of protest in liberal circles in Norway, and attracted contributions to every major newspaper in the country. Hanging had been abolished by a law of 1905, but the last executions under the previous law had taken place back in 1876, forty years before Hamsun's article. As much as he may have wanted to see it reintroduced it is highly unlikely that Hamsun thought it possible. Nevertheless, he kept at it, and in six articles throughout the course of the year against his many challengers, including the novelist, Sigrid Undset, he defended, and indeed, advanced his position. With a fiendish and unattractive glee, and that willingness amounting almost to a pathological need to shock, and show the completeness of his disregard for 'civilised' opinion, he studded his own contributions with the refrain 'Hang them!'. He wrote without respect for his opponents who were, according to him, 'chiefly the childless, the parents of unwanted children, married people with no desire to be parents, or male and female agitators with no interest in the Family'. Even where a contributor tried to find something good to say about his motives in raising the whole question, he flatly rejected the imputation of humanity: a certain Ragnhild Wiesener tried to honour him for wanting to 'save all life for society', to which he replied that, on the contrary, he wished to 'exterminate and clear away the lives which are hopeless for the benefit of those lives which might be of value'. His own constructive solution to the problem – bigger and better Children's Homes that could take and look after the children of women who would otherwise kill them – also involved him in scorning the liberal protection of other categories of weak people – the old, the crippled, the insane – which, according to him, was at the expense of the protection of children: 'The old have had their turn at being people, and now it's over; others have never been people, and never will be.'[20]

There is no doubt that Hamsun felt the plight of the children very deeply, and was unable, or unwilling, to admit the problems of being an unwed mother living alone and in disgrace in a society; but the furious and bloodthirsty nature of his journalism was a hopelessly misguided attempt to enlist sympathy for his point of view. In his novel from the year following the debate, *The Growth of the Soil*, he returned to the problem. Two separate cases of infanticide play a part in the plot, and by a fairly crude act of editorial insertion, reminiscent of Nagel's resumé of the contents of Hamsun's own literary lectures in 1891 in *Mysteries*, the trial of Barbro for the murder of her child by Axel Strøm takes up a large part of the second half of the novel. As novelist, Hamsun's discussion of the problem is more refined and subtle; and his mouthpiece Geissler confines his reactions to grunting loudly and contemptuously during the delivery of liberal speeches in court in defence of Barbro. Hamsun lifted large tracts of these from his opponents' contributions to the newspaper debate.

Of course, Hamsun's whole approach to the debate may have involved a certain amount of extravagant coat-trailing in a situation in which he knew from the outset that his position was hopeless. 'And I enjoy being reckless, so that decent people open their mouths and gape at me', he had written to Bolette Larsen in 1890.[21] For most of his life he seems to have felt this glee in the idea of others thinking of him as 'that *terrible* Hamsun'. But one does feel sometimes, especially as he got older, that he lost the ability to distinguish himself between those utterances which were meant to shock and tease, and those which were expressions of his true opinion.

Whichever, the whole business is just one of those many occasions on which one wishes Hamsun had managed to hold his peace. A witty and humane journalist, Paul Gjesdal, writing shortly afterwards a tribute to Hamsun on his birthday, expressed the situation well: 'When a wanderer reaches fifty he plays on muted strings' he wrote, recalling the title and mood of Hamsun's

1909 novel, 'And when he reaches sixty, he bangs on the big drum.'

The problems brought on by this experiment in living in which the Hamsuns were engaged were beginning to mount up. Major personal and professional difficulties were caused by the remoteness of Hamarøy. On the personal side, Hamsun had managed to see his daughter Victoria only once since the move, when she visited Skogheim in the summer of 1912, just after the birth of Tore. The journey was too long for her, and father and daughter did not meet again for several years. And during those long periods when Hamsun was away from home trying to write, the family were dependent for communication on a very fallible postal and telecommunications network. Impediments could suddenly rise up from nowhere: while Hamsun was in Sortland trying to work on *The Last Joy*, in March 1912, just as Tore was being born, a strike by English coal-loaders led to drastic cutbacks in the ferry services in north Norway, with corresponding problems for the delivery of letters. Sometimes, as at Kraakmo, there was a telephone; but Hamsun's developing deafness meant that he was never particularly happy with the instrument. Even these periods when he was away from the farm were often spoiled for him by his constant anxieties about how Marie was coping – Has she lifted the potatoes yet? Is the pig penned for the winter? Make sure to lift those two stones we broke the reaper on before the snow covers them! Is the horse eating properly? Get the smith to mend the fire in the living room! Remember to air the potato store! In fact, she seems to have coped marvellously with things in his absence, and kept him supplied with long, reassuring letters that alternate between family news and practical matters:

. . . They shirked for a couple of hours on Monday, but that was all. Lars wants to finish for this year, but says he'll be back next year. He thinks it will be just rain from now on, not enough to do, and would rather do a bit of trading in leather. He's travelling to Bodø today. The boys say they'll carry on, they say they've learned enough now to finish the job alone. Elverhøi has offered them seven kroner per acre (seventy kroner per quarter acre) to clear the wood below the kitchen garden. We got sixty barrels of mixed potatoes, fifty-two barrels of large, ten times what we got last year, so we mustn't grumble. We lifted the turnips yesterday – thirty-three barrels which we've had to put in the housekeeping store, since the cellar is full to the ceiling with potatoes. We're getting hay from Dundas in December . . .

Tore is fine at the moment, clever and sweet-tempered. Every day he has a new trick for us, the latest is a loud cackling laugh which causes all the rest of us to laugh. So everything is going well here. And he doesn't need constant attention any more. He sits for hours alone in his pram and plays with his toys, which he has plenty of, from the egg-whisk to that big india-rubber of mine . . .

But they both suffered from the absences. In February 1915 Hamsun took time off from writing *Segelfoss Town* in Harstad to sigh, in a letter to Marie, that 'if only I had a soundproof hideaway at home I would come back at once and try to continue there'. The hut that they built in the garden of Skogheim in the summer of 1916 was an attempt to provide these kind of isolated work conditions for him. But it was a half-hearted attempt: already in early 1916 Hamsun had advertised Skogheim for sale at 12,000 kroner. Marie, thinking chiefly of the children, protested that a move was impractical and unwise. She had also come to love the place, and Hamsun gave in with a good, if temporary, grace. That a move was inevitable he was quite determined on, and his thinking on possible new places to settle led him, in April 1916, to renew contact with his old friend Erik Frydenlund in Valdres, and sound him out about the possibilities of the family moving there:

I nearly sold my smallholding here earlier this spring, but then my children are so small that my wife won't agree to move with them yet, and she's right enough. But it leaves me here with nothing else to do. The farm is drained, cleared and levelled. Of course, I could keep draining and levelling, but it would be just nonsense, just gentleman farming, and I'm too practical a man to go in for that. I'll have to wait a year and a half until I've got the rough outlying land cleared, and then maybe set to work on the large swamp there. – If you've got a nice piece of land near you then I'll come and buy it, and be a Valdres-man for the rest of my days. It must be land that I can cultivate (which is the best fun I know) and there must be at least enough wood for heating.[22]

Another passing thought of happy days in the past caused him to write a letter to the Neeraas' in Kristiansund, where he had lived briefly in 1892, and ask what the prospects were for buying a house there. But it was the Valdres idea that persisted, and on New Year's Eve 1916 he again wrote to Erik Frydenlund to tell him that he had now absolutely made up his mind that they must move as soon as possible, he could stand no more delay. He had decided that it

must be Valdres, but now he was thinking along the lines of a large
house, not another farm:

> So now please forget about my first question, and devote your
> thought instead to this one. God, if I felt even as well as I did last
> year then I'd go in for farming again, but now I'm destroyed. I'm
> not saying that I intend to fall down and die, but my nerves are
> gone. Once before I was in Aurdal, and the place made a human
> being of me again after a difficult time. I think of those days now,
> and feel I'd like to try again. I've also been thinking about the
> south, Mandal or somewhere like that. But you aren't there, nor
> all the old familiar faces, and that's the strangest thing – that for
> all the rambling about I've done, I feel as though I have a kind of
> home in Aurdal – much more of a home than I have here now.[23]

For all these nostalgic longings, however, Hamsun knew better
than to spoil yet another carefully preserved dream of the remote
past by setting up home in it. Casting around for the solution to his
problem he showed again his old flair for addressing himself to the
right man at the right time, and wrote to a journalist friend on the
editorial board of *Aftenposten*, called Christofersen explaining
what he saw as the major obstacle to his move – that of finding
someone in the north of Norway who could afford to pay the
20,000 kroner he now valued the farm at – and asking whether
Christofersen could help him in any way. The ready response to
his letter shows the extent to which Hamsun was respected and
admired by his contemporaries: Christofersen immediately
proposed, and organised, the formation of a limited company
among fourteen of his friends who each bought a share at 1000
kroner in Skogheim, the editor himself providing the other 6000
kroner, and thus the farm was sold. One year later, the company
sold the farm to Hamarøy commune as a residence for the doctor,
making a profit on each of the shares of precisely eighteen kroner
for the shareholders. Hamsun, meanwhile, had been travelling in
the south of Norway looking at houses, and bought the villa
Solgløtt in the town of Larvik. This was one of a string of upper-
class holiday towns on the south and south-east coast of Norway, a
mere eighty miles south of the capital, instead of Hamarøy's one
thousand miles north. The family packed and left Nordland in
April 1917.

There were other reasons that dictated a move: the fact that
Hamsun and his farm were becoming something of a 'must' for

tourists to north Norway, who took him in along with the mountains and the midnight sun; the difficulties involved in getting the corrected proof copies of his novels to Christiania or Copenhagen in time for the printing (at times he was reduced to *telegraphing* his corrections); and a certain disillusionment with the gossipy and exposed nature of life in a small settlement.

The most pressing was probably that he had begun work on *The Growth of the Soil*, his Nobel Prize-winning novel, in the summer of 1916. To try to get going on it, he had returned to one of the most remote of his retreats, the farm Kraakmo on Sagfjord, a day's rowing up a valley across seven large lakes to Johannes Kraakmo's farm, where he had worked successfully on *Children of the Age* in 1913. When the work-hut at Skogheim was ready later in the summer he tried to carry on there; but in spite of the fact that he had all the major themes clear in his head, and an outline for every chapter, by January 1917 he had produced no more than forty pages of the novel. For this sorry state of affairs he blamed the impossible division of cares between farming and writing. The novel was especially important to him in that he intended it as 'a warning to my generation', as he wrote to Kønig at Gyldendal, adding ironically, 'I know the world can manage quite well without me – but all the same . . .'[24]

In the end it proved so important that he was prepared to sell his farm in order to get it written.

The *Segelfoss* novels rattle and clatter and whistle and bang along; one might almost call them industrial novels. *The Growth of the Soil* is a much quieter book. If in the earlier books he had tried, by depicting the changes that were taking place in Norwegian society during the latter half of the nineteenth and the first half of the twentieth centuries, to give a view of society as it really was, in *The Growth of the Soil* he attempted to show society as he wished it were; unchanging, strong and sure, a solid farm-based culture that succeeding generations affirmed without real question or doubt, one that effortlessly withstood the challenge of town and industry.

The opening paragraph strikes the mythic keynote of the novel:

The long, long road over the moors and up into the forest – who trod it into being first of all? Man, a human being, the first that came here. There was no path before he came. Afterwards, some beast or other, following the faint tracks over marsh and moorland, wearing them deeper; after this again some Lapp gained scent of the path, and took that way from field to field, looking to his reindeer. Thus was made the road through the great Almenning – the common tracts without an owner; no-man's-land.

The man comes, walking towards the north. He bears a sack, the first sack, carrying food and some few implements. A strong, coarse fellow, with a red iron beard, and little scars on face and hands; sites of old wounds – were they gained in toil or fight? Maybe the man has been in prison and is looking for a place to hide; or a philosopher, maybe, in search of peace. This or that, he comes: the figure of a man in this great solitude.

We never find out who this man, Isak, was, nor where he came from, which is perhaps the only link he has with the Hamsun heroes of old, the narrator of *Hunger*, Nagel, Thomas Glahn. Hamsun's point here is that Isak's personal past is wholly unimportant, since what he proposes to give his readers in Isak is a symbol rather than a man.

Isak chooses a place to settle in the wilderness, clears the ground, and begins farming and building there. He sends out a message, via the mystical figure of a wandering Lapp, that he is looking for a woman who is willing to live and work with him, and presently Inger comes to him from over the mountains. She is a woman disfigured by a hare-lip, but a strong and hard-working home-maker and helper, and together they establish the settlement known as Sellanraa. Thereafter Hamsun's visionary, rather than strictly novelistic, concern is to expand and strengthen this new settlement, increase it in livestock and acreage, raise children on it, populate the surrounding areas with other settlers inspired by Isak's initiative – some successful, like Axel Strøm, and some not so, like Brede Olsen – and to keep these humans with their values fixed about the wheel of the seasons, as he sends it slowly and inexorably rolling out of the far end of the book into the safekeeping of an inviolable eternity.

Within this vision, the major roles that Hamsun requires his characters to play are symbolic. Axel Strøm is a variant of Isak, and Isak's son Sivert is a replica of his father. Another son Eleseus carries out a disastrous flirtation with the city and its ways, which turns him into a slightly ridiculous and rather sad figure, neither peasant nor dandy, a misfit whose crime is what Hamsun hints is the only real crime – discontentment, dissatisfaction with one's lot, the compulsion to try to change onself. Another victim of the city is Barbro, daughter of the unsuccessful settler Brede Olsen. Still another corrupted by civilisation is Isak's own wife Inger: sent to prison for the murder of a girl-child born to her with a hare-lip, she spends seven years in a city jail where she nevertheless manages to acquire a veneer of empty sophistication which takes a long while to wear off after her return to Sellanraa. Then there is her sister Oline, a tough spinster who survives into ripe old age, thanks to a sharp ear for the clashing of personalities and a talent for changing sides at the right tactical moment in the little wars and feuds that ensue.

The narration presents all these characters in the style that Hamsun had begun exploring for the first time in genuinely extended form in the *Segelfoss* books, commenting and musing and reacting constantly, exclaiming with delight, muttering with disapproval, shaking the head, abruptly halting in astonishment; the style is intensely verbal, that of a voice playing all the parts. But this narrator seems less Hamsun the author than does the enigmatic character Geissler. Several correspondences identify him with his creator, notably a sudden memory that comes to him 'from the time I was a year and a half; I stood leaning down from the barn bridge at Garmo and noticed a smell'; Garmo was Hamsun's own birthplace. And Geissler's contribution to the court proceedings against Barbro for the murder of two of her children reproduces the more temperate and ironic parts of Hamsun's own comments on the subject of the murder of unwanted children in the newspaper debate of 1915.

Geissler is a development of a figure Hamsun had used once or twice before in his fiction; the lighthouse-keeper Schøning in *Benoni*, and the telegraph operator Baardsen in the *Segelfoss* novels. These characters have in common a slight sense of mystery about them, an identification with providence. And Geissler is a man who functions best by suddenly appearing in the middle of a situation, acting so as to influence its outcome decisively, and disappearing back into his mystery. Of Hamsun's various conjuring of such characters, Geissler is the most distinctly and deliberately mercurial: as the government agent responsible for handling Isak's buying of Sellanraa he lets him have it for a ridiculously cheap price. Later, after he has lost this job, he makes a fortune by selling to some Swedish engineers a mining concession on land he has bought from Isak, and forces them to pay Isak a large sum of money too. On another occasion, when Sellanraa is threatened by drought, he teaches Isak and his son Sivert the principle and practice of irrigation which saves their crops that summer. He presents Isak with a mechanical hayrake, and Axel Strøm, another favoured settler, receives a mowing machine and a harrow. As payment for all this help he asks only that Isak and Axel and the Sellanraa people continue in their cultivation of the same land, and maintain the same values – hard work, human tolerance, humility and respect for nature.

Yet Geissler is a human being, and his powers to astonish and delight in an enigmatic way are only possible on account of his long absences from the scenes of his activities. The narrative often hints that Geissler is suffering from a hangover. He loses his job, and is separated from his wife and family. At times he appears to be so broke that he cannot even pay for his lodging at Sellanraa; and yet suddenly he has the money to give away costly farm machinery as presents. He and his ideas permeate the book. He describes himself as 'a sort of fog', everywhere, but insubstantial, indefinable. Articulate, quick-witted and educated, in a world of inarticulate people, he encourages and exalts them, and is their apologist to the reader. The simple and instinctive rightness of their way of life is something that is no longer possible for him personally, since, as he rather sadly describes himself, he is someone who knows the right thing to do, but does not do it.

Geissler is like a fading trace across the firmament of this vision of Hamsun's Wanderer figure, a Nagel in middle-age maybe. Like Tobias Holmengraa at the end of *Segelfoss Town*, Geissler is allowed to depart from the novel with his mystery intact. The fates of the more obviously mortal characters are calmly delineated in Chapter Six of the second book of the novel, with much use of the historic present to emphasise an overall continuity which will replace them with other, similar characters. During this process Hamsun painstakingly affirms the humanity of all of his characters, and accepts and celebrates them all. Isak's wife Inger has had a hard life which has left her 'a little damaged, a little warped', but she is 'good by nature'. When she betrays Isak with a charming wanderer named Gustav, this is only because she is a 'strong woman, full of weakness, and only following the laws of nature all about her'. Eleseus, who finally vanishes into the thin air of the immigrant's dream of America, was 'not strong, either of body or will, but a thorough good fellow for all that'. Old Oline dies, not mourned by anyone in particular, but accepted, respected for her willingness to use others and in turn let herself be used. The failed settler Brede Olsen, a man too fundamentally sensual for the hard life which he gamely tried to lead, ends up running a coffee shop and lodging-house with his wife in the nearest town, where their fat dog is a living advertisement for the good quality of their food. Even Brede's daughter Barbro, whom the journalist Hamsun would have hung twice for the murders of two of her children is finally not, after all, 'so thoroughly harsh and unlovable'. Hamsun the novelist does not try to explain or excuse her killings as the result of any unendurable social pressure on her, but simply sweeps them up into the general net of humanity which hangs beneath her:

> She has never spared herself, to tell the truth, never been of a lazy sort, and that is why she has her neat figure now and pretty shape. Barbro is quick to learn things, and often to her own undoing; what else could one expect? She had learned to save herself at a pinch, to slip from one scrape to another, but keeping all along some better qualities; a child's death is nothing to her, but she can still give sweets to a child alive. Then she has a fine musical ear, can strum softly and correctly on a guitar, singing hoarsely the while; pleasant and slightly mournful to hear. Spared herself? No; so little indeed, that she has thrown herself away altogether and felt no loss. Now and again she cries, and breaks her heart over this or that in her life – but that is only natural, it goes with the songs she sings, and is the poetry and the friendly sweetness in her; she had fooled herself and many another with the same.

As for Isak, the last picture we get of him realises to the full his mythical status. We see him out sowing in his fields, 'a stump of a man, a barge of a man to look at'. Like the other great settler Axel, and like his own son and heir Sivert, he is expressly a man of peace:

> A tiller of the ground, body and soul; a worker on the land without respite. A ghost risen out of the past to point the future, a man from the earliest days of cultivation, a settler in the wilds, nine hundred years old, and, withal, a man of the day.

Of course, the whole thing was a vision, just a dream, and one that could only be sustained by carefully sparing Isak the agonies of an ordinary human consciousness. But as a dream, it is at times extremely beautiful; and if the narration is at times too pressing, too intimate, too naïve, the novel is rich in Hamsun's ecstatic pantheism, and contains many fine examples of his genius in describing the ways inhibited people nevertheless have of expressing their love for one another.

And in a Europe smashed and exhausted by war, a book with such a powerful message of peace and hope was probably a surprising, and slightly wonderful, thing for a reader to come across.

The Growth of the Soil was an immediate popular success in Norway; published on 1 December 1917, the first edition of 18,000 was sold out before Christmas. Within two years it had sold 36,000 copies, and by 1927 55,000 copies. These were previously un- heard-of sales figures in Scandinavia, and not bad going for an author who had remarked in 1906, in the resigned spirit of his recently published novel *Under the Autumn Star* (a first edition of 3000 copies) that 'I will never sell more books than that. I have my regular readership.'

The Growth of the Soil was 'a warning to my generation' he had written to Kønig. In fact the novel was all part of the message, in artistic form, that Hamsun had been trying to impress upon his countrymen for some years now, in his conscientious but deeply uneasy attempts to fill the role of Poet Laureate. The message was reaction. Go back. His reasons were primarily spiritual, religious: that people growing up in the soulless environment of the city, and expending their labour in factories, were losing contact with their roots in life. The portraits of the new working men in the *Segelfoss* books, Aslak and Konrad, make it clear that he found in industrial- ised man an ill-mannered, selfish, and respectless creation whose only hope of salvation was to refuse to participate in the process of 'progress' and return to an honourable and honest life on the farm. Hamsun also felt that there were sound economic reasons that argued the advisability of Norwegians concentrating on farming at the expense of industry. He outlined his theory in a letter to the editor Christofersen of *Aftenposten* on 17 March 1918.

> I'm convinced that agriculture is the future for us now. Whether the Germans 'win' the war or not, their industry will be more or less boycotted by the rest of the world – and they'll work cheaply, even more cheaply than now. We couldn't possibly compete with them, we'll always be behind, and that's why we'll do better to make a start on cultivating Norway. Did you see that the Insurance Companies have given six million towards new farming projects? Wonderful! There's a gift without precedent!

But for the Hamsuns it was, temporarily at least, a case of 'do as I say, not as I do'. The house in Larvik, bought from a dentist, was not ready for them to inhabit immediately, and so the whole family moved into the luxury quarters provided for them by the owner of Larvik Sanatorium. The owner, a rich socialite with an elegant Swedish wife known locally as 'the Countess', fêted Hamsun shamelessly, and there were dinner parties every night. Hamsun enjoyed the attention hugely. It gave him the opportunity to wear the elegant suit of clothes he had had made up for himself in Bodø the year before in anticipation of his return to civilisation.

At fifty-seven Hamsun was still an extremely attractive man, and it was Marie, twenty-three years younger, who suffered from jealousy, particularly of 'the Countess'. Marie had had three children in the space of five years, and was heavily pregnant with a fourth by the time of the move to Larvik. Much more than her husband she had given herself over to the role of countrywoman, and this new, sophisticated social life intimidated and depressed her. She felt shabby and provincial, doubly shaming for someone who had once been an actress at the National Theatre in Christiania. So her relief must have been considerable when they were eventually able to move into their own house, even though she found it 'costly and banal'.

Here they stayed just one year; time enough for Hamsun to finish the novel, and for their fourth child to be born. So complete was Hamsun's dedication to his work that not even the christening of the new baby was allowed to interfere with his routine. He chose the name for the child – Cecilia – because he said it had silk gliding through it, but was gone early in the morning on the day itself, leaving a note to Marie excusing himself from attendance:

Dear Mother of Cecilia,
    I've taken sandwiches and I'll be away with my fifty people until the evening.
    Tell the Godfathers that even though they're rid of me today they can be sure I'll catch up with them later. And tell them to have a marvellous time.[25]

Even while *The Growth of the Soil* was going through the printers, ideas for the next novel had begun to pile up on his desk. This was to be a novel in polar relationship to that idyll; harsh, cynical, and illusionless. Unable, as usual, to get a decent start on it, he took one of his impulsive and random trips away from home with his papers and his pen, and sailed on a westbound ferry and hopped off at Kragerø a little further down the coast. The trick didn't work on this occasion, and he spent his time instead on a piece of social journalism, *The Neighbouring Town*, another glorification of the past at the expense of the present. Even after his return from Kragerø he was unable to hit the right note on which to start his new novel, and instead devoted some time to writing his most considerable contribution to the debate raging in Norway over the principles which should guide the future development of the Norwegian language.

This debate was one of the most problematic concomitants of the achievement of full independence in 1905. The issue is still a live one in Norway today, in which two related but distinct languages, 'Nynorsk' and 'Riksmål', compete for an ultimate authority and status which, in all likelihood, neither of them will achieve. As a gesture of total commitment to their Norwegianness, certain writers, like Arne Garborg, went over to writing their fiction and poetry in Nynorsk, essentially a written form of the language pruned of Danicisms, and based on the spoken language of the common people of Norway as defined and codified by the philologist Ivar Aasen during the middle of the nineteenth century. This language was considered more purely Norwegian, and in some absolute way, more beautiful. Reverence for tradition was not an important part of Hamsun's advocacy of the past; moreover the new form of the language was incomprehensible to the other Scandinavians, so that for a writer to use it in many ways defeated the object of the exercise – communication – and, in addition, did not make economic common sense.

Thus we have yet another paradox to consider in Hamsun: that linguistically he was a radical, a progressive, and the subjectivity of the journalist Hamsun is, for once, a delight as he sets about the various professors and professional language 'experts' delegated by the Norwegian government to report on advisable language reforms:

> It is not the philologists whom we have to thank for our language. Shakespeare's works contain some pretty weird spellings here and there, but Shakespeare created a world from his language. When it suited his purpose J P Jacobsen tore the Danish language to shreds, but all the same, he has immeasurably enriched that language.

He shuddered at the thought of professors being accepted as authorities on language when 'few of them know anything at all about *language*, although they know all about words and letters', and this dry, passionless approach was what upset him most:

> The whole Committee thinks of language as words. But language is spirit. Writing is the soul manifesting itself in dead things. The Committee has no spiritual relationship to a living language.

Originally published in article form in *Aftenposten* in June 1918, 'Language in Danger' was also published as a pamphlet the same year. Fifty thousand copies were sold, an indication of the interest the subject aroused. Hamsun's common sense and enlightened attitude, not to mention the extraordinary freedom with which he used his own language in his novels, was an important contribution to the enduring good health of the Norwegian language.

Again he tried to get his new novel underway. Marie hired a cottage in the country a few miles away from Larvik and took the four children with her in the summer of 1918. Hamsun stayed at home to work. But just a few days after the holiday began he turned up too, with a suitcase containing all his notes for the book. But he did no work there either – he never even opened the suitcase – and spent his time playing in the grass with the children.

The Larvik move had served its purpose. *The Growth of the Soil* had been written. Now both the Hamsuns began to wonder what they were really doing there when both of them felt a similar fundamental distaste for the social life, and had, on reflection, enjoyed their experience of farm life in Hamarøy so much. Marie seems never to have had any real doubts about the kind of life she wanted. Hamsun had perhaps wished to test the strength and reality of his love of the country by subjecting himself once again to the attractions of civilisation. Certainly he must have felt less of a freak at Larvik than he did in Hamarøy; and the nearness of Christiania was a blessing he had already enjoyed, travelling in to see Victoria again for the first time since 1912.

Almost by a process of elimination, then, he discovered what it was that he did not want, as well as what he wanted. He put the house at Larvik on the market, and opened a correspondence with a friend of his from long, long ago, bank manager Birkenes from Lillesand, whom he had met while working on *Mysteries* in 1890. What he wanted, he told Birkenes, was:

. . . in the first place, somewhere close to the sea, with water and electricity laid on, with a large house, and not too much land (between 80 and 150 Mål cultivatable land), plenty of trees and pasture, near a school, though it needn't be near a town. An old, run-down and neglected mansion house would do, I'd put it back on its feet again, and plough the land.

Another absolute stipulation was that the house should have no near neighbours. Everything had to be right this time because, as he told Birkenes, 'When I buy this time it will be for life for me and my children, and I want somewhere nice.'

Birkenes could assure him that there were plenty of places answering this description, and sent him addresses and photographs to look at, as well as checking out certain places himself.

Unfortunately there was always some slight impediment – there were neighbours too close by, or the house was too far from the sea, or it cost a million kroner. Then in July, after a search that had taken him across three counties, Hamsun saw the place he wanted: a long, large, low, white mansion house built by some long departed member of the Danish aristocracy, standing all on its own, well back from a corner of the country highway running along the end of the garden, affording magnificent views over a lake with tree-clad shores, and beyond, to the skerries and the open sea. The estate was richly afforested, and had plenty of cultivable land, yet was sufficiently run-down to persuade Hamsun that he would get it for a price he could afford. The owner, a man named Longum, had bought the place just a few months earlier, and seems not to have had any particular desire to sell again so soon. In fact, the house was not officially on the market at all. Hamsun asked Longum to name his price. Longum suggested 200,000 kroner (£11,000), a price perhaps intended to put the buyer off, and to his surprise Hamsun accepted immediately. In a characteristically impulsive way he had taken another decisive step in his life. On a rainy day in November 1918, the family moved into Nørholm.

Many changes had taken place in Hamsun's life during the years in Nordland, and the Larvik interlude. As a private individual he had experienced in rich and various forms the pleasures of 'the last joy' – fatherhood – and found in it one answer to the rather existential kind of depression that seems to have plagued him most of his life. In particular he felt that in family life he had found the solution to the problem of what remains after the achievement of achievable goals. His marriage to Marie was unusual, but looked to be successful. The attempt to return to his roots had been perhaps a failure considered from a purely geographical point of view; but in the attempt he had rediscovered more general, less individual roots that restored to him his sense of identity as a countryman.

From now on, Hamsun will claim consistently to be a farmer first, and a writer second. Calling himself a farmer leaves him free to give full vent to the uneasy sense of self-disgust which being a writer seems always to have excited in him. The weird refrain, only one of the wild jangle of paradoxes that made up his personality, was sounded more firmly than ever in a letter he wrote around this time to a Danish woman who had sent her latest publication to him to read and pass his judgement on. One might imagine that his answer came as a considerable surprise to her:

You and I, we shouldn't live from scribbling and emptiness, we ought to have meaning as human beings, marry and have children, make a home and live close to the earth. Think about it. I am old and I know it. I've written maybe thirty books, I don't remember exactly; but I have five children, and that is my real blessing. What do people want with all those books? If it weren't for my children I wouldn't even have the right to a grave.

Chapter 13
1918–1927: The Quiet Years:
Family Man and Psychoanalysis

When Marie Hamsun broke the news to her husband that he had won the Nobel Prize for Literature for 1920, his initial reaction disappointed her. She described the scene in *The Rainbow*:

> He did not look up from his food, and said quietly: It can change nothing for us now.
> Did a shadow suddenly fall across his mind, something from his childhood? The fear in the cemetery at Hamarøy, perhaps. Or did he think then of Tomtegaten, the occasional five kroner pieces, and *Hunger*?
> I said: But Knut, the *honour*?
> Then he looked up, darkly, and said cuttingly:
> So you think I haven't had enough honour!
> What did he have against honour? Yes, honour comes to *old* people.
> Thick and dull, it comes to the old, seated man. To old age, the most loathsome of all, worse than death.
> I crept out again behind his back.

But this initial guarded reaction presently gave way to ordinary pleasure and pride in the award. As a patriot, Hamsun was proud to be the first Norwegian since his old idol Bjørnson to win the prize; and as a farmer, father of four and now the owner of a large, costly and run-down estate, the 136,000 kroner in prize money was particularly welcome.

His literary achievements and his reputation might have earned him the Nobel Prize many years earlier, but not until *The Growth of the Soil* did he produce a book that might be described as idealistic, a condition in the awarding of the prize that was taken seriously in its early days. Ever since the novel's publication there had been talk of the prize, and Hamsun had two champions in Sweden who campaigned vigorously for his nomination – Albert Engström the caricaturist and comic writer whom he had met in Finland with Bergljot in 1899; and the secretary of the Academy himself, Erik Axel Karlfeldt. After a near miss in 1919, when the prize went instead to the Swiss Carl Spitteler, the two finally succeeded in securing it for their man, though the Hamsuns remained blithely unaware of the fact until a reporter on the local newspaper at Grimstad rang Nørholm with the news.

Proud he may have been, but one of Hamsun's first thoughts was of trying to get out of attending the ceremony. He was suffering increasingly from a dislike, and even a fear, of public appearances; and the journey, the ceremony itself, the celebrations, the journalists, the obligation to act as the centre of attraction appeared to him a circus of horrors to be avoided at all costs. He contacted Engström and Karlfeldt, both of whom urged him to attend, promising him protection from press and visitors, and offering to take care of booking the accommodation in Stockholm. Hamsun bowed to the inevitability, and he and Marie began their respective preparations for the ceremony. Hamsun locked himself away to try to write a speech, and Marie took a trip into Christiania to buy herself a new gown. When she returned, and showed her husband what she had bought, he expressed immediate concern about the low neck-line, and was adamant that her health would suffer. Marie, for whom the glamorous days as an actress in the capital were now but a remote memory, sighed stoically as Hamsun improved the dress with a length of black tulle and some scissors to make it 'warmer' for her.

The journey to Stockholm got off to a bad start – their train was stopped by the first day of a sixteen-day national rail strike, a circumstance which did not improve Hamsun's low opinion of socialism and the development of organised trade unions in Norway. They hired a cab to take them to Charlottenberg, and were able to take the Stockholm train from there.

Albert Engström had reserved a room for them at the Grand Hotel Royal in the Swedish capital, and had booked in there himself with his wife, the better to be able to protect Hamsun from unwanted attentions. Engström was an eccentric chap who slept with a skeleton beside his bed; the kind of grim humour that appealed to Hamsun. However, the first meeting between the two old friends, who had not met since 1899, did not get off to a good start as Engström stepped forward and warmly greeted Hamsun with the words 'Goodness me, how old you look!' It was just a

temporary hitch, though. Engström and Hamsun preserved a lifelong friendship, even though they met only twice. Or perhaps it
was because they met only twice.

The prize-giving itself took place on 10 December in the main
hall of the Academy of Music, in the presence of members of the
Swedish royal family. The prizewinners for that year were the
Swiss physicist Charles Guillaume, the German chemist Walter
Nernst, and the Danish physiologist August Krogh. The peace
prize went to the French politician Leon Bourgeois. They sat on the
stage for the speeches, and the prizegiving by Prince Carl, and
then joined the guests below for the banquet. Hamsun's neighbour
was Selma Lagerløf the novelist, herself a former winner of the
literature prize. Hamsun was no great admirer of her work, but she
was a lively and intelligent woman, and the two took an obvious
joy in one another's company. Marie was not so lucky: her
neighbour was August Krogh, discoverer of the regulation of
the motor mechanism of capillaries, who sat wretchedly studying
his speech on a piece of paper held under the tablecloth until
the awful moment to deliver it arrived.

Hamsun gave no sign of nerves, and when he rose to speak won
the hearts of the assembly by being both brief and personal in his
acceptance speech:

Ladies and Gentlemen!
    What can I possibly say to an honour like this? You raise me on
high, I lose my footing. The room floats away with me. It's not
easy to be me this evening. I've been loaded down with honour
and riches, the speech from the stage was like a wave, it made
me sway.
    It occurs to me that I'm lucky that on a previous occasion in my
life, when I was young, I was also at times in a state that made
me sway. I feel tempted to say that everything that happens in
life benefits us in some way or other, in the end.
    But I must refrain from trying to talk wisdom to an audience
such as is gathered here this evening – especially now, when we
have just heard from the world of science. On behalf of my
country I must thank the Academy, and Sweden, for the honour
that has been shown me. I bow my head beneath the weight of
such honour. I am proud that the Academy has shown its faith in
my ability to bear it.
    I write my books, in my fashion; but I have learnt from
everybody, and not least from the last generation of Swedish
lyricists. And if I was really any good at literature then I'd be
making a better speech here, and trying somehow to connect it

Hamsun at Lillehammer in 1895, where he went to relax after overworking in Paris. The painter Johannes Muller attempts to amuse the solemn Miss Konow, while Hamsun may conceivably have resorted to tickling the singer, Miss Lund, in order to win her charmingly toothy smile.

Hamsun and his first wife Bergljot on their wedding day, 16 May 1898. Bergljot was a wealthy, upper-class woman, daring and stylish in her dress. Hamsun's rise from rags to riches should have been complete here with his marriage to a 'princess'. It proved to be not, after all, what he wanted.

Bergljot and Victoria Hamsun. The photo was taken in Christiania (Oslo) in 1906, the year the family broke up.

Hamsun's daughter Victoria. He sent her to France about 1920 in order to learn the language. She joked that his ambition was for her to marry a rich American. However, she chose an Englishman, to her father's intense displeasure.

ABOVE RIGHT Marie, Hamsun's second wife. She had been a schoolteacher and an actress before meeting him, both of them occupations which Hamsun affected to despise.

RIGHT Hamsun and family at Larvik in 1918. Tore, Marie, Arild, Hamsun, Ellinor. Marie is pregnant with a fourth child, Cecilia. Hamsun was fascinated by hands. His own were huge, and in his novels he frequently remarks upon the appearance

Knut Hamsun at Fornebu Airfield on his arrival from Germany, 28 June 1943, after the meeting with Hitler.

Knut Hamsun på besøk i u-båt.

Et interessant islett i ukerevyen denne gang vilde det ikke undre oss om vi får mangen er Knut Hamsuns besøk ombord høre at Hamsun har vært på tokt. en tysk u-båt like før sin 85-års dag. Det ene bilde viser ham i ferd med å Vi får anledning til å følge ham rundt besiktige u-båtens perioskop. om i fartøyet, og overalt er han en like På det andre bildet ser man kominteressert tilskuer såvel oppe på dek mandanten forklare Hamsun forskjellige ket som nede i maskinrommet. Så neste finesser i u-båtens innredning.

Ny lov om Norges Næringssamband og næringsgruppene.

Alle byggende kretser samles i en selvforvaltende organisasjon

Ministerpresidenten har den 7. sep Næringsorganisasjonene sorterer untember d. å. vedtatt og undertegnet en der Næringsdepartementet forsåvidt ny lov om Norges Næringssamband og gjelder de organisasjonsmessige spørsde 10 næringsgruppene. Hermed er slutt mål. Vedtak angående næringsgrupper steinen lagt på et forberedende arbeid som sorterer under annet fagdepartesom har strukket seg gjennom mange ment må Næringsdepartementet treffe år og som på forskjellig måte har søkt med samtykke av dette. Næringssamå styrke samarbeidet mellom de næ bandets og næringsgruppenes presidenringsdrivende og å samle de i nærings ter oppnevnes av Ministerpresidenten.

A propaganda newspaper report of a visit Hamsun made on board a German U-boat in 1944. The visit was filmed for use in cinema newsreels.

Hamsun at his trial in 1948 with Sigrid Stray. The paraffin lamp was provided by his son Arild after he complained that the light in the courtroom was so poor that he could not see to read. Hamsun's dislike of educated women was another of his 'theoretical' prejudices, and Sigrid Stray was both lawyer and valued friend for the last twenty years of his life.

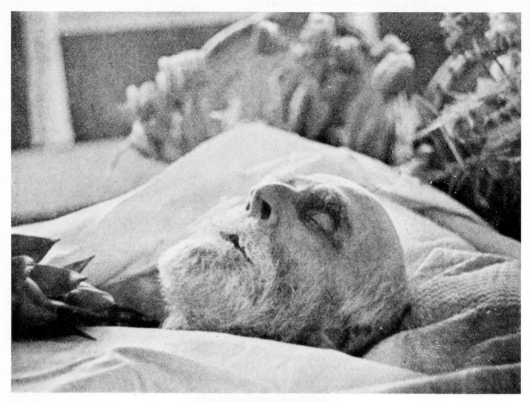

Hamsun on his
deathbed, 19
February 1952.

The room in which
Hamsun died. On
the wall are pictures
of Dostoevsky and
Goethe.

with the preceding speech. And yet that would be just super-ficial cleverness and words, it would not come from the heart. Nor am I young enough for that, I couldn't face it. What I would much rather do now, under all this light, and before a gathering such as this, would be to come to each and every one of you with flowers and verses and gifts. To be young again, and ride the wave. That is what I'd really like to do on such a great occasion, for one last time. But I no longer dare do it, I could not save the picture from caricature. I have been weighted down with honours and riches here in Stockholm today – yes; but I lack the only thing that really matters. I lack youth. There are none of us here so old that we cannot remember it. As we grow older, it is only right that we should give way; but we must do so with honour.

Regardless of what I ought to do now – I don't know – regardless of what would be most fitting – I do not know – I empty my glass for the youth of Sweden, for all youth, for all that is young in life!

This unashamed, melancholic romanticism, laced with self-insight, was quintessential Hamsun. Marie Hamsun reported that one of her neighbours at table, the Academy secretary Karlfeldt, had tears in his eyes afterwards. She herself was profoundly moved on this, the only occasion in her life when she heard her husband speak publicly. When she read the transcript in the newspapers afterwards, she could only compare its relationship to the sound of those same words spoken as that between a pressed flower in a glass case, and that same flower blowing in long, dew-flecked grass. Again one is reminded of the observation, made by so many of those who met Hamsun personally, men and women, that both his physical appearance and his voice were of great manly beauty.

With the formalities over, the serious drinking could begin. Hamsun turned over his wallet to the waiter (it contained all their travel money, and the Nobel cheque) with instructions to keep his own account of what was spent. Marie left him to it in the early hours. Much later he turned up himself, with the assistance of Albert Engström, who explained that Hamsun was 'tired'. Marie tried to undress him, but gave up at the tie, and he slept the night on top of the bed in evening dress. Waking in the morning, he examined himself carefully, and cried in mock distress to Marie: 'Sweetheart, have I slept all night without a tie on?'

Some two weeks before the Hamsuns travelled to Stockholm for the prizegiving, Hamsun published his sixteenth novel, *The Women at the Pump*, written largely in hotels in Lillesand, Arendal, and in one of two deserted cottar's farms that formed a part of the Nørholm estate, fifteen minutes' walk from the main house. He had the usual hellish problems in getting started on it, and his difficulties were exacerbated by an increasingly debilitating shaking of the right hand which he attributed to the pressures of writing with pencil. Many times he told Marie that this would be the last novel. In fact, there were to be five more, and like all of his work in this neo-Dickensian style, all thick books, three or four hundred pages long.

The Women at the Pump forms a remarkable contrast to *The Growth of the Soil*. Had some rich industrialist with a dark sense of humour founded a prize in opposition to Nobel's, for a 'least idealistic work of literature', it might well have led to a clean sweep of prizes for Hamsun in 1920. If we take it as a kind of dark twin to *The Growth of the Soil*, the two together illustrate well the polarity in Hamsun's personality, and heighten the sense of these poles existing not in harmony, but in furious competition with one another.

The novel is a minute description of life in a small Norwegian town on the coast. In many respects it seems to be a deliberate expansion of the short-story *Small Town Life* from the collection *Brushwood*, published in 1903, which was in turn a development of the rather feeble, Twain-inspired story of the same title published in *Bergens Tidende* in 1890. The central character of the short-story, Tønnes Olai, a town layabout and drifter who lives by his wits, reappears in the novel under the name of Oliver, deprived of his manhood in an accident at sea, and yet willing for reasons of pride and economy to accept five children which his wife Petra produces over the course of the years as his own. Oliver is a cripple, a liar, a self-deceiver, a thief, a pimp, and eventually a murderer, and in presenting him as his hero Hamsun's purpose seems to be to make a statement that resolutely affirms life in even its ugliest and least idealistic form.

The novelist Hamsun had been fascinated by cripples all his life, from the shoebinder in *Hunger*, through the midget in *Mysteries*, the doctor in *Pan* and the crippled old pair, Mons and Frederick Mensa in *Benoni*. In *The Women at the Pump* this fascination is given full play, and besides Oliver there is another cripple, the town drunk Olaus, who lost his looks when a dynamite charge blew up in his face, and a short while later lost half an arm in another accident. These cripples are largely an object of horror in Hamsun's gallery, but it may be that it is a horror born out of fear, rather than a genuine lack of humanity. It is certainly worth bearing in mind how much cripples feature in Hamsun's own early life. The most striking example is clearly his uncle Hans, who suffered from paralysis agitans, but other examples from within his own family circle were his sisters Marie, who was lame in one foot, and Sofie, who was crippled in one hip and sat most of her life in a chair. There was also his mother, who had only one eye, and was very deaf. For a poor family, living in a remote rural setting like Hamsund, there could be no question of treatment and operations, and disability could only be viewed as the implacable hand of a largely indifferent God. The charitable explanation of Hamsun's treatment of crippled people in his work might be that it was in the nature of a defiance of God, and perhaps expressed some primitive belief that we ward off what we fear by mockery and loud scorn.

The Women at the Pump is another of what one might call Hamsun's novels of many voices. One voice sees Oliver thus:

> The cripple likewise is on his way home. There is no one, of course, who doesn't keep a wary eye on him, who doesn't hide from him, twisted as he is, so signally mauled, an abomination to his fellow creatures. Can he expect anyone to look at him willingly? His pendulous obesity is appalling, his whole being repulsive, the way he hops along the street insufferable. He is incomplete even as an animal, a quadruped, he is a hollowed-out cripple, an empty husk. Once he was a human being.

Yet this repulsive specimen who lives a lie as a family father, and is not above blackmailing one of the real fathers of the children in order to get himself a job, who lives at times off stolen money, and money simply found, who prostitutes his wife to their chief creditor time and again, this pathetic creature possesses in high degree the most important ability of all, the ability to survive. He watches life with the constant attention of a wild animal, ready at a moment's notice to improvise where an opening occurs for him. Sometimes his inspired scavenging is on the grand scale: he salvages a whole ship on one occasion; on another occasion, on an illegal expedition in his rowing boat to steal down-feathers, he finds huge quantities of paper money from a post-office robbery that have been used by the birds to line their nests. Like Oline in *The Growth of the Soil*, he never gives up. He gets in harness with his destiny, complains of nothing, and fears nothing, except that one day someone will cease to play the game and expose the lies on which his self-respect and his social image are based. When Olaus does this, asking Oliver with that cruel, taunting wit that Hamsun was such a master of, why he even bothers wearing clothes, why doesn't he just walk about the streets in the nude, it costs him his life.

Oliver is posed in harsh contrast to the two idealists in the town, the gentle and philosophical postmaster, and Carlsen the black-smith, a practising Christian. Both of these receive blows that destroy their faith in life and leave them broken men. Oliver, beginning without faith, cannot be destroyed by mere circum-stance:

> An experienced postmaster received one night a thrust in his untested human thought and had been dumb and dim from that moment. Carlsen, the honest old blacksmith, could not endure wickedness, could not endure being suspected of a son who went around with Japanese pictures on his body; he became a child, twitched his lips, thanked God for good and evil and waited for death. Oliver was made of sterner stuff, less delicate and sensitive, more carefree, in short, the right human clay; he could endure life. Who had taken a harder knock than he? But a tiny upward turn in his fortunes, a lucky theft, a successful swindle, restored him to contentment. Did he bear the palm of victory? Oliver had knocked about the world; he had seen palms, they were not the sort of thing to go carrying around.

As in the *Segelfoss* novels, the characters in *The Women at the Pump* fall naturally into small groups. There is an upper class of consuls; a middle class, with a lawyer and a doctor; and a working class composed of fishermen, blacksmiths and seamen. There is no real plot, and in order to keep things moving along Hamsun uses a device that he had exploited as early on in his career as 1892, in *Mysteries*; namely, that of providing the reader with false and misleading information about characters and events. This is a plotting technique curiously similar to that used by the writers of television soap-operas: at any point where the plot seems to be running out of ideas it simply stops, turns, examines its own recent past for some firmly stated fact or event, and now states even more firmly that it did *not* happen, this was *not* to come, thus freeing itself to set off again in pursuit of another definite state-ment which in due course will itself be denied.

For a long time the reader is led to believe that Oliver sustained his crippling injuries when a barrel of whale oil fell on him; not until much later do we discover that this is a lie to protect his reputation, that in fact he carelessly fell from the rigging, and landed astride a derrick. This 'lie' is an essential part of Oliver's character, and a part of the novel's affirmation of the necessary role of the life-lie in normal human society; but when, late on in the story, the fall of the greatest of the consuls, double-consul Johnsen, is heralded by the sinking of his largest and most expensive cargo ship, loaded and uninsured; and when we learn even later that, in fact, the consul's son had after all secretly insured the ship, so that the family fortunes are in fact saved, it does smack rather of Hamsun's simply 'making it up' as he goes along.

The novel relies heavily on this technique; but in the end it all seems simply a part of Hamsun's odd and unpredictable charm as a novelist. Having seen him use rather too frequently the grand, saga-writer's formula 'And the years went by', we might find ourselves beginning to wonder just how old Oliver's two sons are by now. In the midst of describing a love scene between the younger boy Abel and Little Lucy, we find Hamsun beginning to wonder about the same thing, with a disarming openness:

> Mind you, they were not all that old, as people go. Suppose he was nineteen, that would make her a mere seventeen or so. Or if we were to tell the truth and say he was only sixteen, that would make her still less – what age would that be? And there they stood.

This daringness is one of the pleasures of Hamsun the narrator. Elsewhere he makes free use of the technique he had discovered in *Mysteries*, and which later came to be called 'stream of consciousness', wherein the narration suddenly swoops from its flight around the head of a character and passing inside the head goes into a direct relation of the character's thoughts. Hamsun also extensively uses a device apparently borrowed from the layout of a play-script: in the middle of an ordinary conversational exchange we get this characteristic formulation:

> The pharmacist (still evasive, but nervously eager): 'Another new specimen? Well, what is one to say?'

The novel is speckled with Hamsun's own special brand of insolent, folksy humour: someone tells the carpenter Mattis that his nose is so big he ought to build a stable for it; Oliver, when singing the praises of Petra's sexuality, tells her 'So help me God, you don't need to find out what sex you are by having a peep – you have it in you!' And the gentle blacksmith has the following absurd exchange with his family:

> Afterwards he would exchange quiet, low-keyed banter with his daughter:

'Yes indeed, we two men have got through a lot of work today, but what about you? I can't see that you've touched a thing – the chairs are still all in one piece.'

They laugh at this, and the daughter replies: 'Ah, but unfortunately I've broken two plates today.'

'Is that all?' says her father, 'In that time I could have broken a dozen!'

This gentle charm is always cropping up at the oddest moments, keeping a steady warmth glowing in the book despite its harshness and its cruelties. Some of the most charming writing occurs in descriptions of Abel, Oliver's younger son. Abel's elder brother, Frank, has been corrupted by his education, and become a vain philologist, fatuously proud of the number of languages he can speak. According to Hamsun, Frank has risen far above his station, 'and now he talked like a savage. He could make himself understood to no-one but himself; he couldn't even, like a magpie, make himself understood to other magpies. Where would it end?' But Abel has his feet firmly on the ground: he has apprenticed himself to the blacksmith, and earns his living in an honest way. His native intelligence is presented as clearly superior to Frank's acquired smartness. He mocks Frank so subtly that Frank does not even realise it. There is a clear echo in this relationship of that in Ludvig Holberg's play *Erasmus Montanus*, between the educated 'Rasmus Berg' and his unpretentious brother Jacob. Abel is a lovely character, and probably has much of Hamsun's own boyhood in him. He even owns the watch chain without a watch which Hamsun himself had owned as a boy, at Walsøe's store in Tranøy.

Elsewhere in the novel, Hamsun continues his attack on the English. The robbery on the post office which works so unexpectedly in Oliver's favour is carried out by crew members of an English ship on a temporary visit; one is the blacksmith's son Adolf, married and resident in England, and the other the son of the postmaster. Adolf's degeneracy has been further increased by the Japanese, who covered his body in lewd tattoos. The betrayal by the son of the postmaster is particularly poignant. With his oriental philosophy of detachment, and his belief in karma and the transmigration of souls, the postmaster seems close to Hamsun's self-portraiture in the *Wanderer* novels of 1907 and 1909 as Knut Pedersen. He is also oddly at variance with his philosophy of detachment, but entirely in accord with Hamsun's own well-known views on the subject, violently anti-English and given to long speeches criticising English imperialism. According to him, the English 'enslave one people after another, take their independence from them, castrate them, make them fat and placid, and then turn righteous and give these eunuchs something the English call self-government.' These speeches by the postmaster are the bitterest expression of anglophobia in all Hamsun's work, and appearing in his first novel after the end of the First World War they indicate clearly his disappointment at its outcome. They indicate even more clearly that the German defeat and English victory intensified rather than resolved his passionate concern for the eventual outcome of this power struggle.

Most of Hamsun's money from the Nobel Prize was spent on restoring Nørholm to something of its former glory. Longum, the previous owner, had speculated in the estate, and in the few months in which he was its owner he had cleared and sold timber to the value of 120,000 kroner. The farm itself, buildings and land, was badly neglected, and the Hamsuns set briskly to work on renovation and recultivation. Hamsun invited his nephew Ottar from Hamarøy to join them on the farm with his new wife Hilde, and act as farm manager. A fine new house was erected for them in the grounds, although, like the main house, it was without electricity until 1921.

Skogheim in Hamarøy had been a small holding; Nørholm, with its eight hundred acres, its forests, and its collection of outhouses which included two cottar's farms, gave Hamsun the chance to play Isak from Sellanraa on the grand scale. There were often up to eight or ten men at work on various parts of the estate, mining, ditching, road-making, building, digging. Three large moors were drained, and sown with rye, and two barns raised to house the yield. A huge programme of reforestation was carried out, to make good the damage done by the previous owner. Old roads and paths were restored to a usable standard, and new roads built. The herd of dairy cattle was increased, and a new milking parlour built to house them all. The entire estate was fenced, and four strong gates put in to keep out tourists and sightseers, and the garden, which became Marie's particular hobby – and sometimes her anodyne as well – was completely redesigned, to the extent of rechannelling a stream that ran through it. They also built a small bridge over the stream which an unusually high tide swept away one day.

Hamsun derived a tremendous enjoyment out of all this, and took an active part in much of it. His family background, and the rich and various experiences of the wandering years of his early manhood had given him a wide variety of practical skills which his new life as the squire of Nørholm gave him plenty of opportunity to practise once again. He particularly enjoyed the experience of road-making, which he had last practised in Gjøvik in 1880, after the final failure of his first mini-career as a writer. Yet the farming was really no more than a vast toy which his success as a writer had enabled him to afford, and no matter how often he pointedly described himself as a farmer first, and a writer second, it was the writing that took precedence whenever a book began to move inside him. His nephew Ottar returned to Hamarøy in the spring of 1921, sick with tuberculosis, like all his brothers and sisters, and like them, fatally; and in 1922 Hamsun handed over the running of the farm to two young Danes, leaving him free from the cares of the practical side of life which had made his twin careers as farmer and writer so difficult for him at Skogheim.

Naturally, he was still the boss of the farm when he was freed from the demands of writing, and he maintained a special interest in a number of projects. He was by all accounts a good, but engagingly eccentric, farmer; a cow with a good nature he liked as much as a cow with a rich yield, and at his insistence, the beasts were arranged in their stalls in descending order of size. When disasters occurred, he took them well. The larger they were, the better he took them. Always a man extremely susceptible to charm, he once allowed a fast-talker and his friends to build him a road across one of his reclaimed moors, which they did in record time. They took their money and disappeared in record time too, and a short while after the Hamsuns stood and watched their road slowly sinking back into the mud. Marie was furious at the thought of the lost kroner, but Hamsun merely remarked that people were only honest as long as they could afford to be, and hadn't the man a large family to support? And when a few months later one of the road-builder's children died, Hamsun paid for the funeral.

He showed a similar orientalism on a later occasion when a Swedish engineer, a 'genius' who had discovered a new way of building barns out of the very earth on which they stood, was invited by Hamsun to come and stay at Nørholm and personally supervise the erection of one of these miraculous new buildings. The 'genius' was given his own room, and spent a lot of time looking at his papers, and measuring land in preoccupied silence. Many men were required to assist on the day when the revolutionary barn was finally erected; but it was all in vain, the very next day the barn had crumbled to the earth again, and the engineer was gone. A passing farmer had met him bright and early that morning, hitching a lift on the road outside Nørholm, and had taken him into Grimstad.

Hamsun, the enemy of 'modern times', was nevertheless willing to make use of revolutions in agricultural technology. He bought one of the first tractors in Norway, and was first among the local farmers to invest in silos. In the course of the 1920s and '30s he turned Nørholm into a model farm, but at the cost of his profit – the farm was subsidised by literature.

The 1920s was Hamsun's most peaceful decade. He had problems, of course; but the Nørholm estate was large, so he could lose himself in making and carrying out projects. 'Happy' is not really a word that springs readily to mind when thinking about Hamsun, but one feels that there were times during these years when he came close to being happy. His children were growing up, and of an age to be a companion to their father. He was a good father to them, firm but kind, imaginative and eccentric and fun, and he spoiled them to death. All his life he retained a strong element of the childlike, and he empathised with all the curious and intense sufferings and joys that he saw his own children going through, that he had once experienced himself. 'Now the slavery begins', he remarked to Marie as he watched his son Tore set off for the first day at school. And at meals he let them run off as soon as they had finished eating, remembering the hell of having to sit and wait for the adults to catch up. When they grew old enough he bought a boxer puppy for the girls, and boxing gloves for the boys. The girls were also given a whole railway carriage for use as a doll's house, equipped with scaled-down copies of the furniture in the house, and with electricity laid on; and later on – a rare luxury – a gramophone. He gave his sons Arild and Tore fatherly advice: 'Be kind to those who are smaller than you and to those who are kind to you. Hit back – hard – at those who torment you. An eye for an eye, a tooth for a tooth', and encouraged them in the art of self-defence. But he rebuked Tore firmly when he heard that he had been boxing in front of an audience, and gave him the benefit of his advice about sports generally:

I hear you've been boxing in public with Sigurd Hoel. You can cut that out straightaway. It's all very well to learn the art of self-defence in case you should ever find yourself in a tight corner, but the whole idea of fighting in general is an abomination, and to box in public for the amusement of a horde of gawking spectators is something no decent person would do.

Nor should you think that sport in general makes you healthier. This is mere superstition. People in Anglo-Saxon lands don't live any longer than anybody else; quite the contrary, in fact. I've never seen anything more stupid than the expression on the faces of 'sports' people when they grab hold of some newspaper and tear through it looking for the 'sports' results . . .

Neither were the children spared instruction in the further failings of 'people in Anglo-Saxon Lands': 'Slice the cheese neatly, children', he used to tell them, 'Only Englishmen and commercial travellers hack at the cheese.' He also warned Tore against the indulgence of shameless personal vanity: 'Never let it be said of a son of mine that he is too interested in his clothes.'

As for the outside world, it was kept resolutely at bay. The lifelong ambivalence about personal publicity, the longing for the limelight, and the aversion to the limelight, and the self-contempt on both counts, had grown heavier on the side of reclusion. To fence in the entire estate was regarded as an anti-social act, and newspapers reports began to refer to 'the hermit of Nørholm'. An experience with an unsympathetic journalist, Anker Kirkeby, during his year at Larvik had left Hamsun with a pathological contempt for the profession of which he, as a 'great man' in a very small country, undoubtedly saw the worst side. Kirkeby pestered Hamsun relentlessly for an interview, and when he got it was deliberately provocative in his questioning, asking Hamsun about the rumour that he was Bjørnson's son, which Hamsun saw now only as a slur on his mother, and trying to provoke him into further 'outrageous' comments on what he referred to as Hamsun's 'favourite subject' – child murder. Nor did he let Hamsun see the resulting article before it was printed in *Politiken*, as he had promised he would.[1] Hamsun found reporters stupid as well as rude; newspapers regularly carried long interviews with neighbours who happened to have exchanged a nod with him as he was out wandering on the estate. And the more reclusive he became, the more the press sought to breach his privacy. Certain old friends were welcome at Nørholm – Hans Aanrud, Vilhelm Krag who lived nearby, Johannes V Jensen, his publisher Christian Kønig – but it was writing, to which he seems to have existed increasingly in the relationship of slave to master, that continued to dominate Hamsun's life.

He pulled down one of the cottar's homes on the estate and had it rebuilt at the back of the main house, well away from it, but within sight, and turned this into a library and workroom. No one was allowed to disturb him here, not even the children. Even so, he continued his habit of impulsively travelling away and lodging at some remote hotel or boarding-house when he felt that he was getting bogged down in his work. His general health was excellent, but he continued to have hellish problems with what he referred to as his 'nerves'. Marie Hamsun wrote that an exhausting or boring conversation, an unsympathetic stopover in a hotel, or a tiresome train ride could put him to bed for three days with these 'nerves'. And the shaking in his right hand continued. Too late in the day, he went over to writing the first drafts of his novels in ink, after years of using pencil only, and reserving ink for the final copies. Many parts of the five long novels he had still to write after *The Women at the Pump* were written with two hands, the right hand holding the pen, and the left holding the right down on to the page. His hearing was also very bad now. He had travelled to see two specialists in Christiania about it, but was obliged to accept as final their verdict that nothing could be done to restore it. Yet his deafness did not spare him the agonies of *every* kind of unwanted noise when he sat in his writing hut and tried to concentrate on the day's work: one day in 1923, while working on *Chapter the Last*, he was disturbed by the clucking of a hen which had somehow managed to find its way from the farm to the grass in front of his hut. Marie – the guardian of the silence at Nørholm – heard it aghast, dropped everything and came running. She arrived too late, and could only stand and watch as her husband chased after the bird with a stick, swiping fiercely at it until finally a blow landed which silenced it forever. Marie wrote that he was mortified afterwards, and could write nothing for the rest of the day.

Often when working at home Hamsun would take long walks round Nørholm, going the rounds of various small trees that he was taking a particular interest in, to see how they were getting along. He always carried a pocketful of string with him on these walks, to make on-the-spot repairs to saplings whose branches had broken beneath the weight of snow, or whose roots had been tilted by ground frost. Sometimes Marie accompanied him, and if the writing was going well he might be talkative and happy and full of nonsensical fun; if he were in trouble the walks would take place in an iron silence. Marie remarked a strange fondness in him during these walks for the screeching of seagulls, and puzzled over it until one day he happened to mention to her that they were now the only birds he could hear.

His children were growing up strong and healthy; Marie had her garden and had also, encouraged by her husband, begun to write as a hobby. She published a collection of short poems in 1921, and wrote a number of children's books during the years at Nørholm which were extremely successful. As for Hamsun himself, he had won the Nobel Prize for Literature, and was beginning to be spoken of as the greatest living writer in the world. He was the owner of a beautiful home, and proprietor of a model farm. At times, in consideration of all this, he might have come close to being happy, had he not been particularly plagued during these years by the thought of death.

Chapter the Last, published on 27 October 1923, is the result of a long and uneasy speculation on the subject which might have been brought on by the death of his mother in Hamarøy, in January 1919. It is undoubtedly the most interesting and thought-provoking of all his late novels as he examines once more the profoundly existential problems which he had first studied in *Mysteries* in 1892. Indeed, in one of the novel's three main characters, Leo Magnus, known as the Suicide, he creates a character who is, uniquely among his later creations, capable of speculation on the same intellectal and metaphysical level as Johan Nilsen Nagel. Features of Hamsun's later fiction are also present in plenty – the contempt for education, the hatred of the English, the exalting of the life of the blood over the life of the mind – but the presence of the Suicide creates an atmosphere and a mood quite different from that of the *Segelfoss* novels, *The Growth of the Soil*, and *The Women at the Pump*.

Daniel, a smallholder living alone on a mountain farm, is visited one day by two businessmen from the city who plan to open a sanatorium in the district. The situation of Daniel's farm seems ideal to them, and they make him an offer for it. He refuses, but they manage to acquire a neighbouring property on which they erect a number of large and vulgar buildings which are soon occupied by a gallery of sickly grotesques from the city. The novel concentrates on the fate of a dozen or so of these patients, most of whom turn out to be swindlers, cheats, liars, and possibly murderers. There are plenty of deaths on and around the premises, but the novel's grim joke is that the dead are either people simply visiting patients at the sanatorium, or members of the staff, or victims of bizarre accidents. One old woman is gored to death by a runaway bull, and an engineer is killed by a piece of falling rock. A maid dies of food poisoning, and a doctor who goes out skating on the frozen lake at midnight, in order to set a good example to the patients, falls through the ice and dies three days later of pneumonia. The flag flying over the main building gets stuck at half-mast, and none of the patients die.

Hamsun's heroine is a pretty and pretentious city girl, Julie d'Espard, who 'knows nothing to speak of, talks the colourless Norwegian of the middle class, can't sing more than anyone else, has never learnt to keep house, can't do a day's work and make her own blouses; but she can click at a typewriter and she has learnt French'. 'Poor Julie d'Espard', sighs Hamsun.

She falls in love with a consumptive Finnish Count, and becomes pregnant by him. He turns out to be wanted for fraud, and disappears, leaving her with a fat envelope of money to look after. She begins desperately looking round for someone to marry and be a father to the child, but an accident leaves her with a scar on her face, and obliges her to lower her sights in her search for a man. While she and the Count were lovers, they often used to walk over to the fields to visit Daniel on his farm: the unpretentious and simple atmosphere of Daniel's home always had a tonic effect on the Count. Now Julie resumes her visits alone. She likes Daniel; he works hard, eats properly, and she thinks he would be quite nice-looking if he washed a bit more often. Without much trouble she seduces him, and the two lay plans to get married.

To the other women at the sanatorium, Julie is an outsider, hated for her popularity with men. She is particularly friendly with the Suicide and his friend, Anton Moss. There are several instances of twinning in *Chapter the Last*, correspondences of fact and in-versions of fact which link each of the three main characters, Julie, the Suicide, and Daniel, with each other, and fleetingly with other minor characters. The strange relationship between the Suicide and Anton Moss is the first of these twinnings, and is reminiscent of the relationship between Nagel and his 'other Self', the midget in *Mysteries*: Anton Moss is diseased on the outside, afflicted with a hideous skin disease which is developing across his face and threatening to take his sight; the Suicide is almost obscenely healthy in body, but his mind is sick, and he is obsessed by the wish to kill himself. These two are inseparable friends, but mask their deep concern for one another beneath an intercourse that consists of scrupulously wrought and extremely offensive insults. Since both understand intuitively the rules of the game, no misunderstandings occur between them. They are fighting to save each other from collapsing, Hamsun tells us: 'They nursed their bitterness so as not to whimper, they gnashed their teeth so as not to burst into tears.'

Eventually Anton Moss is taken away to an isolation hospital, leaving the Suicide alone. The other patients at Torahus sana-torium regard him as insane, and have as little to do with him as possible. When he does enter spontaneously into a conversation, he does so with the same unnerving and upsetting violence with which Nagel addressed social gatherings in his little Norwegian coastal town. Rector Frank Oliver, the eldest son of Oliver from *The Women at the Pump*, and now a school headmaster, turns up at the sanatorium with his two sons. His polite attempts to patronise the Suicide are flatly rejected, and he has to listen to the first of several tirades from him on the theme of the fatuity and the downright unnaturalness of the idea of educating children. The Suicide, who also shares his creator's horror of tinned food, delivers the most thought-provoking of Hamsun's many attacks on the evils of education. Hamsun's attitude can often seem psychologically conditioned by his own feeling of inferiority in the face of professors and the possessors of large, formal educations; a simple, bitter and irrational form of self-assertion. On this occasion his statements have a striking formal likeness to similar criticisms of education in Taoist philosophy: 'Schooling means going against Nature, turning the pupil into a side-track which runs in quite a different direction from the primary one.' He claims that 'Our personality is not rich in proportion to what we have learnt from books; on the contrary, it is rich in the degree in which we have been able to dispense with book-learning.' This line of thought baffles and irritates the rector, to the Suicide's huge enjoyment.

The Suicide and Julie d'Espard often talk together, and in the absence of Anton Moss the Suicide's conversation is much less guarded; he shows his feelings much more openly. He tells her at length about his disastrous marriage. A few years after the wedding he discovered that his wife had a lover. Hamlet-like, he brooded, and did nothing. He became obsessed by the idea that the affair had begun even before he married his wife, and that their daughter Leonarda was not his child. At length he left home and moved into the sanatorium, while the lover moved in with his wife. Now he is determined to commit suicide; but, because of a peculiar theory that suicide is inferior to murder, he is hindered from carrying out the act until he can find a way of doing it sufficiently unusually to exalt the manner of his death. Julie comforts him, and dismisses the idea that the betrayal might have begun even before the wedding. Yet shortly afterwards Hamsun pairs her with the Suicide by reintroducing the Finnish Count, Fleming. Cleared of the charges against him, he has returned to the sanatorium to resume his search for health, and to find Julie again. By this time her child has been born, Fleming's child, and at the innocent Daniel's insistence the boy has been christened Julius. Fleming and Julie resume their old relationship and betray Daniel in various places about the farm. Thus, finally, Daniel and the Suicide – who never actually meet – arrive in a paired situation.

This final pairing is the critical one. Daniel finds out that he is being betrayed, and warns Fleming and Julie. They ignore his warnings, and the next time he finds them together he shoots and kills Fleming. He flees to the hills with his gun, and a manhunt ensues. Finally Daniel returns to his farm and lays his gun down. Like Glahn about to face his death, he washes and dresses in his best clothes and calmly awaits the arrival of the sheriff. He is sentenced to seven years' imprisonment, but his fate is ultimately good: Julie drops her pretensions, throws away her French novels, and sets about becoming a farm-wife and a mother to Julius. She will wait for Daniel.

There is no such joy for the Suicide, the man who thought too much, who strayed too far too long ago from his instincts, and found himself trapped in a hell of metaphysical speculation. Hamsun shares with his character a knowledge of this hell: 'Where is the road ahead?' the narration asks. 'Nowhere. But then, where is the road back? Nowhere.' And in spite of an overt physical cause for his state of mind in the infidelity of his wife, the existential nature of the Suicide's problem appears forcefully over and over again throughout the book. In a moment of weakness with Anton Moss he mentions the possibility of praying to God for salvation, only to subject his own suggestion to bitter mockery a moment later. Life seems pointless to him, and God nothing but a blind, implacable and impassive system. His long speech to Julie d'Espard contains the essence of his thought, and probably much of Hamsun's own thought as he entered his sixties:

This night a Saviour is born unto you. I don't say that by way of bombast, it's quite possible that there is something in that side of the question too, I mean as to the Saviour and salvation – salvation from the existence that has been given us without our asking, salvation from a life that we've been bounced into without the slightest wish on our part. Oh God, how mysterious it all is, though I don't say it's entirely incredible on that account; some people, you know, can believe just because it's absurd. Here we are, led with a rope around our neck to destruction, and we go willingly, but dead against our own interest. We hear about the wise scheme of existence, but as to seeing it, perceiving it – no. I don't know which is the right way to take it, some men are serious and wouldn't think of making fun of life. But there we go along the road. We are led without a stop, whatever part of us time and old age do not completely destroy, they at any rate render unrecognisable. When we have travelled for a time, we travel awhile longer, then we go on for one day more, after that a night, and finally in the grey dawn of the next morning the hour has come and we are killed, killed in earnest and for good. That is the romance of Life, with Death as chapter the last.

Yet for a while it looks as though things may turn out well for the Suicide after all. His wife seeks him out at the sanatorium, and informs him that she has thrown her lover out. More decisive than he, she has come to discuss the possibility of a divorce; but in the course of their evening together a change comes over them both, and it seems as though their individual sufferings may after all have brought them together again. She abandons her plans to leave the following morning, and retires to bed. So that she will not have to be woken up again to lock her door, the Suicide offers to lock it for her from the outside, and then goes to his own room with the key in his pocket. Some of the other guests are having a drinking party. A fire breaks out, and within moments the sanatorium is consumed in flames. Leo Magnus, the Suicide, in his longing to survive, makes a fantastical and hair-raising escape; but the flames prevent him from reaching the room where his wife is locked in. Briefly her face is seen at the window, with her hair in flames, and then it disappears. The building is burnt to the ground.

Thus all of the following day, in one of Hamsun's most extraordinary images, the Suicide wanders about the mountain with a key in his pocket to a locked room that does not exist. He gets hold of a rope and sets off into the forest to look for a suitable tree from which to hang himself. In his search a pine needle gets stuck in his sock and begins to chafe: he sits down, removes his boot, and relieves the chafing. The first decent-looking branch he finds breaks under his weight. A second would hold, but instead of committing suicide Leo Magnus sits down and begins to cry. And later, as though waking from a trance, full of self-contempt, but alive, he wanders away from the mountain and disappears.

Nagel thought often of committing suicide, and finally drowned himself; Glahn deliberately tormented a fellow hunter into shooting him; but Leo Magnus is too cravenly addicted to a life he despises to take the logical consequences of his feelings. He is a ghost from the 1890s, and his shabby disappearance is Hamsun's last comment on the fate of the intensely romantic gospel of life which he expounded so passionately during those years. Much of the cynicism which these later novels exhibit might perhaps stem from a sense of powerful personal disillusionment, and perhaps even self-disgust, at being, in spite of all, still alive at sixty-five. Yet Hamsun carefully ends the novel on a positive note, an image of profound normality, with Julie going about her daily routine on the farm at Torahus. *Chapter the Last* shows more clearly than most of

Hamsun's later novels that when he announces happiness in the form of the simple life, such as Isak of Sellanraa and Daniel enjoy, and such as Julie is learning to value, it is the imagined happiness of *other people* that he is describing, not his own. Cursed by the disease of consciousness, he finds at best a vicarious contentment in the thought of other lives mercifully free from the disease.

Hamsun's work on the novel was frequently interrupted during its later stages by a rather curious court case in which he was involved, along with his younger brother Thorvald, and Thorvald's son Almar. Alone among the Hamarøy Pedersens, Thorvald had begun using the name Hamsun in the wake of Knut's literary success in the 1890s. He was married under the name of Peder Thorvald Hamsun on 6 April 1895, and his son was duly christened Thorolf Oskar Hamsun shortly after being born on 4 December 1898.

Hamsun did not particularly like his younger brother. Thorvald worked for a while as a detective in the Christiania police force in the 1890s, and his activities during the investigation into the persecution of Hamsun by anonymous letters in 1898 seem to have hindered rather than helped Hamsun's case. So Hamsun, at any rate, believed, and there had been no contact whatsoever in the intervening years between the brothers. Thorvald, meanwhile, had changed his job, and was working as a customs inspector in Narvik, while Almar, after the fashion of Hamsun's 'other' uncle, Vetltrayein, was leading a restless and unsettled life. In the course of his wanderings and his sometimes dubious enterprises he seems to have run up debts for the payment of which, in time, irate creditors began to apply to Hamsun. Hamsun may not have liked his brother's adoption of a name to which he felt an almost mystical attachment after the restless experimentation of his early years with Knut Pedersen, Knut Hamsunn, *et al*, but he did not feel moved to do anything about it until he felt that Almar's activities were bringing direct disgrace on the name. His first move was to try to get third parties to persuade Thorvald and Almar to renounce the name voluntarily, and when this failed he took them both to court.

The proceedings here were quite extraordinarily protracted, and dragged on with numerous postponements and adjournments from 16 November 1922 until the judgement on 5 January 1925. Thorvald and Almar, by virtue of the fact that they had used the name without hindrance for over twenty years, stood in a strong position. Surprisingly, Hamsun repeated for the court the myth that the name had come into being accidentally, as the result of a misprint in his 1885 article for the *New Illustrated Times* on Mark Twain, when in fact he had used it himself as early as 1880, in a letter of 24 March to Zahl at Kjerringøy. The case was complicated by the fact that it was common practice among Norwegians who emigrated from their home communities, either to the city or to America, to adopt the name of their place of origin as their surname. The whole thing seemed to many people not a little ridiculous, and many felt that it was acting in very poor taste indeed for Hamsun to sue his own brother over such an issue, particularly in view of the fact that one was a world-famous and wealthy man, while the other was an obscure public servant with a monthly wage of 260 kroner. Hamsun's target was Almar, but if the thing was to be done legally, clearly it would have to include Thorvald.

One journalist pointed out a wicked irony in the whole business: in his 1915 novel, *Segelfoss Town*, Hamsun devotes considerable effort to the mockery of a certain peasant boy, Lars Larsen, whom Willatz Holmsen has helped to an education, and ultimately to the priesthood. In celebration of his rise in the world (or fall, as Hamsun came to view it), he changes his name from Larsen to the much more refined, slightly Swedicised 'Lassen'. With his education he becomes a great man to the local people, and his name becomes known all over the north of Norway. As usual whenbrothers crop up in a Hamsun novel, his brother Julius is his opposite – earthy, realistic, true to his roots, and with a natural command of his wits which makes him every bit the equal of his book-learned brother in the wisdom of life. This Julius runs a hotel in Segelfoss, and thinking to cash in on his brother's reputation, he proposes to write on his signboard that this is 'Lassen's Hotel'. The priest pompously refuses to give his permission, for which he is mercilessly satirised by Hamsun. It made Hamsun's own case in 1922 look rather silly. Yet without necessarily claiming that it does not do so, it is as well to remember that in satirising Larsen/Lassen in the first place, Hamsun was quite deliberately mocking aspects of his own rise from poverty. In the fabulous merchant Tobias Holmengraa, Hamsun created a kingly incarnation of himself; in Lassen he created a monkey of himself.

The judgement fell on 5 January 1925, in Oslo Municipal Court.* Under dissent, Almar and Thorvald were found to be entitled to use the name Hamsun. Hamsun appealed to the High Court; but in the meantime the matter was settled by private arrangement. Hamsun offered Thorvald 3000 and Almar 5000 kroner to abandon the use of the name, and they accepted.

* In 1925 the name of the capital was changed from Christiania to Oslo.

The case left a legacy of bitterness. Many people were shocked by Hamsun's behaviour, and regarded it as arrogant. Thorvald continued to use the name, sometimes with and sometimes without the 'd', but felt himself humiliated. He even made rather pathetic enquiries to the Department of Justice about the possibility of legally annulling a state of brotherhood.[2] Almar took the name Bjørnefjell, and continued in his restless and unsettled ways. In 1937 he published a book, *Almar Hamsun Who Died*, but it was not the sensational success he hoped it would be. Nor did a later volume of memoirs which incorporated this earlier book under the title *Almar Hamsun Who Died – Lives* do much better for him when it was published in 1971.

The whole business was rather sad and pathetic. It damaged the harmlessly pretentious Thorvald, and it fuelled the growing suggestions that Hamsun's aloofness at Nørholm was predominantly an expression of sovereign contempt for the world. The rumours cut through Hamsun's isolation and wounded him deeply. Marie Hamsun wished that he had never raised the case, and by the time it was all over he might privately have wished so too. But it was not Hamsun's way to turn back. Right or wrong, he would follow a stated course, into the heart of complete disaster, if so be it, rather than admit a mistake.

In spite of such problems, however, these were in the main some of the most troublefree years of Hamsun's life. Outwardly, things seemed to be going well for him; but as he wrote in *Pan*, 'it is within oneself that the sources of joy and sorrow are to be found', and beginning in 1920 one finds him making curious and uncharacteristic references in letters to some intensely private form of distress that he was undergoing. His long letter of thanks to Albert Engström of 30 December 1920, in which he expressed his joy at seeing his old friend again in Stockholm during the Nobel festivities, included this sad observation:

> Being with you again was a party and a blessing. I can't think of anything that has cheered me up so thoroughly, because I was very depressed, and afraid of everybody.

Two years later, while staying at the Grand Hotel in Arendal and working on the novel *Chapter the Last*, he wrote to Marie at 10 pm on Friday 13 October 1922:

> Sad and awful here. More and more I feel I need a nursemaid or a nurse; I sit here and feel afraid of everything, even though I keep the door locked. . . . I wish that you could be here, I don't

believe I've ever felt so terrible before. But it must surely pass. Thank God, I don't know anyone here at the hotel, so no one disturbs me.

Now I'll go straight out and post this and so to bed. A lousy letter, but I just wanted to write a few lines –

Goodnight, my sweet. I don't *need* you, you understand – it's just that I feel myself alone.

Chapter the Last, his book about death, drained him physically and creatively. In the months that followed its publication he sought with increasing desperation for a theme for his next novel, and found none. His old trick of dodging past a block in his consciousness by leaving home on sudden impulse, failed to work for him this time. In February 1925 he travelled to Bergen, and lived a while in Room 45 at the Hotel Norge, using the name of Dr Hansen in a hopeless attempt to preserve his privacy; but there was no spark, no light, and after a few days he invited Marie to join him, and the visit turned into a holiday, with sightseeing in Bergen, and outings to the big shops.

'To write is to sit in judgement over oneself', Henrik Ibsen wrote in a poem. It is a remark that may be applied to the writing of every one of Hamsun's novels. The physical act of writing them was an enormous struggle for him, a fight, a challenge to do battle with raging chaos; and for all his talk, later on, of being a farmer first and a writer second, his reaction to the possibility of being faced with a writer's block shows clearly that this was only a public pose; that his self-respect, in its entirety, depended upon his being able to meet the challenge of writing books. Away from home, during the difficult early stages of a book, at least one of his letters to Marie would always contain a formulation along the lines of 'And now we'll see what kind of stuff I'm *really* made of', as he contemplated the struggle ahead of him. The award of a Nobel Prize had no effect whatever on the wholly private nature of this relationship between his literary talent and his self-respect: working on *Chapter the Last* at the Ernst Hotel in Kristiansand, he wrote to Marie in January 1923: 'Now we'll see what I'm fit for, life, death, or putrefaction.' Now, as time went by, and the great light which had always shone for him in the past shone no more, no book came, and he felt his self-respect ebbing away.

Hamsun's passionate faith in the value of the unknown, the irrational, the mysterious in life, so fervently preached by Nagel in *Mysteries*, was a genuine part of his everyday approach to life. When Victoria Hamsun fell ill not long after she was born, Hamsun held her body for long periods against his naked chest, and claimed that it was the animal warmth of his body that had saved her life. On a later occasion he was an enthusiastic wearer of a large zinc belt round his waist, known as the 'Reiersen Belt', and corresponded keenly with the manufacturers about whether the belt actually *produced* blood, or merely made existing blood circulate in a more lively fashion. He dutifully sent his belt back to them for 'rezincing', and abandoned faith in it only after a long struggle which included charging the belt with stronger batteries, and even wearing two belts at once. When now on 4 January 1926 he went into a full-scale psychoanalysis, as one of the first people in Norway to do so, it was a further gesture of his faith in the importance of the irrational, and evidence that at sixty years of age his taste for the experimental and the different remained as strong as ever. His analyst, Johannes Irgens Strømme, practised in Oslo, and at his insistence Hamsun moved to the capital, and for the six months of his analysis lived at the Victoria Hotel in the centre of town.

Strømme was the son of a priest from Marie Hamsun's home-town of Elverum; in the course of his medical studies in the 1890s he had come across articles by Freud which had decided him to devote himself full-time to the study of the new science of the mind. In 1913 he worked in Zurich as assistant to Eugen Bleuler, the inventor of the term 'schizophrenia', and a pioneer in the study of this illness. He returned to Norway, and from 1916 onwards had a private practice in the capital.[3] He wrote a book *Nervøsitet*, and sent a copy to Hamsun. Hamsun was fascinated by the book, and after a short correspondence, he agreed to analysis. It was a characteristic expression of Hamsun's openness where theories of the mind and the nature of the workings of consciousness were concerned; for psychoanalysis was, in 1926, in Norway, viewed with considerable suspicion. A newspaper report of a case in 1930, in which Strømme was sued by the ex-husband of a patient of his, described his as 'a name which most of us connect with the rather obscure concept of *psychoanalysis*, a kind of miracle doctor, an exclusive Marcello Haugen',* and added that it was 'particularly difficult to accept his "immoral methods of treatment". He is a naïve man in many ways, and his book on nervousness cannot be accepted as a serious scientific work. Psychoanalysis is a gospel for him, and he looks upon himself as a prophet. But he is a good man.'[4] However, Strømme seems to have inspired total devotion in his patients, and respectful curiosity among the uncommitted. Hamsun saw him daily except Sundays, sometimes twice daily,

* Marcello Haugen was a famous Norwegian medium and faith-healer.

and in letters to a highly sceptical Marie at Nørholm he described with childlike wonder the course of this new adventure:

(6.1.26) I've seen the doctor three times now. It's a queer sort of treatment, and involves me trying to remember with all my might parts of my dream from the night before. Then the doctor 'analyses' them. He is pleased with me. He said again today that he was sure it would be successful. He recommends that I remain sceptical of him, but he has asked me to undertake not to run off and give the whole thing up after the first couple of weeks. He works so hard with me, sometimes I have to feel sorry for him. We'll see how it goes.[5]

(29.1.26) I've had to get rid of that air-pillow I've been using to sit on, it has a leak and is visibly flatter in the morning after simply lying unused on the chair all night. I took it back to the shop and got two razorblades instead, because the doctor says that part of my problem is that I don't shave *every day*. He says it's laziness, and I must work on myself. Think of it – when I come home again I'll be shaving every day – I who sometimes go a week without shaving!

Apart from this it's the same as usual as the doctor's. I go once a day as a rule, but sometimes twice, when he isn't finished. He is remarkably kind and conscientious. He said today that he was *extremely* pleased with me, but that my unconscious is offering considerable resistance.

I passed Wang's yesterday, they were having an auction and I went in. It was thick with people, and you would never guess these were hard times, the bidding was astronomical, way up in the hundreds. It was so full of people I couldn't see what they were bidding for, but I saw a table that went for several hundred kroner. They're welcome to it. It wasn't Empire anyway. I bought a tie yesterday, and now I'm very smart. But no hat yet – it takes a long time to wear out a hole. The doctor has lent me that controversial book *Feminism*. It's riotously funny. It's sold out now, but I've been promised a second-hand copy, and I'll send it to you.

(4.2.26) Dear Marie, a month today since I began. I hardly know what to say any more. If I was the first and only one, the guinea pig, then I think I would remain extremely sceptical. But there are so many of us, in so many lands. (I read something about it in *The Times* a few days ago, and you have probably read director Arnesen's review of Dr Strømme's *Nervøsitet* in *Aftenposten*. The doctor told me he had been resident physician at Arnesen's clinic for a couple of years. Arnesen didn't believe in the new treatment; but he had a sister whom he couldn't cure, and when he sent her to Strømme, Strømme cured her. That was seven years ago.

As I was walking home yesterday evening it suddenly occurred to me that I had no reason to be afraid of people any more (you remember the phobia, the fear in the book?)* So I stood up straighter, and walked with head high, and went to bed still feeling the same. Read awhile, slept, and woke with the same feeling, and now I'm going to try and stay like this. I'm going to try to get rid of my phobia. What reason have I got to be afraid of people?

When I told the doctor this today, here is what he said to me: On the 4 January, the same day that you began, a woman, a married woman began. She was thirty something years old, weary of life, afraid of being old, afraid of dying, afraid of going mad. She had always been sexually impotent, but had two children. Today I sent her home, said the doctor. Couldn't you crack her? I asked. – She's cured, he answered. – And will it last? I asked. – In all my fourteen to sixteen years' work I haven't had one relapse, said he. – I questioned him further: she doesn't hang her head any more; she's sexually awakened (he thinks that that is wonderful too), and she's back at work again.

Well, well, now we must see what I can manage. The thing is, I'm worse than her. I'm sceptical, and I resist (this is discussed in the book).

As the treatment continues, Hamsun's perception of his purpose in taking it seems to change slightly. More frequently he focuses on the hope that the sessions with Strømme will release some treasure-house of material locked up in his mind and enable him to write again. The desire to be rid of his fear of people recedes. In any event, whatever the efficacy of Strømme's sessions, these weeks and months in Oslo offered Hamsun a more extensive social life than he had had for many years, and he took full advantage of the opportunity; seeing old friends like Henrik Lund and doing a great deal of relaxed drifting around the city streets and shops. He thought of his early days, and revisited some of the scenes of *Hunger*. It all seemed so long ago to him:

On Sunday I took a stroll round Vaterland and looked at the old haunts from 38 – thirty-eight – years ago. I seemed to recognise one or two of the old houses, but I couldn't be sure. My old

* Probably a reference to a passage in Strømme's book.

place, Tomtegaten II* at any rate was gone. But it was strange to walk around the old streets . . .

He began visiting the cinema, and took a great delight in the experience, particularly enjoying unpretentious adventure films and comedies. He went with the head-waiter from the Victoria to see a film about a lightning-swift pickpocket which he found 'extremely interesting', and on another occasion went to a cinema where children were admitted and saw a film 'about a man who knocked over everything he touched, even the walls of houses fell down on him'. It was just nonsense, he told Marie, but he enjoyed it, and enjoyed even more the laughter of the children in the cinema.

After a while he thought he began to notice some progress:

> . . . Tonight was the first time – I think, for about a year – that I have been able to write down a note, scribble a few lines towards the thing I'm working on. It wasn't the discovery of any great 'source', far from it. But it showed me that I'm not stone dead, and that cheered me up. When I told the doctor this he said he was glad, but he didn't overestimate things either. Naturally he asked me if I thought I knew why it was, and I said that I thought it was because I was expecting a visit from you any day now . . .

And when he despaired, Strømme encouraged him with the certainty of success:

> (27.4.26) My dear Marie, what wonderfully good, warm newsy letters you write to me. Here's thanks and a hug, as we used to say when I was a child. God knows, I hope I can pay all this back to you some day. It all seems so strange, here I am being treated by a doctor for my inability to write, when all I really want is to be back home and working away in my writing hut writing good books and earning fat royalties to keep us all. Months go by, and I'm wasting time and wasting money. But this *will* succeed, the doctor says. He is so totally convinced of it. If even once he were to say·*might* I would feel maybe a little uncertainty, but he says it *will*. But for the time being life is wretched for me.

He had lost his appetite, and not even an early lunch and an eight-hour walk could bring it back. But he was dreaming fiercely now, and with a rather touching pride told Marie of a dream 'which left

* Tomtegaten II was where Hamsun lived in 1880; the narrator of *Hunger* also lives there.

even the doctor speechless'.

Finally, in June, Hamsun decided to call it a day. Marie had all along been opposed to the treatment, and even though he didn't necessarily feel 'cured', he felt that he had made a certain amount of progress. Visits to the theatre for the first time in fifteen years had done nothing to alter his low opinion of the whole art of drama. He left after one and a half acts of Galsworthy's *Loyalties*, partly because he couldn't hear it, partly because he found the seats too warm, partly because he found it unspeakable. A later visit to a play called *Dunungen* (*The Fledgling*) encouraged him to think seriously again about writing a play, he told Marie:

> I'll tell you why it is I want to write a play: I saw a bit of *Gentlemen*, and later on I met Hedqvist who recommended *Dunungen* to me. Fine – I bought two tickets, and Gundersen and I went to see it. I couldn't hear much better on this occasion, but whenever the public laughed Gundersen told me what the joke was, and Christ above, it was pitiful. People are grateful for so little! At one point a woman sits down in a chair and chats elegiacally to herself for fifteen minutes! I'm sure I could have done it better. And I understand now how important it is to have tension, which is something I've never bothered about before.

But the main point of this letter of 13 June is to announce that he is coming home, and to try to take some of the sting out of Marie's anger in advance – she was bitterly jealous of this social life of his, and deeply resentful of his visits to the despised world of the theatre from which he had struggled so fiercely to wrest her in the first days of their courtship:

> I've made up my mind to stop this and come home, and I'll be giving the doctor a little hint about this. For *every* reason I can't carry on here like this for the rest of my life. I am convinced that I am much more inwardly resolute, and that I will be able to write again. I haven't found any 'source', no, but when I've had expensive dreams analysed for more than five months without discovering any source, then in God's name it's time to call a halt. *I'll be home in fourteen days, if not before.*
>
> It's a shame I wrote that about Tore,* because you may already have mentioned it to him. But you can explain it by saying that I am finished here earlier than I thought I would be. And then there's you. If you could try to be a little more inwardly resolute

* Had had proposed in an earlier letter that Tore might join him in Oslo and continue his schooling there.

as well, and try to be a bit more cheerful – not just for the first few days, but always – then I think I'll be able to work again. God knows, all this I've been through here is for the sake of all of us, you absolutely must understand this. There are so many wives who have to help the head of the family by easing his burden all they can to keep hunger and want away, but you don't, and I think you ought to be able to laugh and dance instead of being depressed, and making me depressed with you. When it comes down to it, what have you got to feel sad about? That I won you, that you haven't been obliged to keep body and soul together in some flat here in town? Believe me, there's some lovely clowns [ie actors] here – it's really something to get sentimental about! More and more grease on the wrinkles on their foreheads, more and more booze to give them a lift, some of them lesbians, some homosexuals, all of them owing money on the clothes they stand up in. – We lead a lonely life at Nørholm, and it is not *all* to the good for either of us. We should get more help, take on a housekeeper so that you're not sitting on pins and needles every time someone visits us. We could cover the expense by trying to be a bit more cheerful, both of us – and I'll be able to work.

Hamsun had his last session with Strømme on 18 June and returned to Nørholm.*

The 'treatment' was successful: installed in his writing-hut back home at Nørholm once more, he set to work at once on *Wayfarers*, the first part of his trilogy about the wandering adventurer, August, writing half of the novel in a burst of creative activity in what remained of the summer.

In the autumn, the whole family of six moved into a rented villa on Bygdøy, an isthmus on the Oslo-fjord near the capital. Part of the purpose in this temporary move from Nørholm was to enable Marie Hamsun to take *her* cure from Strømme. This was something that Hamsun, backed by the doctor, had been urging on her almost from the beginning, and after a hopeless attempt at resistance she agreed to take a treatment that she neither wanted, needed, nor believed in. Her relationship with Strømme got off to a bad start, and deteriorated. She found his obsession with sexual

---

* Strømme's stenographic transcripts of the sessions with Hamsun still exist, and in 1978 were handed over to Gyldendal with a view to possible publication. However, Strømme's shorthand, using a Swiss system, has proved impossible to decipher satisfactorily. Ethical objections to the project were also raised. Strømme entrusted the manuscript in 1958 to his own publisher, Theodor Myklestad, and told him that the main theme of the analysis was Hamsun's 'limitless jealousy' of Marie.[6]

symbolism ridiculous, but gritted her teeth and stayed the course. Hamsun was working again – that was all that mattered. It was a typical act of self-sacrifice.

Hamsun resumed his own analysis on 3 January 1927. Sometimes the two met one another on the stairs up to Strømme's office. Only smiles and nods by way of greeting were allowed; they were not to converse. Hamsun rented a hut near the villa on Bygdøy, and wrote steadily throughout the winter. *Wayfarers* was finished in the spring, Hamsun's analysis was complete on 8 March, Marie heaved a great sigh of relief, and they all travelled back to Nørholm. As with the move to Larvik which got *The Growth of the Soil* written, one sometimes has the slightly dizzying feeling in the middle of all this that the whole earth was being moved to enable the writer to produce another one of his books.

Chapter 14
1927–1933: The Height of Fame:
the *August* Trilogy

The opening chapter of *Wayfarers*, the first part of the trilogy known as the *August* trilogy, is a masterpiece. Two dark and exotic men, one of them blind, arrive one day in a small village. The blind man sets up a barrel-organ on a pole and begins to play it. A crowd gathers around them, mostly women and children, since the men are all away for the winter fishing in the Lofoten Islands. Presently the two strangers begin to argue. The sighted man insists that they move on, that there is no money to be had from an audience like this, while his partner, the blind musician, wants to stay and entertain the people. The sighted man loses his temper and hits his partner, drawing blood from a wound inflicted on his face. The audience protests, and a boy of thirteen named Edevart runs foward and knocks the bully to the ground. He picks himself up, shakes his fist a couple of times and runs off. The sympathetic audience now dip into their pockets for coins for the blind man. Suddenly he astonishes them by pressing a secret button on the organ which causes doors to open up on it revealing a tiny world with figures that move and turn in time to the music. Napoleon in the centre lifts a telescope to and from his eye. He is flanked by two generals, and in front of them is a small, laughing beggar boy with a bowl in his hand. Whenever a coin is put into his bowl, he jerks it into a box. This magical little theatre enchants the villagers. When the flow of money dries up a little girl steps forward and puts a bright, treasured button into the bowl. At this the boy makes a jerk in the opposite direction and the button is cast far out into the snow. The audience thinks this is wonderful too, and they begin putting stones and nails and wood-shavings into the bowl until the boy goes haywire and rattles his bowl so violently that nothing at all will stay in it. The organist stops the show and closes up the doors on the little theatre again. The women of the village then feed him and give him some warm socks, and he sets off on his way again. The boy Edevart, still captivated by the show, follows after him in secret. The man discovers him and angrily orders him to go home. Now the sighted partner steps out from behind a tree and asks what's going on. The blind man, who is clearly not blind at all, wipes the fake bloodstain from his cheek and whispers to him, and the men both laugh. Edevart is completely confused. The men shoo him away while they count up the takings, and then wave goodbye to him. He returns to the village, Polden, realising that he has been tricked.

This classic description of the loss of innocence prefigures all that follows. Young Edevart shortly afterwards teams up with an older youth named August, an orphan from the next village who has been a seaman and has already travelled in exotic lands like Burma. August is a fantasist, a liar, a charmer and a con-man who wears gold caps on his teeth. The introverted Edevart is drawn to him, and the two set off adventuring together in north Norway, like Huck Finn and Tom Sawyer on the Mississippi, or like Hamsun's own earlier pairing of the reckless charmer Munken Vendt and the more sensitive and withdrawn student Frederick Parelius. They salvage a murdered skipper's fishing boat and sail it south to Bergen, putting in at various ports along the way. At one remote stopover, a farm called Doppen, they meet a young mother bringing up two children alone. She says her husband has gone away to America. Edevart rescues one of her sheep for her, and when he and August sail on again he cannot forget the woman. He takes a job on Knoff's trading settlement, based on Zahl and his settlement at Kjerringøy, and works in the store there in order to be close to her. Knoff favours him, and later gives him command of a fishing-sloop. Edevart makes a successful fishing trip, and he dries his catch afterwards at his home town of Polden, thereby starting an important new enterprise there. But the woman at Doppen, Lovise-Magrete, is always in his mind, and one day he returns there. They become lovers and lead an idyllic and happy life for a few weeks until a letter arrives for her. She had been lying, her husband was not in America at all but serving a jail sentence in Trondheim for a crime of violence. The letter announces his unexpected and imminent release, and Edevart has to leave. He returns to Knoff's trading post and the job in the store again. Sometimes he sees Lovise-Magrete when she comes to the settlement on a shopping expedition with her husband Håkon. Her husband is a drinker and a womaniser, and she seems to be still attracted to Edevart. Håkon gets drunk and provokes a fight

with Edevart, and although she realises she loves Edevart more,
her loyalty is to her husband. The impossibility of the situation
wears Edevart down. He and August carry on adventuring, and he
continues to receive instruction from August in the arts of hustling
and cheating and enjoying life on the wing. He meets other
hustlers too along the way, like Knoff's corrupt old skipper Solem,
and the old watchseller Papst. For August and Solem and Papst,
their way of life is the natural one, and only reflects the way of the
world, but Edevart can never get rid of his sense of shame. The
world goes sour for him gradually. Everything that happens seems
to be a taint on life. On a journey back to his home town he finds it
different and in some obscure way spoiled. Ragna was a childhood
sweetheart, the little girl who put her button in the beggar boy's
bowl. Now she has given birth to an illegitimate child, and it seems
as though her grandmother has strangled the child and passed the
death off as a stillbirth. Edevart tries hard to be more like August,
to stop objecting to life, to overcome its banalities and sorrows with
tall tales and wonderful lies. He tries to break his dangerous
addiction to his life of feelings, but finds that he cannot because,
like Lieutenant Glahn, he is not only in love, but in love with a
dream of love, and a dream of innocence. When Edevart and
August had sailed away from Doppen after that first meeting with
Lovise-Magrete, August asked Edevart if he'd kissed her. Edevart
tried to laugh off the question and be brave, but it struck him as a
cruel question, and made him feel 'as though a painting or a
rainbow were being torn apart within him'. When later on Lovise-
Magrete comes to him and asks him to lend her money, so that she
and Håkon and the children can return to America and try to make
a fresh start, Edevart does so. They leave. Edevart becomes
depressed. He can think of no good reason to stay in the old haunts
anymore, and shortly afterwards he resolves to try America
himself. He goes quietly, taking leave of no old friends.

Thus ends the first part of *Wayfarers*. It is complete in itself, a fine
short novel about the pain of the loss of innocence, containing a
love story in many ways as moving as *Pan*, or *Victoria*. Edevart's
decision to leave at the end reminds one of Glahn's similar decision
at the end of *Pan*, when with the hopeless love affair with Edvarda
behind him, he longs to be away from the scene of it all, and travels
to India.

'I don't know where my inspiration comes from', Hamsun told a
German psychologist in 1929, 'I do nothing consciously to arouse
it. A dream, a sentence in a newspaper, a note on the piano, a child

laughing can start it up.'[1] Perhaps he should have kept his dreams to himself instead of going back to Dr Strømme with them in the autumn of 1926 after completing this first part of the novel. The sad fact is that the second part, written while continuing his analysis, is much inferior to the first. Edevart does not, in fact, go to America after all, a point which leaves the reader feeling slightly cheated, especially in view of the extremely low-key way in which the reversed decision is communicated. He resumes instead his life of peddling and wandering with August, whose personality, exploits and enterprise are increasingly what Hamsun relies on to sustain interest in the novel now that the love story is over. Part two turns into a less interesting repetition of part one, and shows the beginnings of the tendency that seriously mars the second volume of the trilogy, and ruins the third, namely the affliction of the Great Idea.

Hamsun had made his protest against progress and the 'spirit of the age' in *Children of the Age* and *Segelfoss Town*. In *The Growth of the Soil* he had suggested a solution, and in *The Women at the Pump* he showed that he understood that his 'solution' was in fact really just a lovely dream – but that life was still not to be despised, for all its shabbiness and cruelties. In *Chapter the Last* he had written a highly personal meditation on the depressive illness that is human consciousness, and produced a novel full of profound despair that still managed to affirm life, and to celebrate its small joys. All of these novels to some extent reflect the conscious attempt Hamsun consistently made after 1910 to act as a kind of spokesman or advisor for the Norwegian people, following in the tradition of Henrik Wergeland and Bjørnstjerne Bjørnson, and all of them contain the seeds of portentousness. But none are marred by their 'message', since Hamsun's instinctive control of his art was enough to keep them well above the level of mere propaganda. But in the *August* trilogy, beginning with the second part of the first novel, that art is in decline, and the Message comes bustling forward, and an undertaking that began so well ends eventually very badly indeed.

The first Great Idea in the trilogy is that emigration is a bad thing which destroys human beings as individuals. This is demonstrated by a description of the further fate of Edevart. He takes the long-postponed trip to America at the end of *Wayfarers*, to join Lovise-Magrete whose husband has left her again, and in volume two, called *August*, the pair return to Norway. Edevart is depicted as an ever more depressed and rootless failure, and Lovise-Magrete as a pretentious suburbanite who wears make-up, despises her origins, and affects to be more at home speaking English than Norwegian.

Authors are in a uniquely advantageous position when appearing to be wise before the event like this. The mining conditions that Emile Zola protested so fiercely about in *Germinal* had in fact largely been rectified some years before his literary 'protest' against them appeared. In the same way, emigration was already an established historical fact of Norwegian life long before Hamsun began delivering these warnings against its effects. In fact, back in 1892, he had already commented on the theme of emigration in a short story for the Danish magazine *Christmas Roses* called *Christmas on the Farm*.

Perhaps taking his cue from an experience with Peter, the eldest Pedersen boy, who had emigrated to America at the age of sixteen in 1867, and who had proved such a let-down to his younger brother Knut when he followed him out there in 1881, Hamsun describes how a family Christmas on a poor mountain farm is transformed by the arrival of a parcel from the eldest son Timian in America which contains a beautiful fur cape. This is the softest and most beautiful thing ever seen on the farm, and the children stand around touching and admiring it for a long, long time before going to bed. The parents decide that the next oldest boy, Rinaldus, shall have the honour of owning it. With an awful care he wears it just twice that winter, both times to church. The story ends abruptly with the information that with the coming of summer, hairs began falling out of it and worms could be seen wriggling in the tufts, a single image that says as much about the experience of the American Dream as all the rambling asides of the trilogy about Edevart and Lovise-Magrete.

The trilogy's other Great Idea is that 'progress' is axiomatically a bad thing, and to demonstrate this Hamsun rather awkwardly begins turning August from an interesting and stimulating fabulist into a symbol of the modern age. It is his Yankee enterprise, we are told, that brings such aspects of modern life as banking, factories, and the postal system to Polden. He does not cease to be the irreverent and whimsically warm-hearted charmer, nor does he cease to be very funny sometimes – one of his boasts is that he has so much lead in his body from bullet wounds that once, in Barbados, they refused to let him go up in a flying-machine – and Hamsun's artistic problem, which remains unsolved throughout the trilogy, is how to reconcile his own huge delight in August at the same time as he attempts to censure him for the effects he has on the stable community.

The final volume, *The Road Leads On*, revisits the characters of volume two, twenty years on, with August an old man in his seventies. Like the final volume of Hamsun's other trilogy, the *Wanderer* books of 1906–12, the setting is different from that of the first two volumes. We meet August in a resolutely twentieth-century Segelfoss town, which now boasts a cinema, a Grand Hotel and a bank. He is a childless and unwed odd-job man working for Gordon Tidemand, the son of the enterprising young storekeeper, Theodor, whose social and economic stars were in the ascendant as the last *Segelfoss* novel from 1915 ended. Theodor went on to become the town's leading citizen, and moved into the mansion once owned by the aristocratic Holmsen family. In fact Tidemand, Theodor's son and heir, is not his son at all, but the result of an affair between his mother and a gypsy, Otto Alexander. August still has something of his old charm and his love of yarning, but he is as frequently an irritated old man who struggles with indifferent success to contain an overwhelming contempt for the mediocrity of everyone around him. He continues to air wild and inspired schemes for new enterprises, one of which is to farm sheep on a huge scale in the mountains up above Segelfoss, but spends most of his time supervising workers who are building a road up into the mountains for Gordon Tidemand. It is along this road that he is walking one day when his sheep are stampeded. The flock bears down on him, and his is swept to his death over the edge of a cliff by the animals.

The Road Leads On is one of the worst of Hamsun's twenty-three novels. His attempt to turn August into a symbol of the 'spirit of the age' is unsuccessful, largely because he tries too hard to overcome his own ambiguous feelings for the character in his determination to press home his reactionary message. In the absence of any plot, his characteristic narrative devices, particularly the posing of clusters of rhetorical questions in order to arouse curiosity about some matter, become windy mannerisms. There is also a limit to the degree of curiosity a reader is prepared to feel about whether or not a post office or a herring factory are going to be built; or whether or not an Englishman will visit Gordon Tidemand; and how, if ever, August is going to get hold of a fortune in lottery winnings which is being held for him back in Polden. Lacking in genuine inspiration, the novel subsists on bad temper, ugly and unconvincing scenes of violence, and racial slurs on Jews, gypsies and Lapps.[2] Six years of work on the trilogy, and over a thousand pages, had drained the riches from Hamsun's literary personality, and left only its dregs.

However, despite the artistic failings of *The Road Leads On*, the

August trilogy was a sensational success, breaking all sales records for Gyldendal in Norway between 1927 and 1933, the succeeding volumes selling respectively 30,000 copies, 25,000 copies, and 27,500 copies. This last figure was nearly double that of Hamsun's nearest competitor, Johann Bojer with 15,000. And as for August, he became a folk-hero among Norwegian people to rival Ibsen's Peer Gynt. Of course, it was the fabulous, life-loving side of August that people responded best to, not the sour and bitter old man, in much the same way that Hamsun is loved for the best in him, not the worst. And despite the artistically weaker second half, *Wayfarers* remains a book that can be read with immense enjoyment.

Gyldendal needed these successes very much. In 1925 they had set up business in Oslo as Gyldendal Norwegian Publishing, having bought the name from the Danish parent company which had been Hamsun's regular publisher from 1902 onwards. The purchase was made possible by a loan from Hamsun which left him the major shareholder in the company with 200 of the 1200 shares. It was also the occasion for a good deal of national pride in the now twenty-year-old Norway, in that it meant that the rights to publish the works of the 'four greats', Ibsen, Bjørnson, Kielland and Lie, finally returned to their homeland.

The agreement with Danish Gyldendal was that the Oslo company would complete payment on the deal within seventeen to twenty years. Not least because of the phenomenal success of the first two volumes of the *August* trilogy, Harald Grieg was able to repay the debt after just six years, in 1931. Gyldendal were, to put it mildly, beholden to Hamsun. And the situation worked greatly to his advantage when, in March 1931, he began trying to sell his rights to his publishers. Danish Gyldendal had bought up the 'four greats' between 1906 and 1907; but in gambling further and buying up the rights of two lesser-known authors, Thomas Krag and Andreas Haukland, they had lost heavily, and Harald Grieg opposed the idea. Hamsun insisted, and Grieg eventually gave way in a gesture that was probably prompted more by gratitude than by strict economic good sense.

On 12 May 1931 the two parties signed a contract which gave Gyldendal Norwegian Publishing full rights to everything Hamsun had written, in all languages, and which made Hamsun richer to the tune of 200,000 kroner (roughly £10,000 at contemporary exchange rates). The money was paid over to him immediately. Now he could indulge a desire to play Croesus which had probably been with him ever since his encounter with the fabulous Zahl from Kjerringøy in 1879, and the huge gift of money that had enabled him to take the first real steps towards realising his dream of becoming a writer.

Within a month of receiving the money from Gyldendal he had given half of it away in the form of three large donations – 25,000 to the Norwegian Society of Authors, 25,000 to the Society of Painters, and 50,000 to two selected Children's Homes. Less than two years later he was back in Grieg's office again and insisting that he be allowed to buy himself back. Grieg, who has stated categorically that Hamsun was one of the two most handsome men he ever met, describes in his memoirs how Hamsun stood before him, put his head on one side, and with a fluttering motion of his large hands down his body explained that he did not like the feeling of not owning himself, that it made him feel naked. Grieg humoured him again. But when Hamsun wrote to him six years later, on 4 August 1938, and calmly declared that Grieg must now 'seriously begin thinking about "buying" me back again', Grieg put a stop to it. The situation in Europe, he explained, had made the different currencies wildly unstable, and he was not prepared to take the risk. Hamsun accepted his decision with a good grace. He had come to trust and like his publisher, although it had taken over eleven years before he had begun addressing him by the intimate pronoun 'du', a step he had taken during an all-night poker session back in the summer of 1931.[3]

Hamsun's fame was now world-wide. His books were available in twenty-seven languages, including Esperanto and Hebrew, and as his seventieth birthday approached in 1929, literary Europe began making its preparations to celebrate the occasion. He was threatened with a biography on five fronts. The prospect filled him with genuine horror.

The bad publicity he had received in the Norwegian press in the 1890s, particularly the repeated suggestion that he was even more skilled in the arts of self-promotion than of writing, had developed in him a horror of publicity which his own natural shyness had turned into a phobia. In 1894 he had begged Langen not to use a photograph of him in the German edition of *Pan*, certain that this would be construed as further proof of the accusation, and in July 1905 he answered Langen's requests for biographical details thus:

Begin on August 4 1860 when I was born, and carry on with a lot of flattering words up to the present. I can do nothing. What can be done? Deep down I think that people are weary of these pictures and biographies of authors all over the world. There are so many of us.[4]

For his friend Bolette Larsen in Bergen in 1894 he had produced a short account of his wandering life up until the breakthrough with *Hunger* in 1890. It is a witty and dismissive document, punctuated here and there with the short refrain, 'Wrote some rubbish or other',[5] which showed clearly that he didn't think any of it mattered very much.

In 1908 he answered a list of questions presented to him by Langen, giving the wrong birthdate, the information that his forebears were 'probably peasants, I don't know', and that he had had 'No schooling'.[6] A similar request for detailed information from a Russian would-be biographer at about the same time was ignored.

Yet the books came. First in the field was the German Carl Morburger's short biographical and literary study from 1910, published in a Norwegian translation in the same year. The Swede John Landquist wrote a study in 1917, and in 1922 came short works by two Americans, Josef Wiehr, and Hanna Astrup Larsen. The first psychoanalytic study of Hamsun through his work, by Eduard von Hitschmann, appeared in Vienna in 1924, and another biographical study by the Swede C D Marcus in 1926. 1929 was the peak year, naturally, and no less than five full-length studies appeared: Landquist produced a revised extension of his earlier book; Cai Woel wrote a study for Hamsun's Danish readership; and a young Norwegian psychologist Trygve Braatøy produced a full-length analysis of Hamsun based on his published writings, a book which Hamsun's analyst Strømme condemned, in a newspaper review of it, for giving a 'distorted and incorrect picture of Hamsun' owing to its 'strongly Adlerian orientation'. The two best books were by Einar Skavlan, a Norwegian writer approved of by Hamsun who enjoyed the advantage of good personal contact with his subject, and Walter A Berendsohn's scholarly biography for Langens in Germany.

Berendsohn's thoroughness particularly at first astonished and then dismayed Hamsun. In written answers to Berendsohn's enquiries he expressed a grudging admiration for the way in which he had unearthed long-forgotten newspaper articles, and even helped him with information about articles written in his earliest years under pseudonyms like W T* and Ego. For the sake of his publisher, he allowed Professor Berendsohn to visit Nørholm, and spend three days researching there, though he was careful to be away himself at the time. But when he found out later that Berendsohn had written to Bergljot and Victoria, requesting details

* Hamsun lived briefly on Waldemar Thranes gate in 1890, and may have got the idea to write under the initials W T from this.

of his early life, he wrote a letter sternly rebuking him, complaining that this had nothing to do with the study of literature, this was merely gossip and scandal.[7] Berendsohn further upset him by unearthing a woman in Fredriksvern who claimed to have 'comforted' Hamsun in Paris,[8] and by a number of assertions and speculations about Hamsun's relationships with other writers, which Hamsun irritably denied – he had never read a single line by Frank Wedekind;[9] he had never denied that he had been influenced by Dostoevsky;[10] and he most emphatically denied that he had been influenced by a reading of Thomas Mann's *Buddenbrooks* in 1903. In fact, he had not read the book until 1927. Thomas Mann, in one of his many long tributes to Hamsun, specifically stated, in any case, that the influence was all in the other direction.

Hamsun read none of these books written about him. As he wrote to Langens in 1928, 'I'm not a Wonder of the World, or a Tourist Attraction.' The whole idea of a literary biography seemed contemptible and ridiculous to him, 'Dear God, I who go into hiding when strangers come walking along the road to "stare at the animal", who refuse to meet journalists and who often go three days at a time without shaving.'[11]

All kinds of honours were offered to him in 1929. Some were fended off, others – a few – accepted. Publicly Hamsun refused to accept a silver cross which the Norwegian Society of Authors tried to present to him, a refusal which again struck sections of the Norwegian press as evidence of arrogance. Privately, a short while later, he accepted the cross. At Dantchenko's invitation, he also accepted Honorary Membership of the Moscow Arts Theatre, calling it 'the finest theatre in the world',[12] but refused a similar invitation from the Academy of Science and Arts. He also refused an Honorary Doctorate from the University of Cologne, explaining both refusals in the same terms – that it was because he was a farmer and a writer, and had nothing to do with seats of learning and academies. This rejection of public honours was nothing new for him: in 1910 he had rejected an invitation to become a Knight of the Order of St Olav, and in 1914 refused an honorary membership offered him by the Theatre School in Düsseldorf.

The two festschrift which were presented to Hamsun on 4 August indicate together the real extent of the influence that he had had on his European contemporaries since 1890. Langens' book, a single copy bound in goose skin, contained over a hundred tributes from some of the leading names in German cultural life: Thomas Mann, Hermann Hesse, Robert Musil, Arthur Schnitzler, Jacob Wassermann, Stefan Zweig, Martin Buber, Arnold Schoenberg, Albert Einstein. The writers paid tribute to

Hamsun's influence on their own literary development. Einstein praised his courageous individuality, as did Schoenberg:

> Let us not complain about the age we live in. A train can pull over a thousand men; but a spiritual giant is still capable of thinking a thought so great that the masses in their millions are not able to follow him in thinking it. But you know this, Knut Hamsun, so much better than I.

All of the German tributes have in common this celebration of the spiritual aristocrat in Hamsun. For the contributors he stands as the great example of the unyielding and uncompromising artist, indifferent to misunderstanding, one who sacrificed everything for his art, and won the victory. A melancholy irony is that, within a few short years, all of these prophets of individuality, most of them Jews, were to be driven from their positions and their homes by the man whom their hero, Hamsun, was later to describe as 'a warrior for mankind' and 'a reformer of the highest rank'.

Gyldendal's Norwegian festschrift contained messages of congratulation from a number of Hamsun's Norwegian contemporaries, as well as tributes from Maxim Gorky, Gerhard Hauptmann, Heinrich Mann, Thomas Mann, the first president of the Czech Republic T G Masaryk, George Sautreau, Stefan Zweig and André Gide. Gide likened Hamsun to Dostoevsky, but described him as 'perhaps even more subtle' than the Russian. Gorky's and Thomas Mann's tributes are article-length contributions, and Gorky was particularly fulsome in his tribute. He seems to have been obsessed by Hamsun, and regarded him as a kind of magician. In 1927 he had written to Hamsun calling *The Growth of the Soil, Chapter the Last,* and *The Women at the Pump* 'works of genius', and added 'I will tell you this quite sincerely: at this moment you are the greatest artist in Europe; there is no one who can compare with you.'[13] In an earlier letter in 1923 he had written that 'Leo Tolstoy and scores of other Russian writers have sung the praises of labour; Wladyslaw Reymont, a Pole, wrote a huge epic novel, *A Year,* dedicated to village life, but all this and much more takes second place after your splendid and powerful work [*The Growth of the Soil*].'

Gorky remained loyal to Hamsun long after the latter's open avowal of national socialism, and continued to recommend him to young Soviet writers as living proof of the fact that the novel form could be renewed on its own existing terms, without recourse to the experimentation of a Proust or a Joyce.

Another Russian contributor, Aleksandra Kollontai, confirmed the importance Hamsun had had for a whole generation of Russian writers: Andrejev, Bunin, Zajtsev, Sologub were all 'bewitched' by Hamsun, she wrote. In fact, hardly a single great name in Russian literature from the first half of the twentieth century had not at some time or other been influenced by Hamsun: Pasternak, Paustovsky, Aleksander Blok, Illya Ehrenburg and Andre Bely were all confessed admirers, as were a whole host of lesser names.[14] The wave of enthusiasm which had reached a first peak in 1910 with the publication of three separate editions of Hamsun's *Collected Works* did not break with the appearance of the new, social novels after 1912. No less than four rival editions of *Chapter the Last* appeared in 1924, although the chaotic copyright situation prevented Hamsun from reaping the financial rewards of all this.

Like their German counterparts, the Russians looked on Hamsun with an almost disbelieving wonder, and seem to have regarded him as a seer, a visionary, someone who had penetrated deep towards the heart of life's mysteries. Kollontai willingly embraced the paradox in this fondness of Soviet writers for someone so passionately reactionary as Hamsun.

The names of Thomas Mann and Hermann Hesse are probably the most striking among the list of celebrants of Hamsun's seventieth birthday, but it is also interesting to realise what a significant effect Hamsun had on Musil and Bely, two authors whose claims to literary greatness in the twentieth century are growing all the time. Kafka, dead in 1924, was another writer of high standing who read Hamsun keenly. Brecht was another still, in his youth.

In America, writers like Ernest Hemingway and Sherwood Anderson were reading everything by Hamsun they could get their hands on. In 1925 Hemingway recommended *The Growth of the Soil* to F Scott Fitzgerald, and Henry Miller was to affirm that everyone was reading him at that time. He described him as a Dickens for American writers in the 1920s and '30s.[15]

Of English writers, only Galsworthy and Wells were represented in the festschrift. His reception in England was cool, and has remained so. *The Growth of the Soil* was universally acclaimed in the wake of the Nobel Prize by English critics in 1920, but the subsequent attempt to market Hamsun in England – the third, after the failure of *Hunger* in 1899, and *Shallow Soil* in 1914 – was another failure. The problem for English critics was that the Nobel novel was for most of them their introduction to Hamsun, and as successive novels appeared in the course of the next ten years, in stilted translations that captured nothing of the subtlety of Hamsun's style, and without regard for their place in his *oeuvre*, the same critics found themselves increasingly baffled by the great dissimilarities in style and subject matter. They did not realise that Hamsun at sixty was not a 'new' writer, and that *The Growth of the Soil* was an exceptional rather than a characteristic Hamsun novel.

The publishers did not help matters by giving little or misleading information about the books. *Victoria* was described on the jacket of the 1923 translation as the 'new' novel from Knut Hamsun. the *Times Literary Supplement* critic doubted his seriousness in writing it at all, and described it as 'completely out of keeping with his more important and characteristic works. We take *Victoria* to be a juvenile experiment.' Another reviewer described *Wanderers* (*Under the Autumn Star* with *A Wanderer Played on Muted Strings*) as an incoherent, trivial, indistinct tale about a 'squalid matrimonial intrigue without the least moral significance', and complained that Hamsun took three hundred pages to describe a situation de Maupassant would have rendered adequately in fifteen. The novel was compared, unfavourably and meaninglessly, with *The Growth of the Soil*, as was *Children of the Age*. The Nobel label had hypnotised them all.

A review of *Chapter the Last* in the *TLS* for 9 October 1924 was kind, but made a valid point about the overall similarity, bordering at times on sameness, between Hamsun's later, hefty novels: 'certain traits in the book are curiously – one is tempted to say unwarrantably – reminiscent of *The Growth of the Soil*. The sanatorium is, as it were, built on the site of it. The effect in parts is that of a palimpsest; a new story written across the manuscript of the author's greatest work.'*

Relatively unimportant works by Hamsun like *Benoni* (1926) and the play *In the Grip of Life* (1924) were published and duly slaughtered, although *Mysteries* (1927) received a good and perceptive review which noted the Dostoevskian cast to the novel, and described Nagel as a cross between Stavrogin and Myshkin. Hamsun's other masterpiece, *Pan* (1920) was ignored. Other works by Hamsun published and reviewed in England in the 1920s were *Rosa*, *The Women at the Pump*, and *Segelfoss Town*.

Sometimes the critics attributed the novels' failure to move them to technical incompetence on the author's part, but there were also reactions based on an instinctive aversion to the picture of life Hamsun painted. One critic described the characters in *Chapter the Last* as seen through 'Herr Hamsun's diminishing glass', while a reviewer of *The Women at the Pump* wrote of characters who are

* Reviewing it in Germany, Hermann Hesse called it 'Far and away the best book I have read recently. Hard and cool, without the familiar lyricism of Hamsun's earlier novels, but tempered and composed in the fires.'

'treated with the contempt of one who regrets and apologises for his material'. He concluded that 'Even Strindberg had a little pity for the sins and foibles of those he so passionately despised'.

This lack of sympathy among the English for Hamsun's work has lasted well into the second half of the century, surviving even the appearance in 1955 of James McFarlane's translation of *Pan* in a style that finally did justice to the original. The *TLS* brushed it aside with the patronising comment that it 'might appeal to the admirers of Mary Webb'.* Furthermore this reviewer described the action of the novel as taking place 'somewhere near the sea in southern Norway', ignoring the fact that the opening line firmly locates the action in the far north of Norway, and that one of the most important elements in the plot is the parallel between the characteristically brief and intense nature of the spring and summer north of the polar circle and the love between Glahn and Edvarda. *Pan* has suffered more than most from hair-raising English ignorance of Scandinavia: an illustration to the first English edition showed Glahn striding along outside a cricket pavilion intended to represent his hut in the forest, and wearing a pair of cricket trousers. *Victoria* suffered somewhat too – one illustrator showed her tripping along a path in deep snow wearing a light summer frock.

The lack of interest from English writers was not total: both John Galsworthy and H G Wells contributed to the Norwegian festschrift, and between Hamsun and Wells at least, the admiration was mutual. Galsworthy as first president of the English PEN Club had enrolled Hamsun as an honorary member in 1921, and a year later invited him to England to address the club. Hamsun was at work on *Chapter the Last*, and instructed Marie to decline the invitation in her best English, because Galsworthy was a 'great man'. It is unlikely that he would have made the trip to England now under any circumstances, given his feelings after the end of the First World War, though Galsworthy presumably knew nothing of Hamsun's anglophobia.

Another English writer who was at least aware of Hamsun was Hall Caine. He had written to him in 1914, and asked him for a contribution to a King Albert's Book, in honour of the King of the Belgians. The letter arrived too late for Hamsun to reply in time to meet the deadline, but he wrote to Hall Caine assuring him that he would otherwise certainly have contributed to the book. 'Life repeats itself', he concluded, and referring to the Boer War he

* Mary Webb (1881–1927) was the best-selling author of the bucolic novel *Precious Bane*.

added, 'Then Germany was the conscience of the world. Now it's England's turn.' With a note of surprised pride he mentioned the invitation in a letter a few days later to Alette Gross, remarking that Hall Caine 'must certainly know that I have never been well-disposed towards the English'. In fact, it is unlikely that anyone outside Norway at this time knew of this peculiarity of Hamsun's, and the comment may indicate a kind of wishful thinking on his part. Perhaps he was hoping that the tactic of aggressive writing which had successfully brought him to the attention of those he considered his enemies in Norway, and brought him close enough finally to win them over, would also work with the English. Perhaps the English would presently become aware of the fact that in Norway there lived a writer who hated them with an unusual and fanatic passion. To be ignored, after all, and for his opinions to be a matter of indifference, was the one thing Hamsun found intolerable.

It is not unthinkable that a more positive reaction to him from England and Englishmen, particularly during the 1920s, might have taken the edge off his fanaticism, and led to his taking a less narrowly personal view of the historical developments in Europe between the wars. But even luck was against any improvement in the relationship. In 1920 *The Times* invited him to fill out a short biographical questionnaire for a planned series, 'Celebrities Of *The Times*'. Hamsun duly answered what he could and returned the form. It makes tragicomic reading as the English establishment and the primitive genius collide over the questions. Questions about 'Clubs. Not Exceeding Three In Number, Please', and 'Education. Please State Schools And Colleges. It Is Not Desired To Confine These To The Big Public Schools And Universities. Degrees And Distinctions Should Be Added' are left respectively blank, and answered with the single word 'none'. Question Ten: 'Career. (Positions Held, Sporting Events, Directorships. Books Written Should Be Confined To The Three Or Four Most Important)' is answered 'Schoolteacher, road-worker, shop assistant and postal official in Norway. Farm labourer, tram conductor, shopkeeper and occasional lecturer in America. Currently a farmer. For the foreseeable future a farmer.' There is no mention here of any books, most important or otherwise.[16] Alas, the planned series was abandoned. A trivial thing, of course – but one of Hamsun's deepest understandings of life was that it is a mosaic made up of trivialities.

There was another such 'near-miss' in the spring of 1929. Hamsun had asked Harald Grieg at Gyldendal to find him a new English publisher as he was dissatisfied with the sales from

England. Grieg went to some lengths to persuade Hamsun to accompany him on the proposed trip,[17] although he shared Hamsun's pessimistic view of the probable outcome. Hamsun refused to be persuaded, and would only recommend to Grieg that he get in touch with Wells for help and advice when in England, and so another opportunity for Hamsun and the English to get to know one another went begging. It all left Hamsun's personal experience of the homeland of the people he detested so passionately confined to a single train journey from Hull to Liverpool back in the remote 1880s.

George Bernard Shaw was among those who declined to contribute to the festschrift, excusing himself with the explanation that he had himself been subjected to seventieth birthday celebrations recently, and was unwilling to add to Knut Hamsun's suffering on the occasion. Hamsun anyway, in preparation for what he always referred to as the 'wretched' 4th of August, had already laid plans to flee Nørholm and the inevitable journalists some days in advance. He, Marie and Tore drove off to an undisclosed destination in their seven-seater Cadillac, with Marie doing the driving, as usual. Fifteen-year-old Arild was left at Nørholm in charge of receiving all the mail and the flowers, and disappointing the press.

The party of three spent the day itself in a small private hotel in Flekkefjord, a small town further along the south coast from Grimstad. Some journalists tracked them down there the following day, but there were no interviews, and the press angle on the great day was the by now familiar one that Hamsun had become an engimatic hermit. The burden of being a 'great man' in Norway, which had increasingly fallen on him since the death of Christian Michelsen (the hero of 1905) in 1925, and the disappearance of Roald Amundsen on a rescue flight in 1928, was something that Hamsun would only accept on his own terms. Where the outside world tried to dictate the terms, he reacted simply by hiding from it.

One feels that a part of him, at least, regarded his 'greatness' as his own invention. He possessed it, as though it were something that he had created quite independently of the thousands of Norwegians who had bought his books. When the Hamsuns left Flekkefjord, their landlady paid her own special tribute to him, setting apart the chair he had sat on in the lounge, and describing it on a placard pinned to the wall under a photograph of him as 'Knut Hamsun's Chair'. The story says so much about the complex relationship between the man and the people. Touching and ridiculous at the same time, it shows how Norwegians insistently made a demi-god of him, and explains how he, in his vanity, could fall into that impatient and rather contemptuous acceptance of the role which found its expression in the respectless arrogance of some of his journalism between 1910 and 1920, and onward through the 1930s to the war.

But the unhappy result of these developments was still some years in the future. For the time being, life at Nørholm continued quietly. The young Danes who had taken over the running of the farm in 1922 had turned it into a model enterprise, and when they left Hamsun had briefly taken over the running of it again. But already in the autumn of 1928, after just a few months, he had begun having ideas for *August*, and resumed his habit of 'walking alone' with a book, as he called it. This second volume of the trilogy was written largely at home in his writing-hut, although he continued to change the scenery whenever he felt it necessary. The Hotel Norge in Lillesand was a popular choice; he always used the same room there, Room 302. He also spent some weeks in the spring of 1929 as the only guest at a remote inland hotel at Vråliosen.

In 1927 Hamsun had written to his old friend Erik Frydenlund in Valdres, and suggested that first Tore, and later Arild, should attend middle-school there under Erik's guardianship. He had renewed contact with Frydenlund in 1922 after a lapse of five or six years; Erik had visited Nørholm, and to Hamsun's obvious delight the old friendship had survived. The surviving correspondence between the two men – Hamsun's side – is eloquent testimony to the warmth and charm and generosity and gentle wit of which Hamsun was capable if he were really fond of someone. Frydenlund was a postmaster, and it is no coincidence that the postmen and postmasters and telegraphists who crop up all over Hamsun's fictional universe are almost always attractive and humane characters.

Frydenlund had agreed to look after the boys. When Arild began to suffer from homesickness after a while, Hamsun travelled to join his boys in the spring of 1930, and lived for a while in Frydenlund's house while he continued work on *August*. Between the years 1927–30, Valdres became a kind of meeting place for the Hamsuns. The eldest daughter Ellinor was sent to a convent in Germany at the age of fourteen, but spent her holidays with the family there. All of the Hamsun children, in fact, spent time in Germany. Hamsun's commitment to the culture was consistent and practical, although the arrangements that he and Marie came to with regard to the education of the children generally are a classic illustration of the wild paradox which riddles all consideration of his personality:

the man who considered the learning of foreign languages to involve the victim in some kind of irreversible spiritual corruption sent his children not only to Germany, but to Belgium and to France, with specific instructions that they were to learn the languages there. And their ambitions, when shortly they became of an age to have them, showed no trace of their father's literary gospel of the simple life, but were the usual refined ambitions of rich children everywhere – Ellinor wanted to be a film star, Tore and Cecilia wanted to paint, and Arild wanted to write.

Valdres was where Hamsun had come on his honeymoon with Bergljot in 1898. After the divorce the couple had remained in contact through Victoria, and in 1919 Hamsun sent his daughter to France to learn the language. But she did something even worse than that, and fell in love with an Englishman, Déderick Charlesson, the son of the English consul in Honfleur, in Normandy. The couple travelled to England, and after two years returned and married and settled in Honfleur. In 1923 Bergljot sold her house in Drøbak and emigrated to France to join them, and from that time onwards contacts between the two branches of the family had been sporadic. In 1930 Hamsun began thinking about Bergljot again. He wrote to her sister Alette in Germany, and asked her to ask Bergljot to write to him 'now and then'. He was anxious to know whether she was happy in France, and offered to help with money if she wished to travel to Vienna to see her daughter by Eduard Goepfert. 'Vesla' was at the start of a career as a popular novelist there, where she had returned with her father after the breakup of the marriage in 1897. Alette seems to have interpreted this show of concern, and the offers of money, as evidence that Hamsun was feeling guilty, and she took the opportunity to rebuke him for the casual indifference of his attitude towards her sister. When Bergljot reckoned up the sum of her experiences with Hamsun, she wrote, her reckonings would leave her with a 'bitter answer'. Yet she was wrong to think that Hamsun had felt guilty; he had only wanted to offer whatever practical assistance he could to Bergljot; and he rejected the invitation to feel guilt:

> I don't really understand your letter. I know of no case where a divorce did not 'degenerate into a mere financial arrangement' – and at the same time there's usually squabbling over the children. What other answer could there be than a bitter one? There's no point in even discussing it. What's done is done.[18]

In the autumn of 1930, a week or two after writing this letter,

Hamsun was admitted to hospital in Arendal with arteriosclerosis. The surgeon made it clear to him that the operation was risky, and recognising that he might die Hamsun made haste to settle his financial affairs with Victoria. Her marriage to Déderick had been much against his will, and he had ceased to support her with money afterwards. In 1927 he had corresponded briefly with her, and made her an offer of a lump sum of money in the hope that she would accept, and so avoid any possibility of squabbling over his money when he was dead. She did not accept, but now in 1930 Hamsun revived the offer. The French currency had grown weaker in the intervening years, and Victoria was now willing to negotiate with her father. However, the matter was conducted by lawyers, and in a short while an acrimonious atmosphere developed. Victoria's lawyers worked out that her share in Hamsun's fortune ought to be 28,000 kroner. Hamsun replied, through his lawyers, that this was too little, and offered her 45,000. His intention was as before, that this settlement would be final; but Victoria's lawyers advised her against signing away her rights to shares in the royalties from Hamsun's books. Victoria travelled to Norway, and meetings took place between various lawyers and intermediaries. She and Marie Hamsun met briefly, and parted deadly enemies. Finally, through Harald Grieg, Hamsun made a last offer of 50,000 kroner (about £5000) which Victoria again rejected on the advice of her lawyers. There the matter rested for a year, during which the French currency continued to decline. In 1931 Victoria contacted her father again. She was so poor, she wrote, she had not even a sheet to call her own – would Hamsun stand by his 'final' offer to her? He had to write back and tell her that the huge donations he had made as a result of selling his books outright to Gyldendal meant that he was no longer in a position to give her the 50,000 kroner. She kept at him, reasoning, perhaps, that a certain amount of wounded pride had to be taken into account, and finally, in February 1932, father and daughter entered into an agreement whereby he gave her 40,000 kroner in return for a guarantee that she would waive all further claims on his estate.[18] It was all rather depressing proof of the truth of Hamsun's remarks in his letter to Alette Gross in September 1930, and at the same time evidence of Hamsun's developed sense of financial responsibility towards his family.

Hamsun was not the only member of his family to be ill in 1930. Marie lay in bed for eight weeks in the spring, and in the summer Ellinor was ill. She was Hamsun's admitted favourite among the children, a rather wild girl who suffered throughout her adolescence from periodic bouts of anorexia nervosa. In her mixture of wildness and sensitivity and stubbornness she had qualities reminiscent of her father, and typically it was for her stubbornness, in which she resembled her father most of all, that Hamsun chided her most. When Marie was visiting Ellinor and Cecilia in Düsseldorf, he told her to:

> Ask Ellinor if she doesn't feel ashamed of herself for causing us all this worry because she is so stiff-necked and obstinate. We all of us only want what's best for her, but she, *alone against everybody*, insists that she knows what is best for her!

Ellinor was treated to Hamsun's miracle cure, and sent to Erik Frydenlund in Valdres to get her appetite back. In November Tore fell ill with meningitis, and in January 1931 a sort of double convalescence trip was arranged. Hamsun had been told that he must consider himself convalescent for the three years following his operation, so he, Marie and Tore, plus Tore's tutor Trygve Tveteraas, set off on a trip to southern Europe.

They travelled by rail across Sweden, Denmark and Germany, and spent three days in Berlin, with Hamsun encamped in his hotel, and the German press encamped in the lobby. His pro-German sentiments were a well-known fact in Germany, and his visit regarded as an honour and a confirmation of his feelings; yet not even his high regard for the Germans could overcome his suspicion of journalists. In fact, his personal experience of Germany at that time was hardly more extensive than his experience of England. He had spent two months in Munich in 1896, and made a brief business trip to Munich and Vienna in 1920, and that was it. Like most passions, his love for the country, like his hatred of England, thrived best as a property of the mind, untarnished by contacts with reality.

From Germany they travelled on through Switzerland to Milan, and crossed the Italian-French border at Ventimiglia on 19 January. Here a ridiculous customs scene ensued. Hamsun became annoyed when a French customs officer began unpacking all their luggage, and he instructed Marie to complain to the man. The officer merely redoubled his efforts to find something to tax, and finally noticed that Hamsun was smoking a pipe: had he any tobacco with him? Hamsun, fairly deaf, unable to speak French and disliking the man, ignored him for some time, but finally produced two tins of Tiedemann's Mixture from his pocket and cast them on the table. The customs officer snapped them up, disappeared, and returned five minutes later with an official demand for twenty francs. In disgust Hamsun took up the tobacco and threatened to throw it out of the window rather than pay tax on it – the tins had travelled tax-free across the whole of Europe with him, and he was damned if he was going to pay twenty francs for them now. The customs officer, having summoned several colleagues, now threatened to arrest Hamsun. At this point Tore intervened diplomatically, and with a few words and a small gift settled the matter to the satisfaction of all parties – except Hamsun. His son's tactful intervention irritated him. He *wanted* the situation to proceed without recourse to tact or diplomacy. He probably even *wanted* to be arrested. Tore Hamsun's account of this winter trip of theirs in 1931 shows that whatever else the old man may have been, he was never boring. In cafés and hotels he behaved consistently with that peculiar kind of petulant eccentricity which is at times consciously and irresistibly hilarious, at other times merely irritating, and occasionally hateful. He was, according to the testimony of many of those who knew him personally, like Albert Engstrøm, extremely like his books.

Arrived at Nice, the party stayed briefly at a large hotel along the Avenue Caravadossi, where Hamsun bemused the staff by speaking to them in Norwegian and refusing point blank to give any tips. The inevitable result was that the party were not favoured guests. Tore and Marie tried to rescue the situation by secret tipping. On the last day Hamsun astonished and delighted the staff by handing out fabulous tips all round. Like Nagel, nothing pleased and amused him more than to create a bad image of himself, let it harden for a while, and then suddenly destroy it with a sudden grand and unexpected gesture. He loved to demonstrate that things are not what they seem to be, that he could not be predicted like other people. It made him a memorable figure, like someone from a fairy-tale, like Geissler from *The Growth of the Soil*. Certainly he must have looked very distinguished as he strolled along the Promenade des Anglais in his grey suit and soft hat and stick – a party of tourists rushed up to him one day and accused him of being a famous American automobile manufacturer.

After a few days in Nice, the party motored the few kilometres up the road to Beaulieu-sur-mer, where they stayed at Marcellin's *pension*. Here Hamsun ran into an old friend from Paris and the days of his first marriage, Peter Egge. He may have hoped for some company from him, but Egge was hard at work on the final stages of a novel he was writing, and the two saw little of each other. Egge says that Hamsun stayed in his room and played patience most of the time, while the three other members of the party were shown around the town by his wife, Fru Egge.[20]

Tore and his tutor stayed behind when the Hamsuns returned home – Hamsun asked Peter Egge to keep an eye on the pair of them – and Knut and Marie travelled back the way they had come. Hamsun claimed not to have enjoyed the trip much, although the rather sour mood of a letter to Erik Frydenlund of 27 January may have been influenced by his recent operation:

Dear E K F – Marie and I are on board a train which is jolting like hell. We've installed Tore at Nizza and he should get better there. You've overfed him these last three years, and he's a fine physical specimen, but he's not all that strong.

We left Nizza about midday, and I'm scribbling this between Marseille and Lyon, and the train is shaking about all over the place! What we won't do for the children. This trip has been a bloody nuisance for Marie and me. Sure, we've seen palm trees and vineyards, and orange trees with lovely fruit and glorious sunshine and all this, but I've seen it all before. Besides, the sun isn't warm here. I've got influenza and am sitting here with three pairs of trousers on.[21]

Back in Norway again he occupied himself with various hobby-like undertakings. As the major shareholder in the new Gyldendal Norwegian publishing house Hamsun could have exercised considerable power in the running of the company had he so chosen, but in matters pertaining to the technical side of running a publishing company he let himself be guided by Harald Grieg. However, he did make frequent recommendations to Grieg to publish certain books he was enthusiastic about. Rufin Piotrowski's *A Polish Refugee's Story*, which he had first read in an edited translation in the days when he was writing *Hunger*, and which had made a deep impression on him, was published in a full translation at his instigation in 1934, with a foreword by Hamsun, although he was less successful in trying to persuade Grieg to publish an American book about lunatic asylums, called *Pick up the Pieces*, which he called 'the strangest and one of the most talented things I have read from America'. He complained that Gyldendal were not promoting Marie's children's books and her books of verse enthusiastically enough. With commendable loyalty he described her 1934 collection *Wintergreen* as 'the only real poetry that has been written this year'. His unhappy interest in race, and the concept of 'racial hygiene' also, led him to press the work of a certain Dr Konrad Simonsen on Gyldendal. Harald Grieg was able to resist the pressure.

Another hobby was keeping his lawyer, Sigrid Stray, busy. Here was a further paradox of classic proportions – Hamsun, who affected to detest educated women, not only married one (who was an actress into the bargain), but chose one as his lawyer. Through her he raised again the question of the identity of the author of the anonymous letters with which he had been persecuted back in 1897. With the co-operation of the Norwegian police the world's leading handwriting expert, a Dr Locard, from Lyons in France, was called in and after extensive study of the fading letters Locard declared categorically that the writer was indeed Anna Munch, as Hamsun had known it was all along.[22] Another case Fru Stray handled for him had certain similarities with the name case of 1922–25 against his brother Thorvald and nephew Almar. This time he sued the previous owners of Nørholm, the family who had owned the house before selling it to the property speculator Longum from whom Hamsun had bought it in 1919.

The case was a peculiarly Norwegian affair, hinging on the right of a property owner to style himself after the name of his property, in this case the farm Nørholm. Hamsun's aim in raising it was to stop the previous owners, ironically enough named Petersen, from calling themselves Petersen-Nørholm now that they no longer had any connection with the estate. In an address to the court, Hamsun claimed that he would never have bought the farm at all had the Petersen family styled themselves 'Nørholmen' on their contract of sale with Longum. 'I am passionate about name cases', he declared. He had asked Harald Grieg to be present in court as an impartial witness of the proceedings. Grieg duly attended on 27 April 1933, and with some surprise heard Hamsun claim that he had 'often' thought of changing his name to Nørholm himself,* but that he would now be unable to do so unless the law would prevent the Petersen family from also using it. The court's decision of 5 May was unanimous: the six members of the Petersen family were all forbidden to call themselves either Nørholmen or Petersen-Nørholm. The whole thing was really no more than the clashing of petty snobbery. Hamsun also showed somewhat dubious morality afterwards in presenting the Chief Magistrate, Halfdan Schelderup, with a leather-bound set of his _Collected Works_, and the two lay magistrates, both local farmers, with copies of _The Growth of the Soil_ as an expression of his gratitude.[23]

Litigation like this cost Hamsun time and money; so did the most

---

* Hamsun claimed to the court that Almar's swindling drove him to thoughts of changing his name to Nørholm. But both Almar and Thorvald had settled out-of-court in 1925, before Hamsun's appeal against the verdict was heard, and with the settlement the argument that he needed another name disappeared.

enjoyable of all his hobbies – running the farm Nørholm. It was as well for him that he was still able to produce best-selling novels to finance it all.

In October 1933 *The Road Leads On* was published, and Hamsun's ten-year long involvement with August was over. The public grieved over his death. Some readers even expressed the hope that the sheep had been so soft to land on that August had survived the fall, and would one day turn up again. The long-term project of the trilogy was now completed, and with the children gone, Nørholm seemed quiet and empty. Perhaps in an attempt to fill these gaps, the Hamsuns took to travelling frequently, sometimes together in the Cadillac, but usually alone. In the spring of 1934 Hamsun travelled to Juan Les Pins to visit Arild and Ellinor, and spent the summer months at Lillesand and Kristiansand. The Goethe Institute awarded him their prize that year. He accepted the medal, but refused the 10,000 marks prize money, explaining that the Germans were recovering, rebuilding, and that he wished to show his support for their efforts.[24] In 1935 he was again in Germany and France, and worked on what was to be his last novel, *The Ring is Closed*. He worked steadily at home at Nørholm, but there were trips again to Hotel Norge in Lillesand.

At the beginning of 1936 Ellinor was involved in a serious car accident in Germany, and Marie travelled to Berlin to be with her. Hamsun stayed behind at Nørholm to write, but found it hard to concentrate for worrying about his favourite child. Yet his work meant so much to him that he reacted with slight surprise to Marie's suggestion that he travel to Berlin to be with them. Had she considered whether he would be able to work in Berlin, he asked her? Presumably she had not. However, he wrote to Ellinor, and offered to come if she wanted him to.

Later in the year he travelled to Egerøya, where he had worked successfully on the last part of the *August* trilogy, and on 19 June the book was finished. It was in the shops by 1 October, in time, as usual, for the Christmas market.

The Ring is Closed marks a return to something like form after the disappointments of *August* and *The Road Leads On*. In conception, execution, and title, it looks like a conscious 'last statement' from Hamsun the novelist. On 19 June he wrote to Harald Grieg that the title means 'that the last link in the chain connects with the first',[25] and there are indeed many remarkable connections between this novel and *Hunger*, published forty-six years earlier. The words of the Norwegian title themselves, *Ringen Sluttet*, incorporate and engulf *Sult*, as in the image of the snake that engulfs its own tail.

The action of the novel takes place in a small coastal town in the south of Norway, clearly not far from Oslo. The hero is a philosophising layabout named Abel Brodersen, and the interest of the novel is in high degree concentrated on him. There are a dozen or so secondary characters, largely preoccupied with sex and money, whose function in the novel is to illuminate, by the different forms of their contact with him, the many sides of Abel's personality.

Abel is the only child of an old, rich lighthouse-keeper and an alcoholic mother. When his mother dies, his father marries a young woman, Lola, who has seduced him to achieve financial security. Abel goes to sea, and after a period in Australia and New Zealand, he settles in America. He rarely writes, and never answers letters sent to him, although he does reveal that he has got married out there.

Presently old Brodersen dies, and Abel inherits his fortune. Despite repeated requests that he come home to Norway and claim the inheritance, he does not do so; he is living a simple life in Green Ridge, Kentucky, and cannot be bothered with the money. Some months later his new wife, Angèle, dies, and shortly afterwards Abel returns to Norway. He has immediate success with the women there, not that it seems to matter much to him. However, the husband, Alex, of one of these conquests, Lili, catches Abel and Lili in bed together and shoots Abel twice, in the foot and in the arm. The wounds are only flesh wounds, and like the hero of an Icelandic saga, Abel finishes tying his shoelaces before attending to them. He feels neither guilt nor shame at being caught like this with another man's wife, and even turns angrily on Alex and rebukes him for having stolen the gun – he recognises it as his own weapon.

Abel continues in his amoral ways, although his amorality seems neither to shock nor surprise the other inhabitants. The fortune inherited from his father is soon gone; given away, squandered, or lent. Abel shows a sublime indifference to material comforts, and presently moves into a deserted railroad shack. There is a pane of glass missing from the window, and no lock on the door.

Several love tangles appear. Lola, Abel's stepmother, is besotted by him. Abel is still in love with his first love, Olga. Olga loves Abel secretly, but will never admit it publicly. Lawyer Clemens, who has been married to Olga, really loves Lola.

Lola desperately wants Abel to 'be somebody'. With money inherited from Old Brodersen she becomes a major shareholder in the local ferry-boat *The Sparrow*, specifically so that Abel can become the captain. Abel has failed to get the hang of the book-learnt navigation at the Seaman's School, but he has a natural talent for picking things up by experience, and he makes a great success of the captaincy. But it is just this talent that makes life hard for him. Nothing ever really seems very difficult for him. He suffers greatly from boredom, and one day he removes his uniform, gives Lola the slip, and disappears again to America. Months go by, and one day he turns up again, penniless and in rags, but still infuriatingly content with the drifting, goalless, resolutely meaningless nature of his existence. He survives a last hard winter in his railroad hovel, stealing his food when he can't pay for it, stealing sometimes just for the excitement of it, offered sex by a number of women, turning them down sometimes, and sometimes accepting them.

It turns out in the course of a conversation Abel has with Olga that he probably murdered his own wife Angèle when he found her with his best friend, the Irishman Lawrence; it was Lawrence he meant to kill, but the bullet went astray. Lawrence took the blame for the murder and went to the electric chair. His relatives later came across a letter that revealed the true facts of the case, and towards the end of the novel we hear that the authorities in America have been in touch with the Norwegian police about Abel, and would like to interview him to hear his side of the story. Even before hearing this news, Abel has been planning his return to America. He expresses neither fear nor relief at the prospect of being brought to justice. Like other Hamsun heroes such as telegraphist Baardsen, and Willatz Holmsen III, and like the classic heroes of the saga literature Hamsun always admired, Abel has a fatalistic and unspoken intuition of his own coming death which leads him to tidy up his personal affairs. His last acts before sailing are to buy a child a promised bicycle, and to pay a photographer's bill.

It must be admitted that here, as indeed in all of Hamsun's novels from *Children of the Age* onwards, there is a tendency to garrulousness which is not always successfully controlled. But the technical details of Hamsun's prose style are always interesting, and at seventy-seven he can still write at times with the irresistible and convincing freedom of the man who invented the art. As he is about to describe the wrecking of *The Sparrow* he spontaneously addresses a few remarks directly to the doomed boat. And when Abel receives payment of an old debt from Tollmaster Robertsen, with no extra punctuation or preparatory remarks Hamsun suddenly slips into the first person to give us a couple of Abel's thoughts on the matter, before resuming in the third person. He does this only once in a book of 320 pages. A similar unique jolt occurs when the narration briefly addresses Lola directly as 'you'.

Hamsun also makes use of one of his most highly characteristic devices, that of suddenly switching tenses, usually from the past into the present, and sometimes in the middle of a sentence. He often did this in order suddenly to step up the tension as some difficult undertaking is about to be embarked upon, or some dramatic event about to happen, but with equal frequency did it for no discernible reason that can be found in the text. The effect always seems right, however, and demonstrates Hamsun's instinctive and masterly control over the varying degrees of intensity of his prose. *The Ring is Closed* also contains one of the finest examples of his brazenness in changing his mind about what he intended to write next, so that instead of the whole business being hidden from us by a rewriting, we get this:

> Clemens did not misunderstand her; naturally it never occurred to him that she had come to offer to work for him again. Or rather, did this occur to him? Absolutely! In one brief exquisite flash, he felt it within his heart.

The Ring is Closed is by far Hamsun's sexiest novel, and includes in Olga a striking portrait of a woman suffering the mind-perversion of her erotic instincts. The thought that Abel might be a killer causes her to seek him out in order to have sex with him. The novel is also largely free from those editorial insertions reflecting the author's own personal prejudices which characterise most of Hamsun's later fiction, although democracy is ridiculed briefly in the scene in which *The Sparrow* runs aground while the three crew members who are supposed to be in charge of her are quarrelling over who should wear the Captain's hat. Elsewhere Abel dismisses with weary contempt the attentions of elderly women who have reached an age when 'the sex-life has gone to smash for them' and who devote themselves instead to religion, charity, and politics. Hamsun presumably failed to recognise the irony in satirising old women for their attention to matters of which at least two – charity and politics – had been hobbies of his for some time by 1936.

Hamsun's main aim this time, though, is not destructive satire, and the novel's secondary characters are neither particularly grotesque nor hateful. It is in fact a strange and provocative blend of two superficially opposed tendencies. On the one hand it can be read as a straightforward affirmation of the master-morality in which Abel does what he wants and beds whom he pleases simply because he feels no guilt in doing so, and because there is no one who cares or dares to stop him. On the other hand it can be understood as a creative attempt to depict a life wisdom in operation, in which Abel is a personification of the rejection of all accepted values of western society. Like a Taoist sage, he is *in* the dust, but not *of* the dust.

Time and again the essentially paradoxical nature of Abel's existence, the paradoxical and amoral statements he makes, remind us of the riddling style of Lao Tzu or Chuang Tzu. More than any other Hamsun creation he is the *deliberate* engima, the living Zen-riddle from whom all orthodox moral and cultural understanding recoils in irritated wonder, and there is little doubt that, in Abel, Hamsun intended to depict the wise man, the man who had found the Way. The nature of the life he leads, flowing like water, refusing to strive, living beyond the limitations imposed on the mind by verbally defined concepts of 'right' and 'wrong', is close to the ideal life of the Taoist sage. If we pursue this coincidence with an ancient Chinese philosophy even further, we come across an even more interesting coincidence. The philosophers known as the Realists, whose most famous representative was Han Fei Tsu (d 233 BC), were early versions of the Nazis. They did not believe that man was possessed of a moral sense, and taught that frightening punishments and large material rewards were the way in which to keep a people under control. Anti-intellectual and anti-merchant, but passionately military, they honoured the farmer, but above all the soldier. Curiously, the Realists found in Taoism a metaphysical basis for their philosophy. The famous sinologist Arthur Waley explains this peculiar ideological alliance by pointing out that many of the incidental tenets of Taoism could be accepted as they stood by the Realists. Taoists and Realists concurred in their contempt for hsien (people of superior morality), for book-learning, for morality and benevolence, for commerce and 'unnecessary' contrivances. Both schools decried ceremony and advocated the return to simple ways of life.

This description accords strikingly with the ideal Hamsun promoted throughout his life and work, and with particular vigour in later novels like *The Growth of the Soil*. The aspects of Taoism which the Realists could not use, such as its insistence on the autonomy of the individual, they either ignored or, as in the case of the main Taoist tenet, 'Cling to the Unity', turned into a political maxim – the absolute unification of everything in the state. Nor had they much use for the Taoists' ecstatic pantheism. This 'mystic basis of Realism', as Arthur Waley calls it, gives us one of the few clues we have for an understanding of the co-existence in Hamsun of two so apparently incompatible strains of thought as oriental

Quietism and western Fascism. These tendencies drove him with equal vigour but in opposite directions, never towards one another. Only in the light of this paradox can we understand how Rebecca West could speak of Hamsun's having 'the completest omniscience of the human soul', and another English admirer of his novels claiming that they showed 'the clearest possible understanding of the human world', while the object of their praises could devote so much of his literary energy in later life to the public demonstration of a lamentably constricted view of the human soul.

The Ring is Closed contains a number of echoes of other Hamsun novels. Abel's return from America wearing his brown ulster reminds us of Nagel's arrival by steamer in the little coastal town, wearing his yellow suit; and when Abel works for a while as odd-job man for Fru Gulliksen, he reminds us of Knut Pedersen the Wanderer, both in his inventive approach to the solution of a practical problem such as how to transplant two large chestnut trees, and in the erotic fascination he exerts over his lusty, middle-aged employer. There are echoes of Glahn in Abel's living in a hut, and in his love of solitude, and his pantheism. Above all, the links are with *Hunger*, the first in Hamsun's long chain of novels.

Hunger seems to be, in some way, contained within *The Ring is Closed* – or rather, a dream or memory of *Hunger*, which is suggested by a number of parallels between the central figures of the two novels, whereby Abel's actions echo those of the narrator of *Hunger*. He visits a second-hand clothes dealer to try to sell his socks and underwear to raise money for food. Having given a cake-seller a lot of money, he returns later, when starving, and claims cakes on account from her. He begs meat from a butcher for a non-existent dog. He finds a bone and takes it back to his hovel with him. (Hamsun specifically points out to us that when Abel breaks it open to get at the marrow, it is *not* to eat it, as the hero in *Hunger* did, but to provide grease for his door.) At the end of Abel's last winter in Norway, Hamsun tells us that he 'had probably never before had such a struggle; a continuing lack of nourishment had rendered him, as it were, inscrutable, in both expression and contacts with people.' But where once it was horses and carriages that splashed through the Christiania mud beside the strange, self-obsessed narrator, it is motor cars that whizz by Abel.

The single great difference between the narrator of *Hunger* and Abel, is that Abel lacks – wilfully – the one thing that drove the *Hunger* hero on, his sense of ambition. Like the starving young writer, Abel performs an act of blasphemy. Not out of passionate and awed hatred for God, but rather to show his familiarity, almost his contempt for Him, he steals a couple of bracelets from an icon of Jesus as a present for a woman he loves. It is all as though Hamsun is saying that he wishes he had never taken life quite so seriously, a confession similar in spirit to Ibsen's last work, *When We Dead Awaken*. Abel comes into some money and buys himself a new winter outfit, and then asks himself, 'What's the difference between yesterday and today? What do I have that I didn't have before? A few clothes.' That's to say, nothing.

Like *Mysteries'* Nagel, the meaning of Abel's existence is apparent only in terms of its deviation from all normally accepted standards and codes of conduct. He is the Artist as Repudiator, as Provoker. He is Paradox, Truth standing on its head in order to attract attention. In the middle of the same old race, along the same old road, towards the same old goals of sex, and more sex, and money, and more money, and more and more meaningless complications, Abel dreams of returning to the life he led with Angèle in the black shanty town at Green Ridge, Kentucky. A woman once asked him in shocked tones, if what she had heard was true, this his wife Angèle had been a negress? 'No she wasn't', Abel had replied, and added, 'But after all, what if she had been?'

He described his life in Green Ridge thus to Lola:

'I was well off. She was lovely to me. I had sunk to the depths, and so had she – so together we took up life down there on the bottom. Just as all the others about us had done. There we all were, crawling around on the bottom, some with only a bottle of milk perhaps, others with only an ear of corn to eat, others suffering only from cold – and no one to expect certain things from Angèle and me. After six months or a year I received a letter. It was brought me by a negro who couldn't read it, so I just let it lie. I suppose you think it's pretty hard to go without food and clothes, but we aren't really dependent upon such things – we were as blissful as two wild beasts only to be together. Down though we were, we had each other and could crawl into bed and sleep. We did not speak when we woke, just got up and went off – wherever one of us might go, the other would follow along. We had chosen the same road through life and followed by each other's side. Now and then I might fill her with joy by bringing her a chicken from the farmer. But he was a stingy brute and stood guard. Once he took a shot at me, and after that I was scared to go near his place. But what of it? There were plenty of fish in the streams around Green Ridge, and in the fall there was everywhere fruit. And I also planted a bushel of potatoes.'

Lola appeared dejected. 'Couldn't you have lifted yourself out of all that?' she asked. 'It can't be so pleasant to live like a wild beast.'

'Oh yes – it was nice.'

To a bewildered Olga, he tried to explain his attitude towards life but succeeded only in confusing her still more:

'You developed, you were telling me. One meal a day – God preserve me! There's no doubt that the effect of that is wearing upon you, and if that's the way you choose to live, it must be because you lack the will to do anything.'

'What if that were a special faculty, Olga?'

She started: 'A special faculty? I've never heard anything like it, how clever you've become at talking! A faculty? You may be right in what you say; and I wouldn't care in the least if you were – if only it weren't you, Abel, who are going to the dogs.'

'That sounds strange coming from you', he said, 'but when I sit in the sun I don't require much in the way of food. I've seen in the tropics how they live from day to day, from hand to mouth, live on almost nothing, except sunshine. Millions live like that. With them the thought of "coming up" is meaningless; they do not think in terms of money and dining-room tables, their lives are simple, they wear flowers for their adornment. They were so beautiful to look at, such a pleasant sight for the eyes! We stopped at the Islands and got acquainted with them; they had no need of anything we might have had in our pockets; we had nothing they wanted to buy, and they didn't beg. We went up in the interior; they were dancing and laughing, they were friendly and gave us fruit, they had beautiful brown bodies, they wore almost no clothes. We were there two nights – '

They stayed only two nights in this paradise. What links the two dream existences is that the shadow of consciousness never falls across them. Consciousness is hell, Hamsun intimates many times throughout his fiction. Yet not to have one is an unthinkable dream. Among the enduring joys of his writing are tiny fragments of this dream which nevertheless, suddenly and quite unexpectedly – often in the middle of some particularly dark passage – flash out from the surface of the prose. Some bright, still miracle seen with the rapt intensity of a child's eye, like a bee sleeping inside a flower, or a seal that turns its head and looks at a boy rowing a boat.

If we include the by no means ridiculous *Bjørger* from 1879,

Hamsun's career had spanned fifty-seven years, and produced twenty-two full-length novels, five stage plays, one verse drama, a book of cultural history, a travel book, and three collections of short-stories. In America, Scandinavia and Germany he was widely regarded as the greatest living writer, and was probably the most admired and imitated literary figure of his day. Now should have been the time to relax and enjoy the last days of his life of truly heroic industry. He had his wife and his beautiful farm, and four grown-up children who might in the course of time produce grandchildren to lighten his last days. Yet it would seem as though the price of the achievement had been too great. Obsessed by his writing, he had taught himself never to give more of himself than he could spare, not even to his wife and children. When the time came when he no longer needed to reserve himself to quite such an extreme degree for his books, he found that he had lost the talent to open himself voluntarily. Instead of he and Marie becoming companions in old age (though Marie was still in fact only in her fifties), their relationship became increasingly characterised by hostility and aggression. Hamsun's two periods of psychoanalysis with Strømme in the 1920s perhaps indicate a clear realisation on his part that important normal sides of the Hamsun family relationship were suffering serious neglect on account of his fanatic dedication to his writing. His letters to Marie bear this out, with their repeated refrain that changes should and must be made, that he should try to join more in family life. He had promised to start going to the cinema in Grimstad with Marie and the boys, and he encouraged Marie to take dancing lessons, so that she could teach him the steps afterwards, and they could go out dancing together. In one letter he had written:

It's enough to drive a person mad, never to meet anyone, never to leave one's room. I want to go into Grimstad sometimes together with you and the children, and go on longish walks sometimes. And we won't be afraid of people. On the contrary we'll be happy, and we'll thank God, and the world.

But in a life which seemed to him without absolute meaning beyond the simple ability, like Oliver or Abel, to survive it, his total absorption in the act of writing was a psychic necessity at the deepest level, and as soon as the *August* trilogy was safely under way with *Wayfarers* in 1926, these good resolutions to be more sociable and accessible had disappeared. Marie gave way to an increasing bitterness. In a secret letter to a friend of Hamsun's from the very old days, the widower of Bolette Larsen in Bergen, she wrote:

By way of explaining Hamsun's attitude, I can tell you that he has not a single so-called friend, that he cannot be bothered to write letters to friends, and that in the course of time all people have become a matter of indifference to him. This may be a fault, but it is simply how Hamsun *is*. . . . Perhaps you cannot understand how a person could change so much. I can't either. But there it is. His work is his only friend, his only love, and the rest of us just have to accept this.

I have written this letter behind Knut's back. He would be very angry if he found out I had sent you these lines by way of explanation. Might I ask you to burn this letter, and pretend that you have never received it?[26]

She added that Hamsun used her to write all his letters for him, and that he had even made her practise forging his autograph. All over the world, people were probably treasuring forged Hamsun autographs.

That was in 1928. She expressed herself similarly to a journalist five years later, in an interview in March 1933:

Yes, I like living here. But Hamsun is not interested in people, and we don't get many visitors. There are times when I feel as though I live in a hermetically sealed world.[27]

In the immediate pre-war years, her bitterness became pathological. Always jealous of her husband, she became obsessed by the idea that he had betrayed her with a Danish actress at some point in the early 1930s. Her fears were understandable; Hamsun's life of travelling and writing, his need for solitude, must have given plenty of scope for her suspicions to feed on while she remained bound to the home by the children and the cares of the estate. They argued frequently and fought. Sometimes fists were raised, and the children had to come between them. Marie often stormed away from conversations threatening suicide. On one occasion she even made a half-hearted attempt to kill her husband, and instructed her daughter Cecilia to crumble some slimming tablets in his sandwiches in hopes of killing him with an overdose. They didn't kill him, but at least they slowed him down for a while, which Marie thought was all to the good.[28]

Hamsun reacted by disappearing whenever possible. He was capable of taking off from Nørholm and staying away for days on end without a word of explanation, and in 1938 he travelled to southern Europe again, living for several months in Italy and Yugoslavia. Back home again he moved out of Nørholm and lived alone for many months in a room in the Bondeheimen Hotel in Oslo. He was bored and depressed and hated getting old.

Marie's fears that Hamsun had betrayed her were probably groundless. Hamsun preserved his looks and his vigour to a quite astonishing degree until he was over eighty, but the picture of his personality we have is not that of a promiscuous man. Apart from the confession of that single act of adultery during his marriage to Bergljot, and Anna Munch's pathetic outpourings in 1897, there is little sexual scandal in his life. But jealousy is a madness, after all, and in 1945 Marie could claim that in his old age Hamsun had begun to show an interest in young girls, and had been unfaithful to her on several occasions.[29] She made the claim to a psychiatrist at Vindern Clinic in Oslo, where her husband was being held for examination. Her long statement to the doctor about her marriage was undoubtedly influenced by fear – fear of the authority vested in him, fear for her husband's fate, as well as fear for her own, since she was also being held pending charges of treason. She painted a very bad picture of the marriage, assuming, probably correctly, that the idea was not to talk about good days and happiness under those particular circumstances. Yet even allowing for the circumstances under which she described their life together, the evidence is that their relationship had never been worse than in the late 1930s. Hamsun's lawyer, Sigrid Stray, to a large extent his confidante during these years, confirms this in her memoir of the period. There was talk on both sides of a divorce. Marie had made several attempts to leave Hamsun which came to nothing. The only thing the pair really had in common, throughout the 1930s, was a political attitude.

Chapter 15
1933–1940: Hamsun's Politics

'I do not understand politics'[1] Hamsun confessed in 1945,* a knowledge which had not prevented him from making a series of statements of an intensely political nature about Hitler and Nazi Germany during the 1930s and during the German Occupation of Norway.

Outside Norway – and to some extent within Norway – there is a widespread and comfortable myth that these statements and the favourable attitude expressed in them were the views of a man suffering from senile dementia. This is as a direct result of the findings of the two psychiatrists who examined Hamsun after the war at the request of the Norwegian government, and found him to be suffering from 'permanently impaired mental faculties'. An acceptance of these findings removes the moral problem posed by reading and being moved by the works of an admirer of Fascism who found in Hitler a brave and stirring figure. This was the solution that the critic and musicologist Hans Keller, for example, adopted in order to preserve his love for Hamsun and his belief in his genius. In a newspaper review of *The Wanderer* in the *TLS* in 1975 he confessed that Hamsun's Nazism 'worried me greatly, until the other week a colleague of mine, the head of music of Norwegian Radio, told me that nobody outside Norway knew quite how senile Hamsun had become. After he had visited Nazi Germany, he was asked, in a radio interview, whether he had met Hitler: "You know, I met so many people, I can't really remember".'[2] A week or two later the translator of *The Wanderer*,

* The details of Hamsun's psychiatric examination were leaked consistently after the war. A book called *Prosessen Mod Hamsun* (1978) by the Danish writer Thorkild Hansen contained so many references to details of the report that the psychiatrists involved, Gabriel Langfeldt and Ørnulv Ødegård decided to publish the full transcript in the hope of preventing misunderstandings and misconstructions of their findings. (Hereinafter referred to as 'the report'.)

Oliver Stallybrass, wrote a letter to the *TLS* explaining that the reply was in fact a prime example of Hamsun's sly and diffident humour, an explanation which drew a further letter from Keller in which he stated with some bewilderment that it seemed to him 'inappropriate' that a Nazi would joke about meeting Hitler. A personality that was capable of this clearly baffled Keller. The unfortunate fact is that Hamsun was demonstrably not senile during the period in question, and indeed, did not become so until the last few weeks before his death in 1952.

In fact, Hamsun's Fascism was a genuinely held political conviction, and although his personality is ultimately simply too complicated to fit comfortably within the description, it responded enthusiastically to a very great deal of what Fascism had to offer in the 1930s. In 1953 Thomas Mann went so far as to claim that Hamsun's Nazism 'could surprise none who recalled his ridicule of Victor Hugo and Gladstone. But what in 1895 was an interesting point of view aesthetically speaking, a literary paradox, becomes a very political position in 1933, and casts a dark and unhappy shadow over Hamsun's reputation as poet and writer.'[3]

Hamsun's aesthetics and his politics were complex and at times fantastical structures. An important element in both was that hatred of the English which found its first expression in Hamsun's writing in the travel book *In Wonderland*, from 1903. It appeared again in the grotesque caricature of Sir Hugh Trevelyan in the *Benoni* and *Rosa* novels of 1908, and reappeared with startling violence in *The Last Joy* in 1912 where two English tourists are more or less accused by the author of bestiality and pederasty. Most of Hamsun's novels thereafter contain more or less extended attacks on the English which are sometimes directed at the arrogant disdain of the individual Englishman for all whom he meets on his travels, and sometimes at England's arrogant and imperialistic conduct of her foreign affairs. The First World War increased this hatred of the English, and at the same time strengthened his ties with Germany. Personal friends like Nils Kjær, Hjalmar Christensen, Sven Elvestad and Sigurd Bødtker were all similarly well-disposed towards Germany, but none of them shared this darker flipside of his enthusiasm.

Though the 1920s was a quiet decade for international affairs as far as Hamsun was concerned, when the activities of the Nazi Party in Germany after their rise to power in January 1933 began to arouse the disapproving attention of certain sections of the international community, Hamsun's dormant sympathies woke up, and he leapt to the defence of the new regime, both in private letters and in newspaper articles. Invariably, in his contributions, he draws England into the picture, sometimes by a fantastical stretch of the imagination. As part of the campaign in Norway to secure the award of the 1934 Nobel Peace Prize for Carl von Ossietzsky, a pacifist journalist being held by the Nazis in Sachsenhausen concentration camp, a letter was sent to the leading authors in Norway soliciting their support. This campaign will be discussed more fully later, but here it is enough to note that in his letter of reply refusing to help, Hamsun devotes a considerable amount of space to making a strictly speaking quite irrelevant point to the committee:

> Do you think that England would respond to an insolent attempt like this to influence her policy in India? Would England tolerate it if a conspiracy of enemies established a court in Berlin to observe and correct a case being tried in an English court? Have England and the rest of the world sent a horde of hostile journalists to Russia to witness the recent butchering of state officials?[4]

And he concludes his letter on a similar note:

> I don't delude myself that my words will make the slightest impression on you or your London-lobby. But I imagine that neither you nor the others object to my little explanation of my refusal.

This Germany-England polarity dominated his view of political events. In January 1935 he sent a greeting to the magazine *Der Norden*, the organ of the Nordic Society, over the question of the return of Saarland to Germany. Saarland had been administered by the League of Nations since 1919, and by a plebiscite in January was reunited with Germany. Hamsun wrote:

> When the German Saarland is once again reunited with the motherland, an irritant between nations will disappear. A new irritant will arise if French policy – with the approval of England – tries once more to bind Germany fast in continued humiliation.[5]

Eleven months later, at the conclusion of a second unsuccessful campaign to secure the Nobel Peace Prize for Ossietzsky, Hamsun publicly protested at these campaigns in a newspaper article in *Tidens Tegn*, and asked whether Ossietzsky really wanted to see his land 'crushed and humiliated among other lands, thanks to the mercy of the French and the English?'. This article appeared on 22 November; but the English had already for some time been trying to dissociate themselves from the keenness of the French in upholding the terms of the Treaty of Versailles, and on 18 June that same year had signed an agreement with Germany over the question of naval re-armament which tacitly recognised Hitler's reintroduction of military conscription some months earlier. Hamsun chose to ignore these English overtures towards Hitler. There was no way in which they could be allowed to influence his by now hardened picture of Germany as a brave nation trying to rise to its feet again after the desperate reversals of the war and the Depression, and trying to do so in the face of the united opposition of Europe, with England still firmly in the role of decisive enemy. This scheme of things was confirmed with manic zeal in the foreword that Hamsun wrote to a book by a Dr Karl Hans Fuchs which argued the case for the inclusion of Danzig in a German empire. Hamsun wrote:

> The Poles are alright – in Poland. This is not what the argument is about. The Poles are a clever people, and realised at an early stage that they would not keep Danzig, a German town in Germany. They found another gateway to the sea, and built their own harbour at the mouth of their own river.
>
> Fine.
>
> But when England, true to her old habits, began once again to encircle Germany, the Poles showed their cleverness once again by volunteering their land as a link in the English ring. They thought that this would enable them to hold on to the German town.
>
> But in this case the Poles were too clever. Danzig will leave them. No power on earth can prevent Danzig from leaving them.
>
> The Poles are a clever people, and by and large a sensible people. In the course of time they'll realise themselves how silly they have been over the Danzig question. They put their reliance on the shred that is left of the Treaty of Versailles, and they put their faith in Albion's 'guarantee'. They would have done better to put their faith in their own port Gdynia. Other lands have put their faith in the Treaty of Versailles and in England's promises –and been betrayed. The Poles should rather have listened to Germany's offer of a friendly solution to the problem.
>
> Danzigers, hold on! You are fine people as well, you are Prussians and members of the great German nation. One day yourselves and your city will return to the Fatherland.

His foreword is dated 15 August 1939, just fourteen days before the German invasion of Poland.

This anti-Englishness, with its forty-year pedigree, is an important factor in the analysis of Hamsun's attitude during the developing European crisis of the 1930s and the subsequent war. Together with his understandable sense of economic and cultural gratitude to Germany, it carries a great deal of weight with those who seek to minimise the extent to which it was Fascism as a political ideology that attracted Hamsun to Hitler. In this way it becomes possible to define Hamsun's as the 'eccentric and unpredictable artist' type of response, in which he is cast as a political analphabetic foolishly mingling with spiritual gangsters, and innocent of any deep commitment to the most unpleasant values of their cause. Unfortunately, other evidence makes it clear that his reponse also contained elements common to all of those who in the 1930s saw a solution in Fascism and a saviour in Hitler.

He understood Left and Right in politics, he told Dr Ødegård, one of the two psychiatrists examining him after the war, but he had never understood socialism.[6] It seemed to him worthless, since it destroyed personal initiative. The report quotes him as saying 'They form a group opinion on things', and records that 'He mentions irritably the endless strikes over the least thing'. 'I hate communism', he added, 'with great vehemence', according to the report. Norwegian society was indeed, like most European societies in the 1920s, in a politically restless and turbulent state. The Russian Revolution of 1917 – and Russia and Norway share a common border in the extreme north – had repercussions in Norway that were probably more extreme and intense than in any other European country. Already in March 1918 the Labour Party Conference passed a resolution reserving for itself 'the right to resort to revolutionary mass action in the struggle for the economic emancipation of the working class'. Uniquely among pre-war socialist parties outside the Russian Empire, the Labour Party adhered to the Comintern, thus placing itself directly under supervision from Moscow. This state of affairs lasted until the formation of a separate Communist Party in 1923. The 'endless strikes' to which Hamsun referred accounted for an average of a million working days lost every year between 1919 and 1939, and the first of them was the sixteen-day 1920 rail strike which had hindered the Hamsuns' trip to Stockholm that year for the Nobel Prize ceremony. In 1921 there was an attempted General Strike which involved about 150,000 workers, and in 1923 a strike of iron workers which developed to involve other workers, so that eventually 75,000 workers were on strike for six months. The first organised reaction from the Right to this was the formation of the formally non-political Fatherland League in 1925, on the initiative of Fridtjof Nansen and the hero of 1905, Christian Michelsen. The aim of the League was to rally 'national' elements against 'international', by which was meant socialism. The different factions of the Labour Party responded by offering a policy that was still so far to the Left that communists could with a good conscience join it, and in the election of 1927 the party secured fifty-nine seats in the Storting, enough to enable them to form a minority government in January 1928 which was brought down after just two weeks. Its short life was only an extreme example of the outstanding characteristic of Norwegian political life during the period between 1920 and 1940 which saw altogether twelve different governments.

The polarisation of political opinion reached its heights in the early years of the 1930s. In 1931 the most violent and alarming of all strikes occurred at the Norsk Hydro plant at Menstad, in Telemark. A hundred and twenty state police sent to disperse workers picketing the plant were routed by the workers, the violence reaching such a pitch that in the end troops and naval vessels were sent in to overawe the workers. Vidkun Quisling was the Defence Minister in the right-wing government under Peder Kolstad at the time, and took responsibility for the decision to use force, a decision which made a hero of him in the eyes of many, including Knut Hamsun. In fact Quisling had nothing to do with it. Justice Minister Lindboe was present at the cabinet meeting in question and records in his diaries that Quisling played no part in taking the decision at all. His reputation as a strong man was thus based on a false assumption. However, he did distinguish himself in sessions of the Storting by the ferocity of his attacks on the Labour Party in which he denounced their every socialist suggestion as 'treason'.

Matters looked to be heading towards a crisis of unmanageable proportions between Left and Right. The cost of living in Norway had fallen by fully one-half between 1920 and 1933, and in December 1932 forty-two per cent of trade unionists were without work. One month after Hitler came to power in January 1933, Quisling was proposing a dictatorship as the only solution to the problem, in the Agrarian Party's organ *Nationen*, and in May the same year he formed his own Nazi Party, Nasjonal Samling, in time for the autumn election. Neither then nor in subsequent elections did the party have any noteworthy success. In fact, the Labour Party had taken the sting out of any potential class war by restoring the democratic pledge to its programme for the 1933 election, and with the rise to power in 1935 of the socialist statesman Johan Nygaardsvold, the crisis was effectively over. By 1939 a hard core of eighteen per cent of trade unionists remained unemployed, but the real value of a day's wage had risen by fifteen per cent during the decade.

All of this happened too late to impress Hamsun. Neither he nor Marie had in any case much sympathy with the plight of the working man. Both of them seemed to believe that life was supposed to be hard, and in an interview with a journalist in March 1933 Marie declared her belief 'that a person instinctively achieves more when he has a knife against his throat'. It was in this same interview that she had described Hamsun as 'not interested in people' and herself as living 'in a hermetically sealed world'. In fact, Hamsun was rather proud of the fact that he kept abreast of political events, and in addition to conservative newspapers like *Aftenposten* and *Tidens Tegn*, and the Fatherland League's *ABC*, he also took *Towards The Day*, an extreme left-wing publication put out by an organisation of the same name. Yet he was still a hermit, by reason of inclination, work, and deafness, and the vision of the outside world he formed from the remote fastness of Nørholm, and the more remote fastness of his own head, was only the crude caricature created for him by these newspapers. Observing far-away events like the battle at Menstad Quay made him angry, and frightened. In the spring of 1932 Quisling delivered a thunderous speech in the Storting on the Labour Party's armed subverting of Norwegian society, and Hamsun was one of over two hundred signatories of a petition of support for Quisling which was subsequently delivered to the Storting. In the same year Hamsun contributed a Foreword to a book *The Politics of Revolution and Norwegian Law*, by Herman Harris Aall, in which Aall argued that the Labour Party's revolutionary activity was illegal, and that the party should be outlawed.

Aall was Hamsun's favourite intellectual. In addition to being anti-communist he was fiercely anti-English, and back in 1915 Hamsun had written an enthusiastic review of a pamphlet by Aall, 'The Danger for Scandinavia'. The 'danger' was the threatened engulfment of Norway in the interests of England's foreign policy. In his Foreword to Aall's book on Norway, Hamsun wrote:

What is happening in our country? Violence, law-breaking, and all the revolution that barbarism and lack of leadership will allow. This is not the flaring of a moment's anger. The idea is to create lasting fear and chaos among the people. It is a plan, with the destruction of life, law and justice as its goal. Here we see physical violence against the police, the guardians of our society. There armed bands of men appear and forbid people to work. Here they use knives. There the gun. Violence. Lawlessness. Revolution.

I lay aside the day's newspapers and await new outrages in tomorrow's. Am I living in Norway?

Complex man that he was, Hamsun longed for simple answers. Among his early literary heroes both Nagel and Ivar Kareno express something of this longing in their prophesying 'the great terrorist', the man who dispenses with debate, discussion and doubt with a single slash of his sword. The psychiatric report notes, following on Hamsun's dismissal of socialism because 'They form a group opinion on things', that 'He himself is more a supporter of the old patriarchal system', by which he meant characters like Zahl at Kjerringøy, and Walsøe at Tranøy, and his godfather Torstein Hestehagen at Lom. It was twentieth-century versions of these born leaders of old that he was looking for in the critical first years of the 1930s. Already in 1932, before the rise of Hitler, he thought he had found one of them. The Italian government sent out invitations in that year to winners of Nobel Prizes from the Nordic countries to visit Italy and meet Mussolini. Hamsun declined the invitation, offering the by now familiar excuse that he could not speak the language. Yet he would like to have gone, he told Harald Grieg in a letter of 5 November 1932:

I would like to have had the opportunity of expressing my very great admiration and respect for Mussolini. God save us, what a man in the midst of these confused times![7]

And almost exactly a year later, he expressed a similar admiration for Mussolini's system by name in a greeting to the Fatherland League's *ABC*, on the occasion of its first anniversary. He praised the *ABC* highly, with one serious reservation: 'In one respect I disagree with the paper: I am not scared stiff of Fascism – I am more frightened of Mowinckel's version of parliamentary government.'

Mowinckel was a Liberal Prime Minister who led a government between 1928 and 1931 and concentrated his policies on establishing Norway as a recognisably neutral country, paying little attention to matters of defence. His attitude alarmed Hamsun greatly, since Hamsun's scheme of the development of things after the First World War insisted that there was going to be another major war soon between England and Germany, and that Norway would need an adequate military force if her rights were to be respected by the main participants in the war. And Mowinckel's

strategy for the preservation of Norwegian neutrality involved
attitudes that Hamsun found unacceptable: among other things,
the Prime Minister had stated in a speech in 1929 that 'As regards
sea-strategy, we must remember that it is Britain which rules the
northern seas, and that this will presumably be the case for a long
time to come.' Hamsun could only interpret this as a tacit
undertaking to support Britain against Germany when what he
saw as the inevitable conflict between the two powers flared up
again. Mowinckel, he declared at the end of his greeting to the
ABC, 'is more dangerous than Fascism'.[8] And two months later he
was prophesying in a second newspaper article that Fascism was
inevitable:

> One day, in one form or another, Fascism will also make its way
> into Norway. Only the stone blind are still unable to see a
> difference in the time and the politics between the pre-war days
> and the present. Only types like Austen Chamberlain, Herriot
> and Benes think that things are going along just fine as they are.

He refers to the clearest advantage that a democracy has over a
dictatorship, which is that the leadership can be changed, but then
criticises Mowinckel for having hung on to power without a
mandate from the people. He maintained that this made a mockery
of the claims for the democratic system, and removed its chief
objection to a dictatorship. In effect, Hamsun was trying to
announce the total breakdown of the democratic system; but the
fact is that from 1921 until after the Second World War the
Norwegian government was *always* a minority government, and
no single party ever had a clear majority in the Storting. The system
produced twelve governments in twenty years, but still worked,
even when this involved coalition governments. In his concluding
lines he again prophesies Fascism, with typical use of irony, after
making the elaborate point that it is the Labour Party which
actually has the moral right to form a government. In the same
breath as he makes this point he contrives to convey that such a
state of affairs is unthinkable, and thereby tacitly dismisses the
moral claims implicit in the democratic system:

> For the time being it is the Labour Party which has a right and a
> duty, if not mathematically then morally, to govern the country.
> We may think what we like about this, but it is a fact!
> Parliamentarily speaking it would be dishonest behaviour to
> cheat the party of its right to govern.

Who has thought of cheating them? Why, our unremovable

democrat. He's already making his plans to go on sitting. Unification? he says, No, rather 'co-operation'. Co-operation as before.

It's a little dishonest, a little shameful of the man to carry on in Government now, but he's going to do it.

This is the advantage parliamentary democracy has over Fascism here in Norway.[9]

Hamsun observed an idiosyncratic distinction between Quisling and his Nasjonal Samling Party. To the psychiatrists examining him after the war, he denied that he had been a national socialist in the 1930s, but was happy to confirm that he had been 'Quisling's man' since long before the war. Though he had not met Quisling, Hamsun had formed a good impression of him after his speech in the Storting in the spring of 1932, and after the part he played in the battle at Menstad. In October 1936 Hamsun also contributed an electoral appeal for him in the National Party's organ *Fritt Folk* in which he wrote that 'Had I *ten* votes, he would get them all. His firm character and resolute strength of will are a blessing to us at this particular time.'[10] The party could have used his ten votes, as it happens – their share of the poll in the 1936 election was 1.8 per cent.*

Hamsun's political extremism was now an open secret. However, these two statements of support for Fascism as a political system caused little public stir beyond the small world of the politically interested. The first statement appeared in a special interest paper, the *ABC*, while the second appeared in a provincial newspaper, the *Skien Fylkesavisen*. On 11 March 1934 he answered a letter from a Fascist sculptor, Professor Wilhelm Rasmussen, who had asked him to lend his name to a campaign protesting the cultural boycott of the new Germany, and while doubting that his name would be of any use at all, he gave Rasmussen full authority to use it 'in this good cause'. He does not mention Hitler or Fascism by name in his letter, but writes with warm sympathy of the German nation. 'They have the wind against them now', he wrote, 'but they sail bravely on and will make the harbour.' The eager Rasmussen immediately passed the letter on to Hamsun's German publishers, now called Langen-Müller, and already the Nazi

---

* It is entirely in keeping with Hamsun's irresponsible attitude towards his own public pronouncements that he did not even give NS the one vote he did have. The single vote the party received in the Hamsuns' constituency of Eide in the General Election of 23 September 1936 was that of their local organiser, Marie Hamsun. Hamsun told a policeman questioning him after the war that as far as he could remember, he had never voted in his life.[11]

Party's own unofficial publisher, and from there the letter was blazoned across the front pages of a dozen German newspapers, including the party's own paper, the *Völkischer Beobachter*, providing an early indication of the efficiency of the Nazi propaganda machine, and an example of the way in which Hamsun was resolutely targeted by the machine from the earliest days. The letter was printed, and its gleeful reception in Germany reported, in the Danish *Ekstrabladet*; but again, there seems to have been little comment on the whole business in the Norwegian press.

Hamsun's real 'coming-out' for his Norwegian public occurred with the publication, in 1935, of a newspaper article entitled simply 'Ossietzsky'. Carl von Ossietzsky was a German veteran of the First World War who later in life became a passionate pacifist. He was a journalist on the magazine *Die Weltbühne* from 1924, and its sole editor from 1927. *Aftenposten* cast a common slur on his journalism in referring to it as communist-pacifist, although the magazine was largely devoted to literary matters. However, Ossietzsky kept a close eye on the reviving militarism in Germany in the 1920s, and in 1929 was sentenced to eighteen months in jail, under the treason laws, for broadcasting details of the secret rearmament of the Air Force. In the same year, ironically, *Die Weltbühne* had carried his almost embarrassingly fulsome tribute to Hamsun on his seventieth birthday.[12] He was arrested a second time in 1933, on the day after the Reichstag fire, and interred in Sachsenhausen concentration camp, where he was to spend the next three and a half years. His case was taken up by pacifists all over Europe,* and the campaign to secure the award of the Nobel Peace Prize for him started in 1934. Hamsun's response to an overture from the organising committee has already been mentioned in reference to his anglophobia. In fact his letter to Christopher Vibe, which was not publicised at the time, went considerably further than mere eccentricity in explaining his refusal to participate. He made the always controversial but at least discussible point that the Nobel Prize should not be used to make political gestures in this fashion, but then swiftly passed beyond the bounds of morality to pose a 'might is right' argument:

> Germany is in the middle of a process of recuperation. When the government decides to introduce concentration camps, then

---

* In a letter to *The Times*, Gilbert Murray wrote that Ossietzsky's decision to expose German rearmament was 'morally right', in spite of the fact that it made him technically a traitor. Most moralists, from Plato to Kant, said Murray, would agree with his decision to follow the dictates of his conscience in the matter.

you and the rest of the world ought to understand that it has its good reasons for doing so. Until further notice such witnesses to the truth as *Seger*, and idealistic pacifists along the lines of our own dear *Kullman* are being looked after there.*

Ossietzsky did not get the award for 1934. In 1935 the Norwegian Foreign Minister Koht, and the former Prime Minister Mowinckel were both members of the awarding committee, and to avoid any possibility of the Nobel Prize award being interpreted as official Norwegian government opinion on German home affairs, it was finally decided to award no prize at all that year. Again, a vigorous campaign had been mounted on behalf of Ossietzsky, and Hamsun's contribution to the debate, published simultaneously in *Aftenposten* and *Tidens Tegn* on 11 November 1935, repeated in public the points he had made in private to Christopher Vibe the year before. The mind-numbing simplicity of his attitude towards the case went even further when he suggested that if Ossietzsky did not like what was happening in Germany, then he had for some time before his arrest been quite free to leave the country. The concluding lines of his article show clearly that the moral courage of a man like Ossietzsky was a complete mystery to him:

What if Hr Ossietzsky instead tried to lend a hand during this momentous period of transition, with the whole world baring its teeth at the authorities of that great people to which he belongs? What does he want? Is it the German rearmament he is trying to demonstrate against as a friend of peace? Would this German rather that his land remained crushed and humiliated in the community of nations, thanks to the tender mercies of the French and the English?

This excited an enormous reaction in Norway, principally among Hamsun's fellow writers. The outcry over the 'Hang them' articles in 1915 pales beside it. The first and best response appeared in *Dagbladet* the same day, by the poet and playwright Nordahl Grieg. In a short article he mocked Hamsun where he knew it would hurt him most – on the question of his honour as a man. He characterised the attack for what it was, a cowardly tirade against someone who was in no position to answer back or to defend himself.

* The reference to Kullman is only one example of the many tragic ironies Hamsun's loose tongue involved him in. Olaf Bryn Kullman, a former naval officer turned pacifist, was arrested by the Germans in 1941, and later died in Sachsenhausen, the same camp as Ossietzsky.

The Ossietzsky article was debated throughout the European press,* with further contributions from Hamsun, and occasional articles in support of him, over the next three years, right up until Ossietzsky's death from tuberculosis in 1938. The most dramatic response came on 14 December 1935, when thirty-three of Hamsun's colleagues, including his old friend Peter Egge and his biographer Einar Skavlan, signed a protest letter in *Tidens Tegn*. For the first time for twenty years, Hamsun was again able to enjoy the privileges of the outcast. 'Have you read my article on Ossietzsky?' he wrote to Tore Hamsun 'The Bolsheviks are foaming at the mouth. I've received many letters.' Yet the sheer size of the response may have shocked him slightly.[13]

In February 1936 Marie Hamsun was still in Berlin with the injured Ellinor. Hamsun sent her a letter containing some additional lines on the case which he asked her to translate into German and add to an explanation he had written of his original article. This explanation was for the use of a Zürich editor, René Sonderegger, and the additions constitute a toning down of the original intemperate attitude. He lays added stress on the reasonable point about the political abuse of the Nobel Prize, and concludes:

> The Nobel Peace Prize is not intended for these purposes! It is another matter altogether if the German authorities hopefully one day feel themselves able to release them (Carl von Ossietzsky as well as other curious 'friends of peace' and awkward persons) from jail.[14]

The words in parentheses, if allowed to stand, would considerably spoil the reasonable tone of these lines, and Hamsun seems to have been unsure how he wanted the article to appear. This use of brackets demonstrates a concern for his public image which the rest of his letter to Marie confirms. He tells her that he has decided to remove what he calls 'my tirade against democracy' from the article, and instructs her to 'say with a little smile that I am a poor democrat'.

---

* It was debated privately too. Thomas Mann discussed the melancholy revelation that his old hero had sided with the Nazis in a letter of 12 December 1935 to René Schickele. He said that he had been 'much tempted to write to him' because 'I thought I owed him a warning; but it would lead too far, and I have given up the idea.' One can only regret that Mann changed his mind; Hamsun admired him very much, and would undoubtedly have found any such 'warning' from him unusually thought-provoking (*The Letters of Thomas Mann 1889–1955* tr R C Wilson, London 1985 p 203).

Hamsun backed losers fairly indiscriminately throughout his life, sympathetic or otherwise, and his efforts notwithstanding, on 23 November 1936 Ossietzsky was retrospectively awarded the Nobel Prize for 1935. Hitler responded three months later by forbidding Germans to accept any Nobel Prize at all.

Before leaving the case one has to point out that Hamsun's attitude towards it was by no means uncommon. His point of view was but an extreme version of what a large section of the Norwegian middle class believed. *Aftenposten*, reporting the award of the prize to Ossietzsky on page one of its evening edition of 24 November, carried beside the report an editorial of equal prominence under the headline 'A Mistake'. In deeply regretting that the award had been made, the paper hoped that the Germans would show largesse in the matter, and opined that the Peace Prize was now irrevocably devalued.

Hamsun's whole enterprise in championing the German nation so passionately was, as he perfectly well knew, a lost cause long before the days of the war. His fellow-countrymen's preference for Englishmen over Germans had been a baffling irritant to him for many decades. The psychiatric report quotes a remark from him on 18 October 1945: 'Listen, ninety-eight per cent of the Norwegian people hate the Germans because they're German, and love Englishmen because they're Englishmen. You can shoot me or do what you like with me. I'm not afraid of having my life shortened.'[15] This fondness for the Germans had its roots in the 1890s, and was originally a combination of a feeling of racial kinship with the German people and a sense of tremendous gratitude towards them for recognising and supporting his talent early on in his career. It was German and, for the few short years of his association with Znanije Publishing, Russian royalties that enabled him to live the life of a successful author in Norway for many years before the success of the *Segelfoss* books during the days of the First World War made him a best-selling author among his own countrymen. He told Dr Ødegård: 'There is not a single great name in our land which has not had to go via Germany to achieve its success, whether in art or in science. It has meant so much for us to have access to this great linguistic community.' Hamsun also expressed his love and gratitude for the Germans in practical ways. He sent his four children there to be educated when they became old enough, and in 1934 accepted the award of the Goethe Medal, but refused to accept the 10,000 marks prize money as a gesture of friendship and support for the process of social reconstruction which he believed the country was undergoing.

Above all, he was Germany's champion in Norway, in good times as in bad. When the nature of the Nazis' policies began to attract adverse comments in the liberal press after the party's rise to power in 1933, he resumed with pride his old role from the days of the First World War. The Ossietzky article of 1935 was his most dramatic, but not his first appearance as apologist for Nazi Germany. In an article entitled 'Wait And See' in *Aftenposten* on 7 July 1934, an academic named Fredrik Paasche had attacked Nazism and Nazi sympathisers in Norway, and declared that the promised 'ethical revival' in Germany had not, after all, taken place. He described the Brown Shirts as protected gangsters, and claimed that the severe sentences handed out after the in-camera investigations into allegations of brutality in Oranienburg concentration camp indicated clearly the nature of conditions in these camps. Hamsun replied three days later with an article pointing out the size of the German task of social reconstruction, and mocking Paasche's impatience because a society of sixty-six million people had not achieved an 'ethical revival' after just fifteen months under the new regime.

The Nazi propaganda machine realised early on the value for them of these spontaneous expressions of support Hamsun was willing to make for Hitler. Both this article and the letter to Wilhelm Rasmussen appeared in German translation in the pages of the Nordic Society's magazine, *Der Nordische Aufseher*, shortly after Hamsun wrote the originals. And from 1933 onwards the Nordic Society cultivated Hamsun relentlessly. The *Aufseher* for August 1934 was a birthday special devoted to him, with greetings from a host of German writers – but of considerably lesser stature than those who had praised him so handsomely in 1929. Hans Friedrich Blunk, Hermann Claudius, Will Vesper, Ina Seidel and Max Mell were among them. Alfred Rosenberg contributed a short article on Hamsun taken from his book on Nazi philosophy, *The Myth of the 20th Century*. Goebbels, who once nurtured literary ambitions himself, also sent his greetings.

The Nordic Society changed the name of their magazine to *Der Norden* in 1935, without noticeably altering the nature of its contents. The concept of a racially bound community of 'Nordic' artists was endlessly propagated in its pages, and the ceaseless promotion and reportage of Hamsun continued. In 1938 they printed a greetings telegram which he had sent to them on the occasion of their celebrations of 'Nordic Day', 21 June. The telegram, from Dubrovnik, and presumably solicited, read: I am like Bjørnson a Norwegian and a German and as such hail Nordic Day heartily – Knut Hamsun. And on his return journey from

Yugoslavia to Norway later on in the summer, Hamsun and Marie met in Berlin and together visited the Nordic Society's officials at their offices on Schellingstrasse 6. Marie Hamsun, much the more orthodoxly politically active of the two, was also photographed in the magazine attending gymnastic displays in the company of Nazi officials.

On his eightieth birthday in 1939 Hamsun was again greeted by both Rosenberg and Goebbels, and for the first time Hitler himself sent a telegram. There were the usual fulsome tributes to him in the Norwegian press, and a fellow-Fascist, the composer David Monrad-Johansen, wrote a symphonic poem inspired by *Pan* for the occasion. Socialists, however, had more or less given up hope on Hamsun, after a valiant struggle to hold on to their admiration for a writer who went out of his way to pour scorn on their movement, and on its beliefs and adherents. For many on the extreme Left he was now a despised figure, a situation he was well aware of. To a well-wisher who had written to him in 1938 proposing to erect a statue of him he replied that they should not waste their time, the 'mob' would only smash it or throw it into the sea. 'In Oslo the Bolsheviks swear at me as I walk down the road', he wrote, 'At Nørholm once a group of people walking by outside the house shouted up and asked if I were home. Don't bother about him, they ended, He'll soon be dead anyway.'[16] Norwegian *Arbeiderbladet* had been running a series of articles in which it gave the names of various Norwegians whom it accused of being agents in the pay of Nazi Germany – Hamsun was among them – while *Nationen* had run a counter-campaign ridiculing the accusations. In indicating what it took to be the self-evident absurdity of it all, the paper printed the names of three of the accused men, but shielded Hamsun behind an abbreviation m fl (and others). However, Hamsun's last peace-time defence of his beloved Germany consisted of a stout rejection of this anonymity in letters to the editors of *Nationen* and *Aftenposten* published simultaneously on 27 September 1939. 'But, Sir,' he boasted, 'I am not m fl. I am Knut Hamsun. Everyone knows that', and he proudly concluded that the three named honourable men must forgive him if he now insists on being named as the fourth man. There is a grotesque confusion of values here in this attempt to be chivalrous in the service of Nazism; and in his proud insistence on being associated with the regime because 'I am Knut Hamsun. Everyone knows that'; there is a strong hint of the megalomania that was never far beneath the surface in his successful days.

The final point of coincidence between Hamsun's views and those put forward by the Nazis is in the matter of race, and in his attitude towards the old, the weak and the crippled. Back in 1915, during the debate on how mothers who murdered their own children should be punished, he had suggested that more money and more time should be devoted to the care of orphaned children, or the children of mothers too poor to support them. His insistence on discovering a polarity and an opposition in all matters led him to suggest that this better treatment could only be achieved at the expense of the care currently being afforded the old and the mentally defective. 'The old have been people once,' he wrote, 'now it's over. The others never have been people, and never will be.'[17] This cult of youth, health, strength and life was also a central part of Nazi philosophy.

Equally important was the concentration on the idea of a Germanic race, and the commitment to protect the presumed purity of this race from sexual and intellectual contact with other races which would compromise it; a commitment which would unnervingly lead to the Holocaust.

This racial mysticism came to play a central part in Hamsun's thinking – or rather lack of it – on the question of an attitude towards the rise of Nazism and the subsequent war in Europe; to trace its origins we have to look at the changing fashions in racial awareness during the years of his life. A first point to note is that until as late as 1851, eight years before Hamsun was born, Jews were forbidden by Article 2 of the Norwegian Constitution of 1814 from entering the land, a prohibition which was strictly observed particularly during the first years after 1814. Jews who more or less accidentally found themselves in Norway were commonly arrested and imprisoned. The eventual removal of the prohibition from the Constitution was largely the result of an energetic campaign led by the first of the Norwegian poetocrats, Henrik Wergeland, and there seems to have been no extensive residue of anti-Semitism after this.

Hamsun's novel *Wayfarers* includes among its characters Papst, a wandering Jewish watch-seller whom Edevart meets at country fairs during his own career as a pedlar with August. Papst is based on a real person named Pabst who travelled in northern Norway during Hamsun's own boyhood. On his death, Hamsun composed an obituary in a newspaper which describes him as a well-known figure all along the coast, and adds that 'it is doubtful if he left behind a single enemy'. While the picture Hamsun paints of Papst focuses always on his Jewishness – understandably, in view of the exotic nature of Papst's presence in arctic Norway – his final judgement on the character is merely that he is – like everyone else in the world – partly good and partly bad. One could hardly call it anti-Semitic.

Rather than any negative anti-Semitism, the racial cults which were most frequently discussed during Hamsun's boyhood and early manhood were pan-Scandinavianism and the later pan-Germanism. Pan-Scandinavianism was a linguistically and geographically determined cult of the brotherhood of Danes, Swedes and Norwegians. Perhaps its most famous literary achievement is Ibsen's verse-play *Brand*, the play with which he finally made his breakthrough as a writer. *Brand*, written in 1865, was inspired by Ibsen's bitter disappointment at the failure of his countrymen to go to Denmark's aid in the war with Prussia over possession of the duchies of Schleswig and Holstein. It was soon superseded by the more mystical racially-based cult of pan-Germanism which was particularly popular among Norwegian students, artists and intellectuals.

Norway's own campaign for independence from Sweden was gathering momentum during these closing decades of the nineteenth century, and it may be that the greater vagueness of pan-Germanism was preferred to what might have seemed a rather embarrassingly specific commitment to brotherhood with Sweden at that time. Hamsun was attracted by the cult. In a letter to Langen in the 1890s we find him referring to himself as a 'Germanic soul, not as a Romanish'. Another keen believer was his great idol Bjørnson, who wrote in a letter to his friend Ragna Jacobi that he put all his faith in the future of world peace in a union of all Germanic people 'in England, America, Germany, Austria, Holland, Belgium, Switzerland, and in the three Scandinavian lands'. Hamsun was still sufficiently devoted to Bjørnson for such an endorsement to carry considerable weight with him. Both men had probably either read or heard extensively discussed a book published in 1890 by one Julius Langbehn, called *Rembrandt the Educator*. This book preached the gospel of the brotherhood of Germanic artists in all countries, and held up the paintings of peasants by Rembrandt as an inspiration to its readers to seek for truth beyond the surface of the rational, and beyond the superficial culture of a machine-dominated age. Published anonymously in the same year as Hamsun's *Hunger*, it sold an astonishing 100,000 copies in its first few months of publication. The author, writing to thank a Scandinavian critic for a particularly enthusiastic review, suggested that on the analogy of Nietzsche's Übermensch, he might refer to the Scandinavians as 'die Überdeutschen'.[18] This kind of glorious and simplistic nonsense would have made a strong appeal to Hamsun, especially when we consider how much of his later life presents us with a picture of a man engaged in a prolonged attempt to free himself from those intricate agonies of

human consciousness which he portrayed so well in his first two
novels. The teaching might also have seemed to offer a solution to
the problem of rootlessness which he wrestled with for most of his
life, his own as well as that of his fellow countrymen.

A friendship started in Paris in 1894 with a young Norwegian
music student, Alf Mjøen, also played its part in forming
Hamsun's attitude towards race. The Mjøen family was one of the
most prominent in Norwegian society, and when Hamsun
returned from Paris he kept up the friendship, and was a frequent
visitor to the large family home at Gjøvik. The acceptance and
friendship offered him here was invaluable to him at a time when
he was looked upon by certain sections of the Norwegian cultural
and social establishment with considerable hostility. To many he
was still regarded as the jumped-up young man who had dared to
attack Ibsen, Bjørnson, Kielland and Lie in his lectures of 1891, and
the author of two scandalous and ill-mannered novels in 1893.
During the last years of the decade Hamsun was also courting the
rich, upper-class Bergljot Bech, and one feels that this period
generally represents his most determined attempt to find
acceptance at the highest social level. Here at Gjøvik he would
have made the acquaintance of Alf's brother Jon Alfred. Jon Alfred
was a biologist, and the foremost proponent in Norway of the
growing interest in certain circles in theories of 'racial hygiene'.
From 1907 he ran his own biologicial clinic at Vindern in Oslo, and
in 1914 published a book called *Racial Hygiene*. In the 1920s he
attended conferences on race in New York, and established a
reputation for himself in Germany in the 1930s with extended
lecture tours there as the guest of the Nordic Society. The
Norwegian Nazi party, NS, also adopted Jon Alfred Mjøen as their
guide in racial matters, and when anti-Semitism became a major
factor in their policies his intricate classifications and sub-
classifications of degrees of Jewishness were accepted as
authoritative. He was a regular contributor to Norwegian newspapers with articles on racial matters. His wife Clare shared his
interests, and in 1933 she wrote anti-Semitic newspaper articles in
which she defended book-burning and the persecution of the
Jews. In her younger years she also translated much Norwegian
literature into German, including Hamsun's own *In Wonderland* in
1904. Hamsun's special friends within the family were the brothers
Reidar and Alf, and there is no evidence that he was particularly
friendly with Jon Alfred. The point is, however, that strongly
racialist attitudes were not only respectable but actually fashionable in certain circles high up in Norwegian society, and that
whatever racist feelings Hamsun entertained in the 1890s would

undoubtedly have received a powerful degree of both cultural and 'scientific' authority from his contact with the racism of the smart set.

The simple promotion of the alleged virtues and superiority of the Germanic race involved inevitably the denigration of other races, above all the Jews, and Hamsun soon drifted into a vague and semi-respectable form of anti-Semitism. In 1925 a rabidly anti-Semitic magazine editor named Mikal Sylten sent him a copy of his booklet 'Who's Who in the World of Jews' and asked for his comments. Hamsun's answer, along with several others, was printed in Sylten's magazine, the *Nationalt tidsskrift*, as part of the celebration of its tenth anniversary. The Balfour Declaration of 1917 and the conclusion of the conference at St Remo had made the discussion of a Jewish homeland in Palestine a much-debated topic at the time, and Hamsun weighed in with his not very profound observations on the matter. 'Anti-Semitism exists in all lands', he wrote, 'It follows Semitism as the effect follows the cause':

> They are an extremely gifted people. I am not speaking here of my able and sympathetic personal friends among the Jews nor am I thinking of the least sympathetic, those who have inter-married with the native population, particularly their descend-ants, the pushy types found in artistic and political and literary circles, the insolent and arrogant, their abilities are too often so shallow, mere technical virtuosity. Jews in the main are an extremely gifted intellectual people. Where do we find the like of their ancient literature, their prophets, their songs? And what a wonderfully musical people they are, surely the most melodic-ally gifted people on earth.
>
> So what? you might say.
>
> But the answer to that might equally be, So what?[19]

As it happens, Hamsun's reply is the only one of those printed that is prepared to allow the Jews any good qualities at all. Even his praise for the allegedly unusual musicality of the Jews was too much for the hard-core readership – in a later edition of the *Nationalt tidsskrift* a contributor corrected him and pointed out that in fact the Jews were unusually gifted *thieves* of other people's music. Putting his own, highly personal, interpretation on the Balfour Declar-ation, Hamsun concluded that a Jewish homeland was desirable 'so that the white races would avoid further mixture of the blood', but thought that this goal was unlikely to be achieved 'as long as England and France continue to annex colonies they have no need of'. 'For the time being', he added, 'the Jews have no homes but the homes of others, and they must therefore continue to live and work within alien societies, to the mutual misfortune of both parties.' Although Hamsun does not share Sylten's fanatic hatred of the Jews, he is prepared to describe his task as 'thankless', and to credit his beliefs as being of a 'firm and honourable' nature. He had read 'Who's Who in the World of Jews' 'with great interest' he told Sylten, which was a fairly shabby betrayal of old friends and supporters from his early days, like the Brandes brothers and Gyldendal's Peter Nansen, whom Sylten listed in his booklet as 'pornographers' and 'plagiarists'.[20]

The *Nationalt tidsskrift* was probably an important source for Hamsun's racial theories. The first issues in the magazine's early years after 1916 were devoted to demonstrating the power of the Jews in Germany and to promoting the 'knife in the back' theory that it was Jews and communists who were responsible for the German defeat in the war. The prominent role of Jews in the Russian Revolution was also a favourite theme in the early years. In 1918 the magazine pilloried a gentile, Professor Edvard Bull, for his attack on a racist book called *The Modern Human Type*, by a Dane named Konrad Simonsen. Hamsun had read and enjoyed this book. In a parenthetical insert in a long newspaper article in July 1917 he had recommended it to his readers as 'the most marvellous book I have read in these corrupt times'.[21] Hamsun had been aware of Simonsen as early as 1913, when he wrote to thank him for a work in which Simonsen had 'disproved' an assertion that Dostoevsky had a 'criminal-type' face. 'I have his picture on my wall', wrote Hamsun, 'and it is the most beautiful and most soulful epileptic-type face in the world',[22] a remark that was not far from consciously making fun of the whole nonsense.*

The fact of the Holocaust tends to illuminate all anti-Semitic remarks, the casual as well as the extensive, in the same harsh and hellish light. Hamsun was a fanatic, but not a fanatic anti-Semite. The degree of his commitment to the prejudice does not approach that of an Ezra Pound, or a Céline, who could say of himself that what attracted him most about Hitler was the one thing other people disliked most about him – his anti-Semitism. Racist remarks and caricatures crop up sporadically in Hamsun's books, from the childish references to 'black half-apes' in *On the*

---

* As a reminder of how widespread and respectable these post-Darwinian observations on race were, it is interesting to note that the assertion about Dostoevsky came from Georg Brandes. And Carl von Ossietzsky in 1929 described Hitler as looking 'like a gypsy chieftain', clearly not intended as a flattering comparison.

Cultural Life of Modern America to the character of hotelier Vendt in *The Road Leads On* from 1933, who embodies an established article of Norwegian anti-Semitic faith of the 1930s – that homosexuality came into Norway via Jewish Hanseatic merchants in Bergen in the fourteenth century.

In his occasional newspaper articles in the 1930s in support of the new Germany Hamsun once expresses himself anti-Semitically, in the 1934 article 'Wait and See', where he sarcastically suggests that opponents of the new regime in Germany might prefer instead a return to 'the old Germany, when the communists, the Jews, and Bruning ruled in this Nordic land'.[23] But his racism is probably best understood within the context of his blind and unconditional *love* for Germany, and at a deeper level as part of his long and confused search for a way back to the Great Simplicity. The reduction to stark oppositions like Young and Old, Germany and England, are just one expression of this search. And the return to Hamarøy in 1910 represents its physical expression. In literature and journalism there was the relentless preaching of the gospel of the soil and the repeated attacks on education, and in his private life the insistence on male supremacy, and the bitter contempt with which he spoke of literature, even while compulsively engaged in the act of creating it. At some point he had looked into the large, round face of racism and seen its awesome simplicity, without lines, without frowns, and been hypnotised.

An English reviewer of Hamsun's novel *Wayfarers* wrote in 1980 that 'in Hamsun's case, you cannot have the baby without the bathwater, however dirty you may find it', and for most people this aspect of Hamsun's personality will be the dirtiest bathwater of all. Hamsun's wife Marie made a similar kind of observation when she wrote of the attempts that were being made to distinguish between the man and the writer in Hamsun; that it was like peeling an onion in search of its sweet-tasting heart. 'I think it will end as on a previous occasion', she wrote, 'with the onion-peeler sitting empty-handed.'[24]

When the awful results of the racialist way of thinking began to appear in Germany in 1933, the general reaction of the Norwegian Right was one of disbelief. For some time after the April 1933 boycott of Jewish businesses, *Aftenposten* continued to refer to the 'alleged persecution of the Jews in Germany.' Not even the Nuremberg laws of 1935 attracted widespread condemnation. Not until the synagogue-burning of the Crystal Nights in 1938 did the alarm bells sound even in the furthest corners of the respectable Right. Deaf and solitary old Hamsun never heard them. And there was no one near him who could tell him what a fool he was making of himself. Marie Hamsun was an even more committed Nazi than her husband, and an active member of Quisling's NS Party. The Hamsun children all shared the German orientation which their parents had carefully fostered in them, and both sons were also NS members. But had there been such a person near Hamsun, he would not have listened to him anyway. He listened only to people like Hermann Harris Aall, who confirmed and developed his prejudices. Aall was NS' leading political theoretician, and a close personal friend of Quisling's. Like Regierungsrat Bogs, the man responsible for the Nazis' press image in Scandinavia, Aall was quick to see the propaganda value of Hamsun's political inclinations for the cause, and cultivated him carefully. He was a frequent visitor to Nørholm throughout the 1930s, a notable exception in Hamsun's otherwise blanket condemnation of learned men.

Chances for Hamsun to reconsider his position did arise, however. Tore Hamsun writes that the murder of General von Schleicher in 1934 shocked his father deeply. Like a true mono-maniac though, somewhere in his heart he found a reason for it which left the mania intact. A last meeting in 1938 with his old friend Johannes V Jensen at the Bristol Hotel in Oslo might have given him pause for thought. There was still considerable mutual respect between the two men, but in fact they had little to say to one another. Jensen dismissed Mussolini as just another Italian gangster who had forgotten to emigrate, but found Hitler so sinister that he hardly liked to talk about him. In fact, Hamsun was incapable of allowing such episodes to distract him, and even if he felt a certain amount of unease in his mind he could never bring himself to admit it publicly. To do so would have involved admitting that his instincts had been wrong, and a subversion of the basis of the authority of all his pronouncements so complete that psychically he could not have survived it. There is a powerful irony in the fact that Hamsun's novels are in a sense all about the impossibility of making statements that are final, and definite, and absolute, and clear. 'Perhaps' is as far as the novelist will ever allow himself to go. And as though by way of compensation, the basic rule observed by Hamsun the journalist was always to make his statements as mind-numbingly direct as possible. Above all, there must be no room for doubt, no suggestion that he does not know *exactly* what he is talking about. This fear of seeming uncertain is something he seems to have regarded as shaming, and is some-thing he ponders over in *Mysteries*, where Nagel tries to define the secret of a great poet, and comes to the conclusion that he 'is a person without shame, incapable of blushing. Ordinary fools have moments when they go off by themselves and blush with shame; not so the great poet.'*25

Hamsun perhaps tried to adopt this position in his determination to be not only a great poet, but a great man. Bjørnson, for example, was a blindingly self-confident and utterly shameless personality, and it was probably just this shamelessness that Hamsun identified as the secret of being a 'great man'. One would imagine that Bjørnson was totally incapable of blushing. Even as an old man, though, Hamsun was still prone to blush, and it was something he was resolutely determined never to be seen doing in his journalism.

With a melancholy precision, Hamsun had adumbrated his own political fate half a century before the outbreak of war in Norway in 1940. In an article on the writer and journalist Kristofer Randers in 1894 he described a certain type of character.

> On the other hand, he has no confidence in democracy, the choice of the masses, rule by the masses. He is repelled by the mob, and despises its essence. So he wanders his own way under his own power, an independent nature, an aristocrat. The trouble is that this 'own way' of his is so often the way of reaction.
>
> An independent and aristocratic loner has no party. He is repelled by democracy and despises reaction. He is a hapless soul who is denied the bourgeois joy of feeling himself content and at home within one of the ordinary political parties. But his sympathies might just tend in a certain direction, towards one particular party. He wishes for the triumph of this party. He burns for the triumph of this party. He does not usually become reactionary until well out into dusty old age. As long as he's young, and has a head and a heart, he feels himself naturally more drawn to that party which, in spite of its democratic reduction of everything to the same level, is nevertheless on the side of freedom of thought and progress.

These are the facts of Hamsun's politics in the 1930s. By all commonly understood definitions of the terms he was both Fascist and racist. He was frightened to death of communism, a prophet of the dictatorship of the charismatic leader, and he entertained dreams of a Germanic empire in Europe ruled by a race of pure-

---

* The first edition of *Mysteries* in 1892 is even more explicitly cynical in its attitude towards 'greatness': Hamsun originally let Nagel describe the great poet as 'without shame, incapable of blushing *over his own phoneyness*'.

blooded Germans. The amusing youthful pose of the 1890s, the 'shocking of decent people' which Thomas Mann called 'an interesting point of view, aesthetically speaking, a literary paradox' did indeed harden into a moral and intellectual paralysis which by the 1930s was a very political position indeed. Hamsun's views were manifestly not the nonce expressions of senile dementia, although in their hermetic and solipsistic completeness they partake of the mania that feeds all racism. A young Jew wrote to Hamsun in 1933 to tell him what was happening in Germany. Hamsun answered him in a friendly and sympathetic vein, and even tried clumsily to help him. But it was the individual he was trying to help, not the Jew. His reply includes the classic short, circular tour of the hell of racism: 'My understanding of the position is not that Germany is trying to drive the Jews out of the country', he wrote, 'but this is how the situation is being presented by Jewish politicians in England and France, and in the Jewish press.'[26]

Above all, it was Hamsun's own eccentric and fanatical anglophobia which played the decisive role in keeping him true to the German cause through the thick and thin years of five decades, and led ultimately to his appearance in court in 1945 charged with betraying his country. Everything else was simply supplementary detail. His wartime journalism, the psychiatric examination and the trial demonstrate vividly the power of this mania. He paid the price for believing that he had reached a point where he no longer needed to think about things in order to know about them. It had been a fruitful literary theory that had enabled him to produce works of genius brimming with marvellous psychological insight; but in applying it also to the fluid and unpredictable world outside the covers of his books he made a terrible mistake. Confronted with the suggestion in 1945 that he had made anti-Semitic remarks he seemed genuinely shocked, and at one point in his conversation with Dr Ødegård came as close as ever he could to admitting that he had been wrong. The relevant passage of the report, which generally speaking does not present us with the picture of a man intent on saving his own skin, reads:

> He could think of nothing Quisling had done wrong. Well, he says spontaneously, he might have left out that business about the Jews. It's good for us to have a community of Jews like other countries. But there wasn't a word about the Jews in the two newspapers he read. He only found out about it afterwards. Wait – when he was in Germany he saw something – they had yellow benches, and he saw some children who were made to

leave an ordinary bench and go and sit on a yellow one – it was because they were Jews. 'But you must understand, I'm an old man. I just went blindly along with it all because I didn't hear. Stupid of me.'[27]

Chapter 16
1940–1945: Hamsun's War

Three of the Hamsun children married in quick succession in the winter of 1939; Tore in Oslo, Cecilia in Copenhagen, and Ellinor in Berlin. Knut and Marie travelled to Copenhagen for Cecilia's wedding. Afterwards, Marie went on to Germany alone,* and at the invitation of the German Ministry of Propaganda gave public readings from Hamsun's books in a number of German cities. Gyldendal published a collection of Hamsun's more respectable journalism from the years 1889–1928 in honour of his eightieth birthday. Arild Hamsun published his first book and Tore Hamsun had his first exhibition of paintings organised at the Kunstnerforbundet in Oslo. Europe was at war, but Norwegian government policy pursued the same neutral line the country had followed since its independence in 1905. Hitler's regime had created ever stronger pro-British and anti-German feelings throughout the 1930s in the country, and in the event of Norway being dragged into the war, the general feeling was that they must avoid ending up on the 'wrong' side.

On 16 February 1940 a German freighter, the *Altmark*, with 300 British prisoners-of-war on board, took refuge from a pursuing British force in the Jøssingfjord, between Egersund and Flekkefjord on the south-west coast of Norway. Acting on personal orders from Winston Churchill, the destroyer *Cossack* followed her in. After a brief exchange of fire she was boarded and her prisoners liberated. This was a clear breach of Norwegian neutrality, and the Nygaardsvold government delivered formal protests to Britain over the incident. Hitler's suspicions that the British would not hesitate to breach Norwegian neutrality if and when they thought it necessary were confirmed. 'What do you think of the English

* *Aftenposten* 19.12.1939. See also *Der Norden* 1940 p 22.

now?' Hamsun wrote triumphantly to Harald Grieg, who replied that, whatever he might think of the English, he thought much worse of the Germans.[1] Grieg, like Hamsun's other close business associate, his lawyer Sigrid Stray, was a firm opponent of the Nazis.

Vidkun Quisling, by now a leader without a party, had met Hitler in Berlin in December 1939, and stressed for him the possibility that the Allies might occupy Norway. He offered to stage a *coup d'état* in which he would accuse the government of constitutional malpractice, and appeal to the Germans to come to his assistance. Hitler did not encourage Quisling in his plans for a coup, but immediately after the meeting gave his military advisers orders to carry out a study for a possible invasion of Norway. His major concern was to safeguard shipment from the northern Norwegian port of Narvik of vital supplies of high-grade iron ore from the Swedish mines at Kiruna and Luleå. The British and the French were already planning to cut him off from these, and had prepared a landing force of 16,000 men that would advance on the mines after going ashore at Narvik. The legal justification for the breach of Norwegian neutrality was to be that the force was a League of Nations undertaking designed to assist the Finns after the Russian invasion of Finland of 30 November 1939 – the Russian attack had been certified as aggression by the League. On 12 March 1940, however, the querulants made peace, and with the justification for their move gone the Allies had to abandon the planned landing. Hitler, meanwhile, on 21 February, had given General von Falkenhorst orders to organise and lead the invasion of Norway, but on 8 April the British and the French officially informed the Norwegian government that three major west-coast fjords had been mined on the night before. They explained that they felt themselves empowered to do this on the grounds that the war Hitler was waging was in breach of Human Rights, and thus the scene for invasion was set.

The mining, of course, served only as further confirmation for Hamsun of the unscrupulousness of the English. A week before, on 2 April, he had voiced his alarm in the NS newspaper *Fritt Folk*. 'The Bear in the East and the Bulldog in the West are lying in wait for us. We are the prey', he wrote. 'The fact is that quite a few of us live in hopes that Germany will protect us – unfortunately not today, we are led to believe, but when the time is right.'

The time was right sooner than he, or anybody else in Norway expected. On 9 April the Germans arrived by sea, and made landings at seven strategic points along the Norwegian coast. The government and King fled the capital on the same day, and at an extraordinary meeting of the Storting, the government was given power to act for Norway until such time as the Storting could meet again under regular circumstances. A call to mobilise was issued. On the same day, the 9th, Quisling declared himself President and visited General Engelbrecht in his rooms at the Hotel Continental to break the news to him. The General rang the German Embassy, and reported that there was a chap in his room who said he was prime minister of Norway, and could he arrest him?

Quisling's 'government' lasted just five days. He was a hated figure in Norway, and the fierce resistance and sabotage acts that hindered the German Occupation in its earliest phases were due in some measure to outright Norwegian rejection of the idea that a man who had failed so comprehensively at the polls should now elect himself to a leading role in the government of the country. On 15 April the High Court, the only legally constituted authoritative body now remaining in the capital, in co-operation with the German Ambassador Carl Brauer, obliged Quisling to resign and set up in his stead an Administrative Council for the Occupied Areas of Norway. Nygaardsvold's government gave it a qualified recognition – at least it meant that Quisling was kept out of power – but with the appointment on 24 April of Josef Terboven as Reichskommissar, the question of the seat of power became academic. A cool and ruthless veteran of the Nazi street-fighting days, the forty-one-year-old Terboven assumed and retained absolute power in Norway for the duration of the war. King and government, meanwhile, continued a slow and hazardous progress northwards through the country, keeping always just ahead of the German advance. After six days in Molde, during which the town was bombed each day, they boarded HMS *Glasgow* on 29 April and sailed to Tromsø in the extreme north. On 7 May the King issued an appeal in the free newspaper *Lofotposten* to the Norwegian people which was in stark contradiction to the sort of message Hamsun was trying to put across. 'This is not war the Germans are waging', the King wrote, 'but a campaign of arson and murder across Norway', and he urged the people to stand by the King and government. By the beginning of June, however, the Allies had decided to evacuate northern Norway, and on 7 June the King and his government sailed with the troops on board the *Devonshire* from Tromsø to England. Three days later the Norwegian army officially surrendered and demobilised, and the war in Norway was at an end after eight weeks of fighting. Denmark had offered no resistance to the German invasion. Sweden was obliged to protect her neutrality by co-operating with the Germans as long as they had the strength to insist on that co-operation, and

Finland co-operated actively with the Germans, so that with the surrender of Norway on 10 June, the whole of Scandinavia was effectively under German control from the middle of 1940 onwards. The completeness of this domination meant that the Scandinavian peninsular had, militarily speaking, a quiet war right up until the Soviet advances into north Norway in the autumn of 1944. The Germans lived in constant fear of an Allied invasion, and maintained at all times a force of between 300,000 and 500,000 troops stationed in Norway. Troops from the Front were often given tours of duty in Norway to enable them to rest and recuperate from the rigours of the war in the East.

On 14 April, while the King and the government were still in the country, Hamsun sat down and wrote the first of the two dozen or so articles which, spread over the next five years, were to form the basis of the charges of treasonable activity laid against him in 1945. His opening move was to try to destroy the credibility of the man who had masterminded the evacuation of King and government from the capital and issued the call to mobilise – the president of the Storting, C J Hambro – by calling him 'the son of an immigrant family which was allowed to settle here in this country'. He described him as a chatterbox, a talk-machine, and while admitting that he probably had his good points, declared that he was not the man to lead the Norwegian people in 1940. 'He lacks the basic requirement,' wrote Hamsun, 'a Norwegian soul.' This was a coy way of saying, in so many words, that Hambro was not the man for the job because he was a Jew. Then he got on to more familiar territory with an attack on the English. He brought up the tactic of the Hunger Blockade – a shameful weapon of war invented by the British and ruthlessly exploited by them throughout their recent military history – and claimed that 27,000 women and children had been starved to death in concentration camps during the Boer War by the British. This, he boasted, was not propaganda, unlike Carl Hambro's declaration that Norway and Germany were now 'at war'.

With complacent arrogance Hamsun set out his credentials:

I see, and I hear. I do not content myself with information from the speeches of short-sighted shipowners and Storting politicians. This is why I have taken so many newspapers, to enable me to see what the other side thinks too. I have weighed for and against. The Norwegian people are in my opinion unfairly prejudiced against Germany just at the moment. Seamen only realise that they have been torpedoed, they do not realise that the fault is with England.[2]

In conclusion he stated the position he was to hold to firmly for the rest of the war, namely that the Germans had come to *protect* Norway against an English attack and, moreover, had given their word of honour that Norway's independence, integrity and neutrality would be respected.

The article bore the title 'A Word To Us', exactly the title Hamsun had given in his first 'address to the nation' back in 1910, when the death of Bjørnson and his own 'fiftieth' birthday led to his being proclaimed 'dikterkongen' in the land. Clearly, he now saw himself assuming again the role of patriarch, speaking to his countrymen in the hour of their need.

Hamsun followed the progress of the invasion with a passionate interest in the first few months. Marie Hamsun writes that he would meet the postman at the gate at Nørholm and tear the newspapers out of his hands. His journalistic activity was also at its most intense in these early days. On 27 April a short article appeared in *Nationen* in which he poured scorn on a government which gave orders to mobilise, and then ran. The flight of the King and the legally constituted authorities in the land seemed to him self-evident acts of desertion. One week later, on 4 May, came the article which, of everything he wrote during the war, came to be the one which symbolised his treason for the Norwegians:

NORWEGIANS!

When the English in all their monstrous wickedness forced their way into the Jøssingfjord and breached our neutrality you did nothing. When the English later laid mines along our coast in order to bring the war to Norway you did nothing either. But when the Germans occupied Norway and prevented the war coming to our country – *then* you acted. You ganged up with our runaway King and his private government and mobilised. Getting hold of a rifle each and gnashing your teeth at the Germans won't get you anywhere, tomorrow or the next day you'll be bombed. England are in no condition to help you apart from the small band of men who wander up and down the valleys begging for food.

NORWEGIANS! Throw down your rifles and go home again. The Germans are fighting for us all, and will crush the English tyranny over us and over all neutrals.[3]

The major Oslo newspapers were still under Norwegian control and refused to print the article, and it appeared only in the NS *Fritt Folk*. Hamsun had been led to believe that his would be only one of several names that would appear as signatories to the article, but in the event his was the only one printed. He felt that he had been, as he put it, 'nonchalantly treated in the matter', but shrugged it aside. In any event, the colourful language and the massive contempt expressed in the article would have revealed it as his composition no matter how many names appeared under it.

An unpublished literary curiosity from these first few weeks is a direct appeal to the King of Norway that Hamsun wrote on 5 May and sent to the editor of *Nationen*. In it he appealed to King Håkon VII to return and call off the hopeless fight, or to abdicate. 'Many with me note, with the greatest astonishment, that Your Highness appears to intend to continue to fight the greatest military power in the world', he began. He closed the address with a rather self-conscious grandeur: 'Here we have spoken to our King. The matter is serious.' Five days later he called the article back, and it was never published. Hamsun was undoubtedly never far from megalomania throughout the war years, but perhaps such a direct address to the King was too astonishing an act even for his own mania to digest.[4]

In June 1940, Hamsun became involved in an affair involving Norway's territorial rights to East Greenland, once a part of the old Viking empire, but by a treaty of 1814 a Danish protectorate. After Norwegian independence in 1905 an extremist movement campaigned fairly consistently throughout the years for the return of the territory to Norway. The matter finally reached the International Court at The Hague in 1933, where Danish sovereignty over the territory was confirmed. Diehards for the cause refused to accept the judgement, and in May 1940 a lawyer named Gustav Smedal contacted Hamsun in some alarm over a rumour he had heard, that Denmark was planning to sell East Greenland to the United States, and asked him to lend his authority to a campaign to prevent this. Hamsun had always been interested in the East Greenland case, and agreed to help. He wrote to Terboven, and offered to contact Ribbentrop in Berlin, saying that Ribbentrop had been helpful to him on a previous occasion. On 24 July he received a reply to his letter from Ribbentrop, and on 1 September put to Smedal a plan which he himself found slightly astonishing. Marie Hamsun was once again in Germany on a propaganda reading tour; Hamsun's idea was that he would rendezvous with her in Berlin, and that they would go together to speak to Ribbentrop. Marie would act as his interpreter, since for all his mystic kinship with the Germanic people, he could not make himself understood in their language. Smedal was delighted, and not a little surprised that the eighty-two-year-old man would do this for him. He arranged for visas for both Knut and Arild Hamsun, and the two flew to Germany in October. The trip was in vain. No definite invitation had been extended to Hamsun, and when he arrived in Berlin and sought a meeting, Ribbentrop put him off with the news that he could not see him until November. Probably, as Hamsun suspected, he had more pressing things to worry about than East Greenland. Instead, the Hamsuns visited their daughter Ellinor, whose marriage to a Nazi film-director named Richard Schneider-Edenkuben in 1939 had broken up, and stayed a few days in an island house in the mouth of the river Elbe. A portrait painter named Ewald Vetter got wind of their presence, and visited the family there in hopes of painting a portrait of Hamsun. He ate his evening meals with them, and his innocent description of the atmosphere at table tallies with suggestions that the marriage was not happy. Marie Hamsun seems to have talked about her husband to Vetter in the third person, speaking his mind for him and conveying his wishes in the patronising and slightly contemptuous way some people have when speaking of the very old and the very deaf. Hamsun, for his part, sat in complete silence throughout the meal, laughed at something he pretended to have heard on the radio, and got up and left the room before the others.[5]

Back in Norway Hamsun visited Smedal on 22 October and reported on his failure to meet Ribbentrop. Smedal found him tired and complaining of his age. He said that his head was weary, and that he often failed to find the words he was looking for. Rather tactlessly, Smedal asked him again to write something about the East Greenland affair for publication in Denmark. Hamsun refused, saying that it would not be good enough. 'I just live on my name now', he added pathetically.[6] It was the first of three trips in all that Hamsun made to Germany during the war years, and the first of many disappointing attempts to influence German policy in matters ranging from political decisions to mercy pleas.

In August Hamsun had the unusual experience of having a manuscript refused by his publisher Gyldendal. 'I ask you not to ask me', Harald Grieg cabled to him,[7] quoting a formula Hamsun had often used himself when Gyldendal came to him looking for praise in support of their various encyclopedias and lexicons. Grieg describes the rejected manuscript in his memoirs as 'a long article' and says it contained another of Hamsun's attacks on the

English. It may well have been 'A Pauline Word' which he wrote at Nørholm on 17 August and which took the form of an open letter to a journalist named Victor Mogens, a supporter of Hitler, who nevertheless interpreted the German invasion as an act of aggression. In a radio speech Mogens had described the order to mobilise delivered by the King and the government as a natural and defensible act directed against an attacking enemy force. Hamsun's protest, at about 2000 words the second longest of all his wartime articles, restates familiar themes of the journalism of the early war years – the futility of armed resistance against the German forces, the folly of regarding the German occupation as other than a friendly guarantee of Norway's neutrality, and the utter worthlessness of all socialists. He writes about the hate-mail he has been receiving:

> They are from people with itchy fingers. People who must 'take up their pens'. Now I'm getting them in mountainous heaps, perhaps even more than you are getting. But again unlike yours, most of mine have been anonymous. I have not read them, just seen what they are about. One of them begins thus: Traitor and swine! The tone of them on the whole is something I recognise from Tranmæl's congregation, the rabble in the Labour Party, those who are so pleased to call themselves communists.[8]

The main point of 'A Pauline Word' was to persuade people to rally behind Quisling so that a Norwegian administration acceptable to the Germans could be established. Hamsun praises Quisling lavishly as a leader and an administrator of the first rank, and invokes the name of his friend and political advisor, Dr Hermann Harris Aall, to give added authority to the recommendation. His contempt for democracy is clearly expressed in the view that 'a politician of the common or garden Norwegian kind does not need to be anything special', and he mentions Hambro as a proof of this statement. Quisling, by contrast, is 'more than a politician, he is a thinker, a constructive spirit'. If Norway does not accept Quisling's dictatorship, then 'the same thing but different' will start all over again, with all of what Hamsun considered to be the evils of twentieth-century public life – parliamentary democracy, socialism and class war, and contested elections between different political parties.

'A Pauline Word' was important to Hamsun. He travelled to Oslo shortly after writing it and as a courtesy showed it to Victor Mogens before publication. By the time Mogens had read the article, Hamsun had changed his mind anyway about publishing it. The political situation in Norway in the autumn was tense and unpredictable, with rumours that Terboven was about to introduce far-reaching changes in the administration of the country. Hamsun's friendship with Harris Aall meant that he was kept well abreast of such rumours. Quisling in the meantime travelled to Germany and met Hitler again. Here he received assurances that he would in due course be allowed to form and lead a government in Norway when the right time came. In spite of having been set aside by the Germans after just five days in power in April, he returned from this meeting with Hitler with improved prospects. Shortly afterwards, on 25 September, Terboven issued a directive dissolving the existing Administrative Council which had run Norway since the middle of April, and appointed in its stead a Council of Thirteen Departmental Administrative Chiefs. Quisling was not among them, but his party, NS, now became the only permitted political party in the country. The directive stated explicitly that from now on, NS was the 'Norwegian people's only possible way to freedom and independence'. In government or not, Quisling as leader of NS was now in a position of considerable power. Hamsun, after six years of publicly praising and support-ing Quisling, had met him for the first and only time around that autumn, and been disappointed. The full extent of Quisling's contribution to their conversation had been to say 'yes' twice. Yet Hamsun clung to the illusion that this was Norway's charismatic leader, her Caesar, her Great Terrorist. This was a more important concept to him than the policy details of NS, which were of little interest to him. Forty-eight hours after Terboven's directive, with Quisling's star beginning to ascend, and over a month after having written his article, Hamsun again took the train to Oslo with 'A Pauline Word' in his pocket. He went straight to the offices of the Party's newspaper *Fritt Folk*, and the article, with its energetic promotion of Quisling, appeared the following day.[9] Clearly, he was looking to lay claim to a position of power for himself in the middle of the changing situation. Neither he nor Quisling could have realised at the time that Terboven was determined to allow Quisling about as much power in Norway as a head boy has in relation to a headmaster at school.

In the autumn the Nazis visited Gyldendal's offices and began their book confiscations. Among the banned volumes was Thomas Mann's *Buddenbrooks*, the book which stood first on Hamsun's list of Six Greatest Books given to the *New York Times* in 1934.[10] A more extensive list of banned books was drawn up in the autumn of 1941 after the arrest and imprisonment of Harald Grieg. Again, many of these were by authors admired by Hamsun, who in turn admired him. Hamsun's personal isolation, and the restrictions imposed on information by the conditions of the Occupation, led to many startling lacunæ in his knowledge of events during these years. After the war he appeared to have had no idea that the Nazis had banned books. 'They published all kinds of books', he protested during his psychiatric examination.

In January 1941, Hamsun with his son Tore went to see Terboven at his headquarters at Skaugum, the official residence of the Norwegian Crown Prince Olav, to plead for the release of a writer, Ronald Fangen. Fangen, a former Chairman of the Writers' Union, was being held at Gestapo headquarters at Møllergaten 19 for anti-Nazi activities. This was Hamsun's first meeting with the Reichs-kommissar and though Terboven listened to the case for Fangen, he afterwards produced a long document elaborating on his reasons for not agreeing to release him. Fangen was released some six months later, in June, and Hamsun's interest in the case in January may well have played some cumulative part in this. As in all such matters involving pleas for mercy, telegrams, and articles, their direct bearing on matters is well-nigh impossible to gauge, and effect and cause cannot always be related. This lack of documentation and certainty made it difficult for Hamsun at his trial to substantiate his claims that he wrote hundreds of letters and telegrams pleading for prisoners and condemned men during the Occupation.

The only discernible public result of the meeting at Skaugum was another impressive propaganda coup for the Germans. A photographer from the Nazi-controlled *Aftenposten* arrived un-announced in the room and took two photographs of the meeting which the paper duly printed the following day. Hamsun, whose dislike of journalists and photographers was well-known, can clearly be seen trying to avert his head from the camera.[11] Another attempted propaganda exercise was less successful. On the day following the meeting at Skaugum the newspapers could report that Hamsun had been invited to fly to Germany with Terboven in his private plane. The invitation appears to have stemmed originally from Goebbels, a long-time admirer of Hamsun, and such a visit, had it taken place, would have been a major public relations success for the Germans. However, during the course of a ten-day wait for decent flying weather, Hamsun heard from Berlin that he would be expected to pay for his trip by playing the 'great man' and allowing himself to be trundled around the country, and he backed out at the last minute.[12]

The failure to get Ronald Fangen freed was an unexpected disappointment for Hamsun, and seems to have caused him to lose his nerve in regard to Terboven. As with most of the important public figures Hamsun was to meet during the war, the participants did not hit it off personally. Shortly after the meeting, Gustav Smedal wrote to Hamsun, asking whether he would contact Terboven to arrange for the publication in German of a book he had written on the East Greenland affair. Hamsun declined, saying that he dare not, they were not exactly friends, and that his name had been struck off Terboven's list. He felt that he had irritated him by backing out of the trip to Germany.

Hamsun's failure to achieve results from Terboven is instructive. In the first place, his willingness to lend his name to this rather footling East Greenland business probably gave him early on the reputation of being a time-waster, which lessened any influence he might have had on the more important business of saving lives and getting prisoners released. Secondly, his very availability caused him similar problems. He had given himself too easily, too ecstatically to the invaders. The Germans knew that he had been in love with them for years. Unlike the lovers of his own fictional world, he made no attempt to hide this. On the contrary, he broadcast his love frequently and passionately, and found that it had the same effect on the object of the love as his own fictional heroes had always feared their own declarations would – the loved one responded with a delighted contempt. From the start Hamsun had held nothing in reserve over the Germans. He had given himself totally to them, and they had nothing particular to win from him save further declarations of love. Tactically it was a terrible mistake, but given his passionate belief it is hard to see how things could have been otherwise.

If he was beginning to be disillusioned with the realities of war, he would not let it show in his journalism. On 24 January, he was interviewed on the radio, and in among several interesting observations on art and politics* again dismissed the claims of democracy as a system out of hand. He contemptuously rejected the suggestion that the Occupation was in breach of the Norwegian Constitution – 'As though the Law preceded Life! No, it's Life that changes the Law.'[13]

On 30 January the local Grimstad newspaper printed Hamsun's 'Reply to Two Questions' which they had sent him concerning the

---

* Apparently unaware of the irony in the remark, he said: 'I don't believe any artist should practise a political art . . . Is political art capable of achieving anything? Power? No, it is better to be the humble practitioner of one's art. That way maybe the artist leaves behind him a great work after his death.' Clearly, he did not see his journalism as political in the accepted sense.

future of relations between Germany and Norway. Hamsun affected a huge optimism on the matter, and expounded the hair-raisingly banal racial basis for it:

> The preconditions are there, although things will take some time yet. On our side things would certainly have gone much more swiftly if Bjørnson, our great spokesman and pan-Germanist, were still alive and active in our midst. But 'the age is dawning, the time will come.' Just as our lands in an earlier time belonged together as traders, and as scientists, as we spoke the same language and shared the same basic needs in life, so a new and rich golden age of culture will dawn, based on a Germanic vision of life here in Norway and in Norden. The preconditions are there. This is not prophecy but firm wisdom, a historical intuition. It is a deep consciousness of the known and the unknown, rooted in a brotherhood of blood. We are all Germans.[14]

A striking point here is the use of the name of the preceding 'dikterkongen', his old idol, the supremely self-confident Bjørnstjerne Bjørnson, to give authority to his words. It was an odd reference to make, in view of the fact that Bjørnson had been dead for over thirty years, and suggests that Hamsun felt a deep-seated unease about his own handling of the role of patriarch. The weird discrepancy between his own understanding of patriotism and that of the great majority of his countrymen must have puzzled him many times during his life. That he might be wrong, and everybody else right, was of course out of the question. Yet the invocation of the name Bjørnson in this rather absurd fashion suggests almost a small boy who suddenly feels himself exposed and alone, and wishes his father were by his side.*

As the title indicates, the 'Reply to Two Questions' was something that Hamsun was asked to write. After the war he claimed that he had been pestered by newspapers for articles all the time, though he freely admitted that much of what he wrote was entirely on his own initiative. *Fritt Folk* was especially importunate, and bothered him constantly for statements on war developments at home and abroad. Sometimes he responded, sometimes not. He produced on request a short denunciation of Rudolf Hess after his defection to England in May 1941, and in the

---

* Hamsun's appropriation of the name and reputation of Bjørnson did not go unremarked. He received a stinging letter of rebuke from the writer and journalist Ella Anker which popped up again in court in 1947 to refute the claims Hamsun made that no one told him that what he was doing was wrong.

relentlessly cheerful 'We Have Changed Tracks and Are On Our Way in a New Time and a New World' (used in other newspapers under the title 'Why Knut Hamsun Became a Member of NS), he produced a positively surreal description of life as he envisioned it under the Nazis.

> We shall live together in peaceful intercourse with all peoples, working together with them, exchanging goods, art and intellectual ideas. We shall create a society in mutual development with others, enter a world, a system based on helping – in short, national socialism.[15]

All lands, all peoples in the world would be welcome in this new epoch – even the Russians, even the English, even the Americans. 'This', he wrote, 'is more or less how I understand it.' In conclusion he claimed that 'so much has been written by so many about our future – but above all, it is Hitler who has spoken to my heart'. Confronted with this, it is as well to recall the remark made in the earlier 'A Pauline Word', about the abusive letters he has been receiving – 'I have not read them, but just seen what they are about.' He had not read Hitler either.

As the war continued, and became a fact of daily life, its fascination wore off for Hamsun. The rather sensational nature of his war gives it, in a sense, an unwarranted prominence in relating the story of his life during these years. On 30 April he wrote a letter to *Fritt Folk* firmly asking them to stop applying to him for contributions. Death, and his marriage, occupied his thoughts more. In February 1940, ten weeks before the German invasion, he had written in a letter to Harald Grieg that soon he would be very old indeed, and that he would not mind too much if he could leave all of life's troubles behind him. 'I have had a good disposition', he wrote, 'but now I feel it is beginning to crack.[16]

Part of the problem was Marie. At home he had been feeling old and unwanted for some time. Now over eighty years of age, the twenty-two year gap between him and his wife was never greater. With each passing month he grew deafer and wearier and sadder while she, in her late fifties, was still an attractive woman who looked fifteen years younger than her real age. Undoubtedly the war came to her as a kind of liberation after a lifetime of being wife to the artist and mother to the dictatorial child in Hamsun, as well as mother to their own four actual children. As Hamsun did not finally stop writing books until he was seventy-seven, Marie was also never entirely free from the responsibility of the day-to-day running of Nørholm. A bitterness had welled up in her over the years and the long involvement with psychoanalsis did not help their relationship. As she wrote bitterly not long afterwards, Hamsun's books were his only real love and it was this bitterness which made her receptive to the strange mixture of idealistic dreams and over-realism of the Fascist philosophies that proliferated in Europe in the 1930s. Hamsun's own view of life had ended in a similar mixture. But Marie could not, and did not follow the line that Hamsun took all his life, of burning for a cause while contriving to avoid complete commitment to it. He acted like a member of NS. He wrote trumpet-blasting newspaper articles at its behest. He was everywhere believed to be a member of the party, but as regards membership card and subscription, attending meetings and registering votes, he had never joined. Marie joined, though. She was the local organiser at Eide, and threw herself into the social and political side of party political life with a desperate abandon. She used this involvement as a tool to break open the hermetic seal that Hamsun had set around their lives.

Now it was her turn to travel extensively. For four winters in succession, between 1939 and 1943, she was abroad on personal appearance tours of Germany, Denmark, and Austria. She brought greetings from Knut Hamsun and Norway to large audiences, sometimes of soldiers, sometimes of women and the elderly. She read from Hamsun's books and from her own children's books, and on her return to Norway gave interviews to newspapers in which she described her triumphal progress. The same papers now printed long and glowing birthday tributes to her, though they were always careful to mention her husband somewhere or other: 'Like her husband, Fru Marie Hamsun is of incalculable value for the NS movement in Grimstad. She is one of the leading lights there in the struggle for the new Norway', *Aftenposten*'s correspondent wrote on the occasion of her sixtieth birthday.

It was her war, and she worked hard to keep Hamsun out of it. Deafness made it impossible for him to hear the radio, so that he was dependent for his information on the newspapers, and on what Marie would tell him of what she heard on the radio. The strain of coping with his interest wearied her, and she seems to have kept him wilfully underinformed. Once Sigrid Stray, travelling with the couple on the coastal boat to Oslo, overheard a conversation between them. Marie replied to something Hamsun said by telling him that things were going badly for the Germans in Africa. 'But they have Rommel there', protested Hamsun.[17] It was long after Rommel had withdrawn from North Africa, but Marie did not enlighten him.*

Her respect for Hamsun was gone. She had broken the tremendous power that he had, from the beginning of their marriage, worked so hard to exercise over her with his personality. Hamsun realised what had happened, and it broke down some of the pride in him, too. He could even reveal himself to a stranger like Gustav Smedal when he wrote 'My wife has gone abroad. As for her, I understand her when she doesn't yell.' The contact between them was so bad that he did not even know whether she had actually left the country yet, or was still living in the Søstrene Larsens Hotel in Oslo. The family as a whole also tended to ignore him and exclude him from things. Back in 1940 Tore had even written a book on him for the German market which he knew nothing about.[18]

In an effort to assert himself in this situation, Hamsun contacted his lawyer Sigrid Stray and asked her to draw up a contract in which the running of the farm and the management of the finances would become, provisionally, Marie's responsibility. His shares in Gyldendal were to be divided between his children and Marie, and Marie would receive one-third of his income from the royalties on his books. Particularly in the 1930s, these had been very considerable indeed, with monthly cheques from Germany which corresponded to the average yearly wage for a Norwegian.† The arrangement, finalised in June 1941, was Hamsun's way of putting the family on test.

His experiment had disappointing results. The fact was that Marie's new life was simply too important for her to abandon. Her ability to speak German was not the least of her advantages over her husband in the new situation. She took over Nørholm. The farm was on a bend in the main southern coastal highway, the E 18, and German officers soon learnt that they were welcomed there, and treated the place as a refreshment station. The seclusion that Hamsun had worked so hard to create for himself was gone. Soldiers came with copies of his books for him to sign. Marie would disappear with them and return with the copies signed. Hamsun

---

* The easy way in which people around the Hamsuns contrived to overlook the family's Nazism is puzzling to a foreigner. It probably has something to do with the smallness of the country – the population of Norway during the war was about three million – and the fact that the people involved like Sigrid Stray and, to begin with, Harald Grieg, were all privileged members of the intimate Norwegian upper class. Lower down the social scale, the relationship between patriotic Norwegians and Norwegian and German Nazis was one of uncomplicated hatred.

† In 1936 alone 210,000 copies of *The Growth of the Soil* were sold, 95,000 copies of *Victoria*, 68,000 copies of *Wayfarers*, and 49,000 copies of *Pan*. (Source: Anni Carlsson, Edda 1966, p 278).

would not show himself. 'I don't like these Germans coming to the farm', he told Sigrid Stray, 'It's Marie that brings them here.'[19] During one particularly riotous evening at Nørholm he left the house and flagged down a car on the main road and drove away.

By the spring of 1943 he'd had enough, and instructed Sigrid Stray to inform his wife that the arrangement of 1941 between them was now annulled, and that he was once again master of Nørholm. It was all done by letter, since the couple appear not to have been speaking at all at the time. Fru Stray drafted the formal statement, with a long and rather pathetic insertion by Hamsun himself in which he wrote as though he were Fru Stray, reporting a conversation with him:

> Hamsun meanwhile finds it necessary to reopen the question. He says that the situation at home has not improved, but become on the contrary worse and worse. In matters great and small he feels himself set on one side. No one speaks to him the whole day long, he is totally ignored and feels that he has no home. These conditions are most distressing for his mind, they lame his personality. He has thought of leaving home, but with the situation as it is at the moment this would not be easy. The only possibility for him would be to live in Grimstad. Only when he has been living alone at home has he been happy.[20]

Hamsun's other great weapon, besides his money, was his name. Despite Marie's breathlessly keen propaganda activities at home or abroad, their effect could not be compared to what Hamsun could achieve with his occasional journalism. His longest wartime article, under the ironic title 'Real Brotherhood', appeared, in German only, in the Axis periodical *Berlin-Tokio-Rome* in February 1942. It is an extended attack on Bolshevism and the perfidy of Roosevelt and the Allies, and contains the most explicit and sinister statements of Hamsun's anti-Semitism. Roosevelt is described as 'a Jew in the pay of Jews, the dominant figure in America's war for gold and for Jewish power', and the article ends with the statement that 'Europe does not want either the Jews or their gold, neither the Americans nor their country.'[21]

The appearance of the article in Berlin coincided grimly with the onset of the serious persecution of Norwegian Jews. Quisling had at last, in February 1942, been allowed by the Germans to form a government. This was in effect an admission on Hitler's part that the Norwegians were never voluntarily going to accept the German Occupation, and that a campaign of ideological warfare conducted by Norwegian Nazis was the only hope of changing the situation. Terboven continued to be the power in the land, and continued to treat Quisling as he had done all along, like a schoolboy. The persecution of the Jews, however, which had not hitherto been a major factor of the Occupation, could safely be left to him. Six weeks after his nomination as Minister President he revoked the 1851 amendment to Article 2 of the Norwegian Constitution, so that Jews were once again at a stroke an illegal presence in Norway. The grim process was speeded up with a law of 24 October which gave the authorities power to arrest people 'liable to commit treasonable acts', and the detention two days later of all male Jews over fifteen years of age. On 11 November the first list of confiscated Jewish property was published, and two weeks later all Jews, regardless of age and sex, were rounded up and sent to Germany. 762 were sent altogether, forty-two per cent of the Jewish population of Norway. Twenty-three of them returned alive.

On 6 April Hamsun had an apoplectic fit as he sat at the breakfast table, and fell to the floor taking the breakfast dishes with him. He was up and about again after two days, but contracted pneumonia, and was admitted to Grimstad Hospital on 21 April. He stayed for a week. A letter to Tore of 22 April showed that his ability to write was impaired, with inverted and repeated words and syllables.[22] His speech was affected too, and certain simple functions such as doing up his buttons were difficult for a time. He recovered, though the difficulty in writing continued. Over a year later he still had to rewrite letters three times before all trace of his difficulty was eliminated.[23] It put an effective stop to any further journalism for the rest of the year, although he did manage a short intro-duction to Gustav Smedal's book on East Greenland towards the end of October.

Meanwhile he continued to grapple with an unexpected and disturbing side-effect of his special position in the country during the Occupation. As the months went by, he found himself playing a peculiarly schizophrenic version of the role of patriarch. On the one hand he was the ideological dictator quite willing to see the system he believed in imposed on people by force; on the other hand, he was the compassionate man trying to help the same people as they became the victims of that force. He received and responded to many requests for help, not only from the families of influential Norwegian citizens, but from ordinary people. He wrote and telegrammed to Hitler, to Goebbels, to Terboven, and to the hated Norwegian Chief of Police Jonas Lie, the grandson of the writer.[24] As on that first occasion when he had visited Terboven to plead for Ronald Fangen in 1941, it seemed rarely possible for him to achieve anything. He found it a distressing and confusing experience. For the first time in his life, he was placed in a situation which demanded moral definition and commitment, and he could not handle it. He had dispensed with a conventional morality long ago, and relied on feeling his way through life. Publicly he was the Viking, the Tartar, the barbarian, the redskin; privately the concerned and compassionate man. It was a paradox he had enjoyed.

Now the violent simplicities of war exposed his double game. He lost control of the paradoxes, and found himself pleading for the freedom of two of his closest friends, Harald Grieg and Sigrid Stray, when they were arrested by the Germans. His own literary agent in Berlin, Max Tau, was a Jew who had been helped to Norway during the persecutions. He came to Hamsun in the autumn of 1941 and asked him to plead for the lives of five condemned Resistance members, and Hamsun gave him permission to use his name in a telegram to Hitler.[25] Often the supplicants were complete strangers. Only Hamsun knew that he was not the 'miracle man' people believed him to be. For all his efforts, only once does he seem to have succeeded in saving lives. This was as a result of his article 'And Again!', published on 13 February 1943.[26] As usual, he wrote with a withering sarcasm of the efforts of these thirteen condemned patriots to combat the might of Germany, and of the wrong-headed futility of their trust in the eventual arrival of the English to rescue the country. The article was one of those which Norwegians remembered with the greatest bitterness; it was regarded as a kick in the pants on the way to the gallows. Yet its concluding lines closed with a direct admission of how distressing it was to receive pleas for help from the friends and relatives of the condemned men. All thirteen were spared, and according to their lawyer J C Mellbye, Hamsun's article was directly responsible for saving their lives.

Ellinor Hamsun had suffered after the breakdown of her marriage to Richard Schneider Edenkuben, and she had become an alcoholic. On one of her trips to Germany, Marie had put her in a sanatorium in München Gladbach. Bombing raids in the winter of 1942–43 had reduced the place to rubble, however, and Marie found her a temporary place in a home in Baden-Baden.[27] The situation was not satisfactory though, and in January 1943 Marie travelled to Germany again with the intention this time of solving the problem once and for all. The Hamsuns eventually decided to try to persuade her to come home with them to Nørholm. On 17

May, as *Fritt Folk* published Hamsun's National Day greetings to
NS – 'I think it's going really well now, the U-boats are working
night and day.' – Knut and Marie were flying to Berlin to see
Ellinor, and to take up the two-year old invitation to meet Goebbels
which Hamsun had backed out of in 1941.

On 19 May they went to Hermann Goering Street, in the
building next door to the American Embassy where, at his official
residence, they were received by Josef Goebbels. His diary entry
for that day opens with his reactions to the success of the Allies
dam-busting mission, goes on to express sympathy for the Italians
for all the psychological pressure they must be suffering on
account of the English and American successes in Tunisia,
comments on a Hollywood film about the Soviet Union, 'Mission
to Moscow' which 'pleads for friendship with the Soviets in such
an evil-smelling manner that even the American people are
protesting', and regrets the psychological effect of the reduction of
the meat ration by 100 grammes. He then refers to Hamsun's
'exceptionally favourable appeal' in *Fritt Folk*, and goes on to
describe the visit in detail:

> I was deeply touched by this visit. When Hamsun saw me for the
> first time tears filled his eyes and he had to turn aside to hide his
> emotion. I saw before me an eighty-four-year-old gentleman
> with a wonderful head. The wisdom of old age was written on
> his brow. It was exceedingly difficult to converse with him, as he
> is so deaf that he does not understand a word, and his wife had
> to translate everything I said into Norwegian and shout it into
> his ear. Nevertheless I was overwhelmed at his visit. To me he is
> the embodiment of what an epic writer should be, and we may
> consider ourselves fortunate to be his contemporaries. What-
> ever he says makes sense. He speaks only a few words, but they
> reflect the experience of age and of a life rich in struggle. His faith
> in German victory is unshakable. From childhood on he has
> keenly disliked the English, for whom he has nothing but
> contempt. He lived in the United States for a long time and
> describes the people there as completely devoid of culture. He is
> visiting the Reich to look after his daughter Ellinor. I placed
> every facility at his service for his family mission. I am very
> happy that I came to know the famous author personally at this
> late period of his life. He is of a touching modesty that fittingly
> matches the lustre of a great personality.
> Again and again I gazed at the high brow behind which
> sprang into existence the figures of Victoria, of Lieutenant
> Glahn, and all the many other characters who have been my

life-long companions since earliest childhood. Hamsun is a poet who has already transcended good and evil [*der bereits jenseits von Gut und Boese steht*]. He does not describe people as they ought to be; he does not regard them through the spectacles either of optimism or pessimism, but exclusively through the glass of a fascinating realistic objectivity. Undoubtedly he will later be ranked among the great epic writers of the world. It is a disgrace for Sweden, Denmark, and especially his native country, Norway, that the Scandinavian countries no longer publish his books because of his friendship for Germany.

I gave immediate orders to print a new German edition of 100,000 copies of his works. Hamsun very modestly tried to decline. He said he was so near the grave, there was so little paper available, and his works were printed so much that he didn't know whether he deserved such an honour. This great personality again proves that real genius is always coupled with an almost touching modesty. When Hamsun and his wife left me after two hours I felt I had experienced one of the most precious encounters of my life. I hope we shall see the poet at our home very often.

Magda, too, was deeply impressed by his visit, especially since Hamsun had always been one of the favourite writers of our whole family. Hereafter, when I read his books, I shall be able to conjure up the image of the author himself. May fate permit the great poet to live to see us win victory! If anybody deserved it because of a high-minded espousal of our cause, even under the most difficult circumstances, it is he.

Hamsun was equally moved by the visit. After the war he described Dr Goebbels as a refined man, a personality, with six remarkably beautiful children. The sight of them lining up to be presented to him reminded him, he wrote afterwards, of 'a set of organ pipes'.[28]

Back in Norway after the trip he looked for a way to express his appreciation of Goebbels' courtesy in receiving him. He puzzled for some time over the most appropriate gift, and finally hit on the idea of presenting the doctor with the medal which he received for the Nobel Prize in 1920. On 17 June he sent it, along with a short explanatory note:

> To Minister of the Reich Dr Goebbels. I wish to thank you for all the kindness you showed to me on my recent trip to Germany.
> I cannot thank you enough.
> Nobel founded his Award as a reward for the most 'idealistic'

writing during the recent past. I know of no one, Minister, who has so idealistically and tirelessly written and preached the case for Europe, and for mankind, year in and year out, as yourself.

Forgive me for sending you my medal. It is a quite useless thing for you, but I have nothing else to send.

At first sight this seems a strange choice of gift, but Hamsun probably knew what he was doing. Goebbels had once entertained hopes of being a writer himself, but failing to realise them, he had turned instead to politics. As his description of the meeting with Hamsun shows, he felt the not uncommon reverence some people feel for artists, and on 23 June he sent a warm letter of thanks to Hamsun for the gift:

That you now honour me in sending me the Swedish Nobel Prize medal, which is the highest accolade in the field of letters, brings only shame to me.

I could on no account accept this honour if I thought it were meant solely on account of my own public work. I see it rather as an expression of your solidarity with our battle for a new Europe, and a happy society.[29]

Hamsun did not in fact receive the letter until he returned to Norway an eventful five days after Goebbels had sent it. On 23 June he was again on board a plane, this time bound for Vienna where he had been invited to attend, as a guest of honour, the first plenary congress of the Press Internationale organised by Goebbels. Representatives from Germany, Italy and Spain were invited, as well as from Hungary, Rumania, Bulgaria, Croatia, Slovakia, and other occupied countries. With him travelled Hermann Harris Aall, still his friend, mentor, and the archivist and statistician of his anglophobia, and a man named Egil Holmboe who was to act as interpreter. *En route* the plane made a short stopover in Berlin, and at the Adlon Hotel, three-quarters of an hour before they resumed the journey to Vienna, he sat down to write a short letter of comfort to his daughter Victoria. She had written to tell him that his first wife, her mother, Bergljot, had died on 10 June. 'We were not suited to one another', he told his daughter, 'but all the same, we had some happy years together.' The letter continued: 'I'm going to a congress in Vienna, they've dragged me into it. I'm to represent Norway with my name, but I would rather be home. I don't suppose it's much fun for you either with the war on. We all hope things will be better soon.'* He posted the letter, boarded the plane again, and shortly before 5.30 the same day walked into the Vienna Hofburg to a standing ovation from the journalists and dignitaries assembled there. With him were Dr Brauweiler from the Ministry of Propaganda, Abteilungsleiter Moser from the Reichskommissariat, Egil Holmboe and the editor of *Fritt Folk*. The ovation continued as he made his way to the front of the hall and took his place of honour in the front row. A few minutes later he rose and delivered a short, diffident and curiously ambivalent speech:

> Please forgive my presuming to appear before you like this. I am tired of writing, and too old to make speeches. All of Europe is represented here, and I only want to offer a greeting from a writer from far away, from the high northlands. He wrote books before he grew old. Now he can only count on people's benevolence. He is too old.[30]

Hamsun, as fearlessly paradoxical as ever, spoke in English,[31] having never mastered the German language. His actual address to the assembly was delivered for him in German by Arnt Rishovd, editor of *Fritt Folk*. The irony was increased by the fact that this proved to be the fiercest, and most anti-English tirade that Hamsun ever wrote. Goebbels' aim in organising the conference had been to mobilise sympathy for Germany and Italy as the victims of the British and American 'terror' bombing raids. 'Save European culture, threatened by Anglo-Saxon Barbarians and Bolshevists' was the Conference slogan. Hamsun did not let him down. As 'Norwegian, as human being, and as German' he witnessed for the assembled five hundred:

> I hate the English, the British, with a hatred that is deep inside me. I cannot remember ever having felt otherwise. I claim no credit for this. It is simply my point of view. Early in life I left my home country and travelled. I met foreigners, Englishmen too. I read a bit, noticed a few things, and tried to make sense of what I saw. It always seemed so strange to me when people preferred the English to other nationalities. Yet this was not uncommonly

---

* There was another ghost from the past waiting for him after the conference – Bergljot's daughter 'Vesla', Victoria's half-sister, by Bergljot's marriage to Eduard Goepfert. Hamsun had not seen her since the 1890s. She visited Hamsun at his hotel with her two grown-up daughters and presented him with books and photographs. She had become a writer herself.

the case. On the contrary – it was the rule rather than the exception. It was especially noticeable among seamen. I could not understand this attitude. For my part, I had never come across a less lovable people than the English – so self-centred, so arrogant, so exclusive.[32]

He went on to explain that his attitude was the result of a hundred-year campaign by the English of treachery, lies, broken promises, aggression, terror, murder, hypocritical religion, oppression, and – a favourite theme – the activities of the British Secret Service. Only the Germans had held out against this campaign, ever since the days of Bismarck. He then referred briefly to the tragic defeat in the First World War before taking up the thread of anglomania again. As Hamsun saw it, Hitler had every right to the Polish corridor. England refused to be reasonable and grant this right. They wanted to provoke another war. In the end, Hitler had to give them what they wanted:

> No, England insisted on a war, and Hitler drew his sword. He was a crusader, a reformer. He would create a New Age, a New Life, a lasting agreement among individual peoples which would operate in the best interests of every land.

Raising itself to a final pitch of passion, Hamsun's oratory struck chords at the close of the speech that chime eerily with the words and expressions used in his 1914 newspaper articles in support of Germany, and recall the passionate loathing of the prophecy in his 1912 novel *The Last Joy*, that 'England must be punished to the death':

> My faith and my witness is this: that England must be brought to her knees. To win over the Yankees and the Bolsheviks is not enough. It is England that must be conquered, or the world will never know peace. This is not something I have seen in the stars. It is an attitude based on what I have seen of England's voyaging – and her behaviour – all over the whole world. Even my own small hidden-away land has known the taste of English power, the English abuse of power, from generation to generation, to the thumbscrew on our trade and to the terrorising of our shipping, even to the Secret Service within our very own rooms. There is nothing we have not experienced.
> No, I have not seen anything in the stars. But in the course of a long life I believe I have seen that almost all of the troubles in this world, the distress, the exploitation, the broken promises, the

violence and the international conflicts, have their origins in England. Even this war, with its global miseries, is something we can thank England for. England is the cause. England to her knees!

The pithiness of the concluding line shows that Hamsun had written with half an eye to the press coverage the speech would get – and sure enough, 'England To Her Knees!' was the banner headline the following day in newspapers across the Axis countries. In other respects too he demonstrated his literary technique; in discussing the German defeat in the First World War, he attributed it to 'a gradual infiltration of foreign elements which infected and weakened the Germanic spirit of the people'. This characteristically Hamsunian implication recalls the reference to Carl Hambro as someone lacking 'a Norwegian soul' in Hamsun's 1940 article 'A Word To Us', and leaves the listener to take alone the final incriminating step to the word 'Jew'. As such, the two references together represent the absolute low point in all of Hamsun's prostitution of his literary talent.

Besides its coverage in the Axis press, the Vienna speech also made *The Times* in London for 28 June. The report there was considerably longer than the three-line paragraph with which the paper reported the much more dramatic meeting three days later between Hamsun and Hitler.

Hamsun did not know that he was going to meet Hitler when he flew to Vienna. The idea was probably something arranged by Hitler's press secretary Dr Otto Dietrich, who was present at the Vienna congress, and Baldur von Schirach, the Gauleiter of Vienna and the man whom Hitler was grooming to succeed him. Von Schirach and Dietrich hosted a reception for the congress guests after the opening day. Von Schirach had just returned from a visit to Hitler at his mountain hideaway, the Berghof, on 24 June, and in her memoirs of the period, Christa Schroeder, Hitler's personal secretary, writes that it was von Schirach who suggested, at the dinner table, that Hitler might like to meet Hamsun.[33] Hitler apparently opposed the idea at first, but allowed himself to be persuaded. Literature was not among his hobbies, and it is unlikely that he was familiar with Hamsun's books. He knew the details of Hamsun's struggle and rise to fame, though, and felt an identification with him as a self-made man.

As soon as the Norwegian party travelling with Hamsun heard the news, and saw suddenly and unexpectedly opening up before them the clear road to the heart of power, they got together, and under Hermann Harris Aall hastily put together a tactic for the meeting.[34] The main point Hamsun and Holmboe were to put concerned Quisling, and the status of NS in Norway. Quisling and NS believed that, given access to certain Norwegian documents-of-state, they could prove that the neutrality of the Nygaardsvold government in Norway before 1940 was a myth, and that the King and government were both pro-English. Terboven, as part of his campaign to keep Quisling as no more than an important front-figure, had consistently refused him access to these papers. The NS complained that he was thereby making it impossible for Quisling, Aall and the Party generally to make any ideological inroads on the fondness of the average Norwegian for the English. Hamsun and Holmboe were to make this point forcibly to Hitler, in hopes that he would order Terboven to release the relevant papers. Another topic they were to bring up was the status of Norwegian shipping, and the crippling effects on the industry of being forcibly confined to rivers and home waters.

As a good party man, Holmboe was determined that Aall's instructions would be followed. Hamsun, however, was anything but a good party man. In spite of his 'yes and amen' to the instructions, neither Aall nor Holmboe felt – and with good cause, as it turned out – that Hamsun could be relied upon to stick to the script.

On Saturday morning, 26 June, the two men were flown in Hitler's private plane to Obersalzberg. While they waited at a hotel until Hitler was ready to receive them at the Berghof, they ate breakfast. They were offered refreshments. Perhaps to Holmboe's consternation, Hamsun ordered and drank a large beer glass filled with cognac. According to Holmboe, the drink had no noticeable effect on him. Shortly afterward the limousine arrived to take them to the Berghof. As they stepped from the car, Holmboe noticed the sharpshooters on watch up on the roof. Inside the house, SS guards helped them off with their coats.

Hitler was waiting for them in the reception room. He agreed to the request that Holmboe should act as interpreter for the meeting, and the official interpreter, Ernst Züchner, left the room and placed himself at a table behind a heavy door-curtain and prepared to take notes of the meeting. Another German interpreter, Dr Burger, sat with him. Hitler's secretary, Christa Schroeder, joined them. Hamsun, Holmboe and Hitler sat round a low table in front of a large fireplace, while Otto Dietrich and ambassador Walter Hewel, Ribbentrop's liaison man with Hitler, sat at a small table nearby. The conversation opened with pleasantries. Hitler asked about Hamsun's work methods, and volunteered that he did most of his own writing in the evenings. Hamsun did not like talking about writing, and having assured the Führer that he had faith in him, tried to get straight down to the business of putting Aall's points to Hitler. The volume at which he pitched his voice had increased over the years with his deafness, and the conversation that followed was clearly audible to the invisible audience of stenographers and household staff:*

Hitler: In wartime unfortunately it is not possible for shipping to travel freely on the seas.

Hamsun: But the Reichskommissar's opinions on the matter are binding also for the future.

Hitler: Nothing certain can be said about the future at the moment.

Hamsun: But all the same this is being said to Norway, the third largest shipping nation in the world. The Reichskommissar has in other respects hinted that in the future there will not be any Norway at all.

Hitler: But Norway has, after all, by contrast with other occupied lands, its own government.

Hamsun: What happens in Norway is all decided by the Reichskommissar.

Holmboe, sensing already that Hamsun's undiplomatic approach threatened to play havoc with the agreed strategy, then steered the conversation towards the main point Aall wished them to make, and told Hitler at length of the difficulties of NS in Norway. Party members were considered traitors in the eyes of Norwegians, he said, which considerably increased the difficulty of their work. It was a question of breaking down the King's popularity; but the Norwegian people had always been a very monarchist people. No other people were so passionately royalist. It was therefore essential to demonstrate to the people how they had been betrayed. He urged that a commission be established which would form the basis for a wholesale change of opinion in the country:

Hitler: (irritated that the interpreter is carrying on a private conversation with him) You mean a State Tribunal. (there follows a long discussion on the purposes of such a tribunal)

Hamsun: (returns to his real purpose, to attack Terboven. Very

* The transcript reproduced here is based on the separate stenographic notes of the meeting made by Züchner and Burger and on interviews given by Holmboe in 1978. The observations in brackets are taken from Züchner's and Burger's reports.

Hitler:　　emotional) The Reichskommissar's methods do not suit us. His 'Prussianness' is intolerable. And then these executions – we can't put up with it any more. (this last was not translated by Holmboe)

Hitler:　　The military authorities of an occupying force are often more amicably disposed towards the population than the political who have to carry out necessary acts. The Reichskommissar has a difficult task.

Hitler then held forth at some length with hypothetical illustrations of the kind of difficulties Terboven would face if, for example, he were to ask him to build a railway to Narvik within eighteen months; or a road through north Norway in six months. Another example involved the Ukraine. The listening Otto Dietrich recognised the tactic: this was Hitler using one of his most effective conversational weapons to prevent other people from putting points to him which he did not wish to hear. He would seize the initiative in the conversation, talk incessantly and belabour his visitor with words until the reception was drawing to an end and a counter-argument, if by then it was still wanted, had been made practically impossible. 'Only once did I see a visitor from abroad thwart his designs', Dietrich writes in his memoirs,[35] 'It was the Norwegian author Knut Hamsun.' Perhaps it was at this point, with Hitler getting into gear about the Ukraine, that Hamsun sensed what was happening and brought the conversation back to Terboven. Regardless of Aall's instructions, he was determined to try to discredit Terboven:

Hamsun:　　(who had not spoken for some time) Terboven doesn't want a free Norway. He tells us that we're to become a protectorate. Will he be recalled one day?

Hitler:　　The Reichskommissar is a soldier. He is there exclusively for the conduct of war. Afterwards he will be recalled to Essen where he is the Gauleiter.

Hamsun:　　You must not think that we are against the Occupation. It will certainly be necessary for some time to come. But this man is destroying more for us than you can build up. (not translated)

Holmboe:　　(shouting at Hamsun) Don't talk about this. We have the Führer's promise.

Hitler:　　If we do not win this fateful battle we are waging, it will mean the end of all of us.

Again Hitler tried to get a grip on the conversation, and began to lecture his guest on new and improved methods of weapon production, the setting up of new Panzer divisions and related military topics. Again Hamsun lost patience and made further interruptions. As was so often the case, it was not so much *what* he said as the *way* he said it that caused offence. As Holmboe put it afterwards, 'he did not show the friendly tact which is necessary if one hopes to achieve something'.

Hamsun: Why should we in Norway be left in such a state of uncertainty? What is going to happen to us? And to Sweden? Sweden is a part of the brotherhood of Germanic people, and belongs with Germany, and with us. We want to continue together with Sweden. But it drifts further away from us all the time.

Holmboe: (vehemently to Hamsun) What does Sweden have to do with us? We are here to put Norway's case.

Hamsun: Have you ever heard anything like it! Sweden has everything to do with us! The Jews are tricking Sweden away from us more and more as the days go by. (not translated)*

Hitler: Germany did not need to set up a Norwegian government. That we did so is a proof of our goodwill.

Hamsun: We are talking to a brick wall. (not translated)

Hitler: Anyway, all this is quite irrelevant when compared to the sacrifices we have to make. The political sacrifices your people have to make count for little in comparison to what the German people have to bear. In addition to all else there is the huge sacrifice of blood.

Hamsun: We have faith in you, but your wishes are being misrepresented. Norway is not being handled in the right way. It will lead to another war afterwards! (only partially translated)

* This reference has puzzled commentators on the meeting. It is almost certainly a reference to Stortingspresident C J Hambro, who fled to Sweden in the first days after the invasion, and appeared as the government spokesman during the early days of the Occupation. Given the powerfully personality-oriented nature of Hamsun's views generally, it is not unlikely that in this one man Hambro, Hamsun found the necessary legitimation for all his anti-Semitic remarks. As a twenty-year-old literary critic on *Morgenbladet* in 1906, Hambro had slaughtered Hamsun's novel *Under the Autumn Star*, and categorically stated 'Knut Hamsun is dead.' Hamsun never forgot or forgave particularly savage reviewers of his work. In public life and in public adversity, he was without scruples.

At some point in the conversation, Christa Schroeder reports that Hitler snapped 'Be quiet, you know nothing about it.' This was probably true, although he could not have known how little bearing knowing about a thing ever had on Hamsun's willingness to voice an opinion on it. He abruptly ended the interview at this point, stood up muttering, shrugged his shoulders and walked out on to the balcony. Hamsun and Holmboe were left to fetch their own hats and coats. As they were leaving, Hitler asked Holmboe to try to calm Hamsun down, as he appeared considerably over-wrought. Ambassador Hewel made the same request. Hamsun told Holmboe, 'Tell Adolf Hitler: we believe in you', whereupon Hitler politely and coolly bid them farewell.

On the trip back to the airport the two Norwegians sat in the front seat of the staff car, with Martin Bormann and the German interpreter Züchner in the back. Hamsun did not realise that Züchner understood Norwegian, and spoke freely about the meeting to Holmboe. He asked Holmboe if he thought that he had got his message across to Hitler, and whether Holmboe had translated everything he had said. Holmboe assured him that he had done so 'word for word.' Hamsun was clearly not convinced by this, and protested that Holmboe had steered the conversation in other directions. Holmboe defended himself by saying that Hamsun need not so persistently have come back to the question of Terboven after they had received Hitler's assurances that the Reichskommissar would be recalled after the war. At this Hamsun became very angry, called his interpreter a fool and said that he was talking rubbish. The war would last for a long time to come, he prophesied, and Terboven's methods were intolerable. 'The man is *ignorant*', protested Hamsun, 'All this should have been said – regardless.' Holmboe protested in vain that one may not criticise a high-ranking official appointed by the Führer in such a manner, and that proof of Hitler's goodwill towards Norway lay in the fact that it had a Norwegian government. Hamsun would have none of this: 'You're arguing for their side', he burst out, 'Sure we have our own government – about as much as the Danes do.* It's Terboven who decides what happens in Norway. It makes absolutely no difference at all what Quisling says to him. Quisling', he added contemptuously, 'The Man of Few Words. He can't even speak.' After a short pause, as though to himself, he muttered 'How is all this going to end?'

* Denmark was occupied on 9 April 1940, the same day as Norway. There was no initial resistance, and until 23 August 1943 the Danes had their own Danish government under Erik Scavenius. Hamsun's sarcastic remark indicates the truth of the matter, that it was a puppet government. The rise of an organised Resistance led to the Germans assuming full power in the country in August 1943.

Hitler was furious after the visit. Dietrich writes that 'days passed before he was able to digest this conversation'. He gave strict instructions to his staff that he must never again be exposed to 'people like that'. A planned second meeting the following day between Hamsun and Goebbels was cancelled without explanation, and on 29 June Hamsun flew back to Norway. Terboven, the man he had tried so hard to persuade Hitler to get rid of, was waiting to meet him at Fornebu Airport with a staff car bedecked with Nazi flags. A photograph of the occasion shows Terboven fearfully immaculate in uniform, staring through his spectacles at Hamsun with cold courtesy. Perhaps he knew what Hamsun had been up to. Hamsun stands looking old and humiliated, with head bowed, and his felt hat held against his thigh between pinched fingers. From his own point of view, the meeting had been a disaster. His personal hope – to have Terboven removed from office – had not been achieved. As things turned out though, the meeting did show the results of Holmboe's loyal insistence on putting to Hitler Aall's point about the need for a commission to investigate the reality of Norwegian neutrality before the war. Shortly afterwards, Terboven received orders directly from Hitler to release the documents which Quisling was so anxious to have access to, and the commission to investigate on neutrality was indeed set up with Aall as its chairman.

Hamsun tried to retrieve the situation later, and wrote to Dr Dietrich explaining that he regretted having upset Hitler. He explained that he had not understood that Hitler had willingly confirmed that Norway would indeed occupy, after the war, the 'high position and great future in the German Empire' which was Hamsun's dream for his country. Otherwise he would not have persisted with his attack on Terboven. The letter was not acknowledged.

His attitude towards Hitler shows clearly the fundamental unworkability of his double game. Publicly, he continued to speak well of him, and to praise him as a great man. Privately, he told his son that he had not liked him. He complained that he had talked about himself all the time, and given him a long lecture, of which he had understood almost nothing, about a railway line he was thinking of building from Trondheim to somewhere or other. He described him as a small, thick-set man who looked like a labourer. This private doubt, though, was not allowed to show through in public. Hamsun *wanted* to have met a great man, and if the reality turned out to be a disappointment, maybe it was reality that was at fault. The public, anyway, were not going to be let in on the disillusionment.

The ambivalence in this, and in Hamsun's whole personality, is captured perfectly in a comment he made to a radio reporter after landing at the airport. Breathless for revelations, the reporter asked Hamsun to confirm that he had visited Hitler. Hamsun would only parry the question: 'I visited so many people.'[36] Was this an evasion tinged by shame, or disappointment? Or was it merely that he was damned if he would trivialise such an awe-inspiring meeting as that between himself and Hitler by discussing it all with some impertinent radio journalist? It is hard to tell. One wonders sometimes whether, having played his game for so long, Hamsun really knew what he thought himself. Perhaps the public and the private views of Hitler had equal status in his mind, the one taking prominence over the other much as Thursday takes prominence over Wednesday.

The strenuous week had exhausted him, and before returning to Nørholm he lodged at the Søstrene Larsens Hotel for a few days. The day after his return he was visited in his room by former associates of his from Gyldendal with requests for him to plead for the release of the literary historian Francis Bull – the man who had edited the collection of Hamsun's essays which Gyldendal had published in 1939. They found Hamsun looking worn out, smoking a cigar and staring down at the floor. He paused long in his replies and fell into a dreamlike trance now and then. To their request for help he answered with great pathos, 'Yes, my God, of course I'll help you.' They suggested that he try Aall, or one of Quisling's ministers, a man named Schanke. He dismissed Aall as 'too learned', and said he did not know Schanke. On hearing that he was a trained engineer he expressed astonishment that an engineer could manage ministerial work. They then suggested Terboven, but he also dismissed that, 'Terboven does not think highly of me.'* They then mentioned that Marie Hamsun had achieved good results with Terboven,† news which clearly surprised Hamsun. He refused to believe that she could have succeeded with Terboven. He seemed not even to know that she had been in contact with Terboven at all. In fact, she had undoubtedly visited Terboven not once, but on many occasions. As though attempting to explain the situation he described his isolation to his visitors. After the haemorrhage in

---

* In fact, according to Albert Wiesener, the lawyer who defended suspected Resistance members and saboteurs in Oslo during the Occupation, Terboven was 'more afraid of Hamsun than Quisling', although he does not seem to have been particularly afraid of either man.
† In September 1942, she and Tore Hamsun had visited Terboven to plead for Harald Grieg who had been arrested in May 1941. Grieg was released shortly afterwards.

April 1942 he had moved into a small room up on the second floor at Nørholm, which had once been one of the children's rooms. No one spoke to him and he could not hear the radio. He was called down for his meals by a banging on the pipes below. His visitors noticed that he spoke with bitterness, particularly about Marie.[37]

The Allies' victories at Stalingrad and El Alamein towards the end of 1942 had turned the tide of the war, and the process continued throughout 1943 as the Germans and the Italians were ejected from North Africa, and Allied forces crossed the Mediterranean and began to fight their way up through Italy. The Germans clamped down on unrest in occupied countries with increasing harshness. Towards the end of the year, 1200 Oslo University students were arrested and threatened with deportation to labour camps in Germany. Many families were hit, and again people came to Hamsun for help. He telegrammed to Hitler. It was all he could do. Any illusions he may have once entertained about playing the patriarch and wielding power had been finally shattered by the débâcle at the Berghof. Even in small matters he now warranted no more special consideration and respect than anybody else. Two incidents described by Sigrid Stray confirm this. One involved a private meeting between the two at Müller's Hotel in Grimstad at which they hoped to discuss some legal business. Their conversation was interrupted by German officers who knocked brazenly on the door, walked in and in spite of Hamsun's obvious displeasure at their presence, handed round cigars and insisted on turning the meeting into a social occasion. Later in the year he tried to arrange to see her in nearby Arendal, again about a legal matter. His request for travelling permission was refused, and that was the end of that.

The long blustering articles were now a thing of the past, although he still lent his name to the cause in *Fritt Folk* when necessary. There were occasional journalistic obligations of other kinds too. In 1944 Edvard Munch died. The two men had attempted friendship briefly in the 1890s, but Munch quarrelled with everybody he met, and the contact between them faded. Hamsun retained his appreciation of Munch's artistic courage and produced a short piece of doggerel for him in *Aftenposten* on 25 January. The rather fawning editor of the paper, Doery Smith, pestered him for other contributions, and printed a piece of petit-journalism, 'My Friend the Almanac', a rambling meditation on the subject of encyclopedias which is probably the closest thing to the product of senility that Hamsun ever wrote.

In March 1944, he broadcast on the radio a directly treasonable appeal to Norwegian seamen working on Allied ships in which he

urged them to desert and come home to Norway.[38] He appealed in
rather melancholic fashion to the men's homesickness, and spoke
of their loved ones and families ashore who were missing them
too. Perhaps something of his own personal unhappiness showed
through in this. Certainly the appeal shows a much greater
subtlety than any of his earlier propaganda which, when considered as propaganda generally, was curiously inept. If the
primary purpose was to persuade, and to change opinions, then
the tone of jeering, hectoring sarcasm which he usually employed
in his addresses to the people seems more likely to have
marshalled support for opponents of his ideas. Hamsun is one of
the greatest exponents of pure charm in all literature, but his
journalism makes no use of this talent at all. Indeed, in its
contempt, it seems almost as though it sought to drive people away
from ideas which were by implication too magnificent, too
exclusive, too wonderful for the average man ever to understand
or embrace – the mysticism of pan-Germanism, and the dream of
the German Empire, with Norway as a nation of racial and spiritual
aristocrats within this Empire.

As propaganda intended for consumption by the Germans and
by fellow Norwegian Nazis, it was more successful. Goebbels was
particularly appreciative of his efforts, understandably so, since
Hamsun was the only indisputably great writer on his side. He was
especially pleased with Hamsun's 1942 article about Roosevelt. His
diary entry for 28 March 1942 describes it as 'a very witty and
exceptionally biting article against Roosevelt' and its author as 'one
of modern Europe's outstanding intellectuals who has always
stood by the flag of the new order'. Hamsun's appearance at
Vienna was a tremendous coup for Goebbels and the Germans,
and the fact that he was invited to meet Hitler shortly afterwards
indicates the value they put on the use of his name. As we have
seen though, he was so much in love with the Germans, and had
given himself so openly to them from the beginning that he
retained no control over the conditions of use of his PR-aura. His
enormous vanity was titillated by these gestures of esteem; but that
was abroad. At home, at grass-roots level, Terboven easily resisted
his efforts to influence policy. On the other hand, he was beyond
all question Quisling's strongest card throughout the war, and his
support a tremendous morale-booster for the members of NS.
Membership, naturally, had increased after the outbreak of war
and the introduction of the one-party system, and increased even
more dramatically after Quisling's appointment as Minister-
President in February 1942. From a few hundreds before the war,
membership rose to top 40,000.

English language newspapers reported Hamsun's war sporadically. On 3 July 1940 the *Evening News* reported his denunciation of the Norwegian government, and on 8 August 1941 the *New York Times* reported that an hour-long programme broadcast by Norwegian radio in honour of his birthday was 'oddly, not broadcast to the Norwegian people but "to the German army of occupation" '. In 1942, probably prompted by the Roosevelt article, Allied newspapers conducted a small but observable campaign against Hamsun that lasted for about six months. Several newspapers in England, America and Canada carried stories of his books being tossed over the fence at Nørholm by disappointed Norwegians. Another favourite story was that the local post office at Grimstad had had to take on extra staff to deal with the flood of copies of his own books being returned to Hamsun, and a related story described an auction at which Hamsun's *Collected Works* were sold for one krone to a woman who then posted them all back to him. Readers of the paper who had always thought of the Norwegians as being without a sense of humour were advised to think again. The *Palestine Post* in Jerusalem, meanwhile, was the only paper to pick up on the anti-Semitic references to Roosevelt.

The activities of the Hamsun boys also attracted attention, and on 6 September the *New York Times* reported that Norwegian authors had gone on strike in protest against the taking over of Gyldendal by NS in the person of Tore Hamsun. The following year the *New York Herald Tribune* reported Arild Hamsun's enrolment in the Norwegian Legion, and quoted Hamsun as expressing pride that a son of his was going off to fight the Bolshevists.

On occasions the propaganda backfired. *The Times* did not mind in the least reporting the speech at the Vienna Internationale in which Hamsun openly admitted that most of the people in the world liked the English, and presented his own hatred as a highly personal idiosyncrasy. And the *New York Times* report of his article 'And Again', picked up on the day of its appearance in Norway on 13 February 1943, with its reference to thirteen condemned Resistance members and mass pleas for mercy, made useful counter-propaganda. After the war, Hamsun claimed doggedly that his main aim had been to prevent what he considered to be the useless sacrifice of Norwegian lives in armed struggle against the Germans. Given the tone of his address, however, it is unlikely that he persuaded many to listen to him.

Another of his aims, towards the end of the war, was to comfort Germans and NS supporters worried by the way things were going. He produced, on request, a bold message of faith in German indomitability for *Fritt Folk* and *Aftenposten* on 12 June after the D-Day landings, although he admitted after the war that he was by this time quite out of touch with developments. His intuition was that things were going badly. His fear of communism seems to have intensified as the war progressed, and by the end he feared the Russians possibly even more than the English. A letter to Victoria of 3 June 1944, gives that impression:

> We have now heard the fate of our country outlined in straightforward language from Russia. Our treacherous King and his treacherous government in London have sold Norway to the communists and the Bolsheviks in Moscow. You can console yourself with the thought that you no longer have anything to do with Norway. There is nothing left for us but defeat now, if the Germans should fail to save us all. Of course Germany is tremendously strong, but unfortunately it is having to fight for the whole of Europe. All nations ought to come together as one now, stand together and help Germany to save us all from Bolshevism. France too. Perhaps France above all in her own interest ought to draw the sword, for not one land, not one people will avoid the embrace of the Russian octopus if Germany should falter in the gigantic battle she is waging at this moment. Now we are waiting for the invasion, we have great hopes of it, Germany will certainly win! We must wait and see. Perhaps I won't live to see the end of the war, but I live in a warm hope night and day. Naturally I am afraid for the Norwegian people who have to live through these terrible times; and I fear for Norway in the years to come, even though I shall not see them myself. I say, God save us from Bolshevism! I say it to myself when I wake up in the middle of the night.

In August Hamsun visited a Panzer division, and a few weeks later was shown round a German U-boat. Both visits were filmed for inclusion in 'Weekly Round-Up' cinema newsreels for public showing. In the U-boat film he is seen saluting the sailors, peering through the periscope and talking to the captain. The newspapers also made the most of the occasions with illustrated headline articles. One of the captions read 'Knut Hamsun enjoying himself with German tank-soldiers', beneath a photo of him staring at his hat on the table in front of him with an expression of indescribable desolation on his face.

His eighty-fifth birthday on 4 August 1944 was likewise an occasion for rejoicing by everyone save the celebrant himself. He received telegrams from Hitler and Quisling, letters of greeting from Terboven and Goebbels, as well as signed photographs of Hitler and Goebbels. A new edition of his *Collected Works* was published in Norway to mark the occasion, a heroic undertaking in the face of the paper shortage at the time. The Nordic Society presented him with a Rosenthal porcelain hunting falcon, and he received a large and handsome chest carved for him by German troops stationed in Norway. Hans Carossa, leader of the European Writers' Union, announced the establishment of a Knut Hamsun Fund which would award scholarships of 60,000 German marks to enable Scandinavian authors to travel to Germany. On the other side, the Resistance newspaper *Kongespeilet* devoted issue Number 1423 to him, and quoted some of his own sarcastic comments about the frailties and stupidities of old age at him. There were enough of them to choose from. His own words to Bjørnson in 1904 were revived for the occasion: 'You have become old, master . . . if only you had not become old.' They brought up past sins, like the campaign for the return of capital punishment, and even the name case against his own brother.

The object of this attention kept to his small and sparsely furnished room up on the second floor at Nørholm. Even when he tried to lie low, however, scandal of one sort or another continued to seek him out. Astonishingly enough, he was once again receiving anonymous letters accusing him of keeping mistresses, giving money to married women and having irregular sexual relationships. Sigrid Stray discovered who the writer was and had the letters stopped, although her memoirs do not name the culprit.[39]*

The autumn's fraternising with German servicemen marked almost the end of Hamsun's propaganda activities, and he lived a quiet life at Nørholm. In the New Year he had another slight stroke while he was out chopping wood in his yard. He lay where he fell for a while, but was presently able to get up and return to the house. Otherwise he and Marie and Ellinor just waited for the end.

It came on 2 May in the form of the news of Hitler's death in the newspapers. There was no indication that it was suicide. He was described as having 'fallen in the battle against Bolshevism.' Hamsun brooded on this for a while, and then did a quite astonishing thing. To demonstrate that he was a loyal man he wrote, unsolicited, a necrology for Hitler, and sent it in to *Aftenposten*. On 7 May, when the headline story was about four men dead and a number of others blinded by meths drinking in the

* Sigrid Stray relates that the letters mention a Danish mistress whom Hamsun was supposed to be keeping, a circumstance which suggests that the writer might have been Marie Hamsun.

seaport of Stavanger, his eight-line necrology for Hitler appeared on the opposite side of page one. Probably nothing that he ever wrote shows more clearly the dreadful obstinacy of his mind, its frightening and finally catastrophic innocence:

ADOLF HITLER
by Knut Hamsun

I am not worthy to speak his name out loud. Nor do his life and his deeds warrant any kind of sentimental discussion. He was a warrior, a warrior for mankind, and a prophet of the gospel of justice for all nations. His was a reforming nature of the highest order, and his fate was to arise in a time of unparalleled barbarism which finally felled him. Thus might the average western European regard Adolf Hitler. We, his closest supporters, now bow our heads at his death.[40]

If ever there was a time when a great poet should have abandoned all his pretensions, and like some ordinary fool, gone off by himself to blush with shame, it was the day this appeared. Naturally, he did not do so. Instead, like the rest of the Hamsuns, he sat down and waited for the nemesis of democracy.

Chapter 17

1945–1948: Internment,
Examination and Trial

The day after Hamsun's necrology appeared in *Aftenposten*, on 8 May, General Franz Böhme, Hitler's recently-appointed military commander in Norway, formally surrendered to the Allies Cease-Fire Commission at a late-night meeting in Lillehammer. At about the same time as the terms were being presented to Böhme, Reichskommissar Terboven entered his bunker at Skaugum with a keg of gunpowder and blew himself up. The following morning at 7.15, Quisling and his ministers were arrested, and the war in Norway was over. By an act of 15 December 1944, passed by the government in exile in London, membership of NS after 8 April 1940 was made a criminal offence, and the arrests began at once. Tore and Arild Hamsun were picked up within a week of the capitulation, but their parents had to wait a little longer – there were 40,000 party members and the process of arresting them all was clearly going to take some time.

On 14 May, *Aftenposten*, once again under free editorship, carried a report that Hamsun had taken poison and been rushed to Grimstad Hospital for a stomach pump. He was said to have recovered and be recuperating at Nørholm in Marie's care. Like newspaper reports of his suicide back in 1902, it was an exaggeration. A doctor had indeed been called to the house to see him, but whatever the trouble had been, it was cured with a half bottle of cognac.

They continued to wait. On 26 May the police came and placed them both under house-arrest. They returned for Marie on 12 June and took her in custody to Blodekjaer jail, in Arendal. Two days later it was Hamsun's turn. On account of his age – he was now eighty-six – he was not taken to jail but to the hospital in Grimstad. Here he was given a room in the fever-wing, a large, cold room with three iron beds in it and a sofa-bench. He had a degree of freedom at the hospital, and was allowed to go out walking, although he was forbidden newspapers, or to go into Grimstad.

On 20 June Hamsun made a statement to the Desk-Sergeant at Grimstad, the first of the many statements concerning his conduct and attitude that he was to be required to give over the next three years. Here he denied for the first time that he was a paid-up and card-carrying member of NS, a technical point that was to be of decisive importance in the months and years that followed. A pattern is apparent already in this first statement, in which Hamsun firmly stands by everything he has written, while at the same time offering conceivably mitigating information about the circumstances of his private life, and of the writing of the various articles. He claimed to have been contacted by the Reichskommiss-ariat with demands for statements and articles that could be used by the press. The statement continues:

> The accused was telephoned as often as three times in the middle of the night by the Reichskommissariat in Oslo. He declined to write anything, but eventually had to give in. Naturally he (the accused) wished to serve Norway as a means of furthering the interests of Germany. The accused is delighted to confirm his participation.
>
> He has never joined NS, but been led in that direction . . . He has never properly studied NS' programme, nor has he been interested in it. Personally he has never paid a subscription to NS although his wife may have done this. He has had no contact with the Germans apart from the Reichskommissariat.
>
> The accused does not wish to trivialise the extent of his connection with NS and the Germans. On the contrary he would have helped more if he could, since he believed it was in Norway's best interests.
>
> He has never given any support to the front-fighters.
>
> He knows nothing about informers. He has never informed on anyone himself.
>
> The accused declares himself Not Guilty because in good faith he was acting in the best interests of Norway.[1]

At the preliminary hearing three days later in Sand District Court Hamsun said that he had known nothing of the Nazis' atrocities until he read about them in the newspapers after the war, and confirmed to the court that he stood by what he had written during the Occupation in *Aftenposten* and *Fritt Folk*. He made two minor alterations to his statement of the 20th. He had intended to say that he, 'wished to serve *Germany* as a means of furthering the interests of *Norway*.' Nor was he happy with his use of the word 'delighted' – he had exaggerated, he explained, to convey that he was not trying to wriggle out of the charges. The hearing was adjourned until 22 September, and Hamsun returned to Grimstad Hospital. About his own personal fate he was already philosophical. What worried him was what would happen to Nørholm, and the fate of his family.

He enjoyed living at the hospital. He walked about, read, played patience, darned his clothes and smoked cigars. Now and then he had a visitor. On 24 August a dozen of his newspaper articles were shown to him and he formally admitted having written them. A week later, on 2 September, he was moved from the hospital because the room was needed for some poliomyelitis patients, and sent to an Old Folk's Home at a place called Landvik between Lillesand and Grimstad. The Home was large and well-equipped, with a community hall, its own library, telephone, daily postal service, and offices. Hamsun had his own room up on the first floor, and his life continued much as before. He started writing again in a small way – a kind of journal of what was happening to him – but the Sea-change was over him already. The Fascist Jove hurling thunderbolts at the wretches below was washed away. Now he was the ageless Asiatic philosopher, flowing along with life, objecting to nothing, in the dust, but not of the dust. He charmed everyone at the Home, with the disappointing exception of the librarian who refused to let him borrow books. 'Who knows,' he thought, 'perhaps I wrote some of them.'

At the hearing on 22 September the case was postponed to 23 November. The Norwegian authorities were clearly not entirely sure what to do about him. The provisional plan was to proceed against him on two counts, first under the treason act of 15 December 1944 which criminalised membership of NS after April 1940, and the spreading of propaganda on behalf of the NS; secondly, under Section 140 of the Penal Code, for having incited others to commit indictable offences. However, when the Attorney-General approached Dr Gabriel Langfeldt, head of the University's Psychiatric Clinic at Vindern on 13 October, and asked him to make a preliminary statement on whether or not Hamsun was fit to stand trial on these charges, it was not primarily an easy solution to an embarrassing problem he was seeking. The Norwegian general public had been largely unaware of the extent of Hamsun's commitment to Fascism in the 1930s. They had anyway long ago learnt to live with the eccentric and unpredictable side of him, and even to value his incorrigibility. He was first and foremost their great writer, their national pride, a loved and admired, and never quite respectable ancient child. When he so openly and keenly sided with the Nazis after 9 April 1940, many people found this difficult, if not impossible, to accept. There was a widespread assumption that he must have become senile, and was not responsible for what he was saying in these articles. The editor of *Lofotposten*, still in May 1940 a free newspaper in unoccupied northern Norway, wrote that 'the only thing that can excuse Hamsun's articles is that he has become feeble-minded in his extreme old age'.[2] Newspapers abroad took the same line. The Dayton Ohio *News* wrote on 22 May 1943 that 'the mind of the old man of eighty-four, we must suppose to explain the unthinkable, is but the tragic remnant of yesterday's genius'. *Aftenposten's* report of Hamsun's alleged suicide attempt also presumed him to be senile.

Accordingly, on 14 October, Hamsun was taken on a night train from Arendal to Oslo, and driven to Dr Langfeldt's clinic at Vindern. One might imagine that the psychiatrist found irresistible the opportunity to study a genius at close hand. After a preliminary examination he declared that there was indeed some doubt about Knut Hamsun's mental fitness to stand trial, and advised that he be thoroughly examined at the clinic. Sitting on 12 November, Oslo Magistrates Court empowered Langfeldt and his colleague Dr Ødegård to carry out the examination.

Thus began a war between Langfeldt and Hamsun which once again cast Hamsun in the role he was all along best equipped to play in life, that of the desperate but charming loser. It was to go a long way towards modifying the picture of the individual Knut Hamsun, unattractive to the point of irremediable, that would otherwise have been left to posterity. He would spend 119 days in this clinic, a period from which he emerged, in his own phrase, 'a quivering wreck'. The confrontation between the two men is an extraordinary and illuminating clash between the two faces of human psychology; Langfeldt's organised, resolutely rational book-science, and Hamsun's flowing, unpredictable and imaginative art. And in its final form the report was an eighty-three-page document.

It opens with an outline of the brief from the Magistrates Court, a summary of the charges against Hamsun, and a biographical sketch of the subject largely based on Einar Skavlan's 1929 biography. The authors, Langfeldt and Ødegård, state that they have permitted themselves to use, with discretion, Hamsun's own writing as a legitimate tool with which to analyse the subject. They characterise him in general terms, mentioning his self-certainty, his aggression and his eccentricities, such as his contempt for the acting profession. As having perhaps, under the circumstances, special interest, they quote the speech by Ivar Kareno from the 1895 play *At the Gates of the Kingdom*, in which he declares that he believes in the 'born leader, the natural despot, the great commander, the one who is not chosen but who elects himself to mastery over the hordes on the earth. I believe and hope for one thing, and that is the coming again of the Great Terrorist, the Life Force, the Caesar.'

Three long letters written by Hamsun to the President of the Storting in 1898 are then reproduced. These were written at the height of the persecution by anonymous letters which he suffered between 1896–98, when he despaired of the police ever solving the case and were passed on to the psychiatrists by 'an interested colleague'. Oddly enough, Hamsun's earlier psychoanalysis in 1926 by Irgens Strømme is neither discussed nor even mentioned in the report. It may be that it was not known about. In any event, there was no love lost between the rigidly Freudian Langfeldt and the more independent Strømme,* though both were freemasons. Additionally, the report contains no reference to the findings of Dr Locard, when Hamsun himself reopened the case in 1935, that the author of the letters was Anna Munch. Again, it is conceivable that the doctors and the 'interested colleague' knew nothing of these findings. Without this knowledge, however, the letters make strange reading, and the section is described in the report under 'Paranoid Reaction in 1898'. There then follows a series of depositions from relatives like Marie and Tore Hamsun, and others with whom Hamsun had had contact during the war, like Harald Grieg, Sigrid Stray, and the author Christian Gierløff.

Gierløff, who had known Hamsun since 1899, had been on the 'other' side during the war. News of the arrest had filled him with alarm, and he began visiting Hamsun shortly afterwards. He was convinced that anglophobia was the vital factor in the case, and as an old acquaintance he had expert knowledge of it which he passed on to the psychiatrists. In many other ways, personally and professionally, he was to be of assistance to Hamsun during these years. Civil servants, local government officials and neighbours with whom Hamsun had come in contact also gave short statements. The report also included copies of the exchange of letters between Hamsun and Goebbels in 1943. After these

---

* Strømme had developed a psychoanalytic method of his own which was based on Freud, Jung, and Bleuler's findings, and which he called 'bio-psychology'. He ended his days well outside the medical establishment, in spite of his pioneer status as the first practising analyst in Norway.

preliminaries, the rest of the report contains a record of interviews with Hamsun, and secret observations made of him during his free time:

15.10.45 The patient is liable to get angry over the slightest thing. He does not understand the regime here. He swears and is irritated when his temperature is to be taken, his clothes taken from the room, or when he has to go in to the doctor.

16.10.45 The patient is constantly angry and irritable and wants what he demands straightaway. He is abrupt and irritable. Often makes sarcastic remarks.

19.10.45 The patient is in a good temper, polite and manageable. He reads a great deal.

26.10.45 It appears as though the patient is beginning to settle down here. Mostly he sits and reads, although he does speak with the other patients. After he went to bed this evening he lay there talking to himself. He was talking about being too long-lived, he should have died years ago. Several times he calls out, 'if I could only get an answer to my question – and I know he listens to prayers'.

Most of the interviews were conducted by Dr Langfeldt. To begin with these were verbal, in the presence of a stenographer:*

10.11.45 (Why are you in here?)

I was taken in good health from an Old Man's Home and put in here, I don't know why, because I was in good health. I don't know why the police don't just sentence me and let me serve my time. I think I can assure the Attorney-General that I am responsible for my actions.

. . .

Did not know NS was a terror-organisation, don't understand how the Germans could hide these mass graves, believe there would have been a change of heart in NS if they had known about it. Dictatorship has to be modified, but it will become a practicable idea in the future. It wasn't all that bad an idea when you think of the 'enevoldskongene', they did many good things. Hitler's dictatorship was a strange business, I got some rather good impressions of him. It's mass-hypnosis that does it.

---

* At times the stenographer's reporting is direct transcription, at times reported speech. The translation reflects this.

They needed someone special in Germany at that time. Funny that he managed to get everyone to call him 'Mein Führer'. Queer to think that Generals could bring themselves to say that. Mass hypnosis is an awful thing, just look at theatres and circuses. It was a terrible time for writing.

Ødegård, whom Hamsun found a more sympathetic man, only interviewed him twice, for about a quarter of an hour each time. The tone of these interviews is noticeably more relaxed:

'It's the King and his government that has led me into this wretchedness. I have always been a monarchist, and Norway has never been anything other than a kingdom. The bottom fell out of the whole thing for me when the King left the country. I knew nothing at all about the London government. He should've done like his brother in Denmark – he was a sensible man. We would have been spared all that sabotage and destruction.' When it is suggested to him that in Denmark there was just as much sabotage as here he smiles, and says that in Denmark they can afford it, a lot better than we can.

He mentioned often his isolation during the war, and said that he never spoke to his family, and only saw them at meal times. Even then, there was no conversation. He also took up a point which has been much discussed; the extent to which he was aware that his activities were widely regarded as treasonable. The extreme subjectivity of his idea of truth emerges clearly in his admission that he *did* receive letters, but threw them away, because none of them came from 'respectable, trustworthy people'. The fact that people wrote to him at all to criticise him, excluded the possibility for him of their being 'respectable, trustworthy people'. Truth was what he said it was, and he seems to have been mentally unequipped to admit that he had made mistakes. This obstinacy was, after all, one of the ground rules laid down by Nagel for becoming a 'great poet' – he never admits to being wrong, for to be wrong is shameful, and a great poet never feels shame. And Hamsun's response to being corrected by Ødegård is instructive in this respect: corrected over the matter of sabotage in Denmark, he tried to obscure the fact by making a supplementary and irrelevant statement of fact. Later in their conversation, Ødegård drew him on the subject of himself as a writer: 'He believes that he is now a dead man as a writer, and that his books will not be read much from now on.' Again he was asked about his attitude towards Germany:

Of Germany and the Germans he says that they have many good qualities – they are a clean and conscientious people, and have been helpful to us. There is not a single great name in our country which has not had to go through Germany to achieve fame, in Art as in Science. It has meant so much to us to have access to this great linguistic community. He has always been pro-German himself, but as NS during the war he has only come into contact with those Germans who were also NS, and that was just a small per cent of the populace. Everybody had to take part in the war, but they weren't all national socialists. They will rise again, and it would be terrible if they did not. We have had good use for them, we writers. If things had gone as they did in Paris we would have had to pay for it. It was not easy to be Germany either – they were threatled by the whole world (corrects this immediately to threatened, and repeats his correction when he sees that notes are being made – this was the only such mistake in the conversation). Was it any wonder that they resorted to methods like the bullet through the back of the neck and so on that the Russians used against them – it was the Russians who began it, putting bodies in mass graves in long rows, like sardines in a tin. It was the Russians who started that.

Hamsun also remarked, not for the last time, that 'the way things have turned out is probably for the best'. His antipathy to communism, the English, and Roosevelt remained unmodified. Roosevelt was 'an extremely crude man who bombarded towns and lands for years. He was a politician and got his way whatever it cost.' He recalled with enthusiasm Quisling's attack on the communists and striking workers in the Storting in 1932: 'every word was like a bomb'. Ødegård then asked him about the Jews:

He says that he has never had anything against them, and that during the last war he helped German Jews over to America, and that he has many friends among the Jews. On being shown the reference to Jews in Sweden made during his conversation with Hitler he more or less smiles it away. Hitler was obsessed by the Jews, but he does not believe Quisling was. He knew nothing whatever about the persecution of the Jews in Norway and Germany – at least, not that it was as bad as he now realises.

The conversation then took up again the by now familiar theme of his isolation during the war years. Sigrid Stray, Gierløff, Harald Grieg and Marie and Tore Hamsun all spontaneously confirmed that this was very considerable indeed. Hamsun's own literary account of the post-war years, *On Overgrown Paths*, which will be discussed later, adds further confirmation. If Hamsun could ever be said to be looking to excuse himself, it would be in drawing attention to his isolation and his deafness, and the consequences for him of this, that he was out of touch with the realities of Nazism and the real progress of the war. Yet the apology is only tentative, a hint, a deceptively casual attempt to engage sympathy. Hamsun knew a great deal about Nazism before the war. He knew that Hitler murdered his opponents. He also supported concentration camps for political prisoners, and the Nazi aggression against Poland. He must have realised that any strong protestation of innocence based on his isolation would not stand up to thorough investigation. More than most men he knew the value of protesting too little. The report continues:

He has not in any way been influenced by his family, since none of them had the patience to talk to him – especially not his wife – 'our relationship was not like that'. They have so to speak not talked to one another for years. He says this with audible sorrow, a bitter melancholy. But adds keenly and with spirit that he will not allow this to be used as an excuse to try to get him to reveal anything about his marriage, as the professor (Langfeldt) has tried to get him to do. He refuses to say a single word on that.

. . .

He is quite clear that he is guilty as the law now stands – but he maintains that this was not the case before, or at least, he did not know anything about it if it was. Now he just wants to be sentenced in the ordinary way, and does not want any special dispensation. He does not want softer treatment because he is old. Well, of course, there must be some reduction, because 'I won't stay in one piece long enough to serve one of these long sentences that are being handed out to people.'

. . .

The stay in the clinic is a torture to him. You have to go through three locked doors when you go out for fresh air, and through the same three locked doors coming back in again (mimes savagely the locking of each door with his hands). And the time is just wasting away here, he can't get on with serving his sentence, he can't get on with what he has to do.

Now Langfeldt returns, and from this point on the examination is conducted by written question and answer, owing to Hamsun's deafness. Langfeldt's first questions are an attempt to get Hamsun to give his own views of his childhood and his personality and life.

The professor was used to people who respected and responded appropriately to the authority vested in him as a psychiatrist, and he was used to getting answers to his questions. Hamsun, however, felt unable to respect him. Langfeldt came to their meetings, he said, 'equipped with his school-books and his learned works which he had learned by heart and taken his examinations in, but something other than that was required here'. For him, Langfeldt symbolised the institutionalisation of the delicate wisdom which psychology was to the artist in him. He was 'damnation over a living being, regulations lacking mercy and tact . . . a psychology of blank spaces and labels, a whole science bristling defiance'. For obvious reasons, Hamsun tried to control his hostility to the professor, but at one point the two men came to a total impasse. Not satisfied with the answers to one of his questions, Langfeldt put four supplementary questions to his patient. Three of them were fairly innocuous requests for more information about his attitude towards his uncle Hans Olsen, his godfather Torstein Hestehagen, and his time as a pedlar and schoolteacher in his youth. Hamsun submitted further short answers, adding in irritated resignation, 'Professor, I am afraid I cannot manage more thrilling answers to 1, 2 and 3 than this.' Langfeldt's fourth question, in which he asked Hamsun to describe why his first marriage to Bergljot Bech had broken up, and to give an account of his marriage to Marie, with particular reference to the difficulties of their recent past, was simply ignored. Langfeldt persisted. Still Hamsun refused. 'It was not myself I wanted to conceal', he wrote later. 'I wanted to prevent an enormity.' Baulked, Langfeldt then summoned Marie Hamsun to the clinic from Blødkjær jail where she was still being held in custody pending trial. She was a more normal person than Hamsun and was overawed by Langfeldt. In her memoirs in which she describes the meeting,[3] she writes that after some routine questions the professor then asked her certain questions that left her speechless. She asked if it was absolutely necessary for her to answer, and Langfeldt insisted. He told her that it was essential if he were to get a complete picture of her husband. Before proceeding with her answers, she warned that if Hamsun ever found out about it, it would mean the end of their marriage. The doctor assured her that the information she was about to give would be strictly confidential. She then unburdened herself to him, and delivered a full and uncensored account of the last years of their married life together. Since he was seventy-eight, she said, her husband had changed considerably. He had become difficult, impossible to handle, and had begun to show an interest in young girls. She stated categorically that he had been unfaithful to her on several occasions. He showed extreme aggression towards her because he felt that she was trying to take over the power in the house. He misjudged people hopelessly. Even the people who worked at the house could be accused of the wildest things, although she would not go so far as to call this a persecution mania. She stressed the extent to which Hamsun lived an isolated life, and went into some detail about their relationship at home. For her, it was a state of open hostility, with arguments, occasional threats of physical violence, threats of divorce, and threats on both sides to leave. She complained that Hamsun compared her unfavourably with his own mother (a comment that caused Langfeldt to report that Hamsun was 'strongly mother-fixated') and that he expressed from the beginning great disappointment over her as a woman. She paid tribute to his generosity, and mentioned his habit of sending money anonymously to struggling young writers whom he knew needed it. Overall she painted for Langfeldt a hellish picture of their relationship and one that did not take into account the many years of, albeit unusual, happiness that the pair had enjoyed during much of their married life. In giving it she was undoubtedly in thrall to the bitterness, and indeed hatred, with which she had regarded her husband since the late 1930s, and onwards throughout the war.

When the interview was over, she asked Langfeldt if she might see Hamsun. Langfeldt agreed, and she was taken to an empty room to wait while he was called. From afar she heard his astonished voice: 'Wife, you say? You mean *my* wife?' There was no joy in it. When he entered the room he simply stood and stared at her. 'What are you up to now?' he asked. His reaction made her understand what she had not realised before, that Hamsun regarded the professor as his deadly enemy. He knew quite well what Langfeldt had done, and by Marie's guilty and confused expression he also knew that she had betrayed him, and given his enemy the information he wanted. He spoke angrily to her. As he turned to leave he stopped at the door and very calmly said, 'Well then, I say goodbye to you Marie. We will not meet again.'[4] It was a statement of fact, a divorce by proclamation. And he meant what he said – nearly.

With that problem surmounted; Langfeldt continued his investigations. He would submit questions to Hamsun, and Hamsun would work on his answers in his cell by the light of a rather dim and remote bulb. They were literary productions to him, and he took some care over them:

(In the statement I have been asked to give to the Authorities on you I must include a description of the most important aspects of your personality. It will be useful to hear what you yourself think on this matter – in that I assume that you have, in the course of your life, analysed yourself thoroughly. As far as I can see, you have always been aggressive. Can you explain whether you think this is congenital, or has its origins in experiences during your upbringing.

At the same time it is my impression that you are extremely sensitive. Is this correct? What other characteristics do you find in yourself? Are you suspicious? Selfish or generous? Jealous by nature? Pronounced sense of fairness? Are you logical? Emotional or controlled?)

Hamsun: I have not analysed myself other than by in my books having created several hundred different characters, every one of them spun from myself, with faults and virtues such as all created characters have.

The so-called 'Naturalists', Zola and his period, wrote about people with dominant characteristics. They had no use for the more subtle psychology, people all had this 'dominant characteristic' which ordained their actions.

Dostoevsky and others taught us all something different about human beings.

From the time I began I do not think that in my entire output you will find a character with a single dominant characteristic. They are all without so-called 'character'. They are split and fragmented, not good and not bad, but both at once, subtle, and changeable in their attitudes and in their deeds.

No doubt I am also like this myself.

It is very possible that I am aggressive, that I have in me something of all the characteristics which the professor mentions. I am sensitive, suspicious, selfish, generous, jealous, righteous, logical, emotional, controlled. But I don't know that I could say that any one of them was more pronounced than the others in me. In addition I am fulfilled by a grace which has permitted me to write my books. But I cannot 'analyse' that.

Brandes has called it the 'divine madness'.

(Will you write (or dictate) a little more about your religious position. (What you mean by 'God'? Do you believe that there are powers beyond us which we cannot apprehend with our senses?))

Hamsun: Just before I was taken from the Old Folk's Home at

Landvik, a man walked into my room and said something. Because I didn't hear him he wrote it on a slip of paper for me: Are you saved?

I answered him, not quite so importunately: Are you yourself saved?

What I understand by the term God?

I am an autodidact and have not seen so many schoolbooks and learned works. By the grace of God I am still here on this earth in my eighty-seventh year.

(Describe your attitude towards religion. Has there been any change in it?)

Hamsun: Almost indifferent. I am not godless, but like all my friends and acquaintances, indifferent to questions of religion.

No, no change whatsoever. I am not much good at praying to God, but warmly grateful to him when he has been merciful, and saved me from something or other.

(I would like some account from you of the most important difficulties you have had in your life, and of the effect these have had on you)

Hamsun: I have been spared real trouble, and have had little of it in comparison to so many others. I have always been physically well, no illnesses, and a constitution that has tolerated much. Perhaps this is, among other reasons, because from my child-hood onwards I have learnt to do without.

At home, when we came in and complained of something, for an answer we'd get: 'That's nothing! It'll get worse than that!'

Like everyone else I have known hard times, but generally speaking they have had no lasting effect on me. I am a light-hearted man. I like to joke and laugh. I take after my father . . .

As regards opposition, I cannot really avoid mentioning the attacks on me in the newspapers. I made my name late in life, and even in my thirties attacks in the newspapers affected me strongly, I remember. But I did not brood on them.

Nils Vogt wrote in *Morgenbladet* 'The Apostle of humbug in our literature, the arch con-man of the new writing, Knut Hamsun.'

(If you on 9 April 1940 had known what you now know, among other things that the Germans have tortured and killed many of your fellow-countrymen, and that they have exercised a spiritual tyranny wherever they went, would you have written as you did in 1940?)

Hamsun: The question is hypothetical. This would naturally have changed my attitude towards the Germans.

The report concludes with the results of a series of medical tests on Hamsun, including an interesting test of his grasp of various concepts. The psychiatrists' evaluation of his answers shows clearly the very great difference in kind between the minds that devised and interpreted the tests, and the mind that was being tested:

Definition of Concepts is quite satisfactory. Eg: self-denial – 'to do without, to deprive oneself of an advantage'.
   Righteousness: Think right, do right.
   On the other hand he did poorly in identifying the *distinctions and similarities between two concepts*. Eg: what is the difference between a child and a dwarf: Answer: The age. What is the difference between self-confidence and conceit: Answer: Conceit will cause you to lose the job after self-confidence has got you the job.
   In answers to questions on *ethical concepts* certain curiosities cropped up. As, for example, when the patient was asked why one should not be untrue to one's wife he answered, 'Because she could do the same.' To a question on whom he admired above all, he answered, 'To put an end to it, Bjørnson.'

In their summing up, the psychiatrists laid stress on the harsh treatment Hamsun had received between the ages of eight to fourteen at the hands of his uncle Hans Olsen, and on the difficult years of his early manhood as he struggled for his literary breakthrough. The struggle was characterised by a hatred of all authority which they traced back to his years at Olsen's. His suspicious and reserved nature in the presence of strangers was attributed to the harsh nature of his upbringing, and the later literary struggle. His self-irony and self-assurance were defence-mechanisms that developed under the same impulses. They noted his unusual *capacity to endure*, his *extreme sensitivity* and his *powers of empathy* so great that at times they 'seem to have obliterated the distinction between himself and the surrounding world'. His pantheism, *extreme suggestibility*, and his boyhood *hallucinations* were related to this. His lifelong need for solitude puzzled them somewhat. Otherwise they commented on his *aggression*, his *generosity* – particularly to tramps and needy writers – coupled with a *parsimony in household matters* and a *fanatic exactitude in the paying back of even small debts*. His most attractive quality, at a quite personal level, they found to be his *absolute honesty*.

Summing up, they posited an inferiority complex in him which, coupled with guilt feelings brought on by the demanding nature of his instincts, caused strong conflicts within him. Further complications were caused by the fact that he was 'a pronounced leadertype who demanded the complete submission of those near him and around him'. Hamsun's deafness, isolation within the family, and his two apoplectic fits were recalled. In all, they confessed that 'it is rare to come across an eighty-six-year-old man who has such a lively interest in current affairs as the subject'. His mental condition in 1898 they described as a paranoid reaction, possibly induced by his fiancée. Thereafter they hop swiftly and rather unconvincingly to their conclusions – that the two strokes, in 1942 and 1944, weakened his power of judgement and his resistance considerably – and the fact that he presented Goebbels with his Nobel medal was evidence of this. Taken together with the increased emotional incontinence of his old age, and his extremely uncompromising attitude towards his family, they came finally to the two-point conclusion of their investigations:

1) We do not regard Knut Hamsun as insane and presume that neither was he insane during the time when the alleged crimes were carried out.

2) We regard him as a person of permanently impaired mental faculties, but do not consider there to be any realistic danger of his repeating the indictable offences.

Ørnulv Ødegård

Vindern 5/2/1946
Gabriel Langfeldt

On 11 February, Hamsun was released from the clinic, after a stay of 119 days, and although now free to return to Nørholm, he decided instead to return to the Old Folk's Home at Landvik as a paying guest. Marie was still periodically at Nørholm as she awaited a date for her trial, and Hamsun refused to be under the same roof with her. 'She is my bad conscience', he was reported as saying. His rent at Landvik was 150 kroner per month, and the daily regime he followed there the same as it was for other tenants: rise at six and light his stove; morning coffee at seven; lunch at twelve; afternoon coffee at three; and an evening snack at seven. Otherwise he read, walked and wrote. As a paying guest he enjoyed the privilege of having his meals served to him in his room. It was all undoubtedly an interesting experience for him to have been so unceremoniously returned to the world of ordinary human beings again after so many years of not so very splendid isolation, and with the responsibilities of being a 'great man' finally removed from him. The four months at the clinic had worn him out mentally and physically, but he was glad to be free again. As usual, he charmed those with whom he came into personal contact: another tenant, a woman of sixty-three, described him as 'the most stylish man in the Home. If only the others were like him.'[5]

On 18 February the Attorney-General announced that:

> After the findings of the experts, I have decided that the public good will not be served by proceeding with a case against the accused, who will soon be eighty-seven years old and is to all intents and purposes deaf. I thereby drop the charge against him by the authority vested in me in Section 85 of the Penal Code, Part 2 paragraph I.

The country was thus spared the embarrassment of putting Hamsun in the dock, and at the same time could take the opportunity to return a little of the contempt he had showered on his countrymen from his privileged position during the early years of the Occupation. However, the Crown did decide to proceed against him on the lesser charge of being member number 26,000 of NS after 8 April 1940, and to claim compensation from him for his part in the damage done to the country by the Party during the Occupation, a total estimated at 300 million kroner. The charge was filed at Agder on 15 May 1946. After an evaluation of Hamsun's financial situation, it was announced that in due course he would be proceeded against with a claim for half a million kroner. Interestingly, Dr Langfeldt was opposed to the decision. His reasoning was that the Crown should accept all of the logical consequences of his findings on Hamsun, and absolve him also of economic responsibility for his actions during the war.[6] His was a minority viewpoint, though. The press particularly were keen to see Hamsun in the dock.

The Norwegian legal system was still blocked by the dreary passage of others of the 40,000 NS members, and it was to be eighteen months before the case was finally heard. Hamsun, in the meantime, felt keenly the contempt implied in the wording of the psychiatric report on him, that he was 'of permanently impaired mental faculties'. Even more keenly he experienced the dropping of the criminal charges as an insult. In letters to Christian Gierløff he insisted, like Quisling, that everything he had done had been for the sake of Norway. On this one point these two very different men shared a similarity. Both were equally sincere in their patriotism and both equally incapable of comprehending the claims of democracy. Hamsun was adamant that he would take responsibility for everything he had done, though even he would probably have drawn the line if asked to share the price paid by Quisling, executed by firing squad on 24 October 1945. He felt that in dropping the criminal charges, the Attorney-General had, as he put it, 'taken this weapon from my hand'. Somehow he had managed to persuade himself that he would be acquitted, or practically acquitted, before an ordinary court. For three or four months he brooded over the matter, and finally on 23 July sent a long letter to the Attorney-General, which later also appeared in *On Overgrown Paths*. He begins by protesting about the treatment he has received at the clinic, and about the presumed purpose of the examination. If this was indeed to have him declared insane, and so not responsible for his actions, then the Attorney-General has reckoned without him:

> From the first moment of the hearing held on 23 June I had assumed responsibility for what I had done and ever since have maintained that stand unswervingly. I knew, you see, in my heart that if I could speak without hindrance, the wind would turn for me towards acquittal, or as close to acquittal as I would dare go and the court accept. I knew that I was innocent, deaf and innocent; I would have readily got through an examination by the prosecuting attorney solely by relating most of the truth.

There is an extraordinary arrogance in this – complete acquittal is something he '*dare*' not risk; and he expects to get by by relating 'most of the truth'. However, the Attorney-General's action in dropping the charges has rendered him defenceless, impotent:

> Mr Attorney-General! When you announced the experts' judgement of me, you allowed the public at the same time to take for granted that you had broken off legal proceedings against me and withdrew the charges.
> Excuse me, but again you acted without me. You did not consider the possibility of my being dissatisfied with this decision. You forgot that in the hearings and always afterwards I have stood by what I had done and awaited sentencing. Your impulsive course of action caused me to dangle between heaven and earth, and my case was nevertheless not settled. Half of it remained. You thought I benefited thereby, but I did not, and I believe that some people will agree with me. Until recently I was not just anybody in Norway and the world, and it did not suit me to live out the rest of my days in a sort of amnesty from you

without having to answer for my action.

But you, Mr Attorney-General, struck the weapon from my hand.

You no doubt believe you have made amends now – afterwards – by issuing a summons calling me before the district court. This amends nothing. I have been thrust out of my secure and proper position.

In the end, he had to be satisfied with the offer of a civil action against him. This would be a major step towards his goal – the state's acknowledgement that he was indeed of sound mind, and fully responsible for his behaviour during the war.

Hamsun's wife was less fortunate than he. On 24 September 1946, Marie's case came up in Sand District Court. For her active membership of NS, and her very considerable propaganda activities on behalf of the Germans, she was sentenced to three years' labour, less 325 days for the time already served in custody. She was also fined 75,000 kroner, and suffered the temporary withdrawal of certain civil rights. For her part in the damage caused to the country by NS she was required to pay 150,000 kroner in compensation, an unusually large sum clearly based on the fact that she was Knut Hamsun's wife. Her appeal against the sentence was heard at the High Court on 20 September 1947. The decision at Sand was upheld, although the 75,000 kroner fine was waived, and on 9 December she entered Bredtvet jail in Grorud in Oslo.

One week later, on 16 December, it was Hamsun's turn to appear in the dock at Sand. It was at once clear what the central document in the case was going to be. This was a form, a questionnaire which was intended to accompany formal applications to join the Party. Here Hamsun had filled in answers to questions about his parents, confirmed that his wife's family was free from any Jewish blood, that he himself had never been married to a non-Aryan, and that, no, he had never been a freemason or member of any secret society. Under Section F, Special Remarks, he recalled with quiet pride ('it has perhaps not been quite forgotten') the series of newspaper articles he had written in defence of Germany during the First World War. But it was Section D that was to be the cause of all the legal head-scratching, and on which the court finally had to take its stand in order to deliver a judgement. Here the applicant was asked if he had previously been a member of NS, and if so, when had he enrolled? Hamson wrote: 'Have not been enrolled, but I have belonged to Quisling's Party.' It was an absolutely classic statement of the strangely fundamental tentativeness of his attitude towards things, one of the thousand *perhapses* and *maybes* of his novels making a sudden and baffling appearance in the real world of the courtroom. Hamsun signed and dated the form: Nørholm, 15 January 1942. To add to the puzzle, another hand had written at the top of the form 'Enrolled in NS 22/12/40', and stamped it with the membership number 26000. If Hamsun and his lawyer Sigrid Stray could persuade the jury of two lay-judges and one judge's deputy that this document was insufficient evidence to prove that he had been a party member after 8 April 1940, then he could walk from the court with his fortune intact.

Hamsun's position in regard to NS recalls unavoidably his own words in his 1894 article on Kristofer Randers, in which he describes how the passionate independence of the true individual is always characterised, almost in spite of itself, by a burning sympathy for the views of an ordinary political party. The individual burns for the success of that party – and yet never takes the final act of commitment by actually *joining* it. Thus the escape route of withdrawal into total individuality, the freedom to deny absolutely that he meant what he has just said, is always open to him. This is both a mechanism of self-defence, and an affirmation of the right of the creative artist to create and inhabit his own moral universe. One is reminded of a characteristic of Hamsun's fictional heroes, the energetic expression of interest in something – a love affair, or a project – followed by abrupt disavowal of all interest in it. It also characterises *On Overgrown Paths*, with its constant small surges of passion quelled by protestations of indifference. He will not be caught, he refuses to be defined. One of the notes that passed between Hamsun and Sigrid Stray in court illustrates well his attitude:

> I have been asked to become a Freemason, a Rotarian, even a member of a Temperance Lodge – and have refused. No one asked me to be a member of NS – but I would have said no to them also. I belong to no corporation. I am free.[7]

And in his long speech to the court Hamsun tried again to put the case for his freedom:

> What tells against me, strikes me to the ground, is wholly and solely my articles in the newspapers. There is nothing else that can be brought against me. For my part I can give a very simple and clear accounting. I have not informed against anyone, have not attended meetings, have not even got involved in the black

market. I have not contributed to the Front Fighters or any other National Socialist group, which it is now said that I was a member of. Nothing, in short. I have not belonged to the National Socialists. I have tried to grasp what National Socialism means, I have tried to understand what it stands for, but it came to nothing. But it may well be that now and then I did write in a Nazi spirit. I do not know, for I do not know what the Nazi spirit is. But it may well be that I did write in the Nazi spirit, that it might have filtered down a little to me from the newspapers I read. In any case my articles are there for anyone to see. I make no attempt to slight them, to make them less than they are; it is bad enough as it is. On the contrary, I stand behind them now as before and as I always have.

What he is quite unable to understand is that the majority of Norwegians did not share his dream of Norway assuming a position of honour within a new and revitalised Europe under the leadership of Germany. It was for this dream he wrote, for Norway. The language with which he describes it indicates how this dream obsessed him:

That thought appealed to me from the very start. It did more, it enchanted me, it captivated me. I don't know that I was free of it any moment in all the time I sat there in solitude. I believed it to be a great idea for Norway, and I believe to this day that it was a great and good idea for Norway, well worth fighting and working for: Norway, an independent, radiant land on the outskirts of Europe!

Too soon though, developments compromised him:

But my efforts did not work out well at all, not at all. I was all too soon confused in my own mind and fell into the deepest confusion when the King and his government voluntarily left the country and put themselves out of operation here at home. It swept the ground right from under me. I was left dangling between heaven and earth. I had nothing firm to hang on to any longer. So I sat and wrote, sat and telegraphed and brooded. My condition in those times was brooding. I brooded over everything.

He describes how he found himself trying to help both sides, with his telegrams and letters to Hitler and Terboven, and that these efforts of his left him in an even more exposed position during the war years:

. . . it was these same telegrams that finally made the Germans a little suspicious of me. They regarded me as a sort of mediator, a slightly undependable mediator whom they'd best keep their eye on. Hitler himself finally turned down my pleas. They bored him. He referred me to Terboven, but Terboven did not answer me.

For all the subtleties of his situation, and for all the many mitigating half-truths he offers up, including the statement that 'no one told me that it was wrong that I sat there and wrote, no one in the whole country', he does not express any regret or guilt. He was too old, and had been playing the 'great man' for too long to do that. In the most straightforward terms he stated his position for the court. He must have known that his words would not win him any sympathy, that they were indeed a disdainment of sympathy, and to have gone ahead with them as he did was just another sign of that eerily heroic obstinacy with which he pursued the task of being Knut Hamsun throughout his life:

Because I sat there and wrote as best I knew how and sent telegrams night and day, it is said now that I was betraying my country. I was a traitor, it is said. Never mind. But I did not feel it to be so at the time, did not deem it to be so, nor do I deem it to be so today. I am at peace with myself, my conscience is completely clear.

I have rather high regard for public opinion. I have an even higher regard for Norwegian justice, but I do not regard it as highly as I regard my own consciousness of what is right and wrong. I am old enough to have a code of conduct for myself, and it is mine.[8]

The court listened to his speech, and for three days struggled with the niceties of his position, but in the end took their stand on the matter. The judge's Deputy, the foreman of the jury, acquitted Hamsun on all charges, since he found that his membership of NS was not proven. The two lay judges, however, decided that his willingness to be taken for a member of NS, and his many close approaches in statements to the police and the psychiatrists to the effect that he had 'drifted into' the Party, were reason enough to decide that he must bear responsibility for the fact that he was registered as a member from January 1942 onwards. Sentence was passed on 19 December. Hamsun was to pay compensation to the country of 425,000 kroner.

His extreme isolation, especially towards the end of the war, was

taken into account, as was his constant willingness to apply to the
very highest German authorities on behalf of imprisoned and
condemned Norwegians. This, taken with the 150,000 kroner in
compensation claimed by the Crown from Marie Hamsun, was a
ruinously large fine, and was clearly intended to be so. On 29
December he gave notice of appeal against the sentence on two
grounds: that it was a miscarriage of justice to declare, on the
evidence produced by the court, that he had been a member of NS,
and that the compensation claimed was too high, in that his
fortune had been assessed by the Crown at 500,000 kroner,
whereas he and Marie together had been sentenced to pay 575,000
kroner.

After lodging his appeal, Hamsun returned to Nørholm. Consistently, before, during, and after his trial, in letters to family and
friends, he had insisted that his personal fate was a matter of
indifference to him. The fierce realist disappeared. Now, and for
the rest of life, he was the Taoist. Glory had come to him, stayed
awhile and gone its way again. As he reminded the court, 'The
names of everyone present here today will be obliterated from the
earth in a hundred years and will be remembered no more, named
no more. It is our fate to be forgotten.' His sense of economic
responsibility, however, had not deserted him. He felt keenly that
he had brought ruin upon his children, and that he must try to do
something about it. With some justification, he now spoke of
himself as 'a dead man as a writer'.[9] In 1947 in Norway, fifty copies
of his *Collected Works* were sold, sixty-seven copies of *The Growth of
the Soil*, thirty-eight copies of *Hunger*, thirty-eight copies of *The
Wild Choir*, plus isolated copies of other works. Abroad his sales
had come to a similar standstill.

From the time when he was taken from Nørholm and placed in
Grimstad Hospital in June 1945, he had been keeping a kind of
diary or journal of events. He had kept it going at the clinic,
working secretly and writing between the lines of another book
since he was under observation and feared, probably with some
justice, that the staff would confiscate the diary and bring it to the
attention of Langfeldt. Originally he wrote probably to comfort
himself in the face of the thousand small humiliations of insti-
tutional life that he suffered daily at the clinic. His intense privacy
was breached by experiences such as having his clothes removed
from his room at night, and his papers gone through by the staff.
On one occasion a nurse borrowed his shaving equipment without
permission and used it to shave other patients before returning it
damaged. There wasn't much else he could do but write about all
this. Anyway, writing was the only thing he was ever really good

at, the only thing he ever really liked. And now the imposition of these enormous fines suddenly provided him with a purpose to continue; encouraged by Christian Gierløff, he decided that he would turn his journal into a book and try to publish it. Even if its success were only scandalous, it would redeem him in his own eyes as a provider by bringing in money for his children. The idea quickly became an obsession. 'I will go so far as to say', he wrote to Victoria in France, 'that I would most probably already be dead by now if I had not had this book to work on.'[10] There were other driving forces behind it too – a burning hatred of Dr Langfeldt, and a desire to put his 'permanently weakened mental faculties' on public display so that people could make up their own minds about his mental state. As he told Gierløff, 'I feel there is little point in living out the rest of my days with that placard on my back.'[11]

He worked hard on the book at Nørholm while he waited for his appeal to be heard. The physical difficulties involved in the act of writing were now considerable. The shaking in his right hand, and a marked deterioration of his eyesight, meant that on bad days the lines could wander about all over the page; but he kept at it, nevertheless.

Hamsun's appeal was heard at the High Court on 18 and 19 June 1948. He had allowed himself to entertain hopes that the whole case would founder on the technicality of the NS form, particularly in view of the fact that the legally trained member of the bench at his first trial had found him not guilty. He regretted bitterly ever having filled the form out. To him it was merely a dreadful tactical error, a fatal wobble in the middle of a tight-rope walk in which he had accidentally dipped his foot in the water. 'If only I hadn't been so *careless* as to fill out the form', he wrote to Sigrid Stray.[12]

It did indeed prove to be a fatal slip: the High Court confirmed by a unanimous decision the verdict of the district court while Hamsun's point about the discrepancy between the compensation claimed and the estimate of his fortune was granted, and the figure reduced to 325,000 kroner (£16,250).

Thus on 23 June 1948, the long battle between Knut Hamsun and democracy, in which his family had been irresistibly and inevitably caught up, came to an end. In the course of it he had demonstrated to the enemy some of the extraordinary things that could be achieved by an individual brave enough to ignore the crowd. 'It delights me to be reckless, so that decent people drop their jaws and gawp at me', he had written to Bolette Larsen back in 1890. Yet it was a difficult and a dangerous game that had finally got out of control and ended very badly indeed. Democracy showed for years not merely its tolerance, but its keen appreciation of the lessons and joys to be had from his experiment in living: but when he took his contempt too far it showed also that it had contained all along the power to curb him. Even had he triumphed in the court case, he would probably have lived to regret it. It would have left him on a winning side, and the strategy on which he had based his personality and its relationship to society depended always for real success, at the deepest level, on his own defeat. He was not a bully. All his life he had tormented democracy, and there would have been no satisfaction in it for him had democracy, in the end, proved unable to stand up for itself.

Overall, one is left with the feeling that the Norwegian authorities after the war handled a difficult problem with firmness and tact. Bearing in mind Ezra Pound's thirteen years in an American Military Asylum for offences similar to Hamsun's, and the eighteen months Céline spent in jail, Hamsun was leniently treated. Of the other members of the family, the eldest son Tore was fined, while his brother Arild, as a former front-fighter, served a jail sentence which kept him out of circulation until May 1949. Marie was released from prison in the autumn of 1948. Her fine of 75,000 kroner had been waived on appeal to the High Court on 20 September 1947; and on 17 October 1951 the Justice Department released her from the claim for 150,000 kroner in compensation. She lived with Tore and his family at his house in Asker, a suburb of Oslo. Her husband would not have her back at Nørholm. The verbal divorce of December 1945 had not been rescinded.

Hamsun spent the next three days after the appeal brooding over the judgement. He read it over and over again, as though he could not quite believe it. The faithful Gierløff was with him (and planning to write a book about him). 'Where's the proof here?' he kept saying, 'Where's the *proof*?' Then on the fourth day he put it all behind him, telegraphed a thanks to Sigrid Stray for her 'magnificent defence', and devoted himself completely to the task of finishing the book, and the by no means easy matter of finding someone willing to publish it. He was, after all, as he had written to Harald Grieg back in March 1946, 'a dead man in Norway and the world'.[13]

Chapter 18

1948–1952: The Last Years:
On Overgrown Paths

Hamsun's relationships with his publishers had always been personal. Both Harald Grieg and his predecessor Christian Kønig had been his friends as well as his publishers, so that signed contracts were not always necessary to make verbal agreements between them binding. Grieg and Hamsun had also continued a friendly relationship after the Occupation in spite of being on opposite sides, and had even joked about Hamsun's visit to Terboven to plead for Ronald Fangen. Hamsun described how he had pleaded for Fangen's family, whereupon Grieg laughed and said that 'Fangen has no family'.[1] Soon, however, the war took a more serious turn for Harald Grieg. In mid-1941 he was deposed at Gyldendal by the Germans and spent a year in prison before being released, probably as a direct result of the Hamsun family's pleas to the same Terboven. And in December 1943 he lost his talented literary brother Nordahl Grieg in a bombing raid over Berlin. The war thus had deeper immediate personal consequences for him than it did for Hamsun, whose major material privation had been the requisitioning of the family Cadillac by the Germans.

After the war, early in 1946, Hamsun wrote to Grieg with a query about an annuity for Ellinor Hamsun. A tradition established from the very earliest days of the relationship between Hamsun and Gyldendal was that the managing director alone had the honour of corresponding with the illustrious author. When Grieg now delegated the job of replying to one of his subordinates, Hamsun was puzzled, and asked Grieg what the matter was:

> It cannot be my 'treason', so it must be something else. I can't work it out myself, and I would be glad if you would tell me what it is. I know I'm a dead man in Norway and the world, but you

surely can't be trying to impress that upon me. What is it then? I ask you in all sincerity to tell me if it is something I have done, or have left undone.

Grieg replied:

Dear Hamsun,
    You wonder 'what it is that has come between you and I'. The answer is very simple: In a battle for life and death we stood on different sides – and still do. There are few people I have admired as much as you, few I have loved so. None has disappointed me more.

On 5 April Hamsun wrote back:

Dear Grieg,
    I thank you for your letter. It is a gift. I have nothing else to say.
                                                            Your Knut Hamsun

The irony misfired. Hamsun had intended this as a cutting and curt end to the friendship, and with it the business relationship with Gyldendal. Grieg, on the other hand, was pleased by the letter. He took it to be a sincere expression of thanks from Hamsun for his honest answer, an interpretation that seemed to him to be supported by the friendly form of address and salutation. He was surprised when Hamsun, via his lawyer Sigrid Stray, began trying to manoeuvre a legal break with Gyldendal.

    Rather unrealistically, given the post-war climate of opinion, Hamsun now complained that Gyldendal were not marketing him with sufficient enthusiasm.* He claimed that he had been receiving letters from readers who had been unable to buy copies of his books; Gyldendal were clearly defaulting on their agreement with him, and he was justified in regarding their arrangement as at an end. Above all, in his anger with Grieg, he wanted to make sure they would not get his new book, *On Overgrown Paths*. The matter was more complicated than he realised, however. Gyldendal denied that his books were not available to the public, and said that if orders were not coming through to them, this was the book-sellers' responsibility. Moreover, while he was free to go where he

---

* The company owned the legal rights to publish everything he had written. One of the basic obligations a publisher is under to an author is to market his books enthusiastically, and to make sure they are always available to the public via booksellers.

liked with the new book, they had legal rights to all his old books, and intended to keep them.

For a while Hamsun considered the possibility of publishing *On Overgrown Paths* himself. Had he gone ahead and done so it would have marked an eerie closing of a literary circle that had opened seventy years earlier with the publication of *Bjørger* at his own expense in Bodø in 1878. The practical problems were too great, however. He realised that he could die at any time, and that the simplest way forward was the best. The confirmation at the High Court on 23 June of his financial ruin and the problems posed by raising the money to pay the fine were inevitably going to drive him into Grieg's arms anyway.

The book itself was finished shortly after the trial and Hamsun handed the manuscript over to Sigrid Stray. Shortly afterwards she brought Harald Grieg into the picture. Hamsun's huge fine could not be managed without a loan, and on behalf of Gyldendal, Grieg offered to arrange such a loan on condition that the company were given the rights to publish it. He insisted on reading it, however, before making a final decision on whether or not to make an offer for the book. He had no way of knowing what manner of work Hamsun had produced. The firm's reputation might be seriously compromised were they to publish – so soon after the war – anything that smacked of self-defence.

In the event, Grieg found that many of his fears were confirmed. In a long letter of 31 July to Sigrid Stray he praised *On Overgrown Paths* as a unique human document, and recognised that it was a sovereign rebuttal of the description of the author as someone with 'permanently impaired mental faculties'. He was disturbed to find, however, that Hamsun appeared not to have changed his mind about what he had said during the war. He did not appear to have repented. Grieg felt that Norwegian readers would be particularly upset at the frequency with which Hamsun described in the book the many small acts of kindness people had shown to him during the period when he was awaiting trial. He regarded this as an attempt to convey an impression that he was everywhere generally regarded with sympathy. The publication of such a book so soon after the war would, Grieg assured Fru Stray, inevitably provoke an adverse press reaction which would badly damage the book's chances of selling well.

Fru Stray, along with various other people interested in helping Hamsun to get his book published – including Christian Gierløff, Max Tau, and Tore Hamsun – was meanwhile investigating the possibility of finding a home for it abroad. She had succeeded in raising positive interest from Bonniers in Sweden, and for a

German-language edition by a Swiss publisher, Ex-Libris. Yet one feels this manoeuvring was largely to strengthen their own bargaining position in dealing with Grieg. Gyldendal was the one they wanted, and needed, and Gyldendal for their part undoubtedly wanted *On Overgrown Paths* too. Grieg was a good businessman, and no doubt shared Hamsun's own sense that the book would arouse enormous curiosity when published. Where the parties disagreed strongly was over the question of timing. Hamsun wanted it out as soon as possible, before he was dead; Grieg was adamant that bitter memories from the war must be given time to fade slightly. And in addition to his point about the generally unrepentant tone of *On Overgrown Paths*, there were one or two specific points that he was very unhappy about. In the section dealing with Hamsun's internment in the psychiatric clinic at Blindern he felt that the description and discussion of Langfeldt suffered from the intensity of his personal hatred of the man, and damaged the artistic quality of the book. Hamsun the artist agreed with him, and willingly restated his dislike of the professor in more controlled fashion. On another related point though, he was not so co-operative. Grieg wanted him to remove the name Langfeldt from the book. His argument was that the name would mean nothing abroad, and that its inclusion risked characterising *On Overgrown Paths* as a largely personal affair, the pursuit of an obscure personal vendetta. In this he enlisted the support of Fru Stray herself as well as Hamsun's other supporters – notably Gierløff and Tore and Arild Hamsun. Hamsun regarded their position as simple cowardice, and he was probably right that Grieg was nervous about the possible reaction from Langfeldt to being turned into a character in a Hamsun book. For over three months Hamsun was subjected to pressures to change or withdraw the name. Predictably, the more he was pressed, the more he resisted. Finally, in a letter of 9 May 1949 to Sigrid Stray, it became clear that he was in fact willing to forego publication of *On Overgrown Paths* rather than give in on this score:

To Lawyer Fru Stray,
Both you and Grieg should respect an old writer's self-defence, and not interfere when he writes in a way you don't approve of in his last book.
I have my reasons, and I won't humiliate myself.
Let Grieg go back on his word and refuse to publish me, let him keep the proof copy – if need be my real intentions can remain locked away until after my death.
For the last time:

I will not remove Langfeldt's name from my book.

One cannot help feeling that in some ways the matter developed into a power struggle between the two old friends, with both parties at various times trying to express their ultimate independence of each other. As things turned out, a bargaining position appeared. To the first set of corrected proofs Hamsun had returned to Gyldendal he had added an insulting footnote about two named Norwegians, Odd Nansen and Ella Anker. These were people whose wartime letters to him condemning his journalism were produced at his trial to refute his claim to the court that 'no one told me that it was wrong that I sat there and wrote, no one in the whole country.' His footnote to this sentence, reproduced as part of his speech to the court, said that 'I am reminded that I got letters from Ella Anker and a letter from Odd Nansen. But I was getting letters from Iceland and India in those days, I didn't keep rubbish like that.'

Odd Nansen was the son of Fridtjof Nansen, and a Resistance hero who had spent the war from 1942 onwards in prison camps. Grieg found the expression 'rubbish' in connection with his letter unacceptable, and gave Sigrid Stray to understand that unless the footnote were withdrawn, he would refuse to publish the book. However, it emerged in a letter from Hamsun to Sigrid Stray that Hamsun had become worried by the lengths to which Gierløff was taking his role as liaison man between himself and Gyldendal, and suspected him of acting as a private censor. Nor did he like the idea of Gierløff's writing a book about him. He suspected that Gierløff's concern for his material was not entirely altruistic, and had sneaked in the offending footnote as bait in a trap. Having satisfied himself that Gierløff was indeed ignoring his refusal to let him have proof copies of what he was writing by going direct to Gyldendal with his request, Hamsun willingly dropped the footnote. In Grieg's eyes this must have seemed like victory – and on the wave of relief and triumph the name Langfeldt slipped through into the final text of the book. It was at last ready for publication in a form acceptable to all.

There were still disagreements, however, over the exact date of publication. Hamsun, who perhaps never really admitted to himself the true extent of his unpopularity at the time, hoped for some time that Gyldendal could be persuaded to publish the book in honour of his ninetieth birthday on 4 August 1949. Grieg refused, and the compromise formula he suggested instead was accepted. A few days before the 4th, Gyldendal released a statement to the press: 'Knut Hamsun, who will be ninety years old on 4 August, has written a new book which Gyldendal will be publishing in the autumn.' It eventually appeared on 28 September in a first edition of 5000 copies which sold out immediately. A second print run of 7000 copies was ordered a few days later. It was published simultaneously in Sweden, and in three different German-language editions the following year.

On Overgrown Paths is Hamsun's real last book, after the 'false' last book of 1936, *The Ring is Closed*. It covers the three years from the house arrest at Nørholm on 26 May 1945 to the hearing of the appeal at the High Court in June 1948, but as a historical document of the period it must be approached with some caution. Hamsun undoubtedly was, as Grieg suspected, deliberately trying to create an impression that he was generally regarded with sympathy by the people he came across. In fact, of course, he *was* regarded sympathetically by most of those he met in the limited world in which he was then moving, but largely on account of his considerable personal charm, not his political views. Elsewhere in the book he manages, for example, to convey the clear impression that he was effectively a prisoner for the three years that he is writing about, whereas he was in fact a free man after his release from Langfeldt's clinic in February 1946. It was his own choice to return to Landvik Old Folk's Home as a paying guest afterwards. Art, though, has little to do with factual reportage, and with the passage of time the book has taken on an existence independent of its origins in historical fact.

A first-person narration written in Hamsun's best prose-style, swift and deceptively simple, it is eerily unlike every other book he produced from 1912 onwards, and probably has most in common with the two *Wanderer* books of 1906 and 1909 with which it shares the propensity to philosophise while describing the everyday round of life. Gone is the turgidity and prolixity that characterises the worst of the later 'official' work, and gone too, in the main, is the preoccupation with 'great ideas'. The book's real joy is that Hamsun rediscovered at the end of his days his greatest strength – the matchless ability to celebrate the scintillating brilliance of the trivial in life, joy in small things, details, the affirmation of the value of the useless.

Systems and great ideas, all the weighty superstructure with which human consciousness burdens itself in its search for meaning, are lightly abandoned, and he realises again what he had known all along but forgotten – that nothing is more important than the taste of a piece of wall-fern on his tongue. The hurricane of disapproval that blew over him after the war finally managed to move him on after years becalmed in the past, and for the first time in over thirty years he was able to write a book that in spite of its being speckled with remote memories gives an overwhelming sense of being about the present moment. Paradoxically there is also a sense of liberation and release about the description of his life on remand which comes from the fact that people no longer expected anything of him. He was no longer required to play, either for himself or his public, the 'great man' who knew what he was talking about. Fame and respectability had stolen from him one of his most prized possessions – his anonymity. With disgrace he resumed possession of his privacy, and with a sense of release he could lay aside the props of respectability, and stop playing a part that somewhere deep inside himself he had never quite ceased to find ridiculous:

> Naturally, I have hardening of the arteries, but that makes no difference either, does not bother me. When I want to put on airs, I call it gout. It is now more than a year since I quit using a cane. What did I need a cane for? It was merely a kind of affectation, like setting my hat on my head a little rakishly and so on. Was the cane any support to me? No. We had become companions, but nothing more. When we fell, we always lay far far apart from each other in the snow.

So might Chuang Tzu or Lao Tzu have written about the stick and the hat. They were affectations to which Hamsun had been in thrall, in greater or lesser degree, since his fiftieth year and his disastrous election to the post of 'dikterkongen' after the death of Bjørnson in 1910. If one might hazard a single main cause for the fact that his life ended in such disaster, it might well have something to do with this business of affectation, and the relationship that was entered into between the writer and his public in that year. Hamsun's natural vanity, hysterically encouraged by a Norwegian press desperate for a new 'great man of letters' to replace the departed quartet of literary father-figures, Ibsen, Kielland, Lie and Bjørnson, led to his accepting the invitation to play a part for which, as man and writer, he was completely unsuited. His tragedy was that he, essentially the modern, neurotic, outsider type of artist, a traveller in inner landscapes, tried to force himself into the older literary tradition into which he was born, that of the writer as the sane and healthy spokesman for a society. Besides Bjørnson, Hamsun's other early idol as man and stylist was Strindberg. Two more disparate types could hardly be imagined, and it is little wonder that Hamsun's attempts to unify in himself these images of the paternal and the demonic ended in such disaster. Nagel's meditations on the nature of 'greatness' in *Mysteries* make it clear that the wise child Hamsun saw through the whole business and recognised it all as largely a question of acting. As he grew older and stiffer in the mind, and less willing to accept in himself such irreverent views, he began to take the acting seriously. One wonders whether the changeover from first- to third-person narrations after 1912 played a part here; whether in abandoning one of the most characteristic and attractive features of his first-person narrations – the ability to make fun of himself – he lost the psychologically necessary corrective to the megalomania in his personality. His letters to friends and family show that he preserved to the end a matchless ability to ironise over himself and his pretensions – but this was in private – and the willingness to make a fool of himself for his public, to play the clown for his readers, disappeared. Remarkably unchanged, it appears once again in *On Overgrown Paths*. Out walking near Landvik one day he stumbles over the edge of the road and slides on his arse down into a rubbish pit:

> I looked about. From where I was sitting it was no longer so abysmally far to the bottom, not bottomless after all. I felt rather pleased with the lake far below, despised it a little, looked down on it. It was by chance that I had landed here, and I was in no mind to let chance have the victory. I pretended that I was extremely busy poking round in the rubbish; here were interesting things, bits of steel wire and bones and a dead cat and tin boxes. Should someone in a car stop up there on the road, he was not to suppose that I had tumbled down; I would show him that I was looking for something, that I was looking for some important pieces of paper which had been blown out of my hand.

The book is full of this kind of gentle self-mockery, and contains other examples of Hamsun's childlike and often rather sad humour. 'Someone calls to me, I hear it – ' he writes, only to admit in the next line, 'But it is not so, only my imagination. I want to be interesting to myself.' One realises again that one of the most powerful sensations aroused by Hamsun's first-person novels is the sense of the natural loneliness of the main character. Glahn, Nagel, Johannes, and the narrator of *Hunger*, are all lonely men who feel uneasy in company, who seem happiest when alone. In their solitude they find company and comfort and interest in the world of natural and inanimate objects which surround them.

Part of Hamsun's genius as a writer was that he could with

apparent effortlessness show the limitless nature of the potential in trifles. Like a conjuror he could take some small detail and use it as a fulcrum with which to throw a whole life into sudden brilliant relief. While poking about in the rubbish pit into which he has fallen he finds a newspaper buried in a pile, and tries to drag it clear. A single strip comes away in his hand. He pockets it nevertheless and takes it back to his room at the Home and reads it:

Naturally the booty could have been richer, but that is nothing to grumble over. For that matter maybe the booty is not so wretched when I have got a look at it. It was a scrap of newspaper without beginning or end, a rather long text, but unfortunately so badly torn that it had lost any meaning. So far as I could understand, it had to do with a man and his wife who could not get along with each other, a rather ordinary situation from the life of artists. I could have thrown away the paper, but I wanted to have something for having taken it home. In any case I took care not to dramatise the episode. Here I sat with the power to do as I pleased. I could simply reconcile these two people, these rascals. Go home and make up!

That scrap of paper 'without beginning or end', of course, tells the story of his life. Feeling, probably, that he had made his point, and at ninety-one years of age willing at last to embrace inevitable defeat in the battle of the sexes, Hamsun did indeed reconcile these two people, these rascals, and asked Marie to come back to him. She returned to Nørholm in the spring of 1950. There was no discussion of the intervening four years. 'You were gone a long time, Marie,' was all he said to her, 'All the time you've been gone I've had no one to talk to but God.'

She nursed him for the last two years of his life. With the publication of *On Overgrown Paths* the last urgent reason for staying alive was gone from him, and at long, long, long last he accepted that he was a very old man indeed. He even accepted philosophically final indignities such as becoming a target for the entertainment of local children who had discovered what fun it was to ambush him with snowballs as he went stumbling, shrunken and Father-Christmas-bearded, through the woods round Nørholm on his daily walks to the Reddals canal. He simply abandoned the walks. Nor would he give Marie permission to seek the children out and tick them off. The great indifference was upon him.

Yet there was still one part of him that could be touched by the world outside. On 7 March 1951 Sigrid Stray drove to Nørholm in response to a telephone call from Marie Hamsun about some legal business she wished to discuss with her. She took with her a copy of Gyldendal's new catalogue which Grieg had sent her and asked her to show to Hamsun. On one page was a large picture of Hamsun's *Collected Works*, and on another a fine photograph of him with a few lines about his life. She noticed the great changes at Nørholm. The farm was neglected, the paint peeling. The roof of one of the outhouses had collapsed many months before under the weight of a heavy winter's snow, but there was no money to raise it again. The Hamsuns themselves went in rags, and she noticed particularly the change in him, the long white beard, the half-blind eyes, and all trace of the magisterial bearing gone. As they sat indoors over coffee, Hamsun began as usual to thank her for coming out to see them. She then showed him what she had with her from Gyldendal. Hamsun wept with disbelieving joy and relief. 'What news this is you've brought with you', he kept saying, 'That I should have lived to see this day.' He found it difficult to believe that he had been forgiven, that he would live again as a writer. Again he wept, saying 'And Grieg has done this for me'. Presently he recovered enough to apologise, and to see her to the door. He asked her politely about her own affairs, his voice now clear and firm as it had always been. Outside, Marie Hamsun told her how Hamsun passed the days. On fine days they sat out in the garden in their favourite seat under a laburnum tree. In the evenings Hamsun would sit in his chair and read, usually the Bible.*

All his life he had been very particular about knowing what time of day it was. During the last two years his sight failed, so that he could no longer see his watch. Marie bought him a large, round, red wall-clock, and he would sit in his armchair with this in his lap. It had no glass in the face, so that he could feel the fingers with his hands. Sometimes when he nodded off it fell on to the floor, but it never broke.

'What's the worst thing you can imagine?' he was asked once in a questionnaire in Gyldendal's Christmas Catalogue. 'To die!' he replied, 'I wouldn't dream of doing it unless I had to.' Even he had

---

* A preacher, Jørgen Grave, accosted Hamsun once on one of his walks round Landvik Old Folk's Home, and reported the following exchange to a journalist. 'Do you read the Bible, Hamsun?' I shouted into his ear.

'The Bible? Yes, I read it. I've read it many times.'

'What do you think of it?'

'What do I think of it? It's a wonderful book, a wonderful book.'

'It is *the* Book. It shows us the way,' I shouted.

He waved his stick, but did not answer. Then he turned and continued along the path towards the Home.

to go in the end though. One night he protested when Marie tried to move his pillows to make him more comfortable. Then he slept for forty-eight hours, and at midnight on 19 February 1952 he died in his sleep. Marie was sitting by the bed with him, and on the wall above him were pictures of Goethe and his beloved Dostoevsky.

In Norway, a country which can seem almost embarrassingly keen to honour its writers, and erects statues of them, portrays them on stamps and paper money, and names streets after the least of them, Hamsun's life remains largely uncommemorated by official-dom. There is a museum at Lom in Gudbrandsdal, where he was born; and another small museum on the farm at Hamsund where he grew up. On a neighbouring hill, hidden away, stands a bust of him. At the back of nearby Presteid, where he lived with his uncle Hans as a boy, there is a narrow dirt-road, with no houses along it, which is called 'Knut Hamsun's Way'. There is another bust of him as a young man, again in an out of the way spot, at Kjerringøy, the Nordland trading post where in 1879 he met the great Zahl whose money gave him a start as a writer. The city centre statues though, the street names, the squares, and public buildings have continued to elude him. Certain tourist guides to the country and its great men contain no references to him. Perhaps he would have preferred it so. His attitude towards all fame was deeply ambiva-lent, and he was genuinely opposed to the celebration of the dead.

Yet Hamsun remains a living presence in the country. Thought about, written about and talked about, he has become a kind of human koan, a Zen riddle, a question to which the answer may not, after all, be the point. If the paths of great wisdom and great foolishness run close together, then he walked them both with the same kind of fearless helplessness, never quite knowing which one he was on at any given time, and never quite caring. He was more interested in living a life that would describe rather than explain him. Arild Hamsun once told him of a sympathetic newspaper article in which the writer had tried to explain his position during the war. He perhaps thought his father would be pleased, but he only swore and complained that 'they have done nothing but try to "explain" me for the last fifty or sixty years; it makes me sick'.[2] Marie Hamsun seems to have shared his suspicion of explanations. She described him as a unique man who lived out the destiny which his creator intended him for, and gave him the courage to bear. 'He is not to be pitied or forgiven', she said.[3]

Hamsun's real subject as a writer was the functioning of the human mind. Because he was able to describe his own with such accuracy and such insight, his best novels *Hunger*, *Pan*, and

Mysteries, remain remarkably undated. Their central character's obsessive interest in himself, and in the hidden effect of what he says and does on other characters, makes him a peculiarly appropriate hero for the late twentieth century. His view of personality as deliberate invention, and people as actors playing the part of themselves, is predictive of our own fascination with the cult of the image. The discovery made him cynical – in which he is also modern – but not dismissive. As he told Langfeldt:

> From the time I began, I do not think that in my entire output you will find a character with a single dominant characteristic. They are all without so-called 'character'. They are split and fragmented, not good and not bad, but both at once, subtle, and changeable in their attitudes and in their deeds. No doubt I am also like this myself.

Hamsun's Fascism will always compromise his reputation both as a writer and as a man, which makes it important to bear these words in mind when thinking about him. In his case particularly, there is a danger of not seeing the trees for the wood. Moreover, as soon as one starts thinking about his Fascism, the paradoxes begin to appear again. Fascism is humourless and hates life; Hamsun was certainly disillusioned by life, but he never hated it. On the contrary, he loved it, and time and again in his books manages to convey the impression that in spite of the shabbiness and banality of it all, simply to be alive is a wonderful thing. Remarkably few great writers have managed to convey as convincingly as he did this deliberately anti-tragic vision of life. He was also extremely funny, and could laugh at himself and his pretensions in a way that seems quite incompatible with the pompous solemnity of Fascism. Fascism is about obedience and uniformity; but for him, the right to be oneself was the most basic demand of life. He hated communism as much as communism hated him; yet one feels that had he ever lived to experience life under Fascism, he would soon have found himself in just as much trouble there as under any communist regime. In all, he was an unusual man who defies easy categorisation. What can safely be said of him is that he was a great writer, and his contribution to the art of writing has been enormous. On a technical level he was one of the most influential and innovative literary stylists of the past hundred years. There is hardly a living European or American writer who does not consciously or unconsciously stand in his debt.

Notes

Abbreviations used in the Notes:

BM TH	*Brev til Marie* ed Tore Hamsun, Oslo 1970
BUB	Bergen Universitets Bibliotek (University library)
DKB	Det Kongelige Biblioteket, Copenhagen
EKF	Hamsun's letters to Erik Frydenlund between 1885 and 1934, collected and introduced by Harald Naess in *Edda* *1959* p 225–268
GHA	Gyldendal's Hamsun archive. This is an unsorted collection of photocopied letters from Hamsun to Harald Grieg and from Grieg to Hamsun during the years 1925–1940
KH ES	*Knut Hamsun* Einar Skavlan, Oslo 1934
KH TH	*Knut Hamsun* Tore Hamsun, Oslo 1959
KHA HN	*Knut Hamsun og Amerika* Harald Naess, Oslo 1969
KHSHV TH	*Knut Hamsun som han var* ed Tore Hamsun, Oslo 1956. This is a large collection of letters from Hamsun to various correspondents.
OUB	Oslo Universitets Bibliotek (University library)
ØU – SSN	*En ørn i uvaer* Sten Sparre Nilson, Oslo 1960
RB MH	*Regnbuen* Marie Hamsun, Oslo 1953
Report	*Den rettspsykiatriske erklaering om Knut Hamsun* Gabriel Langfeldt og Ørnulv Ødegård, Oslo 1978
SS	*Min klient Knut Hamsun* Sigrid Stray, Oslo 1978
U 123/456	References to the newspaper clipping files in Oslo University Library
UG MH	*Under Gullregnen* Marie Hamsun, Oslo 1959.

References

CHAPTER ONE

1 *Report* p79
2 *KH* TH p14
3 *The Growth of the Soil* London 1979 p314
4 *KH* TH p19
5 *Artikler 1889–1928* Oslo 1968 p11
6 *Report* p60
7 *KH* ES p29
8 *KH* TH p42
9 *Report* p81
10 U251/107
11 *Hamsun, slik jeg kjente ham* Harald Grieg p58
13 *KHSHV* TH p35
12 U 358/9
14 *En forleggers erindringer* Harald Grieg p222
15 *Edda 1977* Article by Arnfinn Engen p255

CHAPTER TWO

1 *Hardanger Årbok* 19.9.1977 Article by Jon Bleie p328
2 *Vesterålen* Sortland 16.8.1960 Article by Welle-Strand
3 *GHA* Letter to Harald Grieg 11.9.1934
4 *Edda 1972* Article by N M Knutsen p321
5 *KHSHV* TH p36
6 *Hunger* tr George Egerton, London 1967 p274
7 *Årbok for Gjøvik historielag 3* 1982 Article by Helge Dahl
8 Quoted in *KHA* HN p15

CHAPTER THREE

1 *KHSHV* TH p37
2 *Aftenposten* 3.8.1984 The poems introduced by Lars-Frode Larsen

3 *KH* ES p80
4 Ibid
5 *KHA* HN p34
6 Ibid p247
7 Ibid p39
8 *Aftenposten* 7.8.9.10 August 1984. Nine letters by Hamsun to Tveraas presented by Harald Næss
9 *Edda 1965* Article by Rolf Nyboe Nettum p27–35
10 *KHSHV* TH p51
11 Letter from Hamsun to Cammermeyer 7.11.1884 in OUB

CHAPTER FOUR

1 *KHSHV* TH p69
2 Details from *Magasinet for alle* 14.3.1962 Article by Eiliv Odde Hauge p31
3 *Polden Poståpneri* Bjørn Storberget p3
4 *EKF* p225
5 Letter reprinted in *Aftenposten* 6.8.1959
6 Letter of 27.10.1884 in OUB
7 *KH* ES p88
8 *Edda 1963* Article by Olaf Øyslebø p143
9 *EKF* p229
10 This is the original version. Hamsun produced another version of the story which was collected in *Brushwood*, 1903
11 *EKF* p231
12 *KHSHV* TH p68
13 Letter reprinted in *Dagbladet* 16.12.1961
14 *EKF* p230

CHAPTER FIVE

1 *EKF* p230
2 Ibid
3 In *Dagbladet* 14.11 and 21.11.1886
4 *Artikler 1889–1928* p145
5 *Sønner af Norge* Minneapolis, Minn 1921 p34
6 Letter reprinted in *Nordisk Tidskrift 40* 1964 p295
7 *Bonniers litterära Magasin 2* Stockholm 1933 p51
8 cf note 5
9 *Recollections of an Immigrant* Andreas Ueland, New York 1929 p63
10 *Hvad jeg har oplevet* Kristofer Janson p222
11 Kroger Johansen's memoir in *Dagbladet* 18.1.1903
12 Loftfield's letter in *Minneapolis Tidende* 11.10.1934
13 *Sett och känt* Axel Lundgård, Stockholm 1925 p100

CHAPTER SIX

1 *EKF* p233
2 *Herman Bang Vol 3* H Jacobsen p58
3 *KHSHV* TH p55
4 Ibid p48
5 Letter to Langens of 25.4.1914, for example, in OUB
6 *KHSHV* TH p97
7 Letter to Georg Brandes of April 1890 in *Strindberg – Brev* Stockholm 1965 p123
8 *KHSHV* TH p58
9 *Olaf Norli – Et Festskrift* Article by Olaf Huseby, Oslo 1933 p27–28
10 Quoted in Øyvind Anker *Boken om Karoline* Oslo 1982 p193
11 The first of them is reprinted in *Artikler 1889–1928*
12 *Før det dages* – Jeppe Aakjær, Copenhagen 1929 p184
13 *EKF* p236
14 *Kringsjaa* Christiania 1904 p500
15 *KHSHV* TH p99, p116
16 Ibid p75
17 Ibid p72
18 Ibid p75
19 *EKF* p238. Also *Hvad jeg har oplevet* Kristofer Janson p225
20 *Norske Intelligenssedler* 13.6.1890
21 *KHSHV* Th p98
22 *Artikler 1889–1928* p34
23 Letter to Bolette Pavels Larsen (no date) OUB
24 Letter to Arne Garborg 10.9. (no year) OUB
25 Letter to Bolette Pavels Larsen (no date) OUB
26 *Artikler 1889–1928* p33
27 *EKF* p241

CHAPTER SEVEN

1 *Minner Vol 1* Peter Egge p211
2 *Samtiden 40* 1929 p353
3 *Kringsjaa* 1904 p500
4 U 351/101–102
5 *Hamsun, Eine Bildbiographie* Marianne Hamsun p67–68
6 *SS* p43
7 *Ord och Bild 63* Stockholm 1954 p25–32
8 Ibid
9 Ibid
10 Ibid
11 Ibid
12 Letter to Marie Herzfeld 7.1.1892 in OUB
13 *KHSHV* TH p53
14 *Aftenposten* 25.9.1892 Review by Kristofer Randers

15 *Litterære Tendenser* Edvard Brandes, Copenhagen 1968 p125–129
16 *KHSHV* TH p83
17 Ibid p84
18 Ibid p141
19 *Report* p82
20 *KHSHV* TH (section entitled 'Plagiat') p138–144
21 *Norkse Intelligenssedler* 15.4.1893
22 *Brevvekslingen mellom Bj. Bjørnson og Amalie Skram 1878–1904* p71, p82,p85
23 Letter to Bolette Pavels Larsen postmarked 14.5.1892 BUB
24 Letter to Bolette Pavels Larsen 10.9.1890 BUB
25 Card to Gerhard Gran (undated) OUB
26 Dated from *Danebrog* 13.4.1893

CHAPTER EIGHT

1 *Litteratur og Lesning omkring 1890* Johs A Dale p30–32
2 *Willy Gretor* Ernst Mentze p109
3 *Danebrog* 8.4.1893
4 Letter to Litleré, 20 January (no year) BUB
5 Letters to Bolette 21.8.1893, 11.10.1893, 6.11.1893 BUB
6 Letter to Bolette (undated)
7 Letter to Victor Nilsson 1.11.1893 OUB
8 Letter to Lybecker 23.7.1893 OUB
9 Letter to Langen 19.4.1895 OUB
10 Letter to Victor Nilsson 5.9.1892 OUB
11 Letter to Bolette 30.10.1893 BUB
12 Letter to Bolette 12.11.1893 BUB
13 Letter to Bolette 6.7.1893 BUB
14 *KHSHV* TH p105
15 *Minner Vol 1* Peter Egge p311
16 Hamsun's letters to Langen in OUB
17 Letter to Bolette 15.6.1894 BUB
18 *Artikler 1889–1928* p14
19 Letter to Bolette 8.4.1891 BUB
20 *Artikler 1889–1928* p19
21 *Læregutt* Johan Boyer p156
22 *Knut Hamsun – Min Far* Tore Hamsun p168–169
23 UG MH p120
24 *KHSHV* TH p147. See also *Erindringer fra et dikterhjem* E Lie p139
25 Letter to Langen 19.4.1895 OUB
26 Letter to Bolette 1.10.1893 BUB
27 *Erinnerungen an das literarische Berlin* S. Przybyszewski p247–251
28 Letter to Bolette 24.2.1895 BUB
29 EKF p234
30 *Norsk Kunstnerliv* Mentz Schulerud p533

CHAPTER NINE

1 Letter to Bolette 30.12.1894 OUB
2 *My Life In Art* Konstantin Stanislavsky, London 1980 p478
3 Letter to Bolette 9.7.1895
4 Letter to Bolette 5.2.1897
5 *KHSHV* TH p87
6 Letter to Bolette 24.7.1896 BUB
7 *Urd 56* Oslo 1952 P525–526
8 This and subsequent material from the *Anonyme Brev* files in the Riksarkiv, Oslo
9 Letter to Bolette 3.5.1897 BUB
10 Letter to Bolette 21.8.1897 BUB
11 *Kringsjaa* Christiania 1904 p500
12 Letter to Bolette 5.2.1897 BUB
13 Letter to Gerda Welhaven 4.8.1897 OUB
14 Letter to Bolette 29.11.1897 BUB
15 *Minner Vol 2* Peter Egge p54
16 *Unsterbliches München* Hanns Arens, Munich 1968 p324
17 Ms in OUB
18 Ingolf Kittelsen's eyewitness account in OUB
19 Letter to Langen 16.6.1898
20 Letter to Langen 29.7.1898
21 Letter to Langen 12.12.1898
22 Letter to Bolette 4.7.1898
23 Letter to Bolette 19.9.1898
24 *KHSHV* TH p104–108

CHAPTER TEN

1 *Menn i motstraum* Johs A Dale, Oslo 1973 p78
2 Letter of 12.4.1899 transcribed by Bergljot's sister Alette Gross in a letter of 26.6.1928 for Walter Berendsohn, in OUB
3 Letter to Slotte 31.5.1899 OUB
4 Letter to Aanrud 16.12.1898 OUB
5 Telegram from Hamsun in Helsinki to Bergljot in Vienna, June 1899, in Déderick Charlesson's archive
6 Letter to Slotte, datable to 1.9.1899 OUB
7 Letter in Bergljot's hand but copying Hamsun's signature to Langen, dated 27.9. with the year 1899 added in pencil. In a letter to Langen 20.10.1899, Hamsun writes of his long journey undertaken 'in the last two months'. The duration of the stay in Russia is unclear
8 Letter to Bergljot dated 7.6. in Déderick Charlesson's archive.
9 *Menn i motstraum* p95
10 Letters to Bergljot, one dated 1901 in Déderick Charlesson's archive
11 *Krig, sult og film Vol 2* Olaf Fønss, Copenhagen 1932 chapter 9
12 Letter of 15.12.1902 transcribed by Alette Gross for Berendsohn cf

note 2. See also *Kjønn og Karakter* Otto Weininger, Oslo 1977 p19
13 *Veien frem, Artikler i utvalg* Nordahl Grieg, Oslo 1947 p80–88
14 Letter to Aanrud 20.5.1904 OUB
15 Letter to Peter Nansen 20.6. in DKB
16 *Minner Vol 2* Peter Egge p267–270
17 *BM* TH p73
18 Letter to Bergljot, undated, in Déderick Charlesson's archive
19 Separation Agreement in Déderick Charlesson's archive
20 *BM* TH p73

CHAPTER ELEVEN

1 *KH* ES p220
2 U 470/121–123
3 Letter to Köhler-Olsen of 1907, reprinted in *Nationen* 6.5.1967
4 Ibid
5 *Hamsun i Russisk Åndsliv* Martin Nag p71
6 See *En dikter og hans oversetter: om Knut Hamsun og P. E. Hansen* Martin Nag, Oslo 1980
7 *KH* ES p222
8 cf note 6 p14
9 *RB* MH p115–119
10 *BM* TH p29
11 Letter to Bolette 23.11.1893 BUB
12 Letter to Peter Nansen (undated) DKB
13 Ibid
14 *Forposten* 5.12.1904 Christiania
15 *Artikler 1889–1928* p74
16 Ibid p98
17 Ibid p104
18 *RB* MH p204
19 *Verdens Gang* 9.8.1910
20 U 410/45
21 U 410/47
22 *KHSHV* TH p63
23 *Aftenposten* 6.9.1910
24 *Hamsun i Russisk Åndsliv* M Nag p159
25 *EKF* p258

CHAPTER TWELVE

1 U 351/99
2 Letter to Christopher Brinchmann 21.3.1911
3 *KH* ES p155
4 *RB* MH p200
5 Ibid p261

6 *BM* TH p136
7 *RB* MH p250
8 Letter to Albert Langen 10.2.1894 OUB
9 Letter to Albert Langen 28.4.1898 OUB
10 Letter to Langens 10.12.1914 OUB
11 *Tidens Tegn* 6.12.1914
12 Letters to Vetlesen 12.1.1915, 26.1.1915, 22.2.1915, 30.3.1915 OUB
13 Letter to Langens 2.9.1915
14 Letter to Langens, 30.6.1917 OUB
15 Letter to Kønig 2.12.1915 in *Vinduet 13* 1959 p94
16 Letter to Nansen 5.4.1913 DKB
17 Letter to Alette Gross 23.11.1914 OUB
18 cf note 15
19 Letter to Langens 16.1.1917
20 Article in Morgenbladet 10.2.1915
21 Letter to Bolette (undated) OUB
22 *EKF* p249
23 Ibid p251
24 cf note 15
25 *RB* MH p284

CHAPTER THIRTEEN

Family background material for this chapter is largely adapted from *RB* MH, *BM* TH, *KH* TH, *Knut Hamsun og Nørholm* ed Arild Hamsun
1 Hamsun's own account of the episode is collected in OUB
2 'Almar Hamsun' Who Died – *Lives* Almar Bjørnefjell, Oslo 1971 p188
3 Biographical details in *Aftenposten* 16.9.1961
4 *Tidens Tegn* 11.10.1930
5 All letters on Hamsun's treatment by Strømme from *BM* TH p203–207
6 Information from a conversation with Strømme's publisher Th Myklestad 6.2.1986 Oslo
7 Information on the proceedings from documents in the Riksarkiv, Oslo

CHAPTER FOURTEEN

1 Quoted in *Edda* 1967 Article by Johs A Dale p147
2 *The Road Leads On* tr Eugene Gay-Tifft p53,p284,p409
3 Details on Hamsun's relationship with Gyldendal from *En Forleggers erindringer* Harald Grieg, also *GHA*
4 Letter to Langen 31.7.1905 OUB
5 *Bergens Tidende* 29.1.1953
6 Letter to Langen 26.3.1908 OUB
7 *KHSHV* TH p112

8 Ibid p113
9 Ibid p113
10 Ibid p114
11 Ibid p112
12 Ibid p210
13 Letter from Gorky to Hamsun dated to 16.3–18.4.1927 by Nag in *Hamsun i Russisk Åndsliv*
14 See *Hamsun i Russisk Åndsliv* M Nag
15 *Aftenposten* 16.11.1971
16 Ms in OUB
17 Letter to Harald Grieg 19.6.1936 in *GHA*
18 Letter to Alette Gross 1.9.1930 in OUB
19 Details on the case from *SS* p61–88, also from letters in Diderick Charlesson's archive
20 *Minner Vol 4* Peter Egge p157–159. See also *Oslo Aftenavis* 28.1.1931
21 *EKF* p266
22 Details from the account in *SS* p37–47, also material in Riksarkivet
23 Details from the account in *SS* p9–29
24 *KHSHV* TH p211
25 Letter to Harald Grieg 19.6.1936 in *GHA*
26 Letter to Larsen 10.1.1928 BUB
27 U 511/107–108
28 *Prossessen mot Hamsun* Thorkild Hansen p417
29 *Report* p35

CHAPTER FIFTEEN

1 *Report* p57
2 *TLS* 5.12.1975
3 My translation from an article in *Folk og Land* 22.8.1953, in itself a translation from 7 *Arts* ed Puma, New York 1953
4 Letter of 18.6.1934 reprinted in *Aftenposten*, 30.10.1978. Article by Kjeld Vibe
5 *Der Norden* January 1935
6 *Report* p70
7 *GHA*
8 Letter of 23.11.1933 in *ABC*
9 *Fylkesavisen* Skien 11.1.1934
10 Ms in OUB
11 *SS* p100
12 Reprinted in *Carl v. Ossietzky* Bruno Frei p256–57. Berlin 1966
13 *Mein Vater* Tore Hamsun, Leipzig 1940 p166
14 Letter to Marie postmarked 4.2.1936 in OUB
15 *Report* p67
16 Letter to Knut Werswick of 18.5.1938 reprinted in *VG* 14.3.1967
17 Article in *Morgenbladet* 10.2.1915

18 Quoted in *Modernism* ed Bradbury and McFarlane, London 1981 p115
19 Letter of 1.12.1925 *to Nationalt tidsskrift* Oslo 1926 p8
20 My thanks to Oskar Mendelsohn for information on Sylten, and for access to his copy of *Hvem er hvem i jødeverden*
21 *Artikler 1889–1928* p123
22 *KHSHV* TH p144
23 *Aftenposten* 10.7.1934
24 *UG* MH p56
25 *Mysteries* tr Bothmer, London 1973 p44
26 *Edda* 1977 Article by Allen Simpson p273
27 *Report* p69

CHAPTER SIXTEEN

1 Letter from Grieg to Hamsun 22.2.1940 in *GHA*
2 *ØU SSN* p198–200
3 Ibid p200
4 Ms in OUB
5 *Tønsberg Bladet* 28.3.1942
6 Correspondence between Hamsun and Smedal collected in OUB
7 *GHA*
8 *ØU SSN* p201–205
9 *Aftenposten* 16.10.1978 Article by Sverre Hartmann
10 Other titles on Hamsun's list of Six Greatest Books were *Les Misèrables* by Victor Hugo, *Devastation* by Tom Kristensen, *San Michele* by Axel Munthe, *The Idiot* by Dostoevsky and *My Life* by Maxim Gorky
11 *Segelfoss Tidende* No 2 ed Doery Smith 1957 p86–87
12 letter from Hamsun to Smedal in OUB
13 *Aftenposten* 24.1.1941
14 *Grimstad Adressetid* 30.1.1941
15 *ØU SSN* p205–206
16 *GHA* letter of 1.2.1940 Hamsun to Grieg
17
   SS p89
18 Ibid p163
19 Ibid p89
20 Ibid p90–95
21 *ØU SSN* p207–213
22 *Report* p45
23 Letter of 3.6.1944 to Victoria in Déderick Charlesson's archive
24 *SS* p119
25 *En flyktning finner sitt land* Max Tau, Oslo 1964 p93
26 *ØU SSN* p213–214
27 *Prosessen mot Hamsun* Thorkild Hansen p121
28 *Report* p61
29 Hamsun's letter and Goebbels' reply in *Report* p52–53
30 Details from U 1012/90

31 Information from Sten Sparre Nilson, Oslo 1986
32 *ØU SSN* p214–216
33 *Er war mein chef* Christa Schroeder, Munich 1985 p194
34 This account of Hamsun's meeting with Hitler is based on three newspaper articles by Sverre Hartmann and Erik Egeland who interviewed Hamsun's travelling companion and interpreter Egil Holmboe in Iceland in 1978 (i) *Berlingske Tidende* 18.10.1978 (ii) *Berlingske Tidende* 19.10.1978 (iii) *Aftenposten* 21.10.1978
35 Extract from *12 Jahre mit Hitler*, Dr Otto Dietrich, printed in *Segelfoss Tidende* Jan/March 1958 p100
36 *Segelfoss Tidende* No. 2, 1957 p71
37 *Report* p77–78
38 *ØU SSN* p217
39 *SS* p97
40 *ØU SSN* p218

CHAPTER SEVENTEEN

Main sources of background material for this chapter are *UG MH*, *SS*, *On Overgrown Paths*

1 *Report* p50
2 *Lofotposten* 3.5.1940
3 *UG MH* p80–81
4 Ibid p82
5 *Dagbladet* 30.3.1946
6 *Samtiden* 67 Oslo 1958 p405–415
7 *SS* p120
8 *On Overgrown Paths* tr Carl L Anderson, New York 1967 p138–147
9 *Report* p71
10 Letter to Victoria of 10.7.1947 in Déderick Charlesson's archive
11 *Knut Hamsuns egen røst*, Christian Gierløff, Oslo 1961 p12
12 *SS* p116
13 *SS* p134

CHAPTER EIGHTEEN

Main sources for material here are *UG MH*, *SS*, *En forleggers erindringer*, Harald Grieg, *On Overgrown Paths*

1 *SS* p135
2 *SS* p172
3 Marie Hamsun in radio interview NRK 12.9.1965

SELECT BIBLIOGRAPHY

I) Books about Hamsun:
Berendsohn, Walter A Knut Hamsun. Das Unbändige Ich und die menschliche Gemeinshaft. Munich 1929
Bull, Francis Knut Hamsun på ny. Oslo 1954
Die Waldhütte. ed Hilde Fürstenberg Mölln in Lauenberg 1964–1978
Gierløff, Christian Kjærlighet og hat i storpolitikken. Særlig om anglomanien og anglofobien. Oslo 1950
Gierløff, Christian Knut Hamsuns egen røst. Oslo 1961
Grieg, Harald En forleggers erindringer. Oslo 1971
(Hamsun) Festskrift til Knut Hamsun. Oslo 1929
Hamsun, Arild Om Knut Hamsun og Nørholm. ed. Arild Hamsun. Oslo 1961
Hamsun, Marianne Hamsun. Eine Bildbiographie. Munich 1959
Hamsun, Marie Regnbuen. Oslo 1953
Hamsun, Marie Under gullregnen. Oslo 1959
Hamsun, Tore Knut Hamsun. Oslo 1959
Hamsun, Tore Knut Hamsun – min far. Oslo 1952
Hamsun, Tore Lebensbericht in Bildern. Munich 1956
Hamsun, Tore Mein Vater. Leipzig 1941
Hamsun, Tore ed Brev til Marie. Oslo 1970
Hamsun, Tore ed Knut Hamsun som han var. Oslo 1956
Hansen, Thorkild Prosessen mot Hamsun. Oslo 1978
Langfeldt, G and Ødegård, Ø Den rettspsykiatriske erklæring om Knut Hamsun. Oslo 1978
Marstrander, Jan Det ensomme menneske i Knut Hamsuns diktning. Oslo 1959
Nag, Martin Hamsun i russisk åndsliv. Oslo 1969
Nettum, Rolf Nyboe Konflikt og visjon. Hovedtemaer i Knut Hamsuns forfatterskap. Oslo 1970
Nilson, Sten Sparre En Ørn i uvær. Oslo 1960
Nilson, T I Bibliografi over Knut Hamsun 1970–1980. Unpublished thesis 1981. Oslo
Næss, Harald Knut Hamsun og Amerika. Oslo 1969
Østby, Arvid Knut Hamsun. En bibliografi. Oslo 1972
Øyslebø, Olaf Hamsun gjennom stilen. Oslo 1964

Segelfoss Tidende editor and publisher Doery Smith. Oslo 1957/58–1959/60
Skavlan, Einar Knut Hamsun. 2nd ed Oslo 1934
Storberget, Bjørn Postmannen og postdikteren Knut Hamsun. Oslo 1963
Stray, Sigrid Min klient Knut Hamsun. Oslo 1978
Svarstad, Christianne Undset Knut Hamsun og fødebygden Lom. Oslo 1960
Wiehr, Josef Knut Hamsun. His personality and outlook on life.
   Northampton, Mass 1922

2) Books and articles containing interesting or useful information about
Hamsun, or providing useful background information:
Aakjær, Jeppe Før det dages. Copenhagen 1929
Aall, Hermann Harris Faren for Skandinavien. Christiania 1915
Anderson, Rasmus B Life Story of Rasmus B Anderson. Written by himself.
   Madison, Wis 1915
Arens, Hans Unsterbliches Munchen. Munich 1968
Askeland, Hallvard Knut Hamsun i Minneapolis. (in Sønner af Norge,
   Minneapolis Minn 1921 P34–42)
Bassøe, Bjarne Stamtavle over familien Bassøe. Oslo 1969
Bjørnefjell, Almar 'Almar Hamsun' som døde – lever. Oslo 1971
Bjørnson, Bjørnstjerne Bjørnstjerne Bjørnsons brevveksling med danske
   1875–1910. Copenhagen 1953
Bly, Robert and Singer, I B Introduction to *Hunger*. New York 1967
Bojer, Johan Læregutt. Oslo 1942
Brochmann, Georg Den norske Forfatterforening gjennom 50 år. Oslo 1952
(*Bull*) Festskrift til Francis Bull på 50 årsdagen. Oslo 1937
Buttry, Dolores Knut Hamsun's supposed anti-semitism: a refutation.
   Edda 2, 1986
Dahl, Helge ed Hamsun's brev til Alf Mjøen (in Samtiden 3, 1983)
Dale, Johs A Garborg-studiar. Oslo 1969
Dale, Johs A Litteratur og lesing omkring 1890. Oslo 1974
Derry, T K A History of Modern Norway. Oxford 1973
Dørsjø, J ed Levende anekdoter. Oslo 1959
Egge, Peter Minner. Vols I–IV. Oslo 1948–55
Engen, Arnfinn Knut Hamsun og Zahl på Kjerringøy. Edda 1977 p255–262
Espeland, Arne Jens Tvedt. Oslo 1959
Fjerdingstad, Trygve Knut Hamsun og Amerika. Unpublished thesis 1941.
   Oslo University Manuscript dept
Fønss, Olaf Krig, Sult og Film. Vol II Copenhagen 1932
Gauguin, Pola Edvard Munch. Oslo 1946
Goebbels, Josef Diaries 1942 and 1943
(*Grieg*) Festskrift til Harald Grieg. Oslo 1950
Grieg, Nordahl Veien frem. Artikler i utvalg. Oslo 1947
Hansen John O Hamsun i Minneapolis. In Minneapolis Journal 12.12.1920
Irving, David Hitler's War. London 1977
Jacobsen, Harry Herman Bang Vol I–IV. Copenhagen 1954–1966
Janson, Kristofer Hvad jeg har oplevet. Christiania 1913
Knutsen, Nils M Tre ukjente Hamsun – brev fra 1880. Edda 1972 p321–327
Krag, Vilhelm Heirefjæren. Oslo 1928

Krigens Dagbok: Norge 1940–1945 ed Per Voksø. Oslo 1984

Krøger, Cecil Knut Hamsun. Hans læreaar. Dagbladet 18.1.1903

Laws, Yngvar Knut Hamsun som jeg kjente ham. (in Sønner af Norge, Minneapolis, Minn 1929 p388–391)

Loftfield, G E Et Hamsun-minde (in Minneapolis Tid. 11.10.1934)

McFarlane, J W The whisper of the blood. A study of Knut Hamsun's early novels. (in Publications of the MLA of America 71, Menasha, Wis. 1956)

Mendelsohn, Oskar Jødenes historie i Norge gjennom 300 år. Oslo 1969

Mendelssohn, Peter de S. Fischer und sein Verlag. Frankfurt am Main 1970

Mentze, Ernst Willy Gretor, født Petersen. Copenhagen 1966

Mjøen, S Da mor var ung. Oslo 1975

Morburger, Carl Knut Hamsun. En studie. Tr Einar Skavlan, Christiania 1910

Morgridge, Barbara G Introduction to The Cultural Life of Modern America. Cambridge, Mass 1969

Munch, Anna To Mennesker. Christiania 1897

Nag, Martin Gorkij i Norge. Sarpsborg 1983

Nilson, Sten Sparre Knut Hamsun, England og Amerika. (in Scandinavica 1, London 1962)

Nilsson, Victor Min Hamsun. (in Bonniers litterära Magasin 2, Stockholm 1933 nr 8)

(Norli) Festskrift for Olaf Norli, Oslo 1933

Næss, Harald ed Brevveksling med postmaster Erik Fryderlund 1885–1934 (in Edda 1959)

Olsen, Frejlif En kjøbenhavnsk Journalist. Copenhagen 1922

Popperwell Ronald G Knut Hamsun og hans bøker på Nørholm. (in Edda 1963)

Przybyszewski, Stanislaw Erinnerungen an das literarische Berlin. Munich 1965

Schulerud, Mentz Norsk kunstnerliv. Oslo 1960

Schulerud, Mentz På Grand i hundre År 1874–1974. Oslo 1974

Seland Johs Macody Lund. Et hjerte i en kruttørne. Oslo 1971

Simpson, Allen Knut Hamsun's Anti-Semitism. Edda 1977 p273–293

Skram A and Bjørnson Bj Brevvekslingen mellom Bjørnstjerne Bjørnson og Amalie Skram 1878–1904 ed Ø Anker og E Beyer. Oslo 1982

Skrede, Magne Omkring Knut Hamsuns unge aar. Smaatræk om slegten og fra hans ophold i Lom. (in Nationen 30.9.1922)

Smedal, Gustav Patriotisme og landssvik. Oslo 1950

Stokland, Johan Hva Hamarøys gamle protokoller forteller (in Segelfoss Tidende 3 Oslo 1959/60)

Strindberg, August Brev Vol X 1894–95. Stockholm 1968

Strindberg, Frida Strindberg och hans andra hustru. Stockholm 1934

Svarstad, Christianne Undset Noen brev fra Knut Hamsun til hans ungdomsvenninne Caroline Neeraas. (in Ord och Bild 63. Stockholm 1954)

Tau, Max En flyktning finner sitt land. Oslo 1964

Wamberg N B Digterne og Gyldendal Copenhagen 1970

Welblund, Aage Omkring den litterære Café. Copenhagen 1951

Welle-Strand, Edvard Den unge Hamsun (in Gads danske Magasin 46, Copenhagen 1952 p90–105)
Welle-Strand, Edvard Knut Hamsun som skolelærer i Vesterålen (in Norges Kvinder, 31.12.1954)
Welle-Strand, Edvard Knut Hamsun (in Vesterålen, Sortland, August 1960)
West, Rebecca The Meaning of Treason. London 1949
Wieslander, Henning Knut Hamsun i brevväxling med Birger Mörner (in Samfundet Örebro stads- och länsbiblioteks vänner. Meddelande 27, Orebro 1959)

Unpublished sources:
Material in the Riksarkiv, Oslo on: the anonymous letters case of 1897; the name case raised by Knut Hamsun against his brother Thorvald 1923–25; the psychiatric examination and trial of Knut Hamsun 1945–1948.
Letter collections in: Oslo University; Bergen University; The Royal Library in Copenhagen.
Déderick Charlesson's archive of letters from Hamsun to Bergljot and Victoria Hamsun.
Gyldendal's archive of photocopied correspondence between Harald Grieg and Knut Hamsun 1925–1940.

KNUT HAMSUN'S WORKS

The Enigmatic One (1877)	(Juvenilia)
Bjørger (1879)	(Juvenilia)
On the Cultural Life of Modern America (1889)	
Hunger (1890)	
Mysteries (1892)	
Editor Lynge (1893)	
Shallow Soil (1893)	
Pan (1894)	
At the Gates of the Kingdom (1895)	(Play)
The Game of Life (1896)	(Play)
Siesta (1897)	(Short-stories)
Evening Glow (1898)	(Play)
Victoria (1898)	
Friar Vendt (1902)	(Verse drama)
Queen Tamara (1903)	(Play)
Brushwood (1903)	(Short-stories)
In Wonderland (1903)	(Travel)
Swarming (1904)	
The Wild Choir (1904)	(Poems)
Striving Life (1905)	(Short-stories)
Under the Autumn Star (1906)	
Benoni (1908)	
Rosa (1909)	
A Wanderer Plays on Muted Strings (1909)	
In the Grip of Life (1910)	(Play)
The Last Joy (1912)	
Children of the Age (1913)	
Segelfoss Town (1915)	
The Growth of the Soil (1917)	
The Women at the Pump (1920)	
Chapter the Last (1923)	
Wayfarers (1927)	
August (1930)	
The Road Leads On (1933)	
The Ring is Closed (1936)	
On Overgrown Paths (1949)	

Index

Compiled by Gordon Robinson

Aaberg, Ola, 71
Aajaer, Jeppe, *Master And Mission*, 109
Aall, Herman Harris, 357, 370, 374, 375, 379, 380
  Hamsun contributes foreword to *Politics of Revolution and Norwegian Law*, 330–1
  Hamsun's favourite intellectual, 330, 346
Aall, Jacob, 13
Aanrud, Hans, 126, 169, 174 fn, 176, 183, 191, 195, 197, 272
Aas, 192
Aasen, Ivar, 256
Abel, Dr Andreas, 69
Across the Sea, 59
adultery, act of, 196, 323
  Maria's accusation, 397
Aftenposten newspaper, 65, 68, 248, 254, 330, 334, 337, 338, 339, 345, 381
  accepts Hamsun's articles, 68, 71
  controlled by Nazis, 359, 363, 384, 388
  criticism of *Mysteries*, 131–2, 149
  'Language in Danger' article, 255–7
  publishes Hamsun's necrology for Hitler, 385–6
  return to free editorship, 387
Aga, Knut, 29
Agder, 402
Ager, W. T., 52, 53, 56, 60, 72, 92
  memoir on Hamsun, 53–4, 54–5
Albert, King of the Belgians, 303
Ålesund, 6
Alexandra, British bombardment of (1882), 234
Altmark, 350
Alvilde, love poem, 169
Alving, Fru, 108
America
  articles on, 68
  departure from, 65
  disillusion with, 94
  emigration to, 47–65
  impressions of, 47, 68, 94, 103–6
  relationship with, 239–40
  Scandinavian emigration to, 7, 44
  return to, 81–95
America magazine, article for, 95, 106
Among the Animals, 9

Amundsen, Roald, disappearance of, 305
Andersen, Marie, 83
Anderson, Sherwood, 301
Anderson, Professor R. B., 40, 45, 47–9, 55, 59, 60, 95
  hatred of Hamsun, 97
  indifference to Hamsun, 50
  meeting with, 48–50
  reports Hamsun as an anarchist to the police, 96
Anderson, Fru, 96
Andrejev, 301
anglophobia of Hamsun, 14, 186, 232–9, 240, 242–3, 268–9, 274, 303, 304, 305, 309, 325, 326–7, 348, 351, 353–4, 356–7, 391
  Vienna tirade in speech, 371–3, 383
Anker, Ella, 361 fn
anxieties for the opinions of others, 82
Arbeiderbladet newspaper, 339
Archer, William, 235, 236, 242
Arendal, 117, 264, 281
  Marie's imprisonment in Blodekjaer jail, 387
aristocratic radicalism, 113, 114
Armour, Philip, financial help from, 85
Arnesen, 284–5
arrogance of Hamsun, 125
Asgjer-Timann, 70
Askeland, Hallvard, 86, 89, 91–2, 94, 95
assistant to town clerk at Bø, 21
assists fellow artists, 144
Aubert, Andreas, 119
August trilogy, 18–19, 288, 290, 293, 294, 296, 306, 313
  sales success, 296, 364 fn
  Wayfarers (1927), 288, 289, 293, 296, 340, 345; synopsis, 290–2
  August (1930), 293–4
  The Road Leads On (1933), 313; synopsis, 294–5
Aulestad, 35, 41, 110, 162
Aurdal, 65, 69, 70, 248
  temporary home at, 73

bad manners, Hamsun's, 141
Baku visit, 184, 188

Balzac, Honoré de, 87, 106, 152
  lectures on, 93
Bang, Herman, 144
Bardu, 225
Basta magazine, 174
Beaulieu-sur-mer visit, 310
Bech, Captain, 171–2, 173
Beckett, Samuel, 112
  The End, 112 fn
Behrens, Carl, 95
  buys article by Hamsun, 97
  publishes extract from *Hunger*, 98
Bely, Andre, 1
  influence of Hamsun, 301
Benes, Eduard, 332
Benoni (1908), 15, 201–2, 228, 232, 238, 251, 264,
  302, 325
  synopsis, 202
Berendsohn, Walter A., biography of Hamsun,
  298–9
Bergen, 17
  lectures at, 122
  offered post of theatre director at National
    Stage, 110
  stay in, 282
Bergens Tidende, 264
Berlin, 135, 159, 217, 309, 313, 336, 350, 351, 358
  cult of Scandinavianism, 119, 163
  Norwegian writers in, 136
  visits to, 339, 356, 368–9, 370
Berlin-Tokio-Rome periodical, 365
Biblical Messenger, 12–13, 43
Birkenes (bank manager), 257
birth of Hamsun at Lom, 8
Bjorger (1879), 18, 23, 25, 26, 33, 59, 178, 320
  published at Hamsun's expense by Knudsen
    of Bodø, 23, 413
  synopsis, 24
Bjørnsen (shoemaker), apprenticed to, 19–20
Bjørnson, Bjørn, 192
Bjørnson, Dagny, marriage to Langen, the
    publisher, 167
Bjørnson, Bjørnstjerne, 13, 21, 33, 41, 49, 53, 54,
  61, 62, 74, 78, 101, 107, 109 fn, 113, 121, 142,
  145, 149, 160, 163, 175, 179, 236, 293, 296,
  338, 342, 361, 385
  acclaims *Mysteries* and *Pan*, 161
  attack on Christianity, 56
  awarded Nobel Prize, 212, 260
  Beyond our Power, 59
  co-founder of Scandinavianism cult, 119
  condemns *Editor Lynge*, 139
  correspondence with Hamsun, 36–7
  criticised by Hamsun, 123, 213
  death, 215, 216, 219, 354, 417
  denounces *On the Cultural Life of Modern
    America*, 106
  first meeting with Hamsun, 35
  helps Hamsun to emigrate to America, 45
  influence on Hamsun, 23–4, 34, 35, 37, 38, 39,
    40, 211
  lecture tour of America, 44, 48, 103
  lectures by Hamsun on, 55, 56, 70–1, 93
  pan-Germanism, 341
  poems in his honour by Hamsun, 192, 212, 215
  praise from Hamsun, 212, 213

  praises Hamsun as the greatest poet, 213
  recommends acting career for Hamsun, 35
  rejects *Frida* manuscript, 35, 54, 68 fn
  shamelessness, 347
Bleuler, Eugen, 283, 391 fn
Blindern Clinic, 389, 395
  protests about his treatment, 403
  psychiatric examination at, 390–401, 414
  release from, 401, 416
Blok, Aleksander, influence of Hamsun, 301
Blunk, Hans Friedrich, 338
Bø, Langøy, 20, 29, 40
  assistant to town clerk at, 21
Böcklin, Arnold, 214 fn
Bodø, 227, 254
  Grand Hotel, 225–6
  published in, 22, 25, 413
  shoemaker's apprentice in, 19–20, 69, 89
Bodø smuggling scandal, 13–14, 236
Bødtker, Sigurd, 325
Boer War, 303, 353
Bogs, Regierungsrat, 346
Böhme, General Franz, surrender to the Allies,
  387
Bojer, Johann, 157, 296
Bolleng, 70
Bonniers publishers, 413
book reviewer, 67–8
Booth, Edwin, 104
Borgen, Johan, 236
Bormann, Martin, 378
Borsch, Maria von, 120, 143, 155
Bøtker, Sigurd, 195
Bourgeois, Leon, 262
Braatøy, Trygve, analysis of Hamsun, 298
Brandes, Edward, 95, 98, 102, 114, 144–5, 344
  criticism of *Mysteries*, 132
Brandes, Georg, 40, 95, 98, 106, 112, 149, 157,
  180, 344, 398
  criticises *Hunger*, 114–15
  influences change and development in literary
    world, 112
  lectures on Nietzsche, 103
  Main Currents in 19th Century Literature, 113
Brauer, Carl, 352
Brauweiler, Dr, 371
Brecht, Bertolt, 1, 301
Brinchmann, Christofer, critical praise for *Pan*,
  156
Brushwood (1903 collection of short stories), 137
  fn, 192, 264
  'A Ghost', 192
  'A Street Revolution', 192
  'A Thorough Rascal', 192
  'Chance', 192
  'The Call of Life', 192
  'Father and Son', 137 fn
  'On Tour', 192
  'Small Town Life', 194
Buber, Martin, tribute from, 299
Budstikken magazine, letter to, 86–7
Bugge, O. C. D., 36
Bull, Edvard, 344
Bull, Francis, 380
Bunin, 301
Burger, Dr, 374, 375 fn

Bye, Fru, 176
Bygdøy, stay at, 288, 289

Caine, Hall, 303–4
Call of Life, The, 167, 168, 174, 192, 233
Cammermeyer, Albert, 65, 67
  publishes *Victoria*, 179
cards and gambling, fondness for, 43, 151, 190,
  195
Carl, Prince of Sweden, 262
Carnations Small, 18
Carnot, President, article on assassination of, 145
Caroline, love affair with, 128
Carossa, Paul, 385
Casselton, 89
ceaseless work and discipline, 160
Céline, Louis Ferdinand, 2, 105, 344
  imprisonment, 410
Chamberlain, Austen, 332
Chance, 120, 192
  accusation of plagiarisation with Dostoevsky's
    The Gambler, 135, 192
Chandler, Raymond, 24
Chapter the Last (1923), 194, 273, 281, 282, 293,
  302
  admired by Hermann Hesse, 302 fn
  book on death, 274
  four rival editions, 301
  praised by Gorky, 300
  synopsis, 274–9
Charlesson, Déderick (son-in-law), 308
  marries Victoria, 307
Chicago, 95, 110
  impressions of, 47
  trials of anarchists after bomb outrage in the
    Haymarket, 94, 96, 104
  work on the railways, 81–5
childhood, 5
  at Lom, 8
  hallucinations, 11–13
  harsh life with Uncle Hans at Presteid, 10–15
  on farm in Hamarøy, 8–10
  schooling, 14
Christensen, Hjalmar, 325
Christiania (later Oslo), 35–8, 65, 74, 75, 95, 116,
  126, 217, 257, 273
  difficulties of life for Hamsun, 76–7, 110–11,
    116
  further stays, 107–10, 121, 159, 169–76, 188,
    190, 191, 197, 203
  Grand Café, 110, 113, 149, 191, 195
  lectures in, 125, 128, 166–7, 184, 200, 238 fn
  literary mood in, 41, 86
  local fame, 107
  name changed to Oslo, 280 fn
  theatre performances of the Kareno trilogy,
    165–6
  see also Oslo
Christmas Roses magazine
  contributes *Christmas on the Farm*, 294
Christofersen, 248, 254
Churchill, Winson, 350
Claudius, Hermann, 338
Collected Novels, 241
Collected Works, 105, 217, 241, 242, 301, 385, 420
Collin, Professor Christen, newspaper debate
  with, 232–6, 242

Cologne University refuses Honorary Doctorate,
  299
Communism, hatred and fear of, 328, 347, 384,
  394, 422
conventional novels, 227–8
Copenhagen, 113, 157, 188, 350
  bombardment by British fleet, 14, 236
  Café Bernina, 101, 113, 137, 140, 195
  cultural capital of Scandinavia, 95
  first visit by Hamsun with manuscript of *Frida*,
    33–5, 36
  introduction to literary society, 101
  literary fashion, 41, 139
  local fame in, 107
  spells in, 96–107, 110, 129, 138, 140
  University lectures by Hamsun, 103, 104, 114
Cossack, HMS, 350
cripples, fascination for, 264–5
culture, views on, 180–1

Dagbladet, 62, 63 fn, 65, 68, 74, 84, 96, 124, 335
  contributions to, 99, 108–9, 110
  critical praise for *Pan*, 156
  provides press card, 80
  publishes *Fragment of Life*, 68, 78
  publishes *On Tour*, 78
  refuses *On Tour*, 77
Dalrymple, Oliver, 89, 90
Dantchenko, 299
Danzig, 327
Darwin, Charles, 113
death of Hamsun at Nørholm, 2, 421
Delius, Frederick, 152, 159
Delius, Jelka, 159
democracy, battle with, 316, 332, 336, 403, 409–
  10
Der Norden magazine, 326
Der Nordische Aufseher, 338
Devonshire, 352
Dickens, Charles
  compared with, 301
  influence of *David Copperfield* on Hamsun, 227
Die Weltbühne magazine, 334
Dietrich, Dr Otto, 373, 374, 376, 379
Dobloug, 80
donations to children's homes by Hamsun, 297
Dostoevsky, Fyodor, 113, 119, 183, 344, 398, 421
  compared with, 1, 300, 302
  Crime and Punishment, 88, 112, 135
  fanaticism, 186
  influence of, 133, 134–5, 299
  Notes from the Underground, 110
  plagiarism of, 88, 135, 232
  The Brothers Karamazov, 135
  The Gambler, 135
  The Insult and the Injured, 135
Drammen, 75, 124, 208
drinking bouts, 140, 151, 159, 190, 191, 195–6
Drøbak, 193, 212, 307
  buys land and builds house at, 196–7
Dubrovnik visit, 338
Dunne, Mary
  infatuation with Hamsun, 117
  Now Spring Has Gone, 117
Düsseldorf, 217, 309
  refused honorary membership of Theatre
    School, 299

Dybfest, Arne, 99
Dybwad, Arne, 125, 174 fn
Dybwad, Christian, 176

East Greenland, Hamsun involved in Norway's
  territorial rights, 355–6, 360, 366
Edelfelt, Albert, 159, 182
Editor Lynge (1893), 133 fn, 137–40, 148, 149, 202,
  212, 224, 242
  Hamsun's description of, 137
  hostile reviews, 139
  popular success, 139, 140
  weakest novel, 139
  written in revenge on Ola Thommessen, 137–8
education, contempt for, 274, 276
Edward VII, 234 fn
Egerøya, stay at, 313
Egge, Fru, 310
Egge, Peter, 99, 125, 150, 174 fn, 175, 195, 310,
  311, 336
  picture of Hamsun, 150–1
Ehrenburg, Illya, influence of Hamsun, 301
Eidsvold, 40, 49
Einstein, Albert, tribute from, 299, 300
Ekstrabladet, 334
Eliot, T. S., 2
Elroy, stay in, 50, 52, 55, 56, 57, 62, 63, 66, 82
Elverum, 217–18, 220, 283
Elvestad, Sven, 325
Emerson, Ralph Waldo, Hamsun's treatment of,
  105
emigration, Hamsun's warnings against the
  effects of, 293–4
Engelbrecht, General, 352
England, lack of sympathy for Hamsun's work,
  301–5
Engstrøm, Albert, 182, 261, 262, 263, 281
  campaigns for award of Nobel Prize to
  Hamsun, 261–2
Enigmatic One, The, (1877), 141
  first prose writing, 19, 21–2, 24, 25, 33, 38
Evening News, 383
Ewald, Carl, 114
Ex-Libris publishers, 414

Faaberg lodgings, 161–2
Fagerstrand, 107
Falkenberg, General von, 351
Fangen, Ronald, Hamsun pleads for his release,
  359, 367
farm work in America, 50–2, 89–91
  article on, 89–90
  short stories about, 90–1
Fatherland League, 329, 331
  ABC journal, 330, 331, 332, 333
Faulkner, William, 2
Fear, 57–8
financial pressures, 217
  assistance from Johan Sorensen, 102, 103
  debts, 75, 79, 82–3, 95, 152, 197, 222; repaying,
  120, 242
  funds raised by friends, 175–6
Fine-Hair, Harald, 7
Finne, Gabriel, 101
first literary efforts, 19, 21–39
  author's disparaging of, 24

First World War, articles in defence of Germany,
  404
  Hamsun's pro-German feelings during, 232–9
Fischer, S. (publishers), 119, 120
  declines *Mysteries*, 135, 143, 242
  publishes *Editor Lynge*, 138
  publishes *Hunger*, 119, 120, 143, 242
  tempting offers from, 242
Flatabø, Captain, 29, 30
Flatabø, Marta, sweetheart at Ostensjo, 31
Flaubert, Gustave, lectures on, 93
Flekkefjord, 305
Florelius, Fru, 176
Fønss, Olaf, 191, 207
Ford, James L., 240
Fragment of a Life, 68, 78, 80, 99
Frederiksen, Professor N. C., loan from, 95
Fredrikstad, 124, 213
Freie Buhne magazine, 119, 120, 135, 136
  accuses Hamsun of plagiarism, 143
Frenssen, Gustav, 228
Freud, Sigmund, 283, 391 fn
Friar Vendt (1902)
  verse drama, 189, 190–1
Frida manuscript, 30, 31, 33, 34, 35, 37, 39, 40,
  41, 77
  disaster with, 35, 54, 68, 97
  rejected by Bjørnson, 35, 54, 68 fn
Fritt Folk, 333, 371
  description by Goebbels of Hamsun's visit to
  Berlin, 368–9
  propaganda articles for, 351, 355, 358, 361,
  381, 384, 388
Frøchen, Just Cato, 122
Fröding, Gustav, 162
From the Unconscious Life of the Mind, 117–18, 120,
  122, 131
Frøsland, Fru, 45
Frøsland, Nikolai, 73, 79
Frøsland, Nils, 43, 45, 47, 73
Frydenlund, 237
  assists at hotel and post office, 69–70
Frydenlund, Erik
  assumes guardianship of Hamsun's sons, 306
  called up for military service, 70
  financial help from, 120
  first meeting with Hamsun, 69
  forms lasting friendship, 69, 71, 73, 100, 115
  Hamsun assists him in the hotel and post
  office, 69
  long correspondence with, 70–1, 74–5, 77, 79,
  81–2, 83, 100–1, 109, 110, 311
  looks after Ellinor after her illness, 309
  renewal of contact with, 168, 247, 306
Frydenlund, Kari, 69, 71
Frydenlund, Nils
  debt owed to, 75, 82–3; repaid, 120
Fuchs, Dr Karl Hans, 327
Fürstenberg, Hilde, proposes to start a Knut
  Hamsun Society in Germany, 2

Gallen, Axel, 182
Galsworthy, John
  admirer of Hamsun, 228, 301, 303
  Gentlemen, 287
Garborg, Arne, 77–8, 101, 106, 119, 145, 156, 175,
  193, 256

assists in publication of *On Tour*, 78
  becomes an enemy, 124, 136, 138–9
  hostile review of *Editor Lynge*, 139
  Peasant Students, 136
  Tired Men, 136
Garmotraedet, 7, 9, 251
Garvey, Marcus, 105
Gauguin, Paul, 142
  meeting with, 159
Gausdal, 162
Gdynia, 327
Geijerstam, Gustaf af, 115
George, Henry, 103
Germany, Hamsun's special relationship with, 2, 119, 143, 232
  fondness for, 337–9, 360, 382, 394
  growth of popularity in, 176, 337
  idea of Germanic race, 340, 341–5, 347–8, 361, 382
  pro-German feelings in First World War, 232–9, 404
  tributes from leading Germans, 299–300
  see also Nazis and Fascism
Ghost, A (1898 short story), 192, 218
  synopsis, 11–12
Gide, André
  likens Hamsun to Dostoevsky, 300
  tribute from, 1
Gierløff, Christian, 391, 394, 402, 409, 410, 413, 414
  biography of Hamsun, 415
Gjesdal, Paul, 245–6
Gjøvik
  lecture at, 74
  navvy at, 40, 67, 168, 199, 270
  visits Mjøen family, 342
Gjøvik's Blad, 43, 44, 50
Gladstone, William Ewart, ridicule of, 325
Glasgow, HMS, 352
Goebbels, Josef, 366, 379, 391
  admirer of Hamsun, 359, 369, 382
  meeting with Hamsun, 368–9
  presented with Hamsun's Nobel Prize medal, 369–70, 401
  sends greetings, 338, 339, 385
Goebbels, Magda, 369
Goepfert, Eduard, 169, 171, 176, 183, 307, 371 fn
Goepfert, Maria ('Vesla'), 169, 183, 307, 371 fn
Goethe, Johann Wolfgang von, 421
  attacked by Hamsun, 148
Goethe Institute, accepts medal from, 313, 337
Gorky, Maxim, 1
  lifelong admirer of Hamsun, 201, 228
  tribute from, 300
Gran, Gerhard, 122
Grave, Jørgen, 420 fn
Gretor, Willy, 142–3, 144
  introduces Hamsun to Albert Langen, 143
Grieg, Edvard, 119, 125
  death of, 216
Grieg, Nina, 125
Grieg, Harald, 304–5, 308, 312, 313, 331, 362, 364 fn, 410, 416
  declines to publish *On Overgrown Paths*, 413, 414, 415
  deposed at Gyldendal by Germans, 411
  depositions on behalf of Hamsun, 391, 394

Hamsun's publisher, 29
  head of Gyldendal publishing house, 24
  imprisoned by Nazis, 358, 367, 411
  includes Hamsun in new catalogue, 420
  on opposite sides during German occupation, 411–12
  opponent of Nazis, 351
  pleas by Hamsun for his release, 367, 411
  rejects manuscript of Hamsun's, 356
  released after plea by Marie and Tore Hamsun, 380 fn
  repays debt to Hamsun, 296
  trust and friendship, 297
  working relationship with Hamsun, 311
Grieg, Nordahl, 193
  death of, 411
  essay *Knut Hamsun*, 238 fn
  mocks Hamsun on the question of his honour, 335
Grimm brothers, 13
Grimstad, 321, 365, 381, 383
  house arrest at hospital, 387–9
  stay in hospital, 366
Gross, Alette, 182, 241, 307, 308
Growth of the Soil, The (1917), 9, 211, 231, 241, 245, 255, 264, 265, 274, 289, 293, 310, 317
  popular success, 253–4
  praised by Gorky, 300
  recommended by Hemingway, 301
  sales of, 253–4, 364 fn
  synopsis, 249–53
  wins Nobel Prize for Hamsun, 249, 260–1
Guillaume, Charles, 262
Gulbransson, Olaf, 167
Gyldendal publishing company, 33, 97, 217, 240, 241, 249, 288 fn, 350, 380, 383, 414, 415–16, 420
  becomes Hamsun's publisher, 193
  borrowing from, 197, 222
  confiscation of books by Nazis, 358
  contract with Hamsun, 296, 308
  distribution of Hamsun's shares, 364
  festskrift from, 300
  Hamsun the major shareholder, 296, 311
  Harald Grieg deposed as head by Nazis, 411
  legal rights to Hamsun's books, 412–13
  payments to Hamsun, 242
  record sales for *August* trilogy, 296
  refusal of manuscript by Hamsun, 356–7
  secret offer to Hamsun, 167
  sets up in Oslo with loan from Hamsun, 296

Haganes, Jul, 69
Håkon VII, 215, 216, 234 fn, 353, 357
  appeal from Hamsun for king's return, 355
  criticised by Hamsun, 384, 393
  flight from Norway to England, 351–2, 354, 406
Halvorsen, Johan, 192
Hamarøy, 7, 16, 29, 114, 188–9, 217, 218, 242, 248, 257, 269, 274, 345
  earliest childhood in, 9–15
  remoteness of, 246
  return to, 220–1, 225, 232
  Skogheim farm, 218–19, 220–3, 225, 226, 227, 246, 247, 248, 269; move to, 218–19; sale of, 248; work-hut at, 249

Hambro, Carl, 357, 377 fn
  attacked by Hamsun, 353, 373
  criticises *Under the Autumn Star*, 377 fn
Hammer, Frøken, 163, 168, 170
Hammett, Dashiel, 24
Hamsun, Almar (nephew)
  Almar Hamsun Who Died, 281
  court case by Hamsun against use of name,
    279–81, 312
Hamsun, Arild (son), 226, 271, 305, 313, 356,
    414, 421
  ambition, 307
  arrest, 387
  attends school in Valdres, 306
  birth of, 225
  enrolment in Norwegian Legion, 383
  first book, 350
  imprisonment, 410
Hamsun, Bergljot (first wife), 128, 180, 181, 217,
    298, 323, 396
  courtship with Hamsun, 171–2, 175, 342
  birth of Victoria Hamsun, 195
  death of, 370
  first marriage to Goepfert and birth of Maria
    Goepfert, 169
  honeymoon period, 176–7, 307
  love at first sight, 169
  marriage to Hamsun, 176, 181, 216; failing,
    196, 197; divorce, 198
  separations from Hamsun, 188–90; separation
    agreement, 197, 222
  travelling companion in Russia, 184–8
  studies to be a midwife, 196
  stays in contact with Hamsun, 307
  unhappiness in Finland, 182–3
  with daughter in France, 307
Hamsun, Cecilia (daughter), 225, 309
  ambition, 307
  birth of, 255
  involved in attempt to kill father, 322
  marriage, 350
Hamsun, Ellinor (daughter), 313, 368, 385
  ambition, 307
  becomes an alcoholic, 367
  birth of, 225
  break-up of marriage, 356, 367
  car accident, 313, 336
  convent in Germany, 306
  father's annuity, 411
  favourite of Hamsun's, 308, 313
  illness of, 308–9
  marriage, 350
Hamsun, Marie (second wife), 198, 209, 215, 217,
    220, 221 fn, 224, 257, 260, 261, 264, 270, 271,
    273, 281, 282, 284, 286, 303, 305, 306, 308,
    309, 310, 311, 345, 385, 388, 391, 394, 395,
    421
  attempt to kill Hamsun, 322
  attends Nobel Prize-giving, 261–3
  birth of children, 225, 255
  committed Nazi, 346
  describes her married life to psychiatrist, 396–7
  despair at separations from Hamsun, 226–7,
    247
  Hamsun refuses to see her after trial, 401
  illness, 308

imprisonment, 387, 396, 404, 408
  lack of sympathy for working man, 330
  local organiser of Nasjonal Samling Party, 333
    fn, 363
  love affair with Hamsun, 203–4
  nurses Hamsun in his last years, 419–21
  personal appearance tours, 363
  propaganda readings in Berlin, 350, 355, 356
  psychoanalysed, 288–9
  jealousy, 225, 227, 255, 287, 322, 323
  reconciliation and return to Nørholm, 419
  relationship with Hamsun becomes hostile,
    321–3, 362–5
  released from prison to live with son Tore and
    family, 410
  running the farm at Skogheim, in Hamsun's
    absence, 246–7
  success with pleas to Terboven, 380
  takes over Nørholm, 364
  verbally divorced by Hamsun, 397, 410
  writings: children's books, 273, 311, 363;
    collection of poems *Wintergreen*, 273, 311;
    memoirs, 3, 354, 396; *The Rainbow*, 208, 260
Hamsun, Thorvald (brother)
  court case by Hamsun against use of name,
    279–81, 312
Hamsun, Victoria (daughter), 196, 197, 199, 201,
    204, 208, 217, 246, 257, 298, 370, 409
  argument over financial settlement with
    father, 308
  birth of, 195
  illness, 282–3
  sent to France to learn language, 307
  settles in Honfleur on her marriage, 307
Hamsund, Peter Pedersen (brother), 7, 49, 50
  immigrant in America, 44, 50, 103, 294
Hamsund, 16, 265
  earliest childhood on father's farm, 8–10
  Hamsun museum, 421
Hanno, Dr von, 203
Hansen, Harald, 119
Hansen, Irgens, 114
Hansen, John O., 86, 88, 95
Hansen, Thorkild, *Prosessen Mod Hamsun*, 324 fn
Hansen, Captain Waldemar, 172–3
Hansson, Ola, 95, 106, 107, 119, 144
Hansteen, Aasta, 124
Harstad, 226
Hart, Harry, 53, 56
Haugen, Marcello, 283
Haugesund, 124
Haukland, Andreas, 296
Hauptmann, Gerhard, tribute from, 300
Hegel, Frederick, 33, 35, 97
Heiberg, Gunnar, 145
Heiberg, Hjalmar, 28
Heidenstam, 156
Heine, Thomas Th., 167
Helsinki visit, 182, 183
Hemingway, Ernest, 1, 228, 301
  comparisons with Hamsun, 24
Herriot, Edouard, 332
Herzfeld, Marie, 119–20, 130–1, 134, 135, 136
Hess, Rudolf, denunciation of, 361
Hesse, Hermann
  admires *Chapter the Last*, 302 fn

tributes from, 1, 2, 228, 299, 301
Hestehagen, Torstein (godfather), 16, 19, 331, 396
Hewel, Walter, 374, 378
Hitler, Adolf, 324, 331, 344, 346, 350, 357, 365, 366, 367, 381, 385, 392–3
  association with, 1, 3
  birthday telegrams from, 339, 384
  comes to power, 329
  communications with, 406–7
  death of, 385
  forbids Germans to accept Nobel Prize, 337
  meetings with Hamsun, 324–5, 373–80
  meets Quisling, 351
  murder of opponents, 395
  necrology from Hamsun, 3, 385–6
  obsession with Jews, 394
  reintroduces conscription, 327
  support from Hamsun, 165, 324, 328, 338, 362, 372
Hitschmann, Eduard von, psychoanalytic study of Hamsun, 298
Hjørundfjord, teaching in, 20–1
Holberg, Ludvig, *Erasmus Montanus*, 268
Holitscher, Arthur, memoirs, 167–8
Hollander, Felix, 135
  accuses Hamsun of plagiarism, 135–6
Holm, Korfitz, 233 fn
Holmboe, Egil, 370, 371, 374, 375, 376, 377, 378, 379
Holst, Lars, 65, 68–9, 78, 107
  assists Hamsun's passage to America, 80
Honfleur, 307
Hooper, George, 52
Hornbeck, 193, 195
Horten, 74
Houens Scholarship for Travel awarded to Hamsun, 193, 196
Hugo, Victor, attacks on, 148, 325
humour, folksy, 267–8
Hunger (1890), 1, 3, 21, 23, 36, 39–40, 41, 68, 76, 102, 103, 109, 110–12, 114, 116, 125, 131, 133, 136, 143, 145, 155, 160, 161, 167, 199, 227, 242, 250, 264, 285, 298, 301, 313, 318, 418, 421
  defence and promotion of, 114–15, 116, 123
  French edition, 161
  Hamsun's pride in, 112
  key to Hamsun's future, 107
  publication of anonymous extract, 98–101
  sales, 163–4
  sensation on publication, 112–15
  translated into German, 118–19
Hyllestad, Carl Christian, 240

Ibsen, Henrik, 48, 55, 61, 71, 74, 101, 106, 113, 120, 125, 156, 163, 175, 179, 211, 236, 282, 296, 342, 417
  A Doll's House, 41, 149
  An Enemy of the People, 31, 41
  Ghosts, 108
  Brand, 341
  censured by Hamsun, 108, 109 fn, 123, 131, 148, 167, 186
  challenged as a playwright, 164
  co-founder of cult of Scandinavianism, 119
  death of, 216

  disliked by Hamsun, 238
  Hamsun's lectures on, 93
  Little Eyolf, 164
  The Master Builde, 238, fn
  The Pillars of Society, 41, 103
  Terje Vigen, 55, 236
  theatre director in Bergen, 110
  verse dramas, 108, 189
  When We Dead Awaken, 109, 319
illnesses, 63–9, 160
  apopletic fit, 366, 401
  arteriosclerosis, 308
  deafness, 246, 273, 362, 363, 375, 395, 401
  given sentence of death by doctors, 63
  nervous disorders, 160–2, 273
  pneumonia, 366
  sciatica, 175
  stroke, 385, 401
impatience, 93
In the Grip of Life (1910), 302
  last and most successful stage play, 217
  synopsis, 217
In Wonderland (1923 travel book), 192, 237, 325, 342
  synopsis, 184–8
inability to control novel, 79
infanticide and hanging debate, 243–5
irony over himself and his pretensions, 72, 418
isolation
  during the war years, 393, 394–5, 407
  need for, 400
  within the family, 401

Jacobi, Ragna, 341
Jacobsen, J. P., 256
  Niels Lyhne, 87–8
Jaeger, Hans, 77, 86, 101, 124, 125
Jaeger, Henrik, 162, 163
Janson, Drude, 60, 63, 64, 78, 88–9
Janson, Kristofer, 21, 57, 62–3, 65, 78, 85, 88–9, 92, 116
  article on, 97
  Children of Hell, 61
  emigration to America, 44–5
  influence of, 23, 44, 59
  lectures by Hamsun on, 93
  meeting with, 59–60
  publishes *Saamanden* magazine, 87
  Unitarianism faith, 59, 60–2, 87
  views defended by Hamsun, 61, 86
  What I Have Experienced, 59–60
Jebe, Halfdan, 159
Jensen, Johannes V., 193, 272, 346
Jews
  anti-Semitism, 342, 343, 348, 365, 377
  attitude towards, 394
  persecution of Norwegian Jews, 365, 366
  prohibited from entering Norway, 340
  tributes to Hamsun from, 300
Johansen, Krøger, 62, 92, 94
Johnson, Anna, romance with, 56
Johnston, Henry M., 52, 55, 56, 57, 58
journalism, Hamsun's
  articles: 'A Word to Us', 214, 373; 'Country Culture', 213; in defence of Germany in First World War, 404; Nazi propaganda leading to charges of treason, 353–8, 360–2,

365, 367, 373, 383, 405–6; 'Theologian in
Wonderland', 213; on impressions of
America, 68, 71–2, 89–91; on Strindberg, 95;
in defence of Janson, 61, 97; on Mark
Twain, 72–3
contempt for, 272
first steps, 30–1, 43–4
most controversial period, 232–45, 255–7
responsible, 213–14
writings for *The Password*, 86
Joyce, James, 112
Ulysses, 132
Juan les Pins, 313
Juel, Dagny, 119, 159
Julson, Dr, 61
Jung, Carl, 391 fn

Kafka, Franz, 1, 112, 168, 228, 301
Castle, 110
Kallum, Mr, 86–7
Kant, Immanuel, 76, 334 fn
Kareno trilogy of plays, 160, 163–6, 168, 174, 202,
208, 237
performances in Christiania and Moscow,
165–6
synopses, 164–5
At the Gates of the Kingdom (1895), 161, 164, 165,
166, 217, 242, 391; adopted by National
Theatre, 163; first play by Hamsun to be
produced, 160
Evening Glow, (1898), 164–5, 166, 180
The Game of Life (1896), 163, 164, 165–6, 174,
204, 217
Karlfeldt, Erik Axel, 263
campaigns for award of Nobel Prize to
Hamsun, 261
Keller, Hans, 324, 325
Kielland, Alexander, 33, 41, 101, 115, 121, 142,
175, 211, 236, 296, 342, 417
death of, 216
debate over grant, 74, 77
Hamsun lectures on, 71, 74, 93
Kipling, Rudyard, 234, 236, 242
Kirkeby, Anker, 272
Kjær, Nils, 195, 325
Kjerringøy, 25, 26, 32
meeting with Zahl at, 29, 421
Knudsen (cousin), plea for shoes, 41
Knudsen, A. F., Hamsun's early publisher
prints *Bjørger*, 23
prints poem 'A Reconciliation', 22
Knut Hamsun Fund established, 385
Knut Hamsun Society, 2
Koestler, Arthur, 24 fn
Koht, Foreign Minister, 335
Kollontai, Aleksandra, praise from, 300–1
Kolstad, Peder, 329
Kongespeilet (Resistance newspaper), 385
Kongsberg, stay in, 200–1, 204
Kønig, Christian, friend and publisher, 249, 254,
272, 411
Konow, Prime Minister, 215
Koppang, 217
Kraakmo farm, Sagfjord, retreat at, 225, 246, 249
Kraakmo, Johannes, 249
Krag, Thomas, 296

Krag, Vilhelm, 40, 159 fn, 204, 272
Kragerø, retreat at, 255
Kringsjaa magazine, 240
critical praise for *Pan*, 156
Kristensen, Brede, 144
Kristiansand, 124, 247, 282
resident in, 128–9, 153–7, 313
Krog, Eli, 23
Krog, Julius, 99
Krogh, August, 262
Krogh, Christian, 77, 86–7, 124, 125
Albertine, 86–7, 105
Kubin, 168
Kullman, Olaf Bryn, 335 fn
Kurella, Dr Hans, 120
Kvartalskrift, article in, 52
Kyseth, Torger, 41, 43, 47, 50
Kyseth, Torger-Maria, 41, 43

Labour Party, Norwegian, 328, 329, 330, 332
Lagerlöf, Selma, 262
Landquist, John, 50
study of Hamsun, 298
Landvik Old Folk's Home, 420 fn
paying guest at, 401–2, 416
stay after arrest, 389, 398–9
Langbehn, Julius, *Rembrandt the Educator*, 341
Lange, Sven, 144, 151, 158, 167
accompanies Hamsun to Paris, 141, 142
Langen, Albert, 126, 137, 145, 153, 154, 155, 157,
159, 164, 177, 181, 196, 232, 297, 298, 341
becomes German publisher after introduction
by Gretor, 143
death of, 233 fn, 242
financial support from, 152, 189, 197
launches *Simplicissimus* magazine in Munich,
167, 174
marries Dagny Bjørnson, 167
organises fund for Hamsun, 175–6, 233
Langens (German publishers), 239, 242
festschrift to Hamsun, 299–300
loyalty to, 242
name changed to Langen-Müller, 333
Langfeldt, Dr Gabriel, 324, 408, 416
Hamsun's hatred of, 409, 414, 415
psychiatric examination of Hamsun, 5, 13, 19,
389, 390–3, 395–401, 422
Lars Oftedal, 144
articles published in book form, 109
Larsen, Bolette Pavels, 146–8, 156, 166, 170–1,
177, 201, 245, 298, 409
admiration for Hamsun, 125
correspondence with, 124, 135, 137, 140, 145
death of, 190 fn
trusted journalist friend, 122
Larsen, Hanna Astrup, study of Hamsun, 298
Larsen, Ole, 163, 321
Larvik interlude, 257, 272, 289
move to, 255
purchase of Villa Solgløtt, 248, 254
Last Joy, The (1912), 194, 199, 225, 234, 246, 325
anglomania in, 234–5, 372
English translation *Look Back on Happiness*, 222
fn
lack of charm, 224
synopsis, 222–4
Lavik, Dore, 204–5

Lawrence, D. H., 2
Laws, Yngvar, 86, 95
League of Nations, 351
lectures by Hamsun, 55–6, 58, 59, 61, 62, 70–1
  adverse reactions to, 123
  Christiania University, 166–7, 184, 200, 238 fn
  Copenhagen University, 103, 104, 114, 138
  earlier tour fiasco in Norway, 74–6, 79
  later tour of Norway, 122–5
  Minneapolis, 92–3, 94, 104
  style of delivery, 93, 125
Liar, A, 77, 78, 100
Lie, Erik, 152, 173, 175
Lie, Jonas, 33, 41, 74, 121, 142, 144, 158, 159, 211,
  236, 296, 342, 417
  death of, 216
  lectures on, 93
Lie, Chief of Police Jonas, 366
Lier, 208
light, passion for, 64–5
Lillehammer
  centre for artists, 162
  convalescence at, 160–3
  German surrender to Allies at, 387
Lillesand, stays at, 116–21, 264, 306, 313
Lillestrøm, 196
Lindberg, August, 108
Lindboe, Justice Minister, 329
Lingjerde, Hans Pedersen, criticised by Hamsun
  in the press, 43–4
Litleré, Mons, 109, 122, 144
Ljan, days at, 163, 168–9, 170, 199
Locard, Dr, 312, 391
Lofotposten, 352, 390
Loftfield, G. E., 92
  description of Hamsun, 92–3
Lofthus, Olav, 122
Lom, 6, 8, 10, 331
  Hamsun museum, 421
  visit to his birthplace, 16
Longum, 258, 312
Lous, Lulli, romance with, 128–9
Louvain, destruction of, 234
love, views on, 24, 179
love affairs, 51–2, 56, 169
  disappointments in, 128–9
Lund, Frøken, 162
Lund, Henrik, 285
Lund, John, 174

macabre, interest in the, 17, 116–17
McFarlane, James, 303
Madelia, 56
  stay in, 57–9
Madison, 47–50
Mandal, 248
Mann, Heinrich, 167
  tribute from, 300
Mann, Thomas, 167, 325, 336 fn, 348
  Buddenbrooks, 299, 358
  tributes from, 1, 2, 228, 299, 300, 301
Mannheim, Baron, 184
Marcus, C. D., biographical study of Hamsun,
  298
Martens, Heinrich, 159
Masaryk, Thomas, tribute from, 300

Maupassant, Guy de, 302
megalomania, 346, 348, 355
Mell, Max, 338
Mellbye, J. C., 367
Menstad Quay, strike at Norsk Hydro plant, 329,
  330, 333
Meyer, Thorvald, 242
Michelsen, Christian, 305, 329
Mill, John Stuart, 180
Miller, Henry, 105
  describes Hamsun as a Dickens, 301
  praised by, 1
Minneapolis
  lectures in, 92–3, 94
  return to, 85–9, 91–4
  stay in, 60–5
Mirbeau, Octave, 145
  praise for Hamsun, 161
Mjøen, Alf, 342
Mjøen, Clare, 342
Mjøen, Jon Alfred, 342
  Racial Hygiene, 342
Mjøen, Reidar, 342
Moe, work in store at, 50
Moestue, Captain, 45–6, 49
Mogens, Victor, 357
Molard, William, 142
Molde, 352
Mollehaugen, Marcelius, 221
Mollergaten Gestapo HQ, 359
Monrad-Johansen, David, 339
Morburger, Carl, study of Hamsun, 232, 298
Morgenbladet, 145, 156, 236, 242, 399
  article on infanticide, 243–5
  unfavourable criticism in book reviews, 146–7,
    148, 180, 377 fn
Mörner, Birger, 156, 157, 182, 183
Moscow, 188
  Arts Theatre, 217; Hamsun accepts
    membership, 299
Moser, Abteilungsleiter, 371
Mowinckel, Prime Minister, 331–2, 335
Munch, Andreas, 13, 33–4, 48
  recommendation from, 34, 37
Munch, Anna, 128, 175
  campaign of persecution against Hamsun,
    169–73, 181, 312, 323, 391
  interviewed by police, 172
  obsessed with Hamsun, 169
  Two People, 169, 172
Munch, Edvard, 119, 142, 159
  death of, 381
  Evening on Karl Johan, 131
  parallel with, 131
Munich, 217, 237, 238, 309
  invitation by Bjørnson to join group, 167
  stay with Langen, 167–8, 174
Murray, Gilbert, 334 fn
Musil, Robert, 1
  influenced by Hamsun, 301
  tribute from, 299
Mussolini, Benito, 346
  admiration for, 331
Myklestad, Theodor, 288 fn
Mysteries (1892), 1, 3, 22, 128, 129, 130–6, 143,
  155, 202, 216, 227, 237, 242, 264, 266, 274,

275, 282, 302, 319, 346–7, 418, 422
acclaimed by Bjørnson, 161
author's description of, 126–7
critical reviews, 131–2, 149
published by Langen, 143

Naerup, Carl, 195
critical praise for *Pan*, 156
names, belief in importance of, 21
anonymity, 76, 99–100
court case against Thorvald and Almar, 279–81
court case against Petersen Nørholm family, 312
experiments with forms of his name, 30, 49, 73, 76, 99
Namur, gambling expedition to, 190
Nansen, Fridtjof, 101, 125, 329, 415
attitude towards, 108
Nansen, Odd, insulted by Hamsun, 415
Nansen, Peter, 195, 212–13, 240, 242, 344
commissions novel from Hamsun, 193
hostile review of *Shallow Soil*, 149
Narvik, 351
Nasjonal Samling (Norwegian Nazi Party), 333, 342, 346, 363, 374, 375, 382, 383, 392, 394
becomes the only permitted party in Norway, 358
fined because of membership, 402
formed by Quisling, 329
Hamsun denies membership, 388
membership becomes a criminal offence, 387, 389
question of Hamsun's membership, 404–5, 407, 408
National Party, Norwegian, 333
National Theatre of Norway
adopts *At the Gates of the Kingdom*, 163
performs *The Game of Life*, 174, 204
performs *Queen Tamara*, 192
Nationalt tidsskrift, 343, 344
Nationen, 329, 339, 354, 355
Nazis and Fascism, Hamsun's commitment to, 92, 114, 324–49, 389, 390, 395
admiration for Mussolini, 331
association and meetings with Hitler, 1, 3, 165, 324–5, 328, 338, 373–80, 384, 406–7
contact with Goebbels, 338, 339, 359, 368–70, 382, 385, 401
fraternising with German servicemen, 384, 385
necrology for Hitler on his death, 3, 385–6
propaganda articles leading to charge of treason, 353–8, 360–2, 365, 367, 383, 405–6
reputation damaged by support for, 1–3, 325, 383, 416, 422
Neeraas, Hans, 128–9, 247
Neeraas, Kalla, 128–9, 130, 247
Neighbouring Town, The, 255
Nernst, Walter, 262
Ny Jord magazine, 95
contribution to, 97
publishes anonymous extract from *Hunger*, 98–101
Ny illustreret Tidende, article by Hamsun on Mark Twain, 72–3, 280
New York Herald, 240
New York Herald Tribune, 383

New York Times, 358, 383
New York, 79, 81
impressions of, 47
Nice, 310, 311
Nietzsche, Friedrich Wilhelm, 95, 103, 106, 113, 119, 180, 222, 341
influence on Hamsun, 114, 133, 134
Nilsson, Victor, 94–5, 97, 106, 110, 115, 141, 145, 150
friendship with, 87–8
reviews Hamsun's lectures, 92, 93
Nobel, Alfred, 185
Nobel Prize, 162, 326, 334, 335–6, 369–70
Nobel Prize for Literature awarded to Hamsun, 260–3
presents Goebbels with the medal, 369–70, 401
speech at the presentation, 262–3
Nordahl, 21, 26, 36, 40
Nordahl, Inger, 21, 28
Norden magazine, accepts Hamsun's poems, 47, 61
Nordic Society, 326, 342
cultivates Hamsun, 338–9
presentation on 85th birthday, 385
Nordstrand lodgings, 199
Nørholm estate, 260, 261, 264, 289, 298, 305, 313, 321, 322, 330, 339, 346, 354, 357, 365, 380, 383, 385, 387, 389, 401, 420
death of Hamsun at, 421
house arrest at, 387, 416
life at, 271–4, 281, 288, 306
move to, 258
name case against Petersen-Nørholm family, 312
restoration into a model farm, 269–71
return after his trial, 408–9
return of Marie after reconciliation, 419
Norske Intelligenssedler, 201
review of *Editor Lynge*, 139
Norway
breach of neutrality by Royal Navy, 350, 351, 354
German occupation, 351–86
independence struggle, 138, 209, 211–12, 216, 341; England's support of, 234 fn
strikes, 328, 329
Norwegian art and artists, cult of, 101, 119
Norwegian language, contribution by Hamsun to debate on its future development, 255–7
Norwegian Society of Authors
donation from Hamsun, 297
refuses, then accepts, silver cross, 299
Nygaardsvold, Johan, 330, 350, 352, 374

obsession to be a writer, 25
Ødegård, Dr Ørnulv: psychiatric examination of Hamsun, 5, 13, 19, 324, 328, 337, 390, 393–5, 401
Oftedal, Lars, 15, 74, 122
attacked by Hamsun, 12–13, 109
involved in scandal, 109 fn
Olaf, King, 7
Olav, Crown Prince, 359
Olsen, Georg, 15, 218, 221
Olsen, Hans (uncle), 5, 6, 19, 20, 21, 36, 109, 116, 140, 192, 218, 396, 400

cruelty to Hamsun, 10–13
death of, 221
Hamsun sent to live with him, 10
influence of, 10
moves north, 7–8
sickness, 10, 15
Olsen, Ola, 69
Olsen, Ole (grandfather), 6, 7, 9
Olsen, Vetltraein (uncle), 8, 50, 279
death of, 16
special friend, 9–10
On the Banks (1891 short story), 19 fn, 54
On the Cultural Life of Modern America (1889), 68, 94, 104–6, 110, 184, 239, 344–5
American attacks on, 118
Strindberg impressed with, 106, 157
On Overgrown Paths (1949), 50–1, 395, 403, 405, 412, 413
difficulties in publishing, 412–15
last book, 416
synopsis, 416–19
On the Prairie, 90, 91
On Tour, 75–8, 80, 99, 111, 136, 192
Garborg assists in its publication, 78
refused by *Dagbladet*, 77
Opeide, 218
Oppegård sanatorium, 176
Oranienburg concentration camp, 338
Orient, interest in the, 116, 176
Oscar II, 38, 39, 40
Oscarsborg fortress, 212
Oslo (earlier Christiania), 280, 339, 346, 350, 358, 364
psychoanalysis in, 283–9
stay in, 323, 380
University students arrested, 381
Vindern Psychiatric Clinic, 5, 323, 342
see also Christiania
Ossietzky, Carl von, 344 fn
death of, 336
exposes German rearmament, 334
Hamsun refuses to help in the award to him of Nobel Peace Prize, 334–7
interned in Sachsenhausen concentration camp, 334
retrospective award of Nobel Peace Prize, 337
Ostensjo, stay at, 29–33, 449
Østre Sørum, lodging at, 67
output, literary, 321

Paasche, Fredrik, 338
Pan (1894), 1, 2–3, 22, 24, 72, 159, 168, 194, 199, 202, 227, 264, 281, 292, 297, 302, 303, 339, 421
acclaimed by Bjørnson, 161
critical praise, 156
establishes Hamsun in literature, 156
inspired by Rousseau and Strindberg, 153, 157
progress of book, 151–2, 153–4
sales of, 364 fn
success of, 161
synopsis, 154–5
paranoia, 401
believes that he is a victim of the Norwegian literary establishment, 136, 145–7, 156
Paris, 141

Café de la Régence, 142, 146, 147, 157, 160
ceaseless work and discipline in, 160
homesickness in, 151–2, 153
meeting with Strindberg, 107 fn, 157
Scandinavian colony and cult, 142, 163
sojourns in, 142–52, 157–60, 162, 232, 342
Parsons, John, 96
Password, The, 86, 92, 97
contributions by Hamsun, 86
Pasternak, Boris, 1
influence of Hamsun, 301
patriotism, Hamsun's understanding of, 361, 402
Paul, Adolf, 144
Paustovsky, influence of Hamsun, 301
Pedersen, Marie (sister), 265
Pedersen, Ole (brother), 220, 221
Pedersen, Hilde, 269
Pedersen, Ottar (nephew), 270
farm manager for Hamsun, 269
Pedersen, Per (father), 17, 20, 29
birth of, 6
death of, 201
economic problems, 8
farming at Hamsund, 9
marriage, 7
respect for, 5, 19
reunited with Hamsun, 188
travelling tailor, 6, 9
Pedersen, Per (grandfather), 6
Pedersen, Sofie (sister), 265
Pedersen, Stine (sister-in-law), 221
Pedersen, Tora (mother), 5, 6, 8, 9, 12, 29, 217, 221
death of, 274
handicaps, 265
marriage, 7
reunion with Hamsun, 188
Pedersen, Ymbjør (grandmother), 6
pedlar, travelling, 18–19
Peerson, Cleng, 7
PEN Club, enrolled as honorary member, 303
persecuted with anonymous letters, 385
abusive letters, 357, 362
campaign by Anna Munch, 169–73, 181, 312, 323, 391
Petersen-Nørholm family, name case against, 312
Philipsen, Gustav, 95, 102, 106, 154, 155
commissions book on America, 103
publishes *Editor Lynge*, 138, 139
publishes *Hunger*, 116, 163
publishes *Shallow Soil*, 148
success with *Pan*, 161
Piotrowski, Rufin, *A Polish Refugee's Story*, 311
plagiarism accusation, 88, 143
damages reputation in Germany, 135
pleas for forgiveness for unspecified crimes, 82
pleas for the release of prisoners of the Nazis, 359, 367–8, 380, 381, 383, 408
polarity in Hamsun's personality, 264
Poles, attitude towards, 327
politics, Hamsun's, 324–49
extremism, 333
Politiken magazine, 98, 132, 151
cutting review of *Shallow Soil*, 149
interview with, 272

post-war retribution for Hamsun
appeal unsuccessful, but compensation
payments reduced, 409
criminal charges dropped, 402–3
house arrest, 387, 416
propaganda articles leading to charge of
treason, 353–8, 360–2, 365, 367, 405–6
psychiatrists' examination and report, 5–6,
324, 328, 333, 337, 348–9, 390–401; findings,
400–1
sentenced to pay compensation, 407
postal assistant, 69–70
Pound, Ezra, 2, 344
treason sentence, 410
press criticism of Hamsun, 125, 131–2, 145–8, 149
Presteid, 8, 17, 218, 421
harsh childhood with Uncle Hans at, 10–15
Prohibition, 86
Przybyszewski, Stanislaw, 119, 159
pseudonym Menz Føyen, 217
psychoanalysed by Strømme, 283–9, 293, 321,
391
psychological literature by Hamsun, 117–18,
122–34, 155
publicity, Hamsun's horror of, 297

Queen Tamara (1903 play), 192
Quisling, Vidkun, 330, 346, 374, 379, 394, 402
allowed to form government, 365
arrested, 387
declares himself President, 352
Defence Minister, 329
execution, 403
forms Norwegian Nazi Party (Nasjonal
Samling), 329
Hamsun his strongest card, 382
meetings with Hitler, 351, 358
obliged to resign, 352
persecution of Jews, 366
plans for a coup, 351
position of power, 358
proposes dictatorship, 329
support from Hamsun, 333, 348, 357, 358
sends telegram on Hamsun's 85th birthday,
384

Råholmen island residence, 182–3
Randers, Kristofer, 347, 405
Rasmussen, Wilhelm, 333, 338
Raufoss, 41, 43
Realist philosophers, 317
recklessness, 245, 409
Reconciliation, A (poem), 22–3, 24
Red Wing, 57
Rejersen of the 'Southern Star', 194
religion, views on, 57, 59–60, 61, 62, 200, 398–9,
420
confirmation at Lom church, 16
Remman, Louis, 72
Revue des Revues, article for, 145
Reymont, Wladyslaw, *A Year*, 300
Ribbentrop, Joachim von, 355, 356, 374
Rilke, Rainer Maria, *Notebooks of Malte Laurids
Brigge*, 110
Ring is Closed, The (1936)
'false' last novel, 313, 416

links with *Hunger*, 318
sexiest novel, 316
synopsis, 314–20
Rishovd, Arnt, 371
Road Leads On, The, 345
road worker, 38, 41–6
Rode, Helge, 193
Rommel, Field Marshal, 363–4
Roosevelt, Franklin D., attacked by Hamsun,
365, 382, 394
Rørdam, Valdemar, 193
Rosa (1909), 15, 199, 202, 204, 228, 232, 238, 302,
325
synopsis, 202–3
Rosenberg, Alfred
greetings from, 339
The Myth of the 20th Century, 338
Rousseau, J. J., 132, 153
Ruh, Pastor, 56
Russia
an important market, 201
blamed by Hamsun for atrocities, 394
success of translations, 217
tributes from, 300–1
Ryder, Ambassador, 96

Saamanden magazine, 87
Saarland, 326
Sachsenhausen concentration camp, 326, 334,
335 fn
St Louis Post-Dispatch, article for, 85
Saltdalen, 225
Samsø island, residence on, 137, 192
Samtiden magazine, 117, 140, 151
Sand District Court
Hamsun's preliminary hearing, 388–9
Hamsun's trial, 404–7
Marie's trial, 404
Sandefjord, 124
Sangstad, Per, 43
Sarpsborg, 125, 127, 128, 171 fn
Sars, Ernst, 40, 107
Scandinavianism, cult of, 119, 142, 163
Scavenius, Erik, 378 fn
Schelderup, Halfdan, 312
Schickele, René, 336 fn
Schiller, Johann von, attacked by Hamsun, 148
Schirach, Baldur von, 373
Schleicher, General von, murder of, 346
Schmelk, Captain, 171
Schneider-Edenkuben, Richard, 356, 367
Schnitzler, Arthus, tribute from, 299
Schoenberg, Arnold, tribute from, 299, 300
Schou, Olaf, 242
Schroeder, Christa, 373, 378
Scribner's Sons publish *Shallow Soil*, 240
Second World War, 350–86
breach of Norwegian neutrality by Royal
Navy, 350, 351, 354
German invasion of Norway, 351
German surrender in Norway, 387
Norwegian surrender, 352, 353
see also Nazis and Fascism
secretary to Janson, Kristofer, 60–3
Segelcke, 152
Segelfoss novels, 228–32, 240, 249, 251, 254, 266,

274, 295, 337; best-selling author with
the publication of, 228
Children of the Age (1913), 225, 227, 230, 231,
232, 239, 249, 293, 302; synopsis, 228–30
Segelfoss Town (1915), 15, 226, 227, 232, 240,
241, 252, 280, 293, 302; synopsis, 230–1
Seidel, Ina, 338
Selmer, Jens, 35, 36
Sengebusch, Ernst, 43, 44, 49, 51
senility, question of Hamsun's, 324, 325, 348,
381, 390
sexual personality, 65, 124–5
Shakespeare, William, 256
dismissed by Hamsun, 123, 148
Shallow Soil (1893), 151, 156, 161, 168, 202 fn, 240,
241, 301
critical disapproval, 148
synopsis, 148–9
Shaw, George Bernard, 305
shoemaker's apprentice, 19–20
Sibelius, Jean, 182
Siesta (1897 short stories), 175, 192
Simonsen, Dr Konrad, 311
The Modern Human Type, 344
Simplicissimus magazine, 167, 176
collection of fund for Hamsun, 175–6, 233
contributes *The Call of Life* short story, 174
Sin (short story), 76, 78, 80, 192
Sinding, Christian, 142, 159 fn
Singer, Isaac Bashevis, praise from, 1
Sivertsen, Inger, 196
Skaar, Jon, 31
Skaar, Nils, 31
Skandinaven (community newspaper), 61
Skaugum, 359, 387
Skautnes, 218
Skavlan, Einar, 37, 78, 336
biography of Hamsun, 298, 390
Skien Fylkesavisen newspaper, 333
Skram, Amalie, 101, 125, 139–40, 145
Skram, Erik, 63–4, 101, 116, 119, 133, 139
Skultbakken, 6
Slaves of Love, 167, 202 fn
Slotte, Alexander, 183, 189
Slotte, Xavier, 189
Smedal, Gustav, 355, 356, 360, 364, 366
Smith, Doery, 381
Social Democrat, article for, 145
Society of Authors, 173–4, 175
Society of Painters, donation from Hamsun, 297
Sollien, 208, 217
Sologub, 301
Sonderegger, René, 336
Søndre Bergenhus Folkeblad, debate on psalm-
singing in, 30–1
Sørensen, Johan, 110
end of association with, 107
financial assistance from, 102, 103
Sortland, 225, 246
Sautreau, George, tribute from, 300
Spitteler, Carl, 261
spokesman for Norwegian people, uneasy role
of, 215, 219, 254, 293, 354, 361, 366
Stallybrass, Gunnvor, 222 fn
Stallybrass, Oliver, 222 fn, 325

Stang, Oberst, 212
Stanislavsky, Constantine
directs Hamsun's plays, 166, 217
My Life In Art, 166
State literary scholarship
awarded, 181
withheld, 173–5
Stavanger, 124, 386
Stockholm, presentation of Nobel Prize, 261–3,
281
Stokmarknes, 18, 31
stores, work in, 16–17, 52, 56–8
Stoughton, 55–6
Strax, 212
Stray, Sigrid, 311–12, 364, 365, 391, 394, 409, 412,
413, 414, 415, 419
defends Hamsun in court, 405, 410
Hamsun pleas for the release of, 367
memoirs, 323, 363–4, 381, 385
opponent of Nazis, 351
Strindberg, August, 41, 87, 95, 106–7, 119, 143,
163, 193, 207, 303
article on, 95, 106
attitude towards, 93
first meeting in Paris, 107 fn, 157
Hamsun lectures on, 71, 74, 93
idolised by Hamsun, 417
impressed with *On the Cultural Life of Modern
America*, 106, 157
Miss Julie, 113
obsession with, 106, 156–7
poverty, 158
relationship with, 157–9, 160
Son of a Servant, 93
Striving Life (1905 collection of short stories), 194
'Alexander and Leonarda', 194
'Blue Man Island', 194
'In the Sweet Summertime', 194
'Under the Crescent Moon', 188, 194
'Vagabond Days', 52, 90, 194
'Win for the Woman, A', 194
Strømme, Johannes Irgens, 298
Nervøsitet, 283, 284
psychoanalysis of Hamsun, 283–9, 293, 321,
391
psychoanalysis of Marie, 288–9
studies of Hamsun, 298–9
Sue, Eugene, 41
Suttestad, 162
Svenska Folkets Tidning, 87, 92, 93
Sverdgny, 25, 26, 29
Sverdrup, Jakob, 174, 175
Swarming (1904), 193–4, 202, 232
synopsis, 194–5
Swedenborg, Emmanuel, 157 fn
Switzerland, contempt for, 214 fn, 240
Sylten, Mikal, 343, 344
'Who's Who in the World of Jews', 343, 344

Taine, Hippolyte, 123
Taoism, 317
Tau, Max, 367, 413
teaching in Hjorundfjord, 20–1
Terboven, Josef, 355, 358, 360, 366, 379, 380, 382
appointed Reichskommissar of Norway, 352
attempts by Hamsun to discredit him with
Hitler, 374–6, 378

communication with, 406–7
greetings from, 385
Hamsun's plea for Ronald Fangen, 359, 367, 411
suicide, 387
Thaulow, Fritz, 40, 101, 144, 145
Thommessen, Ola, 80, 107
attacks Hamsun's lectures, 125–6
Hamsun's revenge, 137–8
Tidens Tegn, 233, 326, 330, 335, 336
Times, The, 334 fn, 373, 383
questionnaire to Hamsun, 304
Times Literary Supplement, 325
reviews of Hamsun's writing, 302, 303, 324
To Bergljot (poem to Bergljot), 176
Tolstoy, Leo, 300
censured by Hamsun, 186
Tonsaasen sanatorium, 168
Tønsberg, 74
Torgeir the Old, 7
Torp, Dr, 162
Toten, road-worker at, 41–6
tourism, Hamsun's article on growing and harmful effect of, 214–15
Towards the Day, 330
tram conductor in Chicago, 81–5
Tranøy, work in Walsoe's store at, 16–17, 236
Trømso, 21, 352
Trondheim, 8, 169
Trykket, Ole, 18
Turkey, journey through, 188
Tveraas, Sven, 56–7, 58–9, 60, 62, 65, 67
Tveteraas, Trygve, 309, 311
Twain, Mark, 186, 194
article in *Ny illustreret Tidende* by Hamsun, 72–3, 280
influence of, 264
Innocents Abroad, 73
respect for, 72–3, 105, 228
Roughing It, 72
The New Pilgrims Progress, 73

Ulrik from Jen's place, 69–70
Undset, Sigrid, 244
Unitarianism, 59, 60–2, 87
Urdal, Mikkel, first publisher, 21, 22

Vågå, 6, 7, 8
Valdres, 82, 83, 237, 247, 248, 309
first stay in, 65–74
holiday in, 109–10
honeymoon, 176–7, 307
meeting place for the Hamsuns, 306
sons attend school at, 306
vanity, 382, 417
Ventimiglia, incident with customs, 309–10
Verdens Gang, 65, 100, 106, 137, 138, 139, 212, 215
article on farm life, 89–90
attacks Hamsun's lectures, 125
hostile review of *Editor Lynge*, 139
gives press card to Hamsun, 80
publishes *Chance*, 135
review of *Pan*, 156
Verlaine, Paul, 167
meeting with, 159
Versailles, Treaty of, 327

Vesper, Will, 338
Vetleson, Thom, 236, 242
Vetter, Ewald, 356
Vibe, Christopher, 334, 335
Victoria (1898), 3, 17, 22, 24, 192, 194, 203, 226, 227, 292, 302, 303
defended by Hamsun, 180–1
honeymoon novel, 177
review, 180
sales, 179, 364 fn
synopsis, 177–9
Victory for the Woman, 83, 84
Vienna, 169, 183, 309
speech at Congress, 371–3, 383
visit to Congress of Press Internationale, 370–4, 382
Vigeland, Gustav, 142, 196
Vignette Picture, A, 55
Villon, François, 167
Vislie, Vetle, 174, 175
Vogt, Nils
attacks on Hamsun, 146–7, 148, 180, 181, 399
unfavourable review of *Victoria*, 180
Völkischer Beobachter, 334
Vråliosen, 306
Vyborg, Constable, 172

Waley, Arthur, 317
Walsøe, Nikolai, 16–17, 18, 179, 221, 236, 331, 392 fn
Walsøe, Laura, 179
adolescent love affair with, 17–18
Wanderer novels, 42, 222, 224, 268, 295, 302, 416
Under the Autumn Star (1906), 199, 201, 222, 302; criticised by Hambro, 377 fn; sales, 254; synopsis, 199–200
Wanderer Plays on Muted Strings, A (1909), 201, 208, 222, 224, 302; synopsis, 208–11
Wassermann, Jacob, 167
tribute from, 299
Webb, Mary, *Precious Bane*, 303
Wedekind, Frank, 143, 144, 167, 168, 299
Weenaas, August, 20, 36
testimonial from, 21
Welblund, Aage, 140
Wells, H. G., 1, 305
admirer of Hamsun, 228, 301, 303
Wergeland, Henrik, 27, 29, 33, 211, 213, 293
campaign against anti-Semitism, 340
Werschowski, 36
West, Rebecca, praise from, 1, 318
Whitman, Walt, attack on, 105
Wiehr, Josef, study of Hamsun, 298
Wiesener, Albert, 380 fn
Wiesener, Ragnhild, 244
Wild Choir (1904 collection of poems), 191, 192
'Fever Poem', 182, 192
'In a Hundred Years It Will All Be Forgotten', 192
'Island Poem', 193
'Letter to Byron in Heaven', 192–3, 213
Willumsen, J. F., 131
Woel, Cai, study of Hamsun, 298
Women at the Pump, The (1920), 273, 274, 275, 293, 302–3
praised by Gorky, 300
synopsis, 264–9

Women's Movement, detested by Hamsun, 124, 149, 209
Woolf, Virginia, 112
working man, lack of sympathy for, 330
world-wide fame, 297
Writers' Union, 359
writing techniques
  alteration in narrative stance for later novels, 227–8
  change from first- to third-person narrations, 418
  plotting techniques of providing reader with false information, 266
  'stream of consciousness', 267
  switching tenses device, 316

Zahl, Erasmus, 30, 221, 331, 392 fn
  correspondence with, 25–6, 27–8, 31–2, 34–5, 37–9, 40, 41, 49, 280
  loans to Hamsun give him a start as a writer, 26, 29, 32, 42, 296
  meeting at Kjerringøy, 29, 421
Zajtsev, 301
Znanije publishing house, 337
  exclusive rights, 201
Zola, Emile
  Germinal, 294
  lectures on, 93, 115, 123, 134, 398
Zorn, Anders, 159
Züchner, Ernst, 374, 375 fn, 378
Zweig, Stefan, tributes from, 299, 300